Teach Yourself
►WordPerfect®5.1◄

Teach Yourself
►WordPerfect® 5.1◄

Mary Campbell

Osborne McGraw-Hill

Berkeley   New York   St. Louis   San Francisco
Auckland   Bogotá   Hamburg   London   Madrid
Mexico City   Milan   Montreal   New Delhi   Panama City
Paris   São Paulo   Singapore   Sydney
Tokyo   Toronto

Osborne **McGraw-Hill**
2600 Tenth Street
Berkeley, California 94710
U.S.A.

For information on translations and book distributors outside of the U.S.A., please write to Osborne **McGraw-Hill** at the above address.

Teach Yourself WordPerfect® 5.1

 234567890 DOC99876543210

ISBN 0-07-881666-1

TAB BOOKS is a McGraw-Hill Company. TAB BOOKS offers software for sale. For information and a catalog, please contact TAB Software Department, Blue Ridge Summit, PA 17294-0850.

To my husband, Dave

►Contents at a Glance◄

► Part I ◄ Essential WordPerfect Features

► Part IV ◄   Appendixes

▶ Contents ◀

3 Printing a Document 65

4 Using Features to Alter the Appearance of Text 87

▶ Part III ◀ Special Features

17 WordPerfect's New Graphics Features 467

18 Creating an Outline 517

▶ Part IV ◀   Appendixes

► Acknowledgments ◄

I would like to extend my thanks to all the people who contributed to producing this book:

Martha Studnicka and Marie Adams of Page Crafters Plus for all of their work on the 5.1 upgrade. Their knowledge of all of WordPerfect's features and attention to detail ensured a smooth and timely conversion of the manuscript.

Gabrielle Lawrence, for all her work on this project. Her ideas helped make this a better book and added variety to chapter examples and exercises.

Cindy Hudson, for her idea to do this series and for all of her behind-the-scenes efforts.

Liz Fisher, for all of her help with the 5.1 upgrade. Madhu Prasher, for coordinating editorial phases; and all the great staff at Osborne who worked on this book: Ilene Shapera, Erica Spaberg, Marcela Hancik, Roger Dunshee, and Lynda Higham.

Roger Stewart, for his work as copy editor. Roger's knowledge of WordPerfect and his positive outlook allowed him to complete the job on a timely basis while still handling all of his other responsibilities at McGraw-Hill.

▶ Introduction ◀

If you have ever tried to learn a new software program on your own, chances are that you were left somewhat frustrated by the experience. Even if you learned to use the program, you probably wondered if you were doing things correctly. Without an expert tutor in the office or the time and money to attend a seminar, you may have felt as if there were no solution. *Teach Yourself WordPerfect 5.1* is designed to provide that solution and to meet the needs of both WordPerfect 5.1 and 5.0 users. Instructions are clearly provided for both pull-down menus and function key approaches to completing tasks.

The short, easy-to-follow lessons in *Teach Yourself WordPerfect 5.1* present basic WordPerfect skills step by step. Each new skill builds on the skills learned previously. Before long, you will be able to create all types of documents.

The book uses a learning-by-example approach and avoids lengthy discussions of features. The chapters are organized by lessons, each focusing on a learning objective. As you master a learning objective, you will acquire a new WordPerfect skill. Each lesson takes about 15 minutes to complete.

Every chapter (except the first) begins with a Skills Check. The Skills Check exercises test your readiness to begin the chapter. The sequences of keystrokes used in the exercises are given in Appendix C, along with the number of the section where the skills were initially covered. If you experience difficulty with an exercise, you will want to go back to the referenced section and work through the examples to improve your skill level before proceeding with the new material.

Once you have mastered the Skills Check, you are ready to tackle the first learning objective. A brief description of the skill is followed by the steps it involves and one or more practical applications. By following these steps you will be able to perform the applications. You will want to enter the examples at your keyboard if at all possible, since reading about the feature does not offer the same reinforcement as trying it out on the computer. The examples are followed by a set of exercises that test your ability to use the feature covered in the learning objective. Appendixes C and D provide the answers for each exercise.

Each chapter concludes with two additional sets of exercises: the Mastery Skills Check and the Integrating Skills Check. Unlike the section exercises, which focus on one learning objective, the Mastery Skills Check tests your skill with all the chapter's objectives. The Integrating Skills Check brings together your new skills and skills mastered in earlier chapters. Appendixes C and D provide the keystrokes and a reference to the chapter and section where skills needed to complete the exercise are covered in detail.

As you complete a chapter, you will find that you can use the skills immediately to create a wide variety of documents. After completing the last chapter, you will have acquired both beginning- and intermediate-level skills with WordPerfect. You will have gained these skills through hard work and repetition but without the frustration so often associated with learning a new package.

HOW THIS BOOK IS ORGANIZED

Teach Yourself WordPerfect 5.1 is divided into 4 parts containing 22 chapters. Parts I and II are designed to be worked through in sequential order. Part I covers the basic skills needed to create WordPerfect documents. Part II covers intermediate-level features that enhance the appearance of your documents and add flexibility to your basic skills. Part III focuses on special topics. You may be interested in all of these topics or just a few. The chapters in Part III can be read in any sequence you choose, according to your need to learn about a topic, since each special topic is not dependent on other special topics.

In Part IV, Appendixes A and B cover installation and hyphenation; Appendixes C and D provide answers to all exercises for both the pull-down menus and the WordPerfect function keys.

CONVENTIONS USED IN THIS BOOK

- *Menu selection approach*   Examples and exercises use the function key approach to feature selections. If you are using 5.1, you have the option of following the installation instructions in Appendix A to make the menus available. The instructions in parentheses show the menu selections you would make to perform the same task.

- *User Input*   Text to be typed into the computer is shown in **bold** type. When entering text, type it continuously, without pressing [Enter] at the end of each line, and do not insert hyphens. In general, use two spaces after a period. You should press [Enter] only at the end of a paragraph or a short line, or as otherwise instructed.

- *Keys*   Keys are shown in keycap symbols (except in Appendixes C and D). Keys to be pressed simultaneously are separated by hyphens. For example: [Shift]-[F3] . The names of function keys are followed by the key you should press. For example: Cancel ([F1]).

- *Answer Key*   Appendixes C and D provide answers to the exercises in the form of menu selections or keystroke sequences. The answers provide one workable solution; others are possible. The keystroke sequences you use may differ from those in

Appendixes C and D depending on the configuration and defaults of your computer system. The system used for developing the answers in this book included an IBM System 2 Model 70 with a VGA monitor and a Hewlett-Packard LaserJet Series II printer.

In the answers for Chapter 1, the entry SPACEBAR is used every time you need to press the spacebar. In subsequent chapters, it is only included where the required keystrokes would not be obvious without it.

In the answer keys, a set of brackets is used to encase function keys. For example: [SHIFT-F3]. A set of braces { } is used to encase descriptive information and directions. For example: {Move the cursor to the top line}. Section references for the Skills Checks, Mastery Skills Checks, and Integrating Skills Checks are found at the outer edge of the page.

OTHER OSBORNE/MCGRAW-HILL BOOKS OF INTEREST TO YOU

We hope that *Teach Yourself WordPerfect 5.1* will assist you in mastering this fine product, and will also pique your interest in learning more about other ways to better use your computer.

If you're interested in expanding your skills so you can be even more "computer efficient," be sure to take advantage of Osborne/McGraw-Hill's large selection of top-quality computer books that cover all varieties of popular hardware, software, programming languages, and operating systems. While we cannot list every title that may relate to WordPerfect and to your special computing needs, here are just a few books that complement *Teach Yourself WordPerfect 5.1*.

Teach Yourself DOS by Herbert Schildt is organized into 15-minute sessions that you can easily fit into your busy schedule. Each DOS technique is presented in hands-on examples and exercises with answers at the back of the book. Schildt also uses skill checks to help you determine whether you need to review material. All the essentials of DOS are presented here.

For all PC-DOS and MS-DOS users, from beginners who are somewhat familiar with the program to veteran users, with any DOS version up to 3.3, see *DOS: The Complete Reference, Second Edition* by Kris Jamsa. This book provides comprehensive coverage of every DOS command and feature. Whether you need an overview of the disk operating system or a reference for advanced programming and disk management techniques, you'll find it here.

1-2-3 Release 2.2 Made Easy by Mary Campbell takes you through all the basics of working with Lotus 1-2-3 Releases 2.0, 2.01, and 2.2, the popular spreadsheets for the IBM PC and compatible computers. From beginning concepts to intermediate techniques, you'll learn 1-2-3 as you follow "hands-on" lessons filled with examples and exercises. Also see *1-2-3 Release 3 Made Easy* if you have Lotus 1-2-3 Release 3.0.

1-2-3: From 2 to 3 by The LeBlond Group helps current users of 1-2-3 Releases 2.0, 2.01, or 2.2 make the jump to Release 3.0. Organized by task, the information you need to use Release 3's commands, features, and functions in business applications can be quickly located.

If you're looking for intermediate-level books on Lotus 1-2-3, see *Using 1-2-3 Release 2.2* by The LeBlond Group or *Using 1-2-3 Release 3* by Martin S. Matthews and Carole Boggs Matthews. Both are fast-paced, hands-on guides that quickly cover basics before discussing intermediate techniques (and even some advanced topics). *Using 1-2-3 Release 2.2* by The LeBlond Group is a book/disk package that also features an add-in word processor to use with Lotus 1-2-3 and is written by Geoff LeBlond, author of the outstanding book on using 1-2-3 that's sold over one million copies.

LEARN MORE ABOUT WORDPERFECT

Here is an excellent selection of other Osborne/McGraw-Hill books on WordPerfect that will help you build your skills and maximize the power of the word processor you have selected.

If you're upgrading from WordPerfect 5.0 to 5.1, you'll quickly discover all the benefits of WordPerfect's latest version with *WordPerfect: From 5.0 to 5.1* by Karen Acerson. All the new features of Release 5.1 are discussed so you'll know exactly how to use them and what has changed. WordPerfect 5.1 commands, features, and functions are described along with tips for best uses and short examples of business applications.

If you are just beginning WordPerfect 5 and are unfamiliar with other word processors (or even unfamiliar with computers), see *Teach Yourself WordPerfect 5* by Mary Campbell, a simple introduction to Word-Perfect 5 essentials with plenty of hands-on exercises.

If you are a beginning WordPerfect 5.1 user looking for an in-depth guide that leads you from basics to intermediate-level techniques, see *WordPerfect 5.1 Made Easy* by Mella Mincberg. If you are using Word-Perfect 5.0, look for *WordPerfect Made Easy, Series 5 Edition* or *WordPerfect Made Easy* if you have release 4.2. Both are by Mella Mincberg.

For a quick-paced book that covers basics before concentrating on intermediate-level skills and even some advanced topics, see *Using WordPerfect, Series 5 Edition* by Gail Todd. If you have WordPerfect for the Macintosh version 1.0, see *Using WordPerfect for the Macintosh* by Daniel Rosenbaum.

WordPerfect 5.1: The Complete Reference by Karen Acerson is ideal for all users. This desktop resource lists *every* WordPerfect 5.1 command, feature, and function along with brief discussions of how they are used. Acerson's *WordPerfect: The Complete Reference, Series 5 Edition* covers release 5.0 and *WordPerfect: The Complete Reference* covers release 4.2.

For a quick reference of only essential commands, see *WordPerfect 5.1: The Pocket Reference* by Mella Mincberg, or Mincberg's *WordPerfect 5: The Pocket Reference*, covering 5.0, or *WordPerfect: The Pocket Reference*, covering release 4.2.

WordPerfect: Secrets, Solutions, Shortcuts, Series 5 Edition by Mella Mincberg is jam-packed with all the tips, tricks, and hints you could want for extending WordPerfect Release 5 capabilities. Whether you're only somewhat familiar with WordPerfect or an experienced user with years of practice, you're bound to learn plenty of new techniques from this book.

If you're an experienced WordPerfect 5 user looking for books to help you refine your skills, see *Advanced WordPerfect, Series 5 Edition* by Eric Alderman and Lawrence Magid, which covers macros, mathematical capabilities, integrating WordPerfect with other software, and more. Also see *Getting the Most from WordPerfect 5* by Ruth Halpern for creating customized macros, handling desktop publishing, and using other sophisticated features.

▸Why◂

This Book Is for You

THIS BOOK'S OBJECTIVES

This book is for you if you are a beginning WordPerfect 5.0 or 5.1 user. If you are new to computers, word processing, or WordPerfect, you will find that this book offers the reinforcement you need to really master the basic features of WordPerfect 5.0 or 5.1. If you would like the benefits of a personal tutor to guide you through the product but lack the time or money for such a class, you can obtain the same benefits with this book. I have used the exercises and examples from the many WordPerfect training classes that I conduct to create the material in this book. You also have advantages in working from this book that classroom participants lack, since you can progress at your own pace at a far lower cost than even the most reasonable training alternatives.

A consistent set of learning techniques has been incorporated into every chapter to ensure that you can actually use WordPerfect features in practical business situations.

1

Unlike books that offer a quick once-over, you will find that this book requires you to try each of your new skills to ensure maximum retention of new information. Each chapter offers the following:

- A series of clear learning objectives that represent the new skills you will learn from the chapter.

- A SKILLS CHECK to test your knowledge of previous material and to ensure your readiness to master the next step.

- Several examples for each new learning objective presented. These examples present each feature in a practical application setting rather than in a theoretical discussion.

- Several exercises for each learning objective that will allow you to practice each new skill.

- A set of mastery exercises at the end of the chapter to test all the chapter objectives.

- A set of exercises that integrate the new skills you learned with skills from earlier chapters.

- Answer keys for both menu and function key solutions, so that there is no need to translate between the two approaches.

Essential WordPerfect Features

►Part I◄

WordPerfect's Basic Components

►1◄

CHAPTER OBJECTIVES

After completing this chapter, you should be able to:

► **Start a WordPerfect session**   1.1

► **End a WordPerfect session**   1.2

► **Clear the screen**   1.3

► **Locate and use special keyboard keys**   1.4

► **Master the use of the Help and Cancel keys**   1.5

► **Control the entry of uppercase and lowercase**   1.6

There are a few basic skills that you need to master before creating WordPerfect documents. You need to learn how to begin and end a WordPerfect session. You will want to become acquainted with the keyboard. Even if you have used a typewriter, you will need to learn how WordPerfect makes use of many of your computer's special keys.

Throughout this book you will receive all the help you need to master the skills presented, regardless of whether you are using WordPerfect 5.0 or Word-Perfect 5.1. If you have WordPerfect 5.1, you will find all the instructions you need for using either the function keys or the menus.

The instructions presented first in each example and exercise are for the 5.1 function key selections. In most cases these are the same function key assign-ments that you find in WordPerfect 5.0. No special mention will be made of 5.0 instructions as long as they are the same. Where different instructions are needed for 5.0, they are provided and clearly labeled.

Alternative pull-down menu instructions are shown in brackets following the function key selec-tions. These instructions assume that you are using WordPerfect 5.1 and have made the necessary choices in Setup to enable menu selections after pressing the [Alt] key. If the [Alt] key does not activate your menu, turn to the installation instructions at the end of Appendix A for additional help. You can also use a mouse to click any of the menu selections shown.

1.1   START A WORDPERFECT SESSION

Computer programs make it possible for your com-puter to perform a specific set of tasks. To use any program, you must load the program into the memory of your computer. WordPerfect is a computer program that provides sophisticated word processing capabilities to your computer. You must load Word-Perfect to make these word processing features available. Once WordPerfect is loaded in your machine, you can think of everything that you do as part of a WordPerfect session.

The process for loading WordPerfect is different for a hard disk than for a floppy disk. In either case, a copy of the operating system (for example, DOS 4.0) must be in your machine, and WordPerfect must already be installed. You will want to consult Appendix A for instructions if you are uncertain of either condition.

The two sets of instructions are for hard disk and floppy disk users who wish to invoke WordPerfect directly. If your screen displays a menu selection to begin WordPerfect, you can skip the directions that follow.

To start a WordPerfect session on a hard disk system:

a. Activate the subdirectory that contains the Word-Perfect files. If you installed WordPerfect according to the directions in Appendix A or the package documentation, you can type **cd \wp51 (cd \wp50** in 5.0) and press (Enter).

b. Type **wp** to start the WordPerfect program.

c. Press (Enter).

To start a WordPerfect session on a floppy disk system:

- ← Cursor

Doc 1 Pg 1 Ln 1" Pos 1"

| FIGURE 1-1. | The initial WordPerfect screen |

a. Type **b:** and press Enter to make drive B the current directory.

b. Place the disk labeled WordPerfect 1 in drive A.

c. Place a formatted disk for storing your word-processing documents in drive B.

d. Type **a:wp** and press Enter .

e. Replace the WordPerfect 1 disk with the Word-Perfect 2 disk when you see the message prompting you to do so.

f. Press any key to continue.

When WordPerfect is loaded, the program displays a blank *document*, as shown in Figure 1-1. A document is WordPerfect's basic structure for letters, reports, and other text entries. Everything you type is held in the current document, which you can store on disk.

The screen displays a blinking rectangle called the *cursor*. As you type, WordPerfect places each character at the cursor location and moves the cursor one position to the right. You can determine the current location of the cursor from the information in the *status line*. The status line indicates the current document, the current page number, and the cursor's distance from the top and left edges of the paper.

EXAMPLES

1. To start WordPerfect on a hard disk system, activate the directory where your WordPerfect files are stored by typing **cd \wp51** (**cd wp\50** in 5.0) and pressing ⌊Enter⌋. Then type **wp** and press ⌊Enter⌋ again to start the program. WordPerfect displays a blank screen like the one in Figure 1-1. Note the initial location of the cursor.

2. On a floppy disk system, place the WordPerfect 1 program disk in drive A and the data disk that will contain your text files in drive B. Type **b:** and press ⌊Enter⌋ to change the current disk drive to drive B. Next, type **a:wp** and press ⌊Enter⌋. At the prompt, replace the WordPerfect 1 disk with the Word-Perfect 2 disk and press any key to continue. WordPerfect is loaded into memory, and the screen looks like Figure 1-1.

EXERCISE

1. Begin a WordPerfect session on your computer.

1.2 | END A WORDPERFECT SESSION

When you have finished using WordPerfect, you end the WordPerfect session by exiting the program. Exiting WordPerfect removes the program from the computer's memory, allowing you to use other programs. When you exit, WordPerfect checks to see if you want to save the current document. If you exit WordPerfect without saving, the text you have in memory will be lost. In Chapter 2, you will learn how to save a document.

To exit WordPerfect:

a. Press the Exit [F7] key [[Alt] File Exit].

b. Type an **n** in response to WordPerfect's prompt for saving the file.

c. Type a **y** in response to WordPerfect's prompt for exiting WordPerfect. When you end a WordPerfect session, you are returned to the DOS prompt. On a hard disk, the prompt might appear as C> or C:\WP51> (C:\WP50 in 5.0). On a floppy disk system, the prompt will probably appear as B>.

EXAMPLES

1. You can exit from WordPerfect at any time. After loading WordPerfect, press the [A] key seven times. The screen looks like this:

aaaaaaa_

Press the Exit ([F7]) key [[Alt] File Exit] to exit. Type an **n** in response to WordPerfect's prompt for saving the document. Type a **y** in response to WordPerfect's prompt for exiting WordPerfect. The DOS prompt appears on your screen.

2. When you load WordPerfect again, the text that was on the screen from an earlier session does not reappear. Type **wp** (for a floppy disk system, **a:wp**) to begin a session. Note that the "a"s do not appear on the screen. Press the Exit [F7] key [[Alt] File Exit] to exit again. Type an **n** and a **y** to return to DOS.

EXERCISE

1. Begin a WordPerfect session. End the current WordPerfect session.

CLEAR THE SCREEN

1.3

You can clear the screen without exiting from Word-Perfect. This feature allows you to create many Word-Perfect documents in a single WordPerfect session. When you want to remove the document on the screen, you clear the screen by telling WordPerfect that you do not want to save the file and you do not want to exit WordPerfect.

To clear the screen:

a. Press the Exit ([F7]) key [[Alt] File Exit.

b. Type an **n** in response to WordPerfect's prompt for saving the file.

c. Type an **n** in response to WordPerfect's prompt for exiting WordPerfect.

These steps provide you with a blank screen identical to the initial screen that appeared when you started your WordPerfect session. In step c, you could press (Enter) instead, since WordPerfect offers **No** as the default response to the prompt.

Remember to clear the screen after each exercise and example throughout the book unless the instructions indicate otherwise. This chapter will include reminders, but after that you're on your own.

EXAMPLE

1. You can remove the text on a screen quickly if you do not need to save it. First, type

this text will be cleared from the screen quickly

Next, press the Exit ((F7)) key [(Alt) File Exit].

Type an **n** in response to WordPerfect's prompt for saving the document. Type an **n** in response to WordPerfect's prompt for exiting WordPerfect, or press (Enter) to accept the default. A blank screen results from your entries.

EXERCISES

1. Type **accounting**, and then clear the screen.

2. Type **trees**, and then clear the screen.

3. Type **1990 holidays**, and then clear the screen.

4. Type **bills, bills, and more bills**. Clear the screen.

LOCATE AND USE SPECIAL KEYBOARD KEYS $\boxed{1.4}$

You must become familiar with some of the special keyboard keys to use WordPerfect effectively. These keys move the cursor around in a document, provide access to WordPerfect features, and help you make changes to text. Figures 1-2 and 1-3 show the location of these keys on two popular keyboards. Table 1-1 lists some of the special keys that you will use when working with WordPerfect documents.

As you move around in a document, WordPerfect indicates the current location in the status line. The **Ln** (line) indicator tells you the position of the cursor from the top of a piece of paper. The **Pos** (position) indicator tells you the position of the cursor from the left edge of the paper. Both line and position are measured in inches in WordPerfect's original setup.

As you become proficient with the basic uses of WordPerfect's special keys, you will want to become familiar with the keys listed in Table 1-1.

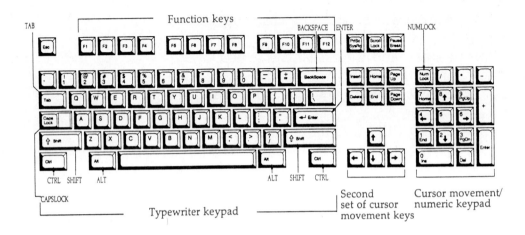

FIGURE 1-2.   The IBM XT and IBM enhanced keyboards

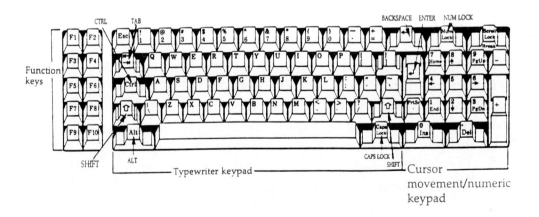

FIGURE 1-3.   The IBM standard keyboard

TABLE 1-1.	WordPerfect's Special Keys

Key Sequence	Action Taken
Enter	Ends a short line or a paragraph
Backspace	Deletes the character to the left of the cursor
↑	Moves the cursor up one line
↓	Moves the cursor down one line
←	Moves the cursor one character to the left
→	Moves the cursor one character to the right
PgUp	Moves the cursor to the preceding page
PgDn	Moves the cursor to the next page
End	Moves the cursor to the end of the line
Home	Moves the cursor in the direction of the arrow key that is pressed next. If you press the Home key once before pressing an arrow key, the cursor moves to the edge of the screen in the direction of the arrow. Using the Home and → key combination moves the cursor to the end of the line rather than to the edge of the screen if the line is not as wide as the screen. Pressing the Home key twice before pressing the ↑ or ↓ key moves the cursor to the top or the bottom of the document
Tab	Moves the cursor to the next tab stop. The initial settings for tabs are every 1/2 inch
Num Lock	Switches the numeric keypad at the side of the keyboard between numbers and the arrow keys
Ctrl Enter	Inserts a hard page break
Esc	Repeats a keystroke a specified number of times
Ctrl - →	Moves the cursor one word to the right
Ctrl - ←	Moves the cursor one word to the left
SCREEN UP (GREY −)	Moves the cursor to the top of the screen; if pressed again, moves the cursor to the previous screen
SCREEN DOWN (GREY +)	Moves the cursor to the bottom of the screen; if pressed again, moves the cursor to the next screen
Ctrl Home	Moves the cursor to a specified character or page
Function keys	The keys on the side or the top of the keyboard, labeled F1 through F10. These keys are used alone or combined with the Shift, Ctrl, and Alt keys to access. These keys are discussed in the chapters where their features are introduced.

NOTE: If you have version 5.1 and have installed a mouse, you can use the mouse to move around the screen.

EXAMPLES

1. You can use the [Enter] key to create blank lines in the document. Beginning with the initial Word-Perfect screen, press [Enter] three times. The cursor moves down three lines from its original position. The **Ln** indicator in the status line shows **1.5"**. Press the Exit ([F7]) key [[Alt] File Exit] and type **n** twice to clear the screen.

2. You can use the [Del] and [Backspace] keys to remove characters from the screen. First, type **abc**. Then press the [Backspace] key to delete the character to the left of the cursor. Next, press the [←] key twice to position the cursor under the letter "a." Press the [Del] key to delete the character above the cursor, leaving only the "b." Press the Exit ([F7]) key [[Alt] File Exit] and type **n** twice to clear the screen.

3. You can enter the same character repetitively with two shortcut features. You can use the [Esc] key to repeat a keystroke; for example, you can create a line of hyphens by using [Esc] to repeat a single hyphen (-). When you press the [Esc] key, the left side of the status line shows the number of times WordPerfect will repeat the character and looks like this:

`Repeat Value = 8`

You can control the number of repeats by typing a new number. For example, type **65** to tell Word-Perfect how many times it should repeat the keystroke that follows, and then type a hyphen. The result looks like this:

```
----------------------------------------------------------- -
```

You can also repeat a keystroke by holding down a key. However, it is more difficult to control the exact number of repeats with this approach. First, press [Enter] to move to the next line. Create another hyphenated line by holding down the hyphen key. After creating the second line of hyphens, press [Enter] to move to the next line. Press the Exit ([F7]) key [[Alt] File Exit] and type **n** twice to clear the screen.

4. You can use the arrow keys to move in any direction on the screen. Type **abc** and press [Enter]. Next, type **def** and press [Enter]. Type **ghi** and press [Enter] to place text on the third line of the document. The screen looks like this:

```
abc
def
ghi
-
```

When you press the [↑] key once, the cursor moves to the "g." When you press the [→] key twice, the cursor moves to the "i." Pressing the [↑] key two more times moves the cursor to the "c." Pressing the [←] key twice moves the cursor to the "a." Press

the ⊡ key once to move to the "d." Press the Exit
(F7) key [Alt File Exit] and type **n** twice to clear
the screen.

5. The numeric keypad keys provide an alternative
when you need to enter many numbers. You can
use the Num Lock key to switch the numeric keypad
between number keys and cursor movement keys.
When you press the Num Lock key to turn it on, the **Pos**
indicator in the status line flashes. Type **46.73** on the
numeric keypad keys and press Enter. When you
press the Num Lock key again, the **Pos** indicator stops
flashing. When Num Lock is not on, you can use the
numeric keypad keys for the functions that are
shown below the numbers. For example, if you
press 8 on the numeric keypad, the keypad
registers an ⊡ to move the cursor back to the line
containing "46.73." Press the Exit (F7) key [Alt]
File Exit] and type **n** twice to clear the screen.

6. Special keystroke combinations make it easy to
move the cursor more than one position at a time
through the document. First, type

a stitch in time saves nine.

Pressing the ⊡ key while holding down the Ctrl
key moves the cursor one word to the left. Press
Ctrl-⊡ six times to move to the word "a." You can
move the cursor one word to the right with the
Ctrl-⊡ combination. Press Ctrl-⊡ six times to
move back to the end of the line. To move to the
end of the line more quickly, press the End key.
Press the Exit (F7) key [Alt File Exit] and type **n**
twice to clear the screen.

7. Three keys, [Alt], [Ctrl], and [Shift], are used in combination with other keys; they normally do not perform any action by themselves. Press the [Alt] key; nothing happens. If you are using WordPerfect's pull-down menu system, pressing the [Alt] key activates the pull-down menu. Press the [Shift] key and then the [Ctrl] key; in both cases, nothing happens. However, when used with other keys, these keys provide features that are not otherwise available. You can press the [Ctrl] key simultaneously with the [Enter] key [[Alt] Layout Align Hard Page] to create a page break. This feature overrides WordPerfect's automatic page breaks and causes a new page to start at the current location. Press the [Ctrl]-[Enter] key combination [[Alt] Layout Align Hard Page] to generate this display:

```
================================================================================
```

WordPerfect displays the current page number after **Pg** in the status line. Press the Exit ([F7]) key [[Alt] File Exit] and type **n** twice to clear the screen.

8. You can use the [PgUp] and [PgDn] keys to move from page to page in a document. Create the first page in a two-page document by typing **existing clients** and pressing [Ctrl]-[Enter] [[Alt] Layout Align Hard Page]. To complete the second page, type **prospective clients**.

When you press [PgUp], you move from page two to page one. When you press [PgDn], you move from page one to page two. WordPerfect displays the first line of the page at the top of the screen. Another way of moving to a different page is using Ctrl - Home [Alt Search Go To]. When you hold down Ctrl and press Home [Alt Layout Align Hard Page], WordPerfect prompts you for the number of the page on which you want the cursor placed. When you type a **1** and press Enter, Word-Perfect moves the cursor to the top of page 1. Press the Exit (F7) key [Alt File Exit] and type **n** twice to clear the screen.

9. You can move from screen to screen in a document with the SCREEN DOWN (GREY +) and SCREEN UP (GREY −) keys. First, type the number **1** 24 times, following each entry with Enter. Next, type the number **2** 24 times, following each entry with Enter. If NUM LOCK is on, press the Num Lock key to turn it off. When you press the SCREEN UP (GREY −) key, WordPerfect moves the cursor to the top of the current screen. When you press the SCREEN UP (GREY −) key again, WordPerfect displays the preceding screen, containing the 1s. If you press the SCREEN DOWN (GREY +) key once, WordPerfect moves the cursor to the bottom of the current screen. If you press it again, WordPerfect moves down to the next screen. Use the entries in this example for the one that follows.

10. You can use the Home key in combination with other keys to move through the entries in the current document. If you press the Home key and then press the ↑ key, the cursor moves to the top

line in the screen. If you press the [Home] key and the [↓] key, the cursor moves to the bottom line of the screen. If the text is too short to fill the screen, the cursor moves to the last line of the document. Press the [Home] key twice and the [↑] key once to move the cursor to the beginning of the document. Press the [Home] key twice and the [↓] key once to move the cursor to the end of the document. Press the Exit ([F7]) key [[Alt] File Exit] and type **n** twice to clear the screen.

11. Once you have a line of text, you can move quickly through it by using the [Home] key in combination with other keys. First, press [Esc], type **20**, and type an equal sign (=). When you press the [Home] key and then the [←] key, the cursor moves to the first character in the line. When you press the [Home] key and then the [→] key, the cursor moves to the end of the line. As you saw in example 7, you can also press [End] to move the cursor to the end of the line. Press the Exit ([F7]) key [[Alt] File Exit] and type **n** twice to clear the screen.

12. The [Tab] key moves the cursor to the next tab stop to the right. Initially, these tab stops are set for every 1/2 inch. You can use the [Tab] key to indent the beginning of an entry. Press the [Tab] key and then type **the meeting is scheduled for the 19th**. Next, press [Enter]. Press the [Tab] key six times. When you do, the **Pos** indicator shows that the cursor is 4 inches from the left edge of the paper. Pressing the [←] key moves the cursor to the preceding tab stop because there is no text be-

tween the cursor location and the previous tab stop. Press the Exit ([F7]) key [[Alt] File Exit] and type **n** twice to clear the screen.

13. Some of the keys can be confused with one another, since they perform similar functions. For example, the [←] key is frequently confused with the [Backspace] key. The [Backspace] key removes the character to the left of the cursor and moves the cursor and the character above it to that position. The [←] key moves the cursor one character to the left but leaves all characters intact. You can see how this works by pressing [Esc], typing **10**, and typing a period. Next, press the [←] key three times. This moves you to the eighth period. Next, press the [Backspace] key three times. This removes three periods. Although the cursor is still below the third period from the end of the line, that period is now the fifth one. Press the Exit ([F7]) key [[Alt] File Exit] and type **n** twice to clear the screen.

14. Two other keys that can be confused with each other are the SPACEBAR and the [→] key. The SPACEBAR inserts a space and moves the cursor and any character above it to the right. All characters to the right of the cursor also move to the right. The [→] key moves the cursor one character to the right but leaves all characters intact. To illustrate how these keys work, press [Esc], type **10**, and type an **x**. To move to the beginning of the line, press the [Home] key and the [←] key. Press the [→] key four times.

Then press the SPACEBAR four times. The text looks like this:

xxx   xxxxx

The SPACEBAR has inserted four spaces and moved the text four characters to the right. The ➡ key moved the cursor four characters to the right but did not insert any spaces or move any characters. Press the Exit (F7) key [Alt File Exit] and type **n** twice to clear the screen.

15. If you are using 5.1 and have installed a mouse according to the directions in Appendix A, you can use your mouse with WordPerfect. If the mouse is installed, rolling it across the desktop will cause a mouse cursor to appear on the screen. This cursor appears as a box and marks your place on the screen. Later you will learn how to click the mouse buttons to perform specific tasks after moving the mouse cursor. Pressing Del, Backspace, or one of the arrow keys causes this cursor to disappear from the screen until you roll the mouse on the desktop again.

EXERCISES

1. Press Enter six times. Use the arrow keys to move to the top of the document and then to the bottom of the document. Clear the screen.

2. Create ten "a"s using the [Esc] key. Create another ten "a"s by holding down the [A] key. Use the [←] and [→] keys to move through this line. Move to the end of the line and press [Enter]. Clear the screen.

3. Use the [Tab] key to move the cursor to 3 inches from the left edge of the page. Use the [←] key to move back to the left side of the screen. Clear the screen.

4. Press [Ctrl]-[Enter] [[Alt] Layout Align Hard Page] four times. Use the [PgUp] and [PgDn] keys to move among the five pages. Use [Ctrl]-[Home] [[Alt] Search Go To] to move to specific pages. Clear the screen.

5. Type

   the early bird gets the worm.

   Press [Enter] and the [↑] key. Use WordPerfect's cursor movement keys to move from word to word and to the beginning and the end of the line. Clear the screen.

6. Create a six-page document with four blank lines on each page. Move a screen at a time to the top and the bottom of the document. Use the [Home] key and the arrow keys to move to the top and the bottom of the document. Check the status line after each move to see where you are. Clear the screen.

7. Use the numeric keypad to enter the following:

   123456789

Clear the screen.

8. Type the following:

abc

Use the [Backspace] key to delete the "c." Use the [←] key to position the cursor under the "a" and delete the "a."

MASTER THE USE OF THE HELP AND CANCEL KEYS

1.5

WordPerfect has two function keys that are useful for all tasks. The Help ([F3]) key [[Alt] Help Help] provides help on any topic. The Cancel ([F1]) key [[Alt] Edit Undelete] cancels a WordPerfect command or recovers deleted text. You can use the Cancel ([F1]) [[Alt] Edit Undelete] key to restore any of the last three deletions you have made. If you accidentally press one of the function keys, you will invoke a WordPerfect command. To cancel a WordPerfect command, press the Cancel ([F1]) key until you are returned to your document.

To use the Help key:

a. Insert the WordPerfect 1 disk in drive B if you are using a floppy disk system.

b. Press the Help ([F3]) key [[Alt] Help Help].

c. Type the first letter of the subject for which you want help, or press the function key for which you want help.

d. Press (Enter) or the SPACEBAR to return to your document.

If you press (F3) twice [(Alt) Help Template], the WordPerfect template displays all the function key assignments.

To use the Cancel key to cancel a command:

a. Press the Cancel ((F1)) key until your document displays on the screen.

To use the Cancel key to restore text:

a. Press the Cancel ((F1)) key [(Alt) Edit Undelete]. WordPerfect displays the most recently deleted text at the cursor location.

b. Type a **2** or a **p** if you want to restore a previous deletion.

c. Type a **1** or an **r** to restore the displayed deletion.

EXAMPLES

1. You can use the Help ((F3)) key [(Alt) Help Help] to display information about the cursor movement keys. Press the Help ((F3)) key [(Alt) Help Help]; then type a **c**, for cursor movement. The screen displays information on features that begin with the letter "c." Type **c** twice to see the second and third screens of topics, where you will find "Cursor Movement." You could also press any of the cursor movement keys to display their functions. Press the SPACEBAR or (Enter) to leave Help.

2. You can use the Cancel ([F1]) key to cancel any command request. You press the Exit ([F7]) key [[Alt] File Exit] to request WordPerfect to save a file. If you change your mind, you can cancel this request by pressing the Cancel ([F1]) key.

3. You can use the Cancel ([F1]) key [[Alt] Edit Undelete] to restore deleted characters. First, type

fourscore and seven years ago

With the cursor at the end of this phrase, press the [Backspace] key until all of the text is removed. Then, press the Cancel ([F1]) key [[Alt] Edit Undelete]. WordPerfect displays the deleted text in a different color or highlighted. To restore this text, type a **1** or an **r**. Press the Exit ([F7]) key [[Alt] File Exit] and type **n** twice to clear the screen.

4. You can restore the most recent deletion or either of the prior two deletions. Type **first** and press [Enter]. Next, type **second** and press [Enter]. Type **third** as the last entry, without pressing [Enter]. Move to the first line and delete the word "first" with the [Backspace] key. Next, press the [↓] key, and delete the word "second" by pressing the [Del] key six times. Press the [↓] key again, and press the [Del] key five times to delete the word "third." When you press the Cancel ([F1]) key [[Alt] Edit Undelete], the word "third" is displayed. If you type a **2**, WordPerfect displays the word "second." Typing a **2** again displays the word "first." Typing a **1** restores this selection. Press the Exit ([F7]) key [[Alt] File Exit] and type **n** twice to clear the screen.

EXERCISES

1. Use the Help (F3) key [Alt Help Help] to determine how to move to the next screen down or up.

2. Type this sentence:

   he suddenly left.

   Delete "suddenly" and use the Cancel (F1) key [Alt Edit Undelete] to place it after the word "left." Clear the screen.

3. Use the Help (F3) key [Alt Help Help] to view the template for the function keys.

4. Use the Help (F3) key [Alt Help Help] to look at the keys used to delete characters.

5. Type the following:

   it was a cold, dark, scary evening

   Delete the word "dark" and the comma and space that follow it. Using the Cancel (F1) key, [Alt Edit Undelete] place it in front of "cold" as the first adjective in the sentence. Clear the screen.

1.6 CONTROL THE ENTRY OF UPPERCASE AND LOWERCASE

When you are typing text in WordPerfect, you will want to make some of the letters uppercase and some lowercase. Your keyboard has two types of keys to change the case of letters that you type. The [Shift] key changes the case of any letter that you type when you are pressing this key. The [Shift] key also enables you to type special characters that appear on the number keys and on other keys. The [Caps Lock] key allows you to switch between typing uppercase and lowercase letters without having to hold down the [Shift] key.

To type a capitalized letter or a special character with the [Shift] key:

a. Press the [Shift] key and hold it down.

b. Type the letter that you want capitalized, or press the key displaying a special symbol above a number or above another character.

c. Release the [Shift] key.

To type capitalized letters with the [Caps Lock] key:

a. Press the [Caps Lock] key.

b. Type the letters that you want capitalized.

c. Press the [Caps Lock] key.

Using the [Shift] key with [Caps Lock] on causes Word-Perfect to enter lowercase characters.

EXAMPLES

1. You can type a series of capital letters with the [Shift] key. Hold down the [Shift] key and type

MEMORANDUM

Press the Exit ([F7]) key [[Alt] File Exit] and type **n** twice to clear the screen.

2. You can capitalize some letters and enter others in lowercase by selectively pressing the [Shift] key. Hold down the [Shift] key and type

ABC C

These letters are entered in uppercase. Release the [Shift] key and type

orporation

These letters appear in lowercase. The screen looks like this:

ABC Corporation_

Press the Exit ([F7]) key [[Alt] File Exit] and type **n** twice to clear the screen.

3. You can use the [Shift] key to type special characters. Hold down the [Shift] key and type

TO:

Without the [Shift] key, the entry would have produced a semicolon (;). The [Shift] key causes Word-Perfect to use the symbol at the top of the key. Press the Exit ([F7]) key [[Alt] File Exit] and type **n** twice to clear the screen.

4. You can use the [Caps Lock] key when you want to type many capitalized letters. First, press [Caps Lock]. The **Pos** in the status line changes to **POS**. For some keyboards, a CAPS LOCK indicator lights up. Type

MEMORANDUM

Press [Caps Lock] again to return to lowercase letter entries. The **POS** in the status line changes back to **Pos**. Using the [Caps Lock] key is easier than holding down the [Shift] key when you have many capital letters to type. Press the Exit ([F7]) key [[Alt] File Exit] and type **n** twice to clear the screen.

5. You can type capital letters and use number keys at the same time. When CAPS LOCK is on, the keyboard still treats the number keys at the top of keyboard as numbers. Press [Caps Lock] and type

SATURDAY 15TH

Even though the letter keys behave as if you are pressing the [Shift] key, the number keys do not. To type the symbols above the numbers, you still must press the [Shift] key while you press the number. Press the Exit ([F7]) key [[Alt] File Exit] and type **n** twice to clear the screen.

EXERCISES

1. Use the [Shift] key to type these characters:

JQLYZBEANL

Clear the screen.

2. Use the (Shift) key selectively to type

The ABC Corporation makes Tiger sedans.

Clear the screen.

3. Without using the separate numeric keypad, type

The lending rate is 15%.
(16*2) + 7 = 39
Profit & Loss Statement

Clear the screen.

4. Use the (Caps Lock) and (Shift) keys to type

CAPITALIZATION CAN EMPHASIZE TEXT
WORDPERFECT makes typing FUN.

Clear the screen.

5. Use the (Caps Lock) key to type

THE LOCAL CAR DEALERSHIP IS OFFERING 16%
APR.
COMPANY PICNIC 8/19/90

Clear the screen.

EXERCISES

1. Exit WordPerfect.

2. Load WordPerfect.

3. Type the following lines. If you make a mistake, use the ⌨Del or ⌨Backspace key.

   August 15th or SEPTEMBER 3RD
   3^2 + (8∗9)

4. Find help on exiting WordPerfect.

5. Clear the screen.

6. Type the following lines. If you make a mistake, use the ⌨Del or ⌨Backspace key.

   10:34 AM
   ACME CORPORATION

7. Exit WordPerfect.

Creating a WordPerfect Document

CHAPTER OBJECTIVES

After completing this chapter, you should be able to:

▶ **Use WordPerfect's defaults to enter text**   2.1

▶ **Save a document**   2.2

▶ **Retrieve a document**   2.3

▶ **Add missing characters (Insert mode)**   2.4

▶ **Replace existing characters (Typeover mode)**   2.5

▶ **Delete characters, words, and lines**   2.6

WordPerfect records your every keystroke in a document. You can create a document for a memo, a letter, a list of names and addresses, a report, and so on. As you type, your document is stored in the memory of your computer system. WordPerfect handles the placement of the words you type on a page and provides default settings that can be used for all your documents. These settings automatically control many features, such as the amount of white space at the edges of your document. After creating a document, you can save it onto a disk for use at a later time.

The ability to recall documents can significantly increase your productivity. No longer will you need to retype an entire document because of an error. You can recall the document and correct the text in error. If you have a document stored on disk that is similar to one you currently need, you can retrieve the document from disk and revise it as necessary. Again, the time required is only a fraction of the time required to type a new document.

SKILLS CHECK

(Do not clear the screen unless instructed to do so.)

1. Start WordPerfect, and type the following exactly as shown:

    A PENNY SAVED IS A penny earned.

    Clear the screen.

2. Type the following:

TO: John Smith
FROM: Mary Brown
SUBJECT: 1990 Holiday Schedule

3. Use the [Esc] key to add a line of dashes under the entries from skills check 2.

4. Add three blank lines after the entry from skills check 3. Then type the following:

    The attached holiday schedule should be circulated to all employees as soon as possible. Note that company holidays have increased to 8.

5. Add a hard page break below your entries and type the following on page 2:

January 1	New Year's Day
January 12	Founders' Day
March 30	Spring holiday
April 3	Easter holiday
May 30	Memorial Day
July 4	Independence Day
November 28	Thanksgiving
December 25	Christmas

6. Move the cursor to page 1 using the [Ctrl]-[Home] option.

7. Move to the end of the document.

8. Move to the beginning of the document.

9. Clear the screen.

10. Review the Help screen for exiting WordPerfect.

11. Exit WordPerfect.

2.1 USE WORDPERFECT'S DEFAULTS TO ENTER TEXT

WordPerfect provides a set of default settings for each new document that you create. Default settings are available to you automatically, without any work on your part. The availability of these settings means that you can begin typing without having to worry about laying out the format for your document. Figure 2-1 shows a printed copy of a WordPerfect page. The white space at the top, bottom, and sides is referred to as the *margins*. WordPerfect allows for a 1-inch margin on all sides of a document. The lines of the document are single-spaced on the page. Later you will learn to change the basic document format, but for now you will need to understand what WordPerfect provides.

When you type on a typewriter, you need to be conscious of the bell that signals the end of a line. With WordPerfect, you can type without regard for the end of the line, since WordPerfect uses a feature called *word wrap*. This feature breaks each line at an appropriate place to maintain the right margin. Word-Perfect moves additional text to the next line without requiring you to press Enter. As you edit the text in a paragraph, WordPerfect automatically adjusts the lines to fit the width of the document. WordPerfect manages the placement of text on the page, creating a professional appearance as in the sample output in Figure 2-1.

Learning To Use WordPerfect

WordPerfect is one of the best word processing packages available today. The short, easy-to-follow lessons in this book are designed to teach you the basic skills. Before long, you will be able to create all types of documents.

This book uses a learning-by-example approach and avoids lengthy discussions of features. The chapters are organized by lessons, each focusing on a learning objective. As you master each learning objective, you will acquire a new WordPerfect skill.

You learned a few basic skills before creating your first document. You learned to begin and end a WordPerfect session. You learned the location of some important keys on the keyboard.

Now that you know a few of the basics, you are ready to create a document. WordPerfect records your every keystroke in a document. You can create a document for a letter, a memo, a list of names and addresses, a report, and so on. As you type your document is stored in the memory of your computer system. WordPerfect handles the placement of words you place on a page and provides default settings that can be used for all of your documents. The settings automatically control many features, such as the amount of white space at the edges of your document. After creating a document, you can save it onto a disk for later use.

You can add emphasis to your text with WordPerfect's special features. Underlining, boldfacing, and centering help to set off text from the rest of your document. WordPerfect changes the appearance of text on the screen to indicate these special features. WordPerfect also adds hidden codes to the document for these features.

If you do not add special features to your text as you type it, WordPerfect allows you to add them later. To add the special feature to existing text, you must first block the text and then have WordPerfect apply the feature.

WordPerfect also allows you to change the appearance of lines of text. You can change the margin settings to allow more or less white space at the left and right edges of the paper. Lines can also be offset from the left and right edges of the paper, allowing you to offset bullet items or other important text.

Normally you will want at least one printed copy of every document you create. Some people prefer to proof first drafts of their documents from printed copies. Also, a printed copy is usually the medium used to share the information in your document with others.

WordPerfect offers a considerable amount of flexibility in its

FIGURE 2-1.   Manuscript printed with WordPerfect's defaults

You can tell WordPerfect exactly where you want a line to end by pressing [Enter]. The next text you type will be placed on a new line. You should use [Enter] to end a paragraph or a short line.

NOTE: On account of typesetting considerations, the lengths of lines in the entries you will type will not exactly match the text shown in the book. When entering text, remember to press [Enter] only at the end of a paragraph or a short line, or as otherwise instructed.

To enter text using WordPerfect's word wrap feature:

a. Type the text without pressing [Enter] at the end of each line.

b. Press [Enter] at the end of each paragraph.

To enter text without using the word wrap feature:

a. Type the text that you want on the line.

b. Press [Enter] to end the line.

EXAMPLES

1. WordPerfect's word wrap feature and default margin settings are automatically applied to the text you type. To see how WordPerfect handles text entries that extend for more than one line, type

ABC's new dryer automatically stops when the clothes are dry. It determines when to stop by checking the humidity inside the dryer. This feature prevents shrinkage that occurs from overdrying clothes.

Since you did not press ⟨Enter⟩, the screen looks like this:

```
ABC's new dryer automatically stops when the clothes are dry. It
determines when to stop by checking the humidity inside the dryer.
This feature prevents shrinkage that occurs from overdrying
clothes. _
```

Depending on the initial settings for your printer, WordPerfect may wrap your text differently, causing your screen to appear different from the examples. Your screen may also appear different if you type only one space, rather than two, after a period. You will use this entry in the next example, so do not clear the screen.

2. Word wrap and margin settings remain in effect when you edit the text entered in example 1. First, press the ⬆ key twice, the ⟨Home⟩ key once, the ⬅ key once, ⟨Ctrl⟩-➡ three times, and the ⬅ key once to move the cursor to the space between "dryer" and "automatically". Next, type a comma, press SPACEBAR, type **Just Dri** as the dryer's name, and type another comma. WordPerfect does not realign the entries on the screen until you move the cursor. After you press the ➡ key, the screen looks like this:

```
ABC's new dryer, JustDri, automatically stops when the clothes are
dry. It determines when to stop by checking the humidity inside the
dryer. This feature prevents shrinkage that occurs from overdrying
clothes.
```

3. Pressing Enter forces WordPerfect to begin a new line even if the first line is not full. Use Enter to type short lines, such as the ones in address labels. First, type

Carol Gallagan

Since this is the only text for this line, press Enter. Next, type

Medical Associates, Inc.

After you type this, end this line by pressing Enter. Enter the street address by typing

4511 Valley Street

To end this line, press Enter. Finally, finish the address information by typing

New Haven, CT 03421

Press Enter to end the line. The screen looks like this:

```
Carol Gallagan
Medical Associates, Inc.
4511 Valley Street
New Haven, CT 03421
```

4. Enter is also used to end paragraphs. First, press Tab and type

Enclosed are the insurance forms that Dr. Wilbur must fill out for my insurance claim. I will stop by next Tuesday to pick them up.

To end the paragraph, press ⌴Enter⌴. For the next paragraph, press ⌴Tab⌴ and type

I have enclosed a check to cover my August 20th visit. Please note this payment on the insurance form.

Since you have finished the second paragraph, press ⌴Enter⌴. The screen looks like this:

```
     Enclosed are the insurance forms that Dr. Wilbur must fill out
for my insurance claim. I will stop by next Tuesday to pick them
up.
     I have enclosed a check to cover my August 20th visit. Please
note this payment on the insurance form.
-
```

If you had not used ⌴Enter⌴ to separate the paragraphs, WordPerfect would have combined them.

EXERCISES

1. Type these lines, using the ⌴Enter⌴ key to separate them:

   January 21, 1991
   The meeting is next Friday.
   They are planning to have lunch at the Cozy Corner restaurant.
   Johnston Company stock is currently selling at 8 3/8.

2. Type this paragraph using WordPerfect's word wrap feature:

   The Stone Corporation is merging with the Johnston Company. The new company's name will be Johnston

Stone Corporation. The Stone Corporation manufactures jewelry. Johnston's main product line, raw stones, ensures the Stone Corporation a constant supply.

3. Type this list, using [Enter] at the end of each item in the list. Allow WordPerfect's word wrap feature to wrap the items that extend for more than one line.

Stones and Their Descriptions
Opal - Comes in various colors and varieties, all of which have an iridescent reflection of light
Garnet - Primarily crimson but also can be brown, green, yellow, or black
Topaz - A yellow, white, green, or blue stone that is transparent or translucent
Sapphire - A blue stone that is almost as hard as a diamond

4. Type the following paragraphs:

One frequent cause of problems is the use of an incorrect word or expression. Incorrect word usage can cause readers to lose part of the meaning in your writing.

"Casual" and "causal" are two words that are sometimes interchanged. "Casual" is synonymous with "relaxed" and "low-key." "Causal" relates to involvement with a cause.

2.2 SAVE A DOCUMENT

As you type a document, it is stored in the memory of your computer system. Although WordPerfect can save documents automatically, it does not normally save documents automatically, it does not normally save them unless you specifically request it to do so. If the power to your system goes off, you will lose your entire document if you have not saved it. If the power is lost after you save a document, you will lose any changes or additions you made since the last time you saved the document. Saving frequently is a way to minimize the risk of losing the text you type.

When you save a WordPerfect file, you must follow the rules of the DOS operating system for naming the file. A filename is a combination of up to eight letters, numbers, and certain symbols. It cannot contain spaces. You can also use an optional one- to three-character filename extension after the filename. If you use a filename extension, you must separate it from the filename with a period (.). Each filename on a disk or in a subdirectory must be unique on that disk or in that subdirectory. To make files easier to find, give each document a name that relates to the document's contents.

To save a document and clear the screen or exit WordPerfect:

a. Press the Exit ([F7]) key [[Alt] File Exit].

b. Type a **y** in response to WordPerfect's prompt for saving the document.

c. Type a filename.

d. Optionally, type a period followed by a filename extension.

e. Press [Enter].

f. Type an **n** or press [Enter] to clear the screen or type a **y** to exit WordPerfect.

To save a document without clearing the document from the screen:

a. Press the Save ((F10)) key [(Alt) File Save].

b. Type a filename.

c. Optionally, type a period followed by a filename extension.

d. Press (Enter).

If you have already named the file, WordPerfect prompts you with the filename when you press the Exit ((F7)) key [(Alt) File Exit] and type a **y** or when you press the Save ((F10)) key [(Alt) File Save]. You can press (Enter) to accept that filename or type a new one before pressing (Enter). If you accept the current filename, you will need to confirm that you want the current document to replace the old contents of the file by typing a **y**.

EXAMPLES

1. You can save a document and clear the screen. First, type the following document:

```
Current Sales      $456,000
Last Year's Sales  $400,000
Growth in Sales    14%
```

To save this file, press the Exit ((F7)) key [(Alt) File Exit]. When WordPerfect asks you whether or not you want to save the document, type a **y**. Next, WordPerfect prompts you for the filename. Type **sales** and press ⏎. The document is saved on your disk. WordPerfect asks if you want to leave WordPerfect. Type an **n**. The screen is cleared.

2. You can save a document without clearing the screen. First, type

```
Memo
To: All Employees
From: Human Resources
Re: Christmas Party
```

Press ⏎ and then the ⇥ key, and type

The company Christmas party will be on December 21 at 6:30 p.m.

Next, press the Save (F10) key [Alt File Save]. When WordPerfect prompts you for the filename, type **xmas** and press ⏎. WordPerfect returns to the document instead of clearing the screen. Also, WordPerfect displays the filename in the status line. You will use this file in the next example.

3. There is one added step when you save a file a second time. Add the following text to the document from example 2:

Dinner will be served at 8. Dancing will begin at 9:30.

Next, press the Exit (F7) key [Alt File Exit] and type a **y** to save the file. WordPerfect displays the filename XMAS, which you used when saving the file the first time. Since this is the correct filename, press ⏎.

WordPerfect prompts you to see if you want to replace the data stored on disk with the data in the current document. Type a **y** to override the default of **No** that would be selected if you pressed `Enter`.

WordPerfect asks if you want to exit WordPerfect. Press `Enter` to accept the default and clear the screen.

4. You can create multiple copies of a document on a disk by saving it under different names. This allows you to create a document and modify a copy of it for another purpose. First, type

Jim Allen
Allen & Associates, CPA's
412 Oakland
Tallahassee, FL 31245

If you need to send two letters to Jim Allen, you can save the name and address with two different filenames to avoid having to type them twice. Press the Save (`F10`) key [`Alt` File Save].

Next, WordPerfect prompts you for the filename. Type **allen1** and press `Enter`.

To save it again, press the Save (`F10`) key [`Alt` File Save].

WordPerfect displays the filename ALLEN1 for the document. Since you want to save the document under a different name, type **allen2** and press `Enter`. After completing the letter in ALLEN1, you can save that document and begin typing the other letter in ALLEN2.

EXERCISES

1. Type the following and save it as STITCH:

   A stitch in time saves nine.

2. Type the following and save it as NAME:

   Jim Allen
   1123 Fork Rd.
   Baltimore, Maryland 21237

   Save this document again as NAME2, and clear the screen.

3. Type the following:

   Insanity is hereditary. You can get it from your kids.
   Sam Levenson

   Save the file as KIDS, and clear the screen.

4. Type the following:

   A man who has never gone to school may steal from a freight car; but if he has a university education, he may steal the whole railroad.
   Theodore Roosevelt

   Save the file as TEDDY. Save it again as SCHOOL, and clear the screen.

RETRIEVE A DOCUMENT

2.3

Documents saved to a disk can be retrieved. If a document is retrieved when the screen is clear, the document in memory will consist of the document from the disk. If there is already text in the current document, the text in the document stored on disk will be added to the text in memory at the position of the cursor.

To retrieve a document:

a. Press the Retrieve (Shift - F10) key [Alt File Retrieve].

b. Type the filename of the document that you want.

c. Press Enter .

After WordPerfect retrieves the file, it displays the filename in the status line. If WordPerfect cannot find the document, it displays a message, such as this one it displayed when it could not find BUDG_RPT:

ERROR: File not found -- BUDG.RPT

EXAMPLES

1. To work with a document you created and saved earlier, you can retrieve it. First, press the Tab key and type the following:

    The next meeting of the WordPerfect User Group is April 20th.

    Press Enter to end the paragraph. Press the Exit (F7) key [Alt File Exit] to save the document and clear the screen. Press Enter , type **user**, and press Enter twice more. The screen is cleared. At this point, you can type a new document or retrieve any document on disk. Press the Retrieve ([Shift]-[F10]) key [[Alt] File Retrieve]. WordPerfect displays this prompt:

Document to be retrieved:

Type **user** and press [Enter]. The document saved as USER appears on the screen like this:

  _   The next meeting of the WordPerfect User Group is April 28th.

The filename appears in the status line. Do not clear the screen.

2. You can retrieve a file with a document already on the screen. Retrieve USER again. There will be two copies of the text on the screen. Clear the screen. Retrieve the ALLEN1 file you saved in section 2.2 by pressing the Retrieve ([Shift]-[F10]) key [[Alt] File Retrieve], typing **allen1**, and pressing [Enter]. Move to the end of the document by pressing [Home], [Home], and the [↓] key. Next, press [Enter] twice to add two blank lines. Retrieve the USER file by pressing the Retrieve ([Shift]-[F10]) key [[Alt] File Retrieve], typing **user**, and pressing [Enter]. The screen looks like this:

Jim Allen
Allen & Associates CPA's
412 Oakland
Tallahassee, FL 31245

  _   The next meeting of the WordPerfect User Group is April 28th.

Before you retrieve a file, be sure that the screen is clear, unless you want to combine files.

EXERCISES

1. Retrieve the file STITCH created in exercise 1 of section 2.2.

2. Retrieve the file NAME created in exercise 2 of section 2.2. Next, retrieve STITCH again without clearing the screen first.

3. Retrieve the file TEDDY created in exercise 4 of section 2.2. Without clearing the screen, retrieve the file a second time. Clear the screen.

4. Type

   Favorite Quotes

   Press Enter and retrieve the file KIDS. Retrieve the file TEDDY. Clear the screen.

2.4 ADD MISSING CHARACTERS (INSERT MODE)

WordPerfect allows you to add a missing character, word, or paragraph at any location in a document. After typing a document, you can edit it to add the information omitted initially. Since WordPerfect's default setting is the Insert mode, you only need to check that the setting has not been changed. The

Insert mode places any character you type to the left of the cursor. If the insertion causes text to extend beyond the right margin, WordPerfect automatically reformats the text to change the word wrap location when you move the cursor.

To use Insert mode:

a. Check to ensure that the left side of the status line displays the filename or is blank. If the word "Typeover" is displayed, press the ⌗Ins⌗ key to set the keyboard for Insert.

b. Type the text you want to insert.

EXAMPLES

1. You can use the insert mode to add a few words to the current document. First, type

   The company is releasing a new product that stops kitchen odors.

   Next, move the cursor to the space between "product" and "that." The screen looks like this:

   The company is releasing a new product_that stops kitchen odors.

   Type **, Odor Gone,**. Now, the screen looks like this:

   The company is releasing a new product, Odor Gone,_that stops kitchen odors.

   When you press any cursor movement key, Word-Perfect adjusts the display.

2. You can use the Insert mode to insert new lines. First, type

Tasks
Review Salary Proposals
Review Budget from Department 439

You can use "Tasks" as a title by inserting a blank line between the word "Tasks" and the first task. Move to the "R" in the second line and press [Enter]. Now the screen looks like this:

Tasks

Review Salary Proposals
Review Budget from Department 439

EXERCISES

1. Type this sentence:

   Company sales reached 1.2 million dollars.

   Insert **ABC** and a space before the word "Company."

2. Type this sentence:

   Cost of goods sold was 135 dollars.

   Change the cost of goods sold to 135,975.

3. Type these sentences:

   The company's sales increased to 1,654,834. Net income after taxes was 60,245.

   Insert the following sentence between the two you just typed:

Cost of goods sold was 983,473.

4. Type the following sentence:

She served cake for dessert.

Change the sentence so it reads

She served rich, warm, chocolate cake and creamy, rich, vanilla ice cream for dessert.

5. Type the following:

Biography is a region bounded on the north by history, on the south by fiction, and on the west by tedium.
Philip Guedalla

Add **on the east by obituary,** in front of "and."

REPLACE EXISTING CHARACTERS (TYPEOVER MODE)

2.5

Sometimes you need to replace the characters in a document with other characters. Typeover mode allows you to replace the character at the current cursor location with another character. If you press the `Ins` key when WordPerfect is in Insert mode, it will change to Typeover mode. Each character that you type will replace a character on the screen until you press the `Ins` key again to switch back to Insert mode. When WordPerfect is in Typeover mode, the word "Typeover" appears at the left edge of the status line.

When you enter text in Typeover mode, the text is not reformatted, since the number of characters in the document does not change. An exception to this is changing a space to a character, or vice versa, since this could change the length of a word at the end of a line. In Typeover mode, the `Backspace` key deletes the character to the left of the cursor and moves the cursor to that space, but it does not move the remaining characters on the line.

To enter replacement characters in Typeover mode:

a. Press the `Ins` key to activate Typeover mode. Check for the indicator in the status line.

b. Type the replacement text.

c. Press `Ins` again to turn off Typeover mode.

EXAMPLES

1. You can use Typeover mode to replace an entry when the replacement is the same length as the original entry. First, type:

   The chairman of the publicity department is Daryl Smith.

   If Daryl Smith resigns and Donna Jones takes his place, you can change this sentence by moving the cursor to the "D" in "Daryl" and pressing the `Ins` key. WordPerfect displays **Typeover** at the left edge of the status line. Now, type

Donna Jones

The screen now looks like this:

The chairman of the publicity department is Donna Jones,

You will use this entry for the next example.

2. The typeover mode can also be used when the new entry is almost as long as the existing entry. The ⟦Del⟧ key can remove the extra characters. You can replace the words "Donna Jones" with the words "Jim Lee." Move to the "D" in "Donna" and press ⟦Ins⟧ if **Typeover** is not displayed in the status line. Type **Jim Lee**. The screen looks like this:

The chairman of the publicity department is Jim Leeones,

Press the ⟦Del⟧ key four times to delete the extra four characters.

3. If the replacement entry is longer than the original entry, Typeover mode will extend the original entry by adding characters before the end of a short line. For example, type

Adele Altourne
114 Marymont Avenue
Sunrise, FL 33252

When Adele moves, you need to change the address. First, move the cursor to the first 1 in 114. Next, press ⟦Ins⟧ to invoke Typeover mode, and type

4756 N.E. 27th Avenue

Since the new street address is longer than the old one, no characters from the old address will need to be deleted. This is a feature that prevents you from typing over more text than you planned. Word-Perfect inserts space for the text you type where you pressed (Enter) in the original entry.

Finally, you can move to the beginning of the third line and type

Fort Lauderdale, FL 33115

The screen now looks like this:

```
Adele Altourne
4756 N.E. 27th Avenue
Fort Lauderdale, FL  33115_
```

EXERCISES

1. Type these sentences:

In the March issue of Growing Businesses, Carol Summers described how she started her metal-etching company as a hobby. Soon her business expanded to creating molds for other manufacturers.

Replace "Carol" with "Ellen".

2. Type this sentence:

The answering machine automatically picks up all calls after 2 rings.

Change the 2 to a 4. Change "picks up all calls" to "answers the phone".

3. Type these sentences:

The company is located at W. 125th and Lorain. The company started in the founder's basement.

Replace the first occurrence of "company" with "J. L. McGregor Corporation".

4. Type the following:

The new prices for copies are

1 to 100	.08 each
101 to 500	.05 each
501 +	.02 each

Change the .08 to .09. Change the .05 to .06 and change the .02 to .03.

5. Type the following:

Your current balance is $789.95.

Change $789.95 to $389.95.

DELETE CHARACTERS, WORDS, AND LINES
2.6

In Chapter 1, you learned how to use the [Del] and [Backspace] keys to remove unneeded characters. Word-Perfect provides some speedy deletion options that are useful when you have a number of characters to remove. You can use these options to delete a word or a sentence.

EXAMPLES

1. To delete the character at the cursor, use the [Del] key. First, type

Joan Kelley is the Assistant Production Manager.

After she is promoted, you need to remove the "Assistant" from her title. First, move the cursor to the "A" in "Assistant."

Next, press the [Del] key ten times. You could also hold the [Del] key down until the word "Assistant" was deleted. Now, the screen looks like this:

Joan Kelley is the Production Manager,

2. An alternative to the [Del] key is the [Backspace] key. First, type

The company's house boat is under repair.

Since "houseboat" is one word, you need to remove the space between the two words. Move the cursor to the word "boat." Then press the [Backspace] key to remove the space. Now the screen looks like this:

The company's houseboat is under repair,

3. When you have to delete several words, you can use [Ctrl]-[Backspace] to remove a word at a time. First, type

John is assuming Katie's position until the end of the year.

If the change becomes permanent, you will want to remove the last six words. Move the cursor to the word "until." Then, hold down [Ctrl] and press [Backspace] six times.

Release [Ctrl]. Finally, press [Backspace] once and type a period. Now the screen looks like this:

John is assuming Katie's position._

4. You can also use the (Ctrl)-(End) key combination to delete several words at one time. Type

Tasks
Review Salary Proposals
Review Budget from Department 439
Prepare Master Budget

When you finish the second task, you can delete the entry. First, move the cursor to the beginning of the word "Review" in the second task.

Next, hold down (Ctrl) and press (End). All of the text in that line disappears. Finally, press the (Del) key to delete the hard return that marks where you pressed (Enter) at the end of the line. The screen now looks like this:

Tasks
Review Salary Proposals
Prepare Master Budget
-

EXERCISES

1. Type this sentence:

The ABC Corporation and the XYZ Corporation are merging together to form the Alphabet Corporation next month.

Use the (Del) key to remove the word together.

Use the (Backspace) key to remove the phrase "next month".

2. Type this paragraph:

The ABC Corporation manufactures personalized license plates, mugs, name plates, and glassware. The XYZ Corporation produces personalized garment tags, shirts, purses, and pillows.

Delete "name plates," and "purses,".

3. Type these lines:

ABC Corp and XYZ slogans:
We'll name anything.
Names are down our lane.
We'll fit any name onto anything.

Delete the second slogan.

4. Type the following:

The major issues to be discussed at the next sales meeting are
      New bonus program
      Smaller sales regions
      Strategies for developing new customers.

Delete the third line.

5. Type the following:

NAME	DEPARTMENT	SALARY
Jan Smith	Biology	25,600
Bill Black	Accounting	29,800
Jeff Jones	Finance	35,400

Delete the word "SALARY" and all the salary figures.

EXERCISES

(Do not clear the screen between exercises unless instructed to do so.)

MASTERY
SKILLS CHECK

1. Type this paragraph:

   At a press conference last Tuesday, XY Graphics Inc. demonstrated its new product, See 'N' Draw. This product is intended for both novices and experts.

2. Insert "June 17" and a comma before "XY Graphics" in the first sentence.

3. Delete "Inc." using the ⌊Del⌋ key.

4. Type "July" over "June".

5. Insert a hard return between the two sentences.

6. Save as SEENDRAW, clearing the screen as you save.

7. Retrieve the file SEENDRAW.

8. Delete the word "both" in the second sentence.

9. Delete the second sentence.

10. Save as DRAW.

(Do not clear the screen between exercises unless instructed to do so.)

INTEGRATING
SKILLS CHECK

1. Type these lines:

CHOCOLATE CHIP COOKIES TASTE GOOD.
However, they are fattening.

2. Use Help to determine which key saves a file.

3. Save as COOKIE.

4. Clear the screen.

5. Type the following line:

   A few of my favorite things:

   Press (Enter), add a line of dashes under the entry, and press (Enter) again.

6. Retrieve COOKIE.

7. Insert the phrase "**AND BUTTERSCOTCH CHIP**" between "CHIP" and "COOKIES."

8. Delete the last line.

9. Save as LIST.

10. Exit WordPerfect.

Printing a Document

CHAPTER OBJECTIVES

After completing this chapter, you should be able to:

▶ Print the current document   3.1

▶ Print a selected page from the current document   3.2

▶ Preview before printing   3.3

▶ Print from a file   3.4

Normally you will want at least one printed copy of every document you create. Some people prefer to proof first drafts of their documents from printed copies. Also, a printed copy is usually the medium used to share the information in your documents with others.

WordPerfect offers a considerable amount of flexibility in its print features. You can print from memory or from a disk file. Even with the basic options in this chapter, you will find that you can print a document while continuing to make changes to the copy in memory. The disk-file option allows you to process a request for a copy of another document while continuing to work in the current document. You can print an entire document or only some of its pages.

To perform any of these tasks, WordPerfect needs an assigned printer. Appendix A covers how to select a printer if one has not already been selected for your system. Chapter 12 covers additional enhancements possible with WordPerfect's print features.

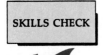

SKILLS CHECK

(Do not clear the screen unless instructed to do so.)

1. Type the following, including the misspelling:

Fourscore and seven years ago our fathers brought forth on this continent, a new nation, conceived in liberty, and dedicated to the propsition that all men are created equal.

Gettysburg Address

2. Delete the first three words, and type **87** in their place.

3. Restore "Fourscore and seven" and delete "87."

4. Change "propsition" to "proposition" by inserting an **o** between the "p" and the "s."

5. Type **Abraham Lincoln** over "Gettysburg Address," using Typeover mode and the ⌨Del key.

6. Save this as LINCOLN.

7. Exit WordPerfect.

8. Load WordPerfect, and retrieve the file LINCOLN.

9. Clear the screen.

PRINT THE CURRENT DOCUMENT

3.1

WordPerfect can print the current document without disrupting your work with the document. You can continue to make changes to the document or save it to disk while WordPerfect is printing. These actions will have no effect on the printed document.

You can use this printed copy to give your eyes a break from the screen as you proof a section of the document, or you might want to give the preliminary version of the document to someone else to review while you continue to make changes.

To print the current document:

a. Press the Print (Shift - F7) key [Alt File Print].

b. Type an **f** or a **1** to print the entire document.

EXAMPLES

1. You can print a document with a single command. First type the following:

Dear Sir:
      According to our records, your balance is past due. Please send the balance of your account, $150, within 30 days to prevent any legal action.

Press Enter twice, press Tab five times, and type **Sincerely,**. Press Enter four times, press Tab five times, and type **Ellen Fitzpatrick**.
      Once you have finished the letter, you can start printing by pressing the Print (Shift - F7) key [Alt File Print] and typing **f**, for full document. Word-Perfect will also accept **1** for this entry, since the options in the print menu, shown in Figure 3-1, are activated by either a letter or a number. The menu disappears, and the document is displayed again as printing begins. You can then edit the document without affecting the print output.
      Save this file as PASTDUE and clear the screen by pressing the Exit (F7) key [Alt File Exit], pressing Enter , typing **pastdue**, and pressing Enter twice more.

2. You can print a multipage document with the same command. First, type

New Hires
Brown, Jim
Scott, Mary

Press `Ctrl`-`Enter` [`Alt` Layout Align Hard Page] to start a new page. Type the following:

Offers Extended
Smith, Jason
Walker, Nancy

Request a printed copy by pressing the Print (`Shift`-`F7`) key [`Alt` File Print] and typing an **f.**

```
Print

    1 - Full Document
    2 - Page
    3 - Document on Disk
    4 - Control Printer
    5 - Multiple Pages
    6 - View Document
    7 - Initialize Printer

Options

    S - Select Printer                          HP LaserJet Series II
    B - Binding Offset                          0"
    N - Number of Copies                        1
    U - Multiple Copies Generated by            WordPerfect
    G - Graphics Quality                        Medium
    T - Text Quality                            High



Selection: 0
```

| FIGURE 3-1. | Print menu |

EXERCISES

1. Retrieve and print the file LINCOLN.

2. Type and print the following letter:

> 12345 Commerce Parkway
> Beachwood, OH 44123
> December 1, 1990

Samantha Koln
Small Business Administration of Cleveland
1235 Public Square
Cleveland, OH 44115

Dear Ms. Koln,

   I am starting a business to manufacture mechanical pencils. Can you provide information on the services that your organization provides to new companies?

> Sincerely,

> Tom Lu
> President, Various Sundries, Inc.

Save the letter as SBA.

3. Type the following:

There is hardly anything in the world that some man cannot make a little worse, and sell a little cheaper.

> John Ruskin

Print a copy of the document. Do not clear the screen.

4. Press (Enter) twice; then add the following quote:

It is just as important that business keep out of government as that government keep out of business.

                          Herbert Hoover

Print the document.

PRINT A SELECTED PAGE FROM THE CURRENT DOCUMENT

3.2

If you make a correction to a single page of a document, there is no need to print pages not affected by your change. WordPerfect allows you to print the current page from a document in memory.

To selectively print a page from a document:

a. Move the cursor to the page that you want printed.

b. Press the Print ((Shift)-(F7)) key [(Alt) File Print].

c. Type a **p** or a **2.**

EXAMPLES

1. You can print a single page from a document. First, type the following document as shown, using the (Esc) key and the equal sign (=) to draw the dividing line.

MEMORANDUM

To: Fran Stoll, Director, Human Services
From: John Smith, Division Manager
Re: Job Opening
= =
Fran:

   Deborah Winters has accepted a position with an-other firm. We need someone to fill her vacancy imme-diately. The following job description can be used for local advertisements.

Next, press [Ctrl]-[Enter] [[Alt] Layout Align Hard Page] to add a hard page break. This places the cursor at the top of the second page of the document. Type the following:

Accountant - Responsibilities include the preparation of budget-analysis and cost-variance data. Must have an MBA or an M.Acct. with 2 years' experience. Salary commensurate with experience.

Move to the first page by pressing [PgUp]. Then press the Print ([Shift]-[F7]) key [[Alt] File Print]. Enter a **2** or a **p** to print the page.

2. You can print any page in a multipage document. First, type the following:

THINGS TO DO TODAY
Complete filing
Prepare budget report

Press [Ctrl]-[Enter] [[Alt] Layout Align Hard Page] to begin a new page, and type

THINGS TO DO NEXT WEEK
Prepare invoices
Order preprinted forms
Complete Part I of Teach Yourself WordPerfect

Press Ctrl-Enter [Alt Layout Align Hard Page] to end the second page and type

END-OF-MONTH ACTIVITIES
Prepare performance reports
Close books

Press Enter to end the last line. Next, press the Print (Shift-F7) key [Alt File Print] and type **p** to print the current page (page 3). WordPerfect prints only page 3. Save this file as TODO.

EXERCISES

1. Retrieve the file SBA created in exercise 2 of section 3.1. Print the document. Add the following paragraph to the end of the letter:

   I have enclosed a notice of our upcoming open house for your monthly newsletter.

   Move to the end of the document, begin a new page, and type

   Attend the Open House Celebration at Various Sundries on May 15 from 7:30 to 9:30 P.M.

   Print a copy of page 2.

2. Assume that you have three sales personnel reporting to you. Their names are John Smith, Mary Brown, and Nancy Caster. Create a document with a page for each employee. Each page should contain "Significant Accomplishments 1990 -" followed by the name of the employee. The first page would look like this:

Significant Accomplishments 1990 - John Smith

After creating the three pages, print a copy of page 3. Do not clear the screen.

3. Print a copy of page 2 from the document created in the previous exercise. Print a copy of page 1.

4. Type the following:

Follow pleasure, and then will pleasure flee;
Flee pleasure, and pleasure will follow thee.

                                        John Heywood

Begin a new page; then type

But pleasures are like poppies spread—
you seize the flower, its bloom is shed.

                                        Robert Burns

Print a copy of page 1.

3.3 PREVIEW BEFORE PRINTING

It can be difficult to imagine exactly what your document will look like when it is printed. If your computer has a graphics card WordPerfect provides a way for you to "preview" your print output without taking the time to print the document. The preview that displays on your screen is an exact duplicate of a WordPerfect printed page.

You can choose to display an overview of a page to see the effect of various formatting selections. You can change the display to view two facing pages at once. If you prefer, you can expand the size of the image to either 100% or 200% to read the words in the document.

To view a document before printing:

a. Press the Print (Shift-F7) key [Alt File Print].

b. Type a **v** or a **6**.

c. To change the size of the image displayed, type **1** for 100%, **2** for 200%, **3** for the default full page, or **4** for facing pages.

d. Press the Exit (F7) key [Alt File Exit] to return to editing the document.

If you choose either of the first two options, you will not be able to see an entire page at once. You can use the arrow keys to move around within a page. You can press PgUp and PgDn to move from page to page in the print image.

EXAMPLES

1. When you preview a document, it displays on the screen exactly as it will appear on the printed page. You can see the margins at the edges of the document and look at how the text will appear on the printed page. First type

Ignio Gonzolez
Italia Buena
765 Coltman Avenue
Cleveland, OH 44106

Dear Ignio,

Thank you for your assistance with the family re-union. Your excellent foods were delightfully prepared, delivery was punctual, and the service was pleasant. We will think of Italia Buena for our next festive occasion.

Press [Enter] twice, press [Tab] five times, and type **Sincerely,**. Press [Enter] four times, press [Tab] five times, and type **Alonzo Benito**.

View the letter to see how it will look when you print it. First, press the Print ([Shift]-[F7]) key [[Alt] File Print]. Next, type a **v**. If you have a graphics card your screen looks like Figure 3-2. While you cannot read the text, you see the general appearance of the letter. Press the Exit ([F7]) key to end this preview. You will use this letter for the next example.

2. You can enlarge the preview of the letter shown in exercise 1. Depending on the type of monitor you have, the expanded size of the words may allow you to read them. Press the Print ([Shift]-[F7]) key [[Alt] File Print] and type a **v**. Type a **1** to expand the current document to its full size. Your screen looks like Figure 3-3. Type a **2** to double the size of the display. Use the arrow keys to move around within the display.

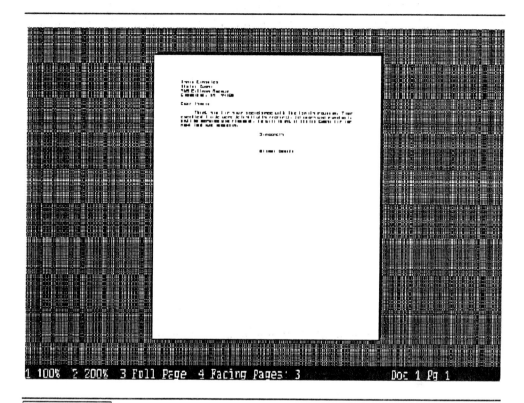

| FIGURE 3-2. | Full-page print preview |

Finally, press the Exit ([F7]) key to return to editing the document. Save the document and clear the screen by pressing the Exit ([F7]) key [[Alt] File Exit], pressing [Enter], typing **ITALIA** as the document name, and pressing [Enter] twice.

EXERCISES

1. Retrieve and view the LINCOLN file created in the skill check in this chapter. Preview the file at the 100% size. Preview the file at the 200% size.

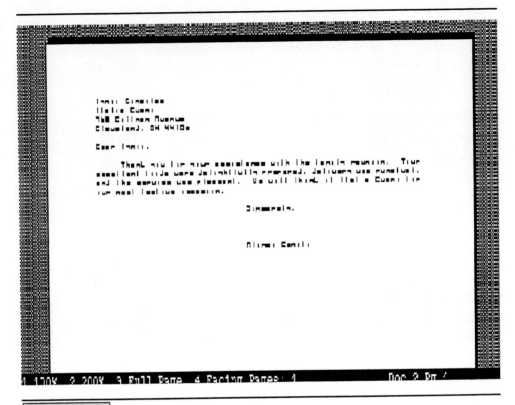

FIGURE 3-3.   Print preview at 100%

2. Type the following document and preview it as a full page, at 100%, and at 200%. Use the [Esc] and equal sign (=) keys to create the dividing line.

To: Sarah Graham, Chief Financial Officer
From: Bob Kelly, Chief Accounting Officer
Re: Financial Statements
= =
Sarah,

Enclosed are the preliminary financial statements. The attached text includes all of the footnotes. If you find any corrections or additions, please contact me immediately.

3. Type the following list of entries:

Meeting on April 20th to discuss new construction.
Make appointment with Harry to discuss new book series.
Meet with marketing to discuss new advertising strategies.

Preview the document. Press (Ctrl)-(Enter) [(Alt) Layout Align Hard Page] at the end of each entry, and preview the document again.

4. Type the following quotations, pressing (Ctrl)-(Enter) [(Alt) Layout Align Hard Page] at the end of each one:

One sees things for the first time only once.

Theodore White

Ignorance is never out of style. It was in fashion yesterday, it is the rage today and will set the pace tomorrow.

Frank Dane

Horatio Alger started by shining shoes and within one year made a million dollars. He must have used very little polish.

Sam Levenson

Nothing is so good as it seems beforehand.

George Eliot

It takes twenty years to become an overnight success.
Eddie Cantor

Preview the document, using the facing-pages view to look at two pages at once. Move to the top of the document and then to the bottom while previewing. Save the document as QUOTES.

3.4   PRINT FROM A FILE

Printing from a file offers convenience since you do not have to interrupt your current activities to print a copy of a document. You can print all the pages of the disk file, or you can specify which pages to print. You have greater flexibility in controlling which pages to print when you print from a file.

To print from a file:

a. Press the Print ([Shift]-[F7]) key [[Alt] File Print].

b. Type a **3** or a **d**.

c. Type the name of the document that you wish to print from disk.

d. Press [Enter] to print the entire document, or type the numbers of the pages that you want printed and then press [Enter].

You can specify one or more pages to print. The page numbers you select are separated by commas. To print a range of pages, you can enter the first page number, a hyphen, and the last page number. You can enter a number preceded by a hyphen to print all pages up to and including that number. Specifying a number followed by a hyphen prints the page specified and all of the pages that follow it. Sample page-number specifications are

1,5-8,12	Prints pages 1, 5, 6, 7, 8, and 12
-5,10-	Prints all pages except 6, 7, 8, and 9
3	Prints page 3

EXAMPLES

1. You can print the file ITALIA created in section 3.3. First, press the Print (Shift-F7) key [Alt File Print]. Next, type a **d** for "Document on Disk." When WordPerfect prompts you for the name of the document, type **italia** and press Enter. Word-Perfect displays **Pages** and prompts you with a default of **All**. Press Enter to have WordPerfect print the entire document.

2. You can print a single page from a document stored on disk. First, create a document that consists of short entries on many pages. Type

   This is page 1.

   and press Ctrl-Enter [Alt Layout Align Hard Page] to begin a new page. Repeat this process, using consecutive page numbers, until you have entered "This is page 7." End this line with Enter. Save the document as PAGES by pressing the Exit (F7) key [Alt File Exit], pressing Enter, typing **pages**, and pressing Enter twice. Press the Print (Shift-F7) key [Alt File Print], and type a **d**. When WordPerfect prompts you for the name of the document on disk, type **pages**, and press Enter. When WordPerfect prompts you for the page numbers to print, type **4**, and press Enter. A copy of page 4 is printed.

3. You can print a range of pages from a document stored on disk. First, press the Print ([Shift]-[F7]) key [[Alt] File Print]. Next, type a **d**. When WordPerfect prompts you for the name of the document on disk, type **pages**, and press [Enter]. When WordPerfect prompts you for the page numbers to print, type **2-5**, and press [Enter]. WordPerfect prints pages 2, 3, 4, and 5.

4. You can exclude a group of pages when printing a document stored on disk. First, press the Print ([Shift]-[F7]) key [[Alt] File Print]. Next, type a **d**. When WordPerfect prompts you for the name of the document, type **pages**. When WordPerfect prompts you for the page numbers to print, type **-3,6-**, and press [Enter]. The 3 represents the last page printed before the group of pages excluded, and the 6 represents the first page printed after the excluded pages. WordPerfect prints pages 1, 2, 3, 6, and 7.

EXERCISES

1. Print the SBA file, created in exercise 2 of section 3.1.

2. Enter the following:

RESIDENTS OPPOSED TO ROAD PAVING
Black
Smith
Campbell
Gilbert
Long
Jackson

Start a new page and enter

RESIDENTS SUPPORTING ROAD PAVING
Wilson
Boswell
Dike

Save the document to disk as ROAD, and clear the screen. Print a copy of the entire document from disk. Print another copy of page 2.

3. Print page 2 of QUOTES, created in exercise 4 of section 3.3.

4. Print pages 2 through 4 of QUOTES.

5. Print pages 1 and 4 of QUOTES.

EXERCISES

(Do not clear the screen unless instructed to do so.)

MASTERY
SKILLS CHECK

1. Type this letter:

To: All Managers
From: Fred Jones, Director of Human Services
Subject: Meetings on the New Benefit Package

    The Human Services Department will be conducting a one-hour information meeting on the new benefit package. We have attempted to schedule these meetings at convenient times. Please route the sign-up sheets to your employees and encourage everyone to attend one of these sessions.

Create four new pages in the same document, with one of the following entries at the top of each page:

Benefit Package meeting - April 5 9:30 A.M.
Benefit Package meeting - April 5 2:30 P.M.
Benefit Package meeting - April 6 8:30 A.M.
Benefit Package meeting - April 6 4:00 P.M.

Preview the letter looking first at the full-page view, then at facing pages, and finally at the two enlarged views.

2. Print this letter and the four attachment pages.

3. Print another copy of page 1.

4. Save the file as BENEFITS and clear the screen. Print the four attachment pages from disk.

INTEGRATING
SKILLS CHECK

(Do not clear the screen unless instructed to do so.)

1. Type this as it appears:

A meeting is scheduled at 5 PM on January 20 to discuss the company's participation in the CLEVELAND CORPORATE OLYMPICS. The meeting will be held in the fourth-floor conference room.

This year, we need a slogan for the banner and a T-shirt design. We also need a list of the employees participating in each activity. Please encourage your staff members to participate.

Interested individuals unable to attend the scheduled meeting should contact Steve Spear. His extension is 3963.

2. Delete the second sentence of the third paragraph.

3. Change the date to the 25th.

4. Print the document.

5. Go to the end of the document.

6. Insert a hard page break.

7. Type this as it appears:

Name	Activity
Sue Marianetti	Bike Race
Sharon Campbell	Tug-of-War
John Peterson	Tug-of-War
Tim Smith	5K Race
Ted McGregor	Tug-of-War
Brandon Leidy	Swimming
Marge Thomas	5K Race
Anne Kettlewood	Bike Race

8. Preview the document.

9. Print page 2.

10. Save this document as OLYMPICS and clear the screen.

11. Begin typing the following in a new document:

CORPORATE SLOGAN SUGGESTIONS
Our Team's the Best

Print page 1 of OLYMPICS; then continue typing these slogans:

The Best at All We Do
Scientific Services Employees Have Brains and Brawn
Sticks and Stones Won't Break Our Bones

Using Features to Alter the Appearance of Text

CHAPTER OBJECTIVES

After completing this chapter, you should be able to:

▶ Underline text as you type   4.1

▶ Boldface text as you type   4.2

▶ Center text as you type   4.3

▶ Reveal the hidden codes for special features   4.4

▶ Search for and delete hidden codes   4.5

▶ Mark and delete block text   4.6

▶ Apply special attributes to blocked text   4.7

WordPerfect's special features can help you add emphasis to text. Underlining, boldfacing, and centering help to set off text from the rest of your document. WordPerfect changes the appearance of your text on the screen to indicate these special features. WordPerfect also adds special hidden codes to the document for each of these features.

If you do not add these special features to your text as you type it, WordPerfect allows you to add them later. To add the special features to existing text, you must first block the text and then have WordPerfect apply the feature.

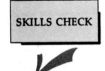

SKILLS CHECK

(Do not clear the screen until instructed to do so.)

1. Type the following, including the mistakes:

   The next meting of the WordPerfect User's Group will be January 5. Each attendeee will receive a free on the use of the new graphics features.

2. Correct the document by changing the spelling of the third word to "meeting," removing the last "e" from "attendeee," and inserting the word "handout" after the word "free."

3. Request help for the function key template. Determine the correct key for saving a document.

4. Save the document as MEETING.

5. Clear the screen.

6. Print the document from disk.

UNDERLINE TEXT AS YOU TYPE

4.1

You can use underlining to add emphasis to words in a document. You should use underlining to maintain the correct form for entries such as book titles. You can also use underlining to represent division in a formula or an equation.

To underline characters as you type:

a. Press the Underline (F8) key. [Alt Font Appearance Underline].

NOTE: Pull-down menu users can produce underlined text by pressing the Alt key and selecting Font Appearance Underline. Because this method requires four keystrokes compared to one, most people prefer to use the Underline (F8) key to underline text. Except for the next example, this book exclusively uses the Underline (F8) key.

b. Type the characters to be underlined.

c. Press the Underline (F8) key [Alt Font Appearance Underline] or press the → key to stop underlining text.

The monitor in your computer system determines the appearance of underlined text on your screen. Some monitors display underlined text with a different background color. Other monitors actually display the underlining beneath the text.

EXAMPLES

1. You can underline text at the beginning of a line. First, press the Underline (F8) key [Alt Font Appearance Underline], and type

Project Review

Next, press the Underline (F8) key [Alt Font Appearance Underline] again or press →. The screen looks like this:

    Project Review_

2. You can underline several words in the middle of a sentence. First, type the following words, which do not require underlining, and include a space after the last word:

The project review committee will meet on

Next, press the Underline (F8) key, and type

Monday, January 4,

Finally, press the Underline (F8) key to end underlining, and type

at 3:00 PM.

The display looks like the following.

The project review committee will meet on `Monday, January 4,` at
3:00 PM._

EXERCISES

1. Create the following bibliography entries:

   Acerson, Karen L., WordPerfect 5.1: The Complete
   Reference, Osborne/McGraw-Hill, 1990.

   Alderman, Eric, and Lawrence J. Magid, Advanced
   WordPerfect, Series 5 Edition, Osborne/McGraw-Hill,
   1988.

   Mincberg, Mella, WordPerfect 5.1 Made Easy,
   Osborne/McGraw-Hill, 1990.

2. Type the following document:

   We will honor employees with more than twenty-five
   years of service at the annual appreciation dinner.
   The following employees are honorees at this year's
   dinner:

EMPLOYEE	YEARS OF SERVICE
J. Smith	25
R. Taylor	35
P. Volker	31

3. Type the following formula:

   $$\text{Cost per square foot} = \frac{\text{Total cost}}{\text{Square feet}}$$

4. Type the following exactly as shown:

   There are many interesting tales in mythology.

The gods, goddesses, and heroes in these stories have unusual names and adventures. The names of each of the gods and other special characters in the following passage are underlined to highlight them.

Aconteus looked at Medusa's head and turned into stone. Medusa was a monster whose hair was made of serpents. Perseus, the son of Danae and Jupiter, killed Medusa. To make himself invisible to Medusa, he wore Pluto's helmet and a pair of winged shoes.

4.2 BOLDFACE TEXT AS YOU TYPE

Bold text is text that is darker than the surrounding text. Using the bold feature can add emphasis to text.

To boldface characters as you type:

a. Press the Bold (F6) key [Alt Font Appearance Bold].

NOTE: Pull-down menu users can produce bold text by pressing Alt and selecting Font Appearance Bold. Because this method requires four keystrokes compared to one, most people use the Bold (F6) key to bold text. Except for the next example, this book exclusively uses the Bold (F6) key.

b. Type the characters you wish to show in boldface.

c. Press the Bold (F6) key [Alt Font Appearance Bold] or press → to stop boldfacing text.

The monitor on your computer system determines the appearance of bold text on your screen. On some monitors, WordPerfect displays bold text with increased intensity. Other monitors display bold text in a different color.

EXAMPLES

1. You can use the Bold feature to highlight a date and time in an entry. First, type the following text, which does not require boldface:

   The next meeting is scheduled for

   Next, add a space after the last word, press the Bold (F6) key [Alt Font Appearance Bold], and type

   11 P.M. on Friday, January 14

   Finally, end the bold text by pressing the Bold (F6) key [Alt Font Appearance Bold] or →, and type a period to end the sentence. When you print the text, it looks like this:

   The next meeting is scheduled for 11 P.M. on Friday, January 14.

2. You can invoke the Bold feature once and continue to type boldface text until you turn it off. To enter a list of bullet items in boldface, request Bold before typing the first bullet item, and turn off Bold after typing the last item. First, type the following text, which does not require boldface:

We will discuss the following topics at the next meeting:

Next, press ⌊Enter⌋ and press the Bold (⌊F6⌋) key. Then, for each bullet item, press the ⌊Tab⌋ key, type the text, and press the ⌊Enter⌋ key:

* **Part-time versus full-time benefits**
* **Training opportunities**
* **Stock option plan eligibility**

Press the Bold (⌊F6⌋) key to end boldfacing. The text looks like this:

We will discuss the following topics at the next meeting:
    * **Part-time versus full-time benefits**
    * **Training opportunities**
    * **Stock option plan eligibility**

3. You can combine Bold and Underline to add extra emphasis to any text. The appearance of boldface, underlined text will vary on different monitors. To begin an entry that uses both Bold and Underline, press the Bold (⌊F6⌋) key, and then press the Underline (⌊F8⌋) key. Type

ANNUAL REPORT

The text should appear different from both underlined text and bold text. The appearance of the text depends on your computer monitor. Next, press the Underline (⌊F8⌋) and Bold (⌊F6⌋) keys or press ⌊→⌋ twice to end both features. The printed text looks like this:

<u>ANNUAL REPORT</u>

EXERCISES

1. Type the following accounts and their balances. Use Bold for all accounts with negative balances (shown in parentheses).

ACCOUNT	BALANCE
Rent	$5,125
Utilities	**(1,250)**
Phone	**(950)**

2. Type the following sentences. Use Bold for "more than 90 days' past due" and "immediately."

   Your account balance is **more than 90 days' past due.** Unless you contact us **immediately**, we will begin legal action to collect the balance of your account.

3. Type the following. Use Bold and Underline for the labels at the top of the columns:

DEPT	**HEAD COUNT**
ACCT	14
FIN	10
MFG	84

4. Type the following, using Bold for the foreign phrases.

   Foreign words can add variety to your writing. When you select foreign phrases, you will want to be certain that both you and your readers understand their meaning. **Deo gratias** means thanks to God. **Dei gratia** means by the grace of God. **Deo volente** means by God's will. **Dieu vous garde** means God protect you.

5. Type the following quotations. Use Bold for the author of each quote and Bold and Underline for the title of each book:

Noble by birth, yet nobler by great deeds.
   Henry Wadsworth Longfellow, <u>Tales of a Way-side Inn</u>
Who fears t'offend takes the first step to please.
   Colley Cibber, <u>Love in a Riddle</u>
The art of praising is the beginning of the art of pleasing.
   Voltaire, <u>La Pucelle</u>

4.3 CENTER TEXT AS YOU TYPE

You can use centering to place a report title in the center of a line in your document. You can also center a company name or department name using the same techniques.

To center characters on a line as you type them:

a. Press the Center (Shift - F6) key [Alt Layout Align Center].

b. Type the characters you wish to center on the line.

c. Press Enter to end centering. WordPerfect displays the text centered on the line.

EXAMPLES

(Do not clear the screen between examples unless instructed to do so.)

1. You can center a company name in the middle of a line by pressing the Center ([Shift]-[F6]) key [[Alt] Layout Align Center]. Next, type the following company name:

ABC COMPANY

Finally, press [Enter] to indicate the end of the entry, producing this result:

ABC COMPANY

___

2. You can center additional lines on a page by invoking the Center feature at the beginning of each line. Press the Center ([Shift]-[F6]) key [[Alt] Layout Align Center], and type

111 North Ave

Press [Enter] to end the line, press the Center ([Shift]-[F6]) key [[Alt] Layout Align Center] and type

Chicago, IL 30211

After you press [Enter], the screen looks like this:

ABC COMPANY
111 North Ave,
Chicago, IL 30211

___

Clear the screen.

3. You can enter text at the left margin on the same line as centered text. First, type

Roger Smith

Next, press the Center ((Shift)-(F6)) key [(Alt) Layout Align Center], and type

ABC Company

After you press (Enter), the results look like this:

Roger Smith   ABC Company
-

Clear the screen.

4. You can use Center with Underline and Bold. Press the Bold ((F6)) key, press the Underline ((F8)) key, and then press the Center ((Shift)-(F6)) key [(Alt) Layout Align Center]. Type

ABC Company

Press the Bold ((F6)) key, the Underline ((F8)) key, and (Enter). If you print the page, the line looks like this:

<u>**ABC Company**</u>

Clear the screen.

EXERCISES

1. Type your name, street address, and city and state on three separate lines, using the Center feature for each line.

2. Using Center and Bold, type **Tinsel Company** on a line.

3. Invoke the Center feature and type the following text, watching the screen as you type:

This text is too long for one line. WordPerfect cannot fit the entire entry on one line. When you print the text, you will notice that WordPerfect centers only the text in the first line.

As you type this text, you cannot see the centering on the screen, because of the length of the lines. Initially, the first characters of the first sentence seem to disappear.

4. Center the following lines as you type them:

ABC COMPANY
PERFORMANCE REPORT
FOR THE QUARTER ENDING JUNE 30, 1990

REVEAL THE HIDDEN CODES FOR SPECIAL FEATURES

4.4

WordPerfect marks special features, such as the end of a line or the end of a page, with hidden codes. The codes provide specific information about each feature used and its exact location within a document. Although some features may be obvious as you look at the screen, others are not apparent unless you reveal the codes within the document. WordPerfect splits the screen to display the codes, using the top window for the normal display and showing the text and codes in the bottom window. You cannot type a new code over an existing code to make a change. You must delete the existing code or insert a new one after it in the document.

To reveal hidden codes in a document:

a. Press the Reveal Codes (Alt-F3) key [Alt Edit Reveal Codes].

b. Use the arrow keys to highlight the codes in the document.

c. Press the Reveal Codes (Alt-F3) key [Alt Edit Reveal Codes] to return to the normal display.

If your keyboard has 12 function keys, you can press the F11 key instead of Alt-F3 to reveal codes.

EXAMPLES

1. Even without using special attributes (such as bold and underlining), your document contains special codes. To see them, use the Reveal Codes feature. Type

ABC Company

ABC Company

ABC Company[HRt]

Doc 1 Pg 1 Ln 1.17" Pos 1"

Press Reveal Codes to restore screen

FIGURE 4-1.   WordPerfect Reveal Codes screen

Next, press Enter. This adds a hidden code for a hard return. Press the Reveal Codes (Alt-F3) key [Alt Edit Reveal Codes] to produce the split screen display shown in Figure 4-1. The [HRt] code represents a hard return where you pressed Enter. WordPerfect inserts a soft return code [SRt] when it uses its word wrap feature to begin the next line. A soft page break is generated when WordPerfect fills a page. The code for a soft page break is [SPg]. When you force WordPerfect to end a page by pressing Ctrl-Enter [Alt Layout Align Hard Page], a hard page break code [HPg] is inserted.

2. You can use Reveal Codes to look at the special attributes in your documents. Press the Bold (F6) key, and type

BUDGET SUMMARY

Press the Bold (F6) key to end Bold. Next, press Enter twice and the Underline (F8) key once. Then type

ACCOUNTING DEPARTMENT

Press the Underline (F8) key to end underlining. To look at the codes for these features, press the Reveal Codes (Alt - F3) key [Alt Edit Reveal Codes]. As you examine the Reveal Codes screen, you will notice that each attribute uses a code at the beginning and at the end of the affected text.

```
{   ▲   ▲   ▲   ▲   ▲   ▲   ▲   ▲   ▲   ▲   ▲   ▲   }   ▲   ▲
[BOLD]BUDGET SUMMARY[bold][HRt]
[HRt]
[UND]ACCOUNTING DEPARTMENT[und]█
```

WordPerfect places [BOLD] and [bold] codes around bold text. It uses [UND] and [und] for underlined text. You can remove the Reveal Codes display from the screen by pressing the Reveal Codes (Alt - F3) key [Alt Edit Reveal Codes] again.

3. You can watch WordPerfect add codes to a document as you type by displaying the Reveal Codes screen before making entries. Press the Reveal Codes (Alt - F3) key [Alt Edit Reveal Codes].

Next, press the Center (Shift - F6) key [Alt Layout Align Center]. Type the following, and press Enter :

ABC Company

WordPerfect places a [Center] code ([Cntr] in 5.0) at the beginning of the centered entry.

EXERCISES

1. Type the following lines, using the Center feature for each line:

ABC COMPANY
BUDGET REPORT
FISCAL 1991

Use Reveal Codes to find the Center codes at the beginning and end of each entry.

2. Type the following, using Bold where indicated:

New Sunday store hours are Noon to 5 P.M.

Use Reveal Codes to locate the Bold codes.

3. Activate Reveal Codes. Type the following, using Bold and Underline:

Overdue Accounts

Note the addition of the codes to the document.

4. Center the following lines:

I think, therefore I am.
$$\text{Rene Descartes}$$

Reveal the hidden codes for Center. Save the file as THINK.

4.5	SEARCH FOR AND DELETE HIDDEN CODES

You do not need to delete text to remove special attributes that you used for the text. You can delete the code for an attribute from either the Reveal Codes display or the normal display. To delete a code from the normal display, you can first search for the attribute code you want to delete. Your search will pinpoint the exact location of the specific code. To remove underlining or boldface codes, you can remove either of the pair of special codes marking the attribute.

To delete a code in the Reveal Codes display:

a. Press the Reveal Codes ([Alt]-[F3]) key [[Alt] Edit Reveal Codes].

b. Use the arrow keys to move the cursor to the code you wish to remove.

c. Press the [Del] key.

d. Press the Reveal Codes ([Alt]-[F3]) key [[Alt] Edit Reveal Codes] to return to the normal display.

You can also delete a code by moving the cursor to the right of the code and pressing the `Backspace` key. When you delete codes after pressing the Reveal Codes (`Alt`-`F3`) key [`Alt` Edit Reveal Codes], Word-Perfect does not ask for a confirmation. If you try to delete a code when it is hidden, WordPerfect prompts you for a confirmation before deleting the code.

To delete codes in the normal display:

a. Press the `Home` key three times and the `↑` key once to move to the very top of the document, before any codes.

b. Press the Search (`F2`) key. [`Alt` Search Forward]

c. Press the function key representing the code, for example, the Bold (`F6`) key.

d. Press the Search (`F2`) key again to begin the search.

e. Press the `Backspace` key to delete the code.

f. Type a **y** to confirm the deletion.

g. Press the Search (`F2`) key twice [or `Alt` Search Forward and then the Search (`F2`) key] to look for the next occurrence of the code. If the search is successful, repeat the procedure from step e.

EXAMPLES

1. You can enter text with a special attribute and later remove the attribute. First, press the Bold (`F6`) key and type

BUDGET REPORT

Next, press the Bold ([F6]) key to end Bold. To look at the codes, press the Reveal Codes ([Alt]-[F3]) key [[Alt] Edit Reveal Codes]. If you position the cursor in the Reveal Codes screen on either the [BOLD] or [bold] code and press [Del], WordPerfect deletes both codes. The text remains on the screen.

Press the Reveal Codes ([Alt]-[F3]) key [[Alt] Edit Reveal Codes] to return to the normal display.

2. You can assign multiple attributes to text and delete any of them without affecting the remaining codes or the text. Press the Bold ([F6]) key and then the Underline ([F8]) key. Next, type

Expenses

Press the Bold ([F6]) key and then the Underline ([F8]) key to end both features. After invoking Reveal Codes by pressing the Reveal Codes ([Alt]-[F3]) key [[Alt] Edit Reveal Codes], use the arrow keys to highlight [und], and press [Del]. This action removes the underlining but retains the text and the boldface. Press the Reveal Codes ([Alt]-[F3]) key [[Alt] Edit Reveal Codes] to return to the normal display.

3. You can use the [Backspace] or [Del] key to remove either text or codes from the normal display. However, unless you search for a specific code, you may have difficulty determining the correct location of a code in this display. Press the Center ([Shift]-[F6]) key [[Alt] Layout Align Center] and type

Lawrence Aluminum

Next, press ⌈Enter⌉ twice, and begin Bold by pressing the Bold (⌈F6⌉) key. Type

Salary Expense

After pressing the Bold (⌈F6⌉) key again, move to the top of the document by pressing ⌈Home⌉, ⌈Home⌉, ⌈Home⌉, and ⌈↑⌉. Press the Search (⌈F2⌉) key [⌈Alt⌉ Search Forward] and then the Bold (⌈F6⌉) key. Press the Search (⌈F2⌉) key again to search for the first Bold code. Press the ⌈Backspace⌉ key to delete the hidden code, and type a **y** to confirm the deletion. To find the next occurrence of Bold, press the Search (⌈F2⌉) key twice [or ⌈Alt⌉ Search Forward and then the Search (⌈Alt⌉) key].

EXERCISES

(Do not clear the screen between exercises unless instructed to do so.)

1. Enter the following text exactly as shown, using Center for the indented lines.

   Quality Corporation is pleased to announce the following Christmas bonus structures:
       Less than 2 years of service - 2% bonus
       2 years or more of service - 5% bonus
   Checks will be available for distribution on <u>December 23</u>.

Find the codes for Bold, Underline, and Center in the Reveal Codes screen. Delete the Center code.

2. Deactivate the Reveal Codes display. Move to the beginning of the document, before any codes, and use the Search feature to locate the Bold code. Clear the screen.

3. Retrieve the file THINK, and delete the code for Center.

4.6 MARK AND DELETE BLOCK TEXT

Normally, the (Del) and (Backspace) keys affect only a single character or code or one pair of codes at a time. Using the Block feature to mark adjacent characters and codes allows you to perform an action on all the marked material at one time.

To mark a block of text:

a. Use the cursor movement keys to position the cursor on the first character or code in the block you wish to define.

b. Press the Block ((Alt)-(F4)) key [(Alt) Edit Block]. If you have a keyboard that has 12 function keys, you can use (F12) instead of (Alt)-(F4) to block text.

c. Use the arrow keys to move the cursor one position past the last character in the block.

The text within the block appears with black letters against a highlighted background. On color monitors, the blocked text may appear with a background color different from that of the normal text. If you wish to remove the highlighting without taking an action, press the Block ([Alt]-[F4]) key [[Alt] Edit Block] again or press the Cancel ([F1]) key. Mouse users can block text by placing the pointer at the beginning of the text to be blocked and depressing the left button while moving the pointer one position past the last character of the block.

EXAMPLES

1. You can block a word in a document and delete it. First, type the following sentence:

   The next loan payment is due January 14.

   Use the arrow keys to move to the "p" in "payment." Next, press the Block ([Alt]-[F4]) key [[Alt] Edit Block]. WordPerfect changes the background display of the position number on the status line to indicate that Block has been activated. Press [Ctrl]-[→] to place the cursor on the "i" in "is." WordPerfect changes the display of the blocked text. The screen looks like this:

   The next loan **payment** is due January 14.

   To delete the blocked text, press the [Del] or [Backspace] key or [[Alt] Edit Delete].

2. You can block larger portions of a document with the same method or with some shortcuts. For example, when Block is activated, typing any character causes everything up to the next occurrence of that character to be included within the block. First, type the following:

The first Advanced WordPerfect seminar is scheduled for February 22, 1990. Employees must complete the exercises in Teach Yourself WordPerfect to be eligible for enrollment.

Next, use the arrow keys to move to the "E" at the beginning of the second sentence. Press the Block (Alt - F4) key [Alt Edit Block] to activate the Block feature. To block the entire sentence, press the • (.) key. Press the Del key [Alt Edit Delete] to remove the sentence. WordPerfect displays a prompt on the status line. Type a **y** to confirm that you want to delete the block.

EXERCISES

1. Type the following. Then block the second sentence.

   New members must pay an initiation fee of $300. In addition, new members must volunteer for association programs a minimum of 25 hours during their first year.

2. Type the following:

An excuse uncalled for becomes an obvious accusation.
                    Law Maxim

Block the word "excuse." Remove the Block feature, and save the file as EXCUSE.

3. Type the following text:

You must submit expense reports by the 15th of the month following travel.

Use the Block feature to block "15th." Turn off the Block feature. Do not clear the screen.

4. Insert the word **previous** before the word "month." Block the new word and delete it.

5. Retrieve the file named THINK. Block and delete "Rene Descartes."

APPLY SPECIAL ATTRIBUTES TO BLOCKED TEXT

4.7

Using special attributes, such as boldface, underlining, and centering is simplest if you invoke the feature before typing the text. However, if you forget, or if you wish to change the appearance of text that has already been typed, you can still add these attributes. You first block the text that you wish to change and then invoke the attribute.

To apply special attributes to a group of characters:

a. Block the text.

b. Press the function key representing the attribute you wish to use, for example, the Underline ([F8]) key.

c. If you are adding a code for centering, you must confirm your request by typing a y when Word-Perfect prompts you for confirmation.

EXAMPLES

1. You can underline text without retyping it. First, complete these entries, pressing [Enter] at the end of each line:

   A few box office hits are:
   Who Framed Roger Rabbit?
   Coming to America
   Bull Durham
   Big

   Press [Enter] after typing the last title. Although you did not underline the movie titles when typing them, you can do so now. Move the cursor to the "W" in the first title, and press the Block ([Alt]-[F4]) key [[Alt] Edit Block]. Use the [↓] key to move the cursor to the line below the last title. Next, press the Underline ([F8]) key. WordPerfect underlines the titles.

2. You can add centering with the same method. First, type:

Productivity Report

Since you can block from either direction, press the Block (Alt - F4) key [Alt Edit Block] and move the cursor to the beginning of the entry. Press the Center (Shift - F6) key [Alt Layout Align Center], and type a **y** to confirm the request. The actions center the entry like this:

Productivity Report

3. You can add more than one attribute to existing text. Type the following:

The last date for renewing your membership at this year's rate is December 31.

You can add both bold and underlining to "last date" and "December 31" by blocking the entries. First, move the cursor to the "l" in "last." Press the Block (Alt - F4) key [Alt Edit Block], and move to the space following the "e" in "date." Press the Underline (F8) key. To add bold, block the data again by pressing the Block (Alt - F4) key [Alt Edit Block]. To return quickly to the first character of the block, hold down Ctrl and press Home twice. Press the Bold (F6) key to add the second attribute. You can repeat this procedure for "December 31". The printed sentence will look like this:

The <u>last date</u> for renewing your membership at this year's rate is <u>December 31</u>.

EXERCISES

1. Type the following:

   After completing this book, you can continue to build your skills with WordPerfect 5.1 Made Easy. Soon you will be your company's WordPerfect expert.

   Use the Block feature to underline "WordPerfect 5.1 Made Easy". Do not clear the screen.

2. Use the Block feature to make "WordPerfect expert" bold.

3. Type the following:

   ACCOUNTS RECEIVABLE AGING

   Underline and center the text without retyping it.

4. Retrieve the file EXCUSE. Add the following at the end of the document:

   A bad excuse is better, they say, than none at all.
                                        Stephen Gosson

   Block the word "excuse" in each quotation, and make it boldface.

5. Type the following:

   A cruel story runs on wheels, and every hand oils the wheels as they run.
                                        Ouida

   Underline and boldface both occurrences of "wheels" after completing the entry.

EXERCISES

(Do not clear the screen between exercises unless instructed to do so.)

1. Underline the following text as you type it:

   Bylaws of the WordPerfect Users Group

   Clear the screen.

2. Enter the following, using Bold for the company name, location, and date:

   ABC Company will hold its annual picnic at the **Loch Raven Pavilion** on **July 17th.**

3. Use Reveal Codes to look at the hidden codes for Bold. Delete the Bold codes for "Loch Raven Pavilion."

4. Move to the top of the document. With Reveal Codes activated, type the following using Center and Underline:

   COMPANY PICNIC ANNOUNCEMENT

5. Add two blank lines. Deactivate Reveal Codes. Use the Search feature to locate the codes for Underline. Print the document, and clear the screen.

6. Type the following memo as shown:

   **ABC COMPANY
   INTERNAL MEMORANDUM**

TO: All staff
FROM: John Smith
SUBJECT: Completion of parking lot resurfacing
DATE: February 15, 1990

The resurfacing of parking lots A and B is complete. Resurfacing of parking lot C is scheduled to begin Monday, February 20.

Your continued cooperation is appreciated.

Use Reveal Codes to remove the hard return before the last line. Save the memo as PARKING.

7. Add bold to the word "complete" in the first sentence. Use Block to mark the second sentence and delete it. Clear the screen.

8. Type the following:

ACCT NO	BALANCE
1204	$12,350
1567	$17,865
2569	$23,789

Use the Block feature to add boldface and underlining to the headings at the top of the columns.

INTEGRATING SKILLS CHECK

(Do not clear the screen between exercises unless instructed to do so.)

1. Type the following document as shown:

ABC BOOKS
1115 Warren Avenue
Cleveland, OH 44017

Mr. John Myers
Winsom Corporation
111 North St.
Akron, OH 43124

Dear Mr. Myers:

   We are holding a copy of Successful Office Management for you. We will hold this book for you until October 12.

Sincerely,

Ralph Jones
Customer Service

2. Save the document as MYERS, and clear the screen. Print a copy of the letter from disk.

3. Retrieve the file, and make the following changes: Use Typeover mode to change "North" to **South**. Add underlining to "Successful Office Management". Add boldface to the date in the last sentence.

4. Activate the Block feature, and block the letter body. Then cancel the Block request.

5. Save the document to disk, replacing the previous copy. Preview the document on the screen. Print a copy.

Changing Line Appearance Within a Document

►5◄

CHAPTER OBJECTIVES

After completing this chapter, you should be able to:

► **Set right and left margins**   5.1

► **Use indentation**   5.2

► **Use the Margin Release feature**   5.3

► **Set tabs**   5.4

► **Use the Flush Right feature**   5.5

► **Change the line spacing**   5.6

► **Alter justification**   5.7

WordPerfect's line-formatting features allow you to change the appearance of one or more lines of text. You can alter the margin settings to add more or less white space at the edges of the paper. Lines can also be indented from the left and right edges of the paper, allowing you to offset bullet items or other important text. You can change the tab settings to conform with the structure of the entries you wish to make.

WordPerfect lets you change the line spacing to provide extra space between lines when printing a draft of a document. Two additional options affect the right margin of a document. The Flush Right feature allows you to place text such as the date or a letter heading at the right edge of a document. Justification affects entire paragraphs of text and allows you to align text with either the left or right margin. You can also choose to align with both margins at the same time. While WordPerfect's default full justification (right justification in 5.0) is designed to provide a consistent right margin when a document is printed, you can change that feature if you desire.

Each of the line-formatting options affects the document beginning at the line in which it is invoked. If you want a formatting change to affect every line in a document, you must invoke the feature at the top of the document.

SKILLS CHECK

(Do not clear the screen until you are so instructed.)

1. Type the following bibliography, centering the heading and underlining the book titles as you type them.

Bibliography

Mincberg, Mella, WordPerfect 5.1 Made Easy, Osborne/
McGraw-Hill, 1072 pages.
Campbell, Mary, 1-2-3 Release 3 Made Easy, Osborne/
McGraw-Hill, 526 pages.

2. Insert the year for each book—1990 and 1989, respectively—between the publisher and the page count.

3. Save the document as BIBLIO.

4. Search for the underline codes and delete them.

5. Clear the screen.

6. Print the file BIBLIO.

SET RIGHT AND LEFT MARGINS   5.1

The left and right margins are the blank area at the left and right sides of a printed page. WordPerfect measures the margins as the number of inches between the edge of the paper and the text and ensures that text entered conforms to the margin settings.

Margin settings can be changed throughout a document. WordPerfect uses the default margin settings unless it finds hidden codes representing other margin specifications. WordPerfect initially has 1″ (1-inch) left and right margins. When you change a margin setting, WordPerfect automatically rewraps the text for the new margin and continues to use that setting unless it finds another hidden code for a margin change.

To change the left and right margins:

a. Press the Format (Shift - F8) key [Alt Layout Line and skip step b].

b. Select Line by typing a letter **L** or a number **1**.

c. Select Margins by typing an **M** or a **7**.

d. Type the number of inches WordPerfect should leave between the left edge of the paper and the text.

e. Press Enter .

f. Type the number of inches WordPerfect should leave between the right edge of the paper and the text.

g. Press Enter .

h. Press the Exit (F7) key to return to the document.

EXAMPLES

1. You can decrease the margins to increase the amount of text that fits on each page. For example, you can decrease the margins to .5". First, type

A presentation on WordPerfect's exciting new graphics features is scheduled for the next meeting of the WordPerfect User Group. This meeting will be held at noon on April 28th.

Move to the top of the document by pressing `Home`, `Home`, and `↑`. Next, press the Format (`Shift`-`F8`) key, and type an L [`Alt` Layout Line] to select the line-formatting options. Type **m** to select the margin-formatting option. Type .5 and press `Enter`. Then, type .5 and press `Enter` again. This allows an additional inch of text on each line. Press the Exit (`F7`) key to return to the document. Then press the `↓` key to make WordPerfect reformat the paragraph. The reformatted lines are shown below:

A presentation on WordPerfect's exciting new graphics features is scheduled for the next meeting of the WordPerfect User Group. This meeting will be held at noon on April 28th.

Press the Reveal Codes (`Alt`-`F3`) key [`Alt` Edit Reveal Codes]. WordPerfect displays [L/R Mar: 0.5",0.5"] as the code for the half-inch-margins setting. Use this entry in the next example.

2. You can increase the margins to decrease the text that fits on each page. If you set the new margins when the cursor is past the hidden code for the current margin setting, you do not have to delete the hidden code. However, if you are changing the margins for the entire document, the best strategy is to eliminate the margin settings that are not needed.

Codes are still revealed from the last example. Press [Home], [Home], and [↑], and press the [Backspace] key to remove the [L/R Mar:0.5″,0.5″] code for the current margin setting. (You can either remain in the Reveal Codes screen or remove it by pressing the Reveal Codes ([Alt]-[F3]) key [[Alt] Edit Reveal Codes] again.) Press the Format ([Shift]-[F8]) key and type an L [[Alt] Layout Line]. Next, type **m** to select Margins. Type a **2** for the left-margin setting, and press [Enter]. Type a **2** for the right-margin setting, and press [Enter] again. Finally, press the Exit ([F7]) key to return to the document. Press the [↓] key to reformat the paragraph. The text now appears with the wider margins, as shown below:

A presentation on WordPerfect's exciting new graphics features is scheduled for the next meeting of the WordPerfect User Group. This meeting will be held at noon on April 28th.

EXERCISES

1. Type the following:

   Some are born great, some achieve greatness, others have greatness thrust upon 'em.
                                         William Shakespeare

   Change the left margin to 2″ and the right margin to 1.5″.

2. Type the following:

What makes us discontented with our condition is the absurdly exaggerated idea we have of the happiness of others.
Proverb

Change the left and right margins to 2". Reveal the hidden codes to see the code for the new margins. Return to the normal screen, and change the margins to 1.5".

3. Type the following:

The plural of most compound nouns is formed by adding "s" or "es" to the main word in the grouping. For example:

   mothers-in-law
   runners-up
   daughters-in-law

Change the left margin to 2.5" and the right margin to 1.5".

4. Type the following lines:

ABC COMPANY - MEMO
Date: Monday, Sept 10, 1990
— —

When using the copier by the coffee machine, only use the paper stacked next to the machine. Since the machine is old, if you use different paper (envelopes, letterheads, etc.), the machine jams.

At the beginning of the document, set the left and right margins to 3". Preview how WordPerfect prints the document. Delete the hidden code for the margin settings.

USE INDENTATION

5.2

WordPerfect allows you to indent a paragraph of text from the left margin. Each time you press the Indent ([F4]) key [[Alt] Layout Align Indent →], Word-Perfect moves one tab stop to the right and establishes a temporary margin at that position. When you press [Enter], the normal margin setting is resumed. This feature allows you to indent bullet items and other special text to set it off from the regular text. The hidden code inserted for Indent is [→ Indent]. If you delete this code, the indentation is removed.

A similar feature allows you to indent the text from both margins at the same time. WordPerfect's Indent Left and Right feature moves the paragraph in from the margins without changing the margins of the remaining text. When you press the Indent Left and Right ([Shift]-[F4]) key [[Alt] Layout Align Indent →←], the margins move in one tab stop from the left edge of the document and an equal amount of space from the right edge. Indentation from both sides may be used to set off a long quote from the body of a letter or report. The hidden code that is added to a document when this feature is used is [→ Indent←].

To indent a paragraph from the left margin:

a. Move the cursor to the beginning of the paragraph that you want to indent.

b. Press the Indent (F4) key [Alt Layout Align Indent ➔] one or more times to move to the tab setting to which you want the paragraph indented.

To indent a paragraph from both margins:

a. Move the cursor to the beginning of the paragraph that you want to indent.

b. Press the Indent Left and Right (Shift - F4) key [Alt Layout Align Indent ➔ ←] one or more times to move to the tab setting to which you want the paragraph indented.

You can perform these steps before or after you type the text.

EXAMPLES

1. You can indent paragraphs from the left margin to set them off from other text. First, type

   On January 3, 1959, Alaska became the 49th state. Congress defeated an earlier bill that would have granted it statehood. Alaska was the first state admitted to statehood since 1912.

   Next, press Enter to end the paragraph. Then, press the Indent (F4) key [Alt Layout Align Indent ➔], and type

   The land was purchased from Russia during Lincoln's administration. The purchase was referred to as Seward's Folly after the secretary of state who supported the purchase.

The second paragraph is indented. The two paragraphs look like the following.

```
On January 3, 1959, Alaska became the 49th state. Congress
defeated an earlier bill that would have granted it statehood.
Alaska was the first state admitted to statehood since 1912.
        The land was purchased from Russia during Lincoln's
        administration. The purchase was referred to as Seward's
        Folly, after the secretary of state who supported the
        purchase.
```

You can display the hidden code for the indent feature by pressing the Reveal Codes ([Alt]-[F3]) key [[Alt] Edit Reveal Codes]. If you delete this code, the indentation is removed.

2. You can indent both sides of a paragraph. This is customary when typing a quotation that uses several lines. To indent both sides of a paragraph, type

Isaac Newton, a mathematician, philosopher and scientist, said:

Next, press [Enter] to end the paragraph. Then, press the Indent Left and Right ([Shift]-[F4]) key [[Alt] Layout Align Indent →◄] and type

I do not know what I may appear to the world, but to myself I seem to have been only like a boy playing on the sea-shore, and diverting myself in now and then finding a smoother pebble, or a prettier shell than ordinary, whilst the great ocean of truth lay undiscovered before me.

After you type the text, the screen looks like this:

Isaac Newton, a mathematician, philosopher and scientist, said:
I do not know what I may appear to the world, but to
myself I seem to have been only like a boy playing on
the sea-shore, and diverting myself in now and then
finding a smoother pebble, or a prettier shell than
ordinary, whilst the great ocean of truth lay
undiscovered before me.

EXERCISES

1. Type the following paragraph after pressing the
   Indent Left and Right ((Shift)-(F4)) key [(Alt) Layout
   Align Indent →←] four times:

   Next Monday, the executive officers are meeting to
   discuss five-year growth projections for the firm. The
   agenda for this meeting will include these topics: financial planning and new debt issues, new product lines,
   the competition, and foreign market opportunities.

2. Type the paragraph used in exercise 1 after pressing the Indent ((F4)) key [(Alt) Layout Align
   Indent→] once. After pressing (Enter) to end the
   paragraph, type the following:

   The meeting is scheduled for 9:00 a.m. in the board
   room.

   o not clear the screen.

3. Reveal the codes, and delete the indent code from
   the first paragraph.

4. Type the following paragraph, pressing the Indent (F4) key [Alt Layout Align Indent→] and the Indent Left and Right (Shift-F4) key [Alt Layout Align Indent→←] where indicated.

> **Frequently saving work in progress is a good habit that all computer users should acquire. It avoids the potential for loss of large amounts of work due to power outages, someone tripping over a power cord, etc.**

5.3   USE THE MARGIN RELEASE FEATURE

WordPerfect's Margin Release feature allows you to type text to the left of the left margin setting. If the text fills more than one line, WordPerfect will wrap subsequent lines to the left margin. You can also use the feature to start the first line of an indented paragraph at the left margin; the other lines will wrap to the designated tab stop. The hidden code for the Margin Release feature is [←Mar Rel].

To use the Margin Release feature:

a. Move to the beginning of the line on which you want to use the Margin Release feature.

b. Press the Margin Release (Shift-Tab) key [Alt Layout Align Margin Rel←] one or more times. WordPerfect moves the cursor one tab stop to the left each time.

c. Type the text.

   You can use Margin Release only when there are tab stops to the left of the cursor. If there are no tab stops to the left, or if the "Pos" indicator on the status line shows that the cursor is at 0″, the cursor stays in its current location.

EXAMPLES

1. You can use the Margin Release feature when you create forms. To create a form, you can use the Margin Release feature to put the labels for the data to the left of the margins. First, press the Margin Release ([Shift]-[Tab]) key [[Alt] Layout Align Margin Rel◄], and type

Name:

Press [Enter] once, and press the Margin Release ([Shift]-[Tab]) key [[Alt] Layout Align Margin Rel◄] twice. Type

Company:

Press [Enter] and the Margin Release ([Shift]-[Tab]) key [[Alt] Layout Align Margin Rel◄]. Type

Dept:

The screen looks like this:

```
  Name:
Company:
   Dept:
```

2. You can use the Margin Release feature to remove the indentation from the first line of an indented

paragraph. Press the Indent (F4) key [Alt Layout Align Indent→] for indentation. To move back to the margin for the first line, press the Margin Release (Shift-Tab) key [Alt Layout Align Margin Rel←]. Then type

When you have an indented paragraph, you may want the first line to align with paragraphs that are not indented. Margin Release allows you to do this.

The paragraph looks like this:

When you have an indented paragraph, you may want the first line
    to align with paragraphs that are not indented. Margin
    Release allows you to do this.

3. When you move the cursor through a line that has a margin release, it may behave unexpectedly. Moving the cursor through lines with Margin Release codes is easier when you reveal the codes. First, press the Margin Release (Shift-Tab) key [Alt Layout Align Margin Rel←] twice. Then type

This line does not start at the left margin.

Press Enter to move to the next line. Press the ↑ key. This moves the cursor to the "d" in "does." Press the → key, the Home key, and then the ← key. This moves the cursor to the "T" in "This." Press the Reveal Codes (Alt-F3) key [Alt Edit Reveal Codes]. Press the ← key. The cursor jumps to the right in the document screen but moves left to cover the [←Mar Rel] code in the reveal codes screen. Press the ← key again. The cursor again jumps to the right in the document screen but moves left in the reveal codes screen to the first [← Mar Rel] code. Because the cursor is located on the first [← Mar Rel] code, the cursor location in the document is on the left margin. Press the ⊕ to move past the first [← Mar Rel] code, and the cursor moves left to the first tab stop left of the margin. Press the Reveal Codes (Alt - F3) key [Alt Edit Reveal Codes] to return to the normal screen display.

EXERCISES

1. Type the following paragraph, first invoking the Margin Release feature until you cannot move the first line any further to the left:

   You can use the Margin Release feature to make an indented paragraph begin at the left margin. You can also use it to fit additional characters on a line.

2. Create an employment application form like the one below. Use the Margin Release feature to align the form labels for the name, address, phone number, and social security number.

```
        Name:
     Address:
Phone Number:
  Soc. Sec. #:
```

SET TABS   5.4

Tab stops provide an easy way to align text at locations other than the left margin. The traditional settings for tab stops are every five characters. This allows you to use the first tab stop for paragraph indentation. You can change the tab stops when you have columns of entries that you want to align. You might also change them when you want to place a column of entries near the middle or right edge of the page. Eliminating unnecessary tab stops allows you to press the ⌜Tab⌟ key once to position the cursor correctly.

When you press the ⌜Tab⌟ key, the cursor moves to the next tab stop and inserts the hidden code [TAB] in your document. Initially, WordPerfect has tab stops at every half inch. These settings conform to the traditional tab stop placement of every 5 characters if you are using 10-pitch type (10 characters to the inch). You can change the tab stops to any positions you want.

To change tab stops:

a. Press the Format (⌜Shift⌟-⌜F8⌟) key [⌜Alt⌟ Layout Line and skip step b].

b. Type an **L** or a **1** to select the line-formatting options.

c. Type a **t** or an **8** to select Tab Set.

d. Using the cursor control keys or the SPACEBAR, move the cursor to where you want a tab stop inserted, and type an **L, r, c,** or **d.**

e. Move the cursor to an existing tab stop that you want to remove, and press the ⌜Del⌟ key.

f. Move the cursor to an existing tab stop that you want to move, and use the ⌜Ctrl⌟-⌜←⌟ and ⌜Ctrl⌟-⌜→⌟ keys to move it.

g. Press the Exit (F7) key when you have finished modifying the tab stops.

To move the cursor in steps d and e, you can press the ← or → key or the SPACEBAR to move one position at a time. Press Home and the ← or → key to move to the edge of the screen and then again to move 3.2″ in that direction. Press Home twice and the ← or → key once to move to the beginning or the end of all tab stops.

The letter you type in step d determines the alignment at the tab stop. "L" left-aligns the text typed at the tab stop. "R" right-aligns the text typed at the tab stop. "C" centers the text typed at the tab stop. "D" right-aligns all characters typed before a decimal point or period.

An alternative to steps d and e is typing the number of the desired tab stop position (for example, **2.5**) and pressing Enter. This inserts a left-aligned tab stop at the specified location and places the cursor there. You can then change the type of tab stop by typing an **r**, **c**, or **d** or delete the tab stop by pressing Del.

When you press the Exit [F7] key after changing tab settings, a hidden code is inserted to indicate the change. The hidden code indicates the locations of the tabs you set but does not identify the type of alignment. It looks like this: [Tab Set:Rel: −1″, −0.5″, +0.5″,+3″] ([Tab Set:0″,0.5″,1.5″,4″] in 5.0).

To remove all the tab stops:

a. Press the Format (Shift-F8) key, type an L [Alt Layout Line], and then type a **t**.

b. Press [Home] twice and the [←] key once. The cursor is at the −1" position (0" position in 5.0).

c. Press the Delete EOL ([Ctrl]-[End]) key.

EXAMPLES

1. When you type lines of numbers, you may want the numbers aligned in a column. You can right-align the numbers by creating a special tab stop. First, press the Format ([Shift]-[F8]) key, type an L [[Alt] Layout Line], and then type a t. The bottom of the screen looks like this:

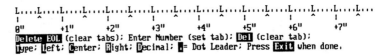

The default left-aligned tab stops at .5-inch intervals are indicated by the "L"s on the Tab Set screen. Each caret (^) between the inch indicators marks a half inch. Press the Delete EOL ([Ctrl]-[End]) key to remove all tab stops to the right of the cursor position. Move the cursor to the .5" position (1.5" position in 5.0), and type an L. Move the cursor to the 5" position, and type an r. The Tab Set screen now looks like this:

```
.....L.......................................R..........................
  !   ^   !   ^   !   ^   !   ^   !   ^   !   ^   !   ^   !   ^
  0"      +1"     +2"     +3"     +4"     +5"     +6"     +7"
Delete EOL (clear tabs); Enter Number (set tab); Del (clear tab);
Type; Left; Center; Right; Decimal; .= Dot Leader; Press Exit when done.
```

Press the Exit (F7) key twice to return to the document. To enter each right-aligned number, press the Tab key twice, type the number, and press Enter.

2. When you type letters, you usually need only two tab stops: one for the beginning of paragraphs and the other for the initial address or the date and the closing. Having extra tab stops can be cumbersome and prevent the address from aligning with the closing. You can remove the extraneous tab stops by pressing the Format (Shift-F8) key, typing an L [Alt Layout Line] and then a **t**. Move the cursor to the right of the .5" position (1.5" position in 5.0). Then, press the Delete EOL (Ctrl-End) key to remove the tab stops to the right. To create a tab stop for the initial address and the closing, type a **3** (**4** in 5.0) and press Enter. You could also create this tab stop by moving the cursor to the 3" position (4" position in 5.0) and typing an L. Now the screen looks like this:

```
.....L...................................R...........................
 !   ^   !    ^   !   ^   !   ^   !   ^   !   ^   !   ^   !   ^
 8"      +1"      +2"     +3"     +4"     +5"     +6"     +7"
Delete EOL (clear tabs); Enter Number (set tab); Del (clear tab);
Type; Left; Center; Right; Decimal; = Dot Leader; Press Exit when done.
```

Press the Exit [F7] key twice to begin typing the letter. Press the Tab key once to start a paragraph and twice to type each line of the first address, the date, or the closing.

3. When you create reports, you often want numbers or text to appear in columns. You can use tab stops

to ensure that the information aligns properly. First, press the Format ([Shift]-[F8]) key, type an L [[Alt] Layout Line] and then a **t**. Once the Tab Set screen appears, press [Home] twice and the [←] key once to move the cursor to the −1″ position (0″ position in 5.0). Then, press the Delete EOL ([Ctrl]-[End]) key to remove the existing tab stops. Next, type **0.5** (**1.5** in 5.0) and press [Enter] to create a left-aligned tab stop for text at .5″ (1.5″ in 5.0). You could also create this tab stop by moving the cursor to the .5″ position (1.5″ in 5.0) and typing an **l**. Next, since you will align numbers with decimals in a column to the right, type a **4**, press [Enter], and type a **d**, or move to the 4″ position and type a **d**. This will align text to the left of the decimal points. Press the Exit ([F7]) key twice to return to the document. Now you can type the following text, pressing the [Tab] key where indicated:

Expenses [[Tab]] Amount
[[Tab]]Insurance [[Tab]]5,600
[[Tab]]Rent[[Tab]]2,135.50
[[Tab]]Salaries[[Tab]]128,937.13

The screen looks like this:

```
Expenses               Amount
    Insurance          5,600
    Rent               2,135.50
    Salaries           128,937.13
```

4. You can set the tab stops to any regular interval. First, press the Format ([Shift]-[F8]) key, type an L [[Alt] Layout Line] and then a **t**. Once the Tab Set screen appears, press [Home] twice and the [←] key once to move the cursor to the −1″ position (0″ position in 5.0).

Then, press the Delete EOL (Ctrl - End) key to remove the existing tab stops. Next, type a **0** (**1** in 5.0), a comma, and **.6**, and press Enter . WordPerfect sets left-aligned tab stops at every .6″ inches, starting at the 0″ position (1″ in 5.0). If you had first typed an **r, c,** or **d** at the 0″ position (1″ in 5.0), the other tab stops also would have been the type that you had indicated.

EXERCISES

(Do not clear the screen between exercises unless instructed to do so.)

1. Add a tab stop at 3.3″.

2. Remove all tab stops after 6″.

3. Create a right-aligned tab stop at 4″.

4. Create a decimal tab stop at 2.5″.

5. Remove all existing tab stops and set stops at 2″ and 4.5″. Type the following entries, using the Tab key to place the names at the 2″ position and the salaries at the 4.5″ position:

   Jones 17,850
   Culver 23,489
   Walker 32,500

   Clear the screen.

6. Change the tab stops to every .75″ starting at 2″.

7. Return the tab stops to WordPerfect's default of every .5" starting at −1" (0" in 5.0).

5.5   USE THE FLUSH RIGHT FEATURE

WordPerfect's Flush Right feature allows you to align a line of text at the right margin. It is normally used for short entries, such as a company name, the date, or an address.

To enter text flush right:

a. Move to the line on which you want to place the flush-right text.

b. Press the Flush Right ([Alt]-[F6]) key [[Alt] Layout Flush Right].

c. Type the text you want aligned at the right margin.

d. Press [Enter]. The hidden code WordPerfect 5.1 inserts for this feature is [FlshRt] ([FlshRt] and [C/A/Flrt] in 5.0).

EXAMPLES

1. You can use the Flush Right feature when you add a date to a document. A special WordPerfect feature can be used to enter the current date. First, press the Flush Right ([Alt]-[F6]) key [[Alt] Layout Align Flush Right]. Next, press the Date ([Shift]-[F5]) key, and type a **1** or a **t** for Date Text [[Alt] Tools Date Text]. Press [Enter]. The screen looks like this:

April 28 · 1990

If the date is not correct, exit WordPerfect, type **date**, press ⌗Enter⌗, type the correct date using the format indicated at the prompt, press ⌗Enter⌗, and reload WordPerfect.

2. The Flush Right feature aligns text only at the right margin. The position of the first character in a flush-right line will depend on the number and size of the characters in the line. Press the Flush Right (⌗Alt⌗-⌗F6⌗) key [⌗Alt⌗ Layout Align Flush Right], type **ABC COMPANY**, and press ⌗Enter⌗. Press the Flush Right (⌗Alt⌗-⌗F6⌗) key [⌗Alt⌗ Layout Align Flush Right] again, type **First Quarter Sales**, and press ⌗Enter⌗. The last characters in the lines are aligned at the right margin, but the first characters are not aligned.

3. You can enter text on the same line as right-aligned text by typing the other text before invoking the Flush Right feature. First, type **Date:**, press the Date (⌗Shift⌗-⌗F5⌗) key, and type a **1** for Date Text [⌗Alt⌗ Tools Date Text]. Then, press the Flush Right (⌗Alt⌗-⌗F6⌗) key [⌗Alt⌗ Layout Align Flush Right], type **ABC Company**, and press ⌗Enter⌗. The text looks like this:

Date: March 30, 1989   ABC Company

EXERCISES

1. Using the Date feature, enter the current date flush right in the top line of a new document.

2. Enter the following text flush right:

ABC COMPANY

3. Type the following memo, using the Date feature to provide the current date.

MEMO
To: All Employees   Date: August 11, 1990
From: Arnold Smith   Re: Cleaning Computer
**   Screens**
– –
Do not use alcohol-based window cleaners to clean your computer screen. Use the special cleaner that is stored with the blank disks.

5.6 CHANGE THE LINE SPACING

Many letters and other types of correspondence use single spacing. Long reports or documents are often double spaced to make them easier to read. You can set the spacing in WordPerfect for an entire document or for a portion of a document. WordPerfect's default is to use single line spacing.

When you change the line spacing, WordPerfect inserts a hidden code into the document that looks like this: [Ln Spacing:3]. The number after the colon indicates the spacing selected.

To set the line spacing:

a. Press the Format (Shift - F8) key [Alt Layout Line and skip step b].

b. Type an **L** or a **1** to select line-formatting options.

c. Type an **s** or a **6** to select Line Spacing.

d. Type the number of spaces you want between lines.

e. Press Enter.

f. Press the Exit (F7) key.

The line spacing selected with these steps begins at the cursor location. The new spacing is used up to the end of the document unless a new line-spacing code is encountered. The change does not affect the text before the cursor location.

EXAMPLES

1. Lengthy documents are often easier to read if they are double spaced. To set double spacing for an entire document, you need to place the hidden line-spacing code at the top of the document. Type the following:

   This text initially displays and prints with single spacing. It is not necessary to retype text to use other spacing. A quick menu selection applies the change beginning at the current location in the document.

   Move to the top of the document by pressing Home, Home, and ↑. Next, press the Format (Shift - F8) key, type an **L** [Alt Layout Line], and then an **s**.

Next, type a **2**. Finally, press ⌜Enter⌟ and the Exit
(⌜F7⌟) key. This inserts blank lines between lines of
text in the document.

2. A lengthy quote in a document can be single spaced
and indented from both sides to set it off from the
rest of the text. First, press the Format (⌜Shift⌟-⌜F8⌟)
key, type an L [⌜Alt⌟ Layout Line], and then an **s** and
a **2**. When you press ⌜Enter⌟ and the Exit (⌜F7⌟) key to
return to the document, WordPerfect inserts a code
to change the text to double spaced. Type

**Quotes from famous people can be fun to read. The
language is often a little different from English as we
know it today.**

Before typing the quote on the next line, press the
Format (⌜Shift⌟-⌜F8⌟) key, type an L [⌜Alt⌟ Layout
Line], an **s**, and a **1**, and press ⌜Enter⌟ and the Exit
(⌜F7⌟) key to change the line spacing. All of the text
after this point will be single spaced. Next, press the
Indent Left and Right (⌜Shift⌟-⌜F4⌟) key [⌜Alt⌟ Layout
Align Indent →←] , and type

**I do not know what I may appear to the world, but to
myself I seem to have been only like a boy playing on
the sea-shore, and diverting myself in now and then
finding a smoother pebble, or a prettier shell than
ordinary, whilst the great ocean of truth lay undiscovered before me.**
Isaac Newton

Press the Format (⌜Shift⌟-⌜F8⌟) key, type an L [⌜Alt⌟
Layout Line], an **s**, and a **2**, and press ⌜Enter⌟ and the

Exit (F7) key to return the document to double spacing after the quote. Press Enter, and type

The diverse interests of some famous individuals may seem surprising. The quote from Isaac Newton is very simplistic when contrasted with some of his scientific theorems.

This last paragraph is double spaced.

EXERCISES

1. Type the following paragraph:

A sense of humor sharp enough to show a man his own absurdities will keep him from the commission of all sins, or nearly all, except those that are worth committing. (Samuel Butler from Life and Habit)

Move to the first character in the paragraph. Change the spacing to double spacing. Next try triple spacing. Then, set the spacing back to single spacing.

2. Type the following paragraphs. Use the default of single spacing for the first paragraph. Change the line spacing to double spacing before typing the second paragraph. Set the line spacing to triple spacing before typing the third paragraph.

   The new Widget maker will expand our current capacity to meet expected demand levels for the next five to ten years. It has a net present value of $25,687.
   The manufacturer gives a 10% trade-in value on

its old Widget maker. This is a slightly lower price than expected in the open market. The capital budgeting plan contains the lower trade-in value, but the company will probably sell the used machine in the second-hand market.

The new Widget maker has many new features. One of these, a free one-year service contract, will save the company $50,000 in the first year.

Make the first and third paragraphs double spaced and the second paragraph triple spaced.

3. Type the following paragraph. After typing the first sentence, set the line spacing to double spacing.

When you set the line spacing, WordPerfect uses it for all lines after the code in the document. If you change the spacing to double spacing in the middle of a paragraph, the lines above the change are single spaced, and the lines after the change are double spaced.

5.7 ALTER JUSTIFICATION

Initially, WordPerfect is set to fully justify (right-justify in 5.0) text when you print it. WordPerfect inserts space between the words in each line so that all full lines end at the right margin. Since Word-Perfect does not display the text fully justified, the printed document will be different from the screen display. If your screen can display graphics, a screen preview of the document will display the text exactly as it will appear when printed. If you want a ragged right edge on the printed document, such as that which you see on the screen display, you can change the setting to left justification (turn justification off in 5.0). WordPerfect 5.1 also allows you to format your text with center justification (each line centered down the page) and right justification (a smooth right margin but a ragged left margin).

To change justification:

a. Press the Format (Shift - F8) key [Alt Layout Line and skip step b].

b. Type an **L** or a **1** to select line-formatting options.

c. Type a **j** or a **3** for Justification.

d. Type an **L** or a **1** if you want left justification, a **c** or a **2** if you want center justification, an **r** or a **3** if you want right justification, or an **f** or a **4** if you want full justification. (Type a **y** if you want the text right justified or an **n** if you want a ragged right edge in 5.0).

e. Press the Exit (F7) key to return to the document.

EXAMPLE

1. You can change the right justification to change the appearance of printed lines. First, type

The company's financial position is improving. The company retired a million dollars of debt this year and will retire another million next year. The company is retiring the debt by buying stock on the open market open market and retiring the certificates. Also, the lag between invoice dates and payment dates has decreased by 3 days.

Move the cursor to the beginning of the paragraph. Press the Format ([Shift]-[F8]) key, type an L [[Alt] Layout Line], a j, and an L (an n in 5.0), and press the Exit ([F7]) key. Now the paragraph will look like this when printed:

```
The company's financial position is improving.  The company
retired a million dollars of debt this year and will retire
another million next year.  The company is retiring the debt by
buying stock on the open market and retiring the certificates.
Also, the lag between invoice dates and payment dates has
decreased by 3 days.
```

EXERCISES

1. Type the following paragraph. If your screen can display graphics, preview the document. Change full justification to left justification (turn off justification in 5.0), and preview the document again. Return the document to full justification (turn justification on in 5.0).

   The Accounts Receivable computer system was installed last January. Due to this new system, the average daily accounts receivable amount dropped by $50. Also, the percentage of bad accounts has dropped from 4% to 2%, mostly due to quicker action on overdue accounts.

2. Type the first paragraph below. Change to left justification (turn off justification in 5.0), and type the second paragraph. Preview how WordPerfect will print the document.

When a paragraph is fully justified, WordPerfect inserts additional space into lines of the printed copy of the document. This creates even left and right margins. The extra spaces appear only in the printed copy and do not appear on the screen.

When a paragraph is left justified, WordPerfect does not insert additional space. The right margin has a jagged appearance.

EXERCISES

1. Increase the right and left margins by 1" each, and type the following paragraph:

Disks store information using magnetized material to hold information. The basic unit of storage is a byte. A byte stores one character of information.

Save this file as DISK.

2. Type the following paragraph, indenting the left margin of the paragraph by an inch.

Disk drives read information from a disk. The disk drive spins the disk quickly. A read/write head above the disk reads the information as it spins past the head.

Save this file as DISKREAD.

3. Remove all tab stops. Set one tab stop at 4", and use the Tab key to create this letter heading:

Acme Corporation
496 Prospect Road
Cleveland, Ohio 44115
January 3, 1990

4. Retrieve the file DISK, and change the line spacing to double spacing. Save the file.

5. Retrieve DISKREAD, and change to left justification (turn off justification in 5.0). Save the file.

6. Enter the following account numbers flush right, with one account number per line:

ACC-9876
HDG-3218
CRC-9873

7. Duplicate the following, using the Margin Release and Indent features:

Campbell, Mary, <u>Teach Yourself WordPerfect 5.1</u>, Osborne/McGraw-Hill, 1990.

INTEGRATING SKILLS CHECK

1. Type the following bibliography entries. Increase the left margin by .5″ so that all of the entries will appear indented. Use the Margin Release feature to make the first line of each entry begin five spaces to the left of the indent position.

Crosby, Samuel, "Mergers and Acquisitions," <u>Business Yearly</u>, (OMB Publishing, 1983), June, p. 46-49.

Lee, Jane and Lifeson, Tom, "Effectively Combining Companies," <u>Journal of Business Results</u>, (AMBA, 1987), vol 36, Fall, p. 101-9.

2. Use Margin Release and other formatting features to create a heading with the following information on a single line:

Acme Corporation
1560 Main Street
Cleveland, Ohio 44103

Place the company name at the left edge of the page. Center the street address. Right align the city, state, and ZIP code. Underline the line.

3. Type the following letter:

Joan Smith
President, Widgets Inc.
7946 Madison Avenue
New York, New York 10061

Dear Ms. Smith:

Enclosed is the pamphlet you requested, Wrapping Consumer Goods. Our products can shrink-wrap any product. If you send the dimensions of the products that you want to shrink-wrap, one of our representatives will prepare a list of the materials and equipment you will need.

Sincerely,

Larry Kennedy
Plastic Covering Co.

Change to left justification (turn off right justification in 5.0) for the letter. Underline the pamphlet name. Reveal the codes, and delete the Underline code. Print the document.

4. Match the following codes with the features they represent:

1. Soft return	a. [Ln Spacing:3]
2. Underline	b. [←Mar Rel]
3. Flush Right	c. [→Indent]
4. Margin Release	d. [BOLD][bold]
5. Indent	e. [UND][und]
6. Hard return	f. [Center] ([Cntr] in 5.0)
7. Hard page return	g. [FlshRgt] ([Flsh Rt] in 5.0)
8. Triple line spacing	h. [→Indent←]
9. Boldface text	i. [HRt]
10. Full justification (Justification on in 5.0)	j. [SRt]
11. Set tabs	k. [Just:Full] ([Just On] in 5.0)
12. Indent Left and Right	l. [HPg]
13. Center text on line	m. [Tab Set:Rel:0",0.5",2.5"] ([Tab Set:0",0.5",2.5"] in 5.0)

5. Enter the date flush right. Search for the Flush Right code and delete it.

Changing the Format
of a Page

▶6◀

CHAPTER OBJECTIVES

After completing this chapter, you should be able to:

▶ Center text on a page   6.1

▶ Adjust top and bottom margins   6.2

▶ Add page numbers   6.3

▶ Change the paper size and type   6.4

Using a pleasing page format can help you create a document with a professional appearance. Rather than continuing to use the default features, you can enhance the presentation quality of your output with page-format changes.

Such options as centering the text between the top and the bottom of the page allow you to create a short document that still presents a professional image. You can alter the margin settings for the top and bottom of the page, add page numbers, and adjust the page length to make additional appearance enhancements.

SKILLS CHECK

(Do not clear the screen until you have completed the last exercise.)

1. Type the following text, using Bold for "Education:".

    John Doe
    23405 Lander Road
    Cleveland, Ohio 44130
    (216)229-8976

    Education: Cleveland State University, Cleveland, Ohio
    Business Administration, August 1983
    Dean's List 7 Quarters, GPA 3.75

2. Center the name, address, and phone number.

3. Boldface the name.

4. Underline the word "Education."

5. At the beginning of the document, create a tab stop at 1.2″ (2.2″ in 5.0), and remove the ones at .5″ and 1″ (1.5″ and 2″ in 5.0).

6. Indent the three lines containing educational information.

7. Move the first line containing educational information back to the left margin using the Margin Release feature.

8. Print the document.

CENTER TEXT ON A PAGE

6.1

A short memo or letter can present a strong impression if it is centered vertically on the page. Such other text as the title page of a report is also most effectively presented centered between the top and the bottom of the page. This feature is different from the line-centering option covered in Chapter 4. It can be used separately or in combination with line-centering features.

The page-centering command adds the hidden code [Center Pg] to your document at the location of the cursor. To remove the feature, you must delete the code.

To center text on a page:

a. Move the cursor to the top of the page on which you want the text to be centered.

b. Press the Format ([Shift]-[F8]) key [[Alt] Layout Page and skip step c].

c. Type a **p** or a **2** to select page-formatting options.

d. Type a **c** or a **1**, then type a **y** to center the text on the page (in 5.0, **y** is automatically entered).

e. Press the Exit ([F7]) key to return to the document.

f. Type the text if it is not already in the document.

g. Press [Ctrl]-[Enter] [[Alt] Layout Align Hard Page] to end the page.

EXAMPLES

1. When you create a title page for a report, you often want the title to appear in the middle of the page. Rather than pressing [Enter] until the cursor is in the middle of the page, you can have WordPerfect automatically center the text for you. First, press the Format ([Shift]-[F8]) key, and type a **p** [[Alt] Layout Page], and then type a **c**; then type a **y** (in 5.0, **y** is automatically entered). Press the Exit ([F7]) key to return to the document. Press the Center ([Shift]-[F6]) key [[Alt] Layout Align Center] and type

   Horton Corporation Financial Statements

   Press [Enter] to move to the next line. Press the Center ([Shift]-[F6]) key [[Alt] Layout Align Center], and type

   As of July 30, 1990

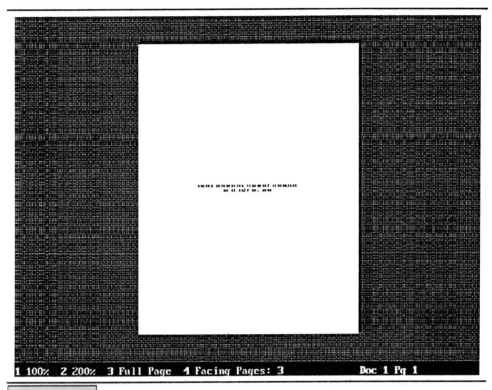

1 100%   2 200%   3 Full Page   4 Facing Pages: 3   Doc 1 Pg 1

| FIGURE 6-1. | Print preview of lines centered on a page |

When you press the Print ([Shift]-[F7]) key [[Alt] File Print] and type a **v** and a **3** to view the full page, your screen looks like Figure 6-1.

2. You can improve the appearance of short business letters by centering them vertically on the page. To center a short letter, press the Format ([Shift]-[F8]) key, type a **p** [[Alt] Layout Page] and a **c**, then type a **y** (in 5.0, **y** is automatically entered). Press the Exit ([F7]) key to return to the document, and type

Tracy Smith
2647 Chillecothe Road
Kirkland, Ohio 44296

Dear Tracy,

   I have enclosed the information you requested.
Please contact me at (212)555-5931 if you have any
questions.

Sincerely,

Darren Jeck

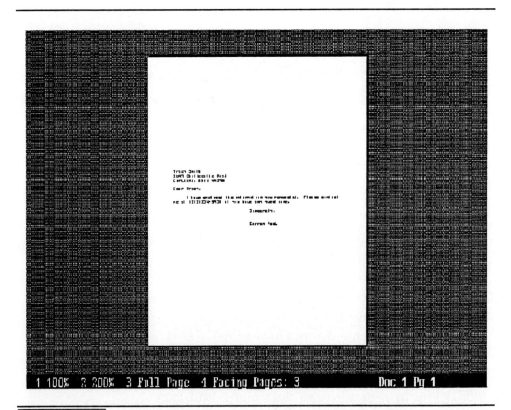

1 100%   2 200%   3 Full Page   4 Facing Pages: 3   Doc 1 Pg 1

FIGURE 6-2.   Print preview of a short letter centered on a page

When you preview this letter before printing, it looks like Figure 6-2.

EXERCISES

1. Create a title page with the following three lines centered horizontally and vertically:

   Investigation into the Physical Properties of Rust
   Dissertation
   Angus McPhearson

2. Create a short thank-you letter to **Jules McBride** at **234 Main Street, Lawrence, PA 28634**, thanking him for promptly sending the information you have requested. Center the letter on the page.

3. Create a title page with the following lines centered horizontally and vertically. Preview how Word-Perfect will print it.

   1990 Financial Statements
   Acme Corporation

4. Create the following memo, centering it on the page. Preview how WordPerfect will print it.

   MEMO:
   To: All Employees
   Re: Paychecks
       To receive a paycheck September 10th, submit your time card to payroll by September 3rd.

ADJUST TOP AND BOTTOM MARGINS   6.2

The top and bottom margins are the white areas at the top and bottom of a printed page. Increasing the size of these margins lessens the amount of text that can be shown on a page. When you are printing on letterhead paper, you may need to increase the top margin to begin printing below the letterhead.

WordPerfect measures each margin as the number of inches from the text to the edge of the paper. WordPerfect initially has 1" top and bottom margins. WordPerfect uses the default margin settings unless it finds a hidden code representing another margin specification. When you change the margins, Word-Perfect inserts a hidden code and adjusts the number of lines that print on each page.

To change the top and bottom margins:

a. Move the cursor to the top of the document or the top of the page on which you wish to change the margins.

b. Press the Format (⟮Shift⟯-⟮F8⟯) key [⟮Alt⟯ Layout Page and skip step c].

c. Select Page by typing a **p** or a **2**.

d. Select Margins by typing an **m** or a **5**.

e. Type the number of inches WordPerfect should leave between the top of the paper and the printed text.

f. Press ⟮Enter⟯.

g. Type the number of inches WordPerfect should leave between the bottom of the paper and the printed text.

h. Press ⟮Enter⟯.

i. Press the Exit ([F7]) key to return to the document.

WordPerfect inserts a hidden code to represent your top and bottom margin settings at the cursor location. For a top margin of 2″ and a bottom margin of 3″, the code looks like this: [T/B Mar:2″,3″]. To see the hidden code, use the Reveal Codes ([Alt]-[F3]) key [[Alt] Edit Reveal Codes].

EXAMPLES

1. You can decrease the margins to increase the amount of text that fits on a page. For example, you can decrease the margins to .5″. First, press the Format ([Shift]-[F8]) key and type a **p** [[Alt] Layout Page] to select the page-formatting options. Next, type an **m** to select the margin-formatting option. Type .5 and press [Enter] to set the top margin. Type .5 and press [Enter] to set the bottom margin. Finally, press the Exit ([F7]) key to return to the document. These changes add an inch of space on each page.

2. You can increase the margins to decrease the amount of text that fits on a page. First, press the Format ([Shift]-[F8]) key and type a **p** [[Alt] Layout Page]. Next, type an **m** to select Margins. Then, type 1.5 to set the top margin, and press [Enter]. Next, type 1.5 to set the bottom margin, and press [Enter]. Finaly, press the Exit ([F7]) key to return to the document. The document has 1″ less space for text on the page.

EXERCISES

1. Change the top and bottom margins to 3″ at the beginning of a document. Determine how many times you can press ⌈Enter⌉ before WordPerfect inserts a page break.

2. Change the top and bottom margins to 0″. Determine how many times you can press ⌈Enter⌉ before WordPerfect inserts a page break.

3. Set the top margin to 9.5″, leaving the bottom margin at 1″. Type the following paragraphs. Preview how WordPerfect will print the document.

> **The top margin determines the space WordPerfect skips on a page when printing a document. You must specify this measurement in inches.**
> **The bottom margin determines the space WordPerfect leaves on a page when printing a document. As WordPerfect prints a document, it determines how much room is left on the page. When the amount of remaining space equals the size of the bottom margin, WordPerfect inserts a soft page break.**

6.3   ADD PAGE NUMBERS

WordPerfect does not print page numbers in a document automatically. This is convenient, since you probably will not want page numbers on letters, memos, and other similar documents. However, you can have WordPerfect add page numbers in a number of locations on a page. If you plan to combine two or more files into one document, you can specify the page number for WordPerfect to use at the beginning of each file to ensure continuous pagination.

To number the pages:

a. Press the Format (Shift-F8) key [Alt Layout Page and skip step b].

b. Type a **p** or a **2** to select the page-formatting options.

c. Type an **n** or a **6** to select the page-numbering options (omit this step in 5.0).

d. Type a **p** or a **4** (**n** or **7** in 5.0) to select the page-number position.

e. Select the number that corresponds to the location where you want WordPerfect to place the page numbers.

f. Type an **n** or a **1** (**n** or **6** in 5.0) to select a new page number if you want the page numbers to start with a number other than the one indicated on the status line. Type the new page number and press Enter.

g. Press the Exit (F7) key to return to the document.

EXAMPLES

1. You can instruct WordPerfect where to place page numbers in a printed document. First, press the Format (Shift-F8) key, and type a **p** [Alt Layout Page], then an **n** (omit for 5.0) to display the Page Numbering menu shown in Figure 6-3. This menu

```
Format: Page Numbering

    1 - New Page Number        1

    2 - Page Number Style      ^B

    3 - Insert Page Number

    4 - Page Number Position No page numbering
```

```
Selection: 0
```

FIGURE 6-3.   Page-numbering menu

allows you to select a location on the page for page numbers. It also provides options like changing the style of page numbers and starting with a number other than 1. These other options are beyond the scope of this book. Next, type a **p** to display the page-numbering format options, as shown in Figure 6-4.

Each number on the screen represents a specific location for page numbers. Selections 4 and 8 put the page numbers at the left on even-numbered pages and at the right on odd-numbered pages. Type a **7** and press the Exit (F7) key. When you

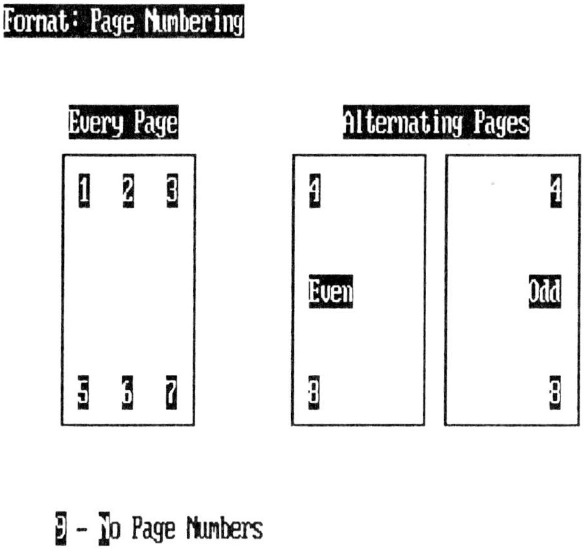

Fornat: Page Numbering

Every Page

1 2 3

5 6 7

Alternating Pages

4

Even

8

4

Odd

8

9 - To Page Numbers

FIGURE 6-4.   Page-numbering options

print the document, WordPerfect will place page
numbers in the lower right corner on every page.

2. You can change the number WordPerfect uses to
start counting page numbers. You can use this
feature when you are combining files. For example,
if you are creating a page to insert at the end of
another document that has 3 pages, you will want
to begin the new document with page number 4.
First, press the format ((Shift)-(F8)) key and type a p
[(Alt) Layout Page], then an **n** (omit for 5.0), and
then a **p**. Type a **4** once to place the page numbers
in the upper left corner on even-numbered pages

and in the upper right corner on odd-numbered pages. Next, type an **n** for the New Page Number option, type a **4**, and press Enter. After you press the Exit (F7) key, you can press the Reveal Codes (Alt-F3) key [Alt Edit Reveal Codes] to see the hidden codes [Pg Numbering: Top Alternating] and [Pg Num:4], which WordPerfect has inserted. Press the Reveal Codes (Alt-F3) key [Alt Edit Reveal Codes] again to remove the codes from view.

Next, type

This is the first page of this document, although we will ask WordPerfect to number it as page 4.

Then, press Ctrl-Enter [Alt Layout Align Hard Page] to create a page break. The status line shows that you are on page 5. Press the Print (Shift-F7) key [Alt File Print] and type an **f** to print the pages.

EXERCISES

1. Instruct WordPerfect to place page numbers in the center at the bottom of each page. Type **Travel Expenses**, and press Ctrl-Enter [Alt Layout Align Hard Page]. Type **Benefits**, and press Ctrl-Enter [Alt Layout Align Hard Page]. Type **Salary Expense**, and press Enter. Preview the document to see where the page numbers will appear.

2. Instruct WordPerfect to number the pages at the bottom center. Next, type the numbers **1** to **5**, pressing Ctrl-Enter [Alt Layout Align Hard Page] between numbers to place each one on a separate

page. Preview the page. Starting with the last page, renumber each page so that WordPerfect numbers them in reverse order; for example, WordPerfect will print page 1 as page number 5.

CHANGE THE PAPER SIZE AND TYPE

6.4

WordPerfect's standard paper size and location are determined when the printer is installed. (See Appendix A for information on installing a printer.) Depending on your printer, you may have a variety of other options available for printing documents.

For example, your printer may be able to print on various sizes of paper, such as legal size sheets and envelopes. Your printer may have more than one paper bin, or location, from which different forms are pulled. These forms could include letterhead, bond paper, cardstock, or mailing labels. Some types of paper may be continuously fed through the printer, while others may have to be manually fed. Usually you will want your documents to be printed in portrait orientation, which prints text across the narrower side of the paper. At other times you'll want the printer to use the paper in landscape orientation, which prints sideways and across the wider side of the paper. Using 8 1/2 by 11-inch paper, portrait mode prints across the 8 1/2-inch side, and landscape prints across the 11-inch side of the sheet. Using Word-Perfect, you can select the size, location, and orientation for printing your documents.

In WordPerfect 5.1, your selection for paper size, type, and orientation is made from one menu called the Format: Paper Size/Type menu. An example of

this menu is shown in Figure 6-5. Your menu will
have a different appearance based on the type of
printer you use and the types of paper that have been
defined for your printer.

In WordPerfect 5.0, your selection for paper size
and orientation is in the Format: Paper Size menu.
This menu is shown in Figure 6-6. Your selection for
the type or location of the document is made from the
Format: Paper Type menu. This menu is shown in
Figure 6-7.

To change the paper format:

a. Press the Format (Shift - F8) key [Alt Layout Page
   and skip step b].

```
Format: Paper Size/Type
                                                   Font Double
Paper type and Orientation    Paper Size    Prompt Loc  Type Sided  Labels

Envelope - Wide               9.5" x 4"      No   Manual Land No
Standard                      8.5" x 11"     No   Contin Port No
Standard                      8.5" x 14"     No   Contin Port No
Standard - Wide               11" x 8.5"     No   Contin Land No
Standard - Wide               14" x 8.5"     No   Contin Land No
[ALL OTHERS]                  Width ≤ 8.5"   Yes  Manual     No
```

```
    1 Select; 2 Add; 3 Copy; 4 Delete; 5 Edit; N Name Search: 1
```

FIGURE 6-5.   Format: Paper Size/Type menu

b. Type a **p** or a **2** to select the page-formatting options.

c. Type an **s** or a **7** (**s** or **8** in 5.0) to select the paper size/type options.

d. In WordPerfect 5.1: Using the cursor keys, highlight the paper selection you will use and press (Enter).

   In WordPerfect 5.0: Select the size of paper you will use from the Format: Paper Size menu and the type of paper from the Format: Paper Type menu.

e. Press the Exit ((F7)) key to return to the document.

Format: Paper Size

   1 – Standard   (8.5" x 11")

   2 – Standard Landscape   (11" x 8.5")

   3 – Legal   (8.5" x 14")

   4 – Legal Landscape   (14" x 8.5")

   5 – Envelope   (9.5" x 4")

   6 – Half Sheet   (5.5" x 8.5")

   7 – US Government   (8" x 11")

   8 – A4   (210mm x 297mm)

   9 – A4 Landscape   (297mm x 210mm)

   0 – Other   -

Selection: 1

| FIGURE 6-6. | Format: Paper Size menu |

```
Format: Paper Type

    1 - Standard

    2 - Bond

    3 - Letterhead

    4 - Labels

    5 - Envelope

    6 - Transparency

    7 - Cardstock

    8 - Other




Selection: 1
```

| FIGURE 6-7. | Format: Paper Type menu |

EXAMPLES

1. You can set the page size and style to print addresses on envelopes. First, press the Format (Shift-F8) key and type a **p** [Alt Layout Page] and an **s**. Next, highlight the envelope selection and type an **s**. (Type an **e** twice in 5.0 to select Envelopes as both the paper size and type.) Finally, press the Exit (F7) key to return to the document. Now you can type addresses on separate pages and have WordPerfect print each address on an envelope. If

you press the Reveal Codes ((Alt)-(F3)) key [(Alt) Edit Reveal codes], you can see the code [Paper Sz/Typ:9.5" x 4",Envelope] at the top of the document. If your printer cannot handle the size or type you select, WordPerfect displays (***requested form is unavailable**) in the page-format menu.

2. When you change the paper size and type, it affects all pages after the code. You can use multiple codes to have pages of a document print on different sizes or types of paper. First, type

Dear Jim,

   Here is the information that you wanted.

To create an envelope for this message, press (Ctrl)-(Enter) [(Alt) Layout Align Hard Page] to start a new page. Press the Format ((Shift)-(F8)) key and type a **p** [(Alt) Layout Page], then type an **s**. Next, highlight the envelope selection and type an **s** (type an **e** twice in 5.0). Press the Exit ((F7)) key to return to the document. Type

Jim Adler
514 Washington Avenue
Columbus, OH 43213

To see how WordPerfect has changed the paper size, press the Print ((Shift)-(F7)) key [(Alt) File Print] and type a **v**. WordPerfect shows the name and address on an envelope-shaped page. When you press (PgUp), WordPerfect shows the letter on a normal page. Press the Exit ((F7)) key to return to the document.

EXERCISES

1. Set the paper size and type for legal-size (8 1/2″ X 14″) standard paper (assuming that your printer supports this size paper). Type **Legal-Size Paper**, and create a hard page break. For the second page, return the paper size and type to standard (8 1/2″ X 11″). Type **Standard-Size Paper**. Preview how Word-Perfect will print the pages.

2. Type the address from the second example in this section in a document set for a half sheet of standard paper (5.5″ X 8.5″). Preview how WordPerfect will print it.

EXERCISES

(Do not clear the screen until you have completed the last exercise.)

1. Type the following, centering each line as well as centering the document on the page:

   Wilbur Horse Supplies
   Financial Statements
   For the Year Ending December 31, 1990

   Preview the document as WordPerfect will print it.

2. Set the top margin to 3″. Preview the document again.

3. Set WordPerfect to print page numbers in the center at the top of each page.

4. Move to the bottom of the document, and enter a hard page break. Set WordPerfect to number the second page of the document as page 10.

5. Change the paper size to half.

(Do not clear the screen until you have completed the last exercise.)

INTEGRATING SKILLS CHECK

1. Center the following lines as you type them:

   Archie's California Grapes
   Production Records
   For the season ending September 30, 1990

2. Center the three lines vertically on the page.

3. Boldface the first line, and underline the second line.

4. Move to the bottom of the document, and insert a hard page break. Set the page numbers to appear in the upper right corner, starting with 1.

5. Change the spacing to double spacing, and type the following paragraph:

   This year's crop is the largest in the last 20 years. It is primarily due to improved fertilization methods and increased rainfall. The plants damaged by last year's drought were replaced.

6. Change the paragraph so that it is not right justified.

7. Print the document.

►7◄

CHAPTER OBJECTIVES

After completing this chapter, you should be able to:

► Search for a word or phrase from the
beginning of a document   7.1

► Search from the end of a document   7.2

► Use the Replace feature   7.3

WordPerfect can assist you in searching through your document to pinpoint the exact location of a word or phrase. This feature provides a significant time savings over visually searching the document and is usually more accurate as well. WordPerfect can search the entire document from the beginning or the end. You can also have it search in either direction from any point in between. In addition to finding an entry, WordPerfect's Replace feature allows you to replace the entry with a new entry. This feature helps you make corrections in several places with ease. Tasks such as correcting the spelling of a name used throughout a document can be handled quickly with this feature.

WordPerfect can find text, numbers, special characters, hidden codes, and any combination of them. Chapter 4 introduced you to searching for hidden codes. You will find that searching for text follows a similar pattern.

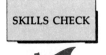

SKILLS CHECK

(Do not clear the screen until you have completed the last exercise.)

1. Type the following paragraph:

Product Announcement

   The XY Graphics Company has announced the release of its new product, See 'N' Draw. This package creates custom pictures by combining existing drawings and advanced graphics features. Since each new feature added to an image is considered a unique layer, you can edit one layer without affecting the others. The

print options offer features unavailable in any competing product.

2. Boldface the title.

3. Center the title.

4. Remove the boldfacing in the title by removing the
hidden codes.

5. Indent the paragraph on both sides.

6. Double-space the paragraph.

7. Center the text on the page.

8. Print the page.

SEARCH FOR A WORD OR PHRASE FROM THE BEGINNING OF A DOCUMENT

7.1

WordPerfect's Search feature can find a match for a
string, or series of characters or codes. You can place
from 1 to 59 characters (including spaces) in the
search string. Since you will be searching forward
(from the beginning to the end), it is important to
begin with the cursor in front of all the text that you
want to include in the search.

If you use one or more capital letters in a search
string, WordPerfect conducts a case-sensitive search.
If you use only lowercase letters in the search string,
WordPerfect ignores case when searching for a match.

If WordPerfect finds a match, it positions the cursor immediately past the matching letter, word, or phrase. If WordPerfect cannot find a match, the computer beeps, the message "∗ Not found ∗" appears on the screen briefly, and the cursor remains where it was. You can also use this feature to search for hidden codes alone or as part of a string.

To have WordPerfect search for a word or phrase:

a. Press the Search (F2) key [Alt Search Forward].

b. Type the word or phrase that WordPerfect should find.

c. Press the Search (F2) key again.

To search for the same word or phrase a second time, press the Search (F2) key twice [Alt Search Forward, F2]. If you have already used the Search command, WordPerfect displays the last string that you searched for. You can edit this text rather than typing the new search text or codes. When Word-Perfect prompts you for the search string, press Ins, Del, or the → key, and change the text displayed in the prompt.

EXAMPLES

1. WordPerfect's Search feature can perform a case-sensitive search. A case-sensitive search matches only words or phrases with the exact capitalization

found in the search string. WordPerfect conducts a case-sensitive search anytime you include capital letters in the search string. First, type the following:

There are many stores that sell computer software. Discount stores, office supply houses, full-service computer stores, and specialized software stores are all options. I prefer to shop at Upgrade Computer.

Next, move the cursor to the beginning by pressing [Home], [Home], [↑]. To find the word "Computer" in "Upgrade Computer," press the Search ([F2]) key [[Alt] Search Forward], and type **Computer**. Then, press the Search ([F2]) key again. WordPerfect moves the cursor to the period following "Computer." WordPerfect skipped the first two occurrences of the word, since they did not begin with a capital "c." Use this paragraph to look at the other Search features in the next two examples.

2. You can conduct a search that ignores the case of entries by entering the search string in lowercase letters. First, move to the top of the document by pressing [Home], [Home], [↑]. Next, press the Search ([F2]) key [[Alt] Search Forward] and type **computer**. When you press the Search ([F2]) key again, WordPerfect positions the cursor on the space following "computer" in the first sentence.

   If you press the Search ([F2]) key [[Alt] Search Forward] again, WordPerfect redisplays the search string. You can type a new entry or press the Search ([F2]) key to use the one displayed. When you reuse the first search string, WordPerfect positions the cursor on the space following "computer" in the second sentence. Pressing the Search ([F2]) key twice [[Alt] Search Forward, [F2]] again positions the cursor on the period following "Computer." If you press the Search ([F2]) key twice [[Alt] Search Forward, [F2]] again, your computer beeps and displays the message "* Not found *."

3. You can use the Search feature to help locate a word or phrase you wish to delete. To find and delete the phrase "office supply houses" in the paragraph, move to the top of the paragraph by pressing [Home], [Home], [↑]. Press the Search ([F2]) key [[Alt] Search Forward], and type

office supply houses,

When you press the Search ([F2]) key again, Word-Perfect positions the cursor at the end of this phrase. Press [Home] and [Backspace] three times to eliminate the phrase.

4. You can use the search feature to find a combination of text and hidden codes. This can help you pinpoint a specific location of a word that may occur many times in a document. First, type the following quote from Shakespeare, adding an underline to the word "His" in the last line:

His words are bonds, his oaths are oracles;
His love sincere, his thoughts immaculate;
His tears, pure messengers sent from his heart;
His heart as far from fraud as heaven from earth.

Move to the top of the entry by pressing [Home],
[Home], [↑]. Press the Search ([F2]) key [[Alt] Search
Forward]. Then, press the Underline ([F8]) key,
type **his**, and press the Underline ([F8]) key again.
The search entry looks like this:

➡️ Srch: [UND]his[und]

The [UND] and [und] symbols are part of the
hidden codes for the document. When you press
the Search ([F2]) key again, WordPerfect finds the
entry "His" in the last line.

5. You can use the Search feature to look for part of a
   word. If you know that you are searching for a
   name that begins with "Smith" but are not certain if
   it is "Smithson," "Smithsonian," or "Smithfield,"
   you can search for "Smith" to find all words that
   begin with "Smith." First, type

   **We have invited the Smithfields and the Harpers for
   dinner on Friday.**

   Press [Home], [Home], [↑] to move to the beginning of
   the document. Press the Search ([F2]) key [[Alt]
   Search Forward], type **Smith**, and press the Search
   ([F2]) key again. WordPerfect places the cursor on
   the "f" in "Smithfield." If you want to find "Smith"
   alone in the middle of a sentence, you can search
   for it by typing Smith for the search string and
   pressing the SPACEBAR. To find any occurrences of
   "Smith" at the end of a sentence, type Smith and a
   period for the search string.

EXERCISES

1. Type the following paragraph. Use the Search feature to locate the name "Jill Smith."

   On Saturday, May 16, XY Graphics is holding a press conference for their new product, See 'N' Draw. At this conference, the public relations director, Jill Smith, will reveal the company's marketing strategy for the product.

2. Type the following lines. Move to the beginning of the file, and use the Search feature to locate the "5" used to specify the number of disks.

   Memory Requirements: 512K
   Storage Space Required: 200K
   Number of Disks: 5
   Tutorial: Yes
   Demo: Yes

3. Type the following text. Then find all occurrences of the word "forgive."

   "I can forgive but I cannot forget," is only another way of saying, "I cannot forgive."
   Henry Ward Beecher

   Forgive! How many will say "Forgive" and find
   A sort of absolution in the sound
   To hate a little longer.
   Alfred, Lord Tennyson

4. Type the following paragraph. Find all occurrences of the three-letter combination "sea." Find all oc-

currences of the word "sea" without finding words that have that letter combination in it.

Searching for seashells is enjoyable. You do not have to leave the seashore or beach to find them. It is a wonderful way to spend your time by an ocean or a sea in any season.

SEARCH FROM THE END OF A DOCUMENT   7.2

WordPerfect can search backward from any point in a document to the beginning of the document. It is important to begin with the cursor past all the text that you want to include in the search. The cursor stops at the position immediately following the match, if one is found. If WordPerfect cannot find a match it beeps and displays the "* Not found *" message, and the cursor remains where it was.

To search backward for a word or phrase:

a. Press the Reverse Search (Shift-F2) key [Alt Search Backward].

b. Type the word or phrase that you want Word-Perfect to find.

c. Press the Reverse Search (Shift-F2) key or the Search (F2) key. (You get the same result, since WordPerfect sets the direction by the command used in step a.)

To search for the same word or phrase a second time, press the Reverse Search (Shift-F2) key twice more [⟨Alt⟩ Search Backward, ⟨Shift⟩-⟨F2⟩]. If WordPerfect does not find the word or phrase, it beeps and displays "* Not found *" in the status line. If the text you type in step b is all lowercase, WordPerfect finds both upper- and lowercase letters. If any part of the search string is uppercase, WordPerfect will find only matches with identical capitalization.

EXAMPLES

1. You can perform a search through a document you have just completed typing without first moving to the beginning of the document by using the Reverse Search (⟨Shift⟩-⟨F2⟩) [⟨Alt⟩ Search Backward] option. First, type the following paragraph:

   The See 'N' Draw package is easy to install. The installation program creates a subdirectory and copies the files to it. After running the installation program, the See 'N' Draw program is ready to run.

   To find where the text mentions "subdirectories," press the Reverse Search (⟨Shift⟩-⟨F2⟩) key [⟨Alt⟩ Search Backward], and type

   subdirector

   Because you did not include the suffix, WordPerfect can find either "subdirectory" or "subdirectories." Press the Search (⟨F2⟩) key. WordPerfect moves the cursor to the "y" in "subdirectory" in the second sentence.

2. You can also use Reverse Search to find hidden codes. For example, when you type a paragraph, you might keep WordPerfect from wrapping the lines correctly by pressing [Enter] at the end of a line that is not the end of the paragraph. You can locate the [HRt] symbol by pressing [Enter] when prompted for the search string. You can locate other attributes, such as centering, boldface, and underlining, just as easily. First, type the following, without pressing [Enter]:

A strong feature of See 'N' Draw is the

Continue the entry on the same line by pressing the SPACEBAR and the Bold ([F6]) key and typing

automatic detection of the hardware components.

Press the Bold ([F6]) key again, press the SPACEBAR twice, and type the following without pressing [Enter]:

When you initially load See 'N' Draw, the program prompts you for information about the equipment you are using. The program determines the proper settings to use for your equipment. You can change these assumptions during installation or later through the menu.

To find the code representing the end of boldfacing, press the Reverse Search ([Shift]-[F2]) key [[Alt] Search Backward]. Since you want the code that turns Bold off, press the Bold ([F6]) key twice, and use the [←] and [Backspace] keys to remove the first Bold code. Next, press the Search ([F2]) key. WordPerfect moves the cursor to the end of the first sentence.

EXERCISES

1. Type the following sentence:

   The entire project was moved to Tobler Hall under the direction of John Tomita.

   Use Reverse Search to find all occurrences of the string "to."

2. Type the following sentences:

   The meeting is Friday, August 11th. <u>All must attend.</u> Discuss previous commitments with Carol Stevens.

   Use Reverse Search to find the ending underline code.

3. Type the following paragraph:

   The next forum for the Secretary's Association is in Buffalo. Since it is close to the Canadian border, they are expecting an increased number of foreigners. The cost, including dinner, is forty dollars.

   Use Reverse Search to find all occurrences of the string "for." Then use Reverse Search to find all occurrences of the word "for" without finding other words that have that letter combination in them.

7.3 USE THE REPLACE FEATURE

In addition to searching for text, WordPerfect can replace a string of characters with another string of characters. Further, this feature provides *global* replacement, meaning that WordPerfect searches the entire document and changes each occurrence of the search string to the replacement string. You can choose to confirm every replacement or allow Word-Perfect to make the replacements without waiting for confirmation. To restrict the text to be affected by the replace operation, you can use the Block feature to mark the text to be searched.

The Replace feature provides a convenient method for correcting names entered incorrectly, incorrect product numbers, or any other information you wish to change. You must supply both the original search string and its replacement.

To have WordPerfect find and replace a word or phrase:

a. Press the Replace ([Alt]-[F2]) key [[Alt] Search Replace].

b. Type a **y** or an **n** to indicate whether you want to confirm each replacement.

c. Press the [↑] key if you wish WordPerfect to proceed with the replace operation toward the beginning rather than the end of the document.

d. Type the word or phrase that WordPerfect should find.

e. Press the Search ([F2]) key.

If the text you type in step d is all lowercase, WordPerfect finds both upper- and lowercase letters. If any part of the search string is uppercase,

WordPerfect finds only matches with identical capitalization.

f. Type the replacement text.

Use the exact capitalization that you wish to appear in the replacement text.

g. Press the Search (F2) key.

If you perform step c and you have already performed a search or replace during the current WordPerfect session, you need to remove the previous search string. You can do so by using the Del or DELETE EOL (Ctrl-End) key. If you begin typing the new search string *before* pressing the ↑ key, however, WordPerfect will delete the first search string automatically.

When WordPerfect replaces text or codes working toward the beginning of the document, it does not reformat the document. You will need to scroll forward through the document after WordPerfect has finished to make it adjust the text.

You can press the Cancel (F1) key at any time during the Replace procedure if you make a mistake or change your mind.

EXAMPLES

1. You can use the Replace feature to change every occurrence of a word or phrase to another word or phrase. First, type the following text.

See 'N' Draw is a product designed for first-time users and artists who want to push the limits of a graphics package. Compared with competitors' products, See 'N' Draw has the easiest user interface to learn. See 'N' Draw is available at most retail software dealers.

Next, to change the package name to "Scene Draw," press the Replace ([Alt]-[F2]) key [[Alt] Search **R**eplace]. WordPerfect displays this prompt in the status line:

w/Confirm? No (Yes)

Type an **n** so that WordPerfect will not prompt you to confirm every replacement. If you typed a **y**, WordPerfect would prompt you at every occurrence of the search string to see if you want it replaced.

Next, since the cursor is at the end of the text, press the [↑] key so that WordPerfect will perform the search and replace toward the beginning of the document. The arrow in the "→Srch" prompt changes to "←." Next, tell WordPerfect what text to find. Remove any previous search string by pressing the DELETE EOL ([Ctrl]-[End]) key, and type

See 'N'

Next, press the Search ([F2]) key. WordPerfect prompts you for the text or codes to replace the search text. Type

Scene

Press the Search ([F2]) key. WordPerfect beeps when it completes the replacements. Press the Scroll Down (GREY +) key to rewrap the paragraph. The paragraph now looks like this:

```
    Scene Draw is a product designed for first-time users and
artists who want to push the limits of a graphics package.
Compared with competitors' products, Scene Draw has the easiest
user interface to learn.  Scene Draw is available at most retail
software dealers.
```

2. You can use search and replace to selectively re-place text or codes. If you have a document in which you have pressed [Enter] at the end of each line, changing the margins might cause the lines to display incorrectly. To correct the problem, you need to remove all the hard returns that do not end a paragraph. This allows WordPerfect to adjust the text correctly within any margin settings you select.

   First, type the following lines, pressing [Enter] at the end of each sentence:

The product will be released on August 17th.
The initial press conference is on August 11th.
The distributors will have the package on August 14th.
A product review in a monthly newsletter was excellent.
The newsletter is considering another article for a later issue.

Next, press the Replace ([Alt]-[F2]) key [[Alt] Search Replace]. WordPerfect prompts you to ask whether you want all replacements confirmed. Type a y. Next, press [Enter]. WordPerfect deletes the previous search string and displays the [HRt] code. Press the

⬆ key to have WordPerfect move backward to perform the search. The search prompt looks like this:

`<- Srch: [HRt]`

Next, press the Search (F2) key. WordPerfect prompts you for the text or codes to replace the search text. Since you want the hard returns replaced with two spaces, press the SPACEBAR twice. Press the Search (F2) key. The cursor stops at the "T" at the beginning of the last line, since that is the first character following the hidden [HRt] code, and WordPerfect displays this prompt:

`Confirm? No (Yes)`

Since you want this replacement made, type a **y**. For each of the successive prompts, type a **y**. Word-Perfect beeps when it is finished. WordPerfect will not rewrap the text until you move down through the document. Press the Scroll Down (GREY +) key to reformat the paragraph. The paragraph now looks like this:

```
The product will be released on August 17th. The initial press
conference is on August 11th. The distributors will have the
package on August 14th. A product review in a monthly newsletter
was excellent. The newsletter is considering another article for
a later issue.
```

3. You can find an exact match for a word by preceding and following the word by a space when typing the search string. If you want WordPerfect to replace the name "Green" with "Lime" and skip

"Greene," "Greenfield," "Greenjeans," and "Greenly," you can type a space before and after "Green" when you identify it as the search string.

First, type

He invited John Greenly, Howard Greensen, Mary Green-field, Beth Greene, and Paul Green to his St. Patrick's Day party.

Move to the top of the document by pressing (Home), (Home), (↑). Press the Replace ((Alt)-(F2)) key [(Alt) Search Replace], and press (Enter) to reject confirmation. Next, type

Green

placing a space on each side of "Green." Press the Search ((F2)) key, and type

Lime

You need to include a space to each side of "Lime" to maintain the proper spacing in the paragraph. When you press the Search ((F2)) key again, WordPerfect performs the replacement. If "Green" had been the last word of the sentence, WordPerfect would not have found it, because the period at the end of the sentence would not have matched the space in the search string.

4. You can restrict the scope of the replacement by blocking the text you wish to be affected. Type

ABC Company had a very profitable year. Five successful new products helped to make 1990 the best year ever for ABC Company. ABC Company performed poorly this year. A record 90 million dollar loss for ABC Company was recorded.

Press ⌜Enter⌟ to end the paragraph. Next, move to the beginning of the third sentence. Block the last two sentences by pressing the Block (⌜Alt⌟-⌜F4⌟) key [⌜Alt⌟ Edit Block] and the ⌜↓⌟ key twice. Next, press the Replace (⌜Alt⌟-⌜F2⌟) key [⌜Alt⌟ Search Replace]. Press ⌜Enter⌟ to accept the default of no confirmation, and type **ABC**. Press the Search (⌜F2⌟) key, and type **XYZ**. When you press the Search (⌜F2⌟) key again, WordPerfect beeps after changing the text to look like this:

```
ABC Company had a very profitable year.  Five successful new
products helped to make 1990 the best year ever for ABC Company.
XYZ Company performed poorly this year.  A record 90 million dollar
loss for XYZ Company was recorded.
```

EXERCISES

1. Type the following paragraph:

   Sam Cook is the production manager. He has five years' experience in this position. Prior to this position, Sam Cook was a sergeant in the army. Sam Cook succeeded Thomas MacNamara in his current position.

   Replace all occurrences of "Sam Cook" with **Daniel Jones**.

2. Type the following text:

   WordPerfect's Replace feature allows you to selectively replace one string of characters with another character string. You can have WordPerfect prompt you before completing each replacement, or you can have it make the changes automatically.

Use the Replace feature to change all occurrences of "WordPerfect" to **WordPerfect 5.1**.

3. Type the following paragraph:

The Public Relations Director for your area is XX. XX has been with the company for many years and can answer your questions.

Replace "XX" with **Nancy Clark**. Then replace "Nancy Clark" with **Martin Smith**.

4. Type the following paragraph:

You can use WP's Replace feature to shorten typing in a ms or doc. In a ms or doc, you type the abbreviations in place of the words and have WP replace the abbreviations with the words they represent.

Replace "ms" with **manuscript**. Replace "doc" with **document**. Replace "WP" with **WordPerfect**.

EXERCISES

(Do not clear the screen between exercises unless instructed to do so.)

1. Type the following paragraph:

WordPerfect lets you search for text. You can search either backward or forward. This means that you do not have to move the cursor to a specific location before you can use this feature.

Go to the top of the paragraph, and use the Search feature to locate each occurrence of the word "search."

2. Go back to the top of the paragraph, and use the Search feature to determine the number of times that the paragraph uses the word "you."

3. Go to the bottom of the paragraph, and use the Reverse Search feature to determine the number of times that the paragraph uses the letter combination "for." Clear the screen.

4. Type the following:

Aeneades was a Trojan prince. He was the son of Diomedes and Achilles. Aeneades married Lavinia.

Replace all occurrences of "Aeneades" with **Aeneas**.

(Do not clear the screen until you have completed the last exercise.)

INTEGRATING SKILLS CHECK

1. Type the following paragraph:

Proposal

The Quick Time division of New Men's Look, Inc., would like to expand their product line to include pocket watches. Adding pocket watches would fit into the division's current production capacity. The plant is operating 30% below capacity. The technology required is already available. This product would also complement the suits produced by another subsidiary, the Taylor division.

Use Search to move the cursor to the hidden code for underlining. Use Reveal Codes to determine the cursor's location in relation to the hidden code.

2. Use Replace to change "Quick Time" to uppercase.

3. Replace "Taylor" with **Tailor**.

4. Center the text on the page.

5. Preview the document as WordPerfect would print it.

Restructuring Your Documents with Copy, Move, and Delete

►8◄

CHAPTER OBJECTIVES

After completing this chapter, you should be able to:

► Move a sentence, a paragraph, or a page   8.1

► Move a block of text   8.2

► Delete a block of text   8.3

► Copy a block of text   8.4

One of WordPerfect's greatest advantages over the use of a typewriter is that it gives you the ability to restructure documents without retyping the text. Moving words, sentences, paragraphs, and pages is easy with WordPerfect's convenient features. Menu options allow you to move a sentence or a paragraph. You can move phrases, multiple sentences, and multiple pages of text by first identifying them with WordPerfect's Block feature. You have mastered the first step in this process already, since you have used Block to underline and boldface text.

The ability to copy a section of text is another useful WordPerfect feature. It allows you to create two similar sections of text by copying the original text and modifying the copy. In addition, a quick method for deleting text is provided, since using the [Del] or [Backspace] key alone is a slow procedure when you have a large amount of text to remove.

SKILLS CHECK

(Do not clear the screen until you have completed the last exercise.)

1. Set all four margins to 2".

2. Set the page numbers to appear in the upper left-hand corner when you print the document.

3. Remove all of the tab stops, and set new ones at every inch.

4. Type the following letter:

Dale Thompson
Birds of a Feather
2398 Manzanita Park
Stanford, CA 94321

Dear Dale,

According to your advertisement in Feathered Friends, you are interested in purchasing two white cockatoos. I own several and would like to sell them. Please contact me at (813) 212-2634.

Sincerely,

Byron Wilson

Underline "Feathered Friends".

5. Use the Replace feature to change "cockatoos" to **parakeets**.

6. Print the document. Center the document on the page and reprint it.

7. Reset all four margins to 1" and tab stops to every .5". Eliminate page numbering.

8.1 MOVE A SENTENCE, A PARAGRAPH, OR A PAGE

Polishing initial drafts of a document can improve the quality and clarity of the writing. Rearranging text is often part of a revision process, since it enables you to place sentences in the most effective order. Word-Perfect makes it easy to rearrange text, since you do not have to retype it. WordPerfect provides options for moving a sentence, a paragraph, or a page.

To move text:

a. Move the cursor to the place in the text where you wish to move.

b. Press the Move (Ctrl-F4) key [Alt Edit Select].

c. Type an **s** or a **1** [Sentence] to select the current sentence, a **p** or a **2** [Paragraph] to select the current paragraph, or an **a** or a **3** [Page] to select the current page as the text to move.

d. Type an **m** or a **1** to select moving the text.

e. Move the cursor to where you want the text placed.

f. Press Enter.

After you perform step d, the text disappears until you press Enter. In step c, selecting Sentence causes WordPerfect to move everything from the beginning of the sentence up to and including the space following a period, question mark, or exclamation point. Selecting Paragraph causes WordPerfect to move everything from the beginning of the paragraph up to and including the hard return before the next paragraph. Selecting Page causes WordPerfect to move everything from the beginning of the page up to and including the hard or soft page break at the end of the page.

EXAMPLES

1. You can move one sentence at a time. First, type

   Please return the books immediately! According to our records, Dave, you were the last one borrowing the department's tax reference books.

   Since this paragraph makes more sense if you reverse the sentence order, move the cursor to any character in the first sentence. Next, press the Move ([Ctrl]-[F4]) key [[Alt] Edit Select]. WordPerfect displays this prompt on the status line:

   `Move: 1 Sentence; 2 Paragraph; 3 Page; 4 Retrieve: 0`

   Select **s** for Sentence. WordPerfect highlights the sentence and displays these selections:

   `1 Move; 2 Copy; 3 Delete; 4 Append: 0`

   Select **m** for Move. The sentence disappears. WordPerfect displays a reminder at the bottom of the screen to press [Enter] where you want the text to be placed. Move the cursor to the end of the remaining sentence. If you did not include two spaces at the end of the second sentence when you typed it,

press the SPACEBAR twice. Press (Enter). The sentence
that was originally first is placed after the other
sentence, and the screen looks like this:

According to our records, Dave, you were the last one borrowing the
department's tax reference books. Please return the books
immediately!

2. Since WordPerfect recognizes a period as the end of
a sentence, you can get some unexpected results
when trying to move a sentence that contains
abbreviations or numbers with decimals. First, type

Dr. and Mrs. Jones bought a St. Bernard puppy.

Press (Home) and the (↑) to move to the beginning of
the sentence. Press the Move ((Ctrl)-(F4)) key and
type an **s** [(Alt) Edit Select Sentence]. Instead of
highlighting the entire sentence, WordPerfect highlights only "Dr." Because the abbreviations in this
sentence require periods, the sentence needs to be
moved with the Block Move procedure covered
later in this chapter.

3. When you move a paragraph, WordPerfect moves
all of the text from the beginning of the paragraph
up to and including the hard return before the next
paragraph. For example, you can create a list of
tasks to perform. Type

To-Do List

**Write instructions for the new subsidiary on the
preparation of financial statements to be submitted to
the parent corporation. They cannot use electronic**

transmission for their information until their system is modified to conform to the parent corporation's accounting system.

Meet with Tom from Purchasing. He wants to streamline the purchasing process for a just-in-time inventory system.

Be sure to press [Enter] at the end of the second paragraph. You can move the first item in the list to make it the second item by moving the paragraph. First, move the cursor to the first paragraph. Next, press the Move ([Ctrl]-[F4]) key and type a **p** for Paragraph [[Alt] Edit Select Paragraph]. WordPerfect highlights the entire paragraph. Next, type an **m** for Move. The paragraph disappears. Move the cursor to the blank line below the paragraph still displayed on the screen, and press [Enter]. Now, the screen looks like Figure 8-1. If you press [Home], [Home], and [↓], you will notice that the second item has a blank line below it. WordPerfect moved the blank line between the two items as part of the paragraph.

To-Do List

Meet with Tom from Purchasing. He wants to streamline the purchasing process for a just-in-time inventory system.
Write instructions for the new subsidiary on the preparation of financial statements to be submitted to the parent corporation. They cannot use electronic transmission for their information until their system is modified to conform to the parent corporation's accounting system.

FIGURE 8-1.   The effect of moving a paragraph

4. You can move a page of text to a new location in a document. First, type

Preparation and Approval of Building Plans

To start a new page, press [Ctrl]-[Enter] [[Alt] Layout Align Hard Page]. Then, type

Construction of the Building Exterior

Next, press [Ctrl]-[Enter] [[Alt] Layout Align Hard Page], and type

Interior Finishing Tasks

Next, type

Site Excavation

Press [Ctrl]-[Enter] [[Alt] Layout Align Hard Page] to end page 4. If you review the pages, you will notice that page 4 ideally should be the second page in the document. Use the [↑] key to position the cursor on page 4, press the Move ([Ctrl]-[F4]) key, and type an **a** for Page [[Alt] Edit Select Page]. All of the text on the page is highlighted. Next, type an **m** for Move. Finally, move the cursor to the first character on page 2, since WordPerfect will insert the text in front of the cursor position. When you press [Enter], WordPerfect moves the page, and the screen looks like Figure 8-2.

EXERCISES

1. Type the following paragraph:

A complex sentence consists of an independent clause, which can stand alone, and one or more dependent clauses. A compound sentence is two or more simple

Preparation and Approval of Building Plans
==
Site Excavation
==
Construction of the Building Exterior
==
Interior Finishing Tasks
==

FIGURE 8-2.   The effect of moving a page

sentences joined by a conjunction, such as "and," "or," "but," or "for." A simple sentence expresses a single action or thought.

Change the sentence order so that the first sentence is third and the third sentence is first.

2. Type the following paragraphs:

The sun's temperature is 11,000 degrees Fahrenheit at the surface and 35,000,000 degrees in the center. It releases 1.94 calories per square centimeter per minute.

The diameter of the sun is 865,000 miles. It is small by comparison to other stars. The sun's proximity to the earth makes it appear larger than other stars.

Move the second paragraph to place it before the paragraph that was entered first.

3. Type the following lines, inserting a hard page break after each line. Move the first page to after the third.

A nebula is a mass of gas in space.
A meteoroid is a small object in space.
A constellation is a group of stars.

4. Type the following paragraphs:

Keyboards usually come in two types. A standard keyboard has ten function keys at the side. An enhanced keyboard has twelve function keys across the top.

With WordPerfect, if you have an enhanced keyboard, you can use F11 in place of ALT-F3. You can also use F12 in place of ALT-F4.

Switch the order of the second and third sentences in the first paragraph. Switch the order of the first and second paragraphs.

8.2 MOVE A BLOCK OF TEXT

You must block text when you want to move part of a document that does not fit WordPerfect's definition of a sentence, a paragraph, or a page. This means that when you have periods within a sentence or [HRt] codes to end short lines in a paragraph, you will need to use Block to move the text. If you wish to move a group of words, several sentences, or half of a page, for example, you will need to block the text first. Although moving blocked text requires this additional step, it provides the ultimate flexibility.

To move blocked text:

a. Move the cursor to the first character or code in the text you want to move.

b. Press the Block ([Alt]-[F4]) key [[Alt] Edit Block].

c. Move the cursor to highlight all of the text and the adjacent codes you want to move.

d. Press the Move ([Ctrl]-[F4]) key [[Alt] Edit Move (Cut) and skip steps e and f].

e. Type a **b** or a **1** to select Block.

f. Type an **m** or a **1** to select Move.

g. Move the cursor to where you want the blocked text placed.

h. Press Enter.

    When you perform step d for menu users or step f for function key users, the block disappears. When you press Enter, WordPerfect inserts the block at the cursor's position, moving everything else down. If your computer has 12 function keys, you can use F12 instead of Alt-F4 [Alt Edit Block] in step b. You can also define a block by starting at the end and moving the cursor to the beginning of the block.

EXAMPLES

1. You can block text to move part of a sentence. Type

> **In order to complete your request, we need the following information: your address, the date of the purchase, your name, and the sales person who handled the order.**

To move the words "your name" to precede the words "your address," move the cursor to the "y" in "your name" and press the Block (Alt-F4) key [Alt Edit Block]. Next, move the cursor to the "a" in "and." The screen looks like this:

```
In order to complete your request, we need the following
information: your address, the date of purchase, your name, and the
sales person who handled the order.
```

Press the Move ([Ctrl]-[F4]) key and type a **b** and an **m** [[Alt] Edit Move (Cut)]. Move the cursor to the "y" in "your address," and press [Enter]. Now, the screen looks like this:

In order to complete your request, we need the following information: your name, your address, the date of purchase, and the sales person who handled the order.

2. You can block text to move it when you have multiple sentences, paragraphs, or pages to move. Type

Last year's sales decreased by 10%. Most of the decrease stemmed from the sale of the Bounce Back Yo-Yo division. Profits increased by 2%.

Be sure to press SPACEBAR twice at the end of the last sentence. You can move the first two sentences to follow the third sentence. First, press [PgUp] to move the cursor to the "L" in "Last." Next, press the Block ([Alt]-[F4]) key [[Alt] Edit Block] and move the cursor to the "P" in "Profits." Press the Move ([Ctrl]-[F4]) key and type a **b** for Block and an **m** for Move [[Alt] Edit Move (Cut)]. Next, press [End] to move the cursor to the second space after the last sentence. Press [Enter], and the text on the screen is reorganized to look like this:

Profits increased by 2%. Last year's sales decreased by 10%. Most of the decrease stemmed from the sale of the Bounce Back Yo-Yo division.

EXERCISES

1. Type this sentence:

See 'N' Draw, XY Graphics' new product, should capture a large part of the graphics market for first-time users.

Move the product name and the comma and space that follow it to after the comma and space that follow "product." The restructured sentence should read

XY Graphics' new product, See 'N' Draw, should capture a large part of the graphics market for first-time users.

2. Type this sentence:

The new machinery funnels the cake mix into preprinted boxes, weighs a predetermined amount of the cake mix, and seals the bag.

Move "weighs a predetermined amount of the cake mix," to come before "funnels the cake mix into preprinted boxes,". The restructured sentence will read:

The new machinery weighs a predetermined amount of the cake mix, funnels the cake mix into preprinted boxes, and seals the bag.

3. Type these lines:

Review meeting agenda.
Nominate potential candidates for new director position.
Review financial statements.
Review minutes from the last meeting.
Introduce new corporate treasurer to board.

Move the last two lines so that they follow the first line.

4. Type this paragraph:

When you move a block, you should check to include any hidden codes in your text. WordPerfect moves all of the codes within the block. If the text that you move is part of a larger block of text that has special print attributes (for example, bold or underline), the special print characteristics appear in both the moved text and the original. To view the codes, press the Reveal Codes (ALT-F3) key [ALT Edit Reveal Codes].

Move the second and third sentences together to the beginning of the paragraph.

8.3 | DELETE A BLOCK OF TEXT

When you edit a document, you may want to delete a section of text. Rather than pressing the ⟨Del⟩ or ⟨Backspace⟩ key until the text disappears, you can save time by blocking the text first. You have several options for deleting a block of text. If the block you wish to delete conforms to WordPerfect's definition of a sentence, paragraph, or page, you can use an even faster procedure for deleting it.

To delete a block of text:

a. Move the cursor to the beginning of the text you wish to delete.

b. Press the Block (Alt-F4) key [Alt Edit **Block**].

c. Move the cursor to highlight all of the text you wish to delete.

d. Press the Del or Backspace key.

e. Confirm that you wish to delete the text by typing a **y**.

Another method for deleting the text offers the use of menu selections. Steps d and e in the above procedure are replaced by steps d through f below.

d. Press the Move (Ctrl-F4) key [Alt Edit **Delete** and skip steps e and f].

e. Type a **b** or a **1** to select Block.

f. Type a **d** or a **3** to select Delete.

To delete a sentence, paragraph, or page:

a. Press the Move (Ctrl-F4) key [Alt Edit **Select**] after positioning the cursor on any character in the text you wish to delete.

b. Type an **s** for Sentence, a **p** for Paragraph, or an **a** for Page as the text to delete.

c. Type a **d** or a **3** to delete the text.

EXAMPLES

1. You can block text and then remove it with the Del key. Type the following sentences, pressing Enter at the end of each one.

Special rules apply to typing numbers:
Numbers of less than three digits are spelled.
Compound numbers less than 100 are hyphenated.
Numbers that represent measurements are expressed
in figures, e.g. 54 miles, 26 feet.

Since the first two rules do not give examples, you can remove the examples from the last entry. Move to the comma after "figures," and press the Block ([Alt]-[F4]) key [[Alt] Edit Block]. Move to the end of the sentence by pressing the [↓] key, and press the [←] key once so that the block does not include the period. Press the [Del] key, and type a y. The blocked text is deleted.

2. You can delete any amount of text by blocking the text you want to delete. First, type

To evaluate investment projects, many companies use
the internal rate of return. The internal rate of return is
the minimum interest rate that a project must earn to
have a net present value of 0.

To remove part of the second sentence, begin by moving the cursor to the period ending the first sentence. Next, press the Block ([Alt]-[F4]) key [[Alt] Edit Block] and move the cursor to the space after "is." Press the Move ([Ctrl]-[F4]) key, type a b for Block and a d for Delete [[Alt] Edit Delete and type a y]. Optionally, you could press the [Del] or [Backspace] key and confirm the deletion by typing a y. After you type a comma and move the cursor down, the screen looks like this:

To evaluate investment projects, many companies use the internal
rate of return, the minimum interest rate that a project must earn
to have a net present value of 0.

3. You can use a shortcut if the block of text you wish
   to delete is a sentence, a paragraph, or a page. Type

John Adams was the second President of the United
States. He served in Europe as the ambassador before
his election as the first Vice President. Following Washington's second term, John Adams succeeded Washington as president. He was ambidextrous and could
write Greek with one hand while writing Latin with the
other.

After pressing Enter, press the ↑ key to move the
cursor to the last sentence. Press the Move (Ctrl-
F4) key [Alt Edit Select], type an **s** for Sentence
and a **d** for Delete.

EXERCISES

1. Type the following paragraph:

The Office of Human Resources reports that hiring has
increased by 14%. This increase is a result of last year's
expansion of the Largo division. The increased hiring,
which created 1000 new jobs, should not affect next
year's personnel needs.

Delete the period ending the first sentence and the
phrase "This increase is." Add a comma after
"14%."

2. Type the following sentence:

As of May 15, the corporation must increase sales by 15,000 units per month, renovate the corporate offices, and divest itself of its Romper division to meet its 1990 objectives.

Delete "renovate the corporate offices" and the comma and space after that phrase.

3. Type the following lines:

Today's Projects
Prepare capital budget request for two computers.
Review receivables older than 90 days.
Prepare next year's forecast.

Block and delete the second and third projects.

4. Type the following paragraph:

Last February, the widget assembler became jammed. While the cause was poor maintenance, the machine's condition requires above-normal maintenance to prevent the problem from recurring. To prevent this problem from recurring, the company should purchase a new machine.

Delete the second sentence.

8.4   COPY A BLOCK OF TEXT

WordPerfect's features for copying text can provide substantial time savings. If you need another copy of existing text, a few menu selections can duplicate the text without any retyping.

Even if you need a modified version of existing text, the Copy feature can provide a better solution than typing. By copying the original text, you can make your modifications more quickly than by typing the entire new section of text.

You can copy a section of text of any size by blocking the text first. If you need to copy a sentence, a paragraph, or a page, you can use an even faster procedure.

To copy blocked text:

a. Move the cursor to the first character in the text you want to copy.

b. Press the Block ([Alt]-[F4]) key [[Alt] Edit Block].

c. Move the cursor to highlight all of the text you want to copy.

d. Press the Move ([Ctrl]-[F4]) key [[Alt] Edit Copy and skip steps e and f].

e. Type a **b** or a **1** to select Block.

f. Type a **c** or a **2** to select Copy.

g. Move the cursor to where you want to place the copied text.

h. Press [Enter].

To copy a sentence, a paragraph, or a page:

a. Move the cursor to the section of text you want to copy.

b. Press the Move ([Ctrl]-[F4]) key [[Alt] Edit Select].

c. Type an **s** for Sentence, a **p** for Paragraph, or an **a** for Page, depending on the amount of text you wish to copy.

d. Type a **c** or a **2** for Copy.

e. Move the cursor to where you want to place the copied text.

f. Press (Enter).

EXAMPLES

1. You can copy a block of any size. First, type the following lines, pressing (Enter) at the end of each one.

   The policy that applies to borrowing the company's 35mm camera is:
   The borrower must return the camera within 24 hours.
   The borrower is responsible for film and development.
   The borrower is responsible for damage or loss.

   To copy the policy, press the Block ((Alt)-(F4)) key [(Alt) Edit Block], and press (PgUp) to move the cursor to the "T" in the first line. WordPerfect highlights all the text. Next, press the Move ((Ctrl)-(F4)) key, and type a **b** for Block and a **c** for Copy [(Alt) Edit Copy].

   Finally, move the cursor to the bottom of the document by pressing (PgDn). Press (Enter) to insert a copy of the text. You can modify the copy to produce a policy for borrowing the company's new video camera.

2. You can also copy a sentence, a paragraph, or a page. To copy a paragraph, first type

The MIS department retains a copy of the manuals for all of the company's software. To borrow a manual, check it out from one of the reference librarians. You may borrow a manual for up to three days.

After pressing Enter, move the cursor to any character in the paragraph. Press the Move (Ctrl-F4) key [Alt Edit Select], and type a **p** for Paragraph. WordPerfect highlights the entire paragraph. Type a **c** for Copy, and press Enter to create the second copy of the paragraph.

3. You can use a special procedure when you need multiple copies of text. First, type

The MIS department retains a copy of the manuals for all of the company's software. To borrow a manual, check it out from one of the reference librarians. You may borrow a manual for up to three days.

The first copy is made with the same procedure you used in example 2. Move the cursor to any character in the paragraph, press the Move (Ctrl-F4) key [Alt Edit Select], and type a **p** for Paragraph. WordPerfect highlights the entire paragraph. Type a **c** for Copy, and move the cursor to where you want the new copy to appear. Press Enter to insert the copy of the paragraph.

To make an additional copy, move the cursor to where you want the next new copy to appear. Press the Move (Ctrl-F4) key, type an **r** for Retrieve [Alt Edit Paste] and a **b** for Block. WordPerfect inserts a copy of the text that you copied last. You can then edit each paragraph to give different instructions for borrowing a manual.

EXERCISES

1. Type the following lines, then place a copy of the lines below the original.

   Name: Patrick Rabbit
   Address: 777 Carrot Lane

   Modify the copy to change the second "Patrick" to **Nancy** and the second street number to **515**. Use the Retrieve and Block options to make an additional copy of the original two lines.

2. Type the following paragraph:

   First, put the correct pens in the plotter. This is an important step. Next, put the paper or transparency in the plotter.

   Copy the second sentence, placing the copy after the third sentence.

3. Type the following lines. Block them, copy them, and make three additional copies.

   Current Month: . . . .
   Sales: . . . .
   Cost of Goods Sold: . . . .

4. Type the following partial paragraph:

Directions to the Cloverleaf Hall: Take the interstate to the Bay Street exit. At the exit, turn right, and take the next left after the light. Stay on this road until you pass the shopping mall on the right. After passing the shopping mall,

Complete the last sentence by blocking and copying "take the next left after the light."

EXERCISES

1. Type the following sentences. Move the first one between the second and third.

   The cost of goods sold is $2,363,782. The beginning inventory is $689,578. The ending inventory is $234,245.

2. Type the following sentences:

   The new and improved widget maker has several features. One of these features is the internal painter. This feature evenly coats each widget and limits the fumes, which reduces the number of employees needed to operate the machine.

   Move the comma and the phrase "which reduces the number of employees needed to operate the machine" to the end of the second sentence. The paragraph should read:

   The new and improved widget maker has several features. One of these features is the internal painter, which reduces the number of employees needed to operate the machine. This feature evenly coats each widget and limits the fumes.

3. Type the following paragraph:

Tuesday, the heads of the accounting, production, and MIS departments will review the steps that they can take to reduce the time between the receipt of an order and its completion.

Block and delete the phrase "that they can take." Then delete the entire paragraph.

4. Type the following paragraph:

Today's weather will be lovely. The temperature will rise to 82 and will cool to an evening low of 70. The low humidity will contribute to the day's pleasant weather.

Block the paragraph and make three copies of it.

INTEGRATING SKILLS CHECK

(Do not clear the screen between exercises unless instructed to do so.)

1. Type the following paragraph:

The ABC widget uses point-of-sale displays as its primary marketing strategy. The new point-of-sale displays are designed to fit at the end of an aisle. As an incentive to the retailer, we are selling the widgets in the aisle pre-packs at a slightly lower cost. Each retailer can choose whether to pass the lower cost on to the customer or increase profits.

Insert a hard page break, and move the paragraph to the second page.

2. Indent the paragraph. Clear the screen.

3. Type the following lines:

   Marketing Strategy
   ABC WIDGETS
   Prepared on July 7, 1990

   Delete the first two words in the last line. Center this information on the page. Preview how Word-Perfect will print the document. Clear the screen.

4. Create a receipt form by typing

   Date:
   Name:
   Amount:
   Explanation:
   Signature:

   Insert a hard page break. Block the lines and the page break, and place a copy below the original.

5. Make three additional copies of the page.

6. Add page numbers in the center at the top of each page, and print the receipt forms.

7. Replace all occurrences of "Explanation" with **For**.

Building on the Basics

►Part II◄

Using the Right Words

►9◄

CHAPTER OBJECTIVES

After completing this chapter, you should be able to:

► Check the spelling of a word   9.1

► Check the spelling of an entire document   9.2

► Find double words   9.3

► Add a word to the supplemental dictionary   9.4

► Delete words from the supplemental dictionary   9.5

► Replace correctly spelled words that are misused   9.6

► Look up a word in the thesaurus   9.7

► Replace a word with a word from the thesaurus   9.8

When you create a document, you hope that it will convey your message in a clear, concise way. Another objective may be to present a professional image of yourself and your firm.

Part of creating a professional image is creating a document that is flawless in spelling and grammar. Although WordPerfect does not as yet have a grammar-checking feature, it has an excellent spelling checker. WordPerfect's Spell feature allows you to check the spelling of a word, a page, or the entire document. It allows you to create personal dictionaries for specialized terminology. WordPerfect's spelling checker will also find occurrences of double words and provide the added bonus of counting the number of words in a document for you.

In addition to spelling the words correctly, to convey your message effectively, you must use the right words to express the meaning you intend. WordPerfect has a Thesaurus feature to help you find the right words easily.

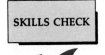

SKILLS CHECK

(Do not clear the screen until you have completed the last exercise.)

1. Change the left and right margins to 2".

2. Add page numbers in the upper left corner of the document.

3. Type the following paragraph:

WordPerfect's Spell feature can find your spelling and typing mistakes. It prompts you with suggested alternatives when it finds a word that is not in one of its dictionaries.

Find all occurrences of "spell" in the text you just typed.

4. Replace all occurrences of the word "it" with **WordPerfect**.

5. Add the following sentence to the end of the paragraph:

WordPerfect's Thesaurus feature can help you find a word that has the exact meaning you need.

Copy the second sentence in the paragraph to the end of the paragraph. Delete "when WordPerfect finds a word that is not in one of its dictionaries," and add **for the word that you look up in its thesaurus**. The completed paragraph should read

WordPerfect's Spell feature can find your spelling and typing mistakes. WordPerfect prompts you with suggested alternatives when WordPerfect finds a word that is not in one of its dictionaries. WordPerfect's Thesaurus feature can help you find a word that has the exact meaning you need. WordPerfect prompts you with suggested alternatives for the word that you look up in its thesaurus.

9.1 CHECK THE SPELLING OF A WORD

If you are uncertain of the correct spelling of a word, you can have WordPerfect check it for you. The ability to check the spelling of a single word is a time-saving feature. Once you have verified it, you can stop questioning the spelling and focus on finishing the document.

To have WordPerfect check the spelling of a word:

a. Move the cursor to the word that you want to check.

b. Press the Spell ([Ctrl]-[F2]) key [[Alt] Tools Spell].

c. Type a **w** or a **1**.

If you spelled the word correctly, WordPerfect moves the cursor to the next word. If WordPerfect does not find the word in its dictionaries, it displays menu options and, in most cases, similarly spelled or pronounced words, labeled with letters for your selection.

d. Select the correct word or one of the menu options if WordPerfect did not move the cursor to the next word.

e. Press the SPACEBAR, [Enter], [Esc], the Cancel ([F1]) key, or the Exit ([F7]) key to return to the document.

EXAMPLES

1. You can use WordPerfect's Spell feature to check the spelling of a few individual words. To illustrate

how the speller works, type the following sentence, including the misspelling of "strategy."

Next Tuesday, the marketing department will present their promotional straegy for the See 'N' Draw package.

To check the spelling of the words "promotional" and "straegy," first move the cursor to the word "promotional." Next, press the Spell (Ctrl - F2) key [Alt Tools Spell]. WordPerfect displays this menu:

Check: 1 Word; 2 Page; 3 Document; 4 New Sup. Dictionary; 5 Look Up; 6 Count: 0

Since you want to check a word at a time, type a **w**. WordPerfect checks the spelling of "promotional." Because "promotional" is spelled correctly, Word-Perfect moves the cursor over to the next word, "straegy." Since you also want to check the spelling of this word, type a **w**. Because it cannot find that word in its dictionary, WordPerfect displays a new menu that looks like this:

Not Found: 1 Skip Once; 2 Skip; 3 Add; 4 Edit; 5 Look Up; 6 Ignore Numbers: 0

It also displays a suggestion for the spelling of the word. Since the suggestion is correct, you can make the replacement by typing an **a**. Since you do not want to check any more words, press the SPACEBAR to leave the Spell feature.

2. When you use the Spell feature on words that are spelled correctly but are not in WordPerfect's dictionary, it still suggests replacements and offers a menu of correction alternatives. You can tell Word-Perfect to ignore correctly spelled words it does not recognize. First, type

Adele Stein is representing the European divisions at the stockholders' meeting.

You can check the spelling of this sentence word by word by moving the cursor to the beginning of the sentence, pressing the Spell (Ctrl-F2) key [Alt Tools Spell], and typing a **w**. WordPerfect highlights "Adele," which it doesn't recognize, and offers suggestions for other spellings. Since you have spelled the name properly, you want WordPerfect to skip this word; type a **2**. By selecting this option, you instruct WordPerfect to ignore "Adele" whenever it finds that word. If you had pressed a **1**, WordPerfect would skip only this occurrence of the word.

3. WordPerfect's Spell feature may offer many alternatives for a word that it does not find in its dictionary. First, type

Lake Erie usualy freezes in November or December.

Next, move the cursor to the word "usualy," press the Spell (Ctrl-F2) key [Alt Tools Spell], and type a **w**. Since you misspelled this word, the screen looks like Figure 9-1. Each of WordPerfect's suggestions has a different letter next to it. Since the replacement word that you want is "usually," type a **b** to have WordPerfect substitute the correctly spelled word. After checking other words in the sentence, press the Exit (F7) key to exit from the Spell feature.

4. When WordPerfect checks the spelling for you, you may need to modify, rather than replace, a word that it does not recognize. First, type

For some misspellings, WordPerfect maynot give appropriate suggestions.

Press (Enter). Then press the (↑) key twice to move to the word "For." Press the Spell ((Ctrl)-(F2)) key [(Alt) Tools Spell]. Type a **w** five times. WordPerfect does not recognize "maynot." You can easily fix this typographical mistake by editing it. Type a 4. Press

---

Lake Erie **usualy** freezes in November or December.

```
=================================================================================
```

A. usual	B. usually	C. usuary
D. acyl	E. assail	F. azalea
G. easel	H. easily	I. icily
J. ocelli	K. osseously	L. osteal
M. ostial		

Not Found: 1 Skip Once; 2 Skip; 3 Add; 4 Edit; 5 Look Up; 6 Ignore Numbers: 0

FIGURE 9-1.   Suggested spelling corrections supplied by the spelling checker the ➡ key three times and the SPACEBAR once. Then press the Exit (F7) key to end editing. WordPerfect checks the modified text. Since the edited words are correctly spelled, WordPerfect moves to the next word. Continue pressing **w** to edit the rest of the sentence. Then press the SPACEBAR to return to the document.

EXERCISES

1. Type the following words:

   Regrdless
   Disinterested
   Paradox
   Momento
   Subsequential
   Torturous

   Use the Spell feature to correct the misspelled ones.

2. Type the following sentence as it appears:

   WordPerfecty can chek a word at a thime, a blok, or an entear document.

   Move to the beginning, and check the sentence's spelling a word at a time.

3. Type the following sentence as it appears:

   Arwena McClellan is th product managr.

   Move to the beginning, and check the sentence's spelling a word at a time. Assume that "Arwena McClellan" is spelled correctly.

4. Type the following:

Ofthe eople, bythe oeople, andfor thepeople.

Move to the beginning, and check the spelling a word at a time. Use the Edit option of the Spell feature to modify the words so that the final result looks like this:

Of the people, by the people, and for the people.

CHECK THE SPELLING OF AN ENTIRE DOCUMENT

9.2

For long documents, pressing keys to check every word whose spelling you are unsure of would be a tedious process. Also, it is likely that you would overlook errors. WordPerfect can check the spelling for the entire document for you with one easy command.

To have WordPerfect check the spelling of a document:

a. Press the Spell ([Ctrl]-[F2]) key [[Alt] Tools Spell].

b. Type a **d** or a **3**.

WordPerfect reviews the entire document. When it finds a word that is not in its dictionaries, Word-Perfect displays its suggestions. After you have instructed WordPerfect how to handle the word it flags as misspelled, it searches for the next misspelled word.

EXAMPLES

1. WordPerfect's Spell feature may find a number of words that are not in its dictionary when you check a document. If you elect to make a replacement for any of these words, WordPerfect makes the correction wherever it finds the misspelling throughout the document. First, type

   The factory's new heeting system uses natural gas. Solar panels assist the heeting system by prividing 20% of the power.

   Next, press the Spell (Ctrl-F2) key [Alt Tools Spell], and type a **d**. The first word WordPerfect flags as misspelled is "heeting." Type an **a** to replace it with WordPerfect's first suggestion, "heating." Since the Spell feature automatically replaces the misspelling wherever it finds the word, Word-Perfect corrects "heeting" in the second sentence.

   The next misspelling that WordPerfect brings to your attention is "prividing." Type an **a** to accept WordPerfect's first suggestion, "providing." Word-Perfect finishes checking the document and displays a word count. Press the SPACEBAR to exit from the Spell feature.

2. When you check a document's spelling, Word-Perfect may question correctly spelled words. Most of the correctly spelled words that WordPerfect will question will be names or technical terms. Type

   Jim Wright
   2209 Sunrise Boulevard
   Ft. Lauderdale, Florida 33304

Dear Mr. Wright,

    We have shipped the supplies that you ordered. You will receive them in a few days. The paper that you ordered is out of stock. We will shipped it once we receive it.

Sincerely,

Adele Stein

To check the spelling of this document, press the Spell ([Ctrl]-[F2]) key [[Alt] Tools Spell], and type a **d** for Document. Because WordPerfect does not have the word "Adele" in its dictionaries, it prompts you with alternate spellings. Since you spelled the name correctly, type a **2** to skip the word. When Word-Perfect finishes checking the document, press the SPACEBAR to leave the Spell features. Notice that WordPerfect does not flag "shipped" as an incorrect word; although it is grammatically incorrect, the spelling is not wrong. The Spell feature is a valuable aid, but it is not a replacement for proofreading your documents.

EXERCISES

1. Type the following paragraph:

The biologicl lab reports that it has created a new hybrid plant called the Panophile. This plant tolerates extreem differences in humidity and temperature pro-vided that it is adequately watered during its first yeer. Its flowers can be red, yellow, white, or purple.

Use the Spell feature to check the paragraph for spelling errors. Assume "Panophile" is correct.

2. Type the following paragraph:

As part of the city's 100-year celabration, thei are having a fiar, the first since before World War II. The fair will emphsize how the city looked 100 years ago.

Use the Spell feature to correct the misspelled words.

3. Type the following paragraph:

Last Tuesday, Markum Products anounced a dividend of $.30 per share. Thes dividend changes its dividend policy, since the lattest dividend equals the total dividends of the last two years.

Use the Spell feature to make necessary spelling corrections. Assume "Markum" is spelled correctly.

4. Type the following paragraph:

When you use the Spell feature, it finds two types of words. The first type is mispelled words. These words are typographical errors or words that you do not know how to spell. The second type is corectly spelled words that the Spel feature does not recognize. Most of thees words are names or technical terms.

Use the Spell feature to find and correct misspellings.

9.3 | FIND DOUBLE WORDS

As you type, you may unintentionally type a word twice. WordPerfect is able to scan your document for

occurrences of repeated, or double, words. Checking
for double words is an automatic function of Word-
Perfect's Spell feature.

WordPerfect allows you to approve the occurrence
of a double-word pair or delete the second occurrence
of the word. It also allows you to edit the document in
case one of the words should be changed. As a final
option, it allows you to disable further checking for
double words in documents in which double words
are intended.

To have WordPerfect find double words:

a. Press the Spell ([Ctrl]-[F2]) key [[Alt] Tools Spell].

b. Type a **d** or a **3**.

When WordPerfect finds a double word, it provides a different set of options than for misspelled
words.

EXAMPLES

1. Double words are easy to overlook. Type the following paragraph, making sure to include the repeated words "a" and "the":

   **As part of the city's 100 year celebration, the city is
   having a a fair, the first since before World War II. The
   fair will emphasize how the the city looked 100 years
   ago.**

   To find the double words, press the Spell ([Ctrl]-[F2])
   key [[Alt] Tools Spell], and type a **d**. WordPerfect

highlights the two "a"s before fair. You can select from the following menu options:

Double Word: **1 2** Skip; **3** Delete 2nd; **4** Edit; **5** Disable Double Word Checking

To remove one of the double words, type a **3**. Next, WordPerfect highlights the two "the"s in the second sentence. Since you want to remove one of them, type a **3**.

Finally, since that was the last spelling error or double word occurrence, press the SPACEBAR to return to the document.

2. WordPerfect's Spell feature automatically searches for double words. When your document contains misspelled words and double words, WordPerfect prompts you for the desired actions for misspellings and double words in the order that WordPerfect finds them. Type the following paragraph, making sure to include the misspellings and the repeated words:

The company is redirecting its resources, while remaining in the the personalized items business. This is due to demigraphic changes in its customer base. Its demigraphic base is aging and and has more disposable income.

Press the Spell (Ctrl-F2) key [Alt Tools Spell], and type a **d**. WordPerfect highlights the two "the"s in the first sentence. Type a **3** to remove the extra word. Next, WordPerfect highlights "demigraphic" as a misspelled word. Type an **a** to substitute WordPerfect's only suggestion. WordPerfect corrects both occurences of the misspelling and highlights the two "and"s in the last sentence. Type a **3** to remove the second "and". When WordPerfect finishes checking the document, press the SPACEBAR to exit from the Spell feature.

EXERCISES

1. Type the following paragraph:

When ABC Corporation combines its corporate offices into a a central location, they expect to to reduce their staff by 30%. Most of the reduction of personnel costs for the first year will be be consumed by severance pay and other employment termination costs.

Use the Spell feature to remove double words.

2. Type the following paragraph:

The employees that have have been invited to to move to the new new corporate headqurters are in the process of moving. Human Resourses is is providing temporary housing and and moving services. Some of of the staff who are not moving to the new new headquarters have already found new jobs.

Use the Spell feature to remove double words and correct spelling mistakes.

3. Type the following paragraph:

Double words often occur with edited text. When you edit text text, you may add a a word to the end of of a phrase you are are adding, not realizing that it it is already there. Double words often happen with with short words.

Use the Spell feature to remove double words.

4. Type the following lines, pressing (Enter) after each line:

WordPerfect does
does not
not check to see if the
the last word of one paragraph is the same word as the
first word word of the next paragraph.

Use the Spell feature to remove double words.

9.4	## ADD A WORD TO THE SUPPLEMENTAL DICTIONARY

WordPerfect's main dictionary contains more than 100,000 words. The words in WordPerfect's dictionary have been identified as the words most commonly used in business writing. Despite the extensiveness of this dictionary, it probably will not contain all the properly spelled words that you will use in your documents. Because of this, there may be occasions when properly spelled words are flagged by Word-Perfect as potential misspellings. You can circumvent this situation by asking WordPerfect to skip the word.

On a one-time basis, this solution can work. However, if you use a word frequently in your writing, you will soon become frustrated by having to tell WordPerfect to skip the word. WordPerfect offers you a supplemental dictionary to overcome this problem. You can use the supplemental dictionary to expand WordPerfect's word list with your own customized additions. You might want to add proper names (names of persons, company names, geographical names, and so on) or technical terms. Rather than skipping such words every time WordPerfect prompts you for an action, you can add them to your dictionary. WordPerfect maintains a supplemental dictionary file, named WP{WP}US.SUP., for these entries.

To add a word to the supplemental dictionary:

a. Check the spelling of the word by pressing the Spell (Ctrl - F2) key [Alt Tools Spell] and typing a **1**.

b. Type a **3** when WordPerfect prompts you for action on a properly spelled word.

EXAMPLES

1. While WordPerfect's dictionary contains many words, it is missing most technical terms. In given areas of business, you might use some of these terms frequently. If you add these words to the supplemental dictionary the first time you encounter them, WordPerfect will recognize the words when checking subsequent documents. First, type

   To assemble the vambrace, align the holes on the largest piece with the holes in the shorter end of the smallest piece. Attach a 2-piece rivet in each hole.

   When you press the Spell (Ctrl - F2) key [Alt Tools Spell] and type a **3**, WordPerfect does not find "vambrace" in its dictionary. Since this word, which describes a type of arm protection, is spelled correctly, you can add it to the supplemental dictionary: Type a **3**. As you create other documents that mention "vambrace," WordPerfect will not stop at that word when checking spelling.

2. You will want to add frequently used names to the supplemental dictionary. WordPerfect recognizes many common names such as John, Nancy, Smith, and Jones. Many other, less common names it does not recognize as correctly spelled words. First, type

Jim Johansen
1209 Sunrise Boulevard
Ft. Lauderdale, Florida 33304

Dear Mr. Johansen,

   We have shipped the supplies that you ordered. You will receive them in a few days. The paper that you ordered is out of stock. We will ship it once our inventory is restocked.

                    Sincerely,

                    Adele Stein

When you check the spelling, WordPerfect does not recognize the name "Johansen." If Mr. Johansen is one of your regular customers and you spelled his name correctly, you can add his name to the supplemental dictionary by typing a **3**. When WordPerfect finds "Johansen" in other documents, it will recognize it as a correctly spelled word.

   Next, WordPerfect suggests that you have misspelled Adele. Since it is spelled correctly, add it to the dictionary by typing a **3**. WordPerfect finishes checking the document. Press the SPACEBAR to end spell checking.

EXERCISES

1. Type the following names and addresses:

   Ann Slater
   2573 Curtiswood
   Plantation, Florida 33145

   Timothy McKee
   8964 Lorain Avenue
   Lakewood, Ohio 44106

   Check the spelling. If WordPerfect flags a proper name as misspelled, add it to your supplemental dictionary.

2. Type your full name. Use the Spell feature to determine if each part of it is in WordPerfect's dictionary. If it is not, add it to your supplemental dictionary.

3. Type the following lines, pressing [Enter] at the end of each one:

   Abbreviations
   ATMOS - Atmosphere
   IDP - Integrated Data Processing
   OCS - Officer Candidate School
   SWAZ - Swaziland

   Check the spelling. If WordPerfect flags a proper name or abbreviation as misspelled, add it to your supplemental dictionary.

4. Type the following paragraph:

Pygmalion was a sculptor who created a beautiful statue called Galatea, which Aphrodite brought to life. George Bernard Shaw wrote a play, called <u>Pygmalion</u>, that relied on this myth for some ideas. The film version of the musical, called <u>My Fair Lady</u>, starred Audrey Hepburn.

Check the spelling. Add any proper names that WordPerfect suggests to your supplemental dictionary.

9.5 | DELETE WORDS FROM THE SUPPLEMENTAL DICTIONARY

As you add more words to your supplemental dictionary, WordPerfect may take longer to check the spelling. If your supplemental dictionary has words that you use infrequently, you should delete them. Since WordPerfect stores all of the words you add in the file WP{WP}US.SUP (WP{WP}EN.SUP in 5.0) , this is the file from which you must remove the words.

To delete words from the dictionary:

a. Clear the screen.

b. Retrieve the file WP{WP}US.SUP (WP{WP}EN.SUP in 5.0).

c. Move the cursor to a word that you want to remove.

d. Press [Ctrl]-[Backspace] and then [Del] to remove the word and the hard return.

e. Repeat steps c and d for each word that you want to delete.

f. Save the file as WP{WP}US.SUP (WP{WP}EN.SUP in 5.0), replacing the one on disk.

The instructions presented assume that the supplemental dictionary is in your default directory. If you installed WordPerfect according to the directions in Appendix A, this will be the correct location. If your dictionary is in another directory, you will need to specify the pathname along with the filename when you retrieve the dictionary in step b.

EXAMPLES

1. In example 2 of section 9.4, you added "Adele" to the supplemental dictionary. If you do not expect to use this name often, you can delete it from the dictionary. First, on a clear screen, press the Retrieve ([Shift]-[F10]) key [[Alt] File Retrieve], type **wp{wp}us.sup** (**wp{wp}en.sup** in 5.0), and press [Enter]. The screen looks like Figure 9-2 . Next, since "Adele" is the first word, press [Ctrl]-[Backspace] and then [Del] to remove the line from the document. Then, press the Save ([F10]) key [[Alt] File Save]. Since WordPerfect prompts you with the correct filename, press [Enter], and type a y to replace the old version of the dictionary with the new version.

2. In example 1 of section 9.4, you saw that WordPerfect's dictionary does not contain some technical terms. You added "vambrace" to the supplemental dictionary. If you do not expect to use "vambrace"

```
adele
aphrodite
atmos
audrey
curtiswood
galatea
idp
johansen
lakewood
lorain
mckee
ocs
pygmalion
slater
swaz
vambrace
```

D:\WP51\WP{WP}US.SUP   Doc 1 Pg 1 Ln 1" Pos 1"

FIGURE 9-2.   WordPerfect supplemental dictionary file

very often, you can delete this word from the dictionary. First, on a clear screen, press the Retrieve ([Shift]-[F10]) key [[Alt] File Retrieve], type **wp{wp}us.sup (wp{wp}en.sup** in 5.0), and press [Enter]. Next, press the [↓] key until the cursor is at the "v" in "vambrace." Press [Ctrl]-[Backspace] and then [Del] to remove the line from the document. Press the Save ([F10]) key [[Alt] File Save]. Since WordPerfect prompts you with the correct filename, press [Enter] and type a **y** to replace the old version of the supplemental dictionary with the revised version.

EXERCISES

1. Remove the words that you added to your supplemental dictionary in the first exercise of section 9.4.

2. Remove the words that you added to your supplemental dictionary in exercise 3 of section 9.4.

3. Remove the words that you added to your supplemental dictionary in exercise 4 of section 9.4.

REPLACE CORRECTLY SPELLED WORDS THAT ARE MISUSED

9.6

WordPerfect's Spell feature checks the spelling in a document; however, it does not check usage. You can have a document with correctly spelled words that are incorrect in usage. Typically, each person makes a mistake or two like this repeatedly. Such habitual mistakes might be caused by a typographical error, for example, typing "form" instead of "from." They might also be caused by the mistaken use of homonyms, as in the use of "their" for "there" or "to" for "too." If you are able to identify any mistakes that you tend to make on a regular basis, you will want to use the Replace feature as part of your document-correction process to check for these potential errors.

EXAMPLES

1. One common mistake that you can make is typing "form" when you want "from" and vice versa. First, type

   Enclosed is the order from received form your department.

   The "form" and "from" are in the wrong places. Since both words are spelled correctly, the Spell feature will not detect the error. To correct this error, press the Replace ([Alt]-[F2]) key [[Alt] Search Replace]. Type a **y** since you will need to confirm each replacement. When prompted for the text for which to search, type **from**, and press the [↑], since you are searching from the bottom of the document. Next, press the Search ([F2]) key. When prompted for the text with which to replace it, type **form**, and press the Search ([F2]) key again. Word-Perfect asks if you want to replace "from" with "form" as the fifth word in the sentence. Type a **y** to confirm the replacement.

   To make the second correction, press [Home], [Home], [↑] to move to the top of the document. Press the Replace ([Alt]-[F2]) key [[Alt] Search Replace], and type a **y** to confirm each replacement. When prompted for the text for which to search, type **form**, and press the Search ([F2]) key. When prompted for the text with which to replace it, type **from**, and press the Search ([F2]) key.

   WordPerfect prompts to see if you want to replace "form" with "from" as the fifth word in the sentence. Since you do not want this replaced, type an **n**. Next, WordPerfect checks to see if you want the second "form" in the sentence replaced. Type a **y** to confirm that you want this replaced.

2. Homonyms present a problem that WordPerfect's Spell feature cannot solve. *Homonyms* are words that sound the same but have different meanings. Examples are "to," "too," and "two." Whenever these words are used in a document, WordPerfect accepts the spelling, although the usage may not be correct. To illustrate the problem, type

   Since the dinner had too speakers, the guests were encouraged not two ask to many questions.

   This sentence has three occurrences of the homonyms, but none is used correctly: "Too" should have been "two," "two" should have been "to," and "to" should have been "too." Checking the spelling does not correct these errors. Since "to" is such a common word, searching a document for every occurrence of the word may require a significant investment of time. You probably would not want to do this unless you made this type of mistake on a regular basis; proofreading each document carefully would be a better solution.

EXERCISES

1. Type the following sentence:

   The fair four the bridge to get to the fare is for dollars.

Replace "fair" and "fare" so that each word is in the correct place. Replace "for" and "four" so that each word is in the correct place.

2. Type the following sentence:

Their demonstrating there new product over they're.

Use the Replace feature to place "their," "there," and "they're" in their proper contexts.

9.7   LOOK UP A WORD IN THE THESAURUS

One important aspect of communicating effectively is using words that convey your exact meaning. Word-Perfect assists you with finding the right words with its on-line Thesaurus feature.

WordPerfect's thesaurus is similar to *Roget's Thesaurus*, with which you may be familiar. Although its function is the same, WordPerfect's Thesaurus feature is much easier to use. When you ask WordPerfect to find a word in its thesaurus, it provides a listing of synonyms, organized by parts of speech, such as noun, verb, and adjective. Some of the words listed will have synonym lists of their own, which you can review to expand the potential replacement options. The Thesaurus feature provides a handy check for words used infrequently. By looking at the list of synonyms for a word you have used, you can verify its correct usage in your sentence.

To find a word in WordPerfect's thesaurus:

a. Move the cursor to a word that you want to find.

b. Press the Thesaurus (Alt-F1) key [Alt Tools Thesaurus].

c. Type the letter of a marked synonym for further synonyms, or select an action from the menu at the bottom of the screen.

d. Press the Cancel (F1) key, the Exit (F7) key, Enter, or SPACEBAR to return to the document.

If the cursor is not on a word, WordPerfect normally uses the next word in the document. If you are at the end of the document or in a blank one, WordPerfect prompts you for the word you want to look up. If it cannot find a word in its thesaurus, WordPerfect prompts you for another word.

EXAMPLES

1. You can use the Thesaurus feature to find a word that you want as you are typing a document. For example, to find words that are similar in meaning to "meet," press the Thesaurus (Alt-F1) key [Alt Tools Thesaurus]. Since the document is blank, WordPerfect prompts you for a word to look up. Type **meet**, and press Enter.

   Now the screen looks like Figure 9-3. As you can see, WordPerfect separates the different parts of speech. Each word with a highlighted dot has its

```
meet-(v)
 1 A ·confront       meet-(n)
   B ·encounter       5    bout
   C ·greet               ·competition
                          ·contest
 2 D ·answer              ·game
   E ·satisfy             tourney
   F ·suffice
                    meet-(ant)
 3 G ·assemble       6    ·avoid
   H  convene             ·disperse
   I ·converge            ·ignore
   J ·gather

 4 K  abide by
   L ·comply with
   M ·fulfill
   N ·observe
   O ·satisfy
1 Replace Word; 2 View Doc; 3 Look Up Word; 4 Clear Column: 0
```

FIGURE 9-3.   Thesaurus entries for "meet"

own entry in the thesaurus. Some entries also list antonyms, as shown in this example.

Once you have looked over the synonyms for the word, press the Cancel ([F1]) key to return to the document, and type the word that you want to use.

2. You can use a word already in a document to find an entry in the thesaurus. First, type **use**. Although the cursor is to the right of the word, WordPerfect looks for "use" in its thesaurus when you press the Thesaurus ([Alt]-[F1]) key [[Alt] Tools Thesaurus]. The screen looks like Figure 9-4. Press the Cancel ([F1]) key to return to the document.

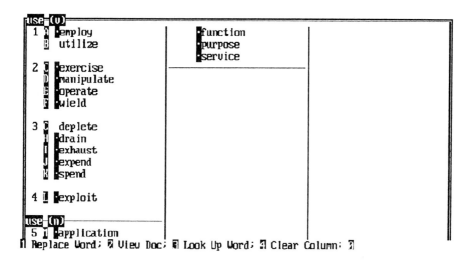

FIGURE 9-4.   Thesaurus entries for "use"

3. You can use synonyms in the thesaurus to find other synonyms. First, type **associate**. Then, press the Thesaurus (⌨Alt⌨-⌨F1⌨) key [⌨Alt⌨ Tools Thesaurus]. The screen looks like Figure 9-5. Several of the words have dots next to them. You can find synonyms for any of those words by typing the letter to the left of the word.

   To find other synonyms for "relate," type an f. Now, the screen looks like Figure 9-6. When you look up a synonym's thesaurus entry, WordPerfect associate

```
┌associate─(v)─────────────────────────────────────────────────┐
│  1 A ·consort         5    ·companion                         │
│    B ·fraternize           ·comrade                           │
│    C ·mingle               ·friend                            │
│                                                               │
│  2 D ·connect         ┌associate─(a)─────────                 │
│    E ·identify with   │  6    ·adjunct                        │
│    F ·relate          │       ·secondary                      │
│                       │       ·subordinate                    │
│  3 G ·affiliate                                               │
│    H ·ally            ┌associate─(ant)────────                │
│    I ·confederate     │  7    ·dissociate                     │
│┌associate─(n)─────────┘       ·alienate                       │
││ 4 J ·assistant                                               │
││   K ·colleague                                               │
││   L  co-worker                                               │
││   J ·partner                                                 │
└┴──────────────────────┴──────────────────────────────────────┘
  1 Replace Word; 2 View Doc; 3 Look Up Word; 4 Clear Column: 5
```

FIGURE 9-5.   Thesaurus entries for "associate"

puts the word's entry in the next blank column or in the rightmost column if all three are full. Only the current column contains letters next to the synonyms. You can select words to look up only from the current column. To change the current column, use the ➡ or the ⬅ key. To remove the current thesaurus entry, type a **4**. As a column is emptied, WordPerfect moves any remaining columns to the left to fill the emptied one. If the thesaurus entry in the rightmost column has more columns to display, it will use the blank column. Press the Cancel (F1) key to return to the document.

associate

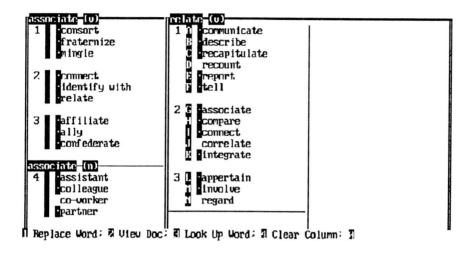

```
associate (u)                 relate (u)
  1   consort                  1  A  communicate
      fraternize                  B  describe
      mingle                      C  recapitulate
                                  D  recount
  2   connect                     E  report
      identify with               F  tell
      relate
                               2  G  associate
  3   affiliate                   H  compare
      ally                        I  connect
      confederate                 J  correlate
associate (n)                     K  integrate
  4   assistant
      colleague                 3  L  appertain
      co-worker                   M  involve
      partner                     N  regard
```

1 Replace Word; 2 View Doc; 3 Look Up Word; 4 Clear Column; 5

FIGURE 9-6.   Using a thesaurus entry to look up another thesaurus entry

---

4. You can also look up synonyms for an entry that is not listed in the current thesaurus entry. You can do this when you find synonyms for one word to be unsatisfactory and want to see synonyms for another word. With this approach, you do not have to exit the Thesaurus, move to the other word, and activate the feature again. First, type **business**. Then, press the Thesaurus ([Alt]-[F1]) key [[Alt] Tools Thesaurus] to display the thesaurus entry for "business."

Next, to find the entry for "product," type a 3, type **product**, and press [Enter]. Now the screen shows entries for both "business" and "product." Press the Cancel ([F1]) key to return to the document.

EXERCISES

1. Find the thesaurus entry for "table."

2. Find the thesaurus entry for "adjoining."

3. Type **rich**, and find the thesaurus entry for that word. Use that entry to find the thesaurus entry for "prosperous."

4. Activate the Thesaurus feature, and find the entry for "limit." Use this entry to find the entry for "bar." Use this entry to find the entry for "board." Use this entry to find the entry for "cabinet." Use this entry to find the entry for "cupboard." Use this entry to find the entry for "press." Remove the "limit" and "bar" entries from the screen.

9.8 | REPLACE A WORD WITH A WORD FROM THE THESAURUS

You can use any of the thesaurus entries to replace a word in your document. The options available in the thesaurus entries allow you to add variety and color to your writing.

To replace a word with WordPerfect's Thesaurus feature:

a. Move the cursor to the word for which you want to find the thesaurus entry, or type the word.

b. Press the Thesaurus ([Alt]-[F1]) key [[Alt] Tools Thesaurus].

c. Type a **1** to select the Replace Word option.

d. Type the letter identifying the word with which you want the original word replaced.

When you replace a word with the Thesaurus feature, WordPerfect inserts the replacement word using the same capitalization as the original word. For example, if the first letter of the original word is capitalized, the first letter of the replacement word is capitalized.

EXAMPLES

1. You can use the Replace Word feature of the Thesaurus when you are editing a document. Type

   Jim Stevens is the newest associate at Stevens & Stevens.

   You can find a replacement word for "associate" by consulting the Thesaurus. First, press [Ctrl]-[←] five times to move the cursor to the word "associate." Then, press the Thesaurus ([Alt]-[F1]) key [[Alt] Tools Thesaurus]. Looking at the selections, you see that "partner" is choice "M." To select this word, type a **1** and an **m**. WordPerfect exits the Thesaurus feature, and the sentence now looks like this:

   Jim Stevens is the newest partner at Stevens & Stevens.

2. Although WordPerfect supplies lettered choices for only the active column, you can change the active column. Type

At the end of the day, the store manager totals the daily sales.

To find another word to use in place of "totals," press [Ctrl]-[←] four times to move the cursor to the word "totals." Next, press the Thesaurus ([Alt]-[F1]) key [[Alt] Tools Thesaurus]. The entries for "totals" use three columns, but only the leftmost column offers lettered choices. Looking through the entries, you can see the verb "add" in the second column. Before you can replace "totals" with "add," you must move the letters from the first column to the second column by pressing the [→] key. The screen now looks like Figure 9-7. To replace "totals" with "add," type a **1** and an **f.** Now, the sentence looks like this:

At the end of the day, the store manager add_the daily sales.

Type an **s** to change "add" to "adds", and the replacement is complete.

EXERCISES

1. Type the following sentence:

The report includes a three-page insert.

Use the Thesaurus feature to find another word for "insert." Replace it.

2. Type the following sentence:

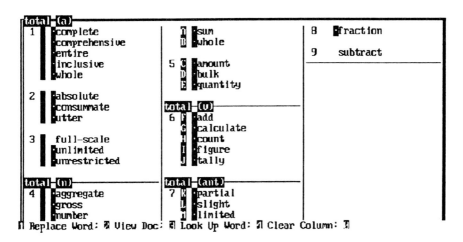

At the end of the day, the store manager **totals** the daily sales.

```
┌total─(a)────────────────────────────────────────────────────────────────┐
│ 1 │complete             A│ sum            8    fraction                   │
│   │comprehensive        B│ whole                                          │
│   │entire                                9    subtract                    │
│   │inclusive        5  C│ amount                                          │
│   │whole                D│ bulk                                           │
│   │                     E│ quantity                                       │
│ 2 │absolute                                                               │
│   │consummate      ┌total─(v)───────────                                  │
│   │utter           6  F│ add                                             │
│   │                   G│ calculate                                       │
│ 3 │ full-scale        H│ count                                           │
│   │unlimited          I│ figure                                          │
│   │unrestricted       J│ tally                                           │
│                                                                           │
│┌total─(n)─────────── ┌total─(ant)───────                                  │
│ 4 │aggregate        7  K│ partial                                        │
│   │gross              L│ slight                                          │
│   │number             M│ limited                                         │
└───────────────────────────────────────────────────────────────────────────┘
 1 Replace Word: 2 View Doc: 3 Look Up Word: 4 Clear Column: 5
```

| FIGURE 9-7. | Thesaurus entries for "total" |

The nylon division reported a 13% increase in sales.

Use the Thesaurus feature to find synonyms for "division." Replace "division" with "branch."

3. Type the following sentence:

The Bargain Business is having a 30% sale.

Use the Thesaurus feature to find synonyms for "business." Replace "business" with "company."

4. Type the following paragraph:

The land holdings include land for raising cattle, land for growing corn, and some land with a high resale value.

Use the Thesaurus feature to replace the four occurrences of "land" with "estate," "ranch," "farm," and "property," respectively. (Naturally, you would also want to add articles to make the sentence read correctly.)

EXERCISES

MASTERY SKILLS CHECK

1. Type the following words as they appear:

   Infomation
   Capitalisation
   Iregardless
   Nevertheless

   Use the Spell feature to check the spelling and correct any mistakes.

2. Type the following paragraph, including the errors:

   Based on the results of a market study, the XYZ Corporation woll market its its personalized hubcaps nationaly. According to the survey, men are four times more likely to to buy them than women. Also, the product appeals primarily to buyers in the 19- to 34-year-old age group.

   Use the Spell feature to correct errors.

3. Type the following letter as it appears:

   Ingram Scott
   536 S. Green Road
   Cleveland Heights, Ohio 44108

Dear Iggy,

    Here is the information that you requested. Please return it when you complete your project.

Sincerely,

Tabitha Marletti

Use the Spell feature to check the spelling. Add the proper names that WordPerfect does not recognize.

4. Remove from the supplementary dictionary the names that you added in exercise 3.

5. Type the following paragraph:

Because of the market study, the XYZ Corporation will market it's personalized hubcaps nationally. According to the survey, men are for times moor likely to buy them than women. Also, the product appeals primarily too individuals 19 two 34 years old.

Several words in the paragraph are homonyms. Use the Replace feature to correct the improper usage.

6. Use the Thesaurus feature to find synonyms for "bar," "block," and "light."

7. Type the following sentence:

Reviewing the data revealed that people thought that the product was overpriced.

Use the Thesaurus feature to find synonyms for "data." Replace "data" with "statistics."

**INTEGRATING
SKILLS CHECK**

(Do not clear the screen until you have completed the last exercise.)

1. Set all margins to 3″.

2. Type the following paragraph, including the errors:

   The company is reducing its products aimed at the do-it-youself market. It is applying these resources towards manufaturing more higher-proced items. The company expects to increace sales by 15% with this stratagy.

   Use the Spell feature to correct errors.

3. Type the following paragraph, including the errors:

   Howard Moore designed an instant-strip wallpaper removr. The product can be used by inexperienced home owners. It removes wallpaper in half the time required for conventonal methods. The trade name for the product is Wall-Off.

   Check the spelling. Add the proper names to the supplemental dictionary if WordPerfect does not recognize them.

4. Move the paragraph created in exercise 3 to precede the paragraph created in exercise 2.

5. Block and copy the paragraph created in exercise 2. Place two additional copies in the document.

6. Type the following sentence:

   All of the McGregors had light complexions.

Use the Thesaurus feature to find synonyms for "light." Replace "light" with **fair.**

7. Print the document.

8. Save the file as WORDS.

9. Remove from the supplemental dictionary the words that you added in exercise 3.

Page Breaks, Paragraph Breaks, and Other Options

▶10◀

The appearance of a document can help convey its message to the reader. This chapter covers some features that provide additional options for controlling the appearance of the text on a page. Widow and orphan protection features prevent single lines of a paragraph from appearing at the top or bottom of a page. By controlling the text placement in this way, you can ensure that your documents have greater clarity for the reader, since an entire paragraph can be presented without the need for the reader to turn the page.

In addition, this chapter introduces headers and footers, which allow you to add fixed lines of text at the top and bottom of every page. You can use these features to include, for example, your name or a report name and number on each page of a document. Footnotes provide the opportunity for removing technical data, equations, and bibliographic references from the main text. WordPerfect's features allow you to automatically number footnotes and print them at the end of your document.

SKILLS CHECK

(Do not clear the screen until you have completed the last exercise.)

1. Type the following paragraph, including the errors:

Cash dividents distribute earnings to the shareholders. Cash dividends have several important dates. The declaraction date is the date the board of directors declares the dividend. The date of record is the date that decides which stockholders are paid the dividend. The date of record is the day used to establish stock ownership. The payment date is the date that the company pays its dividents.

Use the Spell feature to check and correct the spelling.

2. Use the Thesaurus feature to replace "decides" with "determines."

3. Move the first sentence to the end of the paragraph.

4. Use the Search feature to find each occurrence of "date."

5. Delete the last sentence.

CONTROL WIDOW AND ORPHAN LINES

10.1

When you work on a document, the first or the last line of a paragraph may appear by itself on a page with the rest of the paragraph on the next or the preceding page. In WordPerfect, the first line of a paragraph placed alone at the bottom of a page is called a *widow*. The last line of a paragraph placed alone at the top of a page is called an *orphan*. Both can cause the reader to lose the line of thought of the paragraph. Widows and orphans also detract from the appearance of a document. WordPerfect lets you prevent widows and orphans from appearing in a document.

To prevent widows and orphans:

a. Move to the beginning of the document.

b. Press the Format (Shift - F8) key [Alt Layout Line and skip step c].

c. Type an **L** or a **1** to select the line-formatting options.

d. Type a **w** or a **9** to select Widow/Orphan Protection.

e. Type a **y** to activate the feature.

f. Press the Exit (F7) key.

When you enable Widow/Orphan Protection, Word-Perfect adds the hidden code [W/O On] to your document.

EXAMPLES

1. WordPerfect's Widow/Orphan Protection feature prevents the last line of a paragraph from appearing as an orphan at the top of a page. To see the effect of orphans while minimizing typing, you can increase the top and bottom margins to limit the amount of text on a page. If you set the top and bottom margins to 5", only six lines will display on each page. First, press the Format (Shift-F8) key [Alt Layout Page], and type a **p** and an **m**. Type a 5 and press Enter for the top margin, and type a 5 and press Enter for the bottom margin. Press the Exit (F7) key to return to the document.

Next, type

The company picnic is scheduled for July 15 at Waverly Park. A full day of activities is planned for employees and their families. Food, games, clowns, bingo, and prizes are a few of the attractions. This year's food selections include fried chicken, hamburgers, hot dogs, roast beef, cakes, pies, ice cream, and an array of

salads. Please stop by the Human Resources office before July 1 to pick up your tickets.

Now, the screen looks like Figure 10-1. The last line of the paragraph is an orphan at the top of a new page.

Move to the top of the document by pressing [Home], [Home], [↑]. Press the Format ([Shift]-[F8]) key, and type an **L** [[Alt] Layout Line] and a **w** for Widow. Type a **y** to turn on Widow/Orphan Protection. Press the Exit ([F7]) key to return to the

---

The company picnic is scheduled for July 15 at Waverly Park. A full day of activities is planned for employees and their families. Food, games, clowns, bingo, and prizes are a few of the attractions. This year's food selections include fried chicken, hamburgers, hot dogs, roast beef, cakes, pies, ice cream, and an array of salads. Please stop by the Human Resources office before

---

July 1 to pick up your tickets.

Doc 1 Pg 2 Ln 1.83" Pos 1"

FIGURE 10-1.   Orphan line at the top of a page

document. Press the ⬇ key to move to the bottom of the paragraph, which now looks like the one in Figure 10-2. The last two lines of the paragraph are both on the second page.

2. Preventing widows also makes documents easier to read. You can obtain protection from widows with the same procedure. First, clear the current document, and set the top and bottom margins to 5" by pressing the Format (Shift - F8) key and typing a p

---

The company picnic is scheduled for July 15 at Waverly Park. A full day of activities is planned for employees and their families. Food, games, clowns, bingo, and prizes are a few of the attractions. This year's food selections include fried chicken, hamburgers, hot dogs, roast beef, cakes, pies, ice cream, and an

---

array of salads. Please stop by the Human Resources office before July 1 to pick up your tickets.

Doc 1 Pg 2 Ln 5.33" Pos 1"

| FIGURE 10-2. | Orphan eliminated with Widow/Orphan Protection |

[⟨Alt⟩ Layout **P**age] and an **m**. Type a **5**, press ⟨Enter⟩, and type a **5** and press ⟨Enter⟩ again. Press the Exit (⟨F7⟩) key to return to the document. Type

The company picnic is scheduled for July 15 at Waverly Hills Park. A full day of activities is planned for employees and their families. This year's special activities include softball, bingo, horseshoes, an executive dunktank, carnival rides, and a puppet show.
You can pick up ticket books for your entire family any day before July 15. These books include coupons for the carnival rides and door prize registration forms. Special food stands have been set up for employees. Coupons are not required at these stands.

The screen looks like Figure 10-3.

NOTE: It is possible that the lines in your entry will not break in the same place if you use a different printer.

The first line of the second paragraph displays as a widow at the bottom of page 1.

Move to the top of the document by pressing ⟨Home⟩, ⟨Home⟩, ⟨↑⟩. Invoke Widow and Orphan Protection by pressing the Format (⟨Shift⟩-⟨F8⟩) key and type an **L** [⟨Alt⟩ Layout **L**ine] and a **w** for **W**idow/Orphan Protection. Type a **y** to enable the feature, and press the Exit (⟨F7⟩) key to return to the document. When you move the cursor down the screen, the text is rearranged as in Figure 10-4. The widow line now appears on the second page along with the rest of the paragraph.

The company picnic is scheduled for July 15 at Waverly Hills Park.
A full day of activities is planned for employees and their
families. This year's special activities include softball, bingo,
horseshoes, an executive dunktank, carnival rides, and a puppet
show.
You can pick up ticket books for your entire family any day before

---

July 15. These books include coupons for the carnival rides and
door prize registration forms. Special food stands have been set
up for employees. Coupons are not required at these stands.

Doc 1 Pg 2 Ln 1.5" Pos 1"

| FIGURE 10-3. | Widow line at the bottom of a page |

EXERCISES

1. Type the following paragraphs with the top and bottom margins set to 5". Include a blank line between the paragraphs when you type them.

   The company's contingent liabilities are as follows: The company has guaranteed a loan on behalf of a subsidiary that was recently spun off. The loan is for $500,000 and will mature on March 30, 1991.

   Estimated loss from a pending lawsuit is $65,000. The suit should be concluded within the next two months.

The company picnic is scheduled for July 15 at Waverly Hills Park.
A full day of activities is planned for employees and their
families. This year's special activities include softball, bingo,
horseshoes, an executive dunktank, carnival rides, and a puppet
show.

You can pick up ticket books for your entire family any day before
July 15. These books include coupons for the carnival rides and
door prize registration forms. Special food stands have been set
up for employees. Coupons are not required at these stands.

Doc 1 Pg 2 Ln 1.66" Pos 1"

| FIGURE 10-4. | Widow eliminated with Widow/Orphan Protection |

Prevent widows and orphans.

2. Type the following paragraph with the top and bottom margins set to 5":

Cost-flow assumptions affect inventory valuation. If a company uses the LIFO method, it assumes that the last inventory items purchased are the first ones sold. This assumption makes the cost of goods sold closely reflect the current cost of the inventory sold. On the other hand, the ending inventory is valued at prior-period purchase costs. This method is best used when purchase costs are rising and the inventory turnover is low.

Prevent widows and orphans. Save the document as LIFO and clear the screen.

3. Retrieve LIFO. Remove the top and bottom margin settings. Set the margins to 1″ on top and 9″ at the bottom. Press the ⏎ key to reformat the paragraph. Save the document and clear the screen.

4. Retrieve LIFO. Leaving the top and bottom margins intact, reset the left and right margins to 3″ on each side. Press the ⏎ key to reformat the paragraph. Save the document and clear the screen.

10.2   USE HEADERS AND FOOTERS ON PAGES

Headers are lines of text that appear at the top of every page of printed output. *Footers* are lines of text that appear at the bottom of every printed page. Header and footer lines are handy options. WordPerfect provides two headers and footers so that you can use one header or footer on even-numbered pages and another on odd-numbered pages. The first header or footer you create is referred to as header or footer A. The second is referred to as header or footer B. WordPerfect supports many formatting features (for example, bold and centering) in headers and footers.

Neither headers nor footers display on the screen with the text. To keep a header or a footer from printing, or to make changes to either, you need to issue a command.

To include a header or footer on every page:

a. Move the cursor to the top of the first page on which you want a header or footer.

b. Press the Format (Shift - F8) key [Alt Layout **Page** and skip step c].

c. Type a **p** or a **2** to select page-formatting options.

d. Type an **h** or a **3** for Headers or an **f** or a **4** for Footers.

e. Type an **a** or a **1** for header or footer A, or type a **b** or a **2** for header or footer B.

f. Type a **p** or a **2** to have the header or footer appear on every page.

g. Type the header or footer text.

h. Press the Exit (F7) key to return to the page-formatting menu.

i. Press the Exit (F7) key to return to the document.

Headers and Footers do not appear on your screen with the document; they appear only when you print or preview the document. WordPerfect puts the header on the first line after the top margin, using additional lines as required for multiline headers. It adds a blank line between the header and the main part of the document. For a footer, WordPerfect stops printing the body of the document before reaching the bottom margin, skips a line, and prints the footer.

To stop printing a header or footer, move to the beginning of the first page that will not have the header or footer. Perform steps b through e, as you did to create the header or footer, type a **d** or a **1**, and press the Exit (F7) key.

You can also remove a header or footer for an entire document by deleting the hidden code for it. The hidden code for a header is [Header X:Y;Z]. "X" represents either A or B, depending on which header the code represents. "Y" represents the name (or the number in 5.0) that you selected in step f to indicate where the header will occur. "Z" represents the text in the header. It ends with an ellipsis if the header contains more than 50 characters. Footers use the same hidden code, but with the word "Footer" in place of "Header."

EXAMPLES

1. You can use headers to place a repeating line at the top of each page of a document. First, press the Format (Shift - F8) key, type a **p** [Alt Layout **P**age] and an **h**, and type an **a** for header A. Next, type a **p** to have the header appear on every page. Then, type

1990 Financial Report

Finally, press the Exit (F7) key twice to return to the document. The header does not appear on the screen. Type the following lines of text in the document:

Consolidated Changes in Financial Position
Limestone Corporation
Sources of Funds:
  Operations:

When you press the Print ([Shift]-[F7]) key [[Alt] File Print] and type a **v** and a **1**, the screen looks like Figure 10-5. The header that appears on this page will appear on every page in the document.

2. You can use WordPerfect's formatting features in headers and footers. First, press the Format ([Shift]-[F8]) key, type a **p** [[Alt] Layout Page] and an **f**, and type an **a** for footer A. Next, type a **p** to have the footer appear on every page. Press the Center ([Shift]-[F6]) key [[Alt] Layout Align Center] and the Underline ([F8]) key, and type

Prepared on 7/1/90

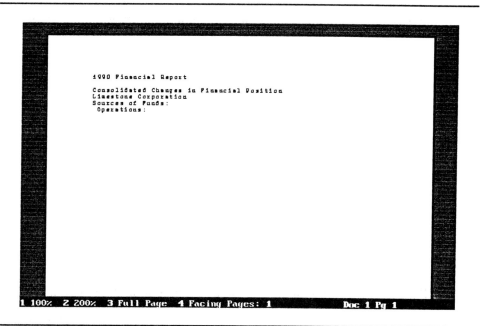

FIGURE 10-5.   View showing header and text

Press the Exit (F7) key twice. Press the Print (Shift-F7) key [Alt File Print], type a **v** and a **1**, and press the Home and ↓ keys to move to the bottom of the page. The screen looks like this:

The footer line on this page will appear at the bottom of each page of the document.

3. You can print page numbers as part of a header or footer. Placing the page number in the header or footer gives you additional control over how Word-Perfect prints the page numbers, since you can add the word "page" or other constants before or after the page number. First, press the Format (Shift-F8) key, type a **p** [Alt Layout Page] and an **h**, and type an **a** for header A. Next, type a **p** to have the header appear on every page. Press the Flush Right (Alt-F6) key [Alt Layout Align Flush Right], type **Page**, and press the SPACEBAR. To have Word-Perfect automatically place page numbers on the line, hold down the Ctrl key and type a **b**. The screen looks like this:

Page ^B

Finally, press the Exit (F7) key twice. When you press the Print (Shift-F7) key [Alt File Print] and type a **v**, the screen looks like this:

WordPerfect replaces "^B" with the appropriate page numbers when it prints documents.

4. You can define two headers or footers for a document. For example, you may want one header on even pages and another on odd pages. First, press the Format (Shift-F8) key, type a **p** [Alt Layout Page] and an **h** and type an **a** for header A. Next, type an **o** to have the header appear on odd-numbered pages. Type: **1990 Financial Report**. Next, press the Exit (F7) key once to return to the page-formatting options. Type an **h** and a **b** for header B. Type a **v** to have the header appear on even-numbered pages. Press the Flush Right (Alt-F6) key [Alt Layout Align Flush Right], type **Ace Corporation**, and press the Exit (F7) key twice. Press the Ctrl-Enter key [Alt Layout Align Hard Page] twice to create additional pages in the document. When you press the Print (Shift-F7) key [Alt File Print] and type a **v** and a **4**, the screen looks like this:

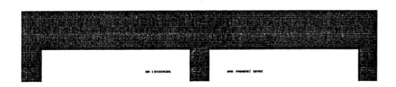

EXERCISES

1. Create a header that says "Acme Inc. Income Statement". Preview how WordPerfect will print it.

2. Create a footer that displays your name in boldface. Preview how WordPerfect will print it.

3. Create a header consisting of the page number encased between hyphens and centered on the page. Preview how WordPerfect will print it.

4. Create a header that prints the page numbers on odd-numbered pages and your name on even-numbered pages. Preview how WordPerfect will print it.

10.3 ADD FOOTNOTES

Footnotes allow you to store supplemental information in notes at the bottom of each page. Financial reports, legal documents, and academic research papers normally contain footnoted text. The footnote may contain explanatory information or a reference to a source for a specific piece of information in the document.

WordPerfect automatically inserts sequential reference numbers for footnotes. Each footnote number is printed as superscript; that is, it appears slightly smaller and higher than the other text on the line. WordPerfect prints each footnote at the bottom of the page containing the footnote reference. If a footnote is long or near the bottom of a page, WordPerfect allows space for a minimum of three lines of footnote text on the page and continues the footnote at the bottom of the next page. A single footnote can contain as many as 16,000 lines.

To create a footnote:

a. Press the Footnote ([Ctrl]-[F7]) key [[Alt] Layout Footnote Create and skip steps b and c].

b. Type an **f** or a **1** for the Footnote options.

c. Type a **c** or a **1** to create a footnote.

d. Type the footnote text.

e. Press the Exit ([F7]) key.

A [Footnote:X;[Note Num] code is inserted in the document at the location of each footnote. "X" represents the footnote number. You can delete a footnote by removing the hidden code or by deleting the footnote number that displays on the screen.

EXAMPLES

1. You can use a footnote to identify the source of a quote. Type

   Getting over the hurdle of learning something new can feel uncomfortable and takes both time and practice, so you must be patient with yourself as you learn Word-Perfect. Work at your own pace. Tackle a chapter or two a day, whatever is appropriate for you. And make sure that you don't just read the chapters, but that you follow along on the computer, step by step. Pretty soon you'll be using WordPerfect like a pro.

Once you have typed this quote, press the Footnote (Ctrl-F7) key, and type an f and a c [Alt Layout Footnote Create] to create a footnote. Next, type a space and the following footnote text:

Mella Mincberg, _WordPerfect 5.1 Made Easy_, Osborne/McGraw-Hill, 1990, pp. xiii-xiv.

Now, the screen looks like this:

        1 Mella Mincberg, WordPerfect 5.1 Made Easy, Osborne/McGraw-
    Hill, 1990, pp. xiii-xiv.

Finally, press the Exit (F7) key. If you are using a color monitor, the footnote number may appear in a different color to indicate that it is superscript.

2. WordPerfect's Footnote feature keeps track of the footnote numbers as you add or delete footnotes. To illustrate this, you need at least two footnotes. First, increase the bottom margin so that you will be able to see the text and the footnotes together in a print preview. Press the Format (Shift-F8) key, type a **p** [Alt Layout Page] and an **m**, and press Enter. Then type an **8**, press Enter, and press the Exit (F7) key. Next, type

The company's EPS is 3.48. The dividend date is August 15.

Move the cursor to the end of the first sentence. Press the Footnote (Ctrl-F7) key and type an f and a c [Alt Layout Footnote Create]. Press the SPACEBAR, and type the footnote text:

$1,169,280 1990 income / 336,000 shares

Press the Exit (F7) key to return to the document. For the second footnote, move to the end of the second sentence, press the Footnote (Ctrl - F7) key, and type an **f** and a **c** [Alt Layout Footnote Create]. Press the SPACEBAR, and type

The date of record is August 1.

Press the Exit (F7) key to return to the document. When you press the Print (Shift - F7) key [Alt File Print] and type a **v** and a **1**, the text and the footnotes look like this:

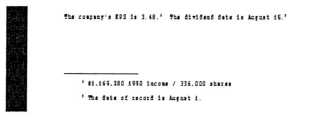

Do not clear the screen. Use these entries in the next example.

3. You can delete a footnote without invoking the menu. When you move or delete a footnote, Word-Perfect automatically adjusts the footnote numbering. To remove a footnote, move the cursor to the footnote number that you want to eliminate, and press Del . Using the footnotes from example 2, move to the first footnote, and press Del . When WordPerfect prompts you for confirmation that it should delete the footnote, type a **y**. Press End to make WordPerfect reformat the other footnote number. Now, the screen looks like this:

The company's EPS is 3.48.   The dividend date is August 15.1

Do not clear the screen. Use these entries in the next example.

4. You can edit footnote text. Press the Footnote ([Ctrl]-[F7]) key, and type an **f**, an **e** [[Alt] Layout Footnote Edit], and a **1** for the number of the footnote that you want to edit and press [Enter]. Next, move the cursor to the "A" in "August 1," press [Ctrl]-[End], and type **July 31** and a period. The screen looks like this:

[] The date of record is July 31.

Press the Exit ([F7]) key to return to the document.

EXERCISES

(Do not clear the screen between exercises unless instructed to do so.)

1. Type the following:

WordPerfect 5.1 Made Easy is written for beginning and intermediate users.

Add a footnote using the following information.

Mella Mincberg,   WordPerfect 5.1 Made Easy, Osborne/McGraw-Hill, 1990, pp. xiii-xiv.

Clear the screen.

2. Type the first line from each of the following pairs of lines, and use the second line in each pair as a footnote:

Once upon a time,. . .
Fairy Tales by the Brothers Grimm

Mary had a little lamb
Mother Goose

The Goose That Laid a Golden Egg
Aesop's Fables

3. Block the first line and its footnote number, and move the line to the end of the document.

4. Edit the footnote for the Grimm Brothers to read "Grimm's Fairy Tales."

EXERCISES

(Do not clear the screen until you have completed the last exercise.)

MASTERY
SKILLS CHECK

1. Set the bottom margin to 9". Type the following:

Preparing a Trial Balance

When you prepare a trial balance, you must make several adjusting entries to properly reflect your income and expenses. You must include prepaid expenses as an asset rather than as an expense. You must include

unearned revenue, such as unredeemed gift certificates, as a liability. You must include accrued expenses
as expenses.

Invoke the Widow/Orphan Protection feature.

2. Insert a page break between the title and the
   paragraph. Add the following footnote at the end of
   the paragraph:

   For example, if half of the period between pay days has
   elapsed, you must include half of the expected salaries
   and wages.

3. Add the following footnote onto the end of the
   second sentence:

   For example, if you pay an insurance premium for two
   years at the beginning of this year, half of what you paid
   is classified as an expense for this year, and half is a
   prepaid expense and classified as an asset.

4. Edit the footnote that you created in exercise 3 so
   that it says

   For example, if you pay a $600 premium insurance for
   two years at the beginning of this year, $300 is classi-
   fied as an expense for last year, and $300 is a prepaid
   expense and classified as an asset.

5. Create a header for every page that consists of the
   title that you typed in exercise 1. Remove the title
   from the body of the text.

6. Create a footer with your name in it to appear on
   odd pages.

   Preview the document. Page through it.

(Do not clear the screen until you have completed the last exercise.)

INTEGRATING SKILLS CHECK

1. Type the following addresses.

Johann Sebastian
390 Market Street
Newport, Rhode Island 01307
Karl Davis
7439 Coral Drive
Stanford, CA 94237
Angus Fuller
764 Ovine Trail
Kansas City, Missouri 12305

Insert a hard page break after each address.

2. Go to the bottom of the first page and type the following letter:

According to our records, we have not received your subscription renewal for our newsletter. To continue to receive this publication, send the enclosed order blank and a check for $35.00.

        Sincerely,

        Elsie Brown
        Secretary, United Dairy Farmers

Use the Thesaurus feature to review synonyms for "continue" and "receive."

3. Use the Spell feature to check the spelling of the letter.

4. Insert the following footnote after the word "publication":

United Dairy Farmers, <u>Dairy Moo-ving</u>

5. Edit the footnote you just typed to include the publisher, Angus Magazines.

6. Block and copy the letter to follow the other addresses on the other pages.

7. Add a right-justified header that contains your name.

Managing Files
►11◄

CHAPTER OBJECTIVES

After completing this chapter, you should be able to:

▶ **Create backup copies** 11.1

▶ **Create subdirectories** 11.2

▶ **Change subdirectories** 11.3

▶ **Delete files** 11.4

▶ **Rename files** 11.5

▶ **Create document summaries** 11.6

▶ **Search for a word within documents on disk** 11.7

▶ **Look at files on disk** 11.8

You have already learned that saving files to disk protects your investment in a document. Once a document is stored on a disk, you can retrieve it again even if the system goes down and you lose the copy of the document in memory. There are other file options that increase your control over the documents you store on disk. Understanding these options gives you the power to manage your resources effectively.

In this chapter, you will learn how to create backup copies. You will learn how to create and manage subdirectories for organizing the many documents you create. You will learn how to rename files on the disk and to delete those you no longer need. You will learn how to search for a file based on text stored within the file. You will see how displaying the contents of the file without retrieving it provides a quick way to verify a file selection. You will learn how to create a document summary to provide an overview of a document.

With so many file options to cover, you will find that this chapter is a little longer than some of the others. Your investment of time will prove worthwhile, however, since you will learn a whole tool kit of skills that can be applied to every WordPerfect document you create.

SKILLS CHECK

(Do not clear the screen until you have completed the last exercise.)

1. Type the following lines exactly as shown:

Companies often issue these types of equity:
Common stock - This stock closely reflects the value of
the company. Stockholders receive a return in value

by an increase in price and dividends. Common stock-holders have voting control of the company.

Preferred stock - This stock must pay a required dividend before the common stockholders receive div-idends. Preferred stockholders frequently do not have voting rights.

Convertible bonds - These are bonds that the bond holders may redeem for other stock.

Move the paragraph about bonds between the two stock paragraphs.

2. Use WordPerfect's Spell feature to check for spell-ing errors.

3. Use the Thesaurus feature to replace "redeem" with **exchange**.

4. Set the top and bottom margins to 5".

5. Prevent widow and orphan lines.

6. Add the following footnote at the end of the convertible bonds paragraph:

Usually in exchange for common stock

7. Save the document as STOCKS, and clear the screen.

CREATE BACKUP COPIES   11.1

A *backup copy* is a second or third copy of a document that you can retrieve if something happens to the original document. Whenever you have a document that would take a significant amount of time to recreate, you should consider creating a backup copy. It is best to create a backup copy of your document on another disk in the event the disk containing the original is damaged. On a hard disk system, this may mean copying the document during a full disk backup or making a copy on a floppy disk: On a floppy disk system, creating a backup means saving a copy of the document to a second floppy disk.

To create a backup copy of a document:

a. Press the List Files (F5) key [Alt] File List Files].

b. Type an = and follow it with by the pathname for the directory of the document you wish to back up if it is different from the one displayed.

c. Press Enter.

d. Move the highlight to the file that you want to back up.

e. Type a **c** or an **8**.

f. Type the drive, directory, and filename under which you want to store the backup of the file.

g. Press Enter.

h. Press the Exit (F7) key to return to the document.

You can also create backups by retrieving a file and saving it under a different name or in a different directory.

EXAMPLES

1. Whether you use a hard disk or a floppy disk system, you can back up a file to a disk and place the backup where it is safe from harm. First, type

   The company is expanding its product line to include more products for the older generation.

   Next, save it as OLDER by pressing the Exit (F7) key [Alt File Exit], pressing Enter , typing **older,** and pressing Enter twice.

   To back up the file, place a disk in drive A, and press the List Files (F5) key [Alt File List Files]. The bottom of the screen looks like this:

   `Dir C:\WP51\*.*`   (Type **=** to change default Dir)

   Since this is the directory that you want, press Enter . The screen now looks like Figure 11-1.

   Next, move the highlight to the file named OLDER. Type a **c.** WordPerfect displays this prompt on the status line:

   `Copy this file to:`

   Type **a:older** for the drive and filename of the backup file, and press Enter . You can use the same filename because you are copying the file to another disk. If you were storing the backup file in the same directory on the hard disk, you would have to use a different name.

```
04-12-90  02:34p              Directory C:\WP51\*.*
Document size:        0  Free:  5,253,120 Used:  4,399,523     Files:      189

.    Current   <Dir>              ..    Parent    <Dir>
LEARN   .       <Dir>  02-22-90 05:43p   114_1   .PIX   1,413  03-18-90 09:49a
116_3   .PIX    1,439  03-18-90 09:55a   118_1A  .PIX   1,835  03-18-90 09:16a
118_1B  .PIX    1,835  03-18-90 10:01a   119_2   .PIX   1,835  03-18-90 10:04a
8514A   .VRS    4,862  01-19-90 12:00p   ALTRNAT .WPK     919  02-07-90 12:00p
ARROW-22.WPG      187  01-19-90 12:00p   ATI     .VRS   6,036  01-19-90 12:00p
BALLOONS.WPG    3,187—01-19-90 12:00p    BANNER-3.WPG     719  01-19-90 12:00p
BIBLIO  .         510  03-18-90 08:57a   BICYCLE .WPG     607  01-19-90 12:00p
BKGRND-1.WPG   11,391  01-19-90 12:00p   BORDER-8.WPG     215  01-19-90 12:00p
BULB    .WPG    2,101  01-19-90 12:00p   BURST-1 .WPG     819  01-19-90 12:00p
BUTTRFLY.WPG    5,349  01-19-90 12:00p   CALENDAR.WPG     371  01-19-90 12:00p
CERTIF  .WPG      679  01-19-90 12:00p   CHARACTR.DOC  43,029  02-07-90 12:00p
CHARMAP .TST   42,530  01-19-90 12:00p   CHKBOX-1.WPG     653  01-19-90 12:00p
CLOCK   .WPG    1,811  01-19-90 12:00p   CNTRCT-2.WPG   2,753  01-19-90 12:00p
CODES   .WPM    7,403  02-07-90 12:00p   CONVERT .EXE 109,049  02-07-90 12:00p
CURSOR  .COM    1,452  02-07-90 12:00p   DEVICE-2.WPG     657  01-19-90 12:00p
DIPLOMA .WPG    2,413  01-19-90 12:00p   DISK    .         743  03-22-90 04:01p
DISKREAD.         755  03-22-90 04:01p   EGA512  .FRS   3,584  01-19-90 12:00p
EGAITAL .FRS    3,584  01-19-90 12:00p ▼ EGASMC  .FRS   3,584  01-19-90 12:00p

1 Retrieve; 2 Delete; 3 Move/Rename; 4 Print; 5 Short/Long Display;
6 Look; 7 Other Directory; 8 Copy; 9 Find; N Name Search: 6
```

| FIGURE 11-1. | List Files screen |

Finally, press the Exit ($\boxed{\text{F7}}$) key to return to the document.

2. You can also create a backup copy on the same disk by using a different filename. You may create this type of backup when you want to make changes to a document yet retain a copy of the original. First, type

The company is instituting a pension plan for all salaried employees. This pension plan will be operated by a trust fund created for this purpose. The pension plan is a defined-contribution plan. The company's contribution is a percentage of each employee's yearly salary. The contract came into effect April 30, 1990.

Next, save it as PENSION by pressing the Save (F10) key [Alt File Save], typing **pension**, and pressing Enter. Press the List Files F5 key [Alt File List Files]. Since you want to back up a file from the directory that WordPerfect displays in the prompt, press Enter.

Next, move the highlight to the PENSION filename. Type a **c**, type **pensions**, and press Enter. Press the Exit (F7) key to return to the document.

3. You can also back up a file by saving it with two different names. You can use this method when you want to back up the file that you are currently using. First, type

The company is paying accrued pension costs over a fifteen-year period and will amortize the costs over a twenty-year period.

Save the file by pressing the Save (F10) key [Alt File Save], typing **accrue**, and pressing Enter. To create a backup copy, press the Save (F10) key [Alt File Save], type **accrue2**, and press Enter.

EXERCISES

1. Type the following paragraph:

The pension plan is expected to earn 6% per year. New employees become vested in the plan after five years with the company.

Save it as PLAN. Clear the screen. Back up the file as EARN.

2. Back up PLAN to another disk.

3. Retrieve PLAN and back it up as VESTED.

4. Back up EARN as PENPLAN.

5. Retrieve VESTED. Back it up to another disk.

11.2   CREATE SUBDIRECTORIES

Subdirectories are logical divisions of a disk that you can create and use to organize data. If you placed all of your documents on a hard disk without any organization, after a while you would have difficulty finding particular documents, since you would need to read through a list of all the files on the disk. To make it easier, you can place related documents or specific types of documents in subdirectories.

You can create just a few subdirectories or many, depending on how many ways you categorize the documents that you create. If you installed Word-Perfect as instructed in Appendix A or your Word-Perfect manual, you already have your first subdirectory, named WP51 (WP50 in 5.0). You can create additional subdirectories on this same level, or you can create subdirectories beneath it.

To create a subdirectory:

a. Press the List Files ([F5]) key [[Alt] File List Files].

b. Type an equal sign (=).

c. Type the name for the new directory.

d. Press [Enter].

e. Type a **y** to create the subdirectory.

Another method for creating a subdirectory is

a. Press the List Files ([F5]) key [[Alt] File List Files].

b. Press [Enter].

c. Type an **o** or a **7** to change directories.

d. Type the name for the new directory.

e. Press [Enter].

f. Type a **y** to create the directory.

g. Press the Exit ([F7]) key to return to the document.

Subdirectories are directories within an existing directory. The first-level directory is the root directory. To indicate the root directory on drive C, you would type **c:**. You use a *pathname* to tell the computer where to find the files in a subdirectory. A full pathname includes the drive, a colon, a backslash, and any subdirectory levels. To indicate a subdirectory named LEGAL in the root directory on drive C, you would type **c:\legal**. If LEGAL were a subdirectory under the WP51 (WP50 in 5.0) subdirectory, you would type **c:\wp51\legal** (**c:\wp50\legal** in 5.0).

EXAMPLES

1. You can create a subdirectory on the same level as WordPerfect. You might do this to put all your budget files into one subdirectory to use with different software packages.

   First, press the List Files (F5) key [Alt File List Files].

   Next, type =c:\budget and press Enter . The screen now displays this prompt:

   `Create c:\budget? No (Yes)`

   Type a **y** to create the subdirectory. The structure of the disk now looks like Figure 11-2.

2. You can create a subdirectory below the Word-Perfect subdirectory. For example, you can create a subdirectory for all of the form letters that you use

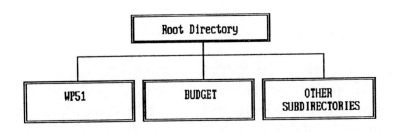

| FIGURE 11-2. | Creating a subdirectory at the same level as WP51 |

in WordPerfect. First, press the List Files ([F5]) key
[[Alt] File List Files]. Type **c:\wp51** (**c:\wp50** in 5.0)
and press [Enter]. Type an **o**. Type **formlett** for the
subdirectory name, and press [Enter]. Since you did
not specify a different pathname, WordPerfect
places the new subdirectory under the current one.
Type a **y** when WordPerfect prompts you to confirm that you want to create the subdirectory. The
screen now looks like this:

```
04-12-90  03:17p              Directory C:\WP51\*.*
Document size:        0   Free:  5,236,736 Used:  4,408,960      Files:      193

.     Current    <Dir>                    | ..    Parent    <Dir>
FORMLETT.         <Dir>  04-12-90 03:14p  | LEARN    .       <Dir>  02-22-90 05:43p
```

The structure of the disk now looks like Figure 11-3.
Press the Exit ([F7]) key to return to the document.

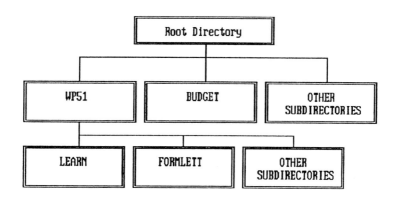

FIGURE 11-3.   Creating a subdirectory under WP51

EXERCISES

1. Create a subdirectory called FINANCE on the same level as the WordPerfect subdirectory.

2. Create a subdirectory called LETTERS beneath the WordPerfect subdirectory.

3. Create a subdirectory of FINANCE called FINC1990.

4. Create a subdirectory of FINANCE called FINC1991.

11.3   CHANGE SUBDIRECTORIES

It is not necessary to work in one subdirectory for an entire WordPerfect session. You can access files without changing subdirectories by typing the full pathname for each file. If you plan to work within a different subdirectory for a while, however, it is easier to make that subdirectory active. You can then save and retrieve files in the subdirectory without having to provide the pathname every time.

To change the subdirectory:

a. Press the List Files ([F5]) key [[Alt] File List Files].

b. Type an equal sign (=) followed by the pathname for the subdirectory that you want to use.

c. Press [Enter].

d. Press (Enter) to have WordPerfect display the list of files for the current subdirectory, or press the Cancel ((F1)) key to return to the document.

Optionally, you can change directories with these steps:

a. Press the List Files ((F5)) key [(Alt) File List Files].

b. Press the (Enter) key.

c. Type an **o** or a **7** to use another subdirectory.

d. Type the pathname of the subdirectory that you want to use.

e. Press (Enter) to have WordPerfect display the list of files for the current subdirectory.

f. Press the Exit ((F7)) key to return to the current document.

You can also change subdirectories by moving the highlight on the List Files screen to the subdirectory that you want and pressing (Enter) twice. This method is more practical when the subdirectory that you want is contained within the current subdirectory.

EXAMPLES

1. You can change directories from the List Files menu. You can use the BUDGET subdirectory that you created in example 1 of section 11.2. First, press the List Files ((F5)) key [(Alt) File List Files]. Next, type **c:**, press (Enter), and type an **o**. Next, type

budget, and press Enter twice. Press the Exit (F7) key to return to the document. When you subsequently save or retrieve a file, WordPerfect will use the BUDGET subdirectory unless you provide a different pathname.

2. You can change directories immediately after pressing the List Files (F5) key [Alt File List Files]. This approach is actually the simplest method to use to make the change. To change to the FORMLETT subdirectory that you created in example 2 in section 11.2, first press the List Files (F5) key [Alt File List Files], and type an equal sign (=). Then type **\wp51\formlett** (**\wp50\formlet** in 5.0), and press Enter twice. WordPerfect displays the contents of this subdirectory. Press the Exit (F7) key to return to the document. When you later save or retrieve a file, WordPerfect will use this subdirectory unless you provide a different pathname.

EXERCISES

1. Change to the FINANCE subdirectory, which you created in exercise 1 in section 11.2.

2. Change to the LETTERS subdirectory, which you created in exercise 2 in section 11.2.

3. Change to the FINC1990 subdirectory, which you created in exercise 3 in section 11.2.

4. Change to the FINC1991 subdirectory, which you created in exercise 4 in section 11.2.

5. Change to the WP51 subdirectory (WP50 in 5.0).

DELETE FILES

Even when you create a document for one-time use, you normally want to save it in case you need another copy of the document. Periodically, you should review the contents of your disk to ensure that it is not cluttered with files that you no longer need. Unneeded files waste disk space and slow access time. WordPerfect provides an easy-to-use option that removes files that are no longer needed.

To delete a file from disk:

a. Press the List Files (F5) key [Alt File List Files].

b. Type the pathname if you wish to change subdirectories.

c. Press Enter.

d. Move the highlight to the file that you want to delete.

e. Type a **d** or a **2.**

f. Type a **y** to confirm that you want to delete the file.

g. Press the Exit (F7) key.

EXAMPLES

1. You can delete a backup file that you no longer need. To delete the backup file that you made in example 2 of section 11.1, first press the List Files ([F5]) key [[Alt] File List Files].

   Next, press [Enter], since WordPerfect displays the subdirectory that you want to use. Move the highlight to the file PENSIONS. When you type a **d**, WordPerfect displays this prompt:

   `Delete C:\WP51\PENSIONS? No (Yes)`

   Type a **y** to confirm that you want to delete this file. Press the Exit ([F7]) key.

2. You can delete a subdirectory with the Delete option in the List Files menu. For example, you can delete the FORMLETT subdirectory created in example 2 in section 11.2. First, press the List Files ([F5]) key [[Alt] File List Files], and press [Enter], since WordPerfect displays the subdirectory that you want to use. Move the highlight to the FORMLETT subdirectory that you want to delete. When you type a **d**, WordPerfect displays this prompt:

   `Delete C:\WP51\FORMLETT? No (Yes)`

   Type a **y** to confirm that you want to delete this subdirectory, and press the Exit ([F7]) key. A subdirectory must be empty before you can delete it. If the FORMLETT subdirectory had contained any files, you would have had to delete all the files in it before you could delete the subdirectory.

EXERCISES

1. Delete the file PLAN, which you created in exercise 2 of section 11.1, from the disk in drive A.

2. Delete the subdirectory LETTERS, which you created in exercise 2 in section 11.2.

3. Delete the subdirectory FINC1990, which you created in exercise 3 in section 11.2.

4. Delete the subdirectory FINC1991, which you created in exercise 4 in section 11.2.

RENAME FILES

11.5

You should always give files names that are meaningful. Using standards that apply to all filenames provides a consistent way to name files. You can rename files on disk that do not conform to the rules that you establish. This renaming process does not require you to recreate the file; the only thing you change is the filename. When you choose the new filename, you need to use a name that is unique for the current disk or subdirectory.

To rename a file:

a. Press the List Files ([F5]) key [[Alt] File List Files].

b. Type the pathname if you wish to change subdirectories.

c. Press [Enter].

d. Move the highlight to the file that you want to rename.

e. Type an **m** or a **3**.

f. Type a new name for the file.

g. Press (Enter).

h. Press the Exit ((F7)) key.

You can edit the filename in step f instead of retyping it. Press the (→) or (End) key to begin the editing process.

EXAMPLES

1. You can rename the OLDER file, which you created in example 1 in section 11.1. First, press the List Files ((F5)) key [(Alt) File List Files]. Press (Enter) to accept the default directory, move the highlight to the file named OLDER, and type an **m**. Type the new filename, **pension1**, and press (Enter). Press the Exit ((F7)) key.

2. You can edit a filename to rename a file. You can rename the ACCRUE file, which you created in example 3 in section 11.1. First, press the List Files ((F5)) key [(Alt) File List Files]. Next, press (Enter) to accept the current directory. Move the highlight to the file ACCRUE, and type an **m**. Press the (End) key to move the cursor to the end of the filename, type a period, and type **pen**. The prompt on the status line looks like this:

New name: C:\WP51\ACCRUE.pen

Press Enter to accept the new name, and then press the Exit (F7) key.

EXERCISES

1. Rename the file PLAN, which you created in exercise 1 in Section 11.1, to PENSION3.

2. Rename the file EARN, which you created in exercise 1 in Section 11.1, to EARNED.

3. Retrieve the file EARNED. Save it as ERN_INC, and clear the screen. Rename ERN_INC to EARN_INC.

CREATE DOCUMENT SUMMARIES

11.6

Document Summaries, a WordPerfect option related to managing files, allows you to store descriptive information about every document file you create. In a document summary, you can provide a Document Name containing as many as 68 characters (in 5.0, it is called a Descriptive Filename and can contain up to 40 characters) to supplement the information conveyed by the filename. Up to 20 characters are allowed to indicate the Document Type (not available in 5.0). You can enter up to 60 characters each (40 in 5.0) for the Author and Typist. The Subject, Account, and

Keywords fields can each contain up to 160 characters of information. (In 5.0, the Subject/Account field can contain up to 40 characters and the Keywords option is unavailable.) The Keywords option can be used to enter words and phrases with which you can search for documents. The Abstract field can contain up to 780 characters of information summarizing the document. (In 5.0, the Comments field can contain up to 400 characters.) Later, you can use this information to provide an overview of the file's contents and use the overview to make decisions concerning the disposition of the file.

To create a document summary:

a. Press the Format ([Shift]-[F8]) [[Alt]] Layout Document and skip step b].

b. Type a **d** or a **3** to select Document.

c. Type an **s** or a **5** to select the Summary option.

d. Select the desired menu option, type the entry, and press [Enter]. When you enter the Abstract field (Comments in 5.0), you must use the Exit ([F7]) key rather than [Enter] to complete the entry.

e. Press the Exit ([F7]) key to return to the document.

In step d, when using Wordperfect 5.1, you can type **d** or a **1** to change the Creation Date. You can type **n** or a **2** to add a document name and change the default document type. You can type **t** or a **3** to input the names of the Author and Typist. Type **s** or a **4** to enter the document's subject. Type **c** or a **5** for the account. Type a **k** or a **6** to enter the keywords to be used to locate the document. Type **a** or a **7** to type in the abstract. (In step d, using WordPerfect 5.0, you can type a **d** or a **1** to add a descriptive filename. You can type an **s** or a **2** to describe the subject or enter an account name. Type an **a** or a **3** for Author and a **t** or a **4** for Typist. Type a **c** or a **5** to enter the Comments section.)

While completing a document summary requires many steps, WordPerfect provides a number of short-cuts to reduce the amount of typing required. First of all, you are not required to fill in all entries of the document summary. Also, by pressing the Retrieve (Shift - F10) key and **y**, WordPerfect will insert the last entered Author and Typist and the first 400 characters of text from the document into the abstract. (In 5.0, the Author, Typist, and Comments are automatically inserted into the summary.) If you choose, you can then edit the Abstract (Comments in 5.0).

If you have not already saved your file when you create the document summary, WordPerfect offers some of the nonspace characters of the Document Name and Type (Descriptive Filename in 5.0) in the prompt that appears when you save it.

EXAMPLES

1. You can create a document summary before creating the document. With a clear screen, press the Format (Shift - F8) key and type a **d** [Alt Layout Document] and an **s**. The screen looks like Figure 11-4.

   Type an **n** to select Document Name, and type

   Pension Plan

Press (Enter), and type

Trust

Press (Enter). (In 5.0, type a **d** to select Descriptive
Filename, and type **Pension Plan** and press (Enter).)
Type a **t** to select Author, and type

Allen Jones

Press (Enter), and for the Typist type

Jim Smith

Press (Enter). (In 5.0, type an **a** to select Author, type
Allen Jones, press (Enter), type a **t** to select Typist,
type **Jim Smith** and press (Enter).) Type an **s** to select
Subject, and type

Acme Corporation

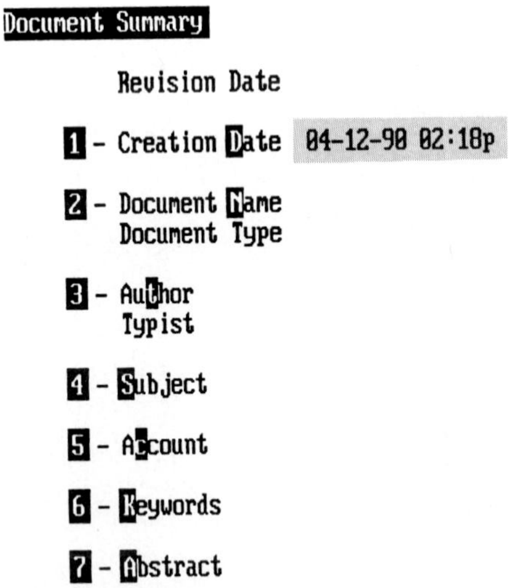

Document Summary

          Revision Date
  1 - Creation Date   04-12-90 02:18p

  2 - Document Name
          Document Type

  3 - Author
          Typist

  4 - Subject

  5 - Account

  6 - Keywords

  7 - Abstract

FIGURE 11-4.   Blank document summary screen

Press ⌈Enter⌉, type a **c** to select Account, and type

10023

Press ⌈Enter⌉. (In 5.0, type an **s** to select Subject/
Account, and type **Acme Corporation/10023**, and
press ⌈Enter⌉.) Type a **k** to select Keywords, and type

contract Acme pension plan

Press ⌈Enter⌉. (In 5.0, skip this step.) Type an **a** to
select Abstract (in 5.0, type a **c** for Comments), and
type

This document contains the original contract on pages
1 through 17. Pages 18 and 19 contain the addendum
passed June 30, 1989.

Press the Exit (⌈F7⌉) key to complete the Abstract
(Comments, in 5.0). The screen now looks like
Figure 11-5. Press the Exit (⌈F7⌉) key to return to the
document. Save and exit this document by pressing
the Exit (⌈F7⌉) key [⌈Alt⌉ File Exit], pressing ⌈Enter⌉,
typing **penscont**, and pressing ⌈Enter⌉ twice.

2. Once you have created one document summary,
   creating others is easy, especially if the other documents already contain text. First, press the Retrieve
   (⌈Shift⌉-⌈F10⌉) key [⌈Alt⌉ File Retrieve], type **pension**,
   and press ⌈Enter⌉. Press the Format (⌈Shift⌉-⌈F8⌉) key,
   and type a **d** [⌈Alt⌉ Layout Document] and an **s**.
   Type an **n** to select Document Name, and type

Acme Corp - Pension Plan

Press ⌈Enter⌉, and type

Press Release

```
Document Summary

        Revision Date

 1 - Creation Date      04-12-90 02:53p

 2 - Document Name      Pension Plan
     Document Type      Trust

 3 - Author             Allen Jones
     Typist             Jim Smith

 4 - Subject            Acme Corporation

 5 - Account            10023

 6 - Keywords           contract Acme pension plan

 7 - Abstract           This document contains the original contract on
                        pages 1 through 17. Pages 18 and 19 contain the
                        addendum passed June 30, 1989.


Selection: 0              (Retrieve to capture; Del to remove summary)
```

FIGURE 11-5. Completed document summary

Press Enter. In 5.0, type a **d** for Descriptive Filename and type

Acme Corp - Pension Plan

Press the Retrieve (Shift - F10) key and **y** to accept the previous Author and Typist names and automatically incorporate text from the document into the abstract. (In 5.0, this is done for you automatically.) Type an **s** to select Subject, and type

Public Announcement 7/1/89

Press Enter, type **c** to select Account, and type

10023

Press [Enter]. (In 5.0, press s to select Subject/Account, type **Acme Corp - Pension Plan/10023**, and press [Enter].) Type a **k** to select Keywords, and type

Pension plan announcement press release

Press [Enter]. (In 5.0, this option is not available.) Press the Exit ([F7]) key to return to the document. Press the Save ([F10]) key [[Alt] File Save], press [Enter], and type a **y** to save this new version.

EXERCISES

1. Create a document summary with this information:

   Document Name (Descriptive Filename in 5.0): **Blank Quit Claim Sales Contract**
   Document Type: **Contract**
   Author: **Jonas Smith**
   Typist: **Karen Polk**
   Subject (Subject/Account in 5.0): **Undeveloped Real Estate**
   Keywords (Omit for 5.0): **Form Contract Quit Claim**
   Abstract (Comments, in 5.0): **This blank contract covers most undeveloped land sales in the state of Florida. This contract has four Xs where you must fill in information. Paragraphs contained in braces are optional. Remove them if they are unnecessary for a particular contract.**

   Save the document as CONTRACT.

2. Type the following new document:

The August 17th meeting discussed the following is-sues:
Installation of new parking lot lights
Hiring of security personnel to patrol the parking lots after dark
Completion of new research and development building
Improved insurance benefits

Create a document summary with the following descriptive title:

August 17th meeting notes

Use the Author and Typist from Exercise 1 and use text from the document for the Abstract (Comments in 5.0). Save the document as ISSUES.

3. Enter the following paragraph:

WordPerfect's Graphics features are among the most advanced in the industry. Investing some time in mas-tering these features could offer a significant payoff for our company. Outside service costs for creating news-letters and brochures can be reduced significantly.

Create a document summary with this information:

Descriptive Filename: **Cut costs with WordPerfect's Graphics**
Document Type (omit in 5.0): **Product Comment**
Abstract (Comments in 5.0): **Reduce newsletter and brochure development costs with Graphics fea-tures. We can recover the cost of the upgrade to 5.1 with the first job.**

Incorporate the Author and Typist entries from the previous document summary.

Save the document as SAVING.

4. Retrieve the ISSUES file. In the document summary, change the name of the typist to **Martha King.**

SEARCH FOR A WORD WITHIN DOCUMENTS ON DISK

11.7

WordPerfect provides a document-search feature that can examine the contents of files on disk. WordPerfect marks the files that contain the word or phrase that you enter for a search string. You can have Word-Perfect check the document summaries, the first page of each document, or the entire text of the documents. Once WordPerfect has marked the files containing your entry, you can use the Look feature to examine them more closely, or you can use other options in the List Files menu.

To search for a word or a phrase in documents:

a. Press the List Files (F5) key [Alt File List Files].

b. Type the pathname containing the files you wish to check if it is different from the one displayed.

c. Press Enter.

d. Type an **f** or a **9** to select Find (**w** or a **9** for Word Search in 5.0).

e. Type a **d** or a **2** to search document summaries, a **p** or a **3** to search the first pages, or an **e** or a **4** to search entire documents. Type a **d** or a **2** to search document summaries, a **p** or a **3** to search the first pages, or an **e** or a **4** to search entire documents. (In 5.0, type a **d** or a **1** to search document summaries, an **f** or a **2** to search the first pages, or an **e** or a **3** to search entire documents.)

f. Type the text for which WordPerfect should search.

g. Press [Enter].

WordPerfect searches through the files and lists the ones that contain the specified word or phrase. (In 5.0, files containing the specified word or phrase are marked with an asterisk.) You can then highlight a file and type an **r** or a **1** to retrieve it, or press the Exit ([F7]) key to return to your current document.

EXAMPLES

1. You can search through files in the current directory to find all of the document summaries that contain the word "contract." First, press the List Files [[Alt] File List Files].

   Next, press [Enter] since WordPerfect prompts you for the current directory.

   Then, type an **f** (a **w** in 5.0), a **d**, and **contract**, and then press [Enter]. After completing its search, Word-Perfect displays the files that have the word "contract" within their document summaries. (5.0 displays asterisks to the right of these filenames.) Some of the files should include PENSION, CONTRACT, and PENSCONT, each of which contains the word "contract" in its document summary.

   Finally, press the Exit ([F7]) key to return to the current document.

2. You can search for a phrase on the first page of each file in the current directory. You can find all of the documents that contain the phrase "pension plan" on the first page. First, press the List Files (F5) key [Alt File List Files].

Next, press Enter , since WordPerfect prompts you for the current directory.

Then, type an **f** (**w** in 5.0) and a **p** (**f** in 5.0). When WordPerfect prompts you for a search string, type a double quote ("), the phrase **pension plan**, and another double quote. Enclosing the phrase in quote marks tells WordPerfect to treat the words in the phrase as a single unit. Press Enter . After completing its search, WordPerfect lists the filenames that meet the search criteria. (5.0 displays asterisks to the right of some of the filenames.)

Finally, press the Exit (F7) key to return to the document.

3. You can search through all the text in documents in the current directory for a specific word, for example, the name "Jones." First, press the List Files (F5) key [Alt File List Files], and press Enter , since WordPerfect prompts you for the current directory. Next, type an **f** (**w** in 5.0), an **e**, and **Jones**. When you press Enter , WordPerfect searches the documents and lists the filenames that meet the search criteria. (5.0 displays asterisks to the right of some of the file entries.) Each of these files contains the name "Jones" somewhere in the document. Finally, press the Exit (F7) key to return to the current document.

4. You can search for more than one word or phrase at a time when you have WordPerfect search your disk files. You can have WordPerfect mark all documents that contain both entries, or you can elect to mark any file that contains either of the entries.

The ability to satisfy multiple conditions uses what WordPerfect refers to as *logical operators*. The semicolon (;) and the comma (,) are the two special operators that WordPerfect uses to join multiple conditions. If you join two words with a semicolon, WordPerfect will search for files that contain both words, since WordPerfect uses the semicolon to imply a logical "and" between the two words. If you join two words with a comma, WordPerfect will search for files containing *either* word, since a comma implies a logical "or."

You can find all documents that contain the word "pension" or "Mary." First, press the List Files (F5) key [Alt File List Files], and press Enter, since WordPerfect prompts you for the current directory. Then, type an **f** (a **w** in 5.0) and an **e**. When WordPerfect prompts you for the search string, type **pension, Mary**, and press Enter. After selecting the files, WordPerfect lists the filenames that meet the search criteria. (5.0 displays asterisks to the right of some of the filenames.) Each marked file contains the word "pension" or the name "Mary," or both, somewhere in the document. Finally, press the Exit (F7) key to return to the current document.

EXERCISES

1. Find all documents that contain the word "August" in the document summary.

2. Find all documents that contain the phrase "Acme Corporation" in the first page.

3. Find all documents that contain the word "plan" in the entire document.

4. Find all documents that contain your first name.

5. Find all documents that contain the words "company" and "product" in the document summary.

6. Find all documents that contain either the word "pension" or the word "contract."

LOOK AT FILES ON DISK

11.8

Sometimes when you are looking for a particular file, you might narrow the choice down to a few files but still be uncertain of the one that you want. A quick way to find the correct file is to use WordPerfect's Look feature. With this feature, you can see a document's contents on the screen without having to retrieve the file. Once you have identified the correct file, you can print it, rename it, delete it, copy it, or retrieve it for editing.

To use the Look feature:

a. Press the List Files ((F5)) key [(Alt) File List Files].

b. Type the pathname if you want to look at files in a different directory.

c. Press (Enter).

d. Move the highlight to the file that you want to view.

e. Type an 1 or a **6**, or press (Enter) to accept WordPerfect's default.

f. Read the document summary (if there is one), or use the cursor-control keys to view the document.

g. Press the Exit ((F7)) key to return to the List Files menu.

h. Press the Exit ((F7)) key to return to the current document.

EXAMPLES

1. You can use the Look feature to display a document without retrieving it. First, press the List Files ((F5)) key [(Alt) File List Files] and press (Enter), since WordPerfect prompts you with the correct directory. Highlight the filename PENSION3, and press

[Enter]. WordPerfect displays the document. You can use the [↑], [↓], SCREEN UP, and SCREEN DOWN keys to view the document.

REMEMBER: Use the GREY+ and GREY- keys for SCREEN UP and SCREEN DOWN, not [PgUp] and [PgDn].

WordPerfect does not let you edit the document. When you finish viewing the document, press the Exit ([F7]) key twice to return to the document in memory.

2. You can use the Look feature to review document summaries when you display documents. First, press the List Files ([F5]) key [[Alt] File List Files], and press [Enter]. Highlight the filename PENSION, and press [Enter]. WordPerfect displays the document summary. If you press a cursor-control key or an l (use only the cursor-control key in 5.0), the text of the document appears. To look at the document summary again, press 3. (In 5.0, the document summary will not reappear; you need to repeat the Look procedure to see it again.)

When you finish viewing the document, press the Exit ([F7]) key twice to return to the current document.

EXERCISES

1. Use the Look feature to view the EARNED file, which you used in exercise 2 in section 11.5.

2. Use the Look feature to view the CONTRACT file, which you created in exercise 1 in section 11.6.

3. Use the Look feature to view the ISSUES file, which you created in exercise 2 in section 11.6.

4. Use the Look feature to view the PENPLAN file, which you created in exercise 4 in section 11.1.

5. Use the Look feature to view the STOCKS file, which you created in the Skills Check in this chapter.

EXERCISES

MASTERY SKILLS CHECK

(Do not clear the screen between exercises unless instructed to do so.)

1. Create a subdirectory named BUDGET91.

2. Type the following lines:

Acme Corporation - 1991 Budget

Estimated Sales	$1,000,000
Fixed Costs	$ 400,000
Variable Costs	$ 400,000
Gross Profit	$ 200,000

Save the document as BUDGET. Clear the screen. Copy the BUDGET file to the BUDGET91 subdirectory under the WordPerfect subdirectory.

3. Make the BUDGET91 subdirectory the current subdirectory.

4. Back up the BUDGET file in the BUDGET91 subdirectory to a file named BDGT1991.

5. Delete the BUDGET file in the BUDGET91 subdirectory.

6. Change the BDGT1991 filename to BDGT91.

7. Retrieve BDGT91, and create a document summary with the following information:

Descriptive Title: **Budget 1991**
Document Type (omit in 5.0): **Budget**
Subject: **Acme Corporation**
Account (omit in 5.0): **10023**
Author: **Jane Smith**
Typist: **John Dow**
Abstract (Comments in 5.0): **Michael McCormick must have this report by September 30, 1990.**

8. Save the file.

9. Search through document summaries for the word "budget."

10. Clear the screen. View the BDGT91 file.

11. Make the WP51 (WP50 in 5.0) subdirectory the current subdirectory.

INTEGRATING SKILLS CHECK

(Do not clear the screen between exercises unless instructed to do so.)

1. Type the following paragraphs:

   Discussions about preferred stock use the following descriptive terms:
   Participation - This feature determines if the preferred stock can receive an additional dividend after the common stock receives a dividend at the same rate of the preferred stock dividend. The additional dividend is determined by whether the stock is fully or partially participating stock.
   Callable - This feature allows the corporation to buy back the preferred stock at a specific price. This feature often places a ceiling on the preferred stock's price.
   Cumulative - This feature determines whether dividends that were not declared in prior years must be paid before current dividends are paid.
   Conversion - This feature allows the stockholder to convert the preferred stock into common stock. If preferred stock has this feature, the stock often fluctuates with the common stock, although not to the same extent.

   Use WordPerfect's speller to determine if you have introduced any spelling errors.

2. Save the document as PREFER.

3. Back up the file as PREFERRD.

4. Create a subdirectory named STOCK.

5. Clear the screen.

6. Back up the PREFERRD file to the STOCK subdirectory.

7. Make the STOCK subdirectory current, and retrieve the PREFERRD file.

8. Rearrange the paragraphs so that the four features are in alphabetical order.

9. Change the top and bottom margins to 5".

10. Prevent widow and orphan lines.

11. Save the file.

12. Delete the PREFER file from the original subdirectory.

13. Use the Search feature to locate the first occurrence of "dividend."

14. Use the Thesaurus to find synonyms for "fluctuates" and "extent."

Changing Print Options

►12 ◄

CHAPTER OBJECTIVES

After completing this chapter, you should be able to:

► Print multiple copies   12.1

► Display the print queue   12.2

► Cancel a print request   12.3

► Rush a print request   12.4

► Affect the print quality   12.5

► Change print fonts   12.6

► Change the size of printed characters   12.7

WordPerfect's print features offer more than just printing a copy of your document. You can request printed copies of many documents at a time. Word-Perfect keeps track of print priorities and sends jobs to the printer in the proper order.

WordPerfect maintains a print queue to manage print requests that have not yet been fulfilled. You can display the jobs in this queue and cancel a job or specify a rush print job.

Another print option allows you to print multiple copies of a document with one print request. You can select from draft-quality to high-quality print output if your printer supports multiple quality options.

WordPerfect provides options for changing the font, size, and color of your printed text. (Naturally, to use these features, your printer must support these options.) WordPerfect's font support allows you to use different character sets. It also supports changes that affect the size of the characters. If your printer has proportional fonts, which use a different amount of space for different characters, WordPerfect sup-ports these as well.

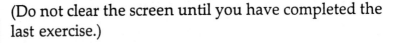

SKILLS CHECK

(Do not clear the screen until you have completed the last exercise.)

1. Type the following paragraph as shown, including the misspellings and repeated words:

In Chapter 3, you learned the basic skills for printiing your your document. This chapter covers other printer

feetures that allow you to customize your document's appearence.

Use the Spell feature to correct spelling errors and eliminate double words.

2. Use the Thesaurus feature to find synonyms for "customize." Replace "customize" with "tailor."

3. Add a header that will print **WordPerfect Print Features**. Add a centered footer that will print **Page** followed by the page number. Preview how Word-Perfect will print this document.

4. Create a document summary with the following:

   Document Name (Descriptive Filename in 5.0): **Describing WordPerfect's Print features**
   Document Type (omit in 5.0): **DOCUMENTATION**
   Author: [your name]
   Typist: [your name]
   Subject (Subject/Account in 5.0): **Teach Yourself WordPerfect**
   Abstract (Comments in 5.0): [Incorporate beginning of document]

5. Save the document as ADVPRINT. Make a copy of this file as PRINTADV. Rename ADVPRINT to PRNTFEAT. Delete PRINTADV.

PRINT MULTIPLE COPIES   12.1

If you need a second copy of a document, you can have WordPerfect create it during your original print request. For a short document, this is usually a quicker solution than a trip to the copy machine.

You can request multiple copies through the Print menu. The number of copies you select remains in effect for the current WordPerfect session.

To print multiple copies:

a. Press the Print ((Shift)-(F7)) key [(Alt) File Print].

b. Type an **n** to select the Number of Copies option.

c. Type the number of copies you want.

d. Press (Enter).

e. Type an **f**, a **p**, or a **d** to start printing.

EXAMPLES

1. You can use this option when you need multiple copies. First, type

   The print options allow you to customize your printer output.

   Next, press the Print ((Shift)-(F7)) key [(Alt) File Print], type an **n** and a **2**, and press (Enter). To start printing, type an **f**. WordPerfect returns to the document and prints two copies. Press the Exit ((F7)) key [(Alt) File Exit], press (Enter), type **printopt**, press (Enter), and type an **n** to save the file and clear the screen.

2. WordPerfect continues to use the multiple-copy setting for the current WordPerfect session. First, type

WordPerfect retains some settings for all documents used in the current session. Other settings are saved with a document and do not apply to other documents.

Next, press the Print ((Shift)-(F7)) key [(Alt) File Print]. The setting that you selected in the first example is still in effect. To print two copies of this new document, type an **f**. WordPerfect prints two copies of the document. Press the Exit ((F7)) key [(Alt) File Exit], press (Enter), type **wpset**, press (Enter), and type an **n** to save the file and clear the screen.

EXERCISES

1. Type the following paragraph:

   You should delete files when you no longer need them. Deleting files frees up needed space on your hard disk or floppy disks.

   Print three copies of the document. Save it as FILEDEL.

2. Type the following paragraph:

   When you save a file, you should use a name that describes the document's purpose. If you do not select meaningful names, you will have difficulty remembering what each document contains. You can rename a file if you wish to change its name.

   Print two copies of the document. Save it as RE-NAME.

3. Print three copies of the file PRINTOPT.

4. Print two copies of WPSET.

5. Print two copies of FILEDEL. Print one copy of WPSET.

12.2 DISPLAY THE PRINT QUEUE

WordPerfect permits you to display the *print queue.* This queue shows the status of the current print job as well as other jobs waiting to print. From the display of print jobs, you can make an assessment of how long it will take to complete the print jobs that you have requested.

To display the print queue:

a. Press the Print ([Shift]-[F7]) key [[Alt] File Print].

b. Type a **c** or a **4** to select the Control Printer option.

c. Press the Exit ([F7]) key to return to the current document.

Each job that is displayed has a number. Word-Perfect starts counting print requests with 1 at the beginning of the session and assigns each subsequent print request the next number. As you will learn in later sections, viewing the print queue allows you to use other WordPerfect Print options.

EXAMPLES

1. When you tell WordPerfect to print a document, it creates a print job for the task. When you display

```
Print: Control Printer

Current Job

Job Number: 4                              Page Number:  1
Status:      Printing                      Current Copy: 1 of 1
Message:     None
Paper:       None
Location:    None
Action:      None


Job List

Job  Document               Destination        Print Options
  4  D:\...\PRINTOPT         LPT 1


Additional Jobs Not Shown: 0



1 Cancel Job(s); 2 Rush Job; 3 Display Jobs; 4 Go (start printer); 5 Stop: 0
```

FIGURE 12-1.   Control Printer screen

the print queue, you can look at the status of every print request that has not yet been fulfilled. First, press the Print ([Shift]-[F7]) key [[Alt] File Print]. Then, type a **d** to print a document on disk, type **printopt**, and press [Enter] twice. You will need to make several additional print requests quickly to create a backlog. Type a **d**, type **printopt**, and press [Enter] twice. Repeat this request one more time. If you proceed quickly to the print queue display, at least one of the print requests should still be in the queue. Type a **c** to select Control Printer from the Print menu. The screen looks like Figure 12-1 if there is one copy left to print. Print jobs usually disappear from the queue quickly, depending on the speed of your computer and printer and the sizes of your print requests.

2. The queue display shows the printer backlog. You can use this display to help you estimate the time it will take to print the jobs in the queue. Even though WordPerfect does not estimate the time requirements for you, if you are familiar with the documents in the queue you will have a good idea of their length and the required time for printing. Temporarily stopping the print process allows you to look at print requests in the job queue. First, take the printer off line (a button on your printer allows you to do this). This stops the printing process until you turn the printer to on line. Press the Print (⸤Shift⸥-⸤F7⸥) key [⸤Alt⸥ File Print]. Then, type a **d** to print a document, type **printopt**, and press ⸤Enter⸥ twice. Then, type a **d** to print a document, type **wpset**, and press ⸤Enter⸥ twice.

Next, type a **c** to select Control Printer from the Print menu. The queue displays both print jobs. Because the printer is off line, the Status message indicates that the printer is not accepting the information that WordPerfect is sending. Turn the printer to on line to make it accept and print the information the computer sends it. As WordPerfect finishes the first job, it removes the job from the queue and changes the information in the top half of the screen to display the print information for the second document. Press the Exit (⸤F7⸥) key to return to the document.

3. The queue display shows some of the print options that you selected, such as the number of copies, rush requests, and print quality. First, press the Print (Shift - F7) key [Alt File Print]. Next, type an **n** and a **4**, and press Enter . Type a **d** to print a document, type **wpset**, and press Enter twice. Type a **c** to select Control Printer from the Print menu. WordPerfect displays the request for four copies in the Print Options column. If your printer prints too fast for you to see the queue, you can turn the printer off before making your request.

EXERCISES

1. Print three copies of the file RENAME, which you created in exercise 2 in section 12.1. Display the print queue while the job is still printing.

2. Print three copies of the file RENAME. Print two copies of FILEDEL, which you created in exercise 1 in section 12.1. Print one copy of the file WPSET. Display the print queue and watch how it changes as WordPerfect prints each job.

CANCEL A PRINT REQUEST

12.3

If you change your mind about printing a document, you can cancel your print request. If the job has already started printing, your printer will continue to print for a page or two: WordPerfect stops transmitting data to the printer when you cancel a job, but it does not clear the printer's memory. The printer continues to print until all the data in its memory has been printed.

To cancel a print request:

a. Press the Print ([Shift]-[F7]) key [[Alt] File Print].

b. Type a **c** or a **4** to select the Control Printer option.

c. Type a **c** or a **1** to select the Cancel Job(s) option.

d. Type the number of the print job that you want to cancel, or type an asterisk (*) to cancel all jobs.

e. Type a **y** to confirm your selection if you typed an asterisk in step d.

f. Press the Exit ([F7]) key to return to the current document.

WordPerfect may display a warning message to initialize the printer if you type an asterisk in step d. To initialize the printer, type an **i** while on the initial print menu screen. Then type a **y** to confirm the message "Proceed with Printer Initialization?"

EXAMPLES

1. You can cancel a print request that is currently printing. First, type

WordPerfect lets you perform several DOS commands with the List Files (F5) key.

Then, press [Ctrl]-[Enter] [[Alt] Layout Align Hard Page] to insert a hard page break. On the second page, type

Using the List Files (F5) key, you can select commands that are equivalent to DOS's COPY, ERASE, RENAME, CD, and TYPE commands.

To print three copies of this document, press the Print ([Shift]-[F7]) key [[Alt] File Print], type an **n** and a **3**, press [Enter] and type an **f**. To cancel this print request, press the Print ([Shift]-[F7]) key, type a **c** twice to select Control Printer and Cancel Job(s). Type the number of the current print job, and press [Enter]. Your printer may continue to print the information the computer has already sent. To return to the document, press the Exit ([F7]) key. Press the Exit ([F7]) key [[Alt] File Exit], press [Enter], type **listfile**, press [Enter], and type an **n** to save the document and clear the screen.

2. You can also cancel all print requests when you have many print jobs. First, you must enter several print requests. Press the Print ([Shift]-[F7]) key [[Alt] File Print]. Type a **d** to print a document, type **printopt**, press [Enter] twice. To print another document, type a **d**, type **wpset**, and press [Enter] twice. Then type a **d** again, type **listfile**, and press [Enter] twice.

   To cancel the print requests, type a **c** twice to select Control Printer and Cancel Job(s). Type an asterisk to cancel all print jobs and a **y** to confirm your choice. If you get a warning message to initialize the printer, press [Enter] to return to the initial print menu, and type an **i** and then a **y**. To return to the document, press the Exit ([F7]) key.

EXERCISES

1. Start printing five copies of the RENAME file, which you created in exercise 2 in Section 12.1. Cancel the print job.

2. Start printing three copies of RENAME, FILEDEL, and WPSET, which you created in section 12.1. Cancel all print jobs.

3. Turn the printer off to temporarily disable Word-Perfect from printing. Request one print of FILE-DEL. Cancel the print job.

4. With the printer turned off, request printouts of WPSET, FILEDEL, and RENAME. Cancel the WP-SET and RENAME print requests. Turn the printer on.

12.4 RUSH A PRINT REQUEST

With the ability to create many print requests at one time, a backlog of print requests can accumulate. WordPerfect provides a way to expedite a print request so that the entire backlog does not have to finish printing before an important job is printed. After requesting a job in the normal fashion, you use an option on the Print menu to specify that the job is a "rush" job. When the current job finishes printing, the rush job is printed before any other jobs in the print queue.

To rush a print request:

a. Press the Print ((Shift)-(F7)) key [(Alt) File Print].

b. Type a **c** or a **4** to select Control Printer.

c. Type an **r** or a **2** to select the Rush Job option.

d. Type the number of the print job that you want to rush.

e. Type a **y** if you want to interrupt the current print job or an **n** if you do not want to interrupt it. RUSH appears in the Print Options column.

f. Press the Exit ((F7)) key to return to the document.

If you interrupt the current print job, WordPerfect finishes the page it is printing, prints the rush job, and then continues printing the interrupted job. If you do not interrupt the current print job, WordPerfect finishes printing it before printing the rush job ahead of other print jobs in the queue.

EXAMPLES

1. You can use the Rush Job option to change the order of the print jobs. Press the Print ((Shift)-(F7)) key [(Alt) File Print]. Type an **n** and a **2**, and press (Enter). Type a **d** to print a document, type **printopt**, and press (Enter) twice. Type a **d**, type **wpset**, and

press (Enter) twice. Type a **d**, type **listfile**, and press (Enter) twice. Press the Exit ((F7)) key to return to the document.

To rush the LISTFILE print job, press the Print ((Shift)-(F7)) key [(Alt) File Print], and type a **c** and an **r**. Then, type the number of the LISTFILE print job. When WordPerfect asks you whether to interrupt the current job, type a **y**. Finally, press the Exit ((F7)) key to return to the document.

2. When you rush a print request, you can direct WordPerfect not to print the rush job until it finishes the current job. Press (Ctrl)-(Enter) [(Alt) Layout **Align Hard Page**] six times to create a multiple-page document. Then, press the Print ((Shift)-(F7)) key [(Alt) File Print], type an **n** and a **1** for copy, and type an **f**. Once the document starts printing, turn the printer off to temporarily halt the printing process. To print a file from disk, press the Print ((Shift)-(F7)) key [(Alt) File Print], type a **d**, type **listfile**, and press (Enter) twice.

To rush the LISTFILE print request, type a **c** and an **r**. Then, type the number of the LISTFILE print job. When WordPerfect asks whether you want to interrupt the current job, type an **n**. WordPerfect will not print LISTFILE immediately, even though it is a rush request. WordPerfect must finish printing the seven blank pages of the current document. Turn the printer back on.

EXERCISES

1. Create a print request for RENAME. Create a print request for FILEDEL. Create a print request for PRINTOPT. Rush the PRINTOPT request, interrupting the current print job.

2. Turn the printer off, and request printouts of WPSET, FILEDEL, and RENAME. Rush the RENAME print request. Turn the printer on.

AFFECT THE PRINT QUALITY

12.5

Many printers support more than one quality of print output. Some printers have a draft mode that prints quickly but is not so high in quality as other modes. WordPerfect supports draft-, medium-, and high-quality print output. It provides separate print-quality selections for text and graphics. These settings also provide a "do not print" option, allowing you to print text and graphics in separate print jobs.

To set the print quality:

a. Press the Print (`Shift`-`F7`) key [`Alt` File Print].

b. Type a **t** to set the text quality or a **g** to set the graphics quality.

c. Type an **n** or a **1** for Do Not Print, a **d** or a **2** for Draft, an **m** or a **3** for Medium, or an **h** or a **4** for High.

d. Type an **f** or a **p** to start printing.

With some printers, the higher the quality, the longer it takes the printer to print. The Do Not Print option in step c can be used for printing text and graphics on a printer that can print one or the other but not both. The options available for graphics are identical to the options for text. They are not discussed here, since they use skills that you will develop in Chapter 17. Text and graphics quality are saved with the files.

EXAMPLES

1. You can set the text quality to draft when you need a quick printed copy. Retrieve PRINTOPT by pressing the Retrieve ([Shift]-[F10]) key [[Alt] File Retrieve], typing **printopt**, and pressing [Enter]. Press the Print ([Shift]-[F7]) key [[Alt] File Print] and type a **t** and a **d**. To see how draft-quality print appears, type an **f**. Use this document in the next example.

2. You use high text quality when you are printing your document for presentation to others. Press the Print ([Shift]-[F7]) key [[Alt] File Print], and type a **t** and an **h**. To see how high-quality text appears, type an **f**.

EXERCISES

(Do not clear the screen until you have completed the last exercise.)

1. Retrieve WPSET. Set the text quality to medium. Print the document.

2. Set the text quality to high. Print the document.

3. Set the text quality to draft. Print the document.

CHANGE PRINT FONTS

12.6

Most printers support multiple fonts. These fonts allow you to use character sets that are created in different styles. Some fonts are proportional; that is, different characters take up different amounts of space on a line. The font options that WordPerfect presents depend on the printer that you are using.

You can change fonts within a document, a paragraph or a line. WordPerfect adjusts the text on the screen and how it is word wrapped to reflect the new font. For example, changing the font does not change the margins. When you change fonts, you can still use other WordPerfect features, such as boldfacing, underlining, and centering. Figure 12-2 is a preview at 100% showing how WordPerfect will print different fonts.

To change the base font:

a. Press the Font (Ctrl-F8) key [Alt Font Base Font and skip step b].

b. Type an **f** or a **4** to choose the Base Font option.

c. Move the highlight to the font that you want, using the cursor-movement keys.

d. Press [Enter].

The fonts available in step c depend upon your printer. When you change the font, WordPerfect inserts the code [Font: font name]. The font name is the font description that you selected in step c.

EXAMPLES

1. You can change the default base font for a Hewlett-Packard LaserJet Series II printer to one with

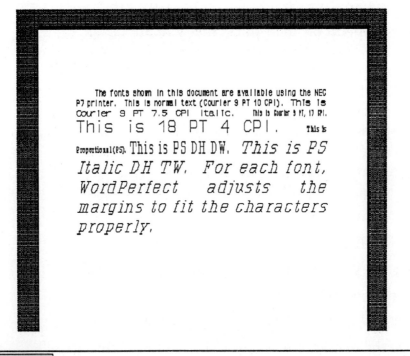

FIGURE 12-2.   Sample fonts

smaller characters than the current font has. If you are using this printer, your choices will be the same as those in this example. First, press the Format (Shift-F8) key, and type an l [Alt Layout Line] and an m. Type a 1, press Enter, type a 4, and press Enter. Press the Exit (F7) key. This increases the right margin so that you can see all the text when you preview the document at 200%. Next, type

Larger characters have smaller pitch numbers.

Press the Font (Ctrl-F8) key, and type an f [Alt Font Base Font]. WordPerfect displays the available base fonts, like these:

```
* Courier 10 pitch (PC-8)
  Courier 10 pitch (Roman-8)
  Courier Bold 10 pitch (PC-8)
  Courier Bold 10 pitch (Roman-8)
  Line Printer 16.66 pitch (PC-8)
  Line Printer 16.66 pitch (Roman-8)
  Solid Line Draw 10 pitch
```

If you have soft fonts or font cartridges for your printer, additional fonts may be available. With other printers, the selections may be quite different. Press the ↓ key to move the highlight to the Line Printer 16.66 pitch (PC-8) font, and press Enter to select this font. Next, type

Smaller characters have larger pitch numbers. Word-Perfect automatically adjusts for the different sizes of characters.

To see how the different fonts appear at 200%, press the Print (Shift-F7) key [Alt File Print] and type a v and a 2. The screen looks like this:

Larger characters have smaller pitch
numbers.   Smaller characters have larger pitch
numbers. WordPerfect automatically adjusts for the different
sizes of characters.

2. If your font options include an italics font, you can
change the base font to italics. In this example,
options for an NEC P7 dot matrix printer are used
to select a font providing large italic characters. The
font selections that are available to you depend
upon your printer. First, type

**Smaller characters have smaller point sizes. Word-
Perfect abbreviates points as PT.**

Press the Font ([Ctrl]-[F8]) key and type an **f** [[Alt]
Font Base Font]. WordPerfect displays the available
base fonts, like the ones for the NEC P7 printer
shown in Figure 12-3. Press the [↓] key to move the
highlight to the Courier 18 PT 7.5 CPI Italic font and
press [Enter]. Next, type

Larger characters have larger point numbers.

Since the characters are larger, WordPerfect fits
fewer characters per line. The italicized characters
probably do not appear as italic on your screen. To
see how the different fonts will appear in print,
press the Print ([Shift]-[F7]) key [[Alt] **File Print**], and
type a **v** and a **1**. The screen looks like this:

Smaller characters have smaller point sizes.   WordPerfect
abbreviates points as PT. *Larger characters have larger*
point numbers.

EXERCISES

1. Type the first sentence of the following paragraph. Change the font to a larger-character base font and type the second sentence. Preview how Word-Perfect will print the document.

   When you change the font, all characters after the font change are affected. Characters before the font change use the initial setting of your printer.

2. Type the first sentence of the following paragraph.

```
Base Font

    Courier  9 PT   5 CPI
    Courier  9 PT   5 CPI Italic
    Courier  9 PT   6 CPI
    Courier  9 PT   6 CPI Italic
    Courier  9 PT   7.5 CPI
    Courier  9 PT   7.5 CPI Italic
  * Courier  9 PT  10 CPI
    Courier  9 PT  10 CPI Italic
    Courier  9 PT  12 CPI
    Courier  9 PT  12 CPI Italic
    Courier  9 PT  15 CPI
    Courier  9 PT  15 CPI Italic
    Courier  9 PT  17 CPI
    Courier  9 PT  17 CPI Italic
    Courier  9 PT  20 CPI
    Courier  9 PT  20 CPI Italic
    Courier 18 PT   4 CPI
    Courier 18 PT   4 CPI Italic
    Courier 18 PT   5 CPI
    Courier 18 PT   5 CPI Italic
    Courier 18 PT   6 CPI

    1 Select: N Name search: 1
```

FIGURE 12-3.   Sample fonts available for an NEC P7 printer

If your printer can print proportional spacing (abbreviated PS), change the base font to a proportionally spaced font. If it cannot, change the font to a smaller-character base font. Type the last two sentences of the paragraph. Preview how WordPerfect will print the document.

Fonts can also be proportionally spaced. In proportionally spaced fonts, each character uses a different amount of space. For example, an l takes less space than an m.

12.7 CHANGE THE SIZE OF PRINTED CHARACTERS

When you select the base font, you are actually changing the default size that the rest of your document will use. WordPerfect has a separate option that changes the size of text without changing the base font. This feature lets you use large characters in a document that has a smaller base font. You can use this feature to create superscript and subscript features. The actual appearance of these characters will depend upon the capabilities of your printer.

To change the size of characters before you type them:

a. Move the cursor to where you want characters to appear in a different size.

b. Press the Font (Ctrl-F8) key [Alt Font and skip step c].

c. Type an **s** or a **1** to choose the Size option.

d. Type the letter or number for the character size that you want [from Superscript through Extra Large on the Font menu].

e. Type the text that you want to appear in that size.

f. To return the character size to normal, press Font (Ctrl - F8) and type an **n** [Alt Font Normal], or press the ➡ key once.

You may notice a change in the color or intensity of the position indicator on the status line when you use different fonts. With a color monitor, text in a different size may appear in a different color.

To change the size of characters that you have already typed:

a. Block the text that you want in a different size.

b. Press the Font (Ctrl - F8) key [Alt Font and skip step c].

c. Type an **s** or a **1** to choose the Size option.

d. Type the letter or number for the character size that you want [from Superscript through Extra Large on the Font menu].

In step d of both methods, WordPerfect provides you with size options. You can type a **p** or a **1** for Superscript, a **b** or a **2** for Subscript, an **f** or a **3** for Fine, an **s** or a **4** for Small, an **L** or a **5** for Large, a **v** or a **6** for Very Large, or an **e** or a **7** for Extra Large, assuming your printer supports these options.

When you change the size of characters, Word-Perfect inserts codes where the special-size text starts and ends. For Superscript, WordPerfect inserts the codes [SUPRSCPT] and [suprscpt]. For Subscript, WordPerfect inserts the codes [SUB-SCPT] and [subscpt]. For Fine, WordPerfect inserts the codes [FINE] and [fine]. For Small, WordPerfect inserts the codes [SMALL] and [small]. For Large, WordPerfect inserts the codes [LARGE] and [large]. For Very Large, WordPerfect inserts the codes [VRY LARGE] and [vry large]. For Extra Large, Word-Perfect inserts the codes [EXT LARGE] and [ext large]. Step f in the first method for changing text size ends the size change by moving the cursor past the end code for the size.

EXAMPLES

1. You can change the size of text that you entered to make it a large heading. First, type

ATTENTION:
The auditors will arrive on Monday. Please provide any assistance and/or answers they require.

Press (Enter) and press the (↑) key three times. Then, press the Block ((Alt)-(F4)) key [(Alt) Edit Block], and press (End). Next, press the Font ((Ctrl)-(F8)) key, and type an **s** and an **e** [(Alt) Font Extra Large] to have the blocked text print as extra-large letters. Finally, press the Print ((Shift)-(F7)) key [(Alt) File Print], and type a **v**. The screen looks like this:

```
ATTENTION:
The auditors will arrive on Monday.  Please provide any assistance
and/or answers they require.
```

2. You can use superscripts and subscripts to type formulas. First, type an **x**. Press the Font ([Ctrl]-[F8])
key, and type an **s** and a **b** [[Alt] Font Subscript] for Subscript text. Then, type a **1**, and press the [→] key. Press the Font ([Ctrl]-[F8]) key, and type an **s** and a **p** [[Alt] Font Superscript] for Superscript text. Then, type a **2** and press the [→] key and the SPACEBAR.

Type a plus sign (+), press the SPACEBAR, and type an x. Press the Font ([Ctrl]-[F8]) key and type an **s** and a **b** [[Alt] Font Subscript] for Subscript text. Then, type a **2**, and press the [→] key. Press the Font ([Ctrl]-[F8]) key and type an **s** and a **p** [[Alt] Font Superscript] for Superscript text. Then, type a **2**, and press the [→] key and the SPACEBAR.

Type an equal sign (=), press the SPACEBAR, and type an x. Press the Font ([Ctrl]-[F8]) key, and type an **s** and a **b** [[Alt] Font Subscript] for Subscript text. Then, type a **3**, and press the [→] key. Press the Font ([Ctrl]-[F8]) key, and type an **s** and a **p** [[Alt] Font Superscript] for Superscript text. Then, type a **2**, and press the [→] key.

This completes the Pythagorean theorem, which states that the square of the longest side of a right triangle is equal to the sum of the squares of the other two sides. Press the Print ([Shift]-[F7]) key [[Alt] File Print] and type a **v**. The screen looks like this:

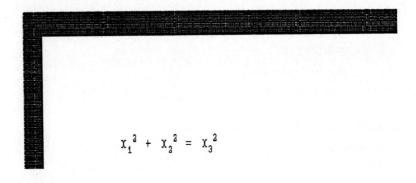

$$x_1^2 \;+\; x_2^2 \;=\; x_3^2$$

EXERCISES

1. Type the following paragraph:

   Always make sure to read the fine print. It may contain information not found in other parts of the document.

   Block the first sentence and change it to fine print. Preview how WordPerfect will print the document.

2. Type the following lines, including the subscript and superscript information as shown. Press [Enter] twice at the end of each line.

   H_2O
   $E = mc^2$
   Subscripted text appears below the normal text.
   Superscripted text appears above the normal text.

   Preview how WordPerfect will print this document.

3. Type the following lines, setting the size of the characters in each line to the size described in the sentence:

   Your printer prints Extra Large text like this.

Your printer prints Very Large text like this.
Your printer prints Large text like this.
Your printer prints Small text like this.
Your printer prints Fine text like this.

Preview how WordPerfect will print this document.

EXERCISES

(Do not clear the screen until you have completed the
last exercise.)

MASTERY
SKILLS CHECK

1. Type the following paragraph.

   WordPerfect uses several abbreviations for font selection. CPI represents the number of characters per inch.
   The larger the number, the smaller the characters.
   Points, or PT, represent the height of the character. The
   larger the number, the larger the characters. Pitch is the
   number of characters that can be printed per horizontal
   inch. The larger the number, the smaller the characters.

   Move to the top of the document, and change the
   base font so that the characters will print as italics.
   (If an italicized font of the same size is unavailable,
   select any other font.)

2. Change the words "CPI," "PT," and "Pitch" to
   appear in large print.

3. Print four copies of the document, using draft print
   quality.

4. Cancel the print request.

5. Print two copies of the document, using high print quality. Print four copies using draft print quality. Rush the draft print job.

(Do not clear the screen until you have completed the last exercise.)

1. Type the following paragraph:

   When you change the size of the characters, you change the number of characters that WordPerfect fits on each line. WordPerfect automatically adjusts word wrapping for fine, extra-large and small fonts. Word-Perfect also automatically adjusts word wrapping for proportionally spaced, larger, and smaller base fonts.

   Check the document for spelling errors.

2. Save the document as WORDWRAP. Create a backup called FONTADJ. Delete the WORDWRAP file.

3. Change the size of the words "fine," "extra large," and "small" so that the words will print in the sizes they describe. Include the punctuation for the words when you change the sizes. View how WordPerfect will print the document.

4. Move to the top of the document, and set the base font to a larger font. Move to the last sentence, and set the base font to a smaller font. View how WordPerfect will print the document.

5. Add the following footnote at the end of the first sentence:

   Changing the font does not change WordPerfect's other default settings, such as margins and page size.

6. Print four copies of the document, using high print quality. Print three copies. Set the text quality to draft, and print two copies. Rush the draft print request.

7. Look at the file FONTADJ on disk.

Working with Two Documents

►13◄

CHAPTER OBJECTIVES

After completing this chapter, you should be able to:

▶ Open and exit from a second document   13.1

▶ Change the size of a document window   13.2

▶ Use two documents at one time   13.3

▶ Copy and move text between documents   13.4

WordPerfect permits you to have two documents in memory at one time. With this feature, you can refer to one document while working on another. You can copy or move information in one document to the other document. You can split the screen to allow part of both documents to be visible on the screen.

WordPerfect maintains the two documents separately; changes to one document do not affect the other. You can switch between documents to edit either one, and you can save the documents in separate files.

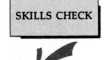

SKILLS CHECK

(Do not clear the screen between exercises unless instructed to do so.)

1. Type the following paragraph:

   In March, the company exchanged 30,000 shares of newly issued common stock for $500,000 principal value of its 6% bonds. It recognized a $145,000 extraordinary gain.

   Add the following footnote at the end of the first sentence:

   These bonds were originally issued to upgrade production facilities.

2. Create a footer containing your name.

3. Create a header that will print the word **Page** followed by a space and the page number.

4. Set the text quality to draft.

5. Set the font to print the document in italics. Save the file as XTRAGAIN, and clear the screen.

6. Create a subdirectory called NOTES below the WP51 (WP50 for 5.0) subdirectory.

7. Back up the file XTRAGAIN to the subdirectory NOTES using the same filename.

8. Print the file XTRAGAIN that is in the subdirectory NOTES.

9. Delete the file XTRAGAIN that is in the subdirectory NOTES.

10. Delete the subdirectory NOTES.

OPEN AND EXIT FROM A SECOND DOCUMENT

13.1

You have been working with only one document at a time in all the WordPerfect tasks you have accomplished thus far. To work in a second document, you need to switch to the second document screen. Once you are in the second document screen, you can begin typing a new document, move or copy text from the first document, or retrieve a document from disk to work with in this screen. The contents of this second document do not affect document 1.

Since WordPerfect stores each document separately in memory, you must exit from each document separately. It does not matter in which order you exit from the documents; for example, you can exit from

document 2 and continue to work in document 1.
When you exit from the remaining document, you
can also exit from WordPerfect.

To open a second document:

a. Press the Switch (Shift - F3) key [Alt Edit Switch
Document].

To exit from a second document:

a. Press the Exit (F7) key [Alt File Exit].

b. Press Enter , type a filename and press Enter if you
want to save the second document; otherwise, type
an **n**.

c. Type a **y** to leave the second document.

EXAMPLES

1. You can type a document in document 2 while you
have a document in document 1. First, type

Rod Taylor
Trenton Inc.
4056 Carnegie Avenue
Cleveland, Ohio 44113

Dear Sir,
Enclosed is an invoice for $278.25. Payment is due by
August 30. This is for the final balance on your account.

Sincerely,

Maud Stevens

After you have typed this letter, you can save it to a file. Press the Save ((F10)) key [(Alt) File Save], type **finalbal**, and press (Enter). To create a second document, press the Switch ((Shift)-(F3)) key [(Alt) Edit Switch Document]. The current document disappears from the screen, and the status line looks like this:

Doc 2 Pg 1 Ln 1" Pos 1"

Doc 2 indicates that you are in WordPerfect's second document screen. For this document, type

The next meeting of the board of directors is December 14.

The first document is still intact, since anything you type in one document does not affect the other.

You can clear this document from memory and remain on this screen by pressing the Exit ((F7)) key [(Alt) File Exit] and typing **n** when WordPerfect asks you whether to save the document and **n** again when WordPerfect asks you whether to exit document 2.

2. You can retrieve a document from disk for document 2. You can retrieve the file that you saved in example 1. First, press the Retrieve ((Shift)-(F10)) key [(Alt) File Retrieve], type **finalbal**, and press (Enter). The screen displays the letter that you created and saved in document 1.. Move to the end of the document, and type

100 Financial Statements	$525.00
6% State tax	$ 31.50
Total	$556.50

Paid to date	$278.25
Total due	$278.25

50% by August 1
Balance upon delivery (August 30)

The original copy in document 1 is still intact. You can see this by pressing the Exit (F7) key [Alt File Exit]. When WordPerfect asks whether you want to save the file, type a **y**, type **final**, and press Enter . When WordPerfect asks whether you want to exit from document 2, type a **y**. The screen displays the original letter that you typed in example 1.

3. You must exit from each document separately. You can create two documents and exit from both of them. First, type

The corporation owns 83,500 shares of Treasury stock.

To switch to document 2, press the Switch (Shift - F3) key [Alt Edit Switch Document]. In document 2, type

25,000 shares of the company's Treasury stock is reserved for stock option plans.

To exit from both documents, first press the Exit (F7) key [Alt File Exit], and type an **n** and a **y**. WordPerfect returns you to document 1. Then, press the Exit (F7) key [Alt File Exit], and type an **n** twice to clear the first document and remain in WordPerfect.

EXERCISES

1. Type the following paragraph:

   Production used 1200 ball bearings to replace the machinery's worn ones.

   Switch to document 2. Retrieve FINAL, and insert a page break between the letter and the text you typed in example 2. Save and exit from document 2. Save document 1 as SKATES.

2. Type the following paragraph:

   The company is using a new printer for the current year's financial statements. This allows the company to include pictures of its executive officers and its main office building.

   Save this document as STMT1. Switch to document 2, and retrieve STMT1. Add the following sentence:

   Management felt that the change was necessary, since the company wants to improve its corporate image.

   Save this document as STMT2. Exit from both documents.

3. In document 1, retrieve STMT2. Switch to document 2, and retrieve STMT1. Exit from both documents.

13.2   CHANGE THE SIZE OF A DOCUMENT WINDOW

WordPerfect normally displays 24 lines in a screen. You can reduce the number of lines displayed in document 1 to allow part of document 2 to be displayed on the screen at the same time. The part of the screen used for each separate document is called a *window*. This window feature allows you to review the contents of a document in one window while you work on a document in the other window.

To set the number of lines WordPerfect uses for a window:

a. Press the Screen (Ctrl-F3) key [Alt Edit Window and skip step b].

b. Type a **w** or a **1**.

c. Type a number from 1 to 24 for the number of lines the current window should use.

d. Press Enter.

WordPerfect uses the number that you provide in step c for the number of lines in the current window and subtracts that number from 22 to determine the number of lines to be displayed in the other window. Each window uses an additional line for the status line. The two windows are separated on the screen by a ruler line, which indicates margin and tab settings for the current window. If you press the Reveal Codes (Alt-F3) key [Alt Edit Reveal Codes], WordPerfect splits the screen to show the codes hidden in the current window and hides the other window.

EXAMPLES

1. You can set the number of lines in a window to allow you to see two documents at once. First, retrieve FINAL by pressing the Retrieve ((Shift)-(F10)) key [(Alt) File Retrieve], typing **final**, and pressing (Enter).

   Next, press the Screen ((Ctrl)-(F3)) key, and type a w [(Alt) Edit Window]. WordPerfect displays this prompt:

   ```
   Number of lines in this window: 24
   ```

   Type **11**, and press (Enter). The screen now looks like Figure 13-1. Each window has its own filename and status line.

   The screen uses 11 lines for document 1 and 11 lines for document 2. The triangles in the ruler line, which represent tab stops, point up, indicating that the cursor is in document 1.

2. You can reset the full screen size for a document by changing the number of lines back to 24. First, press the Screen ((Ctrl)-(F3)) key, and type a w [(Alt) Edit Window]. Next, type **24**, and press (Enter). Although document 2 disappears from the screen, it remains in the computer's memory.

3. You can also set the window size while using the second window. First, press the Switch ((Shift)-(F3)) key [(Alt) Edit Switch Document] to switch to document 2. Press the Screen ((Ctrl)-(F3)) key, and type a w [(Alt) Edit Window].

```
Rod Taylor
Trenton Inc.
4056 Carnegie Avenue
Cleveland, Ohio 44113

Dear Sir,
Enclosed is an invoice for $278.25. Payment is due by August 30.
This is for the final balance on your account.

                Sincerely,
```

```
D:\WP51\FINAL                              Doc 1 Pg 1 Ln 1" Pos 1"
{   ▲   ▲   ▲   ▲   ▲   ▲   ▲   ▲   ▲   ▲   }   ▲   ▲
```

```
                              Doc 2 Pg 1 Ln 1" Pos 1"
```

| FIGURE 13-1. | Two document windows on the screen |

Next, type **15**, and press (Enter). Document 2 now has 15 lines, and document 1 has 7. Document 2 always appears below document 1 on a split screen. When you press the Exit ((F7)) key [(Alt) File Exit] and type an **n** and a **y**, you return to the first document, although the window for document 2 remains on the screen. You can remove it by resetting the window for document 1 to 24 lines.

You will find more details on switching in the next section.

EXERCISES

1. Set the document 1 window to 10 lines. Reset it to 24.

2. Set the document 1 window to 8 lines. Reset it to 18 lines.

3. Set the document 2 window to 14 lines.

4. Set document 2 to 8 lines.

USE TWO DOCUMENTS AT ONE TIME

13.3

You can use the same technique that allowed you to open the second document window to switch back and forth between the two windows. You can use this feature to allow you to read along in one document as you type a response in the second document. You can also use this technique to edit text in either document. Each time you press the Switch (Shift-F3) key [Alt Edit Switch Document], WordPerfect activates the other window.

To switch between documents:

a. Press the Switch (Shift-F3) key [Alt Edit Switch Document].

EXAMPLES

1. You can switch between two documents when you are creating a document that makes use of information contained in another document. You can use the information contained in the file FINAL to write a reminder notice. First, press the Retrieve (Shift-F10) key [Alt File Retrieve], type **final**, and press Enter.

   Next, switch to document 2 by pressing the Switch (Shift-F3) key [Alt Edit Switch Document]. In document 2, type

   Dear Sirs,

   Your account balance of

   To determine the balance due, press the Switch (Shift-F3) key [Alt Edit Switch Document]. You can see from the schedule at the bottom of the document that the client owes $278.25.

   Return to document 2 by pressing the Switch (Shift-F3) key [Alt Edit Switch Document], and type

   $278.25 is overdue. Please remit a check for this amount. As per our agreement, we should have received payment on

   To determine the date the balance was due, press the Switch (Shift-F3) key [Alt Edit Switch Document]. You can see from the schedule at the bottom of the document that the balance should have been paid by August 30. Return to document

2 by pressing the Switch ([Shift]-[F3]) key [[Alt] Edit Switch Document], and type

August 30.

        Sincerely,

        Maud Stevens

2. You can switch between documents to create two closely related documents. For example, when you type a summary letter for a contract, you may need to switch between the contract and the letter to check that both documents use the same facts. First, type

Know all men by these presents, that I, Tom Jones, the undersigned, in consideration of the sum of $40,000, in hand paid, do hereby grant, bargain, sell and convey to Ron Delaney, of Broward County, Florida, the following described real estate situated in the county of Orange, State of Florida, to wit: 1/2 acre lot at the corner of Rio Pinar Drive and Gator Alley, to have and to hold to his heirs and assigns forever.

Then, create the summary letter to send with the contract. Press the Switch ([Shift]-[F3]) key [[Alt] Edit Switch Document], and type

Tom Jones
513 Allworthy Lane
Oxford, CT 09134

Dear Mr. Jones,

Enclosed is the contract to sell your land at the corner of Rio Pinar Drive and Gator Alley to

To check the buyer's name and the price, press the Switch (Shift - F3) key [Alt Edit Switch Document]. The contract states that the buyer is Ron Delaney and the price is $40,000. To return to the letter, press the Switch (Shift - F3) key [Alt Edit Switch Document]. Type

Ron Delaney for $40,000. Sign the contract, notarize it, and return it to our office as soon as possible.

Sincerely,

Jane Perez, Attorney

By creating both documents at once, you can ensure that they both use the same information.

EXERCISES

1. Type the following paragraph. When you get to the four "X"s, switch to document 2, retrieve FINAL, and find the sales tax. Switch to document 1, and type the sales tax in place of the four "X"s.

   The discrepancy between the amount due and what the client believes is the proper amount is the sales tax of XXXX. The client was not aware that sales tax would be added for printing services.

2. Type the following sentence:

The president, Amanda Williams, started with the company as chief production officer fifteen years ago.

Switch to document 2, and type

Ms. Williams' experience includes chief production officer, divisional vice president, production vice president, and president.

Switch to document 1, and type

After four years as production officer, she was promoted to divisional vice president of the appliance division.

Save document 1 as PRESIDNT and 2 as PRES-RESU.ME.

COPY AND MOVE TEXT BETWEEN DOCUMENTS

13.4

You can use the techniques for copying and moving text in one document to perform the same tasks in two documents. This feature allows you to recall a file from disk and use it as the basis for another document. When you move data between documents, the data from the current document is removed and placed in the other document. When you copy text, it is left in its original location, and a copy of it is placed in the other document. Either document 1 or document 2 can contain the data to be moved or copied.

To copy or move text between documents:

a. Move the cursor to a character in the sentence, paragraph, or page that you want to copy or move.

b. Press the Move ((Ctrl)-(F4)) key [(Alt) Edit Select].

c. Type an **s** or a **1** to copy or move a sentence, a **p** or a **2** to copy or move a paragraph, or an **a** or a **3** to move a page.

d. Type an **m** or a **1** to move the highlighted text or a **c** or a **2** to copy the highlighted text.

e. Press the Switch ((Shift)-(F3)) key [(Alt) Edit Switch Document] to switch to the other document.

f. Move the cursor to where you want the text to be placed.

g. Press (Enter).

To copy or move blocked text between documents:

a. Move the cursor to the beginning of the text that you want to move or copy.

b. Press the Block ((Alt)-(F4)) key [(Alt) Edit Block].

c. Move the cursor to the end of the text that you want to move or copy.

d. Press the Move ((Ctrl)-(F4)) key [(Alt) Edit Move (Cut) or Copy and skip steps e and f].

e. Type a **b** or a **1** to select Block.

f. Type an **m** or a **1** to move the blocked text or a **c** or a **2** to copy the blocked text.

g. Press the Switch ((Shift)-(F3)) key [(Alt) Edit Switch Document] to switch to the other document.

h. Place the cursor where you want the blocked text to be copied or moved.

i. Press (Enter).

EXAMPLES

1. You can move text from one document to another. First, press the Retrieve ((Shift)-(F10)) key [(Alt) File Retrieve], type **final**, and press (Enter). Next, switch to document 2 by pressing the Switch ((Shift)-(F3)) key [(Alt) Edit Switch Document]. Press the Retrieve ((Shift)-(F10)) key [(Alt) File Retrieve], type **stmt1**, and press (Enter).

   To move the paragraph in document 2 to document 1, press the Move ((Ctrl)-(F4)) key, and type a **p** [(Alt) Edit Select Paragraph] and an **m**. The paragraph is removed from the current document.

   Next, press the Switch ((Shift)-(F3)) key [(Alt) Edit Switch Document] to return to document 1. Place the cursor below the numbers at the bottom of the document, and press (Enter). WordPerfect inserts a copy of the paragraph from the other document into the current document.

2. You can copy a block of text from one document to another. First, set the number of lines in the document 1 window to 11 by pressing the Screen ((Ctrl)-(F3)) key, typing a **w** [(Alt) Edit Window] and **11**, and pressing (Enter). Then, press the Retrieve ((Shift)-(F10)) key [(Alt) File Retrieve], type **finalbal**, and press (Enter).

To copy the inside address to another document, begin by pressing the Block (Alt-F4) key [Alt Edit Block]. Move the cursor to the blank line before the salutation. Then, press the Move (Ctrl-F4) key, and type a b and a c [Alt Edit Copy]. The highlighting disappears, and the block remains in the current document.

Next, switch to document 2 by pressing the Switch (Shift-F3) key [Alt Edit Switch Document]. Press Enter to place a copy of the block from document 1 in document 2. Now you can type the remainder of the second document. Even though you have completed the Copy procedure, the message **Move cursor; press Enter to retrieve** will remain in the first document's status line until you switch back to that window.

EXERCISES

1. Type the following paragraphs:

   Peter Sullivan is production vice president. He has held this position for the past three years.

   Paula Atchinson is the financial vice president. She has held this position for the past two years.

   Move the first paragraph to document 2 and then clear both documents.

2. Type the following name and address:

Terry Kesley
Kesley Associates
496 Berry Avenue
Newport, Rhode Island 03563

Copy them to document 2.

EXERCISES

(Do not clear the screen until you have completed the last exercise.)

MASTERY
SKILLS CHECK

1. Type the following paragraphs:

The company has made the following accounting changes:
   Inventory valuation now uses the FIFO method instead of the LIFO method. The change to this year's income is $40,000, last year's income is $48,000. The total effect on income from prior years is $88,000.
   Contracts are now accounted for using the percentage-of-completion method rather than the completed-contract method. This increased last year's net income by $40,000 and this year's by $60,000.

Switch to document 2.

2. Set the window for document 2 to 12 lines.

3. Switch to document 1. Set the window for document 1 to 8 lines.

4. Copy the first accounting-change paragraph to document 2.

5. Move the second accounting-change paragraph to the beginning of document 2.

 **INTEGRATING SKILLS CHECK**

(Do not clear the screen until you have completed the last exercise.)

1. Type the following paragraphs:

> The company leases most of its office space and mainframe computer equipment. It owns all of its production facilities.
> Total rental expense is $1,709,000 for the current year, $998,000 for 1989, and $923,000 for 1988.

Save as LEASES. Back up the file as LEASES.BAK.

2. Switch to document 2. Retrieve LEASES.BAK.

3. Add the following paragraph at the bottom of the document:

> The company's minimum lease obligations are $503,000 for 1991, $432,000 for 1992, $401,000 for 1993, $352,000 for 1994, $318,000 for 1995, and $1,293,000 for later years.

Copy the last paragraph to the bottom of document 1.

4. Save document 1 as LEASES.NEW, and switch to document 2.

5. Create a document summary with the following information:

   Document Name (Descriptive Filename in 5.0):
   Notes for financial statements
   Author: [your name]
   Typist: [your name]
   Subject: **For 1990 financial statements**

6. Delete the file LEASES.BAK.

7. Add the following header:

   Financial Statement Notes

8. Create a footer that will print your name.

9. Turn your printer's power switch to the off position. (If you attempted this exercise with your printer on, it is likely that the print job would finish before you could activate the Control Printer screen.) Start a print job to create two copies of the current document. Cancel the print job. Turn your printer on.

Special Features

►Part III◄

Merging Variable
Information into
a Standard Letter

►14◄

CHAPTER OBJECTIVES

After completing this chapter, you should be able to:

▶ **Create a secondary file**   14.1

▶ **Create a primary file**   14.2

▶ **Produce the Merge document**   14.3

▶ **Print the Merge document**   14.4

Sometimes you need to create many documents that are almost identical. The only difference in the documents may be individualized information, such as a customer name and address or an account balance. Such documents are referred to as form letters since each of them follows an identical format. WordPerfect supports the creation of form letters with its Merge features. The Merge features allow you to integrate variable information with a document that is fixed in content and format. This capability allows you to create letters, invoices, and other documents that are similar without having to type each document from scratch.

You can create a base document with special markers entered where variable information is to be inserted. You can create a second document containing the variable information, such as names, addresses, and account balances. At your command, WordPerfect merges the variable information into the base document to create individualized documents.

To merge files in WordPerfect, you must have primary and secondary document files. The *primary file* contains the form letter or other nonchanging text. It also directs WordPerfect to the specific locations at which information should be inserted. The *secondary file* contains the variable information that WordPerfect places into the primary document. When the merge operation is complete, you will have individualized documents for the information in the secondary file. These documents will all be stored in one file in memory.

(Do not clear the screen between exercises unless
instructed to do so.)

SKILLS CHECK

1. Delete the default tab stops and set tabs stops at 0.5"
   and 3" (1.5" and 4" in 5.0). Type the following letter:

   Highland Graphics, Inc.
   24257 N.W. 5th Street
   Sunrise, FL 33146
   305-331-2473

   Mark Scheimer
   Chairman, Education and Development
   Association of Computer Graphic Artists
   1347 S.W. 14 Ave.
   Davie, FL 33136

   Dear Mr. Scheimer,
      Since my company is having a display at your up-
   coming forum, I need the dimensions for the display
   space. I also need the number of electrical outlets
   available for use in my display and the distance from
   the display to these outlets.

      Sincerely,

      Ann Slater
      President, Highland Graphics, Inc.

   Use WordPerfect's Spell feature to check the spelling.

2. Block the name and address information for Mark
   Scheimer.

3. Place a copy of the block in a second document.

4. Return to the first document. Change the window size to 12 lines.

5. Save the document as REQUEST.

6. Print two copies of the letter.

7. Request two printed copies two more times. Then cancel all print jobs.

8. Add the following paragraph to the letter:

I have enclosed a list of the sales representatives who will be attending the forum.

Add a hard page break at the end of the letter. Type the following list of names on the new page:

**Jim Styverson
Karen Acermann
Julie Greenlowe
Paul Hatterfield**

Check the spelling for this page. Add the proper names that are not recognized by the spelling checker to your supplemental dictionary.

9. Add the following header to the second page:

Forum Attendees

10. Make a backup of the REQUEST file LETTER.BK.

11. Switch to the second document screen. Add the following header:

Booth Assignments

Copy the list of names from the first document to the end of the second.

12. Set the tab stops in the second document to have only one tab stop, at 3" (4" in 5.0). Use this tab stop to enter the following times in a column next to the names:

    8:00 - 10:00
    10:00 - 1:00
    1:00 - 3:00
    3:00 - 5:30

13. Set the number of print copies to 1. Request a copy of the original letter in the REQUEST file twice. Request a print of the page containing booth assignments, and have WordPerfect make it a rush job.

14. Save the document as TIMES. Rename the file as BOOTH.

15. Search your default directory for files that contain the name "Karen."

16. Clear both files from memory. Look at the BOOTH file.

17. Retrieve BOOTH, and create a document summary that contains entries for document name (descriptive filename in 5.0), author, and typist.

18. If you have a hard disk, change to and look at the root directory. Look at the files on the disk in the other drive if you have a floppy disk system.

19. If you have a hard disk, create a new subdirectory called TRDESHOW at the same level as the Word-Perfect subdirectory. If you have a floppy disk, create a TRDESHOW subdirectory in the root directory of the floppy disk. In either system, remove the new subdirectory. Return the current subdirectory to WP51 (WP50 in 5.0) if you are using a hard disk.

20. Add a footer to BOOTH that shows the date at the left and the page number at the right, preceded by the word "Page." Save the file and clear the screen. Change the window size back to 24 lines.

21. Remove the names you added to the supplemental dictionary in exercise 8.

14.1 | CREATE A SECONDARY FILE

Secondary files contain the information that you want WordPerfect to substitute in place of markers in a primary file. Each unit of information that Word-Perfect substitutes is called a *field*. WordPerfect has no limit on the amount of text that a field can contain; different fields may contain one word, one line, or multiple lines, or be blank.

WordPerfect refers to each field by a number; for example, the second field is field 2. The set of fields that WordPerfect uses for each part of a Merge document is called a *record*. WordPerfect has no limit on the number of records that your secondary file can contain.

To create a secondary file:

a. Type the information for the first field.

b. Press the End Field (F9) key (Merge R (F9) key in 5.0).

c. Type the information for the additional fields of a record, pressing the End Field (F9) key (Merge R (F9) key in 5.0) each time you finish a field.

d. Press the Merge Codes (Shift-F9) key [(Alt) Tools Merge Codes End Record and skip step e].

e. Type an **e**.

f. Repeat steps a through e for each record.

g. Save the file.

As you perform these steps, WordPerfect adds codes to the file. These special codes do not appear in the Merge document; WordPerfect uses them to mark the ends of fields and records. When you press the End Field (F9) key (Merge R (F9) key in 5.0), WordPerfect puts an {END FIELD} code (^R in 5.0) at the end of the line and moves the cursor to the next line. (The "R" in "Merge R" stands for "return.") When you press the Merge Codes (Shift-F9) key and type an **e** [(Alt) Tools Merge Codes End Record], WordPerfect inserts a an {END RECORD} code (^E in 5.0) and a page break and moves the cursor to the next line. You *cannot* achieve the same result by typing the caret symbol (^) followed by the letter.

EXAMPLES

1. You can create a record containing different fields of data in a secondary file. The record can contain fields for a person's name, the person's title, the person's company, the first line of the person's address, the second line of the address, the person's phone number, and a salutation to use in a form letter to the person. First, type **Mary Ann Kelley**. Next, press the End Field (F9) key (Merge R (F9) key in 5.0). The screen looks like this:

```
Mary Ann Kelley{END FIELD}
-
```

Next, fill in the field for the title by typing **President**. Press the End Field (F9) key (Merge R (F9) key in 5.0). Fill in the field for the company by typing **Kelley Graphics**. Press the End Field (F9) key (Merge R (F9) key in 5.0). The screen now looks like this:

```
Mary Ann Kelley{END FIELD}
President{END FIELD}
Kelley Graphics{END FIELD}
-
```

You can complete the address fields by typing **6035 N.E. 25th Avenue**, pressing the End Field (F9) key (Merge R (F9) key in 5.0), typing **Lighthouse Point, FL 33041**, and pressing the End Field (F9) key (Merge R (F9) key in 5.0) again. Next, type **305-275-6582** and press the End Field (F9) key (Merge R (F9) key in 5.0) to add the phone-number field to the record. You can add the name to be used in a salutation by typing **Mary Ann** and pressing the End Field ([F9]) key (Merge R ([F9]) key in 5.0) to mark the end of that field.

Finally, press the Merge Codes ([Shift]-[F9]) key, and type an **e** [[Alt] **Tools Merge Codes End Record**]. The record now looks like this:

```
Mary Ann Kelley(END FIELD)
President(END FIELD)
Kelley Graphics(END FIELD)
6035 N.E. 25th Avenue(END FIELD)
Lighthouse Point, FL 33041(END FIELD)
305-275-6582(END FIELD)
Mary Ann(END FIELD)
(END RECORD)
==========================================================================
-
```

Press the Exit ([F7]) key [[Alt] **File Exit**] and type **n** twice to clear the screen.

2. You can put multiple lines in a field. The same record that you typed can be entered with two lines in the address field instead of one. First, type **Mary Ann Kelley,** and press the End Field ([F9]) key (Merge R ([F9]) key in 5.0). Next, type **President,** and press the End Field ([F9]) key (Merge R ([F9]) key in 5.0). Then, type **Kelley Graphics,** and press the End Field ([F9]) key (Merge R ([F9]) key in 5.0).

You can use two lines for the address. Type **6035 N.E. 25th Avenue,** press [Enter], type **Lighthouse Point, FL 33041,** and press the End Field ([F9]) key (Merge R ([F9]) key in 5.0). The two lines look like this:

```
6035 N.E. 25th Avenue
Lighthouse Point, FL 33041(END FIELD)
```

To include the telephone number, type **305-275-6582,** and press the End Field ([F9]) key (Merge R

(F9) key in 5.0). The last field in this record is the name to be used in the salutation. Type **Mary Ann,** and press the End Field (F9) key (Merge R (F9) key in 5.0).

Finally, press the Merge Codes (Shift-F9) key and type an e [Alt Tools Merge Codes End Record]. The record now looks like this:

```
Mary Ann Kelley{END FIELD}
President{END FIELD}
Kelley Graphics{END FIELD}
6035 N.E. 25th Avenue
Lighthouse Point, FL 33041{END FIELD}
305-275-6582{END FIELD}
Mary Ann{END FIELD}
{END RECORD}
================================================================================
-
```

Keep this record on the screen to use in the next example.

3. You can create records that do not include information in all fields. However, you must tell Word-Perfect which fields are empty so that it will continue to use the proper fields after it reaches a field you are skipping. Create a record without a title or company. First, type **Scott McGregor,** and press the End Field (F9) key (Merge R (F9) key in 5.0). Next, since he does not have a title, press the End Field (F9) key (Merge R (F9) key in 5.0) again. The record looks like this:

```
Scott McGregor{END FIELD}
{END FIELD}
Scott McGregor{END FIELD}
{END FIELD}
```

The second {END FIELD} code (^R in 5.0) tells WordPerfect that the information to the left of it is for the second field. Since there is nothing to the left of it, WordPerfect will recognize that the second field is blank. Since Scott McGregor does not have a company name, press the End Field ([F9]) key (Merge R ([F9]) key in 5.0) again.

Fill in the address field by typing **503 S.W. 6th Avenue**, pressing [Enter], typing **Pompano, FL 33167**, and pressing the End Field ([F9]) key (Merge R ([F9]) key in 5.0).

To complete the phone number field, type **305-465-6734**, and press the End Field ([F9]) key (Merge R ([F9]) key in 5.0).

To include the first name for a salutation, type **Scott**, and press the End Field ([F9]) key (Merge R ([F9]) key in 5.0).

Finally, since the salutation field is the last one, press the Merge Codes ([Shift]-[F9]) key and type an e [[Alt] Tools Merge Codes End]. The completed record for Scott McGregor looks like this:

```
Scott McGregor{END FIELD}
{END FIELD}
{END FIELD}
503 S.W. 6th Avenue
Pompano, FL 33167{END FIELD}
305-465-6734{END FIELD}
Scott{END FIELD}
{END RECORD}
==============================================================================
```

The document now contains two records that are ready to be combined with a primary file, which you will create in the next section. Save this document as NAMES by pressing the Exit ([F7]) key [[Alt] File Exit], typing **y** and **names**, and pressing [Enter]. Type an **n** to stay in WordPerfect.

EXERCISES

1. Create a secondary file that contains the following four records:

B. J. Smith	231-46-4232
Carroll Lawrence	564-90-5327
Sara Graham	976-95-3194
Ellen Pelton	687-64-6546

2. Retrieve the NAMES file created in example 3. Using the same format, add the following record to the secondary file:

Paul Stevens
Vice President
Stevens & Stevens
635 Dover Street
Daytona Beach, FL 34240
305-287-3863
Paul

3. Add another record to the NAMES secondary file, using your own information. Save the revised file.

14.2 CREATE A PRIMARY FILE

A primary file contains the text that is to appear in each form letter or other Merge document. It also contains Merge codes that instruct WordPerfect where it should place the different fields when it merges with the secondary file. You do not have to use all of the available fields in the primary file; you can use any of the fields you want, in any order you choose. You can also use a field more than once in the primary file.

You might find it worthwhile to print a copy of a secondary file format to help you correctly identify the field numbers when you create a primary file.

To create a primary file:

a. Type the text as you want it to appear in each Merge document. Where the final documents will display individualized information, leave the primary file blank.

b. Place the cursor where you want WordPerfect to substitute one of the fields from the secondary file.

c. Press the Merge Codes ([Shift]-[F9]) key [[Alt] Tools Merge Code Field and skip step d].

d. Type an **f** for Field.

e. Type the number of the field containing the information that you want inserted at that spot.

f. Press [Enter].

g. Repeat steps b through f for each field in the secondary file that you want placed in the primary file when WordPerfect merges the files.

h. Save the file.

When you press [Enter] during this procedure, WordPerfect inserts a {FIELD} n˜ code (ˆFnˆ in 5.0) where n represents the field number you specify.

EXAMPLES

1. You can create a primary file that generates address labels. Since the address labels will include only text that is in the secondary file, the primary file will consist of only field references. First, press the Merge Codes to([Shift]-[F9]) key [[Alt] Tools Merge Codes] to display the options shown here:

1 Field; **2 E**nd Record; **3 I**nput; **4 P**age Off; **5 N**ext Record; **6 M**ore: **0**

Next, type an **f** [[Alt] Tools Merge Codes Field]. When WordPerfect prompts you for a field number, type a **1**, for the field containing the person's name in each record, and press [Enter]. Press [Enter] to move to the next line. The screen now looks like this:

{FIELD}1~

Add the Merge code for the field containing the person's title by pressing the Merge Codes ([Shift]-[F9]) key, typing an **f** [[Alt] Tools Merge Codes Field] and a **2**, and pressing [Enter]. Press [Enter] to move to the next line.
Add the Merge code for the field containing the company name by pressing the Merge Codes ([Shift]-[F9]) key, typing an **f** [[Alt] Tools Merge Codes Field] and a **3**, and pressing [Enter]. Press [Enter] to move to the next line.
Add the Merge code for the field containing the company address by pressing the Merge Codes ([Shift]-[F9]) key, typing an **f** [[Alt] Tools Merge Codes Field] and a **4**, and pressing the Exit ([F7])

key. You use the Exit (F7) key rather than Enter to avoid adding hard returns to the Merge document. Even though the address uses two lines in the secondary file, the primary file requires only one, since WordPerfect will use the hard return in that field when it merges the files. The primary file looks like this:

```
{FIELD}1~
{FIELD}2~
{FIELD}3~
{FIELD}4~
```

Finally, save this document as LABELS by pressing the Exit (F7) key [Alt File Exit], pressing Enter, typing **labels**, pressing Enter, and typing a **y**.

2. You can create a form letter that confirms reservations. The first part of a letter is the inside address. This address is the information contained in the secondary file that you created earlier. First, press the Merge Codes (Shift-F9) key, type an **f** [Alt Tools Merge Codes Field] and a **1**, for the field containing the person's name. Press Enter. The screen looks like this:

```
{FIELD}1~
```

Next, press Enter to move to the next line. Add the field name for the title by pressing the Merge Codes (Shift-F9) key, typing an **f** [Alt Tools Merge Codes Field] and a **2**, and pressing Enter. Press Enter to move to the next line.

Add the Merge code for the field containing the company name by pressing the Merge Codes

([Shift]-[F9]) key, typing an **f** [[Alt] Tools Merge Codes Field] and a **3**, and pressing [Enter]. Press [Enter] to move to the next line.

Add the Merge code for the field containing the company address by pressing the Merge Codes ([Shift]-[F9]) key, typing an **f** [[Alt] Tools Merge Codes Field] and a **4**, and pressing [Enter]. Since WordPerfect will use the hard return in field 4 in the secondary file when it merges the files, you need to use only one line for this field in the primary file. Press [Enter] twice to place a blank line between the inside address and the salutation.

To create the salutation, type **Dear**, press the SPACEBAR, press the Merge Codes ([Shift]-[F9]) key, type an **f** [[Alt] Tools Merge Codes Field] and a **6**, and press [Enter]. Type a comma to end the salutation, and press [Enter] twice. At this point, the screen looks like this:

```
{FIELD}1~
{FIELD}2~
{FIELD}3~
{FIELD}4~

Dear {FIELD}6~,
```

Type the body and closing of the letter as follows, using the 3.5″ tab stop for the closing:

Enclosed are the registration materials for the upcoming forum, Taking Computer Graphics One Step Further. Please return the completed forms no later than the end of the month to insure that you are registered in time.

Sincerely,

Mark Scheimer
Chairman, Education and Development
Association of Computer Graphic Artists

Enc:(3)

This primary file does not use field 5, which contains phone numbers. Save the file as REGIS.

3. You can modify Merge codes in a primary file so that WordPerfect will not include blank secondary file fields. Press the Merge Codes ([Shift]-[F9]) key, type an **f** [[Alt] **Tools Merge Codes Field**] and a **1**, for the field containing the name, and press [Enter]. Press [Enter] to move to the next line.

   Next, press the Merge Codes ([Shift]-[F9]) key, type an **f** [[Alt] **Tools Merge Codes Field**] and a **2**, type a question mark (?), and press [Enter]. The ? after the field number tells WordPerfect to use this field in a Merge only if the field contains information. If the field is blank, WordPerfect will not include it when it merges the record. Press [Enter] to move to the next line. The screen looks like this:

{FIELD}1~
{FIELD}2?~

To include the third field, company name, press the Merge Codes ([Shift]-[F9]) key, type an **f** [[Alt] **Tools**

Merge Codes Field] and a **3**, type a **?**, and press
[Enter]. Press [Enter] again to move to the next line.

For the address, press the Merge Codes ([Shift]-
[F9]) key, type an **f** [[Alt] Tools Merge Codes Field]
and a **4**, and press [Enter]. The address uses two lines,
but the primary file requires only one, since Word-
Perfect will incorporate the hard return in the
secondary file when it merges the two. Press [Enter]
twice to place a blank line between the address and
the salutation.

To create the salutation, type **Dear**, press the
SPACEBAR, press the Merge Codes ([Shift]-[F9]) key,
type an **f** [[Alt] Tools Merge Codes Field] and a **6**,
and press [Enter]. Type a comma, and press [Enter]
twice. The screen now looks like the following.

```
{FIELD}1~
{FIELD}2?~
{FIELD}3?~
{FIELD}4~

Dear {FIELD}6~,
```

Type the body and closing of the letter as follows,
using the 3.5″ tab stop for the closing:

Enclosed are the registration materials for the upcoming forum, Taking Computer Graphics One Step
Further. Please return the completed forms no later
than the end of the month to insure that you are
registered in time.

Sincerely,

Mark Scheimer
Chairman, Education and Development
Association of Computer Graphic Artists

Enc:(3)

If you had not used question marks, WordPerfect would have printed blank lines for Scott McGregor's title and company when it merged this primary file with the secondary file containing his record.

Save this file by pressing the Exit ([F7]) key [[Alt] File Exit], pressing [Enter], typing **register**, and pressing [Enter]. Type an **n** to stay in WordPerfect.

EXERCISES

1. Create a primary file for the following form letter, replacing the information in parentheses with Merge codes for fields. Assume that the secondary file is in the format of the examples in section 14.1.

    The Association of Computer Graphic Artists wishes to thank (person's name) from (person's company) for his or her assistance with the Taking Computer Graphics One Step Further forum.

    Save this file as THANKS.

2. Create a primary file for the following form letter, substituting the information in parentheses with Merge codes for fields. Assume that the secondary file is in the format of example 2 in section 14.1. Use the 3.5″ tab stop for the closing.

    (full name)
    (title)
    (company)
    (address)

Dear (first name),
   To stimulate attendance at your display during the upcoming forum, we are providing cards for you to distribute. These cards are professionally printed on high-quality paper. The format of these cards is as follows:
(company name)
(address)
(phone number)

Contact: (person's name)
          (title)
   If you prefer a different format, call us at (501) 365-2352 by next Monday.

                Sincerely,

                Mark Scheimer
                Chairman, Education and Development
                Association of Computer Graphic Artists

Save the file as CARDS.

14.3 PRODUCE THE MERGE DOCUMENT

Once you have created the primary and secondary files, you are ready to produce the Merge document. When you merge the two files, you create another document that contains a copy of the primary file for each record in the secondary file. The new copies have the information from each field substituted for the Merge code for the field number in the primary file. WordPerfect automatically inserts a page break after merging each secondary file record.

Since WordPerfect creates Merge documents in the computer's memory, you may be limited in the number of records you can have in a secondary file. If a Merge exceeds the computer's memory, break up the secondary file into smaller files, and merge the primary file with each smaller secondary file in turn.

WordPerfect has many other Merge features that are beyond the scope of this book. These features are covered in the WordPerfect manual and in *WordPerfect 5.1: The Complete Reference* (by Karen L. Acerson; Osborne/McGraw-Hill, 1990).

To create a Merge document:

a. Be sure the current document screen is empty.

b. Press the Merge/Sort (Ctrl - F9) key [Alt Tools Merge and skip step c].

c. Type an **m** or a **1** for Merge.

d. Type the name of the primary file, and press Enter .

e. Type the name of the secondary file, and press Enter .

WordPerfect merges the files you specified. It automatically adjusts line spacing and word wrap to accommodate the substitution of the secondary file information for the Merge codes for field numbers.

EXAMPLE

1. You can combine the primary file created in the examples in section 14.2 with the secondary file

created in the examples in section 14.1. Press the Merge/Sort (Ctrl-F9) key to display this menu:

1Merge; **2**Sort; **3**Convert Old Merge Codes: **0**

Type an **m** to select Merge [Alt Tools Merge]. Type **register** for the primary file, and press Enter. Type **names** for the secondary file, and press Enter. Figure 14-1 shows one of the letters that result from WordPerfect's replacing the Merge codes for field numbers in the primary file with the contents of the fields in the second record. The letter containing your name should appear on your screen. Press the PgUp key to view the other letters.

```
================================================================================
Scott McGregor
583 S.W. 6th Avenue
Pompano, FL  33167

Dear Scott,

    Enclosed are the registration materials for the upcoming
forum, Taking Computer Graphics One Step Further.  Please return
the completed forms no later than the end of the month to insure
that you are registered in time.

                Sincerely,


                Mark Scheiner
                Chairman, Education and Development
                Association Of Computer Graphic Artists

Enc:(3)



                        Doc 1 Pg 2 Ln 4.16" Pos 1"
```

FIGURE 14-1.   WordPerfect screen showing a Merge document

Save the Merge document by pressing the Exit
(F7) key [Alt File Exit], pressing Enter, typing
rgstr, and pressing Enter. Type an **n** to remain in
WordPerfect.

EXERCISES

1. Merge the THANKS primary file that you created in
exercise 1 in section 14.2 with the NAMES secondary file. You should save the Merge document as
THANKS.OUT.

2. Merge the CARDS primary file that you created in
exercise 2 in section 14.2 with the NAMES secondary file. Save the Merge document as CARDS.OUT.

PRINT THE MERGE DOCUMENT

14.4

Once you have produced the Merge document, you
can print it. You can print a Merge document from
disk if you've saved it or print it directly from memory. You can use the same print features that work
with printing regular documents.

To print a Merge document:

a. Press the Print (Shift-F7) key [Alt File Print].

b. Type an **f** or a **1** to print the full document.
WordPerfect prints the Merge document.

To print a Merge document from disk:

a. Press the Print (Shift-F7) key [Alt File Print].

b. Type a **d** or a **3**.

c. Type the name of the Merge document that you saved, and press (Enter).

d. Type the numbers of the pages that you want printed and press (Enter), or press (Enter) to print the entire document.

EXAMPLE

1. You can print the Merge document that you created in the example in section 14.3. Press the Print ((Shift)-(F7)) key [(Alt) File Print], type a **d** and **rgstr**, and press (Enter) twice. Figure 14-2 shows a printed

---

```
Paul Stevens
Vice President
Stevens & Stevens
635 Dover Street
Daytona Beach,  FL 34240

Dear Paul,

     Enclosed are the registration materials for the upcoming
forum, Taking Computer Graphics One Step Further.  Please return
the completed forms no later than the end of the month to insure
that you are registered in time.

                    Sincerely,

                    Mark Scheimer
                    Chairman, Education and Development
                    Association Of Computer Graphic Artists

Enc:(3)
```

FIGURE 14-2.   Printed copy of a letter created with the Merge feature page from the Merge document created with the REGISTER primary file and the NAMES secondary file.

EXERCISES

1. Print the Merge document THANKS.OUT, which you created in exercise 1 in section 14.3.

2. Print the Merge document CARDS.OUT, which you created in exercise 2 in section 14.3.

EXERCISES

1. Create a secondary file that contains records with the following information. Each line represents a separate field.

MASTERY
SKILLS CHECK

Karen Simon
34220 Euclid Avenue
Cleveland, OH 44134

Jim Darcy
12353 Carnegie Avenue
Lakewood, OH 44116

Save the file as NAMES2.

2. Create a primary file that creates address labels when merged with the secondary file NAMES2. Save the primary file as LBLS. Merge the primary and secondary files, and print the Merge document.

3. Retrieve the NAMES2 secondary file. Add a field for the first name to be used as a salutation in form letters. Save the revised file as NAMES2.

4. Create a primary file containing a letter to be used with NAMES2. Use the following as the letter body:

According to our records, we cannot finish processing the application until you send two ID-sized photos. Please send these photos so that your application to the Radio Controlled Planes Club may be processed.

Sincerely,

Tim Powers
Membership Director

Save the file as PHOTOS. Merge this file with the NAMES2 secondary file, and print the Merge document.

5. Retrieve the PHOTOS primary file, and modify it so that the person's first name and a comma appear after "According to our records." Save the revised file. Merge the file with the NAMES2 secondary file, and print the Merge document.

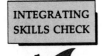

INTEGRATING SKILLS CHECK

(Do not clear the screen between exercises unless instructed to do so.)

1. Create a secondary file that contains records with the following information:

Thomas Douglas
Dept. Manager, Accounting
X3963

Tanya Smith
Dept. Manager, Data Processing
X3959

Save the file as NAMES.TWO. Clear the screen.

2. Create a primary file that contains the following memo. Replace the parenthetical information with a Merge code or fill in the information, as appropriate. Use the format of the secondary file created in exercise 1 for field numbers.

Memo
To: (name)
            (title)
            (phone number)
Date: (today's date)
From: (your name)
Re: Smoking Areas

    In compliance with local ordinances, the company must limit smoking to a designated area. The designated smoking area is the cafeteria's west end. Please inform the staff of your department. This is effective immediately.

3. Center the word "Memo."

4. Place a hyphenated line between "Memo" and "To."

5. Save the file as SMOKERS, and clear the screen.

6. Merge the SMOKERS primary file with the NAMES.TWO secondary file.

7. Print two copies of the Merge document.

8. Clear the screen. Retrieve the secondary file into document 1 and the primary file into document 2. Change the size of the document 2 window to 12 lines.

Adding a Column of Numbers

▶15◀

CHAPTER OBJECTIVES

After completing this chapter, you should be able to:

▶ **Obtain a total for a column of numbers** 15.1

▶ **Use multilevel totals** 15.2

WordPerfect's Math feature is not designed to do heavy-duty calculating like a spreadsheet program. It does, however, have basic math capabilities that can perform simple calculations. In this chapter, you will add a column of numbers to produce a subtotal. You will also add subtotals to produce a total and combine totals into a grand total.

You will want to master the basic math features presented in this chapter to guarantee that expense reports, invoices, and other such documents are accurate.

SKILLS CHECK

1. Clear the default tab stops. Create tab settings at 1.5", 2", and 4". Reset the tab stops to the default setting.

2. Type the following paragraph, using Bold and Underline where indicated:

   We have written several times to inquire about the status of order number 98754. Please check the status of the back-order items. If you are unable to fill the remainder of the order within <u>10 days</u>, please notify us so that we can contact other <u>suppliers</u>.

3. Type the following, using the [Esc] key to draw the line:

   ```
   150
    50
   100
   ───
   300
   ```

4. Type the following, using bold where indicated:

You can use an 's to create the plural of letters, numbers, symbols, and words. For example, you could write that there are four **s's** and four **i's** in **Mississippi**.

Print two copies of the paragraph.

5. Type the following:

Errors, like straws, upon the surface flow;
He who would search for pearls, must dive below.

John Dryden

Use the Block feature to make two more copies of the quotation and author name.

6. Reset the number of copies to one.

OBTAIN A TOTAL FOR A COLUMN OF NUMBERS

15.1

Many of the documents that you create may contain columns of figures. Rather than use a calculator to obtain the correct total at the bottom of a column, you can use WordPerfect's Math features.

WordPerfect's Math features require a bit of advanced planning and a little extra care on your part. You must follow a set procedure, placing the math entries in columns set with tab stops. The Math features use a special symbol to tell WordPerfect that you wish to add the numbers in a column.

Once you have learned the process, abiding by the rules is not difficult. Your reward is column totals that are always accurate, whether you are preparing commission reports, purchase orders, or the company bowling team's scores.

To calculate a total for a column of numbers:

a. Place the cursor where you wish to use the Math features.

b. Set tab stops for the columns you plan to use.

c. Press the Columns/Table ([Alt]-[F7]) key (Math/Columns ([Alt]-[F7]) key and skip step d in 5.0) [[Alt] Layout Math **On** and skip steps d and e].

d. Type an **m** or a **3** to select Math.

e. Type an **o** or a **1** to turn Math On (**m** or **3** in 5.0).

f. Type the column entries for the labels and numbers.

g. Type a plus sign (**+**) where you want the total calculated.

h. Press the Columns/Table ([Alt]-[F7]) key (Math/Columns ([Alt]-[F7]) key and skip step i in 5.0) [[Alt] Layout Math **Calculate** and skip steps i and j].

i. Type an **m** or **3** to select Math.

j. Type a **c** or a **4** for Calculate (**a** or **2** in 5.0).

k. Press the Columns/Table ([Alt]-[F7]) key (Math/Columns ([Alt]-[F7]) key and skip step l in 5.0) [[Alt] Layout Math **Off** and skip steps l and m].

l. Type an **m** or **3** to select Math.

m. Type an **f** or a **2** to turn Math off (**m** or **1** in 5.0).

The hidden codes [Math On] and [Math Off] mark the beginning and ending locations for Math. These steps produce what WordPerfect refers to as a subtotal for the column. WordPerfect uses the special code [+] to mark where it will compute the subtotal. In many documents, the subtotal will be all you need.

EXAMPLES

1. You can use WordPerfect's Math features to add amounts in an invoice. First, type the top of the invoice: Press the Center ([Shift]-[F6]) key [[Alt] Layout Align Center], and type

   ABC COMPANY

   Press [Enter]. Next, press the Center ([Shift]-[F6]) key [[Alt] Layout Align Center], and type

   Invoice Number 889-3452

   Press [Enter]. Then, press the Center ([Shift]-[F6]) key [[Alt] Layout Align Center], and type

   As of August 5, 1990

   Press [Enter] twice. The screen looks like this:

   ```
                     ABC COMPANY
             Invoice Number 889-3452
               As of August 5, 1990
   ```

   You are now ready to set the tabs for the math columns. Since you can store the text descriptions at the left margin, you need only one tab stop for the numeric column. Press the Format ([Shift]-[F8]) key, and type an L [[Alt] Layout Line] and a **t**. Clear all the tabs by pressing the DEL EOL ([Ctrl]-[End]) key. Type **4.5**, and press [Enter]. Type a **d** to change the tab set to a decimal tab, which aligns numbers on their decimal points. Press the Exit ((F7)) key twice.

Press the Columns/Table ((Alt)-(F7)) key (Math/ Columns ((Alt)-(F7)) key in 5.0), and type an **m** and an **o** (just **m** in 5.0) to turn the Math feature on [(Alt) Layout Math On]. WordPerfect displays **Math** at the left edge of the status line. WordPerfect can perform calculations only in an area of the document where the Math feature is on.

Type **Desk**, press the (Tab) key, and type **249.95**. WordPerfect places the decimal point at the tab stop. Press (Enter), type **Chair (side)**, press the (Tab) key, and type **98.75**. Press (Enter), type **Chair (desk)**, press the (Tab) key, and type **185.00**. For the last item, press (Enter), type **Lamp**, press (Tab), type **59.95**, and press (Enter).

You can use a plus sign (+) to make Word-Perfect add the numbers in the column. First, press the (Tab) key to position the cursor in the numeric column. Next, type a **+**. Nothing seems to happen, as the plus symbol only marks the place where you want the calculation; it does not perform the calculation. The screen looks like Figure 15-1. To perform the calculation, you must return to the Math menu. Press the Columns/Table ((Alt)-(F7)) key (Math/Columns ((Alt)-(F7)) key in 5.0). Type an **m** and **c** (**a** in 5.0) to calculate the subtotal [(Alt) Layout Math Calculate]. The result on the screen should match Figure 15-2. When you print this document, the **+** symbol will not appear on the printed copy.

You can now turn off the Math feature. Press the Columns/Table ((Alt)-(F7)) key (Math/Columns ((Alt)-(F7)) key in 5.0), and type an **m** and **o** (**m** in

```
                    ABC COMPANY
              Invoice Number 889-3452
                 As of August 5, 1990

Desk                             249.95
Chair (side)                      98.75
Chair (desk)                     185.00
Lamp                              59.95
                                    +
```

Plus sign used for subtotal

5.0) [(Alt) Layout Math Off]. The Math features are inactive at the current cursor position. A + symbol typed outside of the document area where Math is on will not be effective in totaling a column of numbers.

Use these entries in the next example.

2. You can revise mathematical calculations that have already been defined. Move the cursor to the "8" in "185.00." Notice that the **Math** indicator reappears on the status line. Press the (Ins) key to invoke Typeover mode, type a **7**, and press (Ins) again to

```
                    ABC COMPANY
              Invoice Number 889-3452
                 As of August 5, 1990

Desk                             249.95
Chair (side)                      98.75
Chair (desk)                     185.00
Lamp                              59.95
                                 593.65+
```

Subtotal calculated

turn Typeover mode off. The new number appears in the column, but the subtotal is unchanged. You must invoke the Math menu again to recalculate the subtotal. Press the Columns/Table ([Alt]-[F7]) key (Math/Columns ([Alt]-[F7]) key in 5.0), and type an **m** and **c** (**a** in 5.0) [[Alt] Layout Math Calculate]. The new subtotal appears at the bottom of the column. Use these entries in the next example.

3. You can insert a new item in a column and include its value in the subtotal. First, move the cursor to the "L" in "Lamp." Press the [Enter] key to add a new line, and use the [↑] key to move the cursor to it. Type **Credenza**, and press the [Tab] key. Type **205.75**. Again, the subtotal needs to be recalculated. Press the Columns/Table ([Alt]-[F7]) key (Math/Columns ([Alt]-[F7]) key in 5.0), and type an **m** and **c** (**a** in 5.0) [[Alt] Layout Math Calculate]. The new subtotal, 789.40, appears at the bottom of the column.

Save the file by pressing the Exit ([F7]) key [[Alt] File Exit], pressing [Enter], typing **invoice**, and pressing [Enter]. Press [Enter] again to remain in WordPerfect.

EXERCISES

(Do not clear the screen until you have completed the last exercise.)

1. Set a decimal tab stop at 3", and create math columns for the following entries:

Salaries	50,000
Benefits	8,500
Travel	18,000
Rent	120,000

Since the numbers do not have a decimal point, WordPerfect right-aligns them at the tab stop when you press [Enter]. Calculate a subtotal at the bottom of the column. Turn off the Math feature.

2. Change the "Benefits" amount to **8,900**. Recalculate the subtotal.

USE MULTILEVEL TOTALS

15.2

WordPerfect supports multiple levels of totals. You can calculate subtotals for columns of entries, add subtotals, and even create a grand total. Each level requires a different symbol to indicate which entries you want WordPerfect to add together.

You can place all of your totals in the same column, or you can use the columns to the right of your entries to show different levels of totals. If you elect to use extra columns, you must use another Math feature to define the columns before making your entries.

To create multiple levels of totals:

a. Place the cursor where you wish to use the Math feature.

b. Set tab stops for the columns you plan to use.

c. Press the Columns/Table (Alt - F7) key (Math/Columns (Alt - F7) key in 5.0 and skip step d) [Alt Layout Math Define and skip steps d and e].

d. Type an **m** or a **3** to select Math.

e. Type a **d** or a **3** for Math Define (**e** or **2** in 5.0).

f. Change the settings as appropriate for each column you will use, and press the Exit (F7) key.

g. Type an **o** or a **1** to turn Math on (**m** or **1** in 5.0).

h. Type the column entries for the labels and numbers.

i. Press the (Tab) key to move the cursor to the appropriate column, and type a plus sign (+) to calculate a subtotal, an equal sign (=) to calculate a total from subtotals, or an asterisk (*) to calculate a grand total.

j. Press the Columns/Table (Alt - F7) key (Math/Columns (Alt - F7) key in 5.0 and skip step k) [Alt Layout Math Calculate and skip steps k and l].

k. Type an **m** or a **3** to select Math.

l. Type a **c** or **4** (**a** or a **2** in 5.0) to calculate.

m. Press the Columns/Table (Alt - F7) key (Math/Columns (Alt - F7) key in 5.0 and skip step n) [Alt Layout Math Off and skip steps n and o].

n. Type an **m** or a **3** to select Math.

o. Type an **f** or a **2** (**m** or a **1** in 5.0) to turn Math off.

The special code [Math Def] marks the Math definition in the Reveal Codes screen; [=] marks where

WordPerfect will compute the total; and [*] marks where WordPerfect will compute the grand total.

EXAMPLES

1. You can add subtotals together. You can place this total in the same column as the subtotals or in a separate column to the right. If you wish to use a separate column, you must be sure the column is defined appropriately.

   You can use this feature to find the total of the salaries paid to sales representatives on the East Coast. In addition to defining the columns for the numeric entries and totals, you can define other text columns to allow for the indentation of various levels of entries.

   The first step is to define the tab settings for all of the columns. Press the Format ((Shift)-(F8)) key, and type an L [(Alt) Layout Line] and a t. Press the DEL EOL ((Ctrl)-(End)) key to clear the tab settings. Create left-aligned tab stops at 0.2", 0.4", and 0.6" (1.2", 1.4", and 1.6" in 5.0). Create decimal tab stops at 3.5" and 5.0" (4.5" and 6.0" in 5.0). The tab settings look like this:

```
..L.L.L...................................D................D.............................
     ¦      ^      ¦      ^      ¦      ¦      ^      ¦      ¦      ^      ¦      ^
   0"      +1"      +2"      +3"      +4"      +5"      +6"      +7"
Delete EOL (clear tabs); Enter Number (set tab); Del (clear tab);
Type; Left; Center; Right; Decimal; .= Dot Leader; Press Exit when done.
```

   Press the Exit ((F7)) key twice to return to the document. Next, press the Columns/Table ((Alt)-(F7)) key (Math/Columns ((Alt)-(F7)) key in 5.0), and type an **m** and **d** (**e** in 5.0) to define the Math columns [[Alt] Layout Math Define]. The Math Definition screen looks like Figure 15-3. The letters at the top represent consecutive columns in the document, not including the column at the left margin. You need to define only the columns you plan to use. The type of column is defined in the next line. As the information near the bottom of the screen explains, **1** indicates Text columns, **2** is used for Numeric columns, and **3** is used for columns containing calculated totals. If the setting for a column is incorrect, you will need to change the number under the column letter.

```
Math Definition          Use arrow keys to position cursor

Columns                  A B C D E F G H I J K L M N O P Q R S T U V W X

Type                     2 2 2 2 2 2 2 2 2 2 2 2 2 2 2 2 2 2 2 2 2 2 2 2

Negative Numbers         ( ( ( ( ( ( ( ( ( ( ( ( ( ( ( ( ( ( ( ( ( ( ( (

Number of Digits to      2 2 2 2 2 2 2 2 2 2 2 2 2 2 2 2 2 2 2 2 2 2 2 2
  the Right (0-4)

Calculation    1
  Formulas     2
               3
               4

Type of Column:
     0 = Calculation    1 = Text     2 = Numeric    3 = Total

Negative Numbers
     ( = Parentheses (50.00)        - = Minus Sign  -50.00


Press Exit when done
```

FIGURE 15-3.   Math Definition screen

The next row in the Math Definition screen defines the appearance of negative numbers. For each column, you can choose a minus sign or parentheses. The entries in the next row indicate the number of digits to be placed after the decimal point in each calculation in each column.

For the current example, the first three columns will be Text columns; type a **1** three times to make these changes. The next column will be a Numeric column. Type a **2** for this setting, or press the ➡ key if the column is already set to 2. Type **3** once to set the next column to be a Total column.

Press the ⬇ key twice, press the ⬅ key two times, and type **0** two times to eliminate decimal places in calculations in the Numeric and Total columns (D and E). Figure 15-4 shows the completed entries. Press the Exit (F7) key to accept the Math column definitions. Type an **o** (**m** in 5.0) to turn on the Math feature.

Next, type **Salary Report**, and press Enter twice. Press the Tab key, type **East Coast**, and press Enter twice. Press the Tab key twice, type **New York**, and press Enter. Press the Tab key three times, and type **Bob Jones**. Press the Tab key again, type **25,600**, and press Enter. Press the Tab key three times, type **Jane Doe**, press the Tab key again, type **26,850**, and press Enter.

Since these are the only two employees listed in the New York area, you can compute a subtotal for the salaries for New York. Press the Tab key four times, and type a **+**. WordPerfect displays the + but does not perform the calculation automatically.

```
Math Definition          Use arrow keys to position cursor

Columns                  A B C D E F G H I J K L M N O P Q R S T U V W X

Type                     1 1 1 2 3 2 2 2 2 2 2 2 2 2 2 2 2 2 2 2 2 2 2 2

Negative Numbers         ( ( ( ( ( ( ( ( ( ( ( ( ( ( ( ( ( ( ( ( ( ( ( (

Number of Digits to      2 2 2 0 0 2 2 2 2 2 2 2 2 2 2 2 2 2 2 2 2 2 2 2
   the Right (0-4)

Calculation    1
   Formulas    2
               3
               4

Type of Column:
      0 = Calculation    1 = Text    2 = Numeric    3 = Total

Negative Numbers
      ( = Parentheses (50.00)        - = Minus Sign  -50.00



Press Exit when done
```

FIGURE 15-4.   Defining math columns for text, subtotal, total, and grand total

Press the Enter key twice, press the Tab key twice, type **Washington**, and press Enter. Press the Tab key three times, type **Nancy Smith**, press the Tab key again, type **32,500**, and press Enter. Press the Tab key three times, type **Mary Marvin**, press the Tab key again, and type **24,350**.

To include the subtotal for Washington, press Enter, press the Tab key four times, and type a +.

To make WordPerfect add the subtotals, press the Enter key, press the Tab key four times, and type an =. This symbol represents the total level. Press the Columns/Table (Alt-F7) key (Math/Columns (Alt-F7) key in 5.0), and type an **m** and a **c** (a in 5.0) to have WordPerfect calculate the total [⟨Alt⟩ Layout Math Calculate]. The results look like Figure 15-5.

Use these entries in the next example.

2. You can add a grand-total level to a WordPerfect report. You can add data for the West Coast to the entries in example 1 and use the grand-total level to produce a total of the salaries in all locations.

First, press the ⟨Enter⟩ key twice to begin entering the additional data. Next, press the ⟨Tab⟩ key, type **West Coast**, and press ⟨Enter⟩ twice. Press the ⟨Tab⟩ key twice, type **California**, and press ⟨Enter⟩. Press

```
Salary Report

   East Coast

      New York
         Bob Jones          25,600
         Jane Doe           26,850
                            52,450+

      Washington
         Nancy Smith        32,500
         Mary Marvin        24,350
                            56,850+
                           109,300=
```

Math   Doc 1 Pg 1 Ln 3.17" Pos 4.5"

| FIGURE 15-5. | Using the equal sign to calculate a total |

the ⌜Tab⌟ key three times, and type **Cindy Harper**. Press the ⌜Tab⌟ key again, type **42,870**, and press ⌜Enter⌟. Press the ⌜Tab⌟ key three times, type **Jeff Parker**, press the ⌜Tab⌟ key again, type **39,700**, and press ⌜Enter⌟.

Since these are the only two employees in the California area, you can have WordPerfect calculate a subtotal for the salaries. Press the ⌜Tab⌟ key four times, type a **+**, and press the ⌜Enter⌟ key twice.

Press the ⌜Tab⌟ key twice, type **Nevada**, and press ⌜Enter⌟. Press the ⌜Tab⌟ key three times, type **Joan Carson**, press the ⌜Tab⌟ key again, type **18,750**, and press ⌜Enter⌟. Press the ⌜Tab⌟ key three times, type **Frances Drake**, press the ⌜Tab⌟ key again, type **16,500**, and press ⌜Enter⌟.

To tell WordPerfect where to place the subtotal for Nevada, press the ⌜Tab⌟ key four times, and type a **+**.

To make WordPerfect calculate a total for the two subtotals, press ⌜Enter⌟, press the ⌜Tab⌟ key four times, and type an **=**. Then, press the Columns/Table (⌜Alt⌟-⌜F7⌟) key (Math/Columns (⌜Alt⌟-⌜F7⌟) key in 5.0), and type an **m** and **c** (**a** in 5.0) [⌜Alt⌟ Layout Math Calculate]. WordPerfect calculates the subtotals for California and Nevada and a total for the West Coast.

You can have WordPerfect calculate a grand total for the East and West Coasts. Press ⌜Enter⌟ once, and press the ⌜Tab⌟ key five times. Type an ***** to mark the location of the grand total. Press the Columns/Table (⌜Alt⌟-⌜F7⌟) key (Math/Columns (⌜Alt⌟-⌜F7⌟)

key in 5.0) and type an **m** and **c** (**a** in 5.0) to make WordPerfect calculate the result [⟨Alt⟩ Layout Math Calculate]. Press the Columns/Table (⟨Alt⟩-⟨F7⟩) key (Math/Columns (⟨Alt⟩-⟨F7⟩) key in 5.0) and type an **m** and **f** (**m** in 5.0) to turn off the Math features [⟨Alt⟩ Layout Math Off]. Since WordPerfect shifted the screen display when it calculated, move the cursor toward the top of the report to see all the entries. Figure 15-6 displays the results. You can make changes to the numbers that are in the Math area, but you will need to recalculate to revise the totals.

```
New York
   Bob Jones           25,600
   Jane Doe            26,850
                       52,450+

Washington
   Nancy Smith         32,500
   Mary Marvin         24,350
                       56,850+
                      109,300=

West Coast

California
   Cindy Harper        42,870
   Jeff Parker         39,700
                       82,570+

Nevada
   Joan Carson         18,750
   Frances Drake       16,500
                       35,250+
                      117,820=
                                     227,120*
Math                                 Doc 1 Pg 1 Ln 5.5" Pos 6"
```

FIGURE 15-6.   Using the asterisk to calculate a grand total

EXERCISES

1. Set a left-justified tab at .05" (1.5" in 5.0) and a decimal tab at 4.0". Use the Math features to re-create the following information, with decimal places set to 0:

Machine repairs

Model 5210
    Factory 1   10
    Factory 2   5
Total Repairs 5210   +

Model 6511
    Factory 1   48
    Factory 2   9
Total Repairs 6511   +

TOTAL ALL MODELS   =

Calculate the subtotals and the total.

2. Set left-justified tabs at 0.3" and 0.5" (1.3" and 1.5" in 5.0) and decimal tabs at 4.5" and 5.5". Recreate the following information with the Math features:

EMPLOYEE BENEFIT PARTICIPATION
    Employees in Savings Plan
        Thrift   500
        S&L   250
        Bonds   250
    Total in Savings   +
    Employees in Stock Option Plan
        Plan A   100
        Plan B   100
    Total in Stocks   +
    Total Employees in Investment Plans =
    Employees in Medical Plan

```
        White Cross       500
        Cheap Docs        500
     Total Medical                   +
  Employees in Life Insurance Plan
        Quick Save        100
        High Risk         100
     Total Life                      +

  Total Employees in Insurance Plans   =
TOTAL NUMBERS IN BENEFIT PLANS    *
```

Have WordPerfect calculate the totals.

EXERCISES

Set the tabs and Math features, type the following information, and calculate the subtotal:

MASTERY SKILLS CHECK

HEAD COUNT BY LOCATION

```
Chicago           120
Dallas             38
Denver            105
New York          302

TOTAL                   +
```

Do not clear the screen.

2. Edit "TOTAL" to read "U.S. TOTAL." Add the following information to the list, and calculate the subtotal.

```
Paris                         82
London                       106
```

```
Lisbon                              34
Frankfurt                          192
            FOREIGN TOTAL              +
```

3. Set a left-justified tab at 0.5" (1.5" in 5.0) and a decimal tab at 4.0". Use the Math features to recreate the following information, and calculate the subtotals and total, with decimal places set to 0:

```
Product 1 Sales
    Jim                    12,500
    Fred                   38,900
    Harry                  23,500
Total Product 1                       +


Product 2 Sales
    Jim                    23,450
    Fred                   56,750
    Harry                  78,900
Total Product 2                       +

Total Products 1 & 2                  =
```

4. Set tabs and the Math features, recreate the following information, and calculate the totals:

```
Office Supplies
                           10.00
                           15.50
                           25.60
Total Supplies                        +
Office Furniture
                          345.00
                          545.00
Total Furniture                       +
Total Office Products                 =
Coffee Supplies            25.00
                           15.80
```

Total Coffee	+
Paper Products	
	115.00
Total Paper	+
Total Miscellaneous	=
TOTAL PURCHASES	*

(Do not clear the screen until you have completed the last exercise.)

INTEGRATING SKILLS CHECK

1. Type the following:

   Expenses for 1990 have risen dramatically. Please review the following figures with your managers.

   Add a header with ABC Company at the left and the date at the right. Add a footer with the page number in the middle preceded by the word "Page."

2. Type the following information below the paragraph, using the Math features. Use 3" and 4.5" left-justified tabs for the column headers and 3.5" and 5" decimal tabs for the numbers.

	Last Year	This Year
Travel	52,900	86,900
Consultants	104,585	190,800
Entertainment	3,900	9,800
Supplies	1,200	15,900
Phone	25,000	49,000
TOTALS	+	+

Calculate the totals for the two columns.

3. Turn off Math, reset the tabs, and type

    A meeting has been scheduled for June 20 to discuss emergency measures to cut costs. Please come prepared to offer your suggestions for both proven and innovative cost-cutting measures.

4. Print two copies of the document.

Drawing Lines and Boxes

►16◄

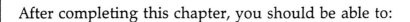

CHAPTER OBJECTIVES

After completing this chapter, you should be able to:

►	Draw a line	16.1
►	Create a box with lines	16.2
►	Erase a line	16.3
►	Move the cursor without drawing	16.4
►	Use a special character for the line	16.5
►	Add text to a box	16.6

WordPerfect's Line Draw feature allows you to add borders, lines, boxes, and graphs to your documents. You can use lines to create your own custom forms or to add a dividing line beneath a letterhead. Organizational charts and flow diagrams are easy to create with the Line Draw feature.

You can use the Line Draw feature in a blank document, or you can type text and add lines around it. WordPerfect's Esc key allows you to control the length of a line. Special characters can be used to add variety to your drawings or to create graphs with multiple data series; you can use a different character line for each data series. You can erase existing lines or move the cursor without extending the current line.

With these features, you have a full set of options for jazzing up your documents with the addition of lines and boxes. If you are using proportionally spaced text on your printer, however, line draw will not produce satisfactory results.

When you draw lines and boxes, WordPerfect uses special codes to describe the symbols. When you reveal codes, these hidden codes appear different from the other codes you have used, but they operate like other keyboard characters.

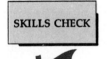

SKILLS CHECK

(Do not clear the screen until you have completed the last exercise.)

1. Create a subdirectory called ACCOUNT on the same level as WP51 (WP50 in 5.0).

2. Create a subdirectory of WP51 (WP50 in 5.0) called LETTERS.

3. Create a line of 55 asterisks with the (Esc) key.

4. On the line below the asterisks, type the following text centered, boldfaced, and underlined:

1990 Statement of Changes in Financial Position

5. Preview the printed document.

6. Block the line of asterisks, and reposition it below the centered text.

DRAW A LINE

16.1

You can draw single or double lines with a simple WordPerfect menu option. The Line Draw feature provides you the means to develop your own set of forms, to which you, can add text. Depending on which direction you move the cursor, you can create lines vertically and horizontally.

To draw a line:

a. Place the cursor where you want the line to start.

b. Press the Screen ((Ctrl)-(F3)) key [(Alt) Tools Line Draw and skip step c].

c. Type an **L** or a **2** to select Line Draw.

d. Type a **1** to draw a single line or a **2** to draw a double line.

e. Move the cursor to where you want the line to end.

f. Press the Exit (F7) key.

An alternative method is

a. Place the cursor where you want the line to start.

b. Press the Screen (Ctrl-F3) key [Alt Tools Line Draw and skip step c].

c. Type an **L** or a **2** to select Line Draw.

d. Type a **1** to draw a single line or a **2** to draw a double line.

e. Press Esc.

f. Type the number of spaces or lines through which you want the drawn line to extend.

g. Press the ↑, ↓, ←, or → key to provide the direction in which the line should be drawn.

h. Press the Exit (F7) key.

As' you move the cursor, WordPerfect draws the line. The arrows that appear on the screen will not be printed. As you draw the line, WordPerfect inserts spaces and hard returns where appropriate to make the line fit the document format.

EXAMPLES

1. You can use vertical lines to set off lines of text. First, type

When you use the drill, remember to:

Next, press (Enter) to move to the next line. Press the
Screen ((Ctrl)-(F3)) key, then, type an L [(Alt) Tools
Line Draw] and a **2**. Press the (↓) key 3 times. This
creates a double line with an arrow at the top and
bottom.

Next, press the Exit ((F7)) key. The screen looks
like this:

When you use the drill, remember to:
↑

|

↓

You can type text to be set off from the vertical line.
Press the (↑) key twice and the (→) key once to
place the cursor next to the first double-line character. Press the SPACEBAR, and type

Wear safety goggles and gloves.

Since WordPerfect inserted a hard return for each
line in which the double line was drawn, you do
not need to press (Enter). Instead, press the (↓) key.
Press the SPACEBAR, and type

Unplug the drill before changing bits.

The screen now looks like this:

When you use the drill, remember to:
↑
| Wear safety goggles and gloves.
| Unplug the drill before changing bits.
↓

When you preview the document at 100% by pressing the Print (⟮Shift⟯-⟮F7⟯) key [⟮Alt⟯ File Print] and typing a **v** and a **1**, the screen looks like this:

```
When you use the drill, remember to:

Wear safety goggles and gloves.
Unplug the drill before changing bits.
```

The actual characters that WordPerfect uses for the lines depend upon your printer.

2. You can use horizontal lines to set off text. First, type

When you use the drill, remember to:

Press ⟮Enter⟯ to move to the next line. Press the Screen (⟮Ctrl⟯-⟮F3⟯) key, and type an **L** [⟮Alt⟯ Tools Line Draw] and a **1**. Press ⟮Esc⟯, type a **5**, and press the ⟮→⟯ key to draw a line 4 characters long with arrows at both ends. Exit from the Line Draw by pressing the Exit (⟮F7⟯) key. The screen looks like this:

```
When you use the drill, remember to:
←——→
```

You can type the first line of text next to this line. Press the ⟮→⟯ key, and type

Wear safety goggles and gloves.

Then, press ⟮Enter⟯ to move to the next line.

   To draw the next line, press the Screen (⟮Ctrl⟯-⟮F3⟯) key, and type an **L** [⟮Alt⟯ Tools Line Draw].

Since WordPerfect retains the last selection from this menu, you do not have to select the type of line you want to draw. Press ⌷Esc⌷, type a **5**, and press the ➔ key. To finish the line drawing, press the Exit (⌷F7⌷) key. Press the ➔ key, and type

Unplug the drill before changing bits.

The screen appears as follows.

```
When you use the drill, remember to:
←——→Wear safety goggles and gloves,
←——→Unplug the drill before changing bits,
```

EXERCISES

1. Type the first paragraph below. Draw a horizontal double line 40 characters long, and type the second paragraph.

   The new accounting system assigns each account a number. The numbers prevent confusion among accounts with similar names but different purposes.
   This change will improve internal control. It should prevent debits and credits to the miscellaneous account that belong in another account.

2. Draw a single line that extends 3 rows down. Then draw a double line 6 characters across. Draw another double line that extends 5 rows down. Preview how WordPerfect will print the lines at 100% and 200%.

16.2 | CREATE A BOX WITH LINES

You can create a box with a series of four connecting lines. The secret to creating boxes with same-length lines on opposite sides is to use the [Esc] key to draw the lines that make up the sides of the box. Word-Perfect automatically adds corners to your boxes as you change directions. Text to the right of the cursor is pushed ahead to make room for the box. Word-Perfect inserts spaces and hard returns to fill blank areas.

To draw a box:

a. Place the cursor where you want the box's upper left-hand corner to appear.

b. Press the Screen ([Ctrl]-[F3]) key [[Alt] Tools Line Draw and skip step c].

c. Type an **L** or a **2** to select Line Draw.

d. Type a **1** to draw a single line or a **2** to draw a double line.

e. Press [Esc], type the number of rows through which the box will extend, and press the [↓] key.

f. Press [Esc], type the number of spaces across which the box will extend, and press the [→] key.

g. Press [Esc], type the number you typed in step e, and press the [↑] key.

h. Press [Esc], type the number you typed in step f, and press the [←] key.

i. Press the Exit ([F7]) key.

EXAMPLES

1. You can use boxes to show where information should be provided in a form. First, type

   Total amount remitted:

   Next, press the Screen (⌷Ctrl⌷-⌷F3⌷) key, and type an L [⌷Alt⌷ Tools Line Draw] and a 1. Then, press ⌷Esc⌷, type a 3, and press the ⌷↓⌷ key. Create the bottom line of the box by pressing ⌷Esc⌷, typing 10, and pressing the ⌷→⌷ key.

   To create the right side of the box, press ⌷Esc⌷, type a 3, and press the ⌷↑⌷ key.

   Complete the box by pressing ⌷Esc⌷, typing 10, and pressing the ⌷←⌷ key. Press the Exit (⌷F7⌷) key. The screen looks like this:

   Total amount remitted:

2. You can combine lines and boxes to create a blank organizational chart. First, type

   Organization Chart

   Press ⌷Enter⌷ to move to the next line, and press ⌷Tab⌷ four times.

   To begin drawing the first box, press the Screen (⌷Ctrl⌷-⌷F3⌷) key, type an L [⌷Alt⌷ Tools Line Draw] and a 2, and press the ⌷↓⌷ key 3 times. To draw the bottom of the box, press the ⌷Esc⌷ key, type 15, and press the ⌷→⌷ key. For the right side of the box, press the ⌷↑⌷ key 3 times. To complete the box, press the ⌷Esc⌷ key, type 15, press the ⌷←⌷ key, and press the Exit (⌷F7⌷) key.

To create a second box, you can block and copy the first one. First, press the ⊥ 3 times, End once, and Enter twice to move below the box. Next, press the ↑ key 5 times and Ctrl-→ to move to the upper left-hand corner of the box. Press the Block (Alt - F4) key [Alt Edit Block], the ⊥ key 3 times, and End once. Then, press the Move (Ctrl - F4) key and type an r [Alt Edit Select Rectangle].

As the highlight shows, blocking a rectangle affects only the area between the cursor's first and last position. When you move, copy, or delete a rectangle, WordPerfect ignores the text or other material that is on the same line as any line of the block but not within the rectangle. Type a c for Copy. Press the ⊥ key twice and Enter once to place the copy of the box below and to the left of the original.

To draw the third box, press End once and Tab 5 times to move to the box's location. Press the Move (Ctrl - F4) key [Alt Edit Paste] and type an r twice for Retrieve and Rectangle. The screen looks like Figure 16-1.

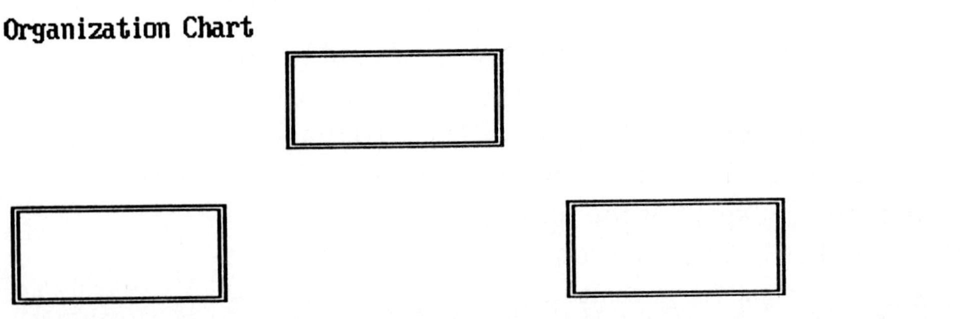

Organization Chart

FIGURE 16-1.   Boxes for an organizational chart

Organization Chart

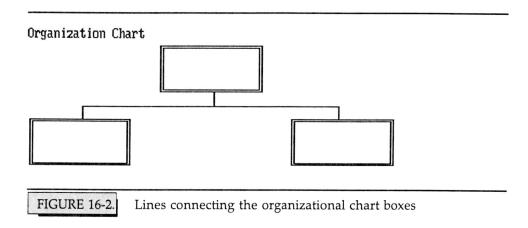

FIGURE 16-2.   Lines connecting the organizational chart boxes

To draw the connecting lines, press (Esc), type a 7, and press the (→) key to move to the middle of the box that you just drew. Next, press the Screen ((Ctrl)-(F3)) key, and type an L [(Alt) Tools Line Draw] and a 1. Press the (↑) key once to draw a line leading up from the box on the right. Press (Esc), type **39**, and press the (←) key to draw a line to the box on the left. Press the (↓) key to connect the line to the box and the Exit ((F7)) key to complete the line drawing.

Next, press the (↑) key, press (Esc), type **20**, and press the (→) key to move to the middle of the line that you created. Then, press the Screen ((Ctrl)-(F3)) key, type an L [(Alt) Tools Line Draw], press the (↑) key to connect all three boxes, and press the Exit ((F7)) key. The organizational chart looks like Figure 16-2.

EXERCISES

1. Create a form that asks for a person's first name and last name. For each place the form prompts for information, create a box to contain the information.

2. Using boxes 5 rows deep and 14 columns wide, draw boxes and lines for a flow chart that looks like this:

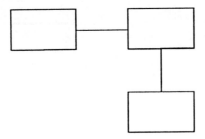

16.3   ERASE A LINE

WordPerfect's erase option in the Line Draw menu lets you correct mistakes without starting over. As you move the cursor over a line, WordPerfect erases that part of the line. You can use this option to shorten or remove a line. WordPerfect adjusts spaces and hard returns to maintain the remaining portions of the line.

To erase a line:

a. Move the cursor to the end or beginning of the part of the line you want to erase.

b. Press the Screen (Ctrl-F3) key [Alt Tools Line Draw and skip step c].

c. Type an L for Line Draw.

d. Type a **5**.

e. Move the cursor along the part of the line you want to erase.

f. Press the Exit (F7) key.

Since WordPerfect erases every character over which you move the cursor when you erase lines, do not move the cursor over part of a line that you want to keep. If you want to move to another line to erase, press the Exit (F7) key first so that you can move the cursor without changing the drawing. You can also erase lines and boxes by pressing Del or typing spaces in Typeover mode.

EXAMPLES

1. You can use the erase option when you have drawn a line incorrectly. First, press the Screen (Ctrl-F3) key, type an L [Alt Tools Line Draw] and a 1, press Esc, type **20**, press the → key, and press the Exit (F7) key.

   To erase part of the end of the line, press the Screen (Ctrl-F3) key, type an L [Alt Tools Line Draw] and a 5, press the ← key twice, and press the Exit (F7) key. You have shortened the line by two characters.

2. You can erase part of a line from the middle. First, press the Screen (Ctrl-F3) key, type an L [Alt Tools Line Draw] and a 1, press Esc, type **12**, press the → key, and press the Exit (F7) key.

Next, press the ← key 6 times to move the cursor to the middle of the line. Then, press the Screen (Ctrl-F3) key, type an L [Alt Tools Line Draw] and a 5, press the → key 3 times, and press the Exit (F7) key. The line now looks like this:

←——→ ←→

3. You can use the Line Draw feature to create boxes representing an office layout and erase part of a box to represent a door between rooms. First, label the drawing by typing

Office Layout

Next, press Enter to move to the next line, press the Screen (Ctrl-F3) key, and type an L [Alt Tools Line Draw] and a 1. To draw the first room, press Esc, type a 4, press the ↓ key, press Esc, type 20, press the → key, press Esc, type a 4, press the ↑ key, press Esc, type 20, press the ← key, and press the Exit (F7) key.

For the second room, press Esc, type a 4, and press the ↓ key. Then, press the Screen (Ctrl-F3) key, type an L [Alt Tools Line Draw] and a 1, press Esc, type an 8, press the ↓ key, press Esc, type 10, press the → key, press Esc, type an 8, and press the ↑ key.

For the third room, press Esc, type an 8, press the ↓ key, press Esc, type 10, press the → key, press Esc, type 8, press the ↑ key, and press the Exit (F7) key. The screen looks like Figure 16-3.

To move to the entrance, press the ↑ key 4 times, press Esc, type 11, and press the ← key. To mark the door, press the Screen (Ctrl-F3) key and

Office Layout

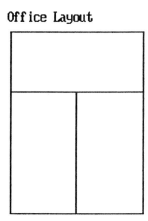

FIGURE 16-3.   Office layout with three rooms

type an **L** [Alt Tools Line Draw] and a **5**, and press
the → key twice.

To move to the next door without drawing or
erasing, press the Exit (F7) key, press the ↓ key
4 times, and press the ← key 7 times. To indicate
the door, press the Screen (Ctrl - F3) key, type an **L**
[Alt Tools Line Draw], and press the → key twice.

To erase the lines for the last door, type a **1** so
that WordPerfect draws a line where you move the
cursor. Next, press Esc , type a **9**, and press the →
key. Then, type a **5** to erase the line, and press the
→ key twice. Press the Exit (F7) key. The screen
looks like Figure 16-4.

EXERCISES

1. Draw a double line 6 characters across. Erase the
   line.

Office Layout

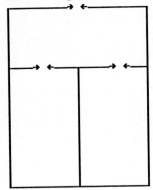

| FIGURE 16-4. | Using the erase option to show doors in the office layout |

2. Create a single-line box that is 5 characters across and 4 rows deep. Erase the middle character in the top and the bottom of the box to split the box in half.

16.4 MOVE THE CURSOR WITHOUT DRAWING

Entering multiple unconnected lines on the screen requires a method for moving the cursor without extending the lines. WordPerfect's Line Draw feature provides a menu option to support cursor movement without line creation.

To move the cursor without drawing (or erasing):

a. Press the Screen (Ctrl-F3) key [Alt Tools Line Draw and skip step b].

b. Type an **L** or a **2** for Line Draw.

c. Draw the first line.

d. Type a **6**.

e. Place the cursor where you want to draw another line.

f. Type a **1** or **2** to draw another line.

WordPerfect adds the necessary spaces and hard returns to allow you to move in a straight direction.

EXAMPLES

1. You can move the cursor around in a document to shorten the steps you must perform when you draw multiple lines. First, type the following lines, pressing [Enter] once after "Name" and "Phone" and twice after "Address":

   ```
     Name:
   Address:
    Phone:
   ```

   To draw a line after each entry, press the [↑] key and [End] to move to the end of the "Phone" line. Next, press the Screen ([Ctrl]-[F3]) key, and type an L [[Alt] Tools Line Draw] and a 1. Press [Esc], type **30**, and press the [→] key. Instead of pressing the Exit ([F7]) key to move to the second "Address" line, type a **6**, and press the [↑] key. WordPerfect automatically inserts spaces at the beginning of the second "Address" line so that you can move up in a straight line.

To draw the line for the second line of the address, type a **1**, press (Esc), type **30**, and press the ⬅ key.

Move to the first "Address" line by typing a **6** and pressing the ⬆ key. To draw the line for the first line of the address, type a **1**, press (Esc), type **30**, and press the ⬅ key.

Move to the "Name" line by typing a **6** and pressing the ⬆ key. To draw the line for the name, type a **1**, press (Esc), type **30**, and press the ➡ key. Press the Exit ((F7)) key. The result looks like this:

```
Name:←————————————————————→
Address:←————————————————————→
         ←————————————————————→
Phone:←————————————————————→
```

2. You can draw a competition list using WordPerfect. For this type of list, some of the lines connect and others do not. To draw the lines for the first set of competitors, press the Screen ((Ctrl)-(F3)) key, type an **L** [(Alt) Tools Line Draw] and a **1**, press (Esc), type **20**, press the ➡ key, press the ⬇ key twice, press (Esc), type **20**, and press the ⬅ key. The screen looks like this:

To draw the lines for other competitors, type a **6**, press the ⬇ key twice, type a **1** to resume line drawing, press (Esc), type **20**, press the ➡ key, press the ⬇ key twice, press (Esc), type **20**, and press the ⬅ key.

Next, draw lines for the finals. First, type a **6**, press the ⬆ key, press (Esc), type **20**, and press the ➡ key to move the cursor to the vertical line. Then, type a **1** to resume line drawing, press (Esc), type **20**, and press the ➡ key. Next, press (Esc), type a **4**, and press the ⬆ key. Press (Esc) again, type **20**, and press the ⬅ key.

To draw a line for the winner, first type a **6**, press the ⬇ key twice, and press the ➡ key until the cursor is at the vertical line. Then, type a **1** to resume line drawing, press (Esc), type **20**, and press the ➡ key. Press the Exit ((F7)) key. The drawing looks like Figure 16-5.

EXERCISES

1. Create a double-line box that is 4 rows deep and 15 characters across. Move 5 spaces beyond the right edge of the box, and create a box that is 2 rows deep and 12 characters across.

2. Make three "I"s using the Line Draw feature. The "I"s should be 10 rows high and 10 characters wide and be 10 characters apart from each other.

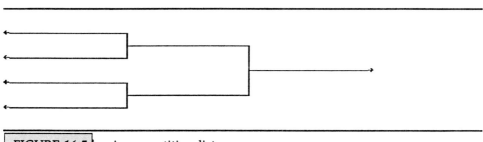

FIGURE 16-5.   A competition list

| 16.5 | USE A SPECIAL CHARACTER FOR THE LINE |

You can draw lines with any character you choose. WordPerfect's default Line Draw menu offers the asterisk (*) as an option for drawing lines when you choose characters other than a single or double line. You can change the setting for this character and draw lines with any character of your choice.

To use the special character to draw a line:

a. Place the cursor where you want the line to start.

b. Press the Screen (Ctrl-F3) key [Alt Tools Line Draw and skip step c].

c. Type an **L** or a **2** to select Line Draw.

d. Type a **3** to draw with the displayed special character.

e. Move the cursor to where you want the line to end, or press Esc, type the number of times you want the special character, and press an arrow key to indicate in which direction to draw the line.

f. Repeat step e for every line you want.

g. Press the Exit (F7) key.

To change the special character:

a. Place the cursor where you want to start drawing with the special character.

b. Press the Screen (Ctrl-F3) key [Alt Tools Line Draw and skip step c].

c. Type an **L** or a **2** to select Line Draw.

d. Type a **c** or a **4** to change the special character.

e. Type the number representing the special character you want or an **o** or a **9** if the one you want is not displayed.

f. Type the character that you want if you typed **9** in step e.

g. Draw your lines with the special character.

EXAMPLES

1. You can create a box of asterisks. First, press the Screen ([Ctrl]-[F3]) key, and type an L [[Alt] Tools Line Draw] and a **3**. Next, press the [↓] key 3 times, the [→] key 4 times, the [↑] key 3 times, and the [←] key 3 times. Finally, press the Exit ([F7]) key. The box looks like this:

```
*****
*   *
*   *
*****
```

2. You can change the special character to a shaded pattern. First, press the Screen ([Ctrl]-[F3]) key and type an L [[Alt] Tools Line Draw] and a **4**. Then, type a **1** to select the character indicated by that number.

3. You can use the special character you have just selected to create a gray box. First, press the Screen ([Ctrl]-[F3]) key, and type an L [[Alt] Tools Line Draw] and a **3**.

Next, press the ⬇ key twice, the ➡ key 7 times, the ⬆ key twice, and the ⬅ key 6 times. Finally, press the Exit (F7) key. The box looks like this:

EXERCISES

1. Set the special character to the number sign (#). Create a box 10 lines deep and 20 characters wide.

2. Set the special character to the solid rectangle (▮). Draw a line 30 characters long.

16.6 | ADD TEXT TO A BOX

If you create organizational charts or flow diagrams, you will need to place text inside your boxes. You can create the text first and draw boxes around the text, or you can draw the box first and add the text. To add text to an existing box, you need to use the Ins key to set WordPerfect to Typeover mode. If you used Insert mode, you would distort the box when you added the text.

To insert text in a box:

a. Press the Ins key.

b. Place the cursor inside the box in which you want to include text.

c. Type the text.

d. Press the [Ins] key.

EXAMPLES

1. You can put text in boxes to set off the text. First, start Line Draw by pressing the Screen ([Ctrl]-[F3]) key and typing an L [[Alt] Tools Line Draw] and a 2. Next, press [Esc], type a 3, press the [↓] key, press [Esc], type 35, press the [→] key, press [Esc], type 3, press the [↑] key, press [Esc], type 35, and press the [←] key. Then, press the Exit ([F7]) key.

   Next, press the [Ins] key, press the [↓] key, press the [→] key twice, and type

   Bill must be paid by August 20th

   For the next line of text, press the [↓] key, [Ctrl]-[←] key combination, and the [→] key twice, and type

   To prevent a late payment penalty

   The final block looks like this:

   ```
   ┌─────────────────────────────┐
   │ Bill must be paid by August 20th │
   │ To prevent a late payment penalty │
   └─────────────────────────────┘
   ```

2. You can use the text and line drawings to create an organizational chart. First, create a box at the top for the president. Press the Screen ([Ctrl]-[F3]) key and type an L [[Alt] Tools Line Draw] and a 2. Then, press [Esc], type a 3, press the [↓] key, press [Esc], type 25, press the [→] key, press [Esc], type a 3, press the [↑] key, press [Esc], type 25, and press the [←] key.

To create a box for the first person who reports to the president, type a **6**, and press ⬇ key 6 times. Then, type a **2**, press (Esc), type a **3**, and press the ⬇ key. Press (Esc) again, type **20**, and press the ➡ key, press (Esc), type a **3**, and press the ⬆ key. To complete the box, press (Esc), type **20**, and press the ⬅ key.

To create a box for the second person who reports to the president, you can copy the box for the first one. First, press the Exit ((F7)) key to end Line Draw. Next, press the Block ((Alt)-(F4)) key [(Alt) Edit Block], the ⬇ key 3 times, and (End). Then, press the Move ((Ctrl)-(F4)) key and type an **r** [(Alt) Edit Select Rectangle] and a **c**. Next, press the ⬆ key 3 times, and press (End) and (Enter) to place the copy of the box next to the original.

To create a box for the third person who reports to the president, press the Move ((Ctrl)-(F4)) key, press an **r** for retrieve [(Alt) Edit Paste] and type an **r** for rectangle.

You can center the president's box with Word-Perfect's Center features. Press (Home) twice, and the ⬆ key once.

Then, press the Block ((Alt)-(F4)) [(Alt) Edit Block] key and the ⬇ key 4 times to highlight the entire box. Press the Center ((Shift)-(F6)) key [(Alt) Layout Align Center], and type a **y**. The screen looks like Figure 16-6.

Once you have created the boxes, you can draw lines between them. First, move the cursor to the bottom left hand corner of the top box. Press (Esc), type **13**, and press the ➡ key to move to the middle of the bottom line of the top box. Then, press the

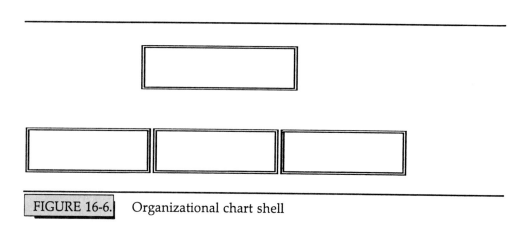

Organizational chart shell

Screen (Ctrl-F3) key, and type an **L** [Alt Tools Line Draw] and a **1**. To draw the first line, press the ↓ key 3 times. To draw the second line, type a **6**, and press the ↑ key twice. Then, press Esc, type **22**, and press the ← key. Press the ↓ key twice. Next, type a **1**, press the ↑ twice, press Esc, type **44**, and press the → key. Then, press the ↓ key twice. Since this completes the line drawings, press the Exit (F7) key. The screen looks like Figure 16-7.

Now you can add text to the boxes. First, press the

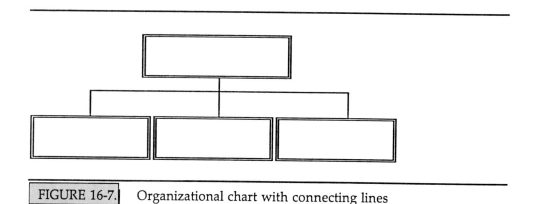

FIGURE 16-7.   Organizational chart with connecting lines

[Ins] key to switch to Typeover mode, and move to the top box by pressing the [↑] key 5 times, the [Ctrl]-[←] key combination twice, and the [→] key 7 times. Then, type **Paula Stevens**, press the [Ctrl]-[←] key combination twice and the [↓] key once, and type **President**.

Next, press the [↓] key 5 times, the [Ctrl]-[←] key combination twice, and the [→] key 5 times to move to the first box in the second row. Type **Tom Packard**, press the [Ctrl]-[←] key combination twice, press the [↓] key, and type **Marketing**.

Next, press the [Ctrl]-[→] key combination, the [↑] key, and the [→] key 6 times to move to the next box. Type **Sue Kegley**, press the [Ctrl]-[←] key combination twice, press the [↓] key, and type **Controller**.

Next, press the [Ctrl]-[→] key combination, the [↑] key, and the [→] key 5 times to move to the last box. Type **George Adams**, press the [Ctrl]-[←] key combination twice, press the [↓] key, and type **Production**.The final organizational chart looks like Figure 16-8,

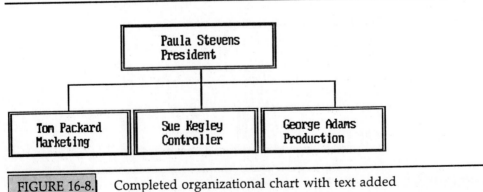

FIGURE 16-8.   Completed organizational chart with text added

3. You can add the boxes after you type the text. You can use this feature to create, for example, a diagram of subdirectories, such as a diagram of a root directory containing the WP51 subdirectory and an ACCOUNT subdirectory. The WP51 subdirectory has its own subdirectory, called LETTERS. First, press (Enter) three times to create space to draw the boxes later. Then, press (Tab) 4 times, and type **Root Directory**. Next, press (Enter) 4 times, press (Tab), type **WP51**, press (Tab) 8 times, and type **ACCOUNT**. Then press (Enter) 3 times, press (Tab), type **LETTERS**, and press (Enter).

To draw a box for the root directory, press (Esc), type a **9**, press the (↑) key, and press (Tab) 3 times. Then, press the Screen ((Ctrl)-(F3)) key, and type an **L** [(Alt) Tools Line Draw] and a **2**, press the (↓) key twice, press (Esc), type **23**, and press the (→) key. To complete the box, press the (↑) key twice, press (Esc), type **23**, and press the (←) key. The "y" in "directory" may temporarily disappear, but it will reappear as you work on the document.

To draw the box for the WordPerfect subdirectory, type a **6**, and press the (↓) key 4 times. Type a **2**, press (Esc), type **15**, press the (←) key, press the (↓) key twice, press (Esc), type **15**, and press the (→) key. To complete the box, press the (↑) key twice.

To draw the box for the ACCOUNT subdirectory, type a **6**, press (Esc), type **26**, and press the (→) key. Then, type a **2**, press the (↓) key twice, press (Esc) type **15**, press the (→) key, press the (↑) key twice, press (Esc), type **15**, and press the (←) key.

To draw the box for the LETTERS subdirectory, type a **6**, press the (↓) key 3 times, press (Esc), type

50, press the ⏎ key, and type a **2**. Then, press the ↓ key twice, press Esc, type **15**, press the → key, press the ↑ key twice, press Esc, type **15**, and press the ⏎ key. Some letters may temporarily disappear, but they will reappear when you move the cursor. The screen looks like Figure 16-9.

Once you have drawn the boxes, you can draw lines to connect them. First, type a **6**, press Esc, type an **8**, press the → key, type a **1** and press the ↑ key. Next, type a **6**, press the ↑ key twice, type a **1**, press the ↑ key, press Esc, type **40**, press the → key, and press the ↓ key to connect the WordPerfect and ACCOUNT subdirectories. To connect the root directory to the subdirectories, press the ↑ key, press Esc, type **20**, press the ⏎

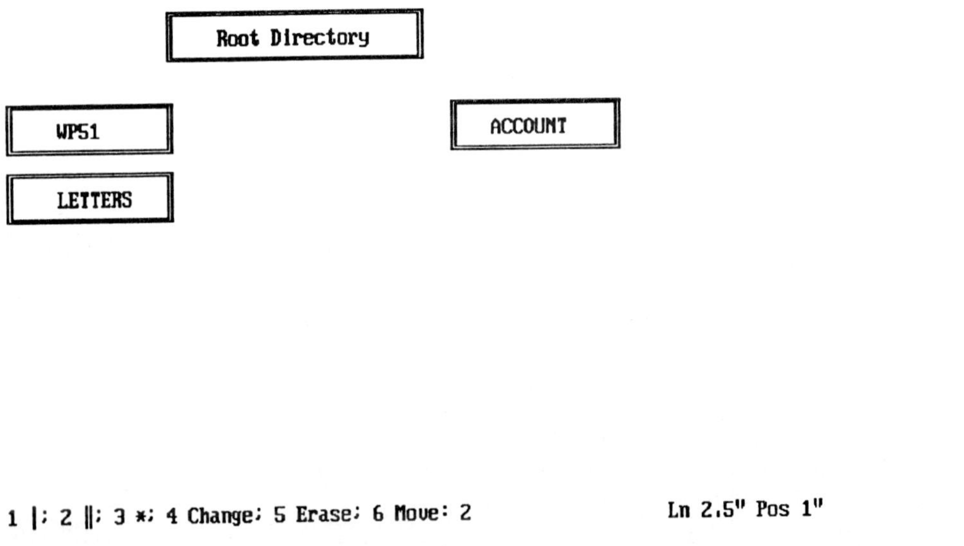

```
              ┌─────────────────┐
              │  Root Directory │
              └─────────────────┘

┌──────────────┐              ┌──────────────┐
│    WP51      │              │   ACCOUNT    │
└──────────────┘              └──────────────┘
┌──────────────┐
│   LETTERS    │
└──────────────┘
```

1 |: 2 ‖: 3 ∗: 4 Change: 5 Erase: 6 Move: 2   Ln 2.5" Pos 1"

FIGURE 16-9.   Boxes added around text

key, and press the ⬆ key. Since this completes the diagram, press the Exit (F7) key. The screen looks like Figure 16-10.

4. You can combine text, lines, and boxes to create a graph like the one shown in Figure 16-11. First, insert blank lines at the top of the screen by pressing Enter 3 times and pressing the SPACEBAR 8 times to leave blank space at the left. Next, press the Screen (Ctrl-F3) key, and type a 2 [Alt Tools Line Draw] for Line Draw. Select a single line by typing a **1**, and press Esc, type **18**, and press the ⬇ key. Press Esc, type **55**, and press the ➡ key to complete the axes for the graph.

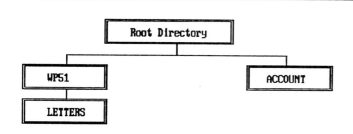

Doc 1 Pg 1 Ln 1.67" Pos 3.8"

FIGURE 16-10.   Completed diagram of subdirectories

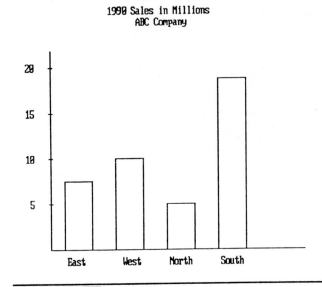

1998 Sales in Millions
ABC Company

FIGURE 16-11.   A bar chart

Type a **6**, and press (Esc), type **55**, and press (←) to move to the intersection of the axes, and press the (→) key 3 times. Type a **1**, and begin drawing the first bar by pressing the (↑) 6 times. Then, press the (→) key 6 times and press the (↓) key 6 times to rejoin the horizontal axis.

To draw the second bar, press the (→) key 5 times, the (↑) key 8 times, the (→) key 6 times, and the (↓) key 8 times. To draw the third bar, press the (→) key 5 times, the (↑) key 4 times, the (→) key 6 times, and the (↓) key 4 times. To draw the fourth bar, press the (→) key 5 times, press (Esc), type **15**, press the (↑) key, press the (→) key 6 times, press (Esc), type **15**, and press the (↓) key.

Next, draw the tick marks on the vertical axis. Press Esc, type **42**, and press ←. Type a **6**, press the ← key, press the ↑ key 4 times, type a **1**, and press the → key twice to draw the first tick mark. To create the next tick mark, type a **6**, press the ↑ key 4 times, type a **1**, and press the ← key twice. For the next tick mark, type a **6**, press the ↑ key 4 times, type a **1**, and press the → key twice. To create the last tick mark, type a **6**, press the ↑ key 4 times, type a **1**, and press the ← key twice. Press the Exit (F7) key to end Line Draw. Each tick mark on the screen looks like a short arrow with an arrowhead at both ends.

To label the tick marks, you must be in Typeover mode. Press the Ins key if **Typeover** is not displayed in the status line, press the ← key 4 times, and type a **20**. For the next tick mark down, press the ↓ key 4 times, press the ← key twice, and type **15**. For the next tick mark, press the ↓ key 4 times, press the ← key twice, and type **10**. For the last tick mark, press the ↓ key 4 times, press the ← key once, and then type a **5**.

To add the labels for the horizontal axis, press the ↓ key 4 times, press End and Enter, then the SPACEBAR 12 times, type **East**, press the SPACEBAR 7 times, type **West**, press the SPACEBAR 7 times, type **North**, press the SPACEBAR 6 times, and type **South**. Move to the top by pressing Home twice and the ↑ key once. Then, press the Center (Shift-F6) key [Alt Layout Align Center], type **1990 Sales in Millions**, and press Enter.

Press the Center (Shift-F6) key [Alt Layout Align Center] again and type **ABC Company**.

When the graph is completed, your screen looks like Figure 16-12.

Although the arrowheads do not appear on the printed graph, their positions are marked by a slight deviation in the straightness of the line on most printers.

You can erase the deviations by replacing the arrows with spaces. First, press the [Ins] key to switch to the Typeover mode if **Typeover** is not displayed in the status line. For each of the arrows you want to remove, move the cursor to an arrow and press the SPACEBAR. When you have removed all the arrows, press the [Ins] key to return to the Insert mode.

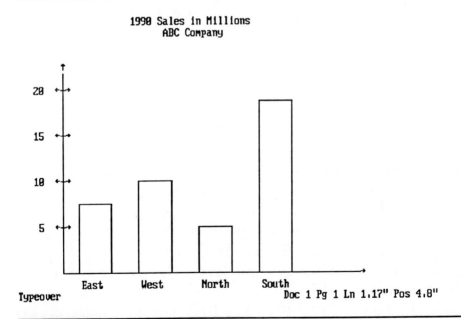

FIGURE 16-12.   A bar chart with lines

EXERCISES

1. Create a subdirectory diagram with three subdirectories under the root directory. Name them BUDGET, PRODUCT, and REPORTS.

2. Create a single-line box that is 50 characters across and 4 rows deep. Type the following text inside the box:

   All of the paintings displayed in this restaurant are for sale on a consignment basis. For more details, see the manager.

EXERCISES

(Do not clear the screen between exercises unless instructed to do so.)

1. Create a single line 40 characters across. Move 20 spaces to the left in the line, and erase the 3 characters to the right. Clear the screen.

2. Create this flow chart:

Clear the screen.

3. Change the special character to colons.

4. Create the following line diagram. Insert a blank line above the diagram, and press ⟨Enter⟩ twice before typing each line of text.

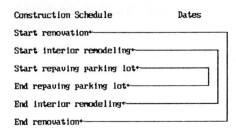

5. Delete the portion of the lines under the "Dates" heading. Then, insert the following dates:

Start renovation	5/1
Start interior remodeling	6/15
Start repaving parking lot	7/1
End repaving parking lot	7/31
End interior remodeling	8/30
End renovation	9/30

6. Draw a box of colon characters around the diagram.

INTEGRATING SKILLS CHECK

1. Create a form for the entry of the following information. After each item, draw a box large enough to contain the information.

Last name:
First name:
Department:
Years with the company:

2. Type the following lines of text:

Acme's Main Product Line
————————————————————
Solder
Silver necklaces
Silver flatware

Add lines that connect the items to the heading "Acme's Main Product Line."

3. Remove the ACCOUNT subdirectory that you created in the Skills Check.

4. Remove the LETTERS subdirectory that you created in the Skills Check.

5. Return the special character for line drawing to asterisks. Create a box 10 lines by 50 characters, and put the following text inside it:

  Clark Corporation is Moving
On Friday the 23rd, Clark Corporation is
closing its Lakewood offices. Its new
headquarters are in Barlow, Florida. It is
moving there to be closer to its prospering
land-development subsidiary.

6. Center the box and the text inside.

WordPerfect's
Graphics Features

▶17◀

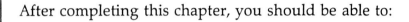

CHAPTER OBJECTIVES

After completing this chapter, you should be able to:

▶ Create a graphics box   17.1

▶ Place text in a box   17.2

▶ Place a figure in a box   17.3

▶ Add a caption   17.4

▶ Position and size a box   17.5

▶ Edit and delete graphics boxes   17.6

▶ Print documents containing graphics   17.7

WordPerfect provides exciting features that allow you to combine text and graphics in a single document. You can use these features to create newsletters, letterheads, customized forms, and other special documents that convey your message with both text and graphics.

You can incorporate graphic images created with computer-aided design (CAD) systems as line drawings and use pictures created with draw packages. If you would prefer not to create the images, third-party developers sell diskettes containing a variety of graphic images. WordPerfect provides a number of sample graphics files that you can use to try out the techniques presented in this chapter.

WordPerfect also enables you to add graphics boxes to a document and display text within the box. Objectives, quotations, sidebars, and other textual materials can be set off from the main text using this method.

WordPerfect 5.1 also has an advanced equations editor that allows you to create complex equations. The equations editor graphics feature is not covered here, but is a feature you may want to look at further if you plan to produce documents that contain equations.

The full set of graphics features offered by this package will require some time to explore. In this chapter, you will be introduced to the basic options to get you started using these exciting new features. Even these basic options will require a little more time to master than some of the other topics in this book. You will find the time investment worthwhile if you want to create professional-looking documents that include text and graphics.

(Do not clear the screen until you have completed the last exercise.)

SKILLS CHECK

1. Type the following paragraph:

   The objective of this chapter is to learn how to incorporate graphics boxes into your document. You will learn how to create these boxes and use options to fill the boxes with images or text. WordPerfect also allows you to create captions for the boxes to provide labels and titles. These boxes can be moved and deleted.

   Underline **objective of this chapter**. Save the document as GRAPHBOX.

2. Switch to the second document. Retrieve GRAPH-BOX, and add the following paragraph:

   Once your document is complete, you can print it. Many printers can print text and graphics simultaneously.

3. Create a header that says **WordPerfect's Graphics Features**.

4. Boldface the words "captions," "labels," and "titles."

5. Preview document 2. Preview document 1.

CREATE A GRAPHICS BOX

17.1

Before you can add a graphics image to a document, you must create a box. Once the box is created, you can access disk files to obtain the text or graphics data to be shown in the box. Graphics boxes are like footnotes in that WordPerfect numbers them in their order of appearance and renumbers them as necessary when boxes are added, deleted, or moved. Graphics boxes can be placed anywhere in a document, including in headers and footers. Once you create a graphics box, you can view how WordPerfect will print it by previewing the page if your monitor and printer support graphics.

To add a graphics box:

a. Press the Graphics ([Alt]-[F9]) key [[Alt] Graphics].

b. Type the option number or letter for the type of box that you want. [Select the type of graphics box, for example, Figure.]

c. Type a **c** or a **1** to create the box [Create].

d. Define or change features of the box, as necessary.

e. Press the Exit ([F7]) key or [Enter] to return to the document.

WordPerfect has five box types: Figure, Table, Text Box, User-Defined Box, and Equation. (Another graphics option, Line, is not used for graphics boxes.) The box type that you select does not affect what can be stored in the box. The differences among the box types are the separate numbering sequences that each type uses and the default settings for each type; these are described in Table 17-1. When you create a graphics box, WordPerfect draws a box on the screen indicating where it will place the graphics box. WordPerfect's default settings keep the document text from overlaying the contents of the box. If WordPerfect cannot fit the entire graphics box on the current page, it moves the box to the next page.

| TABLE 17-1. | Default Settings for Graphics Boxes |

Graphics Box Type	Figure	Table	Text Box	User-Defined Box	Equations Box
Initial caption	Figure #	Table #	#	#	None
Caption position	Below box, outside border	Above box, outside border	Below box, outside border	Below box, outside border	No caption
Numbering	Arabic (1, 2)	Roman (I, II)	Arabic (1, 2)	Arabic (1, 2)	None
Initial size	3.25" × 3.25"	3.25" × 3.71" 3.25" × 3.37" (5.0)	3.25" × 0.625" 3.25" × 0.6" (5.0)	3.25" × 3.25"	6.5"x.333"
Border	Single line on all sides	Thick lines on top and bottom	Thick lines on top and bottom	No border	No border
Alignment	Right	Right	Right	Right	Full

Once you have created a graphics box, you can preview it. To preview it, press the Print (Shift-F7) key [Alt File Print], and type a **v**. This displays your text and graphics as they will print. If the graphics do not display, you most likely have a monitor that cannot display graphics or you have a nongraphics printer. You will have a blank preview screen if you have a user-defined graphics box with nothing in it.

EXAMPLES

1. You can insert a graphics box and add additional information later. First, press the Graphics (Alt-

F9) key, then type an **f** for figure and a **c** to create a figure [Alt Graphics Figure Create]. Press the Exit (F7) key to accept the default settings for this type of box and return to the document. The screen does not show the bottom of the graphics box until you move the cursor down to that area of the document. To see how WordPerfect marks the document area for the graphics box, press Enter several times to move the cursor toward the bottom of the screen. The screen looks like Figure 17-1.

2. When you create a graphics box, WordPerfect wraps text around it unless you specify otherwise. To illustrate this feature, press the Graphics (Alt)-

Doc 1 Pg 1 Ln 4.83" Pos 1"

FIGURE 17-1.   Sample graphics box

[F9]) key, and type a **t** for table and a **c** for create [[Alt] Graphics Table Create]. Press [Enter] to accept the default settings for the table and return to the document. WordPerfect has not drawn the box yet. To see how WordPerfect wraps words around a graphics box, type

WordPerfect allows you to add graphics boxes anywhere in your document. The options let you put graphic images or text into the boxes. You can also move or copy a box or change a box's size.

As you type the text, WordPerfect wraps the words and draws the sides of the graphics box. The screen looks like this:

```
WordPerfect allows you to add     ┌TAB I─────────────────────
graphics boxes anywhere in your   │
document. The options let you     │
put graphic images or text into   │
the boxes. You can also move or   │
copy a box or change a box's      │
size. _                           │
```

3. When you preview your document, WordPerfect displays the graphics box. To preview a text box, press the Graphics ([Alt]-[F9]) key, type a **b** for text box and a **c** [[Alt] Graphics Text Box Create], and press the Exit ([F7]) key. Next, press [Enter] until WordPerfect draws the entire box. To see how WordPerfect will print this box, press the Print ([Shift]-[F7]) key [[Alt] File Print] and type a **v** and a **1**. The text box looks like this:

4. You can create multiple graphics boxes on the same page. As you add additional ones, WordPerfect makes them smaller whenever necessary to accommodate their correct placement. To create two adjacent text boxes, press the Graphics (Alt - F9) key, type a **b** and a **c** [Alt Graphics Text Box Create], and press the Exit (F7) key. Next, press the Graphics (Alt - F9) key, type a **b** and a **c** [Alt Graphics Text Box Create], and press the Exit (F7) key. Because the default position setting for the first box is at the right margin, WordPerfect places the second box to the left of the first. To see how WordPerfect will print these boxes, press the Print (Shift - F7) key [Alt File Print] and type a **v**. The preview of the text boxes look like this:

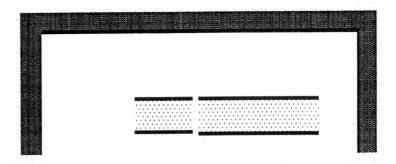

5. You can place graphics boxes below one another in a document. If the boxes are not side by side, WordPerfect does not make the new boxes smaller. To create a figure above a table, press the Graphics (Alt - F9) key, type an **f** and a **c** [Alt Graphics Figure Create], and press the Exit (F7) key. Next, press Enter 21 times. Then, press the Graphics

([Alt]-[F9]) key, type a **t** and a **c** [[Alt] Graphics Table Box Create], and press [Enter]. To see how Word-Perfect will print the figures, press the Print ([Shift]-[F7]) key [[Alt] File Print], and type a **v** and a **3**. The figures look like Figure 17-2.

EXERCISES

1. Create a user-defined box. Press [Enter] until the cursor reaches the line below the bottom of the box.

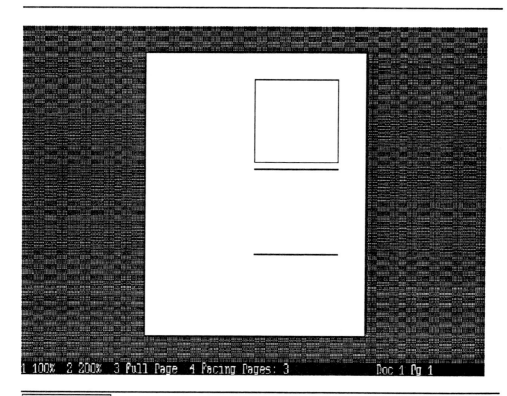

1 100% 2 200% 3 Full Page 4 Facing Pages: 3   Doc 1 Pg 1

FIGURE 17-2.   Two graphics boxes

2. Create a figure. Type the following text, allowing WordPerfect to draw the box and wrap the text as you type it.

   When you create a graphics box, WordPerfect wraps the document text around it. If WordPerfect has not already drawn the box, it draws the box as you type the text. Even as you edit the text that you put next to the box, WordPerfect adjusts the text so that it is still properly wrapped.

3. Create a table. Preview how WordPerfect will print it.

4. Create a text box. Press (Enter) until the cursor reaches the line below the bottom of the box. Create a figure. Preview how WordPerfect will print it.

5. Create a table. Create a figure box next to it. Press (Enter) until the cursor reaches the line below the bottom of both graphics boxes. Preview how Word-Perfect will print them.

17.2 PLACE TEXT IN A BOX

You can display the contents of another document file within a graphics box in the current document. You can also type the text for a graphics box when you define the settings for the box. This can be an effective way to highlight project objectives or to set off quotations or any other important text in the document.

When you use another document as the text for a graphics box, WordPerfect copies the text from the document on disk into the box in the current document. Since the box reflects the disk document's contents at the moment you copy it, it is not updated to include any changes you subsequently make in the original document. Likewise, any changes you make to the duplicate copy in the current document do not affect the original file. When you use a document file in a graphics box, the size of the graphics box changes to accommodate the size of the document.

You can edit or create the text for a graphics box in a screen accessible through the graphics box menu selections. You can preview the contents of a text box using the Print Preview Menu Option.

To use text from a document stored on disk in a graphics box:

a. Press the Graphics (Alt - F9) key [Alt Graphics].

b. Type the appropriate number or letter for the box type that you want to create. [Select the type of graphics box, for example, User Box].

c. Type a **c** or a **1** to create the graphics box [Create].

d. Type an **f** or a **1** to retrieve a file into the graphics box.

e. Type the name of the file containing the text that you want to appear in the graphics box.

f. Press Enter.

g. Press the Exit (F7) key to return to the document.

To enter text in a graphics box or edit a graphics box containing a file:

a. Press the Graphics (Alt - F9) key [Alt Graphics].

b. Type the appropriate number or letter for the box type that you want to create or edit. [Select the type of graphics box, for example, Text Box].

c. Type a **c** or a **1** to create a box or an **e** or a **2** to edit an existing box [Create or Edit].

d. If you typed an **e** or a **2** in the previous step, type the number of the box you want to edit, and press Enter .

e. Type an **e** or a **9** (8 in 5.0) to edit the graphics box.

f. Type the text that you want to appear in the graphics box, or edit the existing text.

g. Press the Exit (F7) key twice to return to the document.

When you place text in a graphics box, Word-Perfect sets the size of the graphics box to the size needed for the text. When you edit the text in a graphics box, you can use all of WordPerfect's formatting features, such as Bold and Underline. If you are using another document in the graphics box, the text contains all of the codes from the document on disk; if this text contains margin codes, you should remove them.

EXAMPLES

1. You can use text in boxes to have the text treated as a unit. First, press the Graphics (Alt - F9) key and type an **f**, a **c** [Alt Graphics Figure Create], and an **e** to enter text for the graphics box. Type

Graphics boxes allow you to treat text as a unit. With text in a box, you can move the box around without affecting the text in it.

Do not press [Enter] at the end of the paragraph. Press the Exit ([F7]) key. WordPerfect changes the size of the graphics box to 3.25″ × .693″ (.69″ in 5.0), assuming your printer is set to print six lines to the inch. Press the Exit ([F7]) key to return to the document, and type

Text in a document containing graphics boxes is automatically moved to accommodate the graphics boxes. As the information in the boxes changes, WordPerfect adjusts the wrapping for the remaining text. Graphics boxes allow some text to be unaffected by the other text.

The screen looks like this:

```
Text in a document containing      FIG 1
graphics boxes is automatically
moved to accommodate the
graphics boxes. As the
information in the boxes
changes, WordPerfect adjusts the
wrapping for the remaining text. Graphics boxes allow some text
to be unaffected by the other text.
```

Press the Print ([Shift]-[F7]) key [[Alt] File Print], and type a **v** and a **1**. The preview of the printed document appears as follows.

```
Text in a document containing    Graphics boxes allow you to treat
graphics boxes is automatically  text as a unit.  With text in a
moved   to   accommodate   the   box, you can move the box around
graphics   boxes.      As   the  without affecting the text in it.
information   in   the   boxes
changes, WordPerfect adjusts the
wrapping for the remaining text.  Graphics boxes allow some text
to be unaffected by the other text.
```

2. You can display text from another document in a text box. First, type

On August 17, 1990, the board of directors approved the company's long-term goals as presented by the Development Committee. The approved goals include: Increase the return on investment from 8 to 10 percent. Renovate the Hamburg facilities and develop a community-responsible attitude in that area.
Focus research and development on the electrochemical market.

Press the Exit (F7) key [Alt File Exit], type a **y**, type **goals**, press Enter, and type an **n** to clear the screen. Press the Graphics (Alt-F9) key, type a **t**, a **c** [Alt Graphics Table Box Create], and an **f**, type **goals**, and press Enter. WordPerfect retrieves that file and places the filename and the word "Text" enclosed in parentheses next to the Filename option. Press the Exit (F7) key to return to the document. Use this document in the next example.

3. You can edit the text in a graphics box without changing the original document that you used. You may want to take this approach to use WordPerfect's formatting features on text for a table. First, press the Graphics (Alt-F9) key, type a **t**, an **e** [Alt Graphics Table Box Edit], and a **1** or an **i**, press Enter, and type an **e**. Change the table's appearance by deleting the first paragraph. Then, press the Bold (F6) key, type **The long-term goals approved by the board of directors are:**, press the Bold (F6) key again, and press Enter. Then, press the Exit (F7) key twice. To view the table, press the Print (Shift-

F7) key [Alt File **Print**] and type a **v** and a **1**. The preview of the table looks like this:

The long-term goals approved
by the board of directors are:
Increase   the   return   on
investment   from   8   to   10
percent.
Renovate the Hamburg facilities
and   develop   a   community
responsible attitude in that
area.
Focus research and development
on the electrochemical market.

EXERCISES

1. Create a table with the following text, typing the text directly into the graphics box:

Project	Date
Systems analysis	5/1
Order equipment	6/15
Design software	7/1
Test software	7/31
Implement software	8/30
Evaluation	9/30

   Preview how WordPerfect will print it.

2. Type the following paragraph:

   Besides creating graphics boxes containing text, you can also create graphics boxes with images. The next section will show you how to create a graphics box with an image. You do not need to create the image first, since WordPerfect provides several ready-made images.

Save the document as PICTURE, and clear the
screen. Create a text box that uses the text from the
PICTURE file. Preview how WordPerfect will print
it.

3. Create a table with the following text, typing the
text directly into the graphics box.

Steps for Creating a Figure with Text in It:
1. Press the Graphics (ALT-F9) key.
2. Type an f for figure.
3. Type a c to create a figure.
4. Type an e to edit the figure's contents.
5. Type the text to appear in the figure.
6. Press the Exit (F7) key to end the edit.
7. Press the Exit (F7) key to return to the document.

Preview how WordPerfect will print the table.

17.3   PLACE A FIGURE IN A BOX

WordPerfect can incorporate graphic images within a
graphics box. The WordPerfect program includes 30
graphic images. You can add your own if you have
graphic images in one of several formats that Word-
Perfect can use. Placing a figure in a box is very much
like placing text in a box. You can view the graphic
images using WordPerfect's print preview if your
computer has a graphics card. If your computer does
not have a graphics card, you can still create graphic
images, although you will not be able to see them
until you print them.

To place a graphic image in a graphics box:

a. Press the Graphics (Alt - F9) key [Alt Graphics].

b. Type the appropriate number or letter for the box type that you want to create or edit. [Select the type of graphics box, for example, Figure].

c. Type a **c** or a **1** to create a graphics box or an **e** or a **2** to edit an existing graphics box [**Create** or **Edit**].

d. If you typed an **e** or a **2** in the previous step, type the number of the box you want to edit, and press Enter .

e. Type an **f** or a **1** to specify the file containing the graphic image.

f. Type the name of the file containing the image that you want to appear in the graphics box, and press Enter .

g. Press the Exit (F7) key to return to the document.

When you place an image in a graphics box, WordPerfect sets the size of the box to fit the image. WordPerfect uses the same height-to-width ratio that was in effect when the image was created.

EXAMPLES

1. You can use WordPerfect's ready-made images, such as the computer image named PC-1.WPG (PC.WPG in 5.0), to enhance your documents. First, press the Graphics (Alt - F9) key, type a **u** for User-defined box, a **c** [Alt Graphics User Box Create], and an **f**. If your WordPerfect graphic images

are in the WP51 (WP50 in 5.0) subdirectory, type **pc-1.wpg** (**pc.wpg** in 5.0) and press Enter. If your graphic images are in a subdirectory of the Word-Perfect subdirectory, type the subdirectory name, a backslash, and the figure name [for example, **\graphics\pc-1.wpg** (**\graphics\pc.wpg** in 5.0)], and press Enter. If your graphics images are not in the WordPerfect subdirectory, type a backslash and the appropriate subdirectory name in the examples and exercises before typing the graphics image filename. WordPerfect finds the file and loads the image into memory. WordPerfect adjusts the graphics box size to a default setting for the image. Press the Exit (F7) key to return to the document. To view the image, press the Print (Shift-F7) key [Alt File Print], and type a **v** and a **3**. The image looks like this:

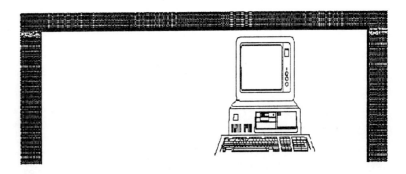

2. You can use WordPerfect images in headers. Press the Format (Shift-F8) key, and type a **p** [Alt Layout Page], an **h**, an **a**, and a **p** to create a header for every page. Press the Graphics (Alt-F9) key, type an **f**, a **c** [Alt Graphics Figure Create], an **f**,

and **balloons.wpg** (**airplane.wpg** in 5.0), and press
[Enter]. WordPerfect finds the file and loads the
image into the header. WordPerfect adjusts the
graphics box size to a default setting for the image.
Press the Exit ([F7]) key three times to return to the
document. To view the header, press the Print
([Shift]-[F7]) key [[Alt] File Print], and type a v and a
1. The screen looks like this:

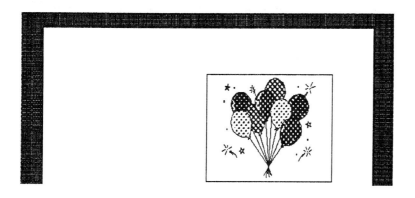

3. WordPerfect can use graphic images from other
packages, allowing you to incorporate graphs and
drawings that you have already made into your
WordPerfect documents. This example requires a
.PIC file from Lotus 1-2-3 and is included because
many users wish to access this type of data. While
you may not have this particular graph or the
spreadsheet with which it was created, these steps
demonstrate the process. If you do not have a Lotus
1-2-3 file, you can use other graphic image files that
various software packages create. You can skip this
example if you do not plan to work with graphs.

To use a Lotus 1-2-3 graph in a WordPerfect document, press the Graphics (Alt-F9) key and type an **f**, a **c** [Alt Graphics Figure Create], and an **f**. To use a Lotus 1-2-3 .PIC file named GRAPH, which is stored in the default directory for 1-2-3, type **c:\123\graph.pic** as the pathname and file-name of the file, press Enter, and press the Exit (F7) key to return to the document. To view this graph, press the Print (Shift-F7) key [Alt File Print], and type a **v** and a **1**. The screen looks like Figure 17-3.

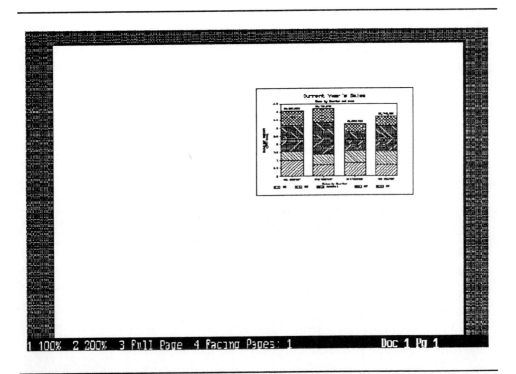

FIGURE 17-3.   Graphics box with Lotus 1-2-3 .PIC file

EXERCISES

1. Create a table that displays the image STAR-5.WPG (MAPSYMBL.WPG in 5.0). Preview how WordPerfect will print it.

2. Create a text box that displays the image named ARROW-22.WPG (ARROW1.WPG in 5.0). Preview how WordPerfect will print it.

3. Create a figure that displays the image BORDER-8.WPG (BORDER.WPG in 5.0). Preview how WordPerfect will print it.

4. Create a user-defined box that displays the image named GAVEL.WPG. Preview how WordPerfect will print it.

ADD A CAPTION

17.4

Once you have created a graphics box, you may want to label it. WordPerfect refers to the box label as a *caption*. As described in Table 17-1, WordPerfect provides default captions, such as "Figure" or "Table" followed by the figure or table number. You can provide additional information in the caption; for example, you can use the caption to provide a title for the graphics box. When you have multiple graphics boxes, the numbers and labels in the captions distinguish the various box entries.

To add a caption to the graphics box:

a. Press the Graphics (Alt-F9) key [Alt Graphics].

b. Type the appropriate number or letter for the box type that you want to create or edit. [Select the type of graphics box, for example, User Box].

c. Type a c or a 1 to create a graphics box or an e or a 2 to edit an existing graphics box [Create or Edit].

d. If you typed an e or a 2 in the previous step, type the number of the box you want to edit, and press Enter.

e. Type a c or a 2 to select the Caption option.

f. Type the text that you want to appear in the caption.

g. Press the Exit (F7) key to return to the Graphics menu.

h. Press the Exit (F7) key to return to the document.

When you add a caption, you can use all of WordPerfect's features, such as Underline and Bold. You can change or remove the initial caption that WordPerfect provides by editing that text. To move the default caption from the beginning to another location within the caption area, delete the caption with the Backspace key and reinsert it by pressing the Graphics (Alt-F9) key. WordPerfect wraps the text in the caption to fit the width of the graphics box. While you can place graphics boxes in headers, footers, footnotes, and endnotes, you cannot use captions in these locations.

EXAMPLES

1. You can use captions to identify graphic images referenced in your text. With captions, a reader browsing through your document can quickly identify the information that each graphics box presents. First, press the Graphics ([Alt]-[F9]) key, type an **f**, a **c** [[Alt] Graphics Figure Create], an **f**, and **globe2-m.wpg** (**usamap.wpg** in 5.0). Press [Enter], and type **c** for Caption. Press the SPACEBAR, type **Acme's Customer Base**, and press the Exit ([F7]) key. Press the Exit ([F7]) key again to return to the document. To view this image, press the Print ([Shift]-[F7]) key [[Alt] File Print], and type a **v** and a **1**. The figure looks like this:

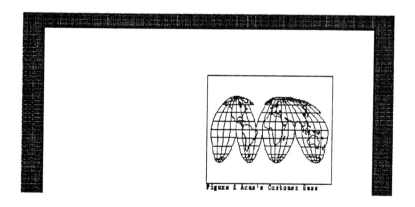

Figure 1 Acme's Customer Base

2. You can also use captions to create titles for tables. First, press the Graphics ([Alt]-[F9]) key, and type a **t**, a **c** [[Alt] Graphics Table Box Create], and an **e**. Then, type

Duct Tape
Electrical Tape
Strapping Tape
Epoxy

Press the Exit (F7) key. Type a **c** for Caption. Press the SPACEBAR, press the Bold (F6) key, type **Acme's Product Line**, press the Bold (F6) key, and press the Exit (F7) key twice. To view this image, press the Print (Shift-F7) key [Alt File Print], and type a **v** and a **1**. The data on your screen looks like this:

Table I Acme's Product Line

Duct Tape
Electrical Tape
Strapping Tape
Epoxy

EXERCISES

1. Create a blank text box with the caption **To be filled in later**. Preview how WordPerfect will print it.

2. Create a table containing the text **insert Ms. Mitchell's picture here** and a caption that says **Susan Mitchell, President**. Preview how WordPerfect will print it.

3. Create a figure with the image named TELEPHONE .WPG (PHONE.WPG in 5.0) and the caption **When It Rings, We Answer**. Preview how WordPerfect will print it.

4. To create a figure with the image named TROPHY.WPG (NO1.WPG in 5.0) and the caption **First in the Business**. Preview how WordPerfect will print it.

POSITION AND SIZE A BOX

17.5

You can control the size and placement of a graphics box on the page. The placement options allow you to specify vertical and horizontal positions. The options for both position settings are dependent on the type of box selected. WordPerfect lets you define a box as a paragraph box, a page box, or a character box. Word-Perfect treats each type of box differently in relation to the text around it. In this chapter, our focus is on the default setting, which is the paragraph type. Paragraph boxes remain with the text that is wrapped around them. For paragraph boxes, the vertical setting is the number of inches that the graphics box is placed from the top of the paragraph. The horizontal settings are left, right, center, and both left and right.

You can accept WordPerfect's calculations for a box size or change the size of a box by altering its height or its width. You can also choose to alter both the height and the width with one menu selection. If you set only one dimension of the box, WordPerfect calculates the other dimension automatically.

To set the horizontal and vertical positions of a graphics box:

a. Press the Graphics ([Alt]-[F9]) key [[Alt] Graphics].

b. Type the appropriate number or letter for the box type that you want to create or edit. [Select the type of graphics box, for example, Text Box].

c. Type a **c** or a **1** to create a graphics box or an **e** or a **2** to edit an existing graphics box [Create or Edit].

d. If you typed an **e** or a **2** in the previous step, type the number of the box you want to edit, and press ⌷Enter⌷.

e. Type a **v** or a **5** (**4** in 5.0) to specify the box's vertical position.

f. Type the number of inches between the top of the paragraph and the box, and press ⌷Enter⌷.

g. Type an **h** or a **6** (**5** in 5.0) to specify the box's horizontal position.

h. Type an **L** or a **1** to have the box align with the paragraph's left margin, an **r** or a **2** to have the box align with the paragraph's right margin, a **c** or a **3** to have the box centered between the paragraph margins, or an **f** (**b** in 5.0) or a **4** to have the box stretch between the left and right margins.

i. Press the Exit (⌷F7⌷) key to return to the document.

The vertical setting is ignored if it prevents the image from fitting on the page.

To set the graphics box's size:

a. Press the Graphics (⌷Alt⌷-⌷F9⌷) key [⌷Alt⌷ Graphics].

b. Type the appropriate number or letter for the box type that you want to create or edit [Select the type of graphics box, for example, Figure].

c. Type a **c** or a **1** to create a graphics box or an **e** or a **2** to edit an existing graphics box [Create or Edit].

d. If you typed an **e** or a **2** in the previous step, type the number of the box you want to edit, and press `Enter`.

e. Type an **s** or a **7** (**6** in 5.0) to specify the box's size.

f. Type a **w** or a **1** to specify the box's width, letting WordPerfect determine the height; an **h** or a **2** to specify the box's height, letting WordPerfect determine the width; or a **b** or a **3** to set both the width and the height, or an **a** or **4** to let WordPerfect determine both dimensions (the last selection is unavailable in 5.0).

g. Type the number of inches for the box's width if you typed a **w**, a **1**, a **b**, or a **3** in step f, and press `Enter`.

h. Type the number of inches for the box's width if you typed an **h**, a **2**, a **b**, or a **3** in step f, and press `Enter`.

i. Press the Exit (`F7`) key to return to the document.

When you set the size of a graphics box that contains a graphic image, WordPerfect changes the size of the image to fill as much of the box as possible. Once the image is as large as possible, remaining space is left blank. When you set the size of a graphics box that contains text, WordPerfect fits as much of the text as possible into the box. If WordPerfect cannot display all of the text in the box, it displays as much as possible and keeps the rest in memory. If the box has more room than the text requires, WordPerfect leaves the remaining space blank.

EXAMPLES

1. You can set the vertical position when you want one or more lines of a paragraph that is wrapped around a graphics box to appear unwrapped above the box. First, type

   Fourscore and seven years ago, our fathers brought forth upon this continent, a new nation, conceived in liberty, and dedicated to the proposition that all men are created equal.

   Next, move the cursor to the "F" in "Fourscore," and press the Graphics (Alt - F9) key, type an **f**, a **c** [Alt Graphics Figure Create], an **f**, and **scale.wpg** (**flag.wpg** in 5.0), and press Enter . WordPerfect finds the file and loads the image. Then, type a **v** and **.2**, and press Enter . Press the Exit (F7) key to return to the document. WordPerfect adjusts the graphics box to fit below the first line of text in the paragraph. To view this image, press the Print (Shift - F7) key [Alt File Print] and type a **v** and a **1**. The screen looks like Figure 17-4. Press the Exit (F7) key. Use this text and the graphics box in the next example.

2. You can set the horizontal position when you want to change how the box aligns with the left or right margin. First, press the Graphics (Alt - F9) key, type an **f**, an **e** [Alt Graphics Figure Edit], and **1** for the figure number that you want to edit, and press

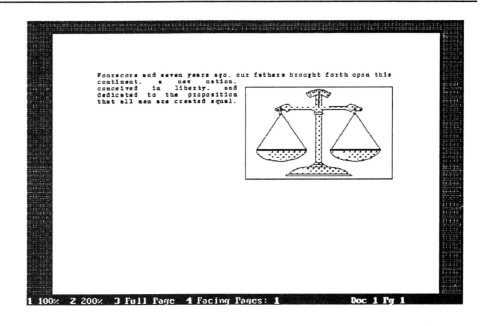

Foursoare and seven years ago, our fathers brought forth upon this
continent,   a   new   nation,
conceived   in   liberty,   and
dedicated   to   the   proposition
that all men are created equal.

1 100% 2 200% 3 Full Page 4 Facing Pages: 1   Doc 1 Pg 1

FIGURE 17-4.   Graphics box with a vertical-position setting

⌨Enter. Type an **h** for Horizontal. To stretch the
graphics box from the right margin to the left
margin, type an **f** (**b** in 5.0), and press the Exit (⌨F7)
key to return to the document. Move the cursor to
the last line of the paragraph. The screen looks like
this:

```
Fourscore and seven years ago, our fathers brought forth upon this
┌FIG 1───────────────────────────────────────────────────────────┐
continent, a new nation, conceived in liberty, and dedicated to the
proposition that all men are created equal.
```

WordPerfect adjusts the graphics box to fit between
the first line of the paragraph and the remaining

lines. Although the graphics box occupies the entire width of the screen, WordPerfect shows only the first line of the graphics box. When the cursor is on the first line of the paragraph, the **LN** indicator in the status line says **1″**. When the cursor is on the second line of the paragraph, the **LN** indicator in the status line says **6.33″** (**4.83″** in 5.0). To view the image, press the Print ([Shift]-[F7]) key [[Alt] File Print], and type a **v** and a **3**. The screen looks like Figure 17-5.

3. For most graphics boxes, you can use the height and width settings that WordPerfect creates. However, you can change the height and width settings for a

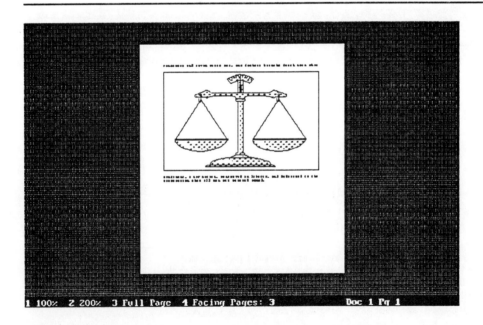

| FIGURE 17-5. | Graphics box with horizontal setting at both left and right margins |

box whenever you wish. First, press the Graphics
(⌈Alt⌉-⌈F9⌉) key, type an **f**, a **c** [⌈Alt⌉ Graphics Figure
Create], an **f**, and **star-5.wpg** (**mapsymbl.wpg** in
5.0), and press ⌈Enter⌉. WordPerfect retrieves the file
and sets the graphics box to a predetermined size.
To change the size, type an **s**, and a **b** to set both
height and width. For the width, type **3**, and press
⌈Enter⌉. For the height, type **1.5**, and press ⌈Enter⌉. To
return to the document, press the Exit (⌈F7⌉) key. To
view the image, press the Print (⌈Shift⌉-⌈F7⌉) key
[⌈Alt⌉ File Print] and type a **v** and a **3**. The screen
looks like this:

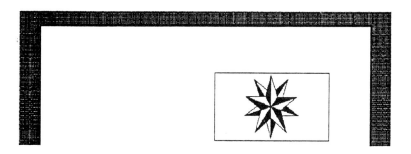

When you change the size, WordPerfect expands or
contracts the image to display it as large as possible
without changing the height-to-width ratio. The
extra space in the box remains empty.

4. When you change the width of a graphics box
   containing text, WordPerfect rewraps the text to fit.
   First, press the Graphics (⌈Alt⌉-⌈F9⌉) key, and type
   an **f**, a **c** [⌈Alt⌉ Graphics Figure Create], and an **e**.
   Then, type

Fourscore and seven years ago, our fathers brought forth upon this continent, a new nation, conceived in liberty, and dedicated to the proposition that all men are created equal.

Then, press the Exit ([F7]) key. Notice that Word-Perfect changed the size of the graphics box to 3.25" by 1.03" (1.02" in 5.0). Press the Exit ([F7]) key to return to the document. To view the figure, press the Print ([Shift]-[F7]) key [[Alt] File Print], and type a **v** and a **1**. The screen looks like this:

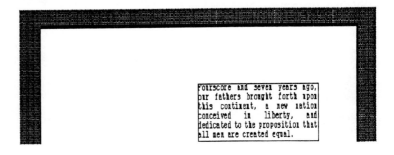

Press the Exit ([F7]) key to return to the document. To change the size of the box, press the Graphics ([Alt]-[F9]) key, type an **f**, an **e** [[Alt] Graphics Figure Edit], a **1**, press [Enter], type an **s**, and a **w**. Type **5**, and press [Enter] for the new width. WordPerfect automatically adjusts the height of the box to accommodate the text. Finally, press the Exit ([F7]) key to return to the document. To view the figure, press the Print ([Shift]-[F7]) key [[Alt] File Print], and type a **v**. The screen looks like this:

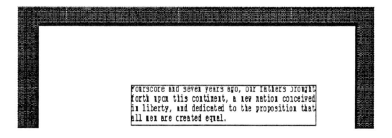

EXERCISES

1. Create a blank text box, setting the vertical position to .4". Now return to the document, and type the following paragraph:

   When you create a graphics box, WordPerfect wraps the document text around it. If WordPerfect has not already drawn the box, it draws the box as you type the text. Even as you edit the text that you put next to the box, WordPerfect adjusts the text so that it is still properly wrapped.

   Preview how WordPerfect will print the document.

2. Create an empty figure at the left margin. Preview how WordPerfect will print it.

3. Create a user-defined box that contains the image named CHKBOX-1.WPG (CHECK.WPG in 5.0). Set the height to 5", and let WordPerfect determine the appropriate width. Preview how WordPerfect will print it.

4. Create a table that contains the following paragraph:

As you change the width of a graphics box that contains text, WordPerfect rewraps the text inside it to fit
the new width. When you set the height of a graphics
box that contains text, WordPerfect fits as much of the
text as possible into the box. If it cannot display all of
the text, the remaining text does not appear, although
WordPerfect remembers it.

Preview how WordPerfect will print the box.
Change the width to 2.5", allowing WordPerfect to
set the height. Preview how WordPerfect will print
the box. Change the width to 3" and the height to 2".
Preview how WordPerfect will print the box.

5. Create a figure that contains the image HANDS-
3.WPG (APPLAUSE.WPG in 5.0). Set the height to
4", allowing WordPerfect to set the width. Set the
horizontal position to center the box. Preview how
WordPerfect will print the box.

17.6 EDIT AND DELETE GRAPHICS BOXES

When you edit a graphics box, you can change any of
the settings established when the box was initially
created. Supplying the same or a new filename updates or changes the contents of a box.

Although you can remove the contents of a box
through the edit option, to eliminate a box, you must
delete the hidden code for the box. You can accomplish this most easily in the Reveal Codes screen. You
can also delete and restore the hidden code to move a
box from one location to another.

To edit a graphics box:

a. Press the Graphics (⌥Alt⌥-⌥F9⌥) key [⌥Alt⌥ Graphics].

b. Type the appropriate number or letter for the box type that you want to edit [Select the type of graphics box, for example, Table Box].

c. Type an **e** or a **2** [Edit].

d. Type the number of the box you want to edit, and press ⌥Enter⌥.

e. Change any options you want changed.

f. Press the Exit (⌥F7⌥) key to return to the document.

Supplying a new filename replaces the old text or image with the contents of the new file.

To delete a graphics box:

a. Press the Reveal Codes (⌥Alt⌥-⌥F3⌥) key [⌥Alt⌥ Edit Reveal Codes].

b. Move the cursor to the code representing the graphics box.

c. Press the ⌥Del⌥ key.

d. Press the Reveal Codes (⌥Alt⌥-⌥F3⌥) key [⌥Alt⌥ Edit Reveal Codes].

When you delete a graphics box, WordPerfect renumbers all of the remaining figures, tables, text boxes, or user-defined boxes.

The hidden codes for graphics boxes are shown in Table 17-2. The number sign (#) represents the figure number. "FILENAME" represents the document name or image name that the graphics box contains.

Table 17-2.		Hidden Graphics Codes

Graphics box type	5.1 Code	5.0 Code
Figure box	[FigBox:#;FILENAME;Caption]	[Figure:#;FILENAME;Caption]
Table box	[TblBox:#;FILENAME;Caption]	[Table:#;FILENAME;Caption]
Text box	[Text Box:#;FILENAME;Caption]	[Text Box:#;FILENAME;Caption]
User-defined box	[Usr Box:#;FILENAME;Caption]	[Usr Box;#;FILENAME;Caption]

"Caption" represents the first 49 characters of the caption that you have provided, which includes [Box Num] for the default caption. The filename and caption are not displayed in the hidden code if the graphics box does not use them.

To move a graphics box:

a. Press the Reveal Codes (Alt-F3) key [Alt Edit Reveal Codes].

b. Move the cursor to the code representing the graphics box.

c. Press the Del key.

d. Place the cursor where you want the graphics box to be moved.

e. Press the Cancel (F1) key [Alt Edit Undelete].

f. Type an r or a 1 to restore the graphics box.

g. Press the Reveal Codes ([Alt]-[F3]) key [[Alt] Edit Reveal Codes].

You can also use the [Backspace] key instead of [Del] if the cursor is to the right of the hidden code for the graphics box.

EXAMPLES

1. WordPerfect places a copy of a document or image from disk into the current document when you specify a filename for a graphics box. The copy of the image or text in the graphics box will not include any changes made to the original document at a later time. By resupplying the filename, you can update the graphics box contents. First, type the following, pressing [Enter] after the colon and after "meeting" in the second line:

   At the next board of directors meeting, they will discuss:
   The upcoming stockholders' meeting
   The company's reaction to the negative press involving the Indiana plant closing

   Press the Exit ([F7]) key [[Alt] File Exit], type a **y**, type **bodmeet**, press [Enter], and type an **n** to save the document and clear the screen. Next, press the Graphics ([Alt]-[F9]) key, type an **f**, a **c** [[Alt] Graphics Figure Create], an **f**, and **bodmeet**, and press [Enter]. Press the Exit ([F7]) key to return to the document. When you preview the document at 100 percent by pressing the Print (⟨Shift⟩-⟨F7⟩) key [⟨Alt⟩ File Print] and typing a **v** and a **1**, the screen looks like this:

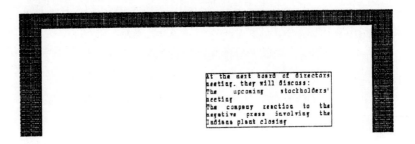

Next, press the Exit (⟨F7⟩) key to return to the document. To show how WordPerfect does not update graphics boxes that use other documents, press the Switch (⟨Shift⟩-⟨F3⟩) key [⟨Alt⟩ Edit Switch Document], press the Retrieve (⟨Shift⟩-⟨F10⟩) key [⟨Alt⟩ File Retrieve], type **bodmeet**, and press ⟨Enter⟩. Press ⟨PgDn⟩ to move to the bottom of the document, press ⟨Enter⟩, and type

Suggestions for new board members to replace Ima L. Shark and Jim Pollack

Press the Exit (⟨F7⟩) key [⟨Alt⟩ File Exit], press ⟨Enter⟩ twice, and type a **y** twice. When you return to the first document and press the Print (⟨Shift⟩-⟨F7⟩) key [⟨Alt⟩ File Print] and type a **v**, the screen does not show the new text that you entered in the BODMEET file. Press the Exit (⟨F7⟩) key to return to the document. To update the figure, press the Graphics (⟨Alt⟩-⟨F9⟩) key, and type an **f**, an **e** [⟨Alt⟩ Graphics Figure Edit], and a **1** for the figure number. Then, press ⟨Enter⟩ and type an **f**. Since Word

Perfect prompts you with the correct filename, press (Enter). When WordPerfect prompts you for a confirmation, type a **y**. Now the figure uses the updated copy of the BODMEET file. Press the Exit ((F7)) key to return to the document. Press the Print ((Shift)-(F7)) key [(Alt) File Print], and type a **v**. The figure looks like this:

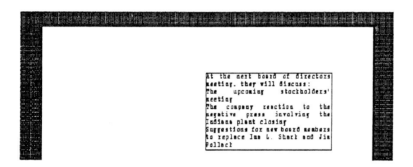

2. You can remove the filename from a graphics box setting. First, press the Graphics ((Alt)-(F9)) key, type an **f**, a **c** [(Alt) Graphics Figure Create], an **f**, and **bodmeet**, press (Enter), and press the Exit ((F7)) key. To remove the filename setting, press the Graphics ((Alt)-(F9)) key, and type an **f**, an **e** [(Alt) Graphics Figure Edit], and a **1** for the number of the graphics box you have created. Press (Enter) and type an **f** for Filename. When WordPerfect prompts you with the current filename, press the DELETE EOL ((Ctrl)-(End)) key, and press (Enter). When WordPerfect prompts you for a confirmation to clear the contents, type a **y**, and press the Exit ((F7)) key to return to the document. To see the empty figure, press the Print ((Shift)-(F7)) key [(Alt) File Print] and

type a **v**. Press the Exit ([F7]) key to return to the document.

3. You can remove a graphics box from a document. Press the Graphics ([Alt]-[F9]) key, type an **f**, a **c** [[Alt] Graphics Figure Create], an **f**, and **bodmeet**, and press [Enter]. Press the Exit ([F7]) key to return to the document. To remove this figure, press the Reveal Codes ([Alt]-[F3]) key [[Alt] Edit Reveal Codes], and press [Backspace]. Press the Reveal Codes ([Alt]-[F3]) key [[Alt] Edit Reveal Codes] to return to the normal screen.

4. You can move a graphics box by using its hidden code. Press the Graphics ([Alt]-[F9]) key, type an **f**, a **c** [[Alt] Graphics Figure Create], an **f**, and **bodmeet**, and press [Enter]. Press the Exit ([F7]) key to return to the document, and press [Enter] until the cursor is at the bottom of the figure. Press the Graphics ([Alt]-[F9]) key, type a **b** and a **c** [[Alt] Graphics Text Box Create], and press the Exit ([F7]) key. Press the [Enter] key five times to create extra room below the text box. To move the figure below the text box, press the Reveal Codes ([Alt]-[F3]) key [[Alt] Edit Reveal Codes], and press [Home], [Home], the [↑] key, and the [←] key to move the cursor to the right of the hidden code for Figure 1. Then, press the [Backspace] key to delete the code.

   To insert the figure at its new location, press [Home], [Home], and the [↓] key. Then, press the Cancel ([F1]) key [[Alt] Edit Undelete]. WordPerfect displays the code for the figure. Type an **r** or a **1** to

restore the figure. Press the Reveal Codes (⌥Alt⌘-
F3) key [Alt Edit Reveal Codes] to return the
screen to normal. To see the figure after it is moved,
press the Print (Shift-F7) key [Alt File Print], and
type a **v**. Press the Exit (F7) key to return to the
document.

EXERCISES

1. Create a table that uses the image named ARROW-
   22.WPG (ARROW1.WPG in 5.0). Preview how
   WordPerfect will print it. Change the image to
   CHKBOX-1.WPG (CHECK.WPG in 5.0). Preview
   how WordPerfect will print it.

2. Create a text box that uses the image CERTIF.WPG
   (CONFIDEN.WPG in 5.0). Preview how Word-
   Perfect will print it. Remove the filename setting.
   Preview how WordPerfect will print it.

3. Create a table with nothing in it. Delete the table.

4. Create a figure that uses the image named
   NEWS.WPG (NEWSPAPR.WPG in 5.0). Press Enter
   until the cursor is below the bottom of the figure.
   Create a figure that uses the image named BULB
   .WPG (PRESENT.WPG in 5.0). Press Enter until the
   cursor is below the bottom of the figure. Move the
   figure with the NEWS.WPG (NEWSPAPR.WPG in
   5.0) image to below the figure with the BULB
   .WPG (PRESENT.WPG in 5.0) image. Move to the
   beginning of the document, and delete the hard

returns until the figure containing the image in BULB.WPG (PRESENT.WPG in 5.0) is at the first line. Preview how WordPerfect will print it.

17.7   PRINT DOCUMENTS CONTAINING GRAPHICS

Many printers can print your graphics boxes as they print your document. A few printers can print graphics and text but not both at one time. If you try to print a document containing text and graphics and one or the other does not print correctly, your printer will not support the combined printing of text and graphics.

Depending on your printer, you may be able to set the quality of the printing. As you improve the quality of text or graphics, especially the latter, you increase the time your printer takes to print the document.

To print a document with text and graphics on a printer that can print both at one time:

a. Press the Print (Shift-F7) key [Alt File Print].

b. Type a **g** to set the graphics quality.

c. Type a **d** or a **2** for Draft, an **m** or a **3** for Medium, or an **h** or a **4** for High.

d. Type a **t** to set the text quality.

e. Type a **d** or a **2** for Draft, an **m** or a **3** for Medium, or an **h** or a **4** for High.

f. Type an **f** or a **p** to start printing the document.

To print a document with text and graphics on a printer that cannot print both at one time:

a. Press the Print (Shift - F7) key [Alt File Print].

b. Type a **g** to set the graphics quality.

c. Type an **n** or a **1** for Do Not Print.

d. Type a **t** to set the text quality.

e. Type a **d** or a **2** for Draft, an **m** or a **3** for Medium, or an **h** or a **4** for High.

f. Type an **f** or a **p** to print the text of the document.

g. When the text is printed, insert the printed pages into the printer so that it will start printing at the beginning of the first page.

h. Press the Print (Shift - F7) key [Alt File Print].

i. Type a **t** to set the text quality.

j. Type an **n** or a **1** for Do Not Print.

k. Type a **g** to set the graphics quality.

l. Type a **d** or a **2** for Draft, an **m** or a **3** for Medium, or an **h** or a **4** for High.

m. Type an **f** or a **p** to print the graphics in the document.

EXAMPLES

1. Printing documents with text and graphics is a simple process with many printers. To create a document with text and graphics, press the Graphics (Alt - F9) key, type an **f**, a **c** [Alt Graphics

Figure Create], an **f**, and **calendar.wpg** (arrow2.wpg in 5.0), and press Enter. Align this image with the left margin by typing an **h** and an **L**. Press the Exit (F7) key to return to the document, and type

At next Tuesday's meeting, several important points will be discussed. It is imperative that you be there.

To print this document, press the Print (Shift-F7) key [Alt File Print], and type a **g**, an **h**, a **t**, and an **h** to set both the graphics and text quality to high. Then, type an **f**. The printed document looks like this:

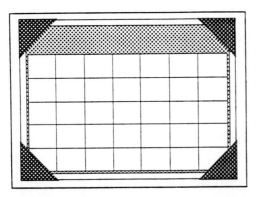

```
At   next   Tuesday's   meeting,
several important points will be
discussed. It is imperative that
you be there.
```

2. If your printer can print text and graphics simultaneously, ignore this example. If you have a printer that cannot print graphics and text at the same time, you must use a different set of steps. First, press the Graphics (Alt-F9) key, type an **f**, a **c** [Alt Graphics Figure Create], an **f**, and **calendar.wpg**

(**arrow2.wpg** in 5.0), and press (Enter). Align this image with the left margin by typing an **h** and an **L**. Press the Exit ((F7)) key to return to the document and type

At next Tuesday's meeting, several important points will be discussed. It is imperative that you be there.

To print this document, press the Print ((Shift)-(F7)) key [(Alt) File Print]. Type a **g** and an **n** to suppress the printing of the graphics, and type a **t** and an **h** to set the text quality to high. Type an **f** to start printing the document.

To print the graphics, reinsert the paper into the paper tray, if your printer uses one, or move the paper back in the traction feeders so that Word-Perfect will start printing the graphics at the beginning of the document. Press the Print ((Shift)-(F7)) key [(Alt) File Print], and type a **t** and an **n** to keep WordPerfect from printing the text. Then, type a **g** and an **h** to set the graphics quality to high, and type an **f** to start printing. WordPerfect will skip over where it printed the text and print the graphics in their appropriate places. The results will look like the illustration from the previous example.

Since this can be a cumbersome process, you may want to perform these steps for one page at a time if only a few pages in your document have graphics.

EXERCISES

1. Create a table with the image named BICYCLE. WPG (AND.WPG in 5.0). Print the document using draft quality for the graphics.

2. Create a text box with the image named PC-1.WPG (KEY.WPG in 5.0). Return to the document, and type the following paragraph:

To check out a key for the computer room, you must register your name with the department secretary, Karen Martin. Then you must sign up for a night on the calendar outside Martin's office. On the day that you have signed up, you must pick up the key by 5:00 p.m.

Print the document with graphics set to medium and text set to high.

3. Create a user-defined box with the image CNTRCT-2.WPG (QUILL.WPG in 5.0). Now return to the document, and type the following paragraph:

Calligraphy is the art of writing beautifully. While some calligraphers use quill pens, you can learn calligraphy using special pens that are available in most art stores. To learn calligraphy, you need a pen, ink, paper, and patience.

Print the document with the graphics quality set to high.

4. Create a figure with the image named BULB.WPG (PENCIL.WPG in 5.0). Without moving the cursor, create a figure with the image named FLOPPY-2.WPG (BOOK.WPG in 5.0). Return to the document, and type the following paragraph.

Each department has a designated person for acquiring office supplies. This person is in charge of ordering and handling the department's transfer of funds for this purpose. Once a year, someone from the internal control department will inspect these records.

Now print the document with the graphics quality set to medium.

EXERCISES

(Do not clear the screen between exercises unless instructed to do so. Preview the document after completing each exercise.)

1. Create a blank figure.

2. Create another blank figure that has a left horizontal position.

3. Edit figure 1 to use the image in MAILBAG.WPG (QUILL.WPG. in 5.0).

4. Edit figure 2 to contain the following text:

   As you graduate:
   A bird is known by its note, and a man by his talk.
   —Proverb
   The secret of success is constancy to purpose.
   —Benjamin Disraeli
   Thrift is too late at the bottom of the purse.
   —Seneca

5. Change the image used in figure 1 to the image named DIPLOMA.WPG (THINKER.WPG in 5.0).

6. Add a caption for figure 1 that says **A few thoughts to ponder**.

7. Change figure 1's height to 2".

8. Change figure 2's width to 3.5".

9. Insert blank lines between the sayings in figure 2.

10. Print the document with text quality set to medium and graphics quality set to high. Clear the screen.

11. Create a left-aligned table with the image named CHKBOX-1.WPG (ARROW1.WPG in 5.0) and with a caption that says **Read This! It Is Important!.**

INTEGRATING SKILLS CHECK

(Do not clear the screen between exercises. Preview the document after each exercise.)

1. Type the following paragraph:

   The images that you use for a graphics box can come from a variety of sources. WordPerfect provides 30 images, all with the .WPG extension. You can also use pictures generated by other software. For example, you can use .PIC files that you generate with Lotus 1-2-3. You can learn more about graphics boxes from WordPerfect 5.1 Made Easy, by Mella Mincberg.

   Save the document as IMAGES. Clear the screen, and create a text box that uses the text in IMAGES. Press (Enter) until the cursor is on the line below the bottom of the text box.

2. Create a table that displays the image CLOCK .WPG. Create a caption that says **A stitch in time saves nine.**

3. Set the table height and width to 4".

4. Switch to the second document. Retrieve IMAGES. Delete the fourth sentence. Save the document.

5. Switch back to the first document. Update the text box to use the new version of IMAGES.

6. Edit the text box to underline "WordPerfect 5.1 Made Easy."

7. Set graphics and text quality to draft. Print the document.

8. Delete the table.

9. At the bottom of the document, create a figure that uses the image that is named HANDS-3.WPG (ANNOUNCE.WPG in 5.0). Press [Enter] until the cursor is on the line below the bottom of the figure.

10. Move the text box to below the figure. Move to the beginning of the document, and remove the blank lines before the figure.

11. Create a header that contains a user-defined box that displays the image named GLOBE2-M.WPG (AIRPLANE.WPG in 5.0). Set the horizontal position to stretch the box from the left to the right margin.

12. Set the graphics quality to high, and print the document.

Creating An Outline

►18◄

CHAPTER OBJECTIVES

After completing this chapter, you should be able to:

▶	**Create an outline**	18.1
▶	**Change the outline**	18.2
▶	**Change the numbering style**	18.3

You can create outlines with WordPerfect. Your outline entries can be complete sentences or just topic words or phrases. You can use these outlines as the basis for a more detailed document with additional, descriptive text. You can also use them to show meeting agendas, project tasks, personnel assignments, and other materials.

If you use WordPerfect's Outline feature as you create your outline, WordPerfect numbers the outline levels automatically. As you add, delete, and move entries in the outline, WordPerfect handles renumbering for you.

WordPerfect supports up to eight levels of outlining, marking each with a different numbering style. Arabic numbers, uppercase letters, lowercase letters, and Roman numerals are combined with periods and parentheses to make each level unique. You can use the default settings for each level, use other predefined style options, or define your own.

SKILLS CHECK

1. Type the following text, indenting it from the left margin:

   WordPerfect has many features that are missing from other word processing packages. Once you master the basics, you will feel comfortable exploring some of the advanced features that WordPerfect offers.

2. Retype the paragraph in exercise 1, indenting it from both margins.

3. Change the tab setting to one tab stop at 4", and type the following:

Joe Jones	Accounting
Paul Balber	Finance
Norlin Rugers	Management
Mary Rogers	Accounting

4. Change the left and right margin settings to 2", and type the following:

WordPerfect's Outline feature makes outline entry and update an easy process. Although each outline entry requires several steps, once the outline is entered, WordPerfect updates level assignments.

Print two copies of the document.

CREATE AN OUTLINE

18.1

An outline can help you organize and focus your thoughts when you have to write a lengthy document. An outline can also serve as a useful end product when you need to share a set of summary data with others.

WordPerfect makes it easy to create outlines. When you turn on the Outline feature, WordPerfect treats each new paragraph as another entry in your outline. You press the `Tab` key to change the next lower outline level. You press the Margin Release (`Shift`-`Tab`) key to move to the next preceding level. Word-Perfect takes care of maintaining perfect order for each level in your outline.

To create an outline in WordPerfect:

a. Position the cursor where you want to begin the outline.

b. Press the Date/Outline ([Shift]-[F5]) key [[Alt] Tools Outline **On** and skip steps c and d].

c. Type an **o** or a **4** to select the Outline feature (skip this step in 5.0).

d. Type an **o** or a **1** to turn on the Outline feature (**o** or **4** in 5.0).

e. Press [Enter] one or more times to insert an outline entry, and press the [Tab] key or Margin Release ([Shift]-[Tab]) key [[Alt] Layout Align Margin Rel ◄—] one or more times to create a different level entry if needed.

f. Press the SPACEBAR or the Indent ([F4]) key [[Alt] Layout Align Indent →], and type the text for the outline entry.

g. Repeat steps d and e as necessary to complete the outline.

h. Press the Date/Outline ([Shift]-[F5]) key [[Alt] Tools Outline **Off** and skip steps i and j].

i. Type an **o** or a **4** to select the Outline feature (skip this step in 5.0).

j. Type an **f** or a **2** to turn off the Outline feature (**o** or **4** in 5.0).

There are differences in the way WordPerfect 5.1 creates outlines as compared to WordPerfect 5.0's method. One of these differences involves step e in the preceding list. When you generate an outline number in 5.1 by pressing the [Enter] key, the new number is at the same level as the previously generated number. If the number is at the proper level, continue making your entry. If not, use the [Tab] key to move to a lower level or the Margin Release ([Shift]-[Tab]) key to move to a higher level.

WordPerfect 5.0 works differently. Whenever you press [Enter], the generated number is always at the highest level. If a lower level number is needed, use [Tab] to move down to the correct level. WordPerfect 5.1's Outline Define menu allows you to turn off the automatic adjustment of the outline numbers to the current level; thus allowing you to make 5.1's outline feature work like 5.0's.

The default numbering that WordPerfect uses for levels in outlines is I., A., 1., a., (1), (a), i), a). If you want to indent the text of an outline entry, press the SPACEBAR before pressing the [Tab] key in step d. The other major difference between WordPerfect 5.1 and 5.0's Outline feature has to do with turning the feature on and off. In WordPerfect 5.1, an [Outline On] code is inserted when you turn the outline feature on and an [Outline Off] code is inserted when you turn it off. Whenever your cursor is located after the [Outline On] code, but before an [Outline Off] code (if any), the message "Outline" appears at the bottom left corner of the screen. In WordPerfect 5.0, the Outline feature works as a toggle switch; that is, you select it once to start it, and you select it again to turn it off. Invoking the Outline feature does not generate a hidden code in the document. Whenever the outline feature is turned on, the message "Outline" appears at the bottom left corner of the screen. In both versions of WordPerfect, pressing [Enter] to create a new entry generates a hidden code. The hidden code generated each time you create an outline entry is [Par Num:Auto].

EXAMPLES

1. You can use WordPerfect's Outline feature to create a topic outline. You might use such an outline to record the various points that you want to discuss at an upcoming management meeting. First, type the following title for the outline:

August 20 Meeting Agenda

Press [Enter] to position the cursor at the beginning of the outline. Press the Date/Outline ([Shift]-[F5]) key, type an **o** to select the Outline feature, and **o** to turn it on (omit one **o** in 5.0) [[Alt] Tools Outline On]. Press [Enter] to have WordPerfect generate the number I. for the first entry. Press the SPACEBAR, and then press the [Tab] key to move to the next tab stop without altering the outline number. Type

Sales bonus program

Press [Enter] and then press the SPACEBAR and the [Tab] key. Next, type

Insurance coverage options

Press [Enter]. Press the SPACEBAR and type

Construction proposals

Pressing the [Tab] key is not necessary: since the number for this entry requires four characters, the SPACEBAR is sufficient to position the cursor.

Press [Enter], the SPACEBAR, and the [Tab] key to generate the number IV. Type

Meeting with security personnel

For the last entry, press [Enter], the SPACEBAR, and the [Tab] key, and type

Position announcements before publication

The completed outline should look like this:

```
August 28 Meeting Agenda

I.   Sales bonus program
II.  Insurance coverage options
III. Construction proposals
IV.  Meeting with security personnel
V.   Position announcements before publication
```

Turn off the Outline feature by pressing the Date/Outline ([Shift]-[F5]) key and typing an **o** and **f** (omit **f** in 5.0) [[Alt] Tools Outline Off].

Save the document by pressing the Exit ([F7]) key [[Alt] File Exit], pressing [Enter], typing **agenda**, and pressing [Enter] again. Press [Enter] to clear the screen and remain in WordPerfect.

2. You can use WordPerfect's Outline feature to create a sentence outline. The Indent ([F4]) key [[Alt] Layout Align Indent →] can be used with the Outline feature to maintain indentation of the text at each level. You can outline project tasks in the order in which they will be completed. First, turn on the Outline feature by pressing the Date/Outline ([Shift]-[F5]) key and typing an **o** and **o** (omit second **o** in 5.0) [[Alt] Tools Outline On]. Press [Enter] to

generate the first outline number, and press the Indent ([F4]) key [[Alt] Layout Align Indent →]. Type

Meet with architect to discuss building plans and zoning requirements.

Press [Enter] to create the next number, press the Indent ([F4]) key [[Alt] Layout Align Indent →], and type

Complete excavation and other site preparation tasks. Complete roadbed preparation.

Press [Enter] to create the next number, press the Indent ([F4]) key [[Alt] Layout Align Indent →], and type

Review architect's drawings, make suggested changes, and discuss construction schedule.

For the last outline entry, press [Enter] to create the number, press the Indent ([F4]) key [[Alt] Layout Align Indent →], and type

Begin construction on main building, drive pilings for pier, and begin paving parking lots.

The outline looks like this:

```
I.   Meet with architect to discuss building plans and zoning
     requirements.
II.  Complete excavation and other site preparation tasks.
     Complete roadbed preparation.
III. Review architect's drawings, make suggested changes, and
     discuss construction schedule.
IV.  Begin construction on main building, drive pilings for pier,
     and begin paving parking lots.
```

Turn the Outline feature off by pressing the Date/Outline ([Shift]-[F5]) key and typing an **o** and **f** (omit **f** in 5.0) [⟨Alt⟩ Tools Outline Off]. Press the Exit (⟨F7⟩) key [⟨Alt⟩ File Exit], press ⟨Enter⟩, type **constrt** as the filename for the document, and press ⟨Enter⟩ twice to clear the screen without leaving Word-Perfect.

3. You can use multiple levels in an outline. The ⟨Tab⟩ and Margin Release (⟨Shift⟩-⟨Tab⟩) keys [⟨Alt⟩ Layout Align Margin Rel →] will indicate to WordPerfect which level you want to use for each entry. You can create an outline structure that shows the winners in a sales contest by region, branch, and employee. The first level of the outline will be the region, the second level the branch, and the third level will be the employee name. First, type the following title for the outline:

Better Boat Brigade Contest

Press ⟨Enter⟩, and turn on the Outline feature by pressing the Date/Outline (⟨Shift⟩-⟨F5⟩) key, typing an **o** and **o** (omit one **o** in 5.0) [⟨Alt⟩ Tools Outline On]. Press ⟨Enter⟩ and the Indent (⟨F4⟩) key [⟨Alt⟩ Layout Align Indent→], and type

Eastern Region

Press ⟨Enter⟩, and press the ⟨Tab⟩ key to create the next level down. Press the Indent (⟨F4⟩) key [⟨Alt⟩ Layout Align Indent→], and type

Boston Branch

Press ⟨Enter⟩ and press the ⟨Tab⟩ key to generate a number one more level down (two ⟨Tab⟩'s in 5.0). Press the Indent (⟨F4⟩) key [⟨Alt⟩ Layout Align Indent→], and type

John Jones

Press (Enter) (press the (Tab) key twice in 5.0), press the Indent ((F4)) key [(Alt) Layout Align Indent→], and type

Mary Smith

To begin another branch entry, press (Enter) and the Margin Release ((Shift)-(Tab)) key once ((Tab) key once in 5.0). Press the Indent ((F4)) key [(Alt) Layout Align Indent→], and type

New York Branch

Press (Enter). To add the names for New York, press the (Tab) key (two (Tab)'s in 5.0), press the Indent ((F4)) key [(Alt) Layout Align Indent→], and type

Nancy Carter

Press (Enter) once, ((Tab) key twice in 5.0), and the Indent ((F4)) key [(Alt) Layout Align Indent→] once, and type

Jeff Greenhoff

The screen looks like this:

```
Better Boat Brigade Contest

I.   Eastern Region
     A.  Boston Branch
          1.  John Jones
          2.  Mary Smith
     B.  New York Branch
          1.  Nancy Carter
          2.  Jeff Greenhoff
```

Complete the entries for the western region with the same approach. Press (Enter) twice and the Margin Release ((Shift)-(Tab)) key [(Alt) Layout Align

Margin Rel ←] twice (omit Margin Release key in 5.0). Pressing [Enter] twice generates a blank line between the entries. Press the Indent ([F4]) key [[Alt] Layout Align Indent →], and type

Western Region

Press [Enter], press the [Tab] key, press the Indent ([F4]) key [[Alt] Layout Align Indent→], and type

Las Vegas Branch

Press [Enter], press the [Tab] key once (twice in 5.0), press the Indent ([F4]) key [[Alt] Layout Align Indent →], and type

Jill Cravens

Press [Enter]. For the last entry, (press [Tab] twice in 5.0), press the Indent ([F4]) key [[Alt] Layout Align Indent →], and type

George Moore

The screen looks like this:

```
Better Boat Brigade Contest

I.  Eastern Region
    A.  Boston Branch
        1.  John Jones
        2.  Mary Smith
    B.  New York Branch
        1.  Nancy Carter
        2.  Jeff Greenhoff

II. Western Region
    A.  Las Vegas Branch
        1.  Jill Cravens
        2.  George Moore
```

Press the Date/Outline (Shift - F5) key, and type an
o and **f** (omit **f** in 5.0) to turn off the Outline feature
[Alt Tools Outline Off]. Save the file and clear the
screen by pressing the Exit (F7) key [Alt File Exit],
pressing Enter , typing **prizes**, and pressing Enter
twice.

EXERCISES

1. Create the following outline:

HIGH SCHOOL SPORTS
I.   BASEBALL
II. FOOTBALL
III. SWIMMING
IV. HOCKEY

Save the file as SPORTS.

2. Create the following outline:

BREEDS OF DOGS
I.   Hounds
     A. Greyhound
     B. Whippet
II. Sporting Dogs
     A. Labrador Retriever
     B. Irish Setter
III. Terriers
     A. Airedale
     B. Welsh Terrier
IV. Working Dogs
     A. Collie
     B. Siberian Husky

Save the file as DOGS.

CHANGE THE OUTLINE

18.2

WordPerfect not only creates the level numbering for an outline, it also maintains it as you change the outline. When you add additional items at any level, WordPerfect assigns the appropriate numbers to those items and renumbers entries affected by the addition. Likewise, if you remove an entry, Word-Perfect adjusts the numbering of the remaining entries in that level. Moving entries by indenting them farther or moving them to new locations also causes WordPerfect to adjust the number assignments.

EXAMPLES

1. You can delete entries in an outline and have WordPerfect maintain the correct numbers for the outline entries. Retrieve the file named AGENDA by pressing the Retrieve (Shift-F10) key [Alt File Retrieve], typing **agenda**, and pressing Enter. The outline created in example 1 of section 18.1 should display on your screen. You can delete the fourth item in the outline by moving to the "I" in "IV.," pressing the DELETE EOL (Ctrl-End) key, and pressing the Del key. Then, press the → key. The revised outline will look like this:

```
August 28 Meeting Agenda

I.   Sales bonus program
II.  Insurance coverage options
III. Construction proposals
IV.  Position announcements before publication
```

Save this revised outline by pressing the Exit (F7)

key once [⟨Alt⟩ File Exit], pressing ⟨Enter⟩ twice, and typing a **y**. Type an **n** to clear the screen and remain in WordPerfect.

2. You can add levels to an existing outline by typing new entries or splitting existing entries. Retrieve the file CONSTRT created in example 2 of section 18.1 by pressing the Retrieve (⟨Shift⟩-⟨F10⟩) key [⟨Alt⟩ File Retrieve], typing **constrt**, and pressing ⟨Enter⟩.

   (In 5.0 only, turn on the Outline feature by pressing the Date/Outline (⟨Shift⟩-⟨F5⟩) key and typing an **o**.) Move to the last outline entry, placing the cursor on the comma that follows "building." Press the ⟨Del⟩ key 3 times to eliminate the comma, the space, and the "d." Type a period, press ⟨Enter⟩, press the Indent (⟨F4⟩) key [⟨Alt⟩ Layout Align Indent →], and type a **D**.

   Move to the comma following "pier," press the ⟨Del⟩ key 7 times, type a period, and press ⟨Enter⟩. Press the Indent (⟨F4⟩) key [⟨Alt⟩ Layout Align Indent →], and type a **B**. WordPerfect automatically assigns the two new outline entries the appropriate level numbers, creating a revised outline that looks like the following.

```
I.   Meet with architect to discuss building plans and zoning
     requirements.
II.  Complete excavation and other site preparation tasks.
     Complete roadbed preparation.
III. Review architect's drawings, make suggested changes, and
     discuss construction schedule.
IV.  Begin construction on main building.
V.   Drive pilings for pier.
VI.  Begin paving parking lots.
```

Use this outline in the next example.

3. WordPerfect adjusts the level numbers when you relocate outline entries. You must be sure to move the required hidden codes along with your entries when you relocate them. The revised outline from example 2 indicates that excavation will start before the architect's plans are approved. To delay this step until after approval, you can rearrange the outline.

Move to the second outline entry. Press the Move ([Ctrl]-[F4]) key, type a **p** for Paragraph [[Alt] Edit Select Paragraph] and an **m** for Move. Press the [↓] key twice to move to the beginning of the next outline entry, and press [Enter]. After you restore the entry, the level numbers initially may not appear correctly. Move down the screen by pressing the [↓] key and the level numbers will be adjusted as shown here:

I. Meet with architect to discuss building plans and zoning
     requirements.
II. Review architect's drawings, make suggested changes, and
     discuss construction schedule.
III. Complete excavation and other site preparation tasks.
     Complete roadbed preparation.
IV. Begin construction on main building.
V. Drive pilings for pier.
VI. Begin paving parking lots.

Save this revised file as CONSTRT by pressing the Save ([F10]) key [[Alt] File Save], pressing [Enter], and typing a **y**.

4. Changing the indentation of an outline entry changes the lettering assigned to the entry. Retrieve the file AGENDA by pressing the Retrieve ([Shift]-[F10]) key [[Alt] File Retrieve], typing **agenda**, and pressing [Enter]. (In 5.0 only, turn the Outline feature on by pressing the Date/Outline ([Shift]-[F5]) key and typing an **o**.) Move to the end of the first outline entry. Press [Enter], press the SPACEBAR, press the [Tab] key, type **Branch managers**, and press [Enter]. Press the SPACEBAR, press the [Tab] key, and type **Sales personnel**. Numbers II and III have been assigned to these two entries. The entry for number III appears to be aligned incorrectly; this will be remedied when its number is adjusted. To change the level of the "Branch managers" entry, move to the beginning of the line, and press the [Tab] key. Press the [→] key, and notice how the number changes. Move to the beginning of the next line, and press the [Tab] key. Press the [↓] key to scroll down the screen. WordPerfect adjusts all of the levels properly, as shown here:

```
August 28 Meeting Agenda

I.   Sales bonus program
     A.  Branch managers
     B.  Sales personnel
II.  Insurance coverage options
III. Construction proposals
IV.  Position announcements before publication
```

You can move an entry back to a higher level by deleting the [Tab] code before the [Par Num:Auto] code.

Save this file as AGENDA by pressing the Save ([F10]) key [[Alt] File Save], pressing [Enter], and typing a **y**.

EXERCISES

1. Retrieve the SPORTS file, created in exercise 1 in section 18.1. Turn on the Outline feature, and add entries for **BASKETBALL** and **TRACK**. Add another level under each sport, and list the names of the team captains. You can use your imagination for these names.

2. Retrieve the DOGS file, created in exercise 2 in section 18.1. Move the entries for "Sporting Dogs" to the end of the outline.

CHANGE THE NUMBERING STYLE

18.3

The default outline numbering style will be adequate for many tasks. If you must conform to a set of established standards, however, you can modify the structure that WordPerfect uses.

You can select from a number of other predefined styles or create your own. Some of the other predefined options will be explored in this section. You will use the legal and bullet styles for marking the levels in an outline.

To change the outline numbering style:

a. Position the cursor at the location where you want to begin using the new style.

b. Press the Date/Outline (Shift-F5) key [Alt Tools Define and skip step c].

c. Type a **d** or a **6** to define a numbering style.

d. Type the letter or number of the numbering style you want.

e. Press the Exit ($\boxed{F7}$) key to leave the definition menu.

In step d, you can type a **p** or a **2** for the paragraph style, an **o** or a **3** for the outline style, an **L** or a **4** for the legal style, or a **b** or a **5** for the bullet style. The hidden code [Par Num Def:] ([Par Num Def] in 5.0) marks the location of the new numbering definition in the document. WordPerfect uses the new paragraph-numbering definition for outline entries after the hidden code.

EXAMPLES

1. The bullet style offers an attractive solution for an outline of ideas or other entries that do not require numbers or letters. To create an outline in this style, press the Date/Outline ($\boxed{Shift}$-$\boxed{F5}$) key, and type a **d** for Define [$\boxed{Alt}$ Tools Define]. WordPerfect displays the Paragraph Number Definition screen shown in Figure 18-1.

Select the bullet style by typing a **b**. Press the Exit ($\boxed{F7}$) key, and turn on the Outline feature by typing an **o** and **o** (omit one **o** in 5.0). Press the $\boxed{Enter}$ key to create the first bullet marker. Then, press the SPACEBAR, press the $\boxed{Tab}$ key, type **Complete filing**, and press $\boxed{Enter}$. Press the SPACEBAR and then

```
Paragraph Number Definition

    1 - Starting Paragraph Number                1
         (in legal style)
                                              Levels
                             1    2    3    4    5    6    7    8
    2 - Paragraph            1.   a.   i.   (1)  (a)  (i)  1)   a)
    3 - Outline              I.   A.   1.   a.   (1)  (a)  i)   a)
    4 - Legal (1.1.1)        1    .1   .1   .1   .1   .1   .1   .1
    5 - Bullets              •    o    —    ■    *    +    .    x
    6 - User-defined

    Current Definition       I.   A.   1.   a.   (1)  (a)  i)   a)
    Attach Previous Level         No   No   No   No   No   No   No

    7 - Enter Inserts Paragraph Number           Yes

    8 - Automatically Adjust to Current Level     Yes

    9 - Outline Style Name



Selection: 8
```

| FIGURE 18-1. | Selecting a numbering style |

the [Tab] key. Type **Create form letter**. Your two
entries should be marked with bullet indicators like
this:

```
•   Complete filing
•   Create form letter
```

Turn off the Outline feature by pressing the Date/
Outline ([Shift] - [F5]) key and typing an **o** and **f** (omit
f in 5.0) [[Alt] Tools Outline Off].

2. The legal style allows you to create outline entries
with each item number displaying all of the levels.

For example, if your entry is the third item under the first section, it will be labeled "1.3." The second item one level below this entry would be labeled "1.3.2." To use the legal style, position the cursor where you want to create the outline, press the Date/Outline ([Shift]-[F5]) key, and type a **d** [[Alt] Tools Define]. Type an **L** for Legal, and press the Exit ([F7]) key. Turn on the Outline feature by typing an **o** and **o** (omit one **o** in 5.0). Press [Enter] to generate a first-level number. Press the Indent ([F4]) key [[Alt] Layout Align Indent →], and type **Easements to Title**. Press [Enter] and the [Tab] key to generate a second-level number. Press the Indent ([F4]) key [[Alt] Layout Align Indent →], and type **Water Rights**. Press [Enter] (press the [Tab] key in 5.0), press the Indent ([F4]) key [[Alt] Layout Align Indent →], and type **Building Rights**. Press [Enter], and press the [Tab] key once (twice in 5.0) to generate a number at the third level. Press the Indent ([F4]) key [[Alt] Layout Align Indent →], type **Special deed rights**, and press [Enter]. (Press the [Tab] key twice in 5.0.) Press the Indent ([F4]) key [[Alt] Layout Align Indent →], and type **Lateral support**. Press [Enter], press the Margin Release ([Shift]-[Tab]) key (press the [Tab] key instead in 5.0), and press the Indent ([F4]) key [[Alt] Layout Align Indent →]. Type **Right of Way**, and press [Enter]. (Press the [Tab] key in 5.0.) Press the Indent ([F4]) key [[Alt] Layout Align Indent →], and type **Way of Necessity**. The completed outline looks like this:

```
1   Easements to Title
    1.1 Water Rights
    1.2 Building Rights
        1.2.1    Special deed rights
        1.2.2    Lateral support
    1.3 Right of Way
    1.4 Way of Necessity
```

Turn off the Outline feature by pressing the Date/Outline (Shift - F5) key and typing an **o** and **f** (omit **f** in 5.0) [Alt Tools Outline Off].

EXERCISES

1. Change the outline style to Legal, and create the following outline:

   ```
   1. Estate Planning
      1.1. Trust
      1.2. Will
   ```

2. Change to the bullet outline style, and create the following entries with the level-four bullet indicators:

   The following employees are being honored for 25 years of service:
   - Jane Parker
   - Bill Black

EXERCISES

(Do not clear the screen between exercises unless instructed to do so.)

MASTERY
SKILLS CHECK

1. Create the following outline with WordPerfect's automatic level-numbering feature.

   PORTFOLIO HOLDINGS
   I.　Zero coupon bonds
   II.　Treasury bills
   III.　Blue chip stocks
   IV.　Mutual fund shares

2. Revise the outline so that "Treasury bills" is the last entry.

3. Add the following entry to the outline with the Outline feature:

   V.　Stock options

   Save the file as INVEST, and clear the screen.

4. Create the following outline:

   I.　New Construction
   　A.　Mayfield Village
   　B.　Highland Heights
   　　1.　1114 Miner Road
   　　2.　4811 Highland Ave.
   II.　Remodeling Projects
   　A.　Gates Mills
   　　1.　112 Sherman Road
   　　2.　230 Saddleback Lane
   　B.　Chagrin Falls

5. Add a new entry for a remodeling project in Solon. Add another entry for a new construction project at 5311 Wilson Mills Road in Highland Heights. Save the file as JOBS.

1. Create the following memo, using the Outline feature for the bullet entries:

From: John Smith
To: George Carson
Subject: Expense Reports

A recent audit of expense reports indicated that several of your employees have exceeded the per diem allowed for travel expense on several occasions. A list of the employees violating this policy is enclosed.

- Jim Miller
- Mary Parker
- Paul Drake

Insert a hard page break above the outline entries, and print a copy of the document.

2. Change Outline options, and create the following outline:

1 WordPerfect's Math Features
   1.1 Add numbers
      1.1.1 Produce a subtotal for a column of
          numbers
      1.1.2 Add subtotals to create totals
      1.1.3 Add totals to produce a grand total
   1.2 Perform formula calculations across columns

Save the outline as MATH.

3. Create the following outline, using Underline for the titles as shown:

I. WordPerfect Books
   A. WordPerfect Made Easy
   B. WordPerfect: The Complete Reference

II. 1-2-3 Books
   A. 1-2-3 Made Easy
   B. 1-2-3: The Complete Reference

Add Teach Yourself WordPerfect 5.1 as item C in the first section. Print two copies of the outline.

4. Create the following outline:

I. Vacation days
II. Sick leave
III. Holidays
   A. Christmas
   B. Thanksgiving
   C. Memorial Day
   D. Halloween
   E. Independence Day
   F. Labor Day

Move the third section with all of its second-level entries to the top of the outline. Delete the entry for Halloween.

Changing the Setup
Parameters

►19◄

CHAPTER OBJECTIVES

After completing this chapter, you should be able to:

► **Change backup options**   19.1

► **Change display options**   19.2

► **Select initial settings**   19.3

Many people use WordPerfect for years without changing the setup parameters that control the package. Not changing these initial settings often leads to having to change the same settings for each new document. By changing WordPerfect's initial settings, you can reset any options you wish to apply to all new documents. In this chapter, you will explore only a few of the many changes that you can make to WordPerfect's initial settings. Since the same process can be used to update other settings, you can explore additional options on your own.

Among the setup parameters is an option for automatically protecting your work. You can have WordPerfect create a backup of the current file at any time interval you select. If your system goes down, you can retrieve the backup file, which will contain any changes you made up to the last time that WordPerfect saved the backup.

WordPerfect's display options allow you to customize the way in which various text styles, sizes, and features are displayed on the screen. You can select from an entire palette of colors for each feature if you have a color monitor.

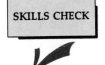

SKILLS CHECK

(Do not clear the screen until you have completed the last exercise.)

1. Type the following lines, using Bold and Underline where indicated:

   WordPerfect allows you to change several settings. You can set WordPerfect to back up files automatically. You

can also change the screen's appearance by selecting the colors WordPerfect uses. These are just a few of the selections available.

2. Save the document as DEFAULT.

3. Rename the DEFAULT file to SETTINGS.

4. Reveal codes to see WordPerfect's code for a soft return.

CHANGE BACKUP OPTIONS

19.1

WordPerfect can create automatic backups of your current document at a fixed time interval. If you request this option, WordPerfect asks you to wait each time it writes your document to disk at the requested interval. If you are working with two documents, it creates files named WP{WP}.BK1 and WP{WP}.BK2, respectively, for them. If your system goes down without warning, you can rename the backup files when you start another WordPerfect session.

To have WordPerfect create automatic timed backups of your work:

a. Press the Setup (Shift)-(F1)) key [(Alt) File Setup Environment and skip step b].

b. Type **e** or a **3** for Environment (omit in 5.0).

c. Type a **b** or a **1** to change the backup settings.

d. Type a **t** or a **1** to change the timed backup settings.

e. Type a **y** to have WordPerfect make timed backups or an **n** to discontinue the feature.

f. If you typed a "y" in step d, type the desired number of minutes between automatic saves, and press [Enter].

g. Press the Exit ([F7]) key to return to your document.

EXAMPLES

1. Timed backups offer protection against power failures or other accidents that remove a document from your computer's memory. To create timed backups, press the Setup ([Shift]-[F1]) key. Next, type an **e** [[Alt] File Setup Environment] (omit in 5.0), a **b**, a **t**, a **y**, and **30**. Press [Enter] and the Exit ([F7]) key. WordPerfect will back up your documents every half hour.

2. If you lose a document, you can rename the backup copy when you start WordPerfect again. First, press the Setup ([Shift]-[F1]) key. Next, type an **e** [[Alt] File Setup Environment] (omit in 5.0), a **b**, a **t**, a **y**, and a **1**, and press [Enter] and the Exit ([F7]) key. To have something to back up, type

WordPerfect has an automatic timed backup feature.

To have WordPerfect back up the document, wait a minute. WordPerfect displays this message on the status line when it saves the file:

`* Please wait *`

To show how you can use this timed backup, reboot the machine without exiting from WordPerfect. First, open the door on drive A if you are using a hard disk system, or place the DOS disk in drive A if you are using a floppy disk system. Next, press the Ctrl-Alt-Del key combination. Once the computer has loaded DOS, load WordPerfect. When you load WordPerfect, it displays this message:

`Are other copies of WordPerfect currently running? (Y/N)`

Type an **n**. When the blank document screen appears, press the Retrieve (Shift-F10) key [Alt File Retrieve], type **wp{wp}.bk1**, and press Enter. The document that WordPerfect backed up for you appears on the screen. Save this file under a new name by pressing the Save (F10) key [Alt File Save], typing **backup**, and pressing Enter. Add the word **efficient** in front of "automatic" to alter the entry and cause WordPerfect to back up the document. When WordPerfect first tries to back up this file in the current WordPerfect session, it will display this message:

`Old backup file exists. 1 Rename; 2 Delete:`

Since you retrieved the data from the backup file and saved it in another file, you can type a **d** for Delete.

EXERCISES

1. Reset the timed backup to 2 hours (120 minutes).

2. Reset the timed backup to 30-minute intervals.

CHANGE DISPLAY OPTIONS

19.2

WordPerfect allows a significant amount of screen customization. If you have a color monitor, you can change the screen colors to make different Word-Perfect features appear different on screen. You can use a special character to display hard returns on your screen. You can also choose whether or not to display the filename of the current document on the screen.

To change the screen colors:

a. Press the Setup (Shift-F1) key [Alt File Setup Display and skip step b].

b. Type a **d** or a **3** to select Display.

c. Type a **c** or a **2** to select color options.

d. Type an **s** or a **1** to select Screen Colors.

e. Move the cursor to the row of the feature that you want to change.

f. Move the cursor to the Foreground or Background column.

g. Type the letter marking the color you want to use.

h. Press the Exit ([F7]) key twice to return to the document.

The colors that are available depend upon the equipment you are using. WordPerfect displays a sample of how the feature appears in the right-hand column of the colors setup screen. Some monitors also include a font column, which allows you to use an alternate font for a feature. If you change your mind while selecting colors, press the Cancel ([F1]) key instead of the Exit ([F7]) key until you return to the document.

To change the character that represents a hard return:

a. Press the Setup ([Shift]-[F1]) key [[Alt] File Setup Display and skip step b].

b. Type a **d** or a **3** to select Display.

c. Type an **e** or a **6** for Edit-Screen Options (omit in 5.0).

d. Type an **h** or a **6** to select Hard Return Display Character.

e. Type the character you want to represent hard returns.

f. Press the Exit ([F7]) key.

The hard return code [HRt] appears as usual when you press the Reveal Codes ([Alt]-[F3]) key [[Alt] Edit Reveal Codes].

To change the display of the filename in the status line:

a. Press the Setup ([Shift]-[F1]) key [[Alt] File Setup Display and skip step b].

b. Type a **d** or a **3** to select Display.

c. Type an **e** or a **6** for Edit-Screen options (omit in 5.0).

d. Type an **f** or a **4** to select the filename option.

e. Type a **y** to display the filename on the status line or an **n** to leave the space blank.

f. Press the Exit ([F7]) key.

EXAMPLES

1. You can change the colors WordPerfect uses to block text. First, press the Setup ([Shift]-[F1]) key. Next, type a **d** [[Alt] File Setup Display], a **c**, and an **s**. If your colors setup screen has a font column, press the [→] key. When the cursor is in the Foreground column, the top of the screen looks like this:

```
Setup: Colors        A B C D E F G H I J K L M N O P
                     ? B C D E F G H I J K L M N O P
Attribute            Foreground  Background  Sample
Normal                   H           B       Sample
Blocked                  P           A       Sample
```

Press the [↓] key, and type an **a** to select black foreground letters. Next, press the [→] key, and type a **c** to select a green background. The new appearance is shown in the sample in the right-hand column. Press the Exit ([F7]) key twice to return to the document. (The available options and the effects they have on your screen depend on your computer equipment.)

2. You can change the character that represents a hard return. WordPerfect's default setting displays a hard return as a blank space. You can change this feature when you are unsure of the location of hard returns and want them to be more obvious. First, type

Hard Return Characters
    Emphasizing the hard return characters allows you to discover where you have pressed ENTER and where WordPerfect has wrapped the text for you.

Next, press [Enter] and the Setup ([Shift]-[F1]) key. Then, type a **d** [[Alt] File Setup Display], an **e** (omit in 5.0), and an **h**. To display the hard return character as a plus sign, type **+**, and press the Exit ([F7]) key. Now the text looks like this:

Hard Return Characters+
    Emphasizing the hard return characters allows you to discover where you have pressed ENTER and where WordPerfect has wrapped the text for you.+

3. You can suppress display of the filename in the status line. First, press the Setup ([Shift]-[F1]) key. Next, type a **d** [[Alt] File Setup Display], an **e** (omit in 5.0), an **f**, and an **n**, and press the Exit ([F7]) key. The filename will no longer appear in the status line after you retrieve a document or save a new document without exiting from it.

EXERCISES

1. Change the foreground color of bold text to black.

2. Set the colors of italic text to the ones for normal text.

3. Change the hard return display character to the "less than" symbol (<).

4. Reset the hard return display character to the space.

5. Set WordPerfect to display the filename in the status line.

19.3 SELECT INITIAL SETTINGS

WordPerfect's initial settings provide additional customization capabilities. You can control the computer's beep with these commands. You can also affect the display of the date and other options.

To change the occurrence of the beep sound:

a. Press the Setup (Shift-F1) key [Alt File Setup Environment and skip step b].

b. Type an **e** or a **3** for Environment (**i** or a **5** for Initial Settings in 5.0).

c. Type an **e** or a **2** (**b** or a **1** in 5.0) for Beep Options.

d. Type an **e** or a **1** to change whether WordPerfect should beep when an error occurs; then type a **y** to have WordPerfect beep or an **n** not to have it beep.

e. Type an **s** or a **3** to change whether WordPerfect should beep when a search fails; then type a **y** to have WordPerfect beep or an **n** to have it not beep when it cannot find a search string.

f. Press the Exit (F7) key to return to the document.

WordPerfect's third beep option, Beep on Hyphen-ation, determines whether WordPerfect beeps when it prompts you to select a location for a hyphen in a word that won't fit on a line. Appendix A discusses hyphenation in detail.

To change the date display:

a. Press the Setup (Shift-F1) key [Alt File Setup Initial Settings and skip step b].

b. Type an **i** or a **5** for Initial Settings.

c. Type a **d** or a **2** for Date Format.

d. Type the appropriate numbers and symbols for the date format you want.

e. Press Enter.

f. Press the Exit (F7) key.

EXAMPLES

1. You can direct WordPerfect to beep when you are searching for text. This alerts you when Word-Perfect cannot find a search string or when it finishes a replace operation. First, press the Setup (Shift-F1) key. Next, type an **e** (**i** in 5.0) [Alt

Setup Environment], an **e** (**b** in 5.0), an **s**, and a **y** to set WordPerfect to beep when a search fails. Finally, press the Exit (F7) key to return to the document. When you search the document for text or codes, WordPerfect will beep when it cannot find the search string.

2. WordPerfect can insert the current date into a document. You can change the date display for WordPerfect's Date feature. First, press the Setup (Shift-F1) key. Then, type an **i** [Alt File Setup Initial Settings] and a **d**. The date format screen provides many options to format dates and times. The screen displays the numbers and symbols you can use. Type the appropriate numbers and symbols to specify a date format. To set the date in the format of MM/DD/YY, type **2/1/5**. Finally, press Enter and the Exit (F7) key. To have WordPerfect insert the date in a document, press the Date/Outline (Shift-F5) key, and type a **t** [Alt Tools Date Text] for Date Text. WordPerfect inserts the date at the cursor's location using the format that you specified.

3. You can use the Date feature to insert the current time in your document. First, press the Setup (Shift-F1) key. Then, type an **i** [Alt File Setup Initial Settings] and a **d**. To set the time in the format of the hour, a colon, and the minute, type **8:9**. Then, press Enter and the Exit (F7) key. To have WordPerfect insert the time in a document, press the Date/Outline (Shift-F5) key and type a **t** [Alt

Tools Date Text] for Date Text. WordPerfect inserts the time at the cursor's location using the format that you specified.

EXERCISES

1. Set WordPerfect not to beep when an error occurs.

2. Set WordPerfect to use the date format of day of the week, a comma, a space, the month, another space, and the day of the month.

3. Type the following sentence. Where the sentence has four "X"s, use the Date feature to insert the current date text.

   On XXXX, the Okra Vegetable company begins marketing its new product line, the Seeing Green frozen foods.

EXERCISES

1. Set the automatic timed backup to every 20 minutes.

2. Set the background for normal text to black.

3. Set the date format to insert the month spelled out, a space, and four digits for the year.

4. Type the following sentence. Where the sentence has four "X"s, use the Date feature to insert the current date text.

Acme Corporation projects that its personnel will increase 5% during XXXX.

5. Set WordPerfect not to beep when it cannot find the text that you want during a search.

(Do not clear the screen between exercises unless instructed to do so.)

1. Set the automatic timed backup to back up your files every minute. Type **Testing Backups**. Wait until WordPerfect backs up your document. Rename the backup file WP{WP}.BK1 to BCKUPTST. Clear the screen without saving the document.

2. Set the automatic timed backup so that it does not back up your files.

3. Set the date format to the month spelled out, a space, the day of the month, a comma, a space, and the year using four digits.

4. Type the following paragraphs. Use the Date feature to replace the four "X"s with the current date text.

The company picnic is on XXXX.
Each person should bring one dish. Please review the schedule, which breaks down the type of dish based upon the person's last name.

5. Make the first sentence boldface. Underline the words "one dish."

6. Set the hard return display character to an asterisk.

7. If you have a color monitor, set the underlined text background to red and the boldfaced text background to light blue.

8. Use the List Files feature to delete the file named WP{WP}.SET. (This restores all of the display settings to their original values.)

9. Save the document as DISH, and exit WordPerfect. Load WordPerfect. Set the automatic timed backup to back up your files every 30 minutes.

Using Styles

►20◄

CHAPTER OBJECTIVES

After completing this chapter, you should be able to:

▶ **Create a paired style**   20.1

▶ **Use a paired style**   20.2

▶ **Create an open style**   20.3

▶ **Use an open style**   20.4

▶ **Modify a style**   20.5

▶ **Save a style library**   20.6

▶ **Use styles from a style library**   20.7

WordPerfect's Styles feature is a useful tool for formatting documents or parts of documents. A *style* is a stored group of codes or text you create that can be retrieved into a document to control its formatting. Most of the usual formatting you are likely to use in a document can be incorporated into a style. Styles can also offer you some expanded capabilities compared to normal formatting.

Styles can simplify the process of creating the formatting for documents (or sections of documents). If, for example, you always change the justification, tabs, and margins for letters, you could create a style to do the same thing for you.

Styles can be used to easily standardize the appearance of documents. Creating sets of styles for each document type you produce can make formatting easier and quicker, and it also allows you to produce a uniform appearance among similar types of documents.

Styles also allow you to easily change the formatting of documents or parts of documents. To change the formatting of text produced with a style only requires changing the codes associated with that style. Within the document all text that is associated with the edited style is automatically modified.

Styles become a part of the document in which they are used. They can also be saved as a style library and later retrieved into and used in other documents.

The capabilities of WordPerfect's Style feature form a powerful tool for formatting documents. This chapter presents the basic features of styles. Once mastered, you can use them to create professionally formatted documents quickly and easily.

(Do not clear the screen between exercises unless instructed to do so.)

SKILLS CHECK

1. Type the following:

   Styles

   Styles are an exciting feature of WordPerfect. Many people use them to simplify document production. One advantage of styles is that they can help you create all types of documents, long or short. Mary Smith of the Accounting Department says:

   "I was afraid that using styles would be too complicated and would take too much time. However, I'm glad I tried them. I'm constantly finding new and better uses for styles."

   As you and your co-workers will discover, styles can be used to simplify document formatting and to create document standards throughout your department.

2. Preview the document.

3. Bold and center the heading.

4. Change the line spacing to double spacing for the first and third paragraphs, but the second paragraph should be single spaced.

5. Delete the quotation marks from the quote and indent the quote from both sides.

6. Underline Mary Smith.

7. Preview the document.

8. Save the document as STYL.DOC and clear the screen.

20.1 | CREATE A PAIRED STYLE

Before you can use styles in your documents, you must first create (or define) them. A *paired style* is a type of style that has a beginning [Style On] and an end [Style Off]. You can place formatting codes in the beginning of the style to affect the entered text. Most codes that are placed in the beginning of the style are automatically turned off by WordPerfect at the end of the style. Sometimes, you will also want codes to occur after the text, because you have other features you will want to invoke.

To create a paired style:

a. Press the Style ([Alt]-[F8]) key [[Alt] Layout Styles].

b. Type a **3** or **c** to create a style.

c. Type a **1** or **n** to select the name option. Type a name for the style (one to twelve characters long) and press [Enter].

d. Type a **3** or **d** to select the description option. Type in a description of the style and press [Enter].

e. Type a **4** or **c** to select the code option. Using the same formatting steps you would use in a document, enter the codes. Press the Exit ([F7]) key when finished.

f. Type a **5** or **e** to select the enter option. Type **1** or **h** to indicate that the [Enter] key should perform as normal, type **2** or **f** to indicate that the [Enter] key should turn the style off, or type **3** or **o** to indicate that the [Enter] key should turn the style off and then back on.

g. Press the Exit ([F7]) key to exit the Edit Styles menu.

h. Press the Exit ([F7]) key to exit the Styles menu.

When you perform step e, you are presented with the Paired Style Codes screen. The screen is split in two to show the Reveal Codes in the bottom half of the screen. The cursor is in the top half of the screen, above the boxed comment. Your entries will be made either above or below this comment. You can look at the codes for these entries in the bottom half of the screen. The Reveal Codes half of the screen includes a [Comment] code. This [Comment] acts as a divider for the formatting codes. You can think of the [Comment] as a placeholder for the text that will be affected by this paired style. The area to the left of the [Comment] is called the Style On area and the area to the right is called the Style Off area. Place formatting codes that you want to affect the entered text before the [Comment] (that is, in the Style On area), and place any codes that are to go into effect after the entered text following the [Comment] (that is, in the Style Off area). Many codes that you turn on in the Style On area are automatically turned off for you by the paired style.

Step f determines how pressing the (Enter) key within the style will affect the style. Often, you will want the (Enter) key to produce a hard return ([HRt]) code, just as it does in the regular document. Sometimes, however, you can save yourself time by changing the function of the (Enter) key, if you know that no [HRt]'s are going to be used within the text affected by the style. Two choices are available: you can use the (Enter) key to turn off the style, or to turn the style off and back on again.

If you choose to have the (Enter) key turn off the style, you will eliminate having to turn off the style yourself. This technique can often be used for headings within documents. Headings are usually short phrases that do not contain [HRt]'s.

Having the (Enter) key turn the style off and then on again can be used for styles in lists where each item in the list is no more than a paragraph long. You'll understand better how this kind of style works when you get to section 20.2.

EXAMPLES

(Do not clear the screen until you have completed the last example and are told to do so.)

1. You are going to create a style for a main heading. This heading is to be centered from left to right on the page and also bolded. Because the style has a

```
Styles

  Name          Type       Description

  Bibliogrphy   Paired     Bibliography
  Doc Init      Paired     Initialize Document Style
  Document      Outline    Document Style
  Pleading      Open       Header for numbered pleading paper
  Right Par     Outline    Right-Aligned Paragraph Numbers
  Tech Init     Open       Initialize Technical Style
  Technical     Outline    Technical Document Style
```

```
1 On; 2 Off; 3 Create; 4 Edit; 5 Delete; 6 Save; 7 Retrieve; 8 Update: 1
```

FIGURE 20-1.   A Styles menu

definite beginning and end, you will use a paired style.

First, press the Style ([Alt]-[F8]) key [[Alt] Layout Styles]. The Styles menu will appear on the screen. An example of the Styles Menu appears in Figure 20-1. Depending on how your WordPerfect program was set up, there may or may not be currently defined styles on this screen. Either way, the process for creating styles is the same.

Second, type c to create the style. The Edit Styles menu, a sample of which is shown in Figure 20-2, will appear on the screen.

To give this style a name, type n for name, then

```
Styles: Edit

    1 - Name

    2 - Type          Paired

    3 - Description

    4 - Codes

    5 - Enter         HRt




Selection: 0
```

FIGURE 20-2.   An Edit Styles menu

type **Main Heading,** and press Enter. (If you did not give the style a name, WordPerfect would assign the style a number.)

Since the type of style chosen is already a paired style, you can skip the second item.

Next, type **d** to describe more fully the purpose of this style, then type **First level of headings for document,** and press Enter. This step is not required, but it makes it easier to identify the style you wish to use.

Next, type **c,** for the codes option. This is where you define what the style actually does. Since the cursor in the bottom half of the screen is already highlighting the [Comment], anything you enter now will come before the [Comment]. You can begin putting in your codes for the heading. First press the Center ([Shift]-[F6]) key [[Alt] Layout Align Center]. The [Center] ([Cntr] in 5.0) code appears to the left of the [Comment]. The other desired formatting for the main heading is to bold it. Press the Bold ([F6]) key. Notice that the [BOLD] code appears to the left of the [Comment], but there is no [bold] code after the [Comment]. Don't worry, the Style Off section of this paired style will automatically turn off the bolding for you.

Press the Exit ([F7]) key to exit the Codes screen.

For this example, you will leave the function of the [Enter] key at its normal setting. To end the definition of this style, press the Exit ([F7]) key twice to return to the document screen.

Remember, do *not* clear the screen. Even though there is no text in your document, the style you created is part of the document. You will want all the styles created in these examples available to you when you do section 20.2.

2. When you use styles, you usually will use more than one of them in a document. You have just created a style for a main heading. Now you are going to create a style for a secondary level heading. This heading will be underlined, and there will always be two [HRt]'s after it.

First, press the Style ([Alt]-[F8]) key [[Alt] Layout Styles]. The Styles menu you left in example 1 will appear on the screen. The Main Heading style that you created will be listed. Second, type **c** to create a style. The Edit Styles menu will appear on the screen.

To give this style a name, type **n**, **Sec. Heading,** and press Enter.

Since the type of style chosen is already a paired style, you can skip the second item.

Next, type **d** to describe more fully the purpose of this style. Type **Secondary level of headings for document**, and press Enter.

Next, type **c**, for the Codes item. This is where you define what the style actually does. Since the cursor is already highlighting the [Comment], anything you enter now will come before the comment. You can begin putting in your underline code for the secondary heading. First, press the Underline (F8) key. Notice the [UND] code appears to the left of the [Comment] but there is no [und] code after the [Comment]. Don't worry, the Style Off section of this paired style will automatically turn off underlining for you.

Then, press the → key to move the cursor to the right of the [Comment]. Press the Enter key twice to insert two [HRt]'s after the [Comment]. These codes will automatically put two blank lines after the secondary heading. Press the Exit (F7) key to exit the Codes screen.

For this example, you will change the function of the Enter key. Type **e** for Enter and type **f** to make the Enter key turn off the style. In section 20.2, you will see how this works.

To end the definition of this style, press the Exit (F7) key twice to return to the document screen.

3. Creating bulleted lists is another instance where styles are useful. Many times, the Tab Settings within a document may change. You cannot count on the tabs always being set properly for specific types of text, such as bulleted lists.

   To do this, first press the Style (Alt - F8) key [Alt Layout Styles]. The Styles menu you left in example 2 should appear on the screen. The Main Heading and Sec. Heading styles should be listed.

   Second, type **c** to create the style. The Edit Styles menu will appear on the screen.

   To give this style a name, type **n**, **Bullet List**, and press Enter .

   Since the type of style chosen is already a paired style, you can skip the second item.

   Next, type **d** to describe more fully the purpose of this style. Type **Indented bulleted lists style**, and press Enter .

   Then, type **c**, for the Codes item. This is where you define what the style actually does. Since the cursor is already highlighting the [Comment], anything you enter now will come before the comment. The first thing you want to do is make sure the tabs have been set for bullets (because you will be using the Indent key to format the list). Press the Format (Shift - F8) key, type **L** for line [Alt Layout Line], and **t** for Tab. Press Home , Home , ← , and the Delete EOL (Ctrl - End) key to delete the current tab settings. Type a 0, Enter , 0.5, Enter , 0.8, and Enter to set the tabs (in 5.0, type **1**, [Enter], **1.5**, [Enter], **1.8**, and [Enter]). Press the Exit ([F7]) key twice to return to the Codes screen.

Press the [Tab] key, type an asterisk (*) for the bullet, and press the Indent → ([F4]) key [[Alt] Layout Align Indent →].

Use the [→] key to move to the right of the [Comment]. Press the [Enter] key twice to create double spacing for the bulleted items. The screen should look like this:

```
   *

┌──────────────────────────────────────────────────┐
│ Place Style On Codes above, and Style Off Codes below. │
└──────────────────────────────────────────────────┘




Style:   Press Exit when done              Doc 1 Pg 1 Ln 1.33" Pos 1"
(      ▲   ▲                                                         )
[Tab Set:Rel: 0",+0.5",+0.8"][Tab]*[→Indent][Comment][HRt]
[HRt]
▮
```

Press the Exit ([F7]) key to exit the Codes screen.

For this example, you will change the function of the [Enter] key. Type **e** for Enter and **o** to make the [Enter] key turn the style off and then on again. In section 20.2, you will see how this works.

To end the definition of this style, press the Exit ([F7]) key twice to return to the document screen.

Once you have returned to the blank document screen, save the document by pressing the Exit ([F7]) key [[Alt] File Exit], typing **y**, **style1.doc**, and pressing [Enter] twice.

EXERCISES

(Do not clear the screen until you have completed the last exercise and are told to do so.)

1. Create a paired style called Header Lvl 1. This style bolds and centers the heading and puts a centered line of 45 asterisks on the next line.

2. Create a paired style called Header Lvl 2. The style turns itself off when you press the [Enter] key. The formatting for the style includes underlining the header and one hard return after the header.

3. Create a paired style called Long Quotes. Define this style to make it set the line spacing to single spacing and indent the paragraph from both sides. Define [Enter] within the style to make it turn the style off when it is pressed.

4. Save the document as STYLE2.DOC and clear the screen.

USE A PAIRED STYLE   20.2

Using a paired style is easy once it has been created. Paired styles can be turned on to affect text as you type it in. Styles can also be used to affect text that is already part of the document. In fact, paired styles work similarly to the way that bold or underline functions do.

To use a paired style on text as you type it in:

a. Press the Style (Alt-F8) key [Alt Layout Styles].

b. Using the ⬆ and ⬇ keys, highlight the style you wish to use.

c. Type a **1** or **o** to turn the style on.

d. Type the text that is to be part of the style.

e. Turn off the style. This step depends on the use you assigned the Enter key. If the Enter key works as normal, either press the Style (Alt-F8) key [Alt Layout Styles] and type **f** for off, or press the ➡ key. If the Enter key turns off the style, just press Enter. If the Enter key turns the style off and then on again, either press the Style (Alt-F8) key [Alt Layout Styles] and type **f** for off, or press Enter, the Backspace key, and **y** to delete the Style code.

To use a paired style on text that already is part of the document:

a. Block the text that is to be affected by the style.

b. Press the Style (Alt-F8) key [Alt Layout Styles].

c. Type a **1** or **o** to turn the style on.

EXAMPLES

(Do not clear the screen until you have completed the last example and are told to do so.)

1. You can use the styles created in the last section to format text of a document that already exists. Retrieve the document called STYLE1.DOC by pressing the Retrieve (Shift - F10) key [Alt File Retrieve], typing **style1.doc**, and pressing Enter .

   Type in the following:

My Summer Vacation

I did some very interesting and fun things this summer. Some of the things I did included working for the city park commission, taking a vacation in Yellowstone National Park, and meeting some new people.

"My Summer Vacation" is the main heading for this paper. To use the Main heading style created for this document, you must first block the text to be included within the style. Move the cursor to the "M" in "My." Press the Block (Alt - F4) key [Alt Edit Block], Enter , and the ← key.

   Press the Style (Alt - F8) key [Alt Layout Styles]. Using the ↑ and ↓ keys, highlight the Main heading style. Type **o** to turn on the style. You are returned to the document. "My Summer Vacation" is now centered and bolded at the top of the screen.

   Press the Reveal Codes (Alt - F3) key [Alt Edit Reveal Codes] and press the ← key to highlight the [Style Off:Main Heading] code. When high-lighted, the code changes to [Style Off:Main Head-ing;[bold]]. When you created the Main Heading style, you did not put in the ending bold code. The paired style automatically created it for you. Now press (Home), (←) to position the cursor adjacent to the Style On code. The code is [Style On:Main Heading]. Press the (←) key one more time so that the cursor is now covering the Style On code. Now the code looks like [Style On:Main Heading;[Cen-ter][BOLD]] ([Style On:Main Heading;[Cntr] [BOLD]] in 5.0). Normally, in Reveal Codes, the Style On and Style Off codes just indicate the name of the style. But when you cover them with the cursor, they also include the formatting codes within the style.

2. Now you will use a style as you type in the text. This time you will use the Sec. Heading style. This style is a paired style that turns the style off when you press the (Enter) key.

First, press (Home), (Home), (↓) to move to the end of the document. Make sure that there are two [HRt]'s after the existing text.

Next, press the Style ((Alt)-(F8)) key [(Alt) Layout Styles]. Highlight the style named Sec. Heading and type o to turn on the style. You will be back at the document screen.

Notice that the cursor is located on top of the [Style Off:Sec. Heading;[HRt][HRt][und]] code. As you type in the secondary heading, the text will be inserted between the Style On and Style Off codes.

Type in the heading:

Working for the City Park Commission

and press Enter. As you press Enter, the cursor moves to the right of the Style Off code and immediately moves down the two [HRt]'s that are part of the code. The cursor moved outside of the Style codes because when you created the style, you reassigned the Enter key to turn off the style.

3. Continue typing the document with the following paragraph:

I learned a lot this summer working for the City Park Commission. I performed a variety of jobs because my main job was to act as a fill-in for regular employees on vacation. Some of my more interesting duties included:

Press Enter twice to get ready to type in some bulleted items. The Bullet List style you created was a paired style where the Enter key turns the style off and then on again.

Press the Style (Alt-F8) key [Alt Layout Styles]. Highlight the Bullet List style and type **o** to turn this style on. Type the following, pressing the Enter key at the end of each item.

Washing the elephants
Selling balloons
Cleaning out animal stalls
Acting as a guide in the monkey pavilion

As you typed in the list, the bullets were created for you. If you are not in Reveal Codes, press the Reveal Codes (Alt-F3) key [Alt Edit Reveal

Codes]. Notice that your cursor is currently located on the Style Off portion of an extra set of style codes. This is because you pressed the `Enter` key after pavilion and WordPerfect automatically generated a new set of style codes. To stop the style at this point, press the `Backspace` key. This deletes the extra pair of Style Codes.

Save the document using SUMMER.JOB as the filename, and clear the screen by pressing the Exit (`F7`) key [`Alt` File Exit], typing **y**, **summer.job**, and pressing `Enter` twice.

EXERCISES

1. Retrieve the file named STYLE2.DOC. Change the line spacing to double spacing. Type in the following text using the Header Lvl 1 style for the main heading, the Header Lvl 2 style for the Department headings, and the Long Quotes style for the quote.

Department Comments and Concerns

****

Accounting Department

Judging from the mail, the Department's main concern has to do with the current conversion from ACME's Word Processor to WordPerfect 5.1. Denise Phelps writes:

> I have been amazed at how quickly we all are learning WordPerfect. It's features seem much more intuitive than our old word processor. Overall, I'm happy with the change.

Sales Department

The Sales Department welcomes a new salesperson. Her name is Carla Miller. She comes to us from Michigan State University where she was a marketing major. Welcome Carla!

Save this document as DEPTNEWS.LTR and clear the screen.

2. Retrieve the document STYLE2.DOC. Type the following text.

Welcome!

We give a warm welcome to the following transferees to our main headquarters.

John Smith
John joins us from our Tucson office, where he was the top salesman for the past three quarters. Congratulations, John!

Jane Brown
Jane comes to us from the New York office, where she managed the MIS department. She joins us here as Chris Robertson's second-in-command in our own MIS department. Welcome!

Use the Header Lvl 1 style on "Welcome!"
Use the Header Lvl 2 style on "John Smith" and "Jane Brown".
Save the document as WELCOME and clear the screen.

20.3 | CREATE AN OPEN STYLE

Open styles are similar to paired styles. Paired styles have a beginning (Style On) and an end (Style Off). Open Styles, however, have only a beginning. The Formatting codes you put into an Open Style stay on for the whole document, or at least until the formatting is either changed within the document or by another style. Open Styles are useful for formatting that affects the entire document. That is why they are often used at the beginning of documents.

To create an open style:

a. Press the Style ([Alt]-[F8]) key [[Alt] Layout Styles].

b. Type a **3** or **c** to create a style.

c. Type a **1** or **n** to select the name option. Type a name for the style (one to twelve characters long), and press [Enter].

d. Type a **2** or **t** to select the type option. Type a **2** or **o** to select the open type.

e. Type a **3** or **d** to select the description option. Type in a description of the style, and press [Enter].

f. Type a **4** or **c** to select the code option. Using the same formatting steps you would use in a document, enter the formatting codes. Press the Exit ([F7]) key when finished.

g. Press the Exit ([F7]) key to exit the Edit Styles menu.

h. Press the Exit ([F7]) key to exit the Styles menu.

There are two main differences between creating a paired style and an open style. The first difference appears in step d, which requires that you tell Word-Perfect that the style is to be an open one. The second difference is that there is no selection for changing the function of the [Enter] key. Because there is no ending to an open style, there is no need to define what the [Enter] key means to the creation of the style.

EXAMPLES

1. One advantage of using styles is to save time. You are now going to create an open style that can be used to start all correspondence from John Smith. Retrieve the document named STYLE1.DOC by pressing the Retrieve ([Shift]-[F10]) key [[Alt] File Retrieve], typing **style1.doc**, and pressing [Enter]. The screen is blank.

   Enter the Styles menu by pressing the Style ([Alt]-[F8]) key [[Alt] Layout Styles] and typing **c** to create a style. The Edit Styles menu that appears will seem familiar. The only difference between this menu and the menu for paired styles is that it does not have the option for redefining the [Enter] key. To give this style a name, type **n** for name, then type **Letter**, and press the [Enter] key. Type a **t** and an **o** to select an open style. Type **d** for the description, then type **Opening of Letter from John Smith**, and press the [Enter] key.

Now you are ready to insert the codes. Type **c** for codes. This takes you into the Open Style Codes screen. Notice that there is no comment to indicate the placement of text affected by the style. With an open style, all text following the Style code is affected by the style.

For this letter, you are going to change the tabs, change to left justification (in 5.0, turn off justification), turn on Widow/Orphan protection, and insert the return address for the letter.

To set the tabs, press the Format (Shift - F8) key, type **L** [Alt Layout Line], and **t** for tabs. Press Home , Home , ← and the Delete EOL (Ctrl - End) key to delete all the tabs. Type **0**, Enter , **0.5**, Enter , **4**, Enter (in 5.0, type **1**, Enter , **1.5**, Enter , **5**, Enter), and press the Exit (F7) key.

To change to left justification, type **j** and **L** (in 5.0, type **n**). To turn Widow/Orphan protection on, type **w** and **y**. Press the Exit (F7) key to return to the Open Style Codes screen.

For the return address, press the Tab key twice and type

John Smith

and press Enter . Press the Tab key twice and type

123 Washington Boulevard

and press Enter . Press the Tab key twice and type

Adrian, Michigan 49221

and press Enter twice. Press the Tab key twice. When you are finished, the screen should look like this:

```
                    John Smith
                    123 Washington Boulevard
                    Adrian, Michigan  49221
```

```
Style:  Press Exit when done                Doc 1 Pg 1 Ln 1.67" Pos 5"
(       ▲                        ▲                          )
[Tab][Tab]123 Washington Boulevard[HRt]
[Tab][Tab]Adrian, Michigan  49221[HRt]
[HRt]
[Tab][Tab]▮
```

Press the Exit (F7) key three times to return to the document screen. To save the document (which currently is blank but in which styles have been defined) and clear the screen, press the Exit (F7) key [Alt File Exit], Enter , type **letter**, and press Enter .

2. Styles are also handy when you know ahead of time that you will eventually want to change the formatting of a document. With this in mind, this example creates an open style designed for the initial drafts of a research paper. Later on in this chapter, you will modify this style for the final version of the research paper.

   The draft of a research paper should be double spaced with a large right margin so there is plenty of room to pencil in corrections and changes. Also, the header of each page should indicate that the document is a draft and include a page number.

   Retrieve the document named STYLE1.DOC by pressing the Retrieve (Shift - F10) key [Alt File

Retrieve], typing **style1.doc**, and pressing Enter. The screen is blank.

To produce this style, enter the Edit Styles menu by pressing the Style (Alt-F8) key [Alt Layout Styles] and type **c** to create. Give the style a name by typing **n** for name, **Research Ppr**, and press Enter. Type a **t** to select type and **o** to select the open style. Type **d**, **Main Document Formatting for Research Paper**, and press Enter to describe the style. Type **c** to enter the Open Style Codes menu.

To create the double line spacing, press the Format (Shift-F8) key and type L [Alt Layout Line], **s**, **2**, and press Enter. To increase the right margin, type **m**, Enter, **2**, and press Enter. Press Enter to exit the line format menu, type **p** for page, **h** for header, **a**, and **p**.

Type **DRAFT**. Press the Flush Right (Alt-F6) key [Alt Layout Align Flush Right], and type **Page**, press SPACEBAR, and Ctrl-B. Press the Exit (F7) key twice.

The Open Style Codes screen should now look like this:

```
Style:  Press Exit when done              Doc 1 Pg 1 Ln 1.33" Pos 1"
[  ^   ^   ^   ^   ^   ^   ^   ^   ^   ]   ^   ^   ^   ^
[Ln Spacing:2][L/R Mar:1",1"][L/R Mar:1",2"][Header A:Every page;DRAFT[Flsh Rgt]
Page ^B]
```

Press the Exit (F7) key three times to return to the document screen. To save the document (which currently is blank but in which styles have been

defined) and clear the screen, press the Exit ([F7])
key [[Alt] File Exit], [Enter], type **research.ppr**, and
press [Enter] twice.

EXERCISES

1. Retrieve the document called STYLE2.DOC. No text
   will appear in the document screen, but the previously defined styles are there.

   Create an open style called Letters that will be
   used frequently for correspondence. Describe it as
   General Correspondence. The left margin should be
   1.5", with a tab set at 0.5" (2" in 5.0). Include within
   the style your name and address for the return
   address, centered from left to right. Skip a line and
   use the Date Code feature to insert the current date,
   centered. Skip 4 lines. Save the document as
   LETTER2.DOC, and clear the screen.

2. Retrieve the document called STYLE2.DOC. No text
   will appear in the document screen.

   Create an open style for Acme Corporation's
   company newsletter named "Newsletter." This is a
   draft format and, therefore, should be double
   spaced. The newsletter heading should be centered
   and say "Acme Corporation Newsletter." Save the
   document as NEWS.LTR, and clear the screen.

USE AN OPEN STYLE

20.4

Using an open style is easy once it has been created.
Open styles work much the same way as adding any

formatting code to a document.

To use an open style in a document:

a. Move the cursor to the location where you want the style to begin.

b. Press the Style (Alt - F8) key [Alt Layout Styles].

c. Using the ⬆ and ⬇ keys, highlight the style you wish to use.

d. Type a **1** or **o** to turn the style on.

e. Continue creating the rest of your document.

In step a, you need to make sure the cursor is located where you want the style to begin. In the case of a style that is intended to format the entire document, you will need to make sure that you are at the beginning of the document. This, of course, is usually easy to do because you will turn on the style before you begin typing the contents of the document.

EXAMPLES

1. You can create a letter from John Smith using the open style created in the previous section. First, you need to retrieve the document LETTER, which contains the style. Press the Retrieve (Shift - F10) key [Alt File Retrieve], type **letter**, and press Enter . The screen will be blank, but it includes the Letter style.

   To start the letter, go into the Style menu by

pressing the Style (Alt-F8) key [Alt Layout Styles]. Using the ↑ and ↓ keys, highlight Letter and type **o** to turn the style on.

Type the following text, pressing Enter four times after you type in the date. Because of the way you defined the style, the date should line up with the return address of the letter. Press the Tab key twice before typing each section of the letter's closing.

April 15, 1990

James T. Brown, President
Consolidated Corporation
1234 Mason Drive
Lansing, Michigan 48913

Dear J.T.:

This letter is to inform you I will no longer be your service representative because I've been transferred to our company's main headquarters. I've turned your account over to the capable hands of Jane Albrecht. She is already familiar with your company and will be contacting you soon.

Sincerely,

John Smith

Preview the letter by pressing the Print (Shift-F7) key [Alt File Print] and typing **v**. Press the Exit (F7) key to return to the document screen. Press the Exit (F7) key [Alt File Exit], then save the file using any filename you wish.

2. You are now ready to start a research paper using the open style you created in section 20.3. Retrieve the document called RESEARCH.PPR by pressing the Retrieve ([Shift]-[F10]) key [[Alt] File Retrieve], typing **research.ppr**, and pressing [Enter]. The screen will be blank but it includes the Research Ppr style.

To start the research paper, go into the Style menu by pressing the Style ([Alt]-[F8]) key [[Alt] Layout Styles]. Using the [↑] and [↓] keys, highlight Research Ppr and type **o** to turn the style on.

Type the following text:

Rocks

There are many different kinds of rocks found on the earth. In fact, the earth is composed primarily of rock. These rocks differ in the minerals they are made of, how they were formed, and their age.

Preview the research paper by pressing the Print ([Shift]-[F7]) key [[Alt] File Print] and typing **v**. Notice the line spacing, the header, and the margins. Press the Exit ([F7]) key to return to the document screen.

Save the document and clear the screen by pressing the Exit ([F7]) key [[Alt] File Exit], [Enter], [Enter], y, and [Enter].

EXERCISES

1. Retrieve the file LETTER2.DOC. Using the open style named Letters, type the following letter. Save the document as TRAVEL.LTR.

Worldwide Travel Agency
12340 Center Parkway
New York, NY 10011

Gentlemen:

We are planning a trip to London, England, in September. Please send me any travel information on hotel accommodations, airfare, and points of interest for sight seeing.

After we have looked the information over, we will arrange an appointment to finalize our plans.

Sincerely,

{type your name}

2. Retrieve the file NEWS.LTR. Using the style Newsletter, create the formatting for the following document. Use the paired style named Header Lvl 2 to format the heading. Type the following:

NEW EQUIPMENT FOR SALES DEPARTMENT

A new microcomputer network will be installed in the Sales Department next month. It will consist of five workstations and a file server with a 150 Mb drive. The configuration also includes two laser printers. The system will run WordPerfect 5.1 and other popular software.

Save the document as NEWSVOL1.DOC.

20.5 | MODIFY A STYLE

So far in this chapter, you have seen how styles can be useful in saving time for formatting documents. You have also seen how styles can be useful in creating consistent formatting for documents and parts of documents. This section will show you what may be the most valuable feature of styles: the ability to modify styles and have the modifications immediately go into effect for your document.

To edit the formatting codes in a style:

a. Press the Style ([Alt]-[F8]) key [[Alt] Layout Styles].

b. Using the [↑] and [↓] keys, highlight the style you want to edit.

c. Type a **4** or **e** to edit the style.

d. Type a **4** or **c** to edit the formatting codes. Modify the formatting codes as required.

e. Press the Exit ([F7]) key when finished editing the formatting codes.

f. Press the Exit ([F7]) key to exit the Edit Styles menu.

g. Press the Exit ([F7]) key to exit the Styles menu.

EXAMPLES

(Do not clear the screen until you have completed the last example and are told to do so.)

1. To explore this feature of styles, you will need to work with a document that already has some styles defined. You will use the document RESEARCH. PPR. To retrieve the document, press the Retrieve ((Shift)-(F10)) key [(Alt) File Retrieve], type **research .ppr**, and press (Enter). The start of the research paper called Rocks will appear in your document screen.

Use the Main Heading style to format the title of the paper. To do this, put the cursor on the "R" in "Rocks." Press the Block ((Alt)-(F4)) key [(Alt) Edit Block] and type **s**. To turn on the style, press the Style ((Alt)-(F8)) key [(Alt) Layout Styles], highlight the Main heading style, and type **o** for on. Rocks will now be centered and in bold.

You will now add text to this research paper, using the other styles you have created. Press (Home), (Home), (↓) to move to the end of the document. To add a secondary heading to the research paper, first press the Style ((Alt)-(F8)) key [(Alt) Layout Styles], then highlight the Sec. Heading style and type **o** for on. Type

Sedimentary Rocks

and press (Enter). When you created the Sec. Heading style, you chose to have the (Enter) key turn off the style. Now type the following paragraph:

Rocks that were formed from dust, sand, seashells, and other materials settling long ago at the bottom of lakes and seas are called sedimentary rocks. Examples of sedimentary rock are:

Press the [Enter] key twice. At this point, you are ready to type a bulleted list. To do this, you will use the style you created called Bullet List. This style turns the style off and back on whenever you press the [Enter] key.

To turn on the Bullet List style, press the Style ([Alt]-[F8]) key [[Alt] Layout Styles], highlight the Bullet List style, and type **o** for on. Type the following three items, pressing [Enter] after each one:

limestone (made from shells)
sandstone (made from sand)
shale (made from clay and mud)

To turn the style off, press the [Backspace] key and type **y** to confirm the deletion of the extra style code.

To type the Metamorphic Rocks section, follow the same process you used to type in the Sedimentary Rocks section of the research paper. Using the Sec. Heading style for "Metamorphic Rocks," and the Bullet List style for the slate and marble items, type in the following:

Metamorphic Rocks
Rocks that have been changed from one kind of rock to another by heat and pressure are called metamorphic rocks. Metamorphic rocks are usually stronger and harder than the rocks they were changed from. Examples of metamorphic rock are:
slate (which comes from shale)
marble (which comes from limestone)

Save the document by pressing the Save ([F10]) key [[Alt] File Save], [Enter], and **y**. Preview the document using the Print ([Shift]-[F7]) key [[Alt] File Print], and type **v**. Notice the line spacing and margins. Press the Exit ([F7]) key to exit the preview screen.

2. Now that you have a document to work with, you are going to see how changing styles can affect the appearance of a document. The Research Ppr style was set up for creating drafts. Let's assume that you have finished modifying the paper and are now ready to put it in final form. To do this, you will need to edit the Research Ppr style.

Press the Style ([Alt]-[F8]) key [[Alt] Layout Styles], highlight the Research Ppr style, and type e to edit. You are taken to the Edit Styles menu. Type c for codes, which takes you to the Open Style Codes screen.

Press the [Del] key three times to delete the line spacing, margins and header codes. Add a page numbering code by pressing the Format ([Shift]-[F8]) key, and typing p [[Alt] Layout Page], n for page number (omit in 5.0), p for position (page numbering in 5.0), and 6 for the bottom center position. Press the Exit ([F7]) key to return to the Open Style Codes screen.

Press the Exit ([F7]) key three times to return to the document. Preview the document using the Print ([Shift]-[F7]) key [[Alt] File Print], and type v. Notice the line spacing and margins. Press the Exit ([F7]) key to exit the preview screen.

3. You will now change the appearance of the secondary headers. Assume that you would prefer the secondary headers to appear on the same line as the following text, underlined, and followed by a colon and two spaces.

Press the Style ([Alt]-[F8]) key [[Alt] Layout Styles], highlight the Sec. Heading style, and type e

to edit. You are taken to the Edit Styles menu. Type
c for codes, which takes you to the Paired Style
Codes screen.

Press the ➡ key twice and the Del key twice to
delete the two [HRt]'s. Press the Underline (F8)
key so the [und] code now appears after the [Com-
ment] code. Type a colon (:) and press the SPACEBAR
twice. Press the Exit (F7) key to return to the Edit
Styles screen.

Press the Exit (F7) key two times to return to
the document. Preview the document using the
Print (Shift-F7) key [Alt File Print], and type **v**.
Notice the change in appearance of the secondary
headers. Press the Exit (F7) key to exit the preview
screen.

Save the document by pressing the Save (F10)
key [Alt File Save], typing **rockdone.ppr**, and
pressing Enter.

EXERCISES

(Do not clear the screen until you have been instructed.)

1. Retrieve the document named NEWSVOL1.DOC.
   Add the following text to the end of the document,
   using the Long Quotes style to format the quote:

   Ron Adams, MIS coordinator states that:

   **"All systems are go. All equipment and cabling has
   been received, assembled and tested. We anticipate no
   problems."**

Training sessions are planned for the next three Fridays at 1:00 pm.

Preview the newsletter and return to the document screen. Save the document using the same name.

2. Assume the document has been edited and is now ready for the final formatting. Modify the Newsletter style by deleting the double spacing code. Bold the Newsletter title. Add a centered line of 27 hyphens underneath the heading.

   Modify the Long Quotes style by indenting the text from both sides a second time.

   Preview the newsletter and return to the document screen. Save the document using the name NEWSVOL1.FIN, and clear the screen.

CREATING A STYLE LIBRARY

20.6

Another powerful feature of styles is that you can save styles in Style Libraries to be used by any or all of your documents. All you need to do is give the set of styles a filename.

To create a style library contained in a document:

a. Retrieve the document which contains the styles you want saved in a style library.

b. Press the Style ((Alt)-(F8)) key [(Alt) Layout Styles].

c. Type a **6** or **s** to save the styles.

d. Type the filename for the style and press (Enter).

e. Press the Exit ((F7)) key to return to the document screen.

EXAMPLES

1. You are going to create a style library from the document named RESEARCH.PPR. First, retrieve the document by pressing the Retrieve ((Shift)-(F10)) key [(Alt) File Retrieve], typing **research.ppr**, and pressing (Enter).

    Press the Style ((Alt)-(F8)) key [(Alt) Layout Styles]. Type an **s** to save the styles, type **research .sty** as the filename and press (Enter). Press the Exit ((F7)) key to return to the document screen.

2. You are going to create a style library from the document named ROCKDONE.PPR. First, retrieve the document by pressing the Retrieve ((Shift)-(F10)) key [(Alt) File Retrieve], typing **rockdone.ppr**, and pressing (Enter).

    Press the Styles ((Alt)-(F8)) key [(Alt) Layout Styles]. Type an **s** to save the styles, type **donepapr .sty** as the filename, and press (Enter). Press the Exit ((F7)) key to return to the document screen.

EXERCISES

1. Create a style library called NEWSLTR.DFT using the styles found in the NEWSVOL1.DOC document.

2. Create a style library called NEWSLTR.FIN using the styles found in the NEWSVOL1.FIN document.

USE STYLES FROM A STYLE LIBRARY

| 20.7 |

Once you have created a style library, you can use it to create other documents. You have the choice of retrieving a style library into either a new or existing document. More than one style library can be incorporated into a single document. Thus you can combine libraries to create additional, larger ones.

To retrieve a style library into your document:

a. Press the Style ([Alt]-[F8]) key [[Alt] Layout Styles].

b. Type a **7** or **r** to retrieve the style library.

c. Type the filename for the style and press [Enter].

d. Press the Exit ([F7]) key to return to the document screen.

EXAMPLES

1. Make sure you have a clear screen by pressing the Exit ([F7]) key [[Alt] File Exit], and typing **n** twice. To retrieve the style library you created called RESEARCH.STY, press the Style ([Alt]-[F8]) key [[Alt] Layout Styles]. Type **r** to retrieve, **research.sty**, and [Enter]. Type **y** in response to the prompt telling you that styles already exist. (There are initial styles

in any new document.) Press the Exit (F7) key to return to the document screen.

At this point, you could create a document using the listed styles.

2. When you retrieve a style library into a document that already contains styles, WordPerfect first checks to see if there are any new styles with the same name. If there are styles with names in common, WordPerfect asks if you want to replace the current styles with the new ones. Type **n** for no if you do not want your current styles to be replaced by the new ones.

Sometimes, it is to your advantage to create two or more style libraries that have style names in common. The research paper about rocks is an example of this.

Make sure you have a clear screen by pressing the Exit (F7) key [Alt File Exit] and typing **n** twice. Retrieve the document named RESEARCH. PPR by pressing the Retrieve (Shift - F10) key [Alt File Retrieve], typing **research.ppr**, and pressing Enter . This is the draft version of your research paper.

Assume that you have finished editing the paper and are now ready to put it in final form. To incorporate the styles for a finished paper, retrieve the style library called DONEPAPR.STY. Go to the Styles menu by pressing the Style (Alt - F8) key [Alt Layout Styles]. Type an **r** to retrieve the style library, type **donepapr.sty**, and press Enter .

WordPerfect asks for confirmation that you want the current styles replaced by the new ones. Type **y** to answer yes. Press the Exit ([F7]) key to return to the document. Notice that the formatting is now for a finished research paper.

EXERCISES

(Do not clear the screen until you have completed the exercises and are told to do so.)

1. Make sure you have a clear screen. Retrieve the style library called NEWSLTR.DFT. Use the Newsletter style to format a newsletter. Type the following:

   An office party to celebrate the coming new year is scheduled for Monday, December 29, at 4:30 pm. All employees are welcome to join in the festivities.

   Print the document.

2. Assume that the newsletter has been edited and is ready to be put in its final form. Retrieve the NEWSLTR.FIN style library into the newsletter, allowing the styles to be overwritten.
   Print the document and clear the screen.

EXERCISES

(Do not clear the screen between exercises unless instructed to do so.)

1. Create a paired style named "Title" that consists of

a centered line of 54 asterisks (*), a [HRt], a centered message, a [HRt], another centered line of 54 asterisks (*), and a [HRt].

2. Create an open style named "Announcement" that sets all four margins at 1.5 inches.

3. Create a document using the Announcement style to set the document formatting. Using the Title style, start the document with the message:

New Medical Reimbursement Procedures

Type the following paragraph:

The application for medical reimbursement has been streamlined. Contact the personnel department for copies of the new forms.

Save the document as ANNOUNCE.DOC but do not clear the screen.

4. Create a style library called STYLE.ANN. Clear the screen.

5. Type the following document:

New Safety Rules Regarding Eye Protection

Anyone caught not wearing goggles in Labs C and D as required will be warned once. Any further infractions will result in the employee being suspended for one day without pay. Any employee breaking this rule four or more times within a one year period will be fired.

Retrieve the style library called STYLE.ANN. Use the Announcement style to format the document. Use the Title style to format the heading.

6. Modify the Title style by eliminating the first row of asterisks (*) and bolding the rest of the style. Clear the screen.

(Do not clear the screen between exercises unless instructed to do so.)

INTEGRATING
SKILLS CHECK

1. Type the following document:

Amalgamated Electronics is pleased to announce the release of its latest computer. The Data-Blaster is the latest and fastest in our series of high speed electronic data crunchers. "No other computer in its price range can compare with the Data-Blaster's performance," says Amalgamated's president, Joshua Miller.

2. Create an open style called Press Rel. that formats a document with double spacing. The style should also include a footer with the message:

PRESS RELEASE – PRESS RELEASE – PRESS RE-LEASE

centered at the bottom.

3. Create a paired style that turns itself off when you press the (Enter) key. Call the style Main Heading. It should consist of bolded, centered text that is followed by one [HRt].

4. Use the Press Rel. style created in Exercise 2 to format the document currently on your document screen.

5. Use the Main Heading style to add a heading at the beginning of the document titled "Data-Blaster Blasts the Competition."

6. Print the press release.

7. Modify the Press Rel. style to include a header that contains the same text as the footer.

8. Print the press release. Clear the screen.

Working with Text Columns

►21◄

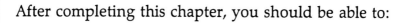

CHAPTER OBJECTIVES

After completing this chapter, you should be able to:

► Define newspaper columns 21.1

► Enter text into newspaper columns 21.2

► Define parallel columns 21.3

► Enter text into parallel columns 21.4

► Modify column entries 21.5

Occasionally, information contained within a document either looks better or is more understandable if it is printed in columns. Sometimes, these columns can be created by setting tabs and using the Tab key to move from one column to the next. This is especially true if the columns consist primarily of numbers or the column entries are very short. However, there are times when you want textual material to appear in a column format. WordPerfect's Column feature is designed to do just that.

WordPerfect provides formatting for two different types of text columns. One type, called *newspaper columns*, is commonly seen in newspapers or magazines. The text displays down a column until it reaches the end of the page and then continues to the start of the next column. Some people refer to newspaper columns as "snaking" columns, because the text snakes from top to bottom through each of the columns.

The other type of column WordPerfect provides is called *parallel columns*. Parallel columns are columns where blocks of text that relate to each other must remain side by side. They are ideal in situations where at least one of the columns contains text that is more than one line long. WordPerfect wraps the text within the columns in the same way it normally wraps text from one page to the next.

You can use both types of columns in a single document, but only one column feature can be used at any one time. You can also use columns at one point in your document, change to normal page formatting, and then change back to column formatting. WordPerfect provides you with a great deal of flexibility.

Both types of columns can be very helpful when you are preparing specialized documents. With WordPerfect, they are also easy to do. Throughout this chapter you may find that your screen does not exactly match the examples since different printer selections will cause different font sizes to be used for defaults and may cause column text to break in different locations.

(Do not clear the screen until you have completed the last exercise.)

SKILLS CHECK

1. Set the top margin to 2″ and the bottom margin to 3″.

2. Change the justification to left justification (in 5.0, turn justification off).

3. Center the following and press ⟦Enter⟧ once:

   Memory Upgrades Available

4. Center 35 hyphens and press ⟦Enter⟧ twice.

5. Type the following paragraph, underlining the word "finally":

   The memory chips we ordered three months ago have <u>finally</u> arrived. Those of you who have been waiting to upgrade your system should schedule a time with MIS Services for swapping memory chips at your earliest convenience.

6. Use WordPerfect's Spell feature to check for spelling errors.

7. Save the document using the filename MEMORY and clear the screen.

21.1   DEFINE NEWSPAPER COLUMNS

Working with text columns in WordPerfect is always a two-step process. You must first tell WordPerfect which column type you are using, and then define how you want the columns to look. The second step requires that you turn the previously defined column feature on. If later in the document you want to stop using columns, you can turn the features off.

When defining columns, there are other considerations besides determining what type of columns you want to use. You need to decide how many columns are going to appear on a page (24 is the maximum), how much space you want between the columns, and the width of the columns. WordPerfect provides defaults which you can choose to accept or change at any time.

To define newspaper style columns:

a. Press the Columns/Table (Alt - F7) key (the Math/ Columns key in 5.0) [Alt Layout Columns Define and skip steps b and c].

b. Type a **1** or **c** to select columns (skip this step in 5.0).

c. Type a **3** or **d** to define columns (type 4 or **d** in 5.0).

d. If you want more than two columns, type a **2** or **n**, the number of columns, and press Enter .

e. If you want to set the distance between columns, type a **3** or **d**, the distance, and press (Enter).

f. If you want to adjust the left and right margins of the columns, type **4** or **m**, and type each margin setting followed by the (Enter) key.

g. Press the Exit ((F7)) key to exit the Text Column Definition screen.

h. Press the Exit ((F7)) key to return to the document.

EXAMPLES

To minimize the amount of typing required to efficiently learn about newspaper columns, you will reduce the size of the page by increasing the bottom margin in each of the following examples.

1. Change the bottom margin to 8″ by pressing the Format ((Shift)-(F8)) key, type **p** for page [(Alt) Layout Page], **m** for margins, press (Enter), 8, (Enter), and press the Exit ((F7)) key. This will shorten the page so that you will be able to see how Word-Perfect automatically scrolls up to the next column when it reaches the end of the first column.

   You are going to define two newspaper columns using WordPerfect's default newspaper columns settings. Press the Columns/Table ((Alt)-(F7)) key (Math/Columns key in 5.0), type **c** to select columns (omit this step in 5.0), and type a **d** to define columns [(Alt) Layout Columns Define].

You are presented with the Text Column Definition menu which looks like Figure 21-1. Since newspaper columns are the default column type, you are going to accept all of the default choices from this menu by pressing the Exit ((F7)) key twice. This returns you to the typing screen.

Press the Reveal Codes ((Alt)-(F3)) key [(Alt) Edit Reveal Codes] to display the [Col Def:Newspaper;2;1",4";4.5",7.5"] code ([Col Def:2;1",4";4.5", 7.5"] in 5.0). This code indicates a column definition for 2 newspaper style columns. The first column's left and right margins are 1" and 4" and the second column's left and right margins are 4.5" and 7.5". To clear the Reveal Codes display, press the Reveal

```
Text Column Definition

    1 - Type                        Newspaper

    2 - Number of Columns           2

    3 - Distance Between Columns

    4 - Margins

    Column    Left    Right    Column    Left    Right
      1:      1"      4"         13:
      2:      4.5"    7.5"       14:
      3:                         15:
      4:                         16:
      5:                         17:
      6:                         18:
      7:                         19:
      8:                         20:
      9:                         21:
     10:                         22:
     11:                         23:
     12:                         24:

Selection: 0
```

FIGURE 21-1. Text Column Definition menu for newspaper columns

Codes (⟨Alt⟩-⟨F3⟩) key [⟨Alt⟩ Edit Reveal Codes]. You will be using the column definition feature in the next section. For now, start a newsletter entry by typing in the heading of the newsletter. Center the heading by pressing the Center (⟨Shift⟩-⟨F6⟩) key [⟨Alt⟩ Layout Align Center] and type:

Acme Corporation Newsletter

Press ⟨Enter⟩. To add a dividing line between the heading and where the columns are to appear, press the Center (⟨Shift⟩-⟨F6⟩) key [⟨Alt⟩ Layout Align Center], press the ⟨Esc⟩ key, type **35**, and press the EQUAL (=) key. Press ⟨Enter⟩ twice.

Save this document to be used in section 21.2 by pressing the Exit (⟨F7⟩) key [⟨Alt⟩ File Exit], typing **y**, **acmecorp.ltr**, and pressing ⟨Enter⟩ twice.

2. For this example, you will define three newspaper columns. Instead of defining the columns at the beginning of the document, you will define them at the location you want the columns to start. Word-Perfect does not care where the definition code is placed, as long as the code occurs before you turn on the columns.

First, change the bottom margin to 8″ by pressing the Format (⟨Shift⟩-⟨F8⟩) key, typing **p** for page [⟨Alt⟩ Layout Page], **m** for margins, pressing ⟨Enter⟩, 8, ⟨Enter⟩, and then the Exit (⟨F7⟩) key. For the heading of this example, press the Underline (⟨F8⟩) key, the ⟨Caps Lock⟩ key, the Center (⟨Shift⟩-⟨F6⟩) key [⟨Alt⟩ Layout Align Center], and type:

pc software trainers club

Press the Underline (⟨F8⟩) key to turn off underlining, the [Caps Lock] key and the [Enter] key twice. Now you are ready to define the columns. Press the Columns/Table ([Alt]-[F7]) key (Math/Columns key in 5.0), type **c** to select columns (omit in 5.0), and type a **d** to define columns [[Alt] Layout Columns Define].

The three columns are all going to be equal in width; however, you will tell WordPerfect that you want them to be 0.4" apart. Type **n** for number of columns, **3**, and press [Enter]. As you press the [Enter] key, the Margins selection will go from settings for two columns to settings for three.

The default distance between columns is approximately 0.5". To change the distance between columns to 0.4", type **d**, **.4**, and press [Enter]. As you press the [Enter] key, notice that the Margin settings again change to immediately reflect the new distance between columns. Accept the margin settings by pressing the Exit ([F7]) key twice. This returns you to the typing screen. Save this document to be used in section 21.2 by pressing the Exit ([F7]) key [[Alt] File Exit], typing **y**, **pcclub.ltr**, and pressing [Enter] twice.

EXERCISES

1. Define two newspaper columns using WordPerfect's default settings on a page with an 8" bottom margin. Start the document by centering the heading:

ACME CORPORATION

Underneath the heading, insert 65 centered equal signs (=) followed by 2 hard returns ([HRt]'s). Save the document using the filename NEWSLTR.DOC and clear the screen.

2. After setting the bottom margin to 8", center and boldface the following heading:

NORTH COAST COMMUNITY NEWS

Center 26 equal signs (=) underneath the heading and include 2 [HRt]'s. Define three newspaper columns spaced 0.3" apart. Save the document using the filename COMMNEWS and clear the screen.

ENTER TEXT INTO NEWSPAPER COLUMNS   21.2

Once newspaper columns are defined, creating the columns is easy. All you need to remember is to turn on the column definition at the location you want columns to begin.

To turn on previously defined columns:

a. Place the cursor at the location where you want columns to begin (making sure the cursor is after the columns definition code).

b. Press the Columns/Table (Alt-F7) key (the Math/ Columns key in 5.0) [Alt Layout Columns On and skip steps c and d].

c. Type a **1** or **c** to select columns (skip this step in 5.0).

d. Type a **1** or **o** to turn columns on (type **3** or **c** in 5.0).

To turn off columns which were previously turned on:

a. Place the cursor at the location where you want columns to end.

b. Press the Columns/Table (Alt-F7) key (Math/Col umns key in 5.0) [Alt Layout Columns Off and skip steps c and d].

c. Type a **1** or **c** to select columns (skip this step in 5.0).

d. Type a **2** or **f** to turn columns off (type **3** or **c** in 5.0).

Once newspaper columns are turned on, WordPerfect treats each column as if it were a separate page. It automatically wraps lines of text to the next line, and moves to the next column when one column is full.

EXAMPLES

1. Retrieve the document named ACMECORP.LTR by pressing the Retrieve (Shift-F10) key [Alt File Retrieve], typing **acmecorp.ltr**, and pressing Enter.

The beginning of the Acme Corporation Newsletter appears on your screen.

Press the [Home], [Home], and [↓] keys to move the cursor to the end of the document. It is now at the location you want to start the newspaper column entries. To turn on the columns feature, press the Columns/Table ([Alt]-[F7]) key (Math/Columns key in 5.0), type a **c** to select columns (omit in 5.0), and an **o** to turn columns on (**c** in 5.0) [[Alt] Layout Columns **On**].

The title for the paragraph is called New Benefits. You can underline and center the title at the beginning of the first column in the same manner as you would a regular page. Press the Underline ([F8]) key and the Center ([Shift]-[F6]) key [[Alt] Layout Align Center], and type

New Benefits

Press the Underline ([F8]) key to turn off underlining and press [Enter] twice. Type the following text as you normally would, allowing WordPerfect to wrap text as usual. As you approach the sentence, "A sign-up card will also be included," note how the text scrolls up to the next column.

Starting June 1, all employees will have a choice in their health plans. Three different plans will be offered. Information will be sent to all departments by May 1st. A sign-up card will also be included. These cards must be filled out and returned to Personnel no later than May 25. The health benefits will begin on June 1. Insurance cards will be mailed the same week. If you have any questions, please call the Personnel office.

When you are finished, the screen should appear

similar to this, although different printers will cause differences in font sizes, thereby affecting column breaks:

```
              Acme Corporation Newsletter
         ===================================

     New Benefits            included.  These cards must be
                             filled out and returned to
Starting June 1, all employees   Personnel no later than May 25.
will have a choice in their  The health benefits will begin
health plans.  Three different   on June 1.  Insurance cards
plans will be offered.       will be mailed the same week.
Information will be sent to all  If you have any questions,
departments by May 1st.  A   please call the Personnel
sign-up card will also be    office.
```

Save the document and clear the screen by pressing the Exit ([F7]) key [[Alt] File Exit], typing **y**, [Enter], **y**, and [Enter].

2. Retrieve the document named PCCLUB.LTR by pressing the Retrieve ([Shift]-[F10]) key [[Alt] File Retrieve], typing **pcclub.ltr**, and pressing [Enter]. The beginning of the PC Software Trainers' Club newsletter appears on your screen.

Press the [Home], [Home], and [↓] keys to move the cursor to the end of the document. It is now at the location you want to start the newspaper column entries. Press the Reveal Codes ([Alt]-[F3]) key [[Alt] Edit Reveal Codes] to display the [Col Def:Newspaper;3;1",2.9";3.3",5.2";5.6",7.5"] code ([Col Def:3;1", 2.9";3.3",5.2";5.6",7.5"] in 5.0). This code indicates a column definition for three newspaper style columns. The first column's left and right margins are 1" and 2.9", the second column's left and right margins are 3.3" and 5.2", and the third is 5.6" and

7.5". To clear the Reveal Codes display, press the Reveal Codes ([Alt]-[F3]) key [[Alt] Edit Reveal Codes].

To turn on the columns feature, press the Columns/Table ([Alt]-[F7]) key (Math/Columns key in 5.0), type a **c** to select columns (omit in 5.0), and an **o** to turn columns on (**c** in 5.0) [[Alt] Layout Columns **On**].

The title for the paragraph is "Featured Speaker". You can underline the title at the beginning of the first column in the same way you would underline on a regular page. Press the Underline ([F8]) key and type

Featured Speaker

Press the Underline ([F8]) key and press [Enter] twice. Type the following text as you normally would, allowing WordPerfect to wrap text as usual.

We are proud to welcome Jan Smithers from Word-Perfect Corporation for our May 15th, 12:00 pm meeting. She will be demonstrating some of the new features of WordPerfect 5.1. Come and see for yourself what all the hoopla has been about these last few months. Send in your reservation card as soon as possible to be guaranteed a good seat. Lunch will be served promptly at 12:15 pm. For members, the fee is $7.00. For non-members, it is $10.00. Bring a friend.

When you are finished, the screen should appear similar to the screen shown on the next page, although font size differences may cause word break differences.

Save the document and clear the screen by pressing the Exit ([F7]) key [[Alt] File Exit], typing **y**, [Enter], **y**, and [Enter].

PC SOFTWARE TRAINERS' CLUB

Featured Speaker

We are proud to welcome Jan Smithers from WordPerfect Corporation for our May 15th, 12:00 pm meeting. She will be demonstrating some of the new features of WordPerfect 5.1. Come and see for yourself what all the hoopla has been about these last few months. Send in your reservation card as soon as possible to be guaranteed a good seat. Lunch will be served promptly at 12:15 pm. For members, the fee is $7.00. For non-members, it is $10.00. Bring a friend.

3. Later on in this chapter you will learn other keystroke combinations that will make editing columns easier. For now, it is sufficient to say that editing text in the normal page format is easier than editing text in newspaper columns. You can create newspaper columns in normal formatting first, and then turn them into columns. For an example of how this is done, type the following text, pressing the (Enter) key twice after the headings and between paragraphs.

EMPLOYEE OF THE MONTH

The employee of the month award at Acme Corporation was awarded to Jessica Lancaster for her outstanding sales performance last month. She sold over $125,000 in office furniture and supplies, setting a new company record. The old record, set in 1985 by Terry Smith, was $120,000. Jessica also increased her customer base by 15%. Congratulations, Jessica!

SOFTWARE FAIR

Last month's PC Software Trainers' Club meeting featured a Mini-Fair. Several vendors set up booths and provided demonstrations on various software packages. These ranged from spreadsheet and database to word processing programs. Sales literature from the participating vendors is available upon request from the club's secretary, Brian Robertson.

```
$125,000 in office furniture
and supplies, setting a new
company record. The old
record, set in 1985 by Terry
Smith, was $120,000. Jessica
also increased her customer
base by 15%. Congratulations,
Jessica!

SOFTWARE FAIR

Last month's PC Software
Trainers' Club meeting featured
a Mini-Fair. Several vendors
set up booths and provided
demonstrations on various
software packages. These
ranged from spreadsheet and
database to word processing
programs. Sales literature
from the participating vendors
is available upon request from
the club's secretary, Brian
Robertson.
                     Col 1 Doc 1 Pg 1 Ln 6" Pos 1"
```

FIGURE 21-2.	Text entries in column 1

Press [Home], [Home] and the [↑] keys to move to the beginning of the document. Now you are ready to define the columns. Press the Columns/Table ([Alt]-[F7]) key (Math/Columns key in 5.0), type **c** to select columns (omit in 5.0), and type a **d** to define columns [[Alt] Layout Columns Define]. Accept the default settings by pressing the Exit ([F7]) key. Type **o** (**c** in 5.0) to turn on the columns. As you press the [↓] key, the document will reformat itself.

Because the page is long enough to contain both paragraphs in column one, if you move to the last line the screen appears like Figure 21-2.

To force the second paragraph to the beginning of the next column, you can press the Hard Page

EMPLOYEE OF THE MONTH

The employee of the month award
at ACME Corporation was awarded
to Jessica Lancaster for her
outstanding sales performance
last month. She sold over
$125,000 in office furniture
and supplies, setting a new
company record. The old
record, set in 1985 by Terry
Smith, was $120,000. Jessica
also increased her customer
base by 15%. Congratulations,
Jessica!

SOFTWARE FAIR

Last month's PC Software
Trainers' Club meeting featured
a Mini-Fair. Several vendors
set up booths and provided
demonstrations on various
software packages. These
ranged from spreadsheet and
database to word processing
programs. Sales literature
from the participating vendors
is available upon request from
the club's secretary, Brian
Robertson.

Col 2 Doc 1 Pg 1 Ln 1" Pos 4.5"

| FIGURE 21-3. | Text entries display in both columns |

(Ctrl - Enter) key [Alt Layout Align Hard Page] (the same way you force a new page). Move the cursor to the end of the first paragraph, just after the exclamation point. Press the Hard Page (Ctrl - Enter) key [Alt Layout Align Hard Page]. Press the Del key twice to delete the two [HRt]'s. The document should now look like Figure 21-3.

Press Home , Home and ↓ to move to the end of the document. Turn the columns off by pressing the Columns/Table (Alt - F7) key (Math/Columns key in 5.0), type c to select columns (omit in 5.0), and type f (c in 5.0) to turn off the columns [Alt Layout Columns Off]. Press the Enter key twice and type]

NORTH COAST GETS POOL

The North Coast Community recreation department is happy to announce the opening of their new swimming pool. The pool is olympic size and features an L-extension that is three feet deep. Pool hours and classes will be posted soon.

Because this paragraph occurs after the [Col Off] code, it is formatted to fit the full width of the page. Preview the document by pressing the Print (Shift - F7) key [Alt File Print], and type v and 3. The screen should look similar to this:

```
set in 1985 by Terry Smith was      Sales    literature    from    the
$120.000.     Jessica     also      participating     vendors     is
increased here customer base by     available upon request from the
15%. Congratulations. Jessica!      club's    secretary.    Brian
                                     Robertson.

NORTH COAST GETS POOL
The  North  Coast  Community  recreation  department  is  happy  to
announce  the  opening  of  their  new  swimming  pool.  The  pool  is
olympic  size  and  features  and  L-extension  that  is  three  feet  deep.
Pool  hours  and  classes  will  be  posted  soon.
```

When you are done previewing the document, press the Exit (F7) key. Save the document by pressing the Exit (F7) key [Alt File Exit], typing y, **pr.doc**, and pressing Enter twice.

EXERCISES

1. Retrieve the document named NEWSLTR.DOC. Turn on the columns at the end of the document and type the following text, centering and under

lining the heading and pressing the (Enter) key twice
after the heading and the first paragraph.

SAFETY SEMINAR

On Saturday, May 5th, the ACME Corporation will host
a seminar on industrial safety for ACME employees.
Frances Wilkens, a well-known speaker from Ohio's
American Red Cross, will be our key speaker. She
offers a wealth of information regarding safety on the
job. Those who attend the seminar will have hands-on
training in first aid skills required in common emer-
gency situations.

The seminar begins at 9:00 am and ends at 4:00 pm.

Save the document using the same filename and
clear the screen.

2. Retrieve the document named COMMNEWS. Turn
on the columns at the end of the document. Type
the following text, centering the heading and pressing the (Enter) key twice after the heading and each
of the following two paragraphs.

KIDDIE CALENDAR

Summer is almost here and our children have much to
look forward to.

With the opening of the new swimming pool, open
swimming hours and swimming classes for the summer
will soon be scheduled. The new schedule will be
included in the next newsletter and posted at the pool.

Games and activities are also scheduled in the Rec hall
every afternoon from Monday through Friday, between
12:00 and 4:00 pm for children ages three to seven.

Save the document using the same filename and clear the screen.

3. Define two newspaper columns. Turn on columns and type the following paragraph in column 1.

Paragraph 1

This is the first paragraph of this exercise.

Force a new column. Type the following paragraph in the second column.

Paragraph 2

This is the second paragraph of this exercise. It appears in column 2.

Turn off the columns and type the following paragraph.

Paragraph 3

This is the third paragraph of this exercise. It should appear below the first two paragraphs.

Preview the document. Save the document as COLUMNS and clear the screen.

DEFINE PARALLEL COLUMNS   21.3

Parallel columns are used to create tables, charts, or other textual material that appears in columnar form but must be read from left to right. When related material that appears in separate columns must remain side by side, the parallel columns feature is a good choice to use.

Parallel columns are defined with a procedure similar to the one you use for newspaper columns. It is more common to vary the width of columns when using the parallel columns feature, however. Often, the amount of text that appears in parallel columns varies depending upon the column's purpose. Usually, you will make columns that contain a lot of text wider than columns with less text.

The Tables feature, available in WordPerfect 5.1 only, can also be used to produce documents with parallel columns. See Chapter 22, "Using 5.1's New Table Features," for more information about Tables.

To define parallel columns:

a. Press the Columns/Table ([Alt]-[F7]) key (Math/ Columns key in 5.0) [[Alt] Layout Columns Define and skip steps b and c].

b. Type a **1** or **c** to select columns (skip this step in 5.0).

c. Type a **3** or **d** to define columns (type **4** or **d** in 5.0).

d. Type a **1** or **t** to select the type of columns. Type a **2** or **p** to select parallel columns, or type **3** or **b** to select parallel columns with the block protect feature.

e. If you want more than two columns, type a **2** or **n**, the number of columns, and press [Enter].

f. If you want to set the distance between columns, type a **3** or **d**, the distance, and press [Enter].

g. If you want to adjust the left and right margins of the columns, type **4** or **m**, and type each margin setting followed by pressing the (Enter) key.

h. Press the Exit ((F7)) key to exit the Text Column Definition screen.

i. Press the Exit ((F7)) key to return to the document.

Step d refers to two different variations of parallel columns. The basic parallel columns format (without block protection) is used for text where one or more columns can run on to the next page. Although the related material must always remain side-by-side, parts of the text may be pushed to the beginning of the next page.

Parallel columns with block protection are used when all related text must remain side-by-side on the *same* page.

EXAMPLES

1. Change the bottom margin to 8.5" by pressing the Format ((Shift)-(F8)) key, type **p** for page [(Alt) Layout Page], **m** for margins, (Enter), 8.5, (Enter), and press the Exit ((F7)) key. This will shorten the page so that you will be able to see how parallel columns work with a minimum of typing.

You are going to define two parallel columns to be used to create a glossary of terms. The first column can be narrower than the second, because the first contains the defined term while the second contains the definition.

Press the Columns/Table ((Alt)-(F7)) key (Math/

Columns key in 5.0), type **c** to select columns (omit in 5.0), and type a **d** to define columns [⟨Alt⟩ Layout Columns **Define**].

You are presented with the Text Column Definition menu, which looks like Figure 21-1. Define the type of column by typing **t** and then **p** to define parallel columns. Leave the number of columns set to 2. Type **m** to set the margins of the two columns.

The cursor moves to the 1″ left margin setting for the first column. Since this setting is acceptable, press ⟨Enter⟩ to move to the next setting. Because you want to narrow the first column, type **2.5** for the right margin of the first column and press ⟨Enter⟩. The cursor moves to the 4.5″ left margin for the second column.

Because you moved the right margin of the first column to the left, there is now room to move the left margin of the second column. Type **3** to allow for half an inch between columns and press ⟨Enter⟩. Press ⟨Enter⟩ again to accept the 7.5″ right margin.

The screen should now look like Figure 21-4. Press the Exit (⟨F7⟩) key twice to return to the main menu.

Press the Reveal Codes (⟨Alt⟩-⟨F3⟩) key [⟨Alt⟩ Edit Reveal Codes] to display the [Col Def:Parallel;2;1″, 2.5″;3″,7.5″] code ([Col Def:2;1″,2.5″;3″,7.5″] in 5.0). This code indicates a column definition for three parallel columns. The first column's left and right margins are 1″ and 2.5″ and the second column's left and right margins are 3″ and 7.5″. To clear the Reveal Codes display, press the Reveal Codes (⟨Alt⟩-⟨F3⟩) key [⟨Alt⟩ Edit Reveal Codes].

```
Text Column Definition

    1 - Type                         Parallel

    2 - Number of Columns            2

    3 - Distance Between Columns

    4 - Margins

    Column   Left    Right    Column   Left    Right
      1:     1"      2.5"       13:
      2:     3"      7.5"       14:
      3:                        15:
      4:                        16:
      5:                        17:
      6:                        18:
      7:                        19:
      8:                        20:
      9:                        21:
     10:                        22:
     11:                        23:
     12:                        24:

Selection: 0
```

FIGURE 21-4.   Text Column Definition menu for parallel columns

---

You will be using this column definition in the next section. For now, start the glossary by typing in the heading. Center the heading by pressing the Center (Shift-F6) key [Alt Layout Align Center] and type:

Flower Glossary

Press Enter twice. Save this document to be used in section 21.4 by pressing the Exit (F7) key [Alt File Exit], typing y, flowers, and press Enter twice.

2. For this example, you will define three parallel columns with block protection turned on. Instead of

defining the columns at the beginning of the document, you will define them at the location you want the columns to start. WordPerfect does not care where the definition code is placed, as long as the code occurs before you turn on the columns.

First, change the bottom margin to 7.5" by pressing the Format (Shift-F8) key, typing **p** for page [Alt Layout Page], **m** for margins, Enter, 7.5, Enter, and pressing the Exit (F7) key. For the heading of this example, press the Underline (F8) key and the Center (Shift-F6) key [Alt Layout Align Center] and type:

Dessert Menu

Press the Underline (F8) key to turn off underlining, and press the Enter key twice. Now you are ready to define the columns. Press the Columns/Table (Alt-F7) key (Math/Columns key in 5.0), type **c** to select columns (omit in 5.0), and type a **d** to define columns [Alt Layout Columns Define].

To define the type of column, type **t** and then **b** to define parallel columns with block protect. Set the number of columns to 3 by typing **n**, **3**, and pressing Enter. As you press Enter, the number of margin settings will change from two to three. Type **m** to set the margins of the three columns.

The cursor moves to the 1" left margin setting for the first column. This setting is acceptable, so press Enter to move to the next setting. Type **2.8** and press Enter to set the first column's right margin. The cursor moves to the left margin for the second column.

Type **3.2** and press Enter for the left margin of

column 2. This leaves .4″ between the two columns. The cursor is now located on the right margin setting for column 2. Type **3.7** and press ⌷Enter⌷. The cursor moves to the left margin for the third column.

Type **4.1** and press ⌷Enter⌷ for the left margin setting. Press ⌷Enter⌷ again to accept the 7.5″ setting for the right margin.

Press the Exit (⌷F7⌷) key twice to return to the document.

Press the Reveal Codes (⌷Alt⌷-⌷F3⌷) key [⌷Alt⌷ Edit Reveal Codes] to display the [Col Def:Parallel/Block Pro;3;1″,2.8″;3.2″,3.7″;4.1″,7.5″] code ([Col Def:3;1″, 2.8″;3.2″,3.7″;4.1″,7.5″] in 5.0). This code indicates a column definition for three parallel columns with block protect. The first column's left and right margins are 1″ and 2.8″, the second column's left and right margins are 3.2″ and 3.7″, and the third column's left and right margins are 4.1″ and 7.5″. To clear the Reveal Codes display, press the Reveal Codes (⌷Alt⌷-⌷F3⌷) key [⌷Alt⌷ Edit Reveal Codes].

Save this document to be used in section 21.4 by pressing the Exit (⌷F7⌷) key [⌷Alt⌷ File Exit], typing **y**, **dessert**, and pressing ⌷Enter⌷ twice.

EXERCISES

1. Create the formatting for a play script using two parallel columns without block protection. The first column's margins are 1″ and 2.5″ and the second

column's margins are 3″ and 7.5″. Center the following headings, pressing [Enter] twice after "Friends" and "Class":

MEETING NEW FRIENDS

A Play Presented By:
Ms. Walker's First Grade Class

Save the document as PLAY.DOC and clear the screen.

2. Set the bottom margin to 8″. Center and bold the following heading, pressing [Enter] twice after the heading:

Name & Address Listing

Define three parallel columns with block protect. Set the first column's left and right margins to 1″ and 2.5″. Set the second column's left and right margins to 3″ and 6″. Set the third column's left and right margins to 6.5″ and 7.5″.
Save the document as N&A.LST.

3. Set the bottom margin to 8.5″. Define an inventory list for the Acme Corporation using three parallel columns with block protect. The three column margins should be set so that column one has margins of 1″ and 1.8″, column two has margins of 2.2″ and 4″, and column three has margins of 4.4″ and 7.5″.

Center the following headings at the top of the page:

ACME CORPORATION
Equipment Inventory

Following Inventory, press Enter twice. Save the document as INVTY.DOC.

ENTER TEXT INTO PARALLEL COLUMNS

21.4

The method for turning on and off parallel columns is the same as for newspaper columns. See section 21.2 for the specific steps required.

Because parallel columns consist of columns with related material displayed side-by-side, the method for entering text into the columns is different than for newspaper columns. The text is entered within the columns from left to right. You enter each individual block of text as ususal, but when the block is finished you immediately press the Hard Page (Ctrl - Enter) key [Alt Layout Align Hard Page]. This jumps the cursor to the next column.

To produce parallel columns after they have been turned on:

a. Type in the first entry for the first column.

b. Press the Hard Page (Ctrl - Enter) key [Alt Layout Align Hard Page]. This jumps you to the next column.

c. Type in the related entry for the second column.

d. Press the Hard Page (Ctrl - Enter) key [Alt Layout Align Hard Page]. This jumps you to the next column (or back to the first column when there are only two columns defined).

e. Continue in the above manner until all entries have been made.

EXAMPLES

1. The best way to learn how parallel columns work is to create a document using them. Press the Retrieve (Shift-F10) key [Alt File Retrieve], type **flowers**, and press Enter to retrieve the document you defined for the flower glossary. Press Home, Home, and ↓ to move to the end of the document. This is where you want to start typing the terms and definitions.

   Turn the parallel columns feature on by pressing the Columns/Table (Alt-F7) key (Math/Columns key in 5.0), typing a **c** to select columns (omit in 5.0), and an **o** to turn columns on (**c** in 5.0) [Alt Layout Columns On].

   Start by typing the column headers. Press the CapsLock key and type **term**, press the Hard Page (Ctrl-Enter) key [Alt Layout Align Hard Page], type **definition**, press the Hard Page (Ctrl-Enter) key [Alt Layout Align Hard Page] again, and press the CapsLock key again. The headers are now in place.

   Type in the following text, pressing only the Hard Page (Ctrl-Enter) key [Alt Layout Align Hard Page] after each section of text. For example, type **Azalea**, press (Ctrl-Enter) [Alt Layout Align Hard Page], type **A shrub . . . acid soil.**, press (Ctrl-Enter) [Alt Layout Align Hard Page], type **Crocus**, press (Ctrl-Enter) [Alt Layout **Align Hard Page**], **and so on.**

Azalea	A shrub with flower blooms of various colors that belongs to the heath family. It thrives in dry, acid soil.
Crocus	A spring-blooming plant of the iris family with grass-like leaves and a yellow, purple, or white flower.
Tulip	A bulb plant with a large, cup-shaped flower. Some of the best varieties are imported from the Netherlands.

When completed, the document screen should look something like like Figure 21-5. If your screen splits sooner due to a different printer font, you can add an extra line to the description for crocus.

Notice, how the definition for crocus is split between pages. This happens because the parallel columns were defined without block protection.

Save the document using the same filename, and clear the screen by pressing the Exit ([F7]) key [[Alt] File Exit], typing y, [Enter], y, and [Enter].

2. Next you will create a document that has block-protected parallel columns. Press the Retrieve ([Shift]-[F10]) key [[Alt] File Retrieve], type **dessert**, and press [Enter] to retrieve the document you defined for the dessert menu. Press [Home], [Home], and [↓] to move to the end of the document. This is where you will start typing the dessert menu.

Turn the parallel columns on by pressing the Columns/Table ([Alt]-[F7]) key (Math/Columns key in

```
                    Flower Glossary

    TERM            DEFINITION

    Azalea          A shrub with flower blooms of various colors
                    that belongs to the heath family. It thrives
                    in dry, acid soil.

    Crocus          A spring-blooming plant of the iris family
    ------------------------------------------------------------
                    with grass-like leaves. Its flowers are
                    yellow, purple, or white.

    Tulip           A bulb with a large, cup-shaped flower. Some
                    of the best varieties are imported from the
                    Netherlands.




                              Col 2 Doc 1 Pg 2 Ln 1.83" Pos 4.2"
```

FIGURE 21-5.   Parallel glossary entries

5.0), typing a **c** to select columns (omit in 5.0), and an **o** to turn columns on (**c** in 5.0) [Alt Layout Columns On].

Type the following text, pressing only the Hard Page (Ctrl - Enter) key [Alt Layout Align Hard Page] after each section of text. (Don't worry if you make a typographical error and can't get back to fix it; this will be discussed in section 21.5.)

Grandpa's Favorite	$3.50	A deep-dish apple pie made from the juiciest apples inside a flaky pie crust. Grandma's secret recipe.

| Patti's Prize | $2.75 | Our prize-winning fudge brownies that melt in your mouth. Loaded with toasted walnuts and covered with rich chocolate icing. A chocolate lover's delight. |
| Bob's Boast | $2.50 | A rich home-made ice cream sundae with your choice of chocolate, vanilla, or butter pecan ice cream. Choose from hot fudge, caramel, or butterscotch sauces. Don't forget the fresh peanuts, whipped cream, and cherry on top. |

When completed, the document screen should look like Figure 21-6.

Notice how Bob's Boast starts at the top of a new page. If you had defined the columns without block protection, part of Bob's Boast would appear at the bottom of page 1, and the rest of column three would appear at the top of page 2. Instead, the entire entry pertaining to Bob's Boast is moved to page 2.

Save the document using the same filename, and clear the screen by pressing the Exit ([F7]) key [[Alt] File Exit], y, [Enter], y, and [Enter].

EXERCISES

1. Retrieve the document PLAY.DOC. Turn the parallel columns on at the end of the document. Center and underline the headings "Character" and "Lines." Type the following text into the columns.

```
                    Dessert Menu

Grandpa's Favorite    $3.50    A deep-dish apple pie made from the
                               juiciest apples inside a flaky pie
                               crust. Grandma's secret recipe.

Patti's Prize         $2.75    Our prize-winning fudge brownies
                               that melt in your mouth. Loaded
                               with toasted walnuts and covered
                               with rich chocolate icing. A
                               chocolate lover's delight.

================================================================================

Bob's Boast           $2.50    A rich, home-made ice cream sundae
                               with your choice of chocolate,
                               vanilla, or butter pecan ice cream.
                               Choose from hot fudge, caramel, or
                               butterscotch sauces. Don't forget
                               the fresh peanuts, whipped cream,
                               and cherry on top.



                    Col 3 Doc 1 Pg 2 Ln 2.17" Pos 5.9"
```

FIGURE 21-6.   Parallel menu entries

(Don't worry if you make mistakes and can't correct them; you'll learn how in the next section.)

Character	Lines
Jane:	"Boy, it sure is lonely coming to a new school. I hope I meet some nice children to play with. I think I'll walk over to that group of girls and say hello. "Hi! My name is Jane and I'm new at this school."
Sarah:	"Hi, Jane! Welcome to our school. My name is Sarah. This is Mary and Betty."

Mary and Betty:	"Hi, Jane! Nice to meet you."
Sarah:	"We are going to play jump rope. Would you like to join us?"
Jane:	"I'd love to. Thanks for being so nice to me."

Save the document using the same filename, and clear the screen.

2. Retrieve the document N&A.LST. Turn the parallel columns with block protect on at the end of the document. For the second column, you will need to press the Enter key after the first line. Press only the Hard Page (Ctrl - Enter) key [Alt Layout Align Hard Page] after the second line of the second column. Enter the following text into the three columns. (Don't worry if you make mistakes and can't correct them; you'll learn how in the next section.)

Sandy Clark	121 S. Main St. Cleveland, OH 44114	287-1120
Joe Kent	2780 Bluebird Lane North Oak, OH 44013	452-7655
Sally Jones	5891 Sunny Vale Little Creek, OH 44410	552-1732

Save the document using the same filename and clear the screen.

3. Retrieve the document INVTY.DOC. At the end of the document, turn on the parallel columns feature with block protection. Enter the following text into the three columns. (Don't worry if you make mistakes and can't correct them; you'll learn how in the next section.)

PART NO	PRODUCT NAME	DESCRIPTION
100459	Personal Computer	1 MB RAM, monochrome mo nitor, 40 MB hard drive, one 5 1/4" floppy diskette drive
122989	Laser Printer	8 pages per minute, 250 page paper tray, envelope feeder
223348	Dot Matrix Printer	300 cps - draft mode, 150 cps -letter quality mode

Save the document using the same filename, and clear the screen.

21.5 MODIFY COLUMN ENTRIES

Editing text within columns is a little different than editing normal text. WordPerfect treats the text within a column similarly to the way it treats text on a page. Jumping from one column to the next thus requires an additional cursor movement combination.

To move from one column of text to another:

a. To move to a column to the right, press the Go To ([Ctrl]-[Home]) key [[Alt] Search Go To] and the [→] key.

b. To move to a column to the left, press the Go To ([Ctrl]-[Home]) key [[Alt] Search Go To] and the [←] key.

Once you are within the column you want to edit, use the cursor movement keys as you would within a normal page.

Changing the width of columns is another common modification made to text columns. If you have already entered text within the existing column definition, you probably want to avoid having to reenter the text. The trick to changing column widths is to make sure the cursor is located after the original column definition but before the code that turns columns on. Place the cursor just to the right of the column definition code.

To change the width of previously created text columns:

a. Find the [Col Def:] code within Reveal Codes, and place the cursor just to the right of it.

b. Press the Columns/Table ([Alt]-[F7]) key (Math/Columns key in 5.0) [[Alt] Layout Columns Define and skip steps c and d].

c. Type a **1** or **c** to select columns (skip this step in 5.0).

d. Type a **3** or **d** to define columns (type **4** or **d** in 5.0).

e. Adjust the column margins by typing **4** or **m**, and type each margin setting followed by pressing the [Enter] key.

f. Press the Exit ([F7]) key to exit the Text Column Definition screen.

g. Press the Exit ([F7]) key to return to the document.

EXAMPLES

1. To experiment with editing columns, retrieve the document ACMECORP.LTR by pressing the Retrieve (Shift-F10) key [Alt File Retrieve], typing **acmecorp.ltr**, and pressing Enter. Press the ↓ key three times so that the cursor is at the beginning of the line where the heading "New Benefits" appears. This puts your cursor at the beginning of the first column.

   You are going to change the due date for submitting the insurance cards from May 25 to May 26. This date appears in the second column. To quickly move to the second column, press the Go To (Ctrl-Home) key [Alt Search Go To] and then the → key. This moves the cursor to the very beginning of the second column.

   Place the cursor on the period after 25. Press the Backspace key to delete the 5, and type 6.

   For more practice, change the second sentence to read "Four different health plans will be offered." Move to the left column by pressing the Go To (Ctrl-Home) key [Alt Search Go To] and then the ← key. This moves you to the left side of the first column. Move to the word "Three." Press the Ctrl-Backspace key to delete the word "Three," type **Four**, and press SPACEBAR. Press Ctrl-→ to move to the beginning of the word "plans," type **health**, and press SPACEBAR. You are now done editing this document.

   Save the document and clear the screen by pressing the Exit (F7) key [Alt File Exit], typing **y**, Enter, **y**, and Enter.

2. To practice editing a three-column document, retrieve the document named DESSERT by pressing the Retrieve ([Shift]-[F10]) key [[Alt] File Retrieve], typing **dessert**, and pressing [Enter].

This example has three parallel columns with block protection. The first editing to be done is to eliminate the word "toasted" from the description of Patti's Prize. Move the cursor by pressing the [↓] key twice. This moves the cursor onto the "G" in "Grandpa's." Move the cursor to the third column by pressing the Go To ([Ctrl]-[Home]) key [[Alt] Search Go To] and the [→] key to move to column two, and then the Go To ([Ctrl]-[Home]) key [[Alt] Search Go To] and [→] key again to move to column three.

Press the [↓] key to move to the line where "toasted" appears. Move to the word "toasted," and delete it by pressing [Ctrl]-[Backspace].

Change the price of Bob's Boast to $2.75. Press the [↓] key four times. Press the Go To ([Ctrl]-[Home]) key [[Alt] Search Go To] and the [←] key to move to column two. Press the [→] key three times, the [Del] key twice, and type **75**. The corrections have been made.

Save the document and clear the screen by pressing the Exit ([F7]) key [[Alt] File Exit], typing **y**, [Enter], **y**, and [Enter].

3. Occasionally, you will want to change the widths of columns after you have entered the text. You will usually also want to avoid retyping the text. To practice editing column margins, retrieve the document named FLOWERS by pressing the Retrieve

(Shift-F10) key [Alt File Retrieve], typing **flowers**, and pressing Enter.

Press the Reveal Codes (Alt-F3) key [Alt Edit Reveal Codes]. Locate the [Col Def;2;1",2.5";3",7.5"] code, and move the cursor just to the right of it.

Press the Columns/Table (Alt-F7) key (Math/ Columns key in 5.0), type a **c** to select columns (skip this step in 5.0), and a **d** to define columns [Alt Layout Columns Define].

The current margins are set to 1" and 2.5" for column one and 3" and 7.5" for column two. Adjust the column margins by typing **m**, pressing Enter to accept 1", typing **2** and pressing Enter to change the first column's right margin, **2.5** and Enter to change the second column's left margin, and pressing Enter again. Press the Exit (F7) key twice to return to the document.

As you press the ↓ key to scroll through the document, the right column adjusts to the new margin settings.

EXERCISES

1. Retrieve the document named COMMNEWS. Make the following editing changes:

Change the starting time in the last paragraph to 2:00 instead of 12:00. Change the title "KIDDIE CALENDAR" to "KIDDIE NOTES."

Save the document using the same filename, and clear the screen.

2. Retrieve the document named N&A.LST. Make the following editing changes:

   Change the second phone number to 555-5555. Change Sally Jones to Sally Smith.
   Save the document using the same filename, and clear the screen.

3. Retrieve the document named PLAY.DOC. Change the right margin of the first column to 2″ and the left margin of the second column to 2.4″.

   Preview the document. Save the document using the same filename, and clear the screen.

EXERCISES

(Do not clear the screen until you have completed the last exercise.)

MASTERY
SKILLS CHECK

1. Define a page with a 4-inch top and bottom margin. Type and center the title **The Greenville Library**. On the next line, center the title **Eager Reader Club**. Skip a line and define newspaper columns using WordPerfect's defaults.

2. Turn on columns. Enter the following text.

   Story Hour

   Eager readers can take part in story hour every Monday from 10:00 to 11:00 am. Every week, we will feature a new story read by everyone's favorite, Mr. Rabbit. After the reading, the children are encouraged to participate in a lively discussion about the story. Mr. Rabbit tries to teach a valuable lesson from every story he reads to our Eager Readers.

Mr. Rabbit is looking forward to seeing you next week.

3. Turn off newspaper columns and add a hard page break.

4. Center the title **The Top Four Favorites**, then skip a line. Define parallel columns using three columns. The first column has margins of 1″ and 3″. The second column has margins of 3.5″ and 6″. The third column has margins of 6.5″ and 7.5″.

5. Turn parallel columns on and center the following headings: **Title**, **Author**, and **Rating**. Enter the following text:

A B C, 1 2 3	Jeffries, Kenneth B.	****
Seven Little Fish	Weston, Meryl Anne	***
The Dancing Flowers	Philips, Jocelyn M.	***
Big Eddie, Little	Duley, Katherine Louise	**
Sam, and Susie		

6. Turn off parallel columns, enter a blank line, then enter the following text that has been indented one tab stop from the left margin.

Book Sale

On May 5th, the Greenville Teen Readers will be sponsoring a book sale of books donated by various members of the community. All are welcome to browse and pick up a few favorites at very low prices. If you have books you would like to donate, please bring them to the library on May 4th during business hours.

7. View the document, then exit, and clear the screen.

(Do not clear the screen until you have completed the last exercise.)

INTEGRATING
SKILLS CHECK

1. Make the following formatting changes: change justification to left justification (turn justification off in 5.0), and set the left, right, top and bottom margins to 1.5".

2. Define two newspaper columns, with the distance between columns set to 0.4".

3. Center and bold the following heading on the page:

   Looking for the Perfect Candy Bar?

   Skip two lines.

4. Turn on the columns.

5. Type the following text. At the end of the first sentence, force the following sentence to the top of the next column.

   Capital Foods announces the release of their first no-calorie, no-cholesterol candy bar called Perfect-Bar.

   The product received rave reviews during its test-marketing. Now you can eat a delicious candy bar guilt free!

6. Turn the columns off. Skip two lines.

7. Center and bold the following heading on the page:

   Perfect-Bar Taste Testers Survey

Skip two lines.

8. Type the following paragraph as normal text, skipping two lines at the end of the paragraph.

Capital Foods test marketed Perfect-Bar in three different areas of the country. The customer

comments were generally favorable. Some of the comments are reproduced below:

9. Define two parallel columns with 1.5″ and 2.5″ margins for the first column and 2.9″ and 7.0″ margins for the second column. Turn on the columns after you have defined them.

10. Type the following text using the parallel columns.

Area A   Tasty nougat center. The chocolate coating is rich and creamy.

Area B   Where did you put the calories? This tastes just like the stuff I'm not supposed to have.

Area C   Anything that tastes this good has to have something wrong with it.

Using 5.1's New Table Features

►22◄

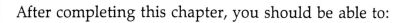

CHAPTER OBJECTIVES

After completing this chapter, you should be able to:

► Define a table   22.1

► Enter text into a table   22.2

► Change the width of a column   22.3

► Add a row or column to a table   22.4

► Join cells   22.5

► Change cell attributes within a table   22.6

► Incorporate simple math features into a table   22.7

The introduction of tables in WordPerfect 5.1 is arguably 5.1's most important addition to WordPerfect's capabilities. The Table features can be used to create a variety of documents including forms, parallel columns, and documents, similar to spreadsheets. Tables can be used to create any document that requires a columns/rows format, and they can perform simple arithmetic calculations similar to spreadsheet programs. Any attributes that can be used within a document (for instance, bolding, right justification, or changing fonts) can be assigned to the entire table, to text within a column or a row, or to the intersection of a row and a column.

These capabilities and others make Tables a very powerful feature of WordPerfect. Unfortunately, the table features are are not available in 5.0. If you are a WordPerfect 5.0 user, read this chapter anyway to see what you are missing. Tables may be the feature that motivates you to upgrade to 5.1!

Using Tables involves a two step process. First, you create the table by defining the number of columns and rows that make up the table. Once you have created the table, you are presented with a Table Editing screen, which allows you to change the way the table looks.

The second step is adding the text and numbers to the table. This editing is done while you are in the regular document screen. After you have created a table, exited the Table Editing screen, and then entered text, you can return to the Table Editing screen to change the table's formatting. Text that already exists within the table immediately conforms to the new format settings. This capability is one of the reasons the Table feature is such a powerful feature of WordPerfect 5.1.

Before you begin working with tables, you must learn the basic vocabulary associated with them. Tables are made up of rows, which run horizontally across the page, and columns, which run vertically. Rows are numbered (starting with number 1 and going down the page), and columns are assigned letters of the alphabet (starting with A).

The location where a row and column intersect is called a *Cell*. Cells are assigned names based on their relative position within the table. The cell located at the intersection of the first column and first row is called A1 because it is in column A and row 1. The cell located at the intersection of the third column and fifth row is called C5 because it is located in column C and row 5. See Figure 22-1 for an example of a table. The row heading "Game 1" is located in Cell A2. The score "201" is located in Cell C3.

	Brian	Ron
Game 1	231	175
Game 2	132	201
Game 3	194	195

FIGURE 22-1. Completed table

This chapter does not cover the full set of features offered by Tables. It does cover basic features that will allow you to produce a large variety of documents. Once you have mastered the concepts covered in this chapter, you will be able to easily master the more advanced and specialized Table features.

Since different printer and font selections affect the number of characters that will display on one line, you may not obtain exactly the same word-wrap breaks shown in this chapter. The examples in this chapter were all developed for use on a Hewlett Packard Laserjet Series II printer using the default Courier font.

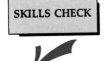

SKILLS CHECK

(Do not clear the screen until you have completed the last exercise.)

1. Remove all tab stops. Set left-justified tab stops at 0″ and 0.5″. Set decimal tabs at 5″ and 6″.

2. Create a centered heading for the document that includes the following information:

Acme Corporation
Statement

On the third line of the heading, enter the current date using WordPerfect's Date/Outline function.

3. Use the ⟨Tab⟩ key to create the following:

Previous Balance	$1,234.56
Expenses	
Rent	400.00
Utilities	119.90

Total Expenses		(519.90)
Income		
Client 012	150.00	
Client 110	1,210.00	
Total Income		1,360.00
Current Balance		$2,074.66

4. Exit the document and clear the screen.

CREATING A TABLE

22.1

As previously noted, a minimum of two steps is required to work with the Table feature. First you must create (define) the table. Afterwards, you can enter the text (data) into the table from the normal editing screen. This section shows you how to do the first step, creating a table.

To create a table:

a. Press the Columns/Table ([Alt]-[F7]) key [[Alt] Layout Tables Create and skip steps b and c].

b. Type a **2** or **t** for Tables.

c. Type a **1** or **c** to create the table.

d. Type the number of columns to be created for the table, and press the [Enter] key.

e. Type the number of rows to be created for the table, and press the [Enter] key.

f. When you are finished editing the formatting for the table, press the Exit ([F7]) key to return to the normal editing screen.

EXAMPLES

1. Creating a table is easy to do. You will start by creating a table that has three columns and four rows. First press the Columns/Table (Alt - F7) key, type **t** for Tables and **c** for Create [Alt Layout Tables Create].

   Type **3** and press the Enter key when prompted for the number of columns to be contained within the table. Type **4** and press Enter when prompted for the number of rows. Once you have done this, the table editing screen appears with the table created. See Figure 22-2 for an example of how your screen should look.

   The cursor is located in the top left hand cell of the table. At the bottom right hand corner of the screen, above the double line, the status line has an additional entry stating that your cursor is located in Cell A1. To the left of the status line, there is a message reminding you that you are currently in the Table Edit screen and that to leave this screen you press the Exit key. Later in this chapter, you will learn about the editing features listed at the bottom of the screen, below the double line.

   Press the Exit (F7) key to leave the table editing screen. You are now in the normal document editing screen, and your cursor is located at Cell A1. Press the Reveal Codes (Alt - F3) key [Alt Edit Reveal Codes] to display the codes inserted for this table. See Figure 22-3 for an example of how your screen should look. The [Tbl Def:I;3,2.17",2.17",2.17"] code is where the table has been defined. Anything

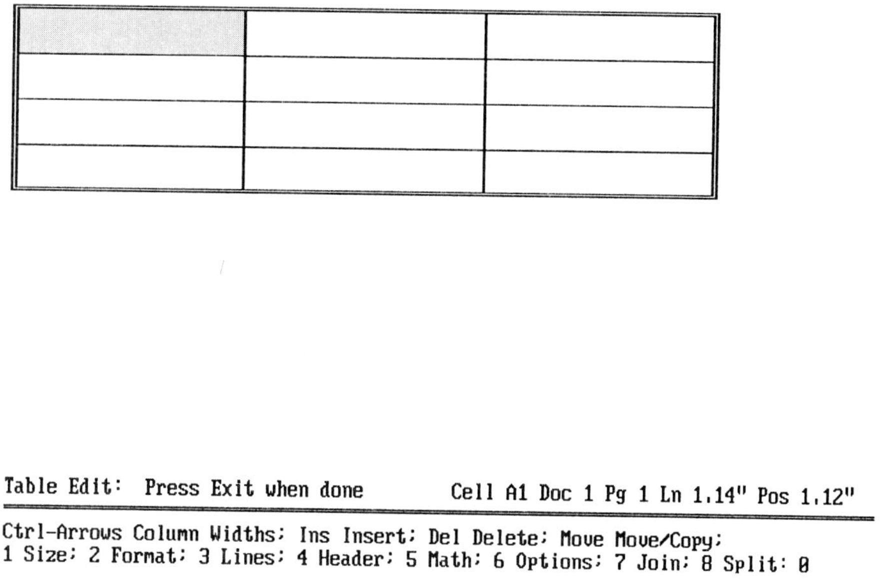

```
Table Edit:  Press Exit when done        Cell A1 Doc 1 Pg 1 Ln 1.14" Pos 1.12"

Ctrl-Arrows Column Widths; Ins Insert; Del Delete; Move Move/Copy;
1 Size; 2 Format; 3 Lines; 4 Header; 5 Math; 6 Options; 7 Join; 8 Split: 0
```

FIGURE 22-2.   Table editing screen

between this code and the [Tbl Off] code is part of the table.

The "I" in the table definition code is a roman numeral, indicating this is the first table within the document. If you created a second table, the code for it would have a "II." The "3" represents the number of columns within the table. The "2.17" repeated three times represents the current width of each of the three columns. The four [Row] lines represent the four rows of the table. And each [Cell] represents the cells within each row. If your cursor

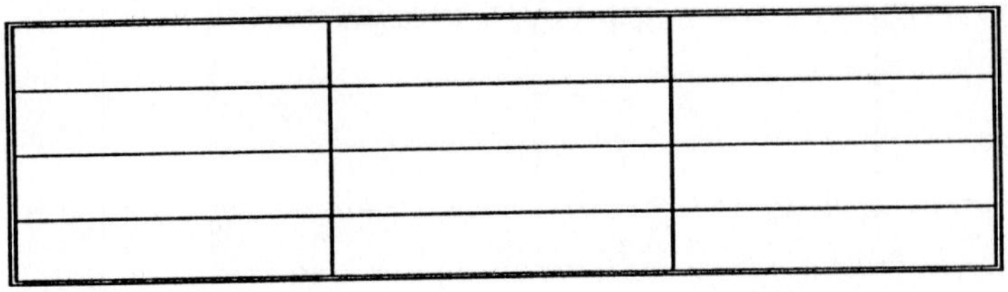

```
                                        Cell A1 Doc 1 Pg 1 Ln 1.14" Pos 1.12"
   {   ▲   ▲   ▲  ] {   ▲    ▲    ▲   ] {   ▲    ▲    ▲   ]
[Tbl Def:I;3,2.17",2.17",2.17"]
[Row][Cell][Cell][Cell]
[Row][Cell][Cell][Cell]
[Row][Cell][Cell][Cell]
[Row][Cell][Cell][Cell][Tbl Off]
```

Press Reveal Codes to restore screen

FIGURE 22-3.   Table codes

is currently located in Cell A1, you'll find it just after the first [Cell] of the first [Row] in the reveal codes screen. Later, as you add text to the table, the [Cell] codes are used to separate the text between each cell.

Turn off the Reveal Codes screen by pressing the Reveal Codes ([Alt]-[F3]) key [[Alt] Edit Reveal Codes]. Move to the end of the document by pressing [Home], [Home], and [↓]. Your cursor will move into a position just below the table. Press [Enter] once and type the following:

The above table lists the scores from last week's series of games for Brian and Ron. The following table lists this week's scores, showing the improvement both players made in one week.

Press the [Enter] key twice, and create a second table similar to the first. First press the Columns/Table ([Alt]-[F7]) key, type **t** for Tables and **c** for Create [[Alt] Layout Tables Create]. Press the [Enter] key twice to accept 3 for the number of columns and 4 for the number of rows. Press the Exit ([F7]) key to leave the table editing screen and return to the normal document editing screen.

Save the document by pressing the Save ([F10]) key [[Alt] File Save], typing **games**, and pressing [Enter].

2. To create a table that contains three columns and five rows, press the Columns/Table ([Alt]-[F7]) key, type **t** for Tables and **c** for Create [[Alt] Layout Tables Create]. Type **3**, and press the [Enter] key when prompted for the number of columns to be contained within the table. Type **5**, and press [Enter] when prompted for the number of rows. The table editing screen appears, showing the created table. Press the Exit ([F7]) key to return to the document screen.

Save the document by pressing the Exit ([F7]) key [[Alt] File Exit], typing **y, 3by5.tbl**, and pressing [Enter] twice.

3. Press the Bold ([F6]) key and type the following title:

1988 OACRS Deductions

Press the Bold (F6) key to turn off bolding, and press the Enter key twice. Create a two-column by four-row table by pressing the Columns/Table (Alt)-F7) key, and typing **t** for Tables and **c** for Create [(Alt) Layout Tables Create]. Type **2**, and press the Enter key when prompted for the number of columns to be contained within the table. Type **4**, and press Enter when prompted for the number of rows. The table editing screen appears with the created table. Press the Exit (F7) key to return to the document screen.

Save the document by pressing the Exit (F7) key [(Alt) File Exit], typing **y**, **oacrs.tbl**, and pressing Enter twice.

4. Create a table by pressing the Columns/Table ((Alt)-F7) key, and typing **t** for Tables and **c** for Create [(Alt) Layout Tables Create]. Type **3**, and press the Enter key when prompted for the number of columns to be contained within the table. Type **2**, and press Enter when prompted for the number of rows. The table editing screen appears with the created table. Press the Exit (F7) key to return to the document screen.

You are now in the normal document editing screen and your cursor is located at Cell A1. Press the Reveal Codes ((Alt)-F3) key [(Alt) Edit Reveal Codes] to display the codes inserted for this table. The cursor is located on the second [Cell] code in the Reveal Codes screen.

Press the Del key. The code is not deleted, but instead the cursor moves one code to the right.

Press the (Del) key again. Again, nothing is deleted, but the cursor now moves to the next code, which is a [Row] code. Pressing the (Del) key while on the [Row] code produces similar results.

Now move the cursor up to the [Tbl Def:] code by pressing (Home), (Home), and the (↑) key. Press the (Del) key. This time, the [Tbl Def:] code is deleted and all the other codes change to [HRt] and [Tab] codes. Specifically, the [Row] codes changed to [HRt] codes, and the [Cell] codes changed to [Tab] codes.

The only way you can delete a table is to delete the [Tbl Def:] code. In this example, you deleted the structure of the table, but left the contents of the table intact. Any text that was in the table remains. (In this example, there was no text contained within the table.) Each Cell's data is separated with a [HRt] or a [Tab] code.

Clear the screen by pressing the Exit ((F7)) key [(Alt) File Exit], typing **n**, and pressing (Enter). Press the Reveal Codes ((Alt)-(F3)) key [(Alt) Edit Reveal Codes] to exit from Reveal Codes.

Create another table with 5 columns and 8 rows by pressing the Columns/Table ((Alt)-(F7)) key, typing **t** for Tables and **c** for Create [(Alt) Layout Tables Create]. Type **5**, and press the (Enter) key when prompted for the number of columns to be contained within the table. Type **8**, and press (Enter) when prompted for the number of rows. The table editing screen appears with the created table. Press the Exit ((F7)) key to return to the document screen.

You are now in the normal document editing screen and your cursor is located at Cell A1. Press the Reveal Codes ([Alt]-[F3]) key [[Alt] Edit Reveal Codes] to display the codes inserted for this table.

This time, you are going to delete the entire table, not just the structure of the table. Press the [Home], [Home], and [↑] keys to move to the [Tbl Def:] code. Press the Block ([Alt]-[F4]) key [[Alt] Edit Block]. Press the [Home], [Home], and [↓] keys to move to a position just after the [Tbl Off] code. (When deleting an entire table, you must be careful to include both the [Tbl Def:] and [Tbl Off] codes within the blocked text.) Press the [Del] key. Type **y** to confirm that you want to delete the block.

5. Center a heading for this document by pressing the Center ([Shift]-[F6]) key [[Alt] Layout Align Center]. Bold the text by pressing the Bold ([F6]) key, and type:

Acme Corporation Employment Application

Press the Bold ([F6]) key, and press [Enter] twice. Create a three-column by four-row table by pressing the Columns/Table ([Alt]-[F7]) key, and typing **t** for Tables and **c** for Create [[Alt] Layout Tables Create]. Type **3**, and press the [Enter] key when prompted for the number of columns to be contained within the table. Type **4**, and press [Enter] when prompted for the number of rows. The table editing screen appears with the created table. Press the Exit ([F7]) key to return to the document screen.

Save the document and clear the screen by pressing the Exit ([F7]) key [[Alt] File Exit], typing **y**, **employee.tbl**, and pressing [Enter] twice.

EXERCISES

1. Type the bolded heading:

   Office Supplies Inventory - Top Shelf

   Insert a blank line. Create a table with 3 columns and 4 rows. Insert a blank line. Type the bolded heading:

   Office Supplies Inventory - Bottom Shelf

   Insert a blank line. Create a table with three columns and five rows. Save the document as SUPPLIES, and clear the screen.

2. Center and bold the heading:

   Faculty Evaluation Form

   Insert a blank line. Type the following paragraph:

   Place an X under the Agree category if you believe the statement regarding the instructor is true. Place an X under the Neutral category if you have no opinion or do not know whether the statement applies to the instructor. Place an X under the Disagree category if you believe the statement regarding the instructor is not correct.

   Insert a blank line. Create a table that contains four columns and five rows. Insert a blank line underneath the table. Type the sentence:

   Return this form to the department's faculty secretary.

   Save the document as FACULTY.TBL, and clear the screen.

3. Type the following:

Attachment C:

Insert a blank line. Create a table with two columns and four rows. Insert a blank line underneath the table. Type:

See page 14-7 for more details.

Save the document as ATTACH.C and clear the screen.

4. Create a table that contains 12 columns and 15 rows. Delete the entire table.

5. Create a table that is two columns wide by four rows long. Save the document as BILL.SHT, and clear the screen.

22.2 ENTERING TABLE DATA

Once the table has been created, entering text into the table is similar to entering text in a normal document. While you are within a cell, you type in the text in much the same way as you would with a normally formatted document. One exception to this is the use of the ⟨Tab⟩ key. Within tables, the ⟨Tab⟩ key is used to move from cell to cell. If you need to use the tab function, press the ⟨Home⟩ key first and then the ⟨Tab⟩ key.

To enter table data:

a. Move the cursor to the cell in which the data is to be entered.

b. Type the text into the cell. Press the [Enter] key to end short lines, but do not press the [Enter] key at the end of the data.

c. Press the [Tab] key to move to the next cell.

The [Tab] key is one method for moving forward from cell to cell. The Margin Release ([Shift]-[Tab]) key will move you backward from cell to cell. Using any of the arrow keys will move you in the direction of the arrow. If your cursor is located at an outer edge of a cell, pressing the arrow key in that direction will move you to the next cell. Pressing the Go To ([Ctrl]-[Home]) key and the [←] or [→] keys moves the cursor from cell to cell (similar to the way the cursor moves within text columns.)

EXAMPLES

1. You will now enter text into a previously created table. Retrieve the document GAMES by pressing the Retrieve ([Shift]-[F10]) key [[Alt] File Retrieve], typing **games**, and pressing [Enter]. Press the [→] key once to move into Cell A1.

   Press the [Tab] key once to move to Cell B1. Type **Brian**, press the [Tab] key to move to Cell C1, and type **Ron**. Press the [Tab] key again, which moves the cursor to cell A2.

   Type **Game 1**, press [Tab], type **231**, press [Tab], and type **175**. Press [Tab], type **Game 2**, press [Tab], type **132**, press [Tab], and type **201**. Finally, press [Tab], type **Game 3**, press [Tab], type **194**, press [Tab], and type **195**. At this point, the screen should like this:

	Brian	Ron
Game 1	231	175
Game 2	132	201
Game 3	194	195

The above table lists the scores from last week's series of games
for Brian and Ron. The following table lists this week's scores,
showing the improvement both players made in one week.

D:\WP51\DOCS\GAMES   Cell C4 Doc 1 Pg 1 Ln 1.98" Pos 5.73"

Using the ⬇ and ⬅ keys, move the cursor to Cell B1 in the second table. Make sure that the status line says "Cell B1" before continuing with this example. You will now enter text into the second table. This time, however, you will use the ➡ key to move from one cell to the next.

Type **Brian**, press the ➡ key, and type **Ron**. Press the ➡ key to move to Cell A2. Type **Game 1**, press ➡, type **220**, press ➡, type **196**, and press ➡. Type **Game 2**, press ➡, type **195**, press ➡, type **212**, and press ➡. Finally, type **Game 3**, press ➡, type **180**, press ➡, and type **194**.

Preview the document by pressing the Print (Shift - F7) key [Alt File Print], and typing v3. The screen should look similar to Figure 22-4.

Press the Exit (F7) key to return to the document screen.

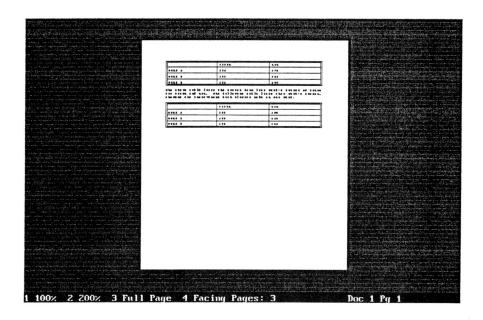

FIGURE 22-4.   Preview of game table

At this point, assume you have discovered a typographical error. In the second table, you realize Brian's first game score should have been 230. Press the ⬆ key twice to move up to Cell C2, and press the Margin Release (Shift - Tab) key once to move to Cell B2. Press the ➡ key twice, then the Del key, and type 0 to change the number to 230.

Print the document by pressing the Print (Shift - F7) key [Alt File Print], and typing f. Save the document using the same file name, and clear the screen by pressing the Exit (F7) key [Alt File Exit], typing y, Enter , y, and Enter .

2. Retrieve the document 3BY5.TBL by pressing the Retrieve ([Shift]-[F10]) key [[Alt] File Retrieve], typing **3by5.tbl**, and pressing [Enter].

In a later section of this chapter, you will create a table heading within the first row of this table. For now, leave this row blank. Press the [↓] key twice. The status line should indicate that the cursor is currently located in Cell A2.

Press the [CapsLock] key, type **team**, press [Tab] to move to Cell B2, type **wins**, press [Tab] to move to Cell C2, type **losses**, and press [Tab]. Your cursor should be located at Cell A3. Press the [CapsLock] key to turn off the Caps Lock feature.

Type **Redmen**, press [Tab], type **10**, press [Tab], type **0**, and press [Tab]. Your cursor should be located at cell A4. Type **Patriots**, press [Tab], type **9**, press [Tab], type **1**, and press [Tab]. Your cursor should be located at Cell A5. Type **Bruins**, press [Tab], type **8**, press [Tab], and type **2**.

Now, add some text before the table. To do this, press [Home], [Home], and the [↑] key. This moves the cursor to the beginning of the document. Type the following:

This year's high school basketball conference has been very exciting for our readership. The following table lists the current standings of our local teams.

Press the [Enter] key to produce a blank line between the paragraph and the table that follows. Print the document by pressing the Print ([Shift]-[F7]) key [[Alt] File Print] and typing **f**.

Save the document by pressing the Exit ([F7]) key [[Alt] File Exit], typing **y**, **baskball**, and pressing [Enter] twice.

3. You can use document formatting features to change the appearance of text within a cell much the same way as in a normal document. If you attempt to use a formatting feature that conflicts with the table formatting defined for the cell, WordPerfect will ignore your attempt. Since you have not yet added formatting to any tables, you need not worry about conflicting formats at this time.

Retrieve the document named OACRS.TBL by pressing the Retrieve (⟦Shift⟧-⟦F10⟧) key [⟦Alt⟧ File Retrieve], typing **oacrs.tbl**, and pressing ⟦Enter⟧. The 1988 OACRS Deductions table should appear on your screen.

Move to Cell A1 by pressing the ⟦↓⟧ key 3 times. The first row is going to contain the headings "Property" and "1988 Deductions." Bold and center the headings as you type them by pressing the Bold (⟦F6⟧) key, the Center (⟦Shift⟧-⟦F6⟧) key [⟦Alt⟧ Layout Align Center], and typing **Property**. Press ⟦Tab⟧, the Bold (⟦F6⟧) key and the Center (⟦Shift⟧-⟦F6⟧) key [⟦Alt⟧ Layout Align Center], and type **1988 Deduction**.

Notice that you needed to press the Bold key for the second column heading because formatting codes do not transfer from one cell to another. For the same reason, you will also not need to turn off the bolding for the second heading.

Press the ⟦Tab⟧ key to move to Cell A2. You are now ready to enter the text. In this example, the text does not fit into one line of the cell. Just type normally, and let WordPerfect wrap the line as needed.

Type **3-year property (fully depreciated)**, press the ⟦Tab⟧ key, and type 0.00. The word "depreciated" scrolls to the second line of the cell, which automatically widens to accommodate the entry. The screen should now look like this:

Property	1988 Deduction
3-year property (fully depreciated)	0.00

Press the (Tab) key so the cursor is located in Cell A3. Type the following four entries, pressing the (Tab) key after each one:

5-year property (21% each year)
9,450.00
10-year property (10% each year)
5,000.00

Notice that when you press the (Tab) key after the "5,000.00" entry, it moves you to the "5" at the beginning of the current cell. This is because there are no remaining cells for the cursor to move to.

Print the document by pressing the Print ((Shift)-(F7)) key [(Alt) File Print] and typing f. Save the document by pressing the Exit ((F7)) key [(Alt) File Exit], typing y, (Enter), y, and (Enter).

4. You are now going to experiment with deleting a table structure and deleting an entire table. You deleted a table structure in section 22.1, but did not have a chance to see what happens when there is data within the table.

Press the Retrieve (Shift-F10) key [Alt File Retrieve], type **games**, and press Enter. Press the Reveal Codes (Alt-F3) key [Alt Edit Reveal Codes] to display the codes and text for this table. The cursor should be located on the [Tbl Def:] code.

To delete the table *structure,* press the Del key. Notice that the [Cell] codes are replaced by [Tab] codes. Because WordPerfect's default tabs are set at every half inch, the headings do not line up with the game scores. If you want to delete the table structure, but retain the text within the tables, it is normally a good idea to adjust the tabs before you delete the [Tbl Def:] code.

To make the correction now, press the Format (Shift-F8) key, type **L** for Line [Alt Layout Line], and **t** for Tabs. This takes you to the line formatting screen. Move the cursor to the "L" at the +.5" mark, and press the Del key. Move the cursor to the "L" at the +1.5" mark, and press the Del key. Press the Exit (F7) key twice to return to the document. The game scores should now line up with the column headings.

The key to deleting an entire table, including its data, is to make sure the [Tbl Def:] code and the [Tbl Off] code are both contained within blocked text.

To delete the bottom table from this document, move the cursor to the [Tbl Def:] code so that the code is highlighted with the cursor. Press the Block (Alt-F4) key [Alt Edit Block]. Press the ↓ key until the cursor is to the right of the [Tbl Off] code. Press the Del key to delete the table. Type **y** to confirm the deletion. The entire table disappears from the document.

Turn off Reveal Codes by pressing the Reveal Codes ([Alt]-[F3]) key [[Alt] Edit Reveal Codes]. Exit without saving the document by pressing the Exit ([F7]) key [[Alt] File Exit] and typing **n** twice.

5. Sometimes the tables you create will not require that text be placed in all of the cells. You may leave some cells empty, to be filled in at a later time; or the document may be used as a form in which someone will be entering information by hand. A sign-up sheet is a good example of this type of table. The following shows an example of a useful table, where some of the cells remain empty.

Retrieve EMPLOYEE.TBL by pressing the Retrieve ([Shift]-[F10]) key [[Alt] File Retrieve], typing **employee.tbl**, and pressing [Enter]. The first column of this table will ask a question. The remaining two columns are used to indicate a yes or no response.

If the answer is yes, the applicant will place a checkmark in column B. If the answer is no, the applicant will place a checkmark in column C. Normally, you want column A to be as wide as possible to accommodate the space required for the questions. Columns B and C should be narrow. You'll learn to do this in a later section of this chapter. For now, the table will look strange because so much of the text of the questions will have to be wrapped within a relatively narrow cell.

Press the ⬇ key until the cursor is located in Cell A1. Press the (Caps Lock) key, and type the following, without pressing (Enter):

answer the following. place a checkmark in the yes column if the answer to the question is yes. place a checkmark in the no column if the answer to the question is no.

Press the (Tab) key, type **yes**, press (Tab), type **no** and press (Tab). The cursor should be located in Cell A2. Press the (Caps Lock) key.

Type the following three questions, pressing the (Tab) key three times after each of the first two questions. (Do not press (Enter).)

Have you ever applied for a position with Acme Corporation before?
Have you ever been convicted of a felony?
Are you a citizen of the United States?

Preview the document by pressing the Print ((Shift)-(F7)) key [(Alt) File Print], and typing **v**. Press the Exit ((F7)) key to return to the document. Save the document by pressing the Exit ((F7)) key [(Alt) File Exit], typing **y**, (Enter), **y**, and (Enter).

EXERCISES

1. Retrieve the document named SUPPLIES. Enter the following data into the first table.

ITEM	TOTAL	UNITS
Pencils	10	Boxes
Pens	8	Boxes
Note Pads	15	Dozen

Enter the following data into the second table.

ITEM	TOTAL	UNITS
Letterhead	3	Boxes
Second Sheet Paper	4	Boxes
Bond Paper	15	Reams
Laser Labels	2	Packages

Print the document, and save it using the same file-name. Clear the screen.

2. Retrieve the document named FACULTY.TBL. Enter the following headings into the four cells of the first row (one heading per cell).

STATEMENT   AGREE   NEUTRAL   DISAGREE

Enter each of the following statements into a separate cell in column A. Leave the remaining cells in columns B, C, and D empty.

1. He/she comes prepared to class.
2. He/she has command of the subject matter.
3. He/she seems genuinely concerned with whether students learn the course material.
4. The course's contents were taught in a manner that promoted learning of the course material.

Print the document, and save it using the same file-name. Clear the screen.

3. Retrieve the document named ATTACH.C. Leave the first row of cells blank. You will be adding a table header later.

   Enter the following information in the indicated cells (leaving cell B4 empty).

   Cell A2: 1988 MACRS deduction: $12,000 $\times$ .20 =
   Cell B2: 2,400.00
   Cell A3: 1989 MACRS deduction: $12,000 $\times$ .32 $\times$
          1/2 year =
   Cell B3: 1,920.00
   Cell A4: Total MACRS deduction:

   Save the document using the same filename, and clear the screen.

4. Retrieve the document named SUPPLIES. Delete the structure of the second table. Adjust the tabs if necessary. Save the document as TOPSHELF.

5. Retrieve the document named BILL.SHT. Enter into Cell A4 the following:

   Total Charges:

   Save the document using the same name and clear the screen.

CHANGING A COLUMN WIDTH

22.3

WordPerfect provides two different methods for changing the width of a column. Both methods require that you be at the Table Edit screen. One method allows you to gradually increase or decrease the width of a specified column and immediately see the results. The other method allows you to specify in inches the new width of a column. With the second method, the reformatting occurs after the column's width has been determined.

To change the width of a column with the Ctrl key method:

a. Move the cursor to a location inside the table. (If you are already in table editing mode, skip steps a and b.)

b. Press the Columns/Table (Alt-F7) key [Alt Layout Tables Edit] to change to the Table Edit screen.

c. Move the cursor to any cell within the column where the width is to be changed.

d. Press the Ctrl-← key combination to make the width of the column smaller or press the Ctrl-→ key combination to make the width of the column larger. Continue until the column's width is acceptable.

e. Press the Exit (F7) key to exit the table editing screen.

In step d, WordPerfect will not let you make the right-most column larger if the table is already the full width of the page. With other columns, WordPerfect will decrease the size of columns to the right to accommodate making a column larger whenever the table is already the full width of the page.

To change the width of a column with the Format Column function:

a. Move the cursor to a location inside the table. (If you are already in table editing mode, skip steps a and b.)

b. Press the Columns/Table ([Alt]-[F7]) key [[Alt] Layout Tables Edit] to change to the Table Edit screen.

c. Move the cursor to any cell within the column where the width is to be changed.

d. Type a **2** or **f** to select the Format feature.

e. Type a **2** or **L** to select the Column feature.

f. Type a **1** or **w** to select the Width feature. You are now within the Format Column Width feature.

g. Type the width for the column in inches. Press the [Enter] key.

e. Press the Exit ([F7]) key to exit the table editing screen.

EXAMPLES

1. You will now have a chance to change the widths of columns in a previously saved table. Retrieve the document GAMES by pressing the Retrieve ([Shift]-[F10]) key [[Alt] File Retrieve], typing **games**, and pressing [Enter]. Press the [→] key once to move into Cell A1 of the first table.

   Since you are currently within the table, activate Table Edit by pressing the Columns/Table ([Alt]-[F7]) key [[Alt] Layout Tables Edit]. Since your cursor is currently located in Cell A1, first decrease the width of column A by pressing the [Ctrl]-[←] key combination ten times. As you do this, the table readjusts itself to reflect each decrease in the size of the column.

Press the ⟶ and the ⬇ keys. Your cursor should be located in Cell B2. Decrease column B's width by eight characters, pressing the Ctrl-⟵ key combination eight times. Press the ⟶ key once so that your cursor is located in Cell C2. Decrease column C's width to be the same as column B's by pressing the Ctrl-⟵ key combination eight times.

Press the Exit (F7) key to leave the table editing screen.

Use this document in the next example.

2. You will now have a chance to decrease the widths of columns using the Format Column Width feature. Move the cursor to any cell within column A of the second table. Activate table editing for this table by pressing the Columns/Table (Alt-F7) key [Alt Layout Tables Edit].

Type **f** for format, **1** for format column and **w** for column width. Type **1.17**, and press Enter to change the width of column A to 1.17". Press the ⟶ key to move to column B.

To change the width of column B, type **f** for Format, **1** for Format Column, and **w** for Column Width. Type **1.37**, and press Enter to change the width of column B to 1.37". Press the ⟶ key to move to column C.

To change the width of column C, type **f** for Format, **1** for Format Column, and **w** for Column Width. Type **1.37**, and press Enter to change the width of column C to 1.37". The widths of the columns in the second table should be the same as the first table in this document. Press the Exit key (F7) to leave Table Edit.

Print the document by pressing the Print (⟨Shift⟩-⟨F7⟩) key [⟨Alt⟩ File Print], and typing f for Full Document. Save the document and clear the screen by pressing the Exit (⟨F7⟩) key [⟨Alt⟩ File Exit], typing y, ⟨Enter⟩, y, and ⟨Enter⟩.

3. You will now experiment with increasing the width of a column where text has wrapped within the cells. Retrieve the document OACRS.TBL by pressing the Retrieve (⟨Shift⟩-⟨F10⟩) key [⟨Alt⟩ File Retrieve], typing **oacrs.tbl**, and pressing ⟨Enter⟩. Press the ⟨↓⟩ key three times to move into Cell A1 of the table.

   Activate table editing by pressing the Columns/ Table (⟨Alt⟩-⟨F7⟩) key [⟨Alt⟩ Layout Tables Edit]. Since your cursor is currently located in Cell A1, first increase the width of column A by pressing the ⟨Ctrl⟩-⟨→⟩ key combination ten times. As you do this, the table readjusts itself to reflect each increase in size of column A. Column B's width decreases to make room for the increased size of column A. Press the Exit (⟨F7⟩) key.

   Print the document by pressing the Print (⟨Shift⟩-⟨F7⟩) key [⟨Alt⟩ File Print] and typing f for Full Document. Save the document and clear the screen by pressing the Exit (⟨F7⟩) key [⟨Alt⟩ File Exit], typing y, ⟨Enter⟩, y, and ⟨Enter⟩.

4. You now have the chance to increase the size of a column where text has wrapped within cells using the format column function. Retrieve the document EMPLOYEE.TBL by pressing the Retrieve (⟨Shift⟩-⟨F10⟩) key [⟨Alt⟩ File Retrieve], typing **employee.tbl** and pressing ⟨Enter⟩. Press the ⟨↓⟩ key three times to move into Cell A1 of the table.

Activate table editing by pressing the Columns/ Table ([Alt]-[F7]) key [[Alt] Layout Tables Edit]. Press the [→] key once to move the cursor into the yes column (column B). Decrease the width of this column by typing **f** for Format, **1** for Format Column, and **w** for Column Width. Type **.5**, and press [Enter] to change the width of column B to .5". Press the [→] key to move to the no column (column C).

Make column C's width the same as column B's. Type **f** for format, **1** for Format Column and **w** for Column Width. Type **.5**, and press [Enter] to change the width of column C to .5".

Now that columns B and C have been decreased in size, it is time to increase column A. Press the [←] key twice to move the cursor to column A. Type **f** for format, **1** for Format Column, and **w** for Column Width. Type **5.5**, and press [Enter] to change the width of column A to 5.5". Press the Exit ([F7]) key.

Print the document by pressing the Print ([Shift]-[F7]) key [[Alt] File Print] and typing **f** for Full Document. Save the document and clear the screen by pressing the Exit ([F7]) key [[Alt] File Exit], typing **y**, [Enter], **y**, and [Enter].

EXERCISES

1. Retrieve the file named SUPPLIES. In the first table, decrease the width of column B by 10 characters. Decrease the width of column C by 5 characters.

   In the second table, use the Format Column feature to change the widths of column B to 1.17" and column C to 1.57".

Preview the document, then save it using the same filename, and clear the screen.

2. Retrieve the document named FACULTY.TBL. Using the Format Column Width feature to change the widths of the four columns, change the width of column D to 1.1″, column C to .9″, column B to .7″, and column A to 3.8″.

   Print the document. Save it using the same filename and clear the screen.

3. Retrieve the document named ATTACH.C. Increase the width of column A by 15 characters. Print the document. Save it using the same filename and clear the screen.

4. Retrieve the document named BILL.SHT. Increase the width of column A by 15 characters. Preview the document. Save it using the same filename and clear the screen.

ADDING A COLUMN OR ROW TO A TABLE 22.4

Sometimes you will find it necessary to add a column or a row to a previously created table. WordPerfect provides two methods for adding columns and rows, depending on where they are to be added.

The first method adds either columns at the right edge of the table or rows to the bottom of the table. Any attributes (formatting) you have assigned to the last row or column of the original table will be copied into the newly created row(s) or column(s).

The second method adds rows or columns at the beginning or in the middle of a table. To add a column, you must first move the cursor to the column just to the right of the location where the new column is to be added. To add a row, you must first move the cursor to the row just below the location where the new row is to be added. In either case, the new column or row takes on the attributes (formatting) of the column or row where the cursor is located.

To add a column or row at the end of a table:

a. Move the cursor to a location inside the table. (If you are already in table editing mode, skip steps a and b.)

b. Press the Columns/Table (Alt-F7) key [Alt Layout Tables Edit] to change to the Table Edit screen.

c. Type a **1** or **s** to select the table size function. Type a **1** or **r** to indicate that rows are to be added, or type a **2** or **c** to indicate that columns are to be added.

d. Type the total number of rows or columns to be in the resulting table, and press Enter.

e. Exit the Table Edit screen by pressing the Exit (F7) key.

To add a column or row at the beginning or in the middle of a table:

a. Move the cursor to a location inside the table. (If you are already in table editing mode, skip steps a and b.)

b. Press the Columns/Table ([Alt]-[F7]) key [[Alt] Layout Tables Edit] to change to the Table Edit screen.

c. If you are adding a row, move the cursor to the row just under the location where the new row is to be inserted. If you are adding a column, move the cursor to the column just to the right of the location where the new column is to be inserted.

d. Press the [Ins] key.

e. Type a **1** or **r** to add a row, or a **2** or **c** to add a column.

f. Type the number of rows or columns to be added, and press [Enter].

g. Exit the Table Edit screen by pressing the Exit ([F7]) key.

EXAMPLES

1. Adding rows and columns to a table is fairly easy. In this example, you will practice adding a row to the bottom and a column to the right edge of a table.

    Retrieve a document by pressing the Retrieve ([Shift]-[F10]) key [[Alt] File Retrieve], typing **games**, and pressing [Enter]. Press the [↓] key once to move to Cell A1 of the first table. Press the Columns/Table ([Alt]-[F7]) key [[Alt] Layout Tables Edit] to turn on the table editing screen.

    To add a row at the bottom of the table, type **s** to select the Table Size function. Type **r** to add a row. WordPerfect prompts you with the current number of rows, which for this example is 4. Since you are adding 1 row, type 5 (4 current rows plus the 1 new row), and press (Enter). The new row appears at the bottom of the table.

To add a column on the right side of the table, type **s** to select the Table Size function. Type **c** to add a column. WordPerfect prompts you with the current number of columns, which for this example is 3. Since you are adding 1 column, type **4** (3 current columns plus the 1 new column), and press (Enter). The new column appears on the right side of the table.

If you have followed the above instructions, your cursor should be located in Cell D1. Exit the table editing screen by pressing the Exit ((F7)) key. Add text to these cells by typing **John**, (↓), **140**, (↓), **151**, (↓), **170**, (↓), and pressing the Margin Release ((Shift)-(Tab)) key three times. Type **Total** in Cell A5. You will have WordPerfect generate the totals in a later section of this chapter.

Edit the paragraph separating the two tables. Move the cursor to the "B" in Brian. Press the Delete Word ((Ctrl)-(Backspace)) key 3 times. Type **the Boomers.**, and press SPACEBAR twice. Move the cursor to the "b" in "both." Press the Delete Word ((Ctrl)-(Backspace)) key twice. Type **the Boomers**, and press SPACEBAR.

Make similar changes to the second table by first moving the cursor to somewhere within it. Press the Columns/Table ((Alt)-(F7)) key [(Alt) Layout Tables Edit] to turn on the table editing screen.

To add a row at the bottom of the table, type **s** to select the Table Size function. Type **r** to add a row. WordPerfect prompts you with the current number of rows, which in this example is 4. Since you are adding 1 row, type **5** (4 current rows plus the 1 new row), and press `Enter`. The new row appears at the bottom of the table.

To add a column on the right side of the table, type **s** to select the Table Size function. Type **c** to add a column. WordPerfect prompts you with the current number of columns, which in this example is 3. Since you are adding 1 column, type **4** (3 current columns plus the 1 new column), and press `Enter`. The new column appears on the right side of the table.

If you have followed the above instructions, your cursor should be located in Cell D1. Exit the table editing screen by pressing the Exit (`F7`) key. Add text to these cells by typing **John**, `↓`, **153**, `↓`, **161**, `↓`, **190**, `↓`, and pressing the Margin Release (`Shift`-`Tab`) key three times. Type **Total** in Cell A5.

Print the document by pressing the Print (`Shift`-`F7`) key [`Alt` File Print] and typing **f** for Full Document. Save the document and clear the screen by pressing the Exit (`F7`) key [`Alt` File Exit], typing **y**, `Enter`, **y**, and `Enter`.

2. In this example, you will practice adding a row and a column in the middle of a table. Retrieve a document by pressing the Retrieve (`Shift`-`F10`) key [`Alt` File Retrieve], typing **baskball**, and pressing `Enter`. Press the `↓` key until you are in Cell A1 of the table. Press the Columns/Table (`Alt`-`F7`) key [`Alt` Layout Tables Edit] to turn on the Table Edit screen.

First, add a row between "Redmen" and "Patriots" to allow room for a new basketball team. Press the ⬇ key three times to move the cursor to Cell A4. Press the [Ins] key and type **r** to indicate you want to add a row. Type **1** and press [Enter] to add one new row. The new row appears inside the table, and the cursor is located within it.

Now, add a column within the table. This column will be located between the TEAM and WINS columns and will list the names of the schools. Press the ➡ once, so the cursor is within the WINS column. Press the [Ins] key, and type **c** to indicate you want to add a column. Type **1** and press [Enter] to add one new column. The new column appears inside the table, and the cursor is located within it.

You want this column to be similar in width to the TEAM column. Press the [Ctrl]-[➡] key combination 11 times to make the new column larger. Leave the table editing screen by pressing the Exit ([F7]) key. Move the cursor to Cell C2 by pressing the ⬆ twice. Type **SCHOOL**, ⬇, **Maple City**, ⬇, **Rochester**, ⬇, **Broadview Heights**, ⬇, and **Cranbrook**. ([Shift]-[Tab]) key once. Type **Warriors**, press the [Tab] key twice, type **9**, [Tab], and **1**.

Preview the document by pressing the Print ([Shift]-[F7]) key [[Alt] File Print] and typing **v** for View. Press the Exit ([F7]) key to return to the document. Save the document and clear the screen by pressing the Exit ([F7]) key [[Alt] File Exit], typing **y**, [Enter], **y**, and [Enter].

3. Retrieve the document OACRS.TBL by pressing the Retrieve ([Shift]-[F10]) key [[Alt] File Retrieve], typing

oacrs.tbl, and pressing (Enter). Press the (↓) key three times to move to Cell A1 of the table. Press the Columns/Table ((Alt)-(F7)) key [(Alt) Layout Tables Edit] to turn on the table editing screen.

Add a row to the bottom of the table by typing **s** for table size, **r** for Row, **5** for the total number of rows, and pressing (Enter).

A row is immediately added to the bottom of the table. Press the Exit ((F7)) key to leave the table editing screen. Type **Total Deduction:** in Cell A5. Leave Cell B5 empty. You will make WordPerfect generate a total in a later section of this chapter.

Preview the document by pressing the Print ((Shift)-(F7)) key [(Alt) File Print] and typing **v** for View. Press the Exit ((F7)) key to return to the document. Save the document and clear the screen by pressing the Exit ((F7)) key [(Alt) File Exit], typing **y**, (Enter), **y**, and (Enter).

4. Retrieve the document EMPLOYEE.TBL by pressing the Retrieve ((Shift)-(F10)) key [(Alt) File Retrieve], typing **employee.tbl**, and pressing (Enter). Press the (↓) key three times to move to Cell A1 of the table. Press the Columns/Table ((Alt)-(F7)) key [(Alt) Layout Tables Edit] to turn on the table editing screen.

You will add a row at the top of this table. This row will be used in a later section of this chapter to add a table heading. Since the cursor is currently in the top row of the table, and the row to be added is above this point, press the (Ins) key. Type **r** for row, then **1**, and press (Enter) to indicate that one row is to be added.

Notice that it appears that the new row has a double line underneath it instead of a single line. The double line comes from the second row because it retains its double line from when it was the top row. Using the line function, you could change the double line to a single line. However, the double line will stay for this application.

You will also add a row at the bottom of this table. To do so, type **s** for Table Size, **r** for row, **6** for the total number of rows, and press `Enter`. A row is immediately added to the bottom of the table. Press the Exit (`F7`) key to leave the table editing screen. Type:

Have you ever served in a branch of the armed services?

Preview the document by pressing the Print (`Shift`-`F7`) key [`Alt` File Print] and typing **v** for View. Press the Exit (`F7`) key to return to the document. Save the document and clear the screen by pressing the Exit (`F7`) key [`Alt` File Exit], typing y, `Enter`, y, and `Enter`.

EXERCISES

1. Retrieve the document named SUPPLIES. Add a column named ORDER NO. between the ITEM and TOTAL columns for both tables. Add a row called "Envelopes" between "Second Sheet Paper" and "Bond Paper" in the second table.

   Add the following column entries in the first table:

ORDER NO.
PX-3
ST-2
RX-5

Add the following column entries in the second table:

ORDER NO.
345
23
X35
RX-34
RX-1

Add the following row entries in the second table:

Envelopes X35 4 Boxes

Preview the document, save it, and clear the screen.

2. Retrieve the document named FACULTY.TBL. Add a row to the bottom of the table. Type in the following statement in column A of the new row:

5. As a student, you were interested in learning the course material.

Print the document, save it, and clear the screen.

3. Retrieve the document TOPSHELF. Add a column named REORDER to the far right of the table. Except for the heading REORDER, leave the other cells blank.

Preview the document, save it using the same filename, and clear the screen.

22.5 | JOINING CELLS

Sometimes the capability of joining two or more cells together to make one cell in a table is very useful. This is especially true for table headings that are used to describe more than one column. WordPerfect provides a simple means for combining cells.

To combine two or more cells into one cell:

a. Move the cursor to a location inside the table. (If you are already in table editing mode, skip steps a and b.)

b. Press the Columns/Table ((Alt)-(F7)) key [(Alt) Layout Tables Edit] to change to the table editing screen.

c. Move the cursor to the first cell to be joined.

d. Press the Block ((Alt)-(F4)) key to turn on the block feature.

e. Use the cursor keys to move to the last cell to be joined. All the cells to be joined together should be blocked.

f. Type a 7 or j to join the cells, and type y to confirm the cells are to be joined.

g. Press the Exit ((F7)) key to leave the table editing screen.

Cells can be joined horizontally, vertically, or both ways. The following examples, however, will only join cells horizontally because creating table headings is the most common application for joining cells.

EXAMPLES

1. Retrieve the document BASKBALL by pressing the Retrieve ([Shift]-[F10]) key [[Alt] File Retrieve], typing **baskball**, and pressing [Enter]. Press the [↓] key until the cursor is in Cell A1 of the table. Press the Columns/Table ([Alt]-[F7]) key [[Alt] Layout Tables Edit] to turn on the table editing screen.

   Now you will join the cells in the first row. Since the cursor is already located in Cell A1, you are ready to block the row of cells. To do this, press the Block ([Alt]-[F4]) key, and then press the [→] key three times. Type **j** to join the cells and **y** to confirm that the cells are to be joined. Press the Exit ([F7]) key to leave the table editing screen.

   Type the following title:

   Local High School Basketball Standings

   Preview the document by pressing the Print ([Shift]-[F7]) key [[Alt] File Print] and typing v for view. Press the Exit ([F7]) key to return to the document. Save the document and clear the screen by pressing the Exit ([F7]) key [[Alt] File Exit], typing **y**, [Enter], **y**, and [Enter].

2. Retrieve the document EMPLOYEE.TBL by pressing the Retrieve ([Shift]-[F10]) key [[Alt] File Retrieve], typing **employee.tbl**, and pressing [Enter]. Press the [↓] key three times to move to Cell A1 of the table. Press the Columns/Table ([Alt]-[F7]) key [[Alt] Layout Tables Edit] to turn on the table editing screen.

   Now you will join the cells in the first row. Since the cursor is already located in Cell A1, you are ready to block the row of cells. To do this, press the Block ([Alt]-[F4]) key, then press the [→] key twice.

Type **j** to join the cells and y to confirm that the cells are to be joined. Press the Exit (F7) key to leave the table editing screen.

Type the following title:

SECTION 5: Background Information

Print the document by pressing the Print (Shift-F7) key [Alt File Print] and typing **f** for Full Document. Save the document and clear the screen by pressing the Exit (F7) key [Alt File Exit], typing **y**, Enter, **y**, and Enter.

EXERCISES

1. Retrieve the document named ATTACH.C. Join the cells in the top row. Type the following title, pressing the Enter key after the first two lines.

Acme Corporation of North America
MACRS deduction calculation for XYZ Gizmo
April 1, 1990

Preview the document, save it using the same filename and clear the screen.

2. Retrieve the document named BILL.SHT. Join the cells in the top row. Type the following title, pressing Enter after the first line.

Service Bill
Please pay upon receipt.

Save the document, and clear the screen.

CHANGING CELL ATTRIBUTES OR JUSTIFICATION

22.6

The Format function provides a large variety of formatting features within the Table feature. With this function you can specify the type style, justification, vertical alignment, underlining, bolding, and other attributes. These attributes can pertain to individual cells, columns, rows, or the entire table.

Once formatting selections have been made, any text that is entered within a cell conforms to the selected formats. These attributes can be set before or after text has been added to a table. The text will always conform to the selected formatting.

In section 22.3 of this chapter, you used the Column Format Width feature to change the width of a column. This section discusses the use of the Format function pertaining to cells.

To change a cell's appearance attribute:

a. Move the cursor to a location inside the table. (If you are already in table editing mode, skip steps a and b.)

b. Press the Columns/Table ([Alt]-[F7]) key [[Alt] Layout Tables Edit] to change to the table editing screen.

c. Move the cursor to the cell where you want to change the attribute.

d. Type a **2** or **f** to select the Format function.

e. Type a **1** or **c** to select the Cell feature.

f. Type a **2** or **a** to select the Attributes category.

g. Type a **2** or **a** to select the Appearance attribute, or type a **1** or **s** to select the Size attribute.

h. Type the corresponding number or letter of the attribute you wish to select.

i. Press the Exit ([F7]) key to exit the table editing screen.

To change a cell's justification:

a. Move the cursor to a location inside the table. (If you are already in table editing mode, skip steps a and b.)

b. Press the Columns/Table ([Alt]-[F7]) key [[Alt] Layout Tables Edit] to change to the table editing screen.

c. Move the cursor to the cell where you want to change the justification.

d. Type a **2** or **f** to select the Format function.

e. Type a **1** or **c** to select the Cell feature.

f. Type a **3** or **j** to select the Justification category.

g. Type the corresponding number or letter of the justification type you wish to select.

h. Press the Exit ([F7]) key to exit the table editing screen.

Whenever a block of cells is to have the same formatting, you can save yourself some work. Modify step c in either of the above sets of instructions by placing the cursor on the first cell to be formatted, pressing the Block ([Alt]-[F4]) key, and using the arrow keys to block the cells to be formatted. Then, continue with the rest of the instructions as written.

EXAMPLES

1. Retrieve the document GAMES by pressing the Retrieve ([Shift]-[F10]) key [[Alt] File Retrieve], typing **games**, and pressing [Enter]. Press the [↓] key once to move to Cell A1 of the first table. Press the Columns/ Table ([Alt]-[F7]) key [[Alt] Layout Tables Edit] to turn on the table editing screen.

   You are going to center the three column headings of this table. Press the [→] key once to move to Cell B1. Press the Block ([Alt]-[F4]) key, then press the [→] key twice. The three cells used for headings are now blocked.

   Type **f** for Format, **c** for Cell, **j** for Justification and **c** for Center. The text within each of the cells is immediately centered.

   You will now right justify the row headers. Move the cursor to Cell A2 by pressing the [↓] key, then the [←] key three times. Press the Block ([Alt]-[F4]) key, and then the [↓] key three times. The four cells used for row headings are now blocked.

   Type **f** for Format, **c** for Cell, **j** for Justification, and **r** for Right Justification. Notice that the text within the cells is immediately right justified.

You will now change the body of the table to decimal alignment. Press the ⮕ key once to move to Cell B5. Press the Block (Alt - F4) key. Press the ⮕ key twice and the ⬆ key three times. Altogether, twelve cells should be highlighted.

Type **f** for Format, **c** for Cell, **j** for Justification, and **d** for Decimal Alignment. Notice that the numbers within the cells are immediately moved to the right. See Figure 22-5 for a picture of how your document should currently look.

Next, you will change the three column headings to bolded text. Move the cursor to Cell D1 by

	Brian	Ron	John
Game 1	231	175	140
Game 2	132	201	151
Game 3	194	195	170
Total			

The above table lists the scores from last week's series of games for the Boomers. The following table lists this week's scores, showing the improvement both players made in one week.

	Brian	Ron	John
Game 1	230	196	153

Table Edit: Press Exit when done Align Cell D5 Doc 1 Pg 1 Ln 2.26" Pos 5.84"

Ctrl-Arrows Column Widths; Ins Insert; Del Delete; Move Move/Copy;
1 Size; 2 Format; 3 Lines; 4 Header; 5 Math; 6 Options; 7 Join; 8 Split: 0

FIGURE 22-5.   Realigned table entries

pressing the ⬆ key. Press the Block (Alt - F4) key. Press the ⬅ key twice. The three headings should now be blocked.

Type **f** for Format, **c** for Cell, **a** for Attribute, **a** for Appearance, and **b** for Bold.

Bold the "Total" header by pressing the ⬅, and then the ⬇ four times. Type **f** for Format, **c** for Cell, **a** for Attribute, **a** for Appearance, and **b** for Bold.

Exit the table editing screen by pressing the Exit (F7) key. Move the cursor to the cell with John's name in it. Delete "John" by pressing the Delete Word (Ctrl - Backspace) key. Type the name **Jack**. Notice that "Jack" is bolded and centered as you type in the text.

Use this document in the next example.

2. Move the cursor to Cell A1 of the second table. Turn on the table editing screen by pressing the Columns/Table (Alt - F7) key [Alt Layout Tables Edit].

Starting with the second paragraph of example 1, follow the directions to change the attributes in this table so that they are identical to the first.

Once you have finished changing the attributes of the second table, print the document by pressing the Print (Shift - F7) key [Alt File Print] and typing **f** for Full Document. Save the document and clear the screen by pressing the Exit (F7) key [Alt File Exit], typing y, Enter, y, and Enter.

3. Retrieve the document BASKBALL by pressing the Retrieve (Shift - F10) key [Alt File Retrieve], typing **baskball**, and pressing Enter. Press the ⬇ key until

the cursor moves to Cell A1 of the table. Press the Columns/Table ([Alt]-[F7]) key [[Alt] Layout Tables Edit] to turn on the table editing screen.

You are going to center the column headings. Press the Block ([Alt]-[F4]) key and the [↓] key once. The first two rows of cells should be highlighted.

Type **f** for Format, **c** for Cell, **j** for Justification, and **c** for Center. Notice that the text within the cells is immediately centered.

Bold the top row heading by first pressing the [↑] key. Type **f** for Format, **c** for Cell, **a** for Attribute, **a** for Appearance, and **b** for Bold. Leave the table editing screen by pressing the Exit ([F7]) key.

Preview the document by pressing the Print ([Shift]-[F7]) [[Alt] File Print] key and typing **v** for view. Press the Exit ([F7]) key [[Alt] File Exit] to return to the document. Press the Exit ([F7]) key, type **y**, [Enter], **y**, and [Enter] to save the document and clear the screen.

4. Retrieve the document EMPLOYEE.TBL by pressing the Retrieve ([Shift]-[F10]) key [[Alt] File Retrieve], typing **employee.tbl**, and pressing [Enter]. Press the [↓] key three times to move to Cell A1 of the table. Press the Columns/Table ([Alt]-[F7]) key [[Alt] Layout Tables Edit] to turn on the table editing screen.

Bold the top row heading by typing **f** for Format, **c** for Cell, **a** for Attribute, **a** for Appearance, and **b** for Bold. Leave the table editing screen by pressing the Exit ([F7]) key.

Preview the document by pressing the Print ([Shift]-[F7]) key [[Alt] File Print] and typing **v** for view. Press the Exit ([F7]) key [[Alt] File Exit] to return to the document. Press the Exit ([F7]) key, type y, [Enter], y, and [Enter] to save the document and clear the screen.

5. Retrieve the document OACRS.TBL by pressing the Retrieve ([Shift]-[F10]) key [[Alt] File Retrieve], typing **oacrs.tbl**, and pressing [Enter]. Press the [↓] key three times to move to Cell A1 of the table. Press the Columns/Table ([Alt]-[F7]) key [[Alt] Layout Tables Edit] to turn on the table editing screen.

You will now decimal justify the dollar amounts under the heading for 1988 deductions. Press the [→] key and the [↓] key, moving your cursor to Cell B2. Turn the Block feature on by pressing the Block ([Alt]-[F4]) key, and then the [↓] key three times. Four cells, including Cell B5, will be highlighted.

Decimal align the blocked cells by typing **f** for Format, **c** for Cell, **j** for Justify, and **d** for Decimal Align. The dollar amounts will immediately move to the right and line up by their decimal points.

Press the Exit ([F7]) key to leave the table editing screen. Save the document and clear the screen by pressing the Exit ([F7]) key [[Alt] File Exit], typing y, [Enter], y, and [Enter].

EXERCISES

1. Retrieve the document named SUPPLIES.
For the first table:
Center the three column headings named OR-DER NO., TOTAL, and UNITS.

Bold all four column headings.

Decimal align the numbers within the TOTAL column.

Do the same for the second table.

Change the total number of boxes of letterhead from 3 to 10.

Print the document, save it using the same filename, and clear the screen.

2. Retrieve the document named FACULTY.TBL. Bold the four column headings.

Save the document using the same filename, and clear the screen.

3. Retrieve the document named ATTACH.C. Center and bold the top row. Decimal align the three cells in the right column that are dollar amounts.

Preview the document. Save the document using the same filename, and clear the screen.

4. Retrieve the document named BILL.SHT. Center and bold the top row of the table. Decimal align the three cells B2, B3, and B4.

Type the following text and numbers in rows 2 and 3:

4.3 hours of typing services	55.90
1 diskette	2.50

Preview the document. Save the document using the same filename, and clear the screen.

ADDING COLUMNS OF NUMBERS

22.7

The Table feature has the capability of doing simple arithmetic. The arithmetic that can be performed in Tables is divided into two categories. The first, adding columns of numbers, is similar to the math feature used with tabular columns. (See Chapter 15, "Adding a Column of Numbers," for more information.) The second category, formulas, allows you to do calculations using addition, subtraction, multiplication, and division, based on the contents of other cells.

Once you have incorporated a math feature into a table, you will need to be conscious that the calculations are not done automatically. Whenever a cell's contents that may affect a calculation are changed, you need to tell WordPerfect to recalculate everything in the table.

Another concern when using the math feature in tables is that tables assume all cell entries are numeric. If you have a cell that falls within the range of cells to be added together, but is not part of the calculation, you must format that cell as a text cell. This will prevent the possibility of generating miscalculations.

This section walks you through the creation of simple math functions. If you are already familiar with WordPerfect's Math feature for tabular columns, you have a head start in learning to use math in tables.

To create a subtotal for a column of numbers:

a. Move the cursor to a location inside the table. (If you are already in table editing mode, skip steps a and b.)

b. Press the Columns/Table (⟦Alt⟧-⟦F7⟧) key [⟦Alt⟧ Layout Tables Edit] to change to the table editing screen.

c. Move the cursor to the cell where you want the subtotal.

d. Type a **5** or **m** to select the Math function.

e. Type a **4** or **+** for a subtotal. (Type **5** or **=** for a total, or type **6** or ***** for a grand total.)

f. Press the Exit (⟦F7⟧) key to leave the table editing screen.

To create a formula:

a. Move the cursor to a location inside the table. (If you are already in table editing mode, skip steps a and b.)

b. Press the Columns/Table (⟦Alt⟧-⟦F7⟧) key [⟦Alt⟧ Layout Tables Edit] to change to the table editing screen.

c. Move the cursor to the cell where you want the result of the formula displayed.

d. Type a **5** or **m** to select the Math function.

e. Type a **2** or **f** to select Formula.

f. Type in the formula and press the ⟦Enter⟧ key. The operators that can be included within the formula are + for addition, - for subtraction, * for multiplication and / for division.

g. Press the Exit (⟦F7⟧) key to leave the table editing screen.

To recalculate all arithmetic within a table:

a. Move the cursor to a location inside the table. (If you are already in table editing mode, skip steps a and b.)

b. Press the Columns/Table ([Alt]-[F7]) key [[Alt] Layout Tables Edit] to change to the table editing screen.

c. Type a **5** or **m** to select the Math function.

d. Type a **1** or **c** to calculate.

e. Press the Exit ([F7]) key to leave the table editing screen.

To change a cell into a text cell:

a. Move the cursor to a location inside the table. (If you are already in table editing mode, skip steps a and b.)

b. Press the Columns/Table ([Alt]-[F7]) key [[Alt] Layout Tables Edit] to change to the table editing screen.

c. Move the cursor to the cell that is to be defined as a text cell. (If there is more than one contiguous cell to be defined as text cells, block the cells first.)

d. Type a **2** or **f** to select the Format function.

e. Type a **1** or **c** to select the Cell feature.

f. Type a **1** or **t** to select the type of cell.

g. Type a **2** or **t** to select the cell type as text.

h. Press the Exit ([F7]) key to leave the table editing screen.

EXAMPLES

1. Retrieve the document named OACRS.TBL by pressing the Retrieve ((Shift)-(F10)) key [(Alt) File Retrieve], typing **oacrs.tbl**, and pressing (Enter). Press the (↓) key three times to move to Cell A1 of the table. Press the Columns/Table ((Alt)-(F7)) key [(Alt) Layout Tables Edit] to turn on the table editing screen.

   Press the (↓) key four times and the (→) key once. This places the cursor in the cell where the total deductions are to be calculated. Type an **m** for Math and a **4** to create a subtotal of the numbers within the column.

   Give this cell a double underlining attribute by typing **f** for Format, **c** for Cell, **a** for Attribute, **a** for Appearance, and **d** for Double Underline.

   Notice that the total 16,438.00 is not the total of the three preceding numbers. 16,438.00 is the total of 1988 from the column heading and the three numbers. To avoid the inclusion of the heading as part of the calculation, you need to define the column heading as a text column.

   Press the (↑) key four times to move the cursor to Cell B2. Type an **f** for Format, **c** for Cell, **t** for Cell Type, and **t** for Text Cell. The result of the calculation remains 16,438. This is because WordPerfect does not automatically produce recalculations. To recalculate, type **m** for Math and **c** to calculate. The total now displays as 14,450.00, which is correct. Press the Exit ((F7)) key to leave Table Edit.

   Print the document by pressing the Print ((Shift)-(F7)) key [(Alt) File Print] and typing **f** for Full

Document. Save the document and clear the screen by pressing the Exit ([F7]) key [[Alt] File Exit], typing **y**, [Enter], **y**, and [Enter].

2. Retrieve the document GAMES by pressing the Retrieve ([Shift]-[F10]) key [[Alt] File **R**etrieve], typing **games**, and pressing [Enter]. Press the [↓] key to move to Cell A1 of the first table. Press the Columns/Table ([Alt]-[F7]) key [[Alt] Layout Tables Edit] to turn on the table editing screen.

   You will add a row to the bottom of the table to compute an average score. To do this, type **s** for Table Size, **r** for Row, **6** for the number of rows in the table, and press [Enter].

   Press the [↑] key and the [→] key once each. To create a subtotal for Brian, type **m** for Math and **4** to create a subtotal. Press the [→] key to move to Ron's column. Type **m** for Math and **4** for a subtotal. Press the [→] key to move to Jack's column. Type **m** for math and **4** for a subtotal.

   Press the [↓] key once. This cell is where the average score for Jack is to appear. Type **m** for Math and **f** for Formula. Type **D5/3** and press [Enter]. This creates a formula that takes the current value located in Cell D5 (Jack's total) and divides it by 3, producing the average.

   Press the [←] key once to move to Ron's column. Type **m** for math and **f** for formula. Type **C5/3** and press [Enter]. Press the [←] key once more to move to Brian's column. Type **m** for Math and **f** for Formula. Type **B5/3** and press [Enter].

   Press the Exit ([F7]) key to leave the table editing screen. Move to Cell A6. Type the word **average**.

Preview the document by pressing the Print ([Shift]-[F7]) key [[Alt] File Print] and typing **v** for View. Return to the document screen by pressing the Exit ([F7]) key.

Move to Brian's third game score by pressing the [↑] key twice and the [Tab] key once. Press the [Del] key to delete the 1 in 194 and type 2 to make the score 294.

Because the numbers have changed, the total and average for Brian are no longer accurate. To recalculate, press the Columns/Table ([Alt]-[F7]) key [[Alt] Layout Tables Edit] to return to the table editing screen. Type **m** for Math and **c** to calculate. The total and average change to reflect the changes made in Brian's score. Press the Exit ([F7]) key to leave the table editing screen.

Print the document by pressing the Print ([Shift]-[F7]) key [[Alt] File Print] and typing **f** for Full Document. Save the document and clear the screen by pressing the Exit ([F7]) key [[Alt] File Exit], typing y, [Enter], y, and [Enter].

EXERCISES

1. Retrieve the document named ATTACH.C. Create a subtotal at the bottom of column B of the table. Define the table header cell as a text cell. Recalculate the subtotal.

   Print the document, and save it using the same file name. Clear the screen.

2. Retrieve the document named BILL.SHT. Add two rows to the bottom of the table.

Make Cell B4 a subtotal of the two previous cells.

Make Cell B5 a sales tax calculation cell by creating a formula that multiplies the contents of Cell B4 by the sales tax rate of .07.

Make Cell B6 a total cell by creating a formula that adds the contents of B4 and B5.

Exit the table editing screen. Type in Cell A6 the phrase:

Sales Tax:

Type in Cell A5 the phrase:

Total Amount Due:

Print the document. Save the document using the same file name and clear the screen.

EXERCISES

1. Create a table with two columns and eight rows.

2. Join the two cells of the first row to form one cell. Define this cell for centering and for text type.

3. Define cells A2 and B2 for centering. Define B2 also for text type.

4. Cells B3 through B8 are decimal aligned.

5. Create a math formula in B8 that adds B6 + B7 and double underline the answer.

6. Create a math formula in B7 that multiplies B6 by .07 and underline the answer.

7. Create a math formula in B6 that is the sum of B3, B4, and B5. Exit table editing.

8. Enter the following information in the table:

JOE'S HARDWARE

Item	Amount
Nails	9.00
Hammer	5.00
Screwdriver	7.00
Subtotal	21.00
Tax @ 7%	1.47
Total	22.47

9. Preview the document, then exit, and clear the screen.

INTEGRATING SKILLS CHECK

1. Create a table with three columns and six rows.

2. In the first row, join all three cells. Center the cell, and define it as text type.

3. In row two, center all three cells, and define cells B2 and C2 as text type.

4. Right-align Cells B3 through B6 and C3 through C6.

5. Cell C6 is the sum of C3, C4, and C5.

6. Cell B6 is the sum of B3, B4, and B5.

7. Cells B5 and C5 are underlined. Exit table editing.

8. Enter the following information in the table.

SALES BY DEPARTMENT

DEPT	JAN	FEB
Clothing	25,000.00	20,000.00
Shoe	15,000.00	12,000.00
Housewares	40,000.00	42,000.00
Total		

Calculate the totals. They should be 80,000.00 and 74,000.00.

9. Add a column at the right edge of the table. Insert the following figures:

MAR
23,000.00
14,000.00
37,000.00

Recalculate the totals. The March total should be 74,000.00.

Appendixes

▶Part IV◀

Installing WordPerfect 5.1 and Selecting a Printer

(These instructions describe the installation of Word-Perfect 5.1. If you need to install WordPerfect 5.0, refer to your WordPerfect 5.0 manual.)

If you do not have WordPerfect installed on your machine, you will need to install the program before you can use it. The process is not difficult and can be completed in a short time if you follow the instructions provided. Part of the installation process involves selecting one or more printers to use with WordPerfect. If your system is already installed, you will need to update the WordPerfect system files to incorporate any new printer you might add to your system. The instructions you should use depend upon the computer system you have. This appendix has the installation steps for two different types of computer systems, instructions for updating your WordPerfect system files, and instructions for adding a printer.

Installing WordPerfect on a hard disk system: Use these instructions if you wish to install WordPerfect on a hard disk.

Installing WordPerfect on a floppy disk system: Use these instructions if you do not have a hard disk and will be running WordPerfect off of floppy disks.

Updating WordPerfect's system files: Use these instructions if you need to install updated WordPerfect system files after WordPerfect has been installed.

Adding printer files: Use these instructions if you need to install a new printer file after WordPerfect has been installed.

The instructions will refer to disk drives by letter names. If your machine has one disk drive, it is drive A. If the computer has two disk drives, the one on the top or the left is drive A, and the one on the bottom or the right is drive B. Drive C is the normal default for a hard disk, although some computers may have hard disks that use other labels.

The instructions are written for 5 1/4-inch disks. If you have a system with 3 1/2-inch disks, these instructions will still work, but you will not need to change disks so frequently. Since the 3 1/2-inch disks have more than double the capacity of 5 1/4-inch disks, one 3 1/2-inch disk will take the place of two 5 1/4-inch disks.

Installing WordPerfect on a hard disk, if available, is strongly recommended. To install WordPerfect on diskettes requires two floppy drives, both with a capacity of 720K or greater. (Check with your computer's manual or your service representative to determine the capacity of your disk drives, if you do not already know.)

Unlike WordPerfect 5.0, you *must* use the installation program to install WordPerfect 5.1. The program files have been compressed on the installation disks and must be expanded using the installation program.

INSTALLING WORDPERFECT ON A HARD DISK SYSTEM   A.1

1. Turn on your computer. The computer loads DOS from the hard disk into your computer's memory.

2. Type the date and the time if the computer prompts you for them, pressing (Enter) after each entry.

3. Insert the WordPerfect installation disk labeled Install/Learn/Utilities 1 disk into drive A.

4. Type **a:install** and press (Enter). WordPerfect displays a screen welcoming you to the WordPerfect 5.1 installation program. You are prompted to type

a **y** or press (Enter) to continue or to type an **n** to abort the installation program. Type a **y**.

5. WordPerfect asks you if you are installing to a hard disk system. Type a **y**.

6. The main WordPerfect 5.1 installation program menu appears. See Figure A-1. Because you are doing a basic system installation of WordPerfect, type a **b** for Basic Installation.

From now until system installation is complete, follow the directions on the screen for inserting disks. You should answer yes to each question regarding installation of particular files. Steps 7 through 23 summarize the steps you will take to install Word-Perfect.

7. Type a **y** and press (Enter) to install the Utility files.

8. Type a **y** to answer yes to the install Learning files prompt. When prompted, replace the installation disk Install/Learn/Utilities 1 disk in drive A with the Install/Learn/Utilities 2 disk and press (Enter) once.

9. Type a **y** to answer yes to the install Help files prompt.

10. Type a **y** to answer yes to the install Keyboard files prompt.

11. Type a **y** to answer yes to the install Style Library files prompt.

```
Installation

    1 - Basic        Perform a standard installation to D:\WP51.

    2 - Custom       Perform a customized installation.  (User selected
                     directories.)

    3 - Network      Perform a customized installation onto a network.
                     (To be performed by the network supervisor.)

    4 - Printer      Install updated Printer (.ALL) File.

    5 - Update       Install WordPerfect 5.1 Interim Release program file(s).
                     (Used for updating existing WordPerfect 5.1 software.)

    6 - Copy Disks   Install every file from an installation diskette to a
                     specified location.  (Useful for installing all the
                     Printer (.ALL) Files.)




Selection: 1
```

FIGURE A-1.   Installation menu

12. Type a **y** to answer yes to the install WordPerfect Program files prompt.

13. Insert the Program 1 installation disk into drive A and press [Enter]. When prompted, insert the Program 2 installation disk into drive A and press [Enter].

14. Type a **y** to answer yes to the install Speller files prompt. Insert the Spell/Thesaurus 1 installation disk into drive A when prompted and press [Enter].

15. Type a **y** to answer yes to the install Graphic Images files prompt.

16. WordPerfect checks your system's CONFIG.SYS file. One of four situations will occur.

   a. If your disk does not have a CONFIG.SYS file, WordPerfect prompts you to create it. Type a **y** and press (Enter) twice.

   b. If your disk contains a CONFIG.SYS file, but the file does not contain the line "FILES = 20" (or greater), WordPerfect prompts you to add the line. Type a **y** and press (Enter).

   c. If your CONFIG.SYS file allows for fewer than 20 files, WordPerfect prompts you to change it. Type a **y** and press (Enter).

   d. If your disk contains a CONFIG.SYS file and it does contain the line "FILES = 20" (or greater), WordPerfect confirms this. Press (Enter).

17. WordPerfect then checks your system's AUTO-EXEC.BAT file. One of two situations are likely to occur.

   a. If your system disk does not contain an AUTO-EXEC.BAT file, WordPerfect prompts you to create it. Type a **y** or press (Enter).

   b. If the AUTOEXEC.BAT file exists, but C:\WP51 is not part of the path command, WordPerfect prompts you to add it. Press (Enter).

18. Open the door for drive A then press the (Ctrl), (Alt), and (Del) keys simultaneously to reboot the system with the newly revised system files. (If the

system files on your system were configured correctly, WordPerfect skips this and the next step, and you therefore should go directly to step 20.)

19. Insert the installation disk called Install/Learn/ Utilities 1 into drive A. At the C> prompt, type **a:install** and press (Enter). Press (Enter) to continue with the WordPerfect installation. WordPerfect takes you to where you left off in the installation program.

20. Insert the installation Printer 1 disk into drive A and press (Enter). Scroll through the list of printers using the (PgUp) and (PgDn) keys to locate the name of your printer. Once located on the screen, press the corresponding number and then press (Enter) twice. You may be prompted to insert a different installation Printer disk and press (Enter).

21. You are asked if you want to install another printer. If yes, type a **y** and repeat step 20. If not, type an **n**.

22. WordPerfect asks you to type in your registration number. This is a good idea because it will be conveniently stored for you within WordPerfect. Your registration number can be found on a card that comes with your WordPerfect user's manual and usually starts with the letters "WP." Type in the number and press (Enter).

23. The screen then displays information about the printers you selected. Press the (F7) key (a function key) to leave the printer information screen(s) when you see the prompt to press any key to exit.

The basic installation of WordPerfect is now complete, but you still must finish defining your printer(s). To do this, you must go into the WordPerfect program.

24. Type **cd c:\wp51** to change to the newly defined WordPerfect directory. Type **wp** and press [Enter].

25. As Chapter 1 explains, the WordPerfect screen appears. Hold down the [Shift] key and press the key labeled [F7]. This is a function key. Type an **s** to select a printer.

26. Use the [↑] and [↓] keys to highlight a printer name. Type a **e** to edit the printer definition.

27. If your printer is not connected to the first parallel port, which is usually labeled LPT1:, type a **p**, and select the appropriate number for the port the printer is connected to. If you select a serial port, WordPerfect displays settings it will use to send information to the printer. If you are unsure of the correct setting to use, check your printer manual to determine the proper baud rate, parity, stop bits, character length, and XON/XOFF protocol. If any of the information displayed is incorrect, type the letter or number next to the option with the incorrect setting, and type the letter or number for the correct setting. When the settings are correct, press the [F7] key.

28. If other printers need to be defined, repeat steps 26 and 27.

29. Press the F7 key three times, type an **n** and a **y**. You are now back in DOS and ready to start learning WordPerfect. Store the original Word-Perfect disks in a safe place.

INSTALLING WORDPERFECT ON A FLOPPY DISK SYSTEM

A.2

You will need 10 formatted, blank disks to install WordPerfect. To format disks, with the DOS disk in drive A and a blank disk in drive B, type **format b:** and press Enter. These disks must have a capacity of 720K or greater.

1. Insert your DOS disk (sometimes called a system startup disk) in drive A. Turn on your computer.

2. Type the date and the time if the computer prompts you for them, pressing Enter after each entry.

3. Remove the DOS or startup disk from drive A, and replace it with the Install/Learn/Utilities 1 disk.

4. Type **install** and press Enter. WordPerfect displays a screen welcoming you to the WordPerfect 5.1 installation program. You are prompted to type a **y** or press Enter to continue or to type an **n** to abort the installation program. Type a **y**.

5. WordPerfect asks you if you are installing to a hard disk system. Type an **n**.

6. You are informed that you need 10 formatted, blank disks labeled as follows: WordPerfect 1, WordPerfect 2, Install/Utilities, Learning/Images, Macros/Keyboards, Speller, Thesaurus, PTR Program, Fonts/Graphics, Printer (.ALL) Files.

   Once you have 10 formatted, labeled disks, press [Enter]. If you do not have the disks, type an **n** and you will exit the installation program and return to the computer system's DOS prompt.

7. The main WordPerfect 5.1 installation program menu appears. See Figure A-1. Because you are doing a basic system installation of WordPerfect, type a **b** for Basic Installation.

From now until system installation is complete, follow the directions on the screen for inserting disks. You should answer yes to each question regarding installation of particular files. Steps 8 through 26 summarize the steps you will take to install Word-Perfect.

8. Insert the disk you labeled Install/Utilities into drive B and press [Enter] three times. WordPerfect copies files to the Install/Utilities Disk.

9. Insert the disk you labeled Learning/Images into drive B and press [Enter] twice. When prompted, replace the installation disk Install/Learn/Utilities 1 disk in drive A with the Install/Learn/Utilities 2 disk and press [Enter] once.

10. Insert the disk you labeled WordPerfect 1 into drive B and press [Enter] twice.

11. Insert the disk you labeled Macros/Keyboards into drive B and press (Enter) twice. When prompted for the styles files, press (Enter) twice.

12. Insert the disk you labeled WordPerfect 1 into drive B (this is the second time) and press (Enter) twice. Insert the installation disk called Program 1 into drive A. Press (Enter) once.

13. When prompted, insert the disk you labeled WordPerfect 2 into drive B and press (Enter).

14. Insert the disk you labeled Speller into drive B and press (Enter) twice. Insert the installation disk labeled Spell/Thesaurus 1 into drive A and press (Enter).

15. Insert the disk you labeled Thesaurus into drive B and press (Enter) twice. When prompted, insert the installation disk labeled Spell/Thesaurus 2 into drive A and press (Enter).

16. Insert the disk you labeled PTR Program into drive B. Press (Enter) twice. Insert the installation disk labeled PTR Program/Graphs 1 into drive A and press (Enter).

17. Insert the disk you labeled Fonts/Graphics into drive B and press (Enter) twice. When prompted, insert the installation disk labeled PTR Program/Graphs 2 into drive A and press (Enter).

18. Insert the disk you labeled Learning/Images into drive B and press (Enter) twice.

19. Insert your DOS disk (or system startup disk) in drive A and press Enter. One of three situations will occur.

    a. If your DOS disk does not have a CONFIG.SYS file, WordPerfect prompts you to create it. Type a **y** and then press Enter twice.

    b. If your DOS disk contains a CONFIG.SYS file, but the file does not contain the line "FILES=20" (or greater), WordPerfect prompts you to add the line. Type a **y** and press Enter.

    c. If your DOS disk contains a CONFIG.SYS file and it does contain the line "FILES=20" (or greater), WordPerfect confirms this. Press Enter.

20. WordPerfect then checks the AUTOEXEC.BAT file on your DOS disk (system startup disk). One of two situations are likely to occur.

    a. If your DOS disk does not contain an AUTOEXEC.BAT file, WordPerfect prompts you to create it. Press Enter.

    b. If the AUTOEXEC.BAT file exists, but A:\ is not part of the path command, WordPerfect prompts you to add it. Press Enter.

21. Insert the diskette labeled Install/Utilities into drive B and press Enter.

22. Insert the DOS system startup disk into drive A. Press the Ctrl, Alt, and Del keys simultaneously to reboot the system with the newly revised system files. (If the system files on your system were

configured correctly, WordPerfect will skip this
and the next step and you therefore should proceed directly to step 24.)

23. Insert the Install/Learn/Utilities 1 installation disk
    into drive A. At the A> prompt, type **install** and
    press (Enter). Press (Enter) to continue with the Word-
    Perfect installation. WordPerfect takes you to
    where you left off in the installation program.

24. Insert the installation Printer 1 disk into drive A
    and press (Enter). Scroll through the list of printers
    using the (PgUp) and (PgDn) keys to locate the name
    of your printer. Once located on the screen, press
    the corresponding number and then press (Enter)
    three times. Insert the disk you labeled Printer
    (.ALL) Files into drive B and press (Enter). You may
    be prompted to insert a different installation
    Printer disk into drive A and then press (Enter).

25. You are asked if you want to install another
    printer. If yes, type a **y** and repeat step 24. If not,
    type an **n**.

26. Insert the disk you labeled Install/Utilities into
    drive B and press (Enter). Insert the disk you labeled
    WordPerfect 2 into drive B and press (Enter). Insert
    the disk you labeled Printer (.ALL) Files into drive
    B and press (Enter).

The basic installation of WordPerfect is now complete, but you still must finish defining your printer(s).
To do this, you must go into the WordPerfect program.

27. Insert your new WordPerfect 1 disk into drive A, type **wp**, and press (Enter). When prompted, insert the new WordPerfect 2 disk into drive A and press (Enter).

28. WordPerfect asks you to type in your registration number. This is a good idea because it will be conveniently stored for you within WordPerfect. Your registration number can be found on a card that comes with your WordPerfect users manual and usually starts with the letters "WP." Type in the number and press (Enter).

29. As Chapter 1 explains, the WordPerfect screen appears. Hold down the (Shift) key and press the key labeled (F7). This is a function key. Type an **s** to select a printer.

30. Type an **a** and an **o**. WordPerfect prompts you for the location of the printer files.

31. Insert the Printer (.ALL) Files disk into drive B. Type **B:** and press (Enter).

32. A list of the available printers appears. Use the (↑) and (↓) keys to highlight your printer. Press (Enter) twice. The printer information is generated and copied to the WordPerfect 2 disk.

33. Press the (F7) key. If your printer is not connected to the first parallel port, which is usually labeled LPT1:, type a **p**, and select the appropriate number for the port the printer is connected to. If you

select a serial port, WordPerfect displays settings it will use to send information to the printer. Check your printer manual to determine the proper baud rate, parity, stop bits, character length, and XON/XOFF protocol. If any of the information displayed is incorrect, type the letter or number next to the option with the incorrect setting, and type the letter or number for the correct setting. When the settings are correct, press the [F7] key.

34. If other printers need to be defined, type an **s** to select a printer and repeat steps 30 through 33.

35. Press the [F7] key three times, type an **n** and a **y**. You are now back in DOS and ready to start learning WordPerfect. Store the original Word-Perfect disks in a safe place.

UPDATING WORDPERFECT'S SYSTEM FILES

A.3

You may need to update the system files after Word-Perfect has been installed. This happens occasionally when WordPerfect comes out with a new release of the same program. The new release may fix problems with the original program or it may enhance the program. To take advantage of the new release, you need to use WordPerfect's installation program to update your system files.

1. Follow steps 1 through 4 of the procedures discussed earlier in this appendix for installing Word-Perfect on your type of system. If you have

WordPerfect installed on your hard drive, use the section called "Installing WordPerfect on a Hard Disk System." If you have WordPerfect installed on floppy disks, use the section called "Installing WordPerfect on a Floppy Disk System." Both methods take you to the main WordPerfect 5.1 installation program menu. See Figure A-1.

2. Type a **u** to indicate you are updating the system files. Insert the updated files disk into drive A. Press Enter to accept the prompt that you are installing the files from the A drive. Press Enter again to accept the location of the system files.

3. You are now in the update installation menu. See Figure A-2 . Using the ↑ and ↓ keys, point to the type of files you are updating and press Enter . (If you are updating more than one of these, select the type of files listed first. Later you will select a type of files that comes next on the screen, and so on.)

4. Type a **y** to answer yes to the install files prompt. You may be prompted to insert one or more installation disks into drive A. Do so and press Enter . If you are a floppy disk system user, you are also prompted to insert one of your system disks into drive B. Do so and press Enter .

5. When finished installing the files, you are returned to the update installation menu.

6. Repeat steps 3 through 5 for any other system files that need to be updated. When finished, press F7 to exit. You are returned to the DOS prompt.

```
Install: Update
 ↳ 1 - Program              Contains the WordPerfect Program,

   2 - Install/Learn/Utilities Contains the Utility Files, Learning Files,
                               Help File, Keyboard Files, and Style Library,

   3 - Spell/Thesaurus       Contains the Speller and Thesaurus,

   4 - PTR Program/Graphics  Contains the PTR Program, Graphic Drivers, and
                             Graphic Images,

   5 - Printer               Contains Printer (,ALL) Files,

   6 - Other

   7 - Exit


Selection: 1
```

| FIGURE A-2. | Update installation menu |

ADDING PRINTER FILES

A.4

If you add a new printer to your system, you will want to check to see if the printer driver is already available on your system. Load WordPerfect onto your computer. If you do not know how to do this, see Chapter 1.

1. While in the document screen, hold down the Shift key and press the F7 key. Type an **s** to get to the Select Printer screen.

2. If you are a hard disk system user, type an **a** to get a listing of the additional printers currently available.

   If you are a floppy disk system user, type an **a** and **o**. WordPerfect prompts you for the location of the printer files. Insert the Printer (.ALL) File disk into drive B. Type **b:** and press (Enter).

3. A list of the available printers appears. Use the (↑) and (↓) keys to scroll through the list of printers. If you find your printer, highlight it and press (Enter) three times. If your printer is not included in the list, skip to step 6.

4. The printer information is generated and added to your WordPerfect system disk. Press the (F7) key.

   If your printer is not connected to the first parallel port, which is usually labeled LPT1:, type a **p**, and select the appropriate number for the port the printer is connected to. If you select a serial port, WordPerfect displays settings it will use to send information to the printer. Check your printer manual to determine the proper baud rate, parity, stop bits, character length, and XON/XOFF protocol. If any of the information displayed is incorrect, type the letter or number next to the option with the incorrect setting, and type the letter or number for the correct setting. When the settings are correct, press the (F7) key.

5. When you are finished, press the (F7) key three times, type an **n** and a **y** to return to the DOS

prompt. You are now finished adding the new printer to WordPerfect.

6. If your printer is not included in the list of installed printer drivers, you will need to use the installation program. Press the F7 key four times, type an **n** and a **y** to exit to DOS.

7. Insert the WordPerfect installation disk labeled Install/Learn/Utilities 1 into drive A. Type **a:install** and press Enter.

8. Type a **y** to affirm that you want to continue into the installation program. You end up in the main WordPerfect 5.1 installation program menu. See Figure A-1.

9. Type a **p** to indicate you are installing printer files.

10. If you are a hard disk system user, follow steps 20, 21, and steps 23 through 29 of the instructions in "Installing WordPerfect on a Hard Disk System" earlier in this appendix.

    If you are a floppy disk system user, follow steps 24 through 27, and 29 through 35 of the instructions in "Installing WordPerfect on a Floppy Disk System" earlier in this appendix.

CUSTOMIZING WORDPERFECT 5.1 FOR MENU AND MOUSE FEATURES   A.5

After installing WordPerfect 5.1 and starting the program, you will want to make some changes to the setup if you will be using a mouse or the pull-down menus. Follow these steps to start WordPerfect and alter the setup of the program:

1. After exiting Install, type **wp** and press (Enter).

2. Press (Shift)-(F1) (Setup) to activate the Setup menu.

3. Type a **d** to select Display.

4. Type an **m** to select Menu Options.

5. Type an **a** to select Alt Key Selects Pull-Down Menu.

6. Type a **y** for Yes.

Without this change you will need to press (Alt)-(−) to activate the menu, rather than just the (Alt) key as indicated throughout the examples in this book.

7. Type a **v** to select Menu Bar Remains Visible.

8. Type an **n** to ensure that the menu bar does not remain visible after it is activated.

9. Press (F7) (Exit) to exit from the Setup menu.

10. Press (Shift)-(F1) (Setup).

11. Type an **m** to select Mouse.

12. Type a **t** to select Type.

WordPerfect provides a list of common mouse types, with representations for PS/2, serial, and bus mouse devices.

13. Highlight your mouse type in the list provided, then type an **s** to select the mouse type.

If the mouse type you have is not visible in the list, you can type an **a** to select Auto-Select. Choosing Auto-Select has the same effect as selecting MOUSE .COM.

Hyphenation

▶ B ◀

Hyphens are used for several purposes when creating word-processed documents. They are used to separate parts of a compound word and can also be used to split long lines. The splitting of words at the end of lines is referred to as hyphenation. Hyphenation splits a word at a syllable break. The first part of a hyphenated word appears at the end of a line, followed by a hyphen (-); the remaining letters appear at the beginning of the next line.

With WordPerfect, you can create documents with or without hyphenation. In documents in which the Hyphenation feature is off, lines always end between words. When you enable Hyphenation, words that occur at the end of lines may be hyphenated. Hyphenation placement is dependent on the version of WordPerfect you are using and the choice(s) regarding hyphenation you have made within WordPerfect. Depending upon the choice you make, you can let WordPerfect hyphenate words for you, you can have WordPerfect prompt you to determine hyphen placement, or you can have WordPerfect prompt you for hyphen placement only when it is unable to determine placement automatically.

Hyphenation can help give your documents a professional appearance. You can add hyphens to your documents yourself for a variety of purposes, or you can have WordPerfect add them for you. When WordPerfect 5.1 hyphenates for you, it uses a hyphenation dictionary to determine hyphen placement. When WordPerfect 5.0 hyphenates for you, it uses a set of rules in an attempt to determine appropriate breaks in a word. Both versions of WordPerfect use a hyphenation zone setting to determine when they should hyphenate a word.

Hyphenation may differ when you use WordPerfect on different systems, depending on the printer that you have selected for each system and the base font that you have selected for each document. Since WordPerfect attempts to display your document on screen as it will appear when printed, the selected printer and fonts will determine the number of characters that will fit on each line of the screen. The examples in this appendix were produced with a Hewlett-Packard LaserJet Series II printer attached to an IBM PS/2 Model 60. The examples use the default font for the LaserJet Series II.

Although hyphenation capabilities exist regardless of the printer type, you may be unable to duplicate the results of the examples in this appendix without identical equipment, as more or fewer characters may fit on each line of your screen and the word breaks may not occur at the same places. However, you can follow the examples to learn the procedure you will use when hyphenating your own text.

In addition to describing the types of hyphens inserted by WordPerfect during hyphenation, this appendix covers the use of hard hyphens and hyphen characters, which you can insert yourself. It also includes instructions for turning Hyphenation on and off and affecting the size of the zone used to decide whether hyphenation is appropriate for an individual word.

HYPHEN CHARACTERS AND HARD HYPHENS

B.1

There will likely be times when you will need to use hyphens in your typing. Since there are several ways to create a hyphen, you will need to know the options. The use of the wrong type of hyphen can cause undesired changes in an edited document.

You can use hyphen characters in compound words. To distinguish hyphens used in compound words from other types of hyphens, WordPerfect requires a special method to create the hyphen character. This instructs WordPerfect to treat the two parts of the word as one. Like other characters, the hyphen character does not have a hidden code associated with it.

To enter a hyphen character:

a. Press the [Home] key.

b. Press the hyphen (-) key.

Compound words use hyphen characters. Using a hyphen character in these words tells WordPerfect that they should be kept together. First, type

The company is changing its write

Then, press the [Home] key, and type a hyphen. Finally, type

off method for receivables.

When you press the Reveal Codes ([Alt]-[F3]) key [[Alt] Edit Reveal Codes], the sentence looks like this:

```
The company is changing its write-off method for receivables.█
```

You can also use a hyphen to break a long word that extends past the right margin. This type of hyphen is called a *hard hyphen*. A hard hyphen has a hidden code: [-]. To create a hard hyphen, simply press the hyphen key. First, clear the screen and type the following line of text.

Companies must report gains and losses from prematurely extin

Since you want this word to continue on the next line, type a hyphen. Then, type the remainder of the sentence:

guishing its debt as an extraordinary gain or loss.

The screen looks like this:

```
Companies must report gains and losses from prematurely extin-
guishing its debt as an extraordinary gain or loss.
```

The hyphen you typed is part of the document, much like the characters in the words. When you edit the sentence, the hyphen stays between the "n" and the "g" in "extinguish." First, move the cursor to the word "must" by pressing the ⬆ key to move to the first line of the sentence, pressing the [Home] key and the ⬅ key to move to the beginning of the line, and pressing the [Ctrl]-➡ key combination to move to the "m" in "must." Next, press the [Ctrl]-[Backspace] key combination to remove the word. After you press the ⬇ key to reformat the paragraph, the screen will look like this:

```
Companies report gains and losses from prematurely extin-guishing
its debt as an extraordinary gain or loss.
```

TURNING HYPHENATION ON AND HYPHENATING A DOCUMENT

B.2

WordPerfect's default setting is for no hyphenation. If you turn Hyphenation on, WordPerfect checks hyphenation as you type each line. If the hidden code for Hyphenation is at the top of your document, or you change the initial setting for Hyphenation to on, WordPerfect checks the entire document for hyphenation when you scroll through. To temporarily disable Hyphenation while you move through large sections of the document or use WordPerfect's features to search for a word or check the document's spelling, you can press the Exit (F7) key in response to the first hyphenation prompt during the operation. Hyphenation resumes when the operation is complete.

During hyphenation, WordPerfect places a soft hyphen in your document. A *soft hyphen* is unlike a hard hyphen or hyphen character in that it disappears if the length of the line changes and the hyphen is no longer needed. Hyphenation operates only on the text following the Hyphenation code. WordPerfect uses the codes [Hyph On] and [Hyph Off] to indicate when Hyphenation is turned on and off. To have hyphenation in effect for the entire document, you need to turn Hyphenation on at the beginning of the document.

B.3 USING HYPHENATION IN WORDPERFECT 5.1

What WordPerfect 5.1 does when you turn Hyphenation on is dependent on how WordPerfect has been configured. There are two options in the Environment Setup menu that pertain to hyphenation. The first option, Hyphenation, tells WordPerfect whether it should use an external hyphenation dictionary to determine hyphen location, or use internal rules for making "educated guesses." The second option, Prompt for Hyphenation, allows you to choose whether and how often WordPerfect should prompt you for hyphenation assistance. Choosing Never means WordPerfect will wrap the word to the next line if it cannot determine hyphen placement. Choosing When Required means WordPerfect will prompt you for hyphen placement when it cannot determine placement on its own or it identifies more than one appropriate hyphen location. Choosing Always means WordPerfect will prompt you with every word it feels should be hyphenated. WordPerfect's default settings for the Hyphenation and Prompt for Hyphenation options are to use the external dictionary and the hyphenation rules, and to prompt whenever required. The following discussions in this chapter will assume these settings.

To turn on hyphenation in WordPerfect 5.1:

a. Press the Format ([Shift]-[F8]) key [[Alt] Layout Line and skip step b].

b. Type an **L** or a **1** for line-formatting options.

c. Type a **y** or a **1** to choose the hyphenation option.

d. Type **y** to turn hyphenation on.

USING HYPHENATION IN WORDPERFECT 5.0

B.4

In WordPerfect 5.0, you can use manual hyphenation, which gives you the opportunity to instruct Word-

Perfect where to place each hyphen. If you prefer, you can use automatic hyphenation, which offers WordPerfect more leeway to make decisions on its own. When hyphenation is set to automatic, Word-Perfect uses a set of rules to make an "educated guess" to determine where it should hyphenate words. It does not use a hyphenation dictionary. If WordPerfect thinks a word should be hyphenated but cannot determine from its rules how to split the word, it temporarily switches to manual hyphenation.

To use automatic hyphenation in WordPerfect 5.0:

a. Press the Format (Shift - F8) key.

b. Type an **L** or a **1** for line-formatting options.

c. Type a **y** or a **1** to enable Hyphenation.

d. Type an **a** or a **3** for automatic hyphenation.

e. Press the Exit (F7) key to return to the document.

To use manual hyphenation in WordPerfect 5.0:

a. Press the Format (Shift - F8) key.

b. Type an **L** or a **1** for line-formatting options.

c. Type a **y** or a **1** to enable Hyphenation.

d. Type an **m** or a **2** for manual hyphenation.

e. Press the Exit (F7) key to return to the document.

B.5 HYPHENATING DOCUMENTS

You can turn Hyphenation on before you type a document to ensure that the entire document will be hyphenated. First, press the Format ((Shift)-(F8)) key, type an L [(Alt) Layout Line], a y, and another y to turn on hyphenation (type a in 5.0 for automatic hyphenation). Next, press the Exit ((F7)) key. To put automatic hyphenation to use, press (Tab) and type

The Donlevy Company recognizes profit on long-term construction contracts using a percentage-of-completion method of accounting. The profit is the percentage of completion multiplied by the difference between the total contract price and the estimated total construction costs. The percentage of completion is the ratio of incurred costs to the estimated total construction cost.

With automatic hyphenation, the paragraph looks like this on the system used for this example:

```
     The Donlevy Company recognizes profit on long-term construc-
tion contracts using a percentage-of-completion method of account-
ing. The profit is the percentage of completion multiplied by the
difference between the total contract price and the estimated total
construction costs. The percentage of completion is the ratio of
incurred costs to the estimated total construction cost.
```

Type the following without first turning on hyphenation.

When a company extinguishes debt before maturity, it recognizes the difference between the cash paid and the book value of the debt, including unamortized bond issue costs, as an extraordinary gain or loss from early extinguishment.

Next, press (Home), (Home), and the (↑) key to move to the beginning of this document. Then, press the

Format ([Shift]-[F8]) key, and type an L [[Alt] Layout Line], and a y twice (m in 5.0). To return to the document, press the Exit ([F7]) key. When you move the cursor down the page, WordPerfect 5.1 hyphenates the existing text automatically. WordPerfect 5.0 prompts you to hyphenate the existing text.

B.6 | WORDPERFECT 5.0—MANUAL HYPHENATION

First, 5.0 displays this prompt:

Position hyphen; Press ESC recog-nizes

Since the hyphen is shown at an appropriate place in the word, press [Esc] to accept WordPerfect's placement. Next, WordPerfect displays this prompt:

Position hyphen; Press ESC extraor-dinary

To put the hyphen at a more appropriate place, between "extra" and "ordinary," press the [←] key twice, and then press [Esc]. The screen now looks like this:

When a company extinguishes debt before maturity, it recognizes the difference between the cash paid and the book value of
the debt, including unamortized bond issue costs, as an extraordinary gain or loss from early extinguishment

OTHER FEATURES OF HYPHENATION

B.7

You can disable hyphenation for a single word. First, clear the screen. Then, press the Format (Shift-F8) key, and type an L [Alt Layout Line], and a **y** twice (**y** and **a** in 5.0). Next, press the Exit (F7) key, and type

Please give my sincerest regards to Mr. and Mrs. Randolph Krinkenheimer. I haven't seen them in years.

When you press the SPACEBAR after "Krinkenheimer," WordPerfect prompts you for how you want "Krinkenheimer" hyphenated. Since proper names generally should not be hyphenated, press the Cancel (F1) key. WordPerfect places the entire word on the next line. When you press the Reveal Codes (Alt-F3) key [Alt Edit Reveal Codes], the lower half of the screen looks like this:

```
[Hyph On]Please give my sincerest regards to Mr. and Mrs. Randolph[SRt]
[/]Krinkenheimer.  I haven't seen them in years. █
```

WordPerfect inserted the [/] code to indicate that "Krinkenheimer" should not be hyphenated.

You can mark a word to prevent hyphenation as you type it. First, clear the screen. Then press the Format (Shift-F8) key, and type an L [Alt Layout Line], and a **y** twice (**y** and **m** in 5.0). Next, press the Exit (F7) key, and type

Outlining, graphics, and merging are three features that

Press the [Home] key and type a slash (/). You do not see a change, but when you type the next word, Word-Perfect will automatically wrap the word to the next line. Type

WordPerfect offers.

When you press the Reveal Codes ([Alt]-[F3]) key [[Alt] Edit Reveal Codes], you can see the [/] code before "WordPerfect."

When you edit hyphenated text, WordPerfect re-members where it hyphenated words. Since these hyphens are soft hyphens, WordPerfect will not use them if they are no longer required. First, clear the screen. Then, press the Format ([Shift]-[F8]) key, and type an L [[Alt] Layout Line], and a y twice (y and a in 5.0). Next, press the Exit ([F7]) key. Type

WordPerfect offers many features, including footnotes and hyphenation.

Then, press the SPACEBAR. WordPerfect hyphenates the word "hyphenation."Accept WordPerfect's sugges-tion by pressing [Esc]. To edit the text, press the [Ctrl]-[←] key combination twice and the [←] key once to move to the end of the word "footnotes." Then, type

, graphics

When you press the Reveal Codes ([Alt]-[F3]) key [[Alt] Edit Reveal Codes], the screen looks like this:

```
[Hyph On]WordPerfect offers many features, including footnotes, graphics and[SRt
]
hyphen-ation.
```

The bold hyphen indicates where WordPerfect hyphenated "hyphenation." This code allows Word-Perfect to hyphenate the word later if necessary, without prompting you for the correct hyphen location again.

You can change WordPerfect's placement of hyphens in words. Using the text just entered, place your cursor on the "n" in footnotes. Press [Ctrl]-[-]. Notice you have just inserted a bolded hyphen similar to the one in the word "hyphenation." This code allows WordPerfect to hyphenate the word "foot-note" later if, during editing, it appears near the end of a line, placing the hyphen where you have indicated.

You can disable hyphenation after invoking it. First, clear the screen. Then, press the Format ([Shift]-[F8]) key, and type an L [[Alt] Layout Line], and a y twice (a in 5.0). Next, press the Exit ([F7]) key, and type

The sum-of-the-years'-digits is one method of accelerated depreciation. This method determines the amount of depreciation expense for a period by multiplying the depreciation by a fraction.

To disable hyphenation, press the Format ([Shift]-[F8]) key, and type an L [[Alt] Layout Line], a y, and a n (f in 5.0). WordPerfect inserts the hidden code [Hyph Off]. Next, press the Exit ([F7]) key, press [Enter], and type

The denominator of the fraction is the sum of the numbers representing each year of useful life. The numerator of the fraction is the number of years of useful life remaining at the beginning of the year.

B.8 HYPHENATION ZONES

WordPerfect uses a setting called the hyphenation zone to determine whether it should hyphenate a word at the end of a line. The hyphenation zone has both left and right zone settings expressed as a percentage of the line length. A small hyphenation zone increases the number of hyphenated words in a document. A large hyphenation zone reduces the number of hyphenated words. WordPerfect's default hyphenation zone setting is 10% and 4%. This means that the last 10% of the line is the left hyphenation zone, and the right hyphenation zone is equivalent to 4% of the line length past the right margin.

If the last word in a line starts before or at the left hyphenation zone and extends to the right hyphenation zone, WordPerfect will hyphenate the word or prompt you for hyphenation. A word that starts after the left hyphenation zone and is long enough to stretch beyond the right zone is wrapped. Figure B-1 shows the hyphenation zone in perspective with the right margin.

To change the hyphenation zone:

a. Press the Format (Shift-F8) key [Alt Layout Line and skip step b].

b. Type an **L** or a **1** for line-formatting options.

c. Type a **z** or a **2** for Hyphenation Zone.

d. Type the percentage of the line to be used for the left hyphenation zone, and press (Enter).

e. Type the percentage of the line to be used for the right hyphenation zone, and press (Enter).

f. Press the Exit ((F7)) key to return to the document.

The hidden code for the hyphenation zone setting is [HZone:X%,Y%]. The "X" represents the left hyphenation zone, and the "Y" represents the right hyphenation zone.

You can decrease the hyphenation zone to increase the number of hyphenated words. First, press the

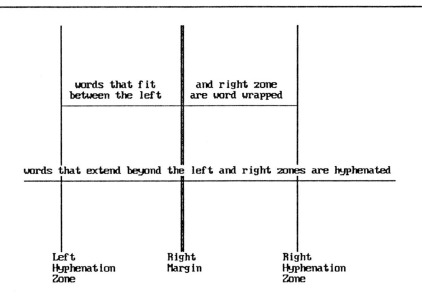

| FIGURE B-1. | Hyphenation zone in perspective with the right margin setting

Format ([Shift]-[F8]) key, and type an L [[Alt] Layout Line] and a z. For the left hyphenation zone, type 5 and press [Enter]. For the right hyphenation zone, type 2 and press [Enter]. To return to the document, press the Exit ([F7]) key. To start automatic hyphenation, press the Format ([Shift]-[F8]) key, type an L [[Alt] Layout Line], a y twice (y and an a in 5.0), and press the Exit ([F7]) key.

To use this new hyphenation zone setting, type

A company often has intangible assets, such as copyrights, patents, and goodwill. These assets do not have a physical shape, like a building, but they have a value. These assets are amortized for a period of not more than 40 years.

As you type the paragraph, hyphens are inserted into "patents" and "amortized." If you have the same system configuration, the paragraph looks like this:

```
A company often has intangible assets, such as copyrights, pat-
ents, and goodwill.  These assets do not have a physical shape
like a building, but they have a value. These assets are amor-
tized for a period of not more than 40 years,
```

You can increase the hyphenation zone to decrease the number of hyphenated words. Without clearing the screen, press the Format ([Shift]-[F8]) key, type an L [[Alt] Layout Line] and a z. For the left hyphenation zone, type 15 and press [Enter]. For the right hyphenation zone, type 8 and press [Enter]. To return to the document, press the Exit ([F7]) key.

To see how the hyphenation differs, press [Enter] and retype the paragraph.

If you wish to use manual hyphenation but are unsure of the correct placement of hyphens, you can refer to almost any dictionary. Words are usually listed with breaks between syllables. Many dictionaries also include a style guide containing information on hyphenation.

Keystroke Answers

The following conventions have been used throughout the answer sections:

Keystrokes are listed in the order they should be entered. Comments and instructions are enclosed in braces {} to distinguish them from keystrokes. Special keys, such as the function keys, are enclosed in brackets [].

References to sections covering the material tested in the skills checks, mastery skills checks, and integrating skills checks are provided in brackets in the margin beside each answer. In the answers for Chapter 1, spaces are indicated by [SPACEBAR]. After Chapter 1, spaces are indicated either by a space in the text or by [SPACEBAR]; the answers use [SPACEBAR] when using a space would cause confusion.

When selections can be made by typing either a letter or a number, the answer gives the letter.

Some exercises have more than one possible solution. Any solution that produces the desired results can be considered correct.

1.1   EXERCISES

1. {for a hard disk system using WordPerfect 5.1}cd\wp51[ENTER]wp[ENTER]{for a hard disk system using WordPerfect 5.0}cd\wp50[ENTER]wp[ENTER]{for a floppy disk system: Place the WordPerfect 1 disk in drive A and a formatted disk for documents in drive B.}b:[ENTER]a:wp[ENTER]{Place the WordPerfect 2 disk in drive A when WordPerfect prompts you, and press any key to continue.}

1.2   EXERCISES

1. {for a hard disk system using WordPerfect 5.1}cd\wp51[ENTER]wp[ENTER][F7]ny{for a hard disk system using WordPerfect 5.0}cd\wp50[ENTER]wp[ENTER][F7]ny{for a floppy disk system: Place the WordPerfect 1 disk in drive A and a formatted disk for documents in drive B}b:[ENTER]a:wp[ENTER]{Place the WordPerfect 2 disk in drive A when WordPerfect prompts you, and press any key to continue.} [F7]ny

EXERCISES ———————————— 1.3

1. accounting[F7]nn

2. trees[F7]nn

3. 1989[SPACEBAR]holidays[F7]nn

4. bills,[SPACEBAR]bills,[SPACEBAR]and[SPACEBAR]more
[SPACEBAR]bills[F7]nn

EXERCISES ———————————— 1.4

1. [ENTER][ENTER][ENTER][ENTER][ENTER][ENTER][UP ARROW]
[UP ARROW][UP ARROW][UP ARROW][UP ARROW][UP ARROW]
[DOWN ARROW][DOWN ARROW][DOWN ARROW][DOWN
ARROW][DOWN ARROW][DOWN ARROW][F7]nn

2. [ESC]10aaaaaaaaaaa{Press the LEFT ARROW and RIGHT
ARROW keys as many times as you like.}[END][ENTER]
[F7]nn

3. [TAB][TAB][TAB][TAB][LEFT ARROW][LEFT ARROW][LEFT ARROW]
[LEFT ARROW][F7]nn

4. [CTRL-ENTER][CTRL-ENTER][CTRL-ENTER][CTRL-ENTER]{Press
PGUP and PGDN as many times as you like.}[CTRL-
HOME]{Type a number from 1 to 5.}[ENTER]{Repeat
until you are comfortable with the CTRL-HOME key
combination.}[F7]nn

5. the[SPACEBAR]early[SPACEBAR]bird[SPACEBAR]gets[SPACE-BAR]the[SPACEBAR]worm.[ENTER][UP ARROW]{Press the CTRL-LEFT ARROW and CTRL-RIGHT ARROW key combinations as many times as you like.}{Press the HOME-LEFT ARROW key combination and the END key as many times as you like.}[F7]nn

6. [ENTER][ENTER][ENTER][ENTER][CTRL-ENTER][ENTER][ENTER][ENTER][ENTER][CTRL-ENTER][ENTER][ENTER][ENTER][ENTER][CTRL-ENTER][ENTER][ENTER][ENTER][ENTER][CTRL-ENTER][ENTER][ENTER][ENTER][ENTER][CTRL-ENTER][ENTER][ENTER][ENTER][ENTER][GREY –][GREY –][GREY +][GREY +][HOME][HOME][UP ARROW][HOME][HOME][DOWN ARROW][F7]nn

7. [NUM LOCK]123456789[NUM LOCK][F7]nn

8. abc[BACKSPACE][LEFT ARROW][LEFT ARROW][DEL]

1.5   EXERCISES

1. [F3]s{for screen}{[ENTER]or[SPACEBAR]to exit Help}

2. he[SPACEBAR]suddenly[SPACEBAR]left.[CTRL-LEFT ARROW][CTRL-LEFT ARROW][LEFT ARROW][DEL][DEL][DEL][DEL][DEL][DEL] [DEL][DEL][DEL][END][LEFT ARROW][F1]1[F7]nn

3. [F3][F3][ENTER]

4. [F3]d[ENTER]

5. it[SPACEBAR]was[SPACEBAR]a[SPACEBAR]cold,[SPACEBAR]
   dark,[SPACEBAR]scary[SPACEBAR]evening[CTRL-LEFT
   ARROW][CTRL-LEFT ARROW][CTRL-LEFT ARROW][DEL][DEL][DEL]
   [DEL][DEL][DEL][CTRL-LEFT ARROW][F1]r[F7]}nn

EXERCISES _____ 1.6

1. [SHIFT-j][SHIFT-q][SHIFT-l][SHIFT-y][SHIFT-z][SHIFT-b][SHIFT-e]
   [SHIFT-a][SHIFT-n][SHIFT-l][F7]nn

2. [SHIFT-t]he[SPACEBAR][SHIFT-a][SHIFT-b][SHIFT-c][SPACEBAR]
   [SHIFT-c]orporation[SPACEBAR]makes[SPACEBAR][SHIFT-t]
   iger[SPACEBAR]sedans.[F7]nn

3. [SHIFT-t]he[SPACEBAR]lending[SPACEBAR]rate[SPACEBAR]is
   [SPACEBAR]15[SHIFT-5].[ENTER][SHIFT-9]16[SHIFT-8]2[SHIFT-0]
   [SHIFT-=]7=39[ENTER][SHIFT-p]rofit[SPACEBAR][SHIFT-7]
   [SPACEBAR][SHIFT-l]oss[SPACEBAR][SHIFT-s]tatement[F7]nn

4. [CAPS LOCK]capitalization[SPACEBAR]can[SPACEBAR]
   emphasize[SPACEBAR]text[ENTER]wordperfect[CAPS
   LOCK][SPACEBAR]makes[SPACEBAR]typing[SPACEBAR][CAPS
   LOCK]fun.[CAPS LOCK][F7]nn

5. [CAPS LOCK]the[SPACEBAR]local[SPACEBAR]car[SPACEBAR]
   dealership[SPACEBAR]is[SPACEBAR]offering[SPACEBAR]
   16[SHIFT-5][SPACEBAR]apr.[ENTER]company[SPACEBAR]
   picnic[SPACEBAR]8/19/89[CAPS LOCK][F7]nn

MASTERY SKILLS CHECK

[1.2]   **1.** [F7]ny

[1.1]   **2.** {for a hard disk system using WordPerfect 5.1}cd\
wp51[ENTER]wp[ENTER]{for a hard disk system using
WordPerfect 5.0}cd\wp50[ENTER]wp[ENTER]{for a
floppy disk system: Place the WordPerfect 1 disk
in drive A and a formatted disk for documents in
drive B.}b:[ENTER]a:wp[ENTER]{Place the Word-
Perfect 2 disk in drive A when WordPerfect
prompts you, and press any key to continue.}

[1.4, 1.6]   **3.** [SHIFT-a]ugust[SPACEBAR]15th[SPACEBAR]or[SPACEBAR][CAPS
LOCK]september[SPACEBAR]3rd[CAPS LOCK][ENTER]3[SHIFT-
6]2[SHIFT-=][SHIFT-9]8[SHIFT-8]9[SHIFT-0]

[1.5]   **4.** [F3]e{Press ENTER or SPACEBAR to leave Help.}

[1.3]   **5.** [F7]nn

[1.4, 1.6]   **6.** 10[SHIFT-;]34[SPACEBAR][SHIFT-a][SHIFT-m][ENTER][CAPS
LOCK]acme = [SPACEBAR]corporation[CAPS LOCK]

[1.2]   **7.** [F7]ny

2

SKILLS CHECK

[1.3, 1.6]   **1.** [CAPS LOCK]a penny saved is a[CAPS LOCK]penny
earned.[F7]n[ENTER]

[1.4, 1.6]   **2.** [CAPS LOCK]to[SHIFT-;][SPACEBAR]j[CAPS LOCK]ohn
[SPACEBAR][SHIFT-s]mith[ENTER][CAPS LOCK]from[SHIFT-;]
[SPACEBAR][CAPS LOCK]ary[SPACEBAR][SHIFT-b]rown
[ENTER][CAPS LOCK]subject[SHIFT-;][SPACEBAR][CAPS LOCK]
1990[SPACEBAR][SHIFT-h]oliday[SPACEBAR][SHIFT-s]chedule

3. [ENTER][ESC]65-   [1.4]

4. [ENTER][ENTER][ENTER][ENTER][TAB]{Type the text as   [1.4]
shown, using the SHIFT key and SPACEBAR where
appropriate.}

5. [CTRL-ENTER][SHIFT-j]anuary[SPACEBAR]1[TAB][TAB][SHIFT-   [1.4, 1.6]
n]ew[SPACEBAR][SHIFT-y]ear's[SPACEBAR][SHIFT-d]ay
[ENTER][SHIFT-j]anuary[SPACEBAR]12[TAB]{Note that
only one tab was required, since the cursor was
already at the first tab stop.}[SHIFT-f]ounders'
[SPACEBAR][SHIFT-d]ay[ENTER]{The remaining entries
follow the same pattern. The lines for November
28 and December 25 will each require only one
tab.}

6. [PGUP]   [1.4]

7. [HOME][HOME][DOWN ARROW]   [1.4]

8. [HOME][HOME][UP ARROW]   [1.4]

9. [F7]nn   [1.3]

10. [F3]e[ENTER]   [1.5]

11. [F7]ny   [1.2]

EXERCISES   2.1

1. {Type the lines as shown, pressing ENTER at the
end of the first line and after each sentence.}

2. {Type the paragraph as shown, pressing ENTER
only at the end of the paragraph.}

3. {Type the text as shown, pressing ENTER after the words "Descriptions," "light," "black," "translucent," and "diamond."}

4. [TAB]{Type the first paragraph as shown.}[ENTER] [TAB]{Type the second paragraph as shown.} [ENTER]

2.2   EXERCISES

1. [SHIFT-a][SPACEBAR]stitch in time saves nine.[F10]stitch [ENTER]

2. [SHIFT-j]im[SPACEBAR][SHIFT-a]llen[ENTER]1123[SPACEBAR] [SHIFT-f]ork[SPACEBAR][SHIFT-r]d.[ENTER][SHIFT-b]altimore, [SPACEBAR][SHIFT-m]aryland[SPACEBAR]21237[F10]name [ENTER][F7]yname2[ENTER][ENTER]

3. {Type the quote as shown.}[ENTER][ENTER][TAB][TAB] [TAB][TAB]Sam Levenson[F7][ENTER]kids[ENTER][ENTER]

4. {Type the quote as shown.}[ENTER][ENTER][TAB][TAB] [TAB][TAB]Theodore Roosevelt[F10]teddy[ENTER][F7] [ENTER]school[ENTER][ENTER]

2.3   EXERCISES

1. [SHIFT-F10]stitch[ENTER]

2. [SHIFT-F10]name[ENTER][SHIFT-F10]stitch[ENTER]

3. [SHIFT-F10]teddy[ENTER][SHIFT-F10]teddy[ENTER][F7]n [ENTER]

4. Favorite Quotes[ENTER][SHIFT-F10]kids[ENTER][SHIFT-F10]teddy[ENTER][F7]nn

EXERCISES _____ 2.4

1. {Type the sentence as shown.}[HOME][HOME][LEFT ARROW][CAPS LOCK]abc[SPACEBAR][CAPS LOCK]

2. {Type the sentence as shown.}[CTRL-LEFT ARROW][LEFT ARROW],975

3. {Type the sentences as shown.}[CTRL-LEFT ARROW][CTRL-LEFT ARROW][CTRL-LEFT ARROW][CTRL-LEFT ARROW][CTRL-LEFT ARROW][CTRL-LEFT ARROW]{Type the new sentence.}[SPACEBAR][SPACEBAR]

4. She served cake for dessert.[CTRL-LEFT ARROW][CTRL-LEFT ARROW][CTRL-LEFT ARROW]rich, warm, chocolate [SPACEBAR][CTRL-RIGHT ARROW]and creamy, rich, vanilla ice cream[SPACEBAR]

5. {Type the quote as shown.}[ENTER][ENTER][TAB][TAB][TAB][TAB]Philip Guedalla{Move to the "a" in "and."}on the east by obituary,[SPACEBAR]

EXERCISES _____ 2.5

1. {Type the sentences as shown; then use the arrow keys to move to the "C" in "Carol."}[INS][SHIFT-e]llen[INS]

2. {Type the sentence as shown.}[CTRL-LEFT ARROW][CTRL-LEFT ARROW][INS]4[CTRL-LEFT ARROW][CTRL-LEFT ARROW][CTRL-LEFT ARROW][CTRL-LEFT ARROW][CTRL-LEFT ARROW][CTRL-LEFT ARROW]answers the phone[DEL][INS]

3. {Type the sentences as shown; then move to the "c" in "company" in the first sentence.}[INS][CAPS LOCK]j. l. m[INS][CAPS LOCK][INS]cGregor Corporation

4. The new prices for copies are[ENTER]1 to 100[TAB][TAB].08 each[ENTER]101 to 500[TAB].05 each[ENTER]501 + [TAB][TAB][TAB].02 each[INS]{Move to each price, typing the new figures over the old.}[INS]

5. Your current balance is $789.95.[CTRL-LEFT ARROW][RIGHT ARROW][INS]3[INS]

2.6   EXERCISES

1. {Type the sentence as shown; then use the arrow keys to move to the "t" in "together."}[DEL][DEL][DEL][DEL][DEL][DEL][DEL][DEL][DEL]{Move to the period at the end of the sentence.}[BACKSPACE][BACKSPACE][BACKSPACE][BACKSPACE][BACKSPACE][BACKSPACE][BACKSPACE][BACKSPACE][BACKSPACE][BACKSPACE][BACKSPACE]

2. {Type the sentences as shown; then move to the word "name" in the first sentence.}[CTRL-BACKSPACE][CTRL-BACKSPACE]{Move to "purses."}[CTRL-BACKSPACE]

3. {Type the lines as shown; then move to the beginning of the second slogan.}[CTRL-END][DEL]

4. {Type the text as shown. Move to the beginning of the third line (before the tab).}[CTRL-END][DEL]

5. {Type the text as shown, using the TAB key to place data in columns. Move to the word "SALARY."}[CTRL-BACKSPACE]

{Move to the first salary figure.}[CTRL-BACKSPACE] {Repeat this process for the remaining two salary entries.}

MASTERY SKILLS CHECK

1. {Type the paragraph as shown. Do not press ENTER until the end of the paragraph.}   [2.1]

2. {Move to the "X" in "XY."}June 17,[SPACEBAR]   [2.4]

3. {Move to the "I" in "Inc."}[DEL][DEL][DEL][DEL][DEL]   [2.6]

4. {Move to the "n" in "June."}[INS]ly[INS]   [2.5]

5. {Move to the "T" in "This."}[ENTER]   [2.4]

6. [F7][ENTER]seendraw[ENTER]n   [2.2]

7. [SHIFT-F10]seendraw[ENTER]   [2.3]

8. {Move to "both."}[CTRL-BACKSPACE]   [2.6]

9. {Move to the beginning of the second sentence.}[CTRL-END][DEL]   [2.6]

10. [F10]draw[ENTER]   [2.2]

INTEGRATING SKILLS CHECK

[1.6]   **1.** {Type the lines as shown, using CAPS LOCK for the first line.}

[1.5]   **2.** [F3]s

[2.2]   **3.** [F10]cookie[ENTER]

[1.3]   **4.** [F7]n[ENTER]

[1.4]   **5.** {Type the line as shown.}[ENTER][ESC]65-[ENTER]

[2.3]   **6.** [SHIFT-F10]cookie[ENTER]

[1.6, 2.4] **7.** {Use the arrow keys to move to the "C" in "COOKIES."}[CAPS LOCK]and butterscotch chip [CAPS LOCK][SPACEBAR]

           8. {Move to the beginning of the last line.}[CTRL-END] [DEL]

[2.2]   **9.** [F10]list[ENTER]

[1.2]   **10.** [F7]ny

3

SKILLS CHECK

[1.4, 1.6, 2.1] **1.** Fourscore and seven years ago our fathers brought forth on this continent, a new nation, conceived in liberty, and dedicated to the propsition that all men are created equal.[ENTER] [ENTER][TAB][TAB][TAB][TAB]GettysburgAddress[ENTER]

2. {Move to "Fourscore."[CTRL-BACKSPACE][CTRL-
BACKSPACE][CTRL-BACKSPACE]87[SPACEBAR]   [2.4, 2.6]

3. [HOME][LEFT ARROW][F1]r[CTRL-BACKSPACE]   [1.4, 1.5]

4. {Move to the "s" in "propsition."}o   [1.4, 2.4]

5. {Move to the "G" in "Gettysburg."}[INS]Abraham   [2.5]
[SPACEBAR]Lincoln[DEL][DEL][DEL][INS]

6. [F10]lincoln[ENTER]   [2.2]

7. [F7]ny   [1.2]

8. {for a hard disk system using WordPerfect 5.1}cd\   [1.1, 2.3]
wp51[ENTER]wp[ENTER][SHIFT-F10]Lincoln[ENTER]{for a
hard disk system using WordPerfect 5.0}cd\wp50
[ENTER]wp[ENTER][SHIFT-F10]lincoln[ENTER]{for a floppy
disk system: Place the WordPerfect 1 disk in drive
A and a disk for documents in drive B.}b:[ENTER]
a:wp[ENTER]{When prompted to do so, replace the
WordPerfect 1 disk with the WordPerfect 2 disk,
and press any key.}[SHIFT-F10]lincoln[ENTER]

9. [F7]nn   [1.3]

EXERCISES ———————————————— 3.1

1. [SHIFT-F10]lincoln[ENTER][SHIFT-F7]f

2. [TAB][TAB][TAB][TAB]12345 Commerce Parkway[ENTER]
[TAB][TAB][TAB][TAB]Beachwood, OH 44123 [ENTER]
[TAB]

[TAB][TAB][TAB]December 1, 1990[ENTER][ENTER][ENTER]
Samantha Koln[ENTER]Small Business Administration of Cleveland[ENTER]1235 Public Square[ENTER]
Cleveland, OH 44115[ENTER][ENTER]Dear Ms. Koln,
[ENTER][TAB]I am starting a business to manufacture
mechanical pencils. Can you provide information
on the services that your organization provides to
new companies?[ENTER][ENTER][TAB][TAB][TAB][TAB]Sin-
cerely,[ENTER][ENTER][ENTER][ENTER][TAB][TAB][TAB][TAB]
Tom Lu[ENTER][TAB][TAB][TAB][TAB]President, Various
Sundries, Inc.[ENTER][SHIFT-F7]f[F10]sba[ENTER]

3. {Type the quote as shown.}[ENTER][ENTER][TAB][TAB]
   [TAB][TAB]John Ruskin[SHIFT-F7]f

4. [ENTER][ENTER]{Type the quote.}[ENTER][ENTER][TAB]
   [TAB][TAB][TAB]Herbert Hoover[SHIFT-F7]f

3.2   EXERCISES

1. [SHIFT-F10]sba[ENTER][SHIFT-F7]f{Move to the end of the
   paragraph.}[ENTER][TAB]I have enclosed a notice of
   our upcoming open house for your monthly
   newsletter.[HOME][HOME][DOWN ARROW][CTRL-ENTER]
   Attend the Open House Celebration at Various
   Sundries, Inc., on May 15 from 7:30 to 9:30
   P.M.[SHIFT-F7]p

2. Significant Accomplishments 1990 - John Smith
   [ENTER][CTRL-ENTER]Significant Accomplishments
   1990 - Mary Brown[ENTER][CTRL-ENTER]Significant
   Accomplishments 1990 - Nancy Caster[ENTER][SHIFT-
   F7]p

3. [PGUP][SHIFT-F7]p[PGUP][SHIFT-F7]p

4. {Type the quotation.}[ENTER][ENTER][TAB][TAB][TAB]
[TAB]John Heywood[ENTER][CTRL-ENTER]{Type the second quotation.}[ENTER][ENTER][TAB][TAB][TAB][TAB]
Robert Burns[ENTER][PGUP][SHIFT-F7]p

EXERCISES _____ 3.3

1. [SHIFT-F10]lincoln[ENTER][SHIFT-F7]v12

2. To: Sarah Graham, Chief Financial Officer[ENTER]
From: Bob Kelly, Chief Accounting Officer[ENTER]
Re: Financial Statements[ENTER][ESC]65 = [ENTER]
Sarah,[ENTER][ENTER][TAB]Enclosed are the preliminary financial statements. The attached text
includes all of the footnotes. If you find any corrections or additions, please contact me
immediately.[ENTER][SHIFT-F7]v312

3. {Type the data as shown.}[SHIFT-F7]v[F7]{Position
the cursor after the period at the end of the first
sentence.}[CTRL-ENTER]{Position the cursor after the
period at the end of the second sentence.}[CTRL-
ENTER]{Position the cursor after the period in the
third sentence.}[CTRL-ENTER][SHIFT-F7]v{Use PGUP and
PGDN to view the document.}

4. {Type the quotes, ending each entry with CTRL-
ENTER to start a new page.}[SHIFT-F7]v4{use PGUP and
PGDN to move within the document.}[F7][F10]
quotes[ENTER]

3.4   EXERCISES

1. [SHIFT-F7]dsba[ENTER][ENTER][F7]

2. [CAPS LOCK]residents opposed to road paving [ENTER]b[CAPS LOCK]lack[ENTER][SHIFT-s]mith[ENTER] [SHIFT-c]ampbell[ENTER][SHIFT-g]ilbert[ENTER][SHIFT-l] ong[ENTER][SHIFT-j]ackson[CTRL-ENTER][CAPSLOCK] residents supporting road paving[ENTER]w[CAPS LOCK]ilson[ENTER][SHIFT-b]oswell[ENTER][SHIFT-d]ike [ENTER][F7][ENTER]road[ENTER]n[SHIFT-F7]droad [ENTER][ENTER]droad[ENTER]2[ENTER][F7]

3. [SHIFT-F7]dquotes[ENTER]2[ENTER][F7]

4. [SHIFT-F7]dquotes[ENTER]2-4[ENTER][F7]

5. [SHIFT-F7]dquotes[ENTER]1,4[ENTER][F7]

MASTERY SKILLS CHECK

[3.3]

1. To: All Managers[ENTER]From: Fred Jones, Director of Human Services[ENTER]Subject: Meetings on the New Benefit Package[ENTER][ENTER][TAB]The Human Services Department will be conducting a one-hour information meeting on the new benefit package. We have attempted to schedule these meetings at convenient times. Please route the sign-up sheets to your employees and encourage everyone to attend one of these sessions.[ENTER] [CTRL-ENTER]Benefit Package meeting - April 5 9:30 A.M.[CTRL-ENTER]Benefit Package meeting - April 5

2:30 P.M.[CTRL-ENTER]Benefit Package meeting -
April 6 8:30 A.M.[CTRL-ENTER]Benefit Package meeting - April 6 4:00 P.M.[ENTER][SHIFT-F7]

2. [SHIFT-F7]f   [3.1]

3. [HOME][HOME][UP ARROW][SHIFT-F7]p   [3.2]

4. [F7][ENTER]benefits[ENTER][ENTER][SHIFT-F7]dbenefits   [3.4]
[ENTER] 2-5[ENTER][F7]

INTEGRATING SKILLS CHECK

1. [TAB]A meeting is scheduled at 5 PM on January   [1.4, 1.6]
20 to discuss the company's participation in the
[CAPS LOCK]cleveland corporate olympics.[CAPS LOCK]
The meeting will be held in the fourth-floor conference room.[ENTER][ENTER][TAB]This year, we need
a slogan for the banner and a T-shirt design. We
also need a list of the employees participating in
each activity. Please encourage your staff members to participate.[ENTER][ENTER][TAB]Interested
individuals unable to attend the scheduled meeting should contact Steve Spear. His extension is
3963.[ENTER]

2. {Move to the "H" in "His."}[CTRL-END]   [2.6]

3. {Move to the 0 in 20.}[INS]5[INS]   [1.4, 2.5]

4. [SHIFT-F7]f   [3.1]

5. [HOME][HOME][DOWN ARROW]   [1.4]

[1.4]

6. [CTRL-ENTER]

[1.4]

7. Name[TAB][TAB][TAB][TAB][TAB]Activity[ENTER][ESC]8-[TAB][TAB][ESC]10-[ENTER]Sue Marianetti[TAB][TAB][TAB]Bike Race[ENTER]Sharon Campbell[TAB][TAB]Tug-of-War[ENTER]John Peterson[TAB][TAB][TAB]Tug-of-War[ENTER]Tim Smith[TAB][TAB][TAB][TAB]5K Race[ENTER]Ted McGregor[TAB][TAB][TAB]Tug-of-War[ENTER]Brandon Leidy[TAB][TAB][TAB]Swimming[ENTER]Marge Thomas[TAB][TAB][TAB]5K Race[ENTER]Anne Kettlewood[TAB][TAB]Bike Race[ENTER]

[3.3]

8. [SHIFT-F7]v3{Use the PGUP and PGDN keys to view both pages.}

[3.2]

9. {Position the cursor on page 2.}[SHIFT-F7]p[ENTER]

[2.2]

10. [F7][ENTER]olympics[ENTER][ENTER]

[1.4, 3.4]

11. [CAPS LOCK]corporate slogan suggestions[ENTER]o[CAPS LOCK]ur Team's the Best[ENTER][SHIFT-F7]dolympics[ENTER]1[ENTER][F7]The Best at All We Do[ENTER]Scientific Services Employees Have Brains and Brawn[ENTER]Sticks and Stones Won't Break Our Bones[ENTER]

4

SKILLS CHECK

[1.4, 1.6]

1. The next meting of the WordPerfect User's Group will be January 5. Each attendeee will receive a free on the use of the new graphics features.

2. {Move to the "e" in "meting."}e{Move to the last   [1.4, 2.4]
"e" in "attendeee."}[DEL]{Move to the "o" in
"on."}handout[SPACEBAR]

3. [F3][F3][ENTER]   [1.5]

4. [F10]meeting[ENTER]   [2.2]

5. [F7]n[ENTER]   [1.3]

6. [SHIFT-F7]dmeeting[ENTER][ENTER][F7]   [3.4]

EXERCISES   4.1

1. Acerson, Karen L.,[SPACEBAR][F8]WordPerfect 5.1:
The Complete Reference[F8], Osborne/McGraw-
Hill, 1990.[ENTER]Alderman, Eric, and Lawrence J.
Magid,[SPACEBAR][F8]Advanced WordPerfect, Series
5 Edition[F8], Osborne/McGraw-Hill, 1988.[ENTER]
Mincberg, Mella,[SPACEBAR][F8]WordPerfect 5.1
Made Easy [F8], Osborne/McGraw-Hill, 1990.

2. We will honor employees with more than [SPACE-
BAR][F8]twenty-five years[SPACEBAR][F8]of service at
the annual appreciation dinner. The following
employees are honorees at this year's dinner:
[ENTER][ENTER][F8][CAPS LOCK]employee[F8][TAB][TAB][F8]
years of service[F8][CAPS LOCK][ENTER]J. Smith[TAB]
[TAB] 25[ENTER]R. Taylor[TAB][TAB]35[ENTER]P. Volker
[TAB][TAB]31

3. Cost per square foot[SPACEBAR]=[SPACEBAR][F8]Total cost[F8][ENTER][TAB][TAB][TAB][TAB][SPACEBAR][SPACEBAR][SPACEBAR]Square feet

4. [TAB]{Type the first paragraph as shown.}[ENTER][TAB][F8]Aconteus[SPACEBAR][F8]looked at[F8]Medusa's[F8][SPACEBAR]head and turned into stone.[SPACEBAR][SPACEBAR][F8]Medusa[F8][SPACEBAR]was a monster whose hair was made of serpents.[SPACEBAR][SPACEBAR][F8]Perseus[F8], the son of[SPACEBAR][F8]Danae[F8]and[SPACEBAR][F8]Jupiter[F8], killed [SPACEBAR][F8]Medusa[F8]. To make himself invisible to[SPACEBAR][F8]Medusa[F8], he wore[SPACEBAR][F8]Pluto's[F8][SPACEBAR]helmet and a pair of winged shoes.

4.2   EXERCISES

1. [CAPS LOCK]account[TAB]balance[CAPS LOCK][ENTER]Rent[TAB][TAB]$5,125[ENTER]Utilities[TAB][F6](1,250)[F6][ENTER]Phone[TAB][F6]([SPACEBAR][SPACEBAR]950)[F6]

2. Your account balance is[F6]more than 90 days past due[F6]. Unless you contact us[F6]immediately[F6], we will begin legal action to collect the balance of your account.

3. [F6][F8][CAPS LOCK]dept[TAB][TAB]head count[F6][F8][ENTER]acct[TAB][TAB]14[ENTER]fin[TAB][TAB]10[ENTER]mfg[TAB][TAB]84[CAPS LOCK]

4. Foreign words can add variety to your writing. When you select foreign phrases, you will want to be certain that both you and your readers understand their meaning.[SPACEBAR][SPACEBAR][F6]Deo gratias[F6][SPACEBAR]means thanks to God.[SPACEBAR][SPACEBAR][F6]Dei gratia[F6][SPACEBAR]means by the grace of God.[SPACEBAR][SPACEBAR][F6]Deo volente[F6][SPACEBAR]means by God's will.[SPACEBAR][SPACEBAR][F6]Dieu vous garde[F6][SPACEBAR]means God protect you.

5. Noble by birth, yet nobler by great deeds.[ENTER][TAB][TAB][F6]Henry Wadsworth Longfellow,[SPACEBAR][F8]Tales of a Wayside Inn [F6][F8][ENTER]Who fears t'offend takes the first step to please.[ENTER][TAB][TAB][F6]Colley Cibber,[SPACEBAR][F8]Love in a Riddle[F6][F8][ENTER]The art of praising is the beginning of the art of pleasing.[ENTER][TAB][TAB][F6]Voltaire,[SPACEBAR][F8]La Pucelle[F6][F8]

EXERCISES _____ 4.3

1. {Substitute your own name and address for the ones in this answer.}[SHIFT-F6]John Smith[ENTER][SHIFT-F6]111 North Ave.[ENTER][SHIFT-F6]Cleveland, OH 44040[ENTER]

2. [SHIFT-F6][F6]Tinsel Company[F6][ENTER]

3. [SHIFT-F6]This text is too long for one line. WordPerfect cannot fit the entire entry on one line. When you print the text, you will notice that

WordPerfect centers only the text in the first line.[ENTER]

4. [CAPS LOCK][SHIFT-F6]abc company[ENTER][SHIFT-F6] performance report[ENTER][SHIFT-F6]for the quarter ending june 30, 1989[ENTER][CAPS LOCK]

4.4   EXERCISES

1. [SHIFT-F6][CAPS LOCK]abc company[ENTER][SHIFT-F6] budget report[ENTER][SHIFT-F6]fiscal 1990[ENTER][CAPS LOCK][ALT-F3]{Look at the codes that cause Word-Perfect to center the text.}[ALT-F3]

2. New Sunday store hours are[SPACEBAR][F6]Noon to 5 P.M.[F6][ALT-F3]

3. [ALT-F3][F6][F8]Overdue Accounts[F6][F8]

4. [SHIFT-F6]I think, therefore I am.[ENTER][SHIFT-F6]Rene Descartes[ENTER][ALT-F3][F10]THINK[ENTER]

4.5   EXERCISES

1. [F6]Quality Corporation[F6][SPACEBAR]is pleased to announce the following Christmas bonus struc-tures:[ENTER][SHIFT-F6]Less than 2 years of service - 2% bonus[ENTER][SHIFT-F6]2 years or more of service - 5% bonus[ENTER]Checks will be available for dis-tribution on[SPACEBAR][F8]December 23[F8].[ALT-F3]

{Use the arrow keys to move around and view the codes. Position the cursor on the first Center code([CNTR] or [C/A/FLRT] in 5.0), and press DEL. Repeat for the second centered line.}

2. [ALT-F3][HOME][HOME][HOME][UP ARROW][F2][F6][F2][F7]nn

3. [SHIFT-F10]THINK[ENTER][ALT-F3]{Move to the code for Center ([CNTR]or[C/A/FLRT]in 5.0) on the first line, and press the DEL key. Repeat for the second line.}

EXERCISES 4.6

1. {Type the text as shown. Move to the "I" in "In."} [ALT-F4].

2. An excuse uncalled for becomes an obvious accusation.[ENTER][TAB][TAB][TAB][TAB]Law Maxim[ENTER] {Move to the first "e" in "excuse."}[ALT-F4][CTRL-RIGHT ARROW][F1][F10]EXCUSE[ENTER]

3. You must submit expense reports by the 15th of the month following travel.{Move to the "1" in "15th."}[ALT-F4][RIGHT ARROW][RIGHT ARROW][RIGHT ARROW][RIGHT ARROW][F1]

4. {Move to the "m" in "month."}previous[SPACEBAR] [ALT-F4][CTRL-LEFT ARROW][DEL]y

5. [SHIFT-F10]THINK[ENTER][DOWN ARROW][ALT-F4][END][DEL]y

4.7

EXERCISES

1. {Type the text as shown. Move to the "W" in "WordPerfect" in the first sentence.}[ALT-F4]y[F8]

2. {Move to the "W" in "WordPerfect" in the second sentence.}[ALT-F4]tt[F6]

3. [CAPS LOCK]accounts receivable aging[CAPS LOCK] [ALT-F4][CTRL-LEFT ARROW][CTRL-LEFT ARROW][CTRL-LEFT ARROW][F8][ALT-F4][CTRL-RIGHT ARROW][CTRL-RIGHT ARROW][CTRL-RIGHT ARROW][SHIFT-F6]y

4. [SHIFT-F10]EXCUSE[ENTER][HOME][HOME][DOWN ARROW] [ENTER]A bad excuse is better, they say, than none at all.[ENTER][TAB][TAB][TAB][TAB]Stephen Gosson {Move to the first "e" in the word "excuse" in the first quotation.}[ALT-F4][CTRL-RIGHT ARROW][F6]{Move to the first "e" in "excuse" in the second quotation.} [ALT-F4][CTRL-RIGHT ARROW][F6]

5. {Type the quotation as shown.}{Move to the "w" in either occurrence of "wheels."}[ALT-F4]s[F6][ALT-F4][CTRL-LEFT ARROW][F8]{Repeat the process for the other occurrence of "wheels."}

MASTERY SKILLS CHECK

[4.1]

1. [F8]Bylaws of the WordPerfect Users Group[F8][F7] nn

[4.2]

2. [F6]ABC Company[F6][SPACEBAR]will hold its annual picnic at the[SPACEBAR][F6]Loch Raven Pavilion[F6] [SPACEBAR]on[SPACEBAR][F6]July 17th[F6].

3. [ALT-F3]{Move to the "L" in "Loch."}[BACKSPACE]   [4.4, 4.5]

4. [HOME][HOME][HOME][UP ARROW][SHIFT-F6][F8][CAPS LOCK]   [4.1, 4.3]
   company picnic announcement[F8][CAPS LOCK]

5. [ENTER][ENTER][ENTER][ALT-F3][HOME][HOME][HOME]   [4.4, 4.5]
   [UP ARROW][F2][F8][F2][SHIFT-F7]f[F7]nn

6. [SHIFT-F6][F6][CAPS LOCK]abc company[ENTER][SHIFT-   [4.2, 4.4, 4.5]
   F6]internal memorandum[ENTER][ENTER]to[SHIFT-;]
   [F6][SPACEBAR]a[CAPS LOCK]ll staff[ENTER][F6][CAPS
   LOCK]from[SHIFT-;][F6][SPACEBAR]j[CAPS LOCK]ohn
   [SPACEBAR][SHIFT-s]mith[ENTER][F6][CAPS LOCK]subject
   [SHIFT-;][F6][SPACEBAR]c[CAPS LOCK]ompletion of parking
   lot resurfacing[ENTER][F6][CAPS LOCK]date[SHIFT-;][F6]
   [SPACEBAR]f[CAPS LOCK]ebruary 15, 1990[ENTER][ENTER]
   The resurfacing of parking lots A and B is com-
   plete. Resurfacing of parking lot C is scheduled to
   begin Monday, February 20.[ENTER]Your continued
   cooperation is appreciated.[ALT-F3]{Move to the "c"
   in "continued."}[BACKSPACE][SPACEBAR][F10]PARKING
   [ENTER]

7. {Move to the "c" in "complete."}[ALT-F4]ee[F6]   [4.6, 4.7]
   {Move to the beginning of the second
   sentence.}[ALT-F4]. [DEL]y[F7]nn

8. [CAPS LOCK]acct no[TAB]balance[CAPS LOCK][ENTER]   [4.6, 4.7]
   1204[TAB][TAB][SHIFT-4]12,350[ENTER]1567[TAB][TAB]
   [SHIFT-4]17,865[ENTER]2569[TAB][TAB][SHIFT-4]23,789
   [ENTER]{Move to the "A" in "ACCT."}[ALT-F4]
   [END][F6][ALT-F4][CTRL-HOME][CTRL-HOME][F8]

INTEGRATING SKILLS CHECK

[1.4, 4.3] **1.** [SHIFT-F6][CAPS LOCK]abc books[CAPS LOCK][ENTER][SHIFT-F6]1115 Warren Avenue[ENTER][SHIFT-F6]Cleveland, OH 44017[ENTER][ENTER]{Type the remainder of the text as shown.}

[1.3, 2.2, 3.4] **2.** [F7][ENTER]myers[ENTER][ENTER][SHIFT-F7]dmyers [ENTER][ENTER][F7]

[2.5, 4.6, 4.7] **3.** [SHIFT-F10]myers[ENTER]{Move to the "N" in "North."}[INS]Sou[INS]{Move to the "S" in "Successful."}[ALT-F4]t[F8]{Move to the "O" in "October."}[ALT-F4]2[F6]

[4.6, 1.5] **4.** [END][ALT-F4][UP ARROW][HOME][LEFT ARROW][F1]

[2.2, 3.1, 3.3] **5.** [F10][ENTER]y[SHIFT-F7]v[F7]f

5

SKILLS CHECK

[4.1, 4.3] **1.** [SHIFT-F6]Bibliography[ENTER][ENTER]Mincberg, Mella, [SPACEBAR][F8]WordPerfect 5.1 Made Easy[F8], Osborne/McGraw-Hill, 1072 pages.[ENTER] Campbell, Mary,[SPACEBAR][F8]1-2-3 Release Made Easy[F8], Osborne/McGraw-Hill, 526 pages.[ENTER]

[1.4, 2.4] **2.** {Move to the 4 in 492.}1990[SPACEBAR]{Move to the 4 in 400.}1989,[SPACEBAR]

[2.2] **3.** [F10]biblio[ENTER]

[4.5] **4.** [HOME][HOME][HOME][UP ARROW][F2][F8][F2][BACKSPACE] y[F2][F2][BACKSPACE]y

5. [F7]nn   [1.3]

6. [SHIFT-F7]dbiblio[ENTER][ENTER][F7]   [3.4]

EXERCISES

5.1

1. Some are born great, some achieve greatness, others have greatness thrust upon 'em.[ENTER][TAB][TAB][TAB][TAB]William Shakespeare[ENTER][HOME][HOME][UP ARROW][SHIFT-F8]lm2[ENTER]1.5[ENTER][F7]

2. What makes us discontented with our condition is the absurdly exaggerated idea we have of the happiness of others.[ENTER][TAB][TAB][TAB][TAB]Proverb[ENTER][HOME][HOME][UP ARROW][SHIFT-F8]lm2[ENTER]2[ENTER][F7][ALT-F3]{The code for the margin change is[L/R Mar:2",2"].}[ALT-F3][SHIFT-F8]lm1.5[ENTER]1.5[ENTER][F7]{Press the DOWN ARROW key to make WordPerfect reformat the paragraph with the new margins.}

3. The plural of most compound nouns is formed by adding "s" or "es" to the main word in the grouping. For example:[ENTER][TAB]mothers-in-law[ENTER][TAB]runners-up[ENTER][TAB]daughters-in-law[ENTER][HOME][HOME][UP ARROW][SHIFT-F8]lm2.5[ENTER] 1.5[ENTER][F7]{Press the DOWN ARROW key to make WordPerfect reformat the paragraph with the new margins.}

4. [CAPS LOCK]abc company - memo[ENTER]d[CAPS LOCK]ate: Friday, Sept 10, 1990[ENTER][ESC]65-[ENTER]

When using the copier by the coffee machine, use only the paper stacked next to the machine. Since the machine is old, if you use different paper (envelopes, letterheads, etc.), the machine jams.[HOME] [HOME][UP ARROW][SHIFT-F8]lm3[ENTER]3[ENTER][F7][SHIFT-F7]v[F7][HOME][HOME][HOME][UP ARROW][DEL]y

5.2   EXERCISES

1. [SHIFT-F4][SHIFT-F4][SHIFT-F4][SHIFT-F4]{Type the paragraph as shown.}[ENTER]

2. [F4]{Retype the paragraph from exercise 1.}[ENTER] The meeting is scheduled for 9:00 a.m. in the board room.[ENTER]

3. [ALT-F3][HOME][HOME][HOME][UP ARROW][DEL][ALT-F3]

4. [SHIFT-F4]Frequently saving work in progress is a good habit that all computer users should acquire. It avoids the potential for loss of large amounts of work due to power outages, someone tripping over a power cord, etc.[ENTER]

5.3   EXERCISES

1. [SHIFT-TAB][SHIFT-TAB]You can use the Margin Release feature to make an indented paragraph begin at the left margin. You can also use it to fit additional characters on a line.

2. Name:[ENTER][SHIFT-TAB][SPACEBAR][SPACEBAR]Address: [ENTER][SHIFT-TAB][SHIFT-TAB]{Depending on the printer: 0, 1, or 2 [SPACEBAR]'s}Phone Number: [ENTER][SHIFT-TAB][SHIFT-TAB]{Depending on the printer: 1, 2, or 3 [SPACEBAR]'s}Soc. Sec.:

EXERCISES _____ 5.4

1. [SHIFT-F8]lt3.3[ENTER][F7][F7]

2. [SHIFT-F8]lt6[ENTER][SPACEBAR][CTRL-END][F7][F7]

3. [SHIFT-F8]lt4[ENTER]r[F7][F7]

4. [SHIFT-F8]lt2.5[ENTER]d[F7][F7]

5. [SHIFT-F8]lt[HOME][HOME][LEFT ARROW][CTRL-END]2[ENTER] 4.5[ENTER][F7][F7][TAB]Jones[TAB]17,850[ENTER] [TAB]Culver[TAB]23,489[ENTER][TAB]Walker[TAB]32,500 [ENTER][F7]nn

6. [SHIFT-F8]lt[HOME][HOME][LEFT ARROW][CTRL-END]2,.75 [ENTER] [F7][F7]

7. [SHIFT-F8]lt[HOME][HOME][LEFT ARROW][CTRL-END] −1, .5 {0,.5 in 5.0}[ENTER][F7][F7]

EXERCISES _____ 5.5

1. [ALT-F6][SHIFT-F5]t[ENTER]

2. [ALT-F6]ABC COMPANY[ENTER]

3. MEMO[ENTER]To: All Employees[ALT-F6]Date: [SPACEBAR][SHIFT-F5]t[ENTER]From: Arnold Smith[ALT-F6]Re: Cleaning Computer Screens[ENTER][ESC]65 [SHIFT-MINUS][ENTER]Do not use alcohol-based window cleaners to clean your computer screen. Use the special cleaner that is stored with the blank disks.[ENTER]

5.6   EXERCISES

1. A sense of humor sharp enough to show a man his own absurdities will keep him from the commission of all sins, or nearly all, except those that are worth committing.[ENTER](Samuel Butler from Life and Habit)[ENTER][HOME][HOME][UP ARROW][SHIFT-F8]ls2[ENTER][F7][SHIFT-F8]ls3[ENTER][F7][SHIFT-F8]ls1 [ENTER][F7]

2. [TAB]The new Widget maker will expand our current capacity to meet expected demand levels for the next five to ten years. It has a present net value of $25,687.[ENTER][SHIFT-F8]ls2[ENTER][F7][TAB]The manufacturer gives a 10% trade-in value on its old Widget maker. This is a slightly lower price than expected in the open market. The capital budgeting plan contains the lower trade-in value, but the company will probably sell the used machine in the second-hand market.[ENTER][SHIFT-F8] ls3[ENTER][F7][TAB]The new Widget maker has many new features. One of these, a free one-year service contract, will save the company $50,000 in the first year.[ENTER]{Reveal the codes, and delete

the line-spacing codes at the beginning of paragraphs 2 and 3. There is no code for paragraph 1,
since the defaults are being used.}[HOME][HOME]
[HOME][UP ARROW][SHIFT-F8]ls2[ENTER][F7]{Move to the
beginning of the second paragraph.}[SHIFT-F8]ls3
[ENTER][F7]{Move to the beginning of the third
paragraph.}[SHIFT-F8]ls2[ENTER][F7]

3. When you set the line spacing, WordPerfect uses
   it for all lines after the code in the document.
   [SHIFT-F8]ls2[ENTER][F7]If you change the spacing to
   double spacing in the middle of a paragraph, the
   lines above the change are single spaced, and the
   lines after the change are double spaced.[ENTER]

EXERCISES
5.7

1. The Accounts Receivable computer system was
   installed last January. Due to this new system, the
   average daily accounts receivable amount
   dropped by $50. Also, the percentage of bad ac-
   counts has dropped from 4% to 2%, mostly due
   to quicker action on overdue accounts.[ENTER]
   [SHIFT-F7]v[F7][HOME][HOME][UP ARROW][SHIFT-F8]ljl{n in
   5.0}[F7][SHIFT-F7]v[F7][SHIFT-F8]ljf{y in 5.0}[F7]

2. [TAB]When a paragraph is fully justified, Word-
   Perfect inserts additional space in lines of the
   printed copy of the document. This creates even
   left and right margins. The extra spaces appear
   only in the printed copy and do not appear on
   the screen.[ENTER][SHIFT-F8]ljl{n in 5.0}[F7][TAB]When

a paragraph is left justified, WordPerfect does not insert additional space. The right margin has a jagged appearance.[ENTER][SHIFT-F7]v[F7]

MASTERY SKILLS CHECK

[5.1] 1. {assumes left and right margins are currently 1"}[SHIFT-F8]lm2[ENTER]2[ENTER][F7]Disks store information using magnetized material to hold information. The basic unit of storage is a byte. A byte stores one character of information.[ENTER][F7] ydisk[ENTER]n

[5.2] 2. [F4][F4]Disk drives read information from a disk. The disk drive spins the disk quickly. A read/write head above the disk reads the information as it spins past the head.[ENTER][F7]ydiskread [ENTER]n

[5.4] 3. [SHIFT-F8]lt[HOME][HOME][LEFT ARROW][CTRL-END]4[ENTER] [F7][F7][TAB]Acme Corporation[ENTER][TAB]496 Prospect Road[ENTER][TAB]Cleveland, Ohio 44115 [ENTER][TAB] January 3, 1989[ENTER]

[5.6] 4. [SHIFT-F10]disk[ENTER][SHIFT-F8]ls2[ENTER][F7][F10][ENTER]y

[5.7] 5. [SHIFT-F10]diskread[ENTER][SHIFT-F8]ljl{n in 5.0}[F7][F10] [ENTER]y

[5.5] 6. [ALT-F6]ACC-9876[ENTER][ALT-F6]HDG-3218[ENTER][ALT-F6]CRC-9873[ENTER]

7. [F4][SHIFT-TAB]Campbell, Mary,[SPACEBAR][F8]Teach   [5.2, 5.3]
   Yourself WordPerfect 5.1[F8], Osborne/McGraw-
   Hill, 1990.[ENTER]

INTEGRATING SKILLS CHECK

1. [SHIFT-F8]lm1.5[ENTER][ENTER][F7][SHIFT-TAB]Crosby,   [4.1, 5.1, 5.3]
   'Samuel, "Mergers and Acquisitions,"[SPACEBAR]
   [F8]Business Yearly[F8], (OMB Publishing, 1983),
   June, p. 46-49.[ENTER][ENTER][SHIFT-TAB]Lee, Jane, and
   Lifeson, Tom, "Effectively Combining Com-
   panies,"[F8]Journal of Business Results[SPACEBAR][F8],
   (AMBA, 1987), vol 36, Fall, p. 101-9.[ENTER]

2. [SHIFT-TAB][SHIFT-TAB]Acme Corporation[SHIFT-F6]1560   [4.3, 4.7, 5.3]
   Main Street[ALT-F6]Cleveland, Ohio 44103[ENTER]
   [ALT-F4][HOME][HOME][HOME][LEFT ARROW][F8]

3. Joan Smith[ENTER]President, Widgets Inc.[ENTER]   [3.1, 4.7, 5.7]
   7946 Madison Avenue[ENTER]New York, New York
   10061[ENTER][ENTER]Dear Ms. Smith:[ENTER][ENTER]En-
   closed is the pamphlet you requested, Wrapping
   Consumer Goods. Our products can shrink-wrap
   any product. If you send the dimensions of the
   products that you want to shrink-wrap, one of
   our representatives will prepare a list of the materials and equipment you will need.[ENTER][ENTER]
   [TAB][TAB][TAB][TAB]Sincerely,[ENTER][ENTER][ENTER]
   [ENTER][TAB][TAB][TAB][TAB]LarryKennedy[ENTER][TAB]
   [TAB][TAB][TAB]Plastic Covering Co.[ENTER][HOME]
   [HOME][UP ARROW][SHIFT-F8]ljl{n in 5.0}[F7]{Move to the
   "W" in "Wrapping."}[ALT-F4][CTRL-RIGHT ARROW][CTRL-

RIGHT ARROW][CTRL-RIGHT ARROW][LEFT ARROW][LEFT
ARROW][LEFT ARROW][F8][ALT-F3][BACKSPACE][ALT-F3]
[SHIFT-F7]f

[1.4, 2.1, 4.1, 4.2,
4.3, 4.4, 4.7, 5.1,
5.2, 5.3, 5.4, 5.5,
5.6, 5.7]

4. 1. j   8. a

2. e   9. d

3. g 10. k

4. b 11. m

5. c 12. h

6. i 13. f

7. l

[4.5, 5.5]

5. [ALT-F6][SHIFT-F5]t[HOME][HOME][HOME][UP ARROW][F2][ALT-
F6][F2][BACKSPACE]y

6

[1.4, 4.2]

SKILLS CHECK

1. John Doe[ENTER]23405 Lander Road[ENTER]Cleve-
land, Ohio 44130[ENTER](216)229-8976[ENTER][ENTER]
[F6]Education:[F6][SPACEBAR][SPACEBAR]Cleveland State
University, Cleveland, Ohio[ENTER]Business Ad-
ministration, August 1983[ENTER]Dean's List 7
Quarters, GPA 3.75[ENTER]

[4.6, 4.7]

2. [HOME][UP ARROW][ALT-F4][DOWN ARROW][DOWN
ARROW][DOWN ARROW][DOWN ARROW][SHIFT-F6]y

[4.6, 4.7]

3. [HOME][UP ARROW][ALT-F4][END][F6]

[4.6, 4.7]

4. [DOWN ARROW][DOWN ARROW][DOWN ARROW][DOWN ARROW]
[DOWN ARROW][HOME][LEFT ARROW][ALT-F4][CTRL-RIGHT
ARROW] [LEFT ARROW][LEFT ARROW][LEFT ARROW][F8]

5. [HOME][HOME][UP ARROW][SHIFT-F8]lt.5{1.5 in 5.0}[ENTER]
   [DEL]1{2 in 5.0}[ENTER][DEL]1.2{2.2 in 5.0}[ENTER][F7][F7] [5.4]

6. [HOME][HOME][LEFT ARROW]{may be omitted in 5.0}   [5.2]
   [DOWN ARROW][DOWN ARROW][DOWN ARROW]
   [DOWN ARROW][DOWN ARROW][F4][DOWN ARROW][HOME]
   [LEFT ARROW][F4][DOWN ARROW][HOME][LEFT ARROW][F4]

7. [UP ARROW][UP ARROW][SHIFT-TAB]   [5.3]

8. [SHIFT-F7]f   [3.1]

EXERCISES ————————————————— 6.1

1. [SHIFT-F8]pcy{omit the y in 5.0}[F7][SHIFT-F6]Investiga-
   tion into the Physical Properties of Rust[ENTER]
   [SHIFT-F6]Dissertation[ENTER][SHIFT-F6]Angus McPhearson[ENTER] {To view the centered text, press SHIFT-F7
   and type a **v.**}

2. {The letter body may be different, and the name
   at the bottom should be your own.}[SHIFT-F8]pcy
   {omit the y in 5.0}[F7]Jules McBride[ENTER]234 Main
   Street[ENTER]Lawrence, PA 28634[ENTER][ENTER]Dear
   Jules,[ENTER][ENTER]Thank you for promptly sending the information I requested.[ENTER][ENTER]
   Sincerely,[ENTER][ENTER][ENTER][ENTER]John Doe
   [ENTER]{To view the centered text, press SHIFT-F7 and
   type a **v.**}

3. [SHIFT-F8]pcy{omit the y in 5.0}[F7][SHIFT-F6]1989
   Financial Statements[ENTER][SHIFT-F6]Acme Corporation [ENTER][SHIFT-F7]v[F7]

4. [SHIFT-F8]pcy{omit the y in 5.0}[F7]MEMO:[ENTER]To: All Employees[ENTER]Re: Paychecks[ENTER][ENTER] [TAB]To receive a paycheck September 10th, submit your time card to payroll by September 3rd. [ENTER][SHIFT-F7]v[F7]

6.2   EXERCISES

1. [SHIFT-F8]pm3[ENTER]3[ENTER][F7]{You can press ENTER approximately 29 times before WordPerfect inserts a page break. The exact number depends upon your printer.}

2. [SHIFT-F8]pm0[ENTER]0[ENTER][F7]{You can press ENTER approximately 65 times before WordPerfect inserts a page break. The exact number depends upon your printer.}

3. [SHIFT-F8]pm9.5[ENTER][ENTER][F7]{Type the paragraphs as shown. WordPerfect inserts page breaks.}[SHIFT-F7]v{Press PGUP and PGDN to switch among the pages.}[F7]

6.3   EXERCISES

1. [SHIFT-F8]pn{omit the n in 5.0}p6[F7]Travel Expenses [CTRL-ENTER]Benefits[CTRL-ENTER]Salary Expense[ENTER] [SHIFT-F7]v{Press PGUP and PGDN to switch among the three pages.}[F7]

2. [SHIFT-F8]pn{omit the n in 5.0}p6[F7]1[CTRL-ENTER] 2
[CTRL-ENTER]3[CTRL-ENTER]4[CTRL-ENTER]5[SHIFT-F7]v
{Press PGUP and PGDN to switch among the pages.}
[F7]{Press PGDN until the **Pg** indicator displays 5.}
[SHIFT-F8]pnn {omit the n in 5.0}1[ENTER][F7][PGUP]
[SHIFT-F8]pnn{omit the n in 5.0}2[ENTER][F7][PGUP]
[SHIFT-F8]pnn{omit the n in 5.0}3[ENTER][F7][PGUP]
[SHIFT-F8]pnn{omit the n in 5.0}4[ENTER][F7][PGUP]
[SHIFT-F8]pnn{omit the n in 5.0}5 [ENTER][F7]

EXERCISES 6.4

1. [SHIFT-F8]psALL OTHERS{omit in 5.0}Ls[F7]Legal-
Size Paper[CTRL-ENTER][SHIFT-F8]psStandard(s in
5.0)[F7] Standard-Size Paper[SHIFT-F7]v{Press PGDN
and PGUP to see how WordPerfect will print the
two pages.}[F7]

2. [SHIFT-F8]psALL OTHERS{omit in 5.0}hs[F7]Jim
Adler[ENTER]514 Washington Avenue[ENTER]Colum-
bus, OH 43213[ENTER][SHIFT-F7]v[F7]

MASTERY SKILLS CHECK

1. [SHIFT-F8]pcy{omit the y in 5.0}[F7][SHIFT-F6]Wilbur   [4.3, 6.1]
Horse Supplies[ENTER][SHIFT-F6]Financial Statements
[ENTER][SHIFT-F6]For the Year Ending December 31,
1990[ENTER][SHIFT-F7]v[F7]

[6.2]

2. [HOME][HOME][HOME][UP ARROW][SHIFT-F8]pm3[ENTER]
[ENTER][F7][SHIFT-F7]v[F7]

[6.3]

3. [HOME][HOME][UP ARROW][SHIFT-F8]pn{omit the n in
5.0}p2[F7]

[6.3]

4. [HOME][HOME][DOWN ARROW][CTRL-ENTER][SHIFT-F8]pnn
{omit the n in 5.0}10[ENTER][F7]

[6.4]

5. [SHIFT-F8]psALL OTHERS{omit in 5.0}hs[F7]

INTEGRATING SKILLS CHECK

[4.3]

1. [SHIFT-F6]Archie's California Grapes[ENTER][SHIFT-F6]
Production Records[ENTER][SHIFT-F6]For the season
ending September 30, 1990[ENTER]

[6.1]

2. [HOME][HOME][HOME][UP ARROW][SHIFT-F8]pcy{omit the y
in 5.0}[F7]

[4.7]

3. [ALT-F4][END][F6][CTRL-RIGHT ARROW][ALT-F4][END][F8]

[6.3]

4. [HOME][HOME][DOWN ARROW][CTRL-ENTER][SHIFT-F8]
pn{omit the n in 5.0}p3n1[ENTER][F7]

[5.6]

5. [SHIFT-F8]ls2[ENTER][F7][TAB]This year's crop is the
largest in the last 20 years. It is primarily due
to improved fertilization methods and increased
rainfall. The plants damaged by last year's
drought were replaced.[ENTER]

6. {Move to the beginning of the paragraph.}
[SHIFT-F8]ljl{n in 5.0}[F7]   [5.7]

7. [SHIFT-F7]f   [3.1]

SKILLS CHECK   *7*

1. Product Announcement[ENTER][ENTER][TAB]The XY   [1.4]
Graphics Company has announced the release of
its new product, See 'N' Draw. This package creates custom pictures by combining existing drawings and advanced graphics features. Since each
new feature added to an image is considered a
unique layer, you can edit one layer without affecting the others. The print options offer features
unavailable in any competing product.[ENTER]

2. [HOME][HOME][UP ARROW][ALT-F4][END][F6]   [1.4, 4.7]

3. [ALT-F4][HOME][LEFT ARROW][SHIFT-F6]y   [4.7]

4. [ALT-F3][UP ARROW]{Highlight the [BOLD] codes.}[DEL]   [4.5]

5. [DOWN ARROW][DOWN ARROW][SHIFT-F4]{Press the DOWN   [5.2]
ARROW key to makeWordPerfect reformat the
paragraph.}

6. [HOME][HOME][HOME][UP ARROW][SHIFT-F8]ls2[ENTER][F7]   [5.6]

7. [SHIFT-F8]pcy{omit the y in 5.0}[F7]   [6.1]

8. [SHIFT-F7]p   [3.1]

7.1 EXERCISES

1. On Saturday, May 16, XY Graphics is holding a press conference for their new product, See 'N' Draw. At this conference, the public relations director, Jill Smith, will reveal the company's marketing strategy for the product.[ENTER][HOME][HOME][UP ARROW][F2]Jill Smith[F2]

2. Memory Requirements: 512K[ENTER]Storage Space Required: 200K[ENTER]Number of Disks: 5[ENTER]Tutorial: Yes[ENTER]Demo: Yes[ENTER][HOME][HOME][UP ARROW][F2]5[ENTER][F2]{or[F2]Disks: 5[F2]}

3. {Type the text as shown.}[HOME][HOME][UP ARROW][F2]forgive[F2][F2][F2][F2][F2][F2]{If you search again, WordPerfect will beep and display the message "* Not found *" in the status line.}

4. {Type the text as shown.}[HOME][HOME][UP ARROW][F2]sea[F2]{Press F2 twice. Repeat until WordPerfect beeps and displays the "* Not found *" message. WordPerfect will find "Searching," "seashells," "seashore," "sea," and "season."}[HOME][HOME][UP ARROW][F2][SPACEBAR]sea[SPACEBAR][F2]{WordPerfect will only find "sea" in the last sentence. If you press F2 twice more, WordPerfect will beep and display the "* Not found *" message.}

EXERCISES _____ 7.2

1. The entire project was moved to Tobler Hall under the direction of John Tomita.[SHIFT-F2]to[F2]{The cursor moves to the "m" in "Tomita."}[SHIFT-F2][F2] {The cursor moves to the "b" in "Tobler."}[SHIFT-F2][F2]{The cursor moves to the space between "to" and "Tobler."}[SHIFT-F2][F2]{WordPerfect beeps and displays the "* Not Found *" message, and the cursor remains in place.}

2. The meeting is Friday, August 11th.[SPACEBAR] [SPACEBAR][F8]All must attend.[SPACEBAR][SPACEBAR][F8] Discuss previous commitments with Carol Stevens.[SHIFT-F2][F8][F8][LEFT ARROW][BACKSPACE][F2]{The cursor moves to the space after the period at the end of the second sentence.}

3. {Type the text as shown.}[SHIFT-F2]for[F2]{Press SHIFT-F2 and F2 again, and repeat until WordPerfect beeps and displays the "* Not found *" message. WordPerfect will find "forty," "foreigners," "for," and "forum."}[HOME][HOME][DOWN ARROW][SHIFT-F2] [SPACEBAR]for[SPACEBAR][F2]{WordPerfect will find "for" in the first sentence. If you press SHIFT-F2 and F2 again, WordPerfect will beep and display the "* Not found *" message.}

7.3   EXERCISES

1. Sam Cook is the production manager. He has five years' experience in this position. Prior to this position, Sam Cook was a sergeant in the army. Sam Cook succeeded Thomas MacNamara in his current position.[ENTER][ALT-F2]n[UP ARROW]{This sets the search and replace to operate from the end. Press DEL to remove any previous search string.}Sam Cook[F2]Daniel Jones[F2]{The paragraph now reads: Daniel Jones is the production manager. He has five years' experience in this position. Prior to this position, Daniel Jones was a sergeant in the army. Daniel Jones succeeded Thomas MacNamara in his current position.}

2. WordPerfect's Replace feature allows you to selectively replace one string of characters with another character string. You can have WordPerfect prompt you before completing each replacement, or you can have it make the changes automatically.[ENTER][ALT-F2]n[ENTER][UP ARROW]WordPerfect [F2]WordPerfect 5.1[F2]

3. The Public Relations Director for your area is XX. XX has been with the company for many years and can answer your questions.[ENTER][ALT-F2]n[UP ARROW]XX[F2]Nancy Clark[F2][ALT-F2]nNancy Clark [F2]Martin Smith[F2]

4. You can use WP's Replace feature to shorten typing in a ms or doc. In a ms or doc, you type the

abbreviations in place of the words and have WP replace the abbreviations with the words they represent.[ENTER][ALT-F2]n[UP ARROW]ms[F2]manuscript [F2][ALT-F2]ndoc[F2]document[F2][HOME][HOME][UP ARROW][ALT-F2]nWP[F2]WordPerfect[F2]

MASTERY SKILLS CHECK

1. WordPerfect lets you search for text. You can search either backward or forward. This means that you do not have to move the cursor to a specific location before you can use this feature. [ENTER][HOME][HOME][UP ARROW][F2]search[F2][F2][F2]   [7.1]

2. [HOME][HOME][UP ARROW][F2]you[F2][F2][F2][F2][F2][F2][F2] [F2][F2]{WordPerfect beeps and displays the "* Not found *" message after finding "you" four times.}   [7.1]

3. [HOME][HOME][DOWN ARROW][SHIFT-F2]for[F2]{The cursor moves to the second "e" in "before" in the second sentence.}[SHIFT-F2][F2]{The cursor moves to the "w" in "forward."}[SHIFT-F2][F2]{The cursor moves to the space between "for" and "text" in the first sentence.}[SHIFT-F2][F2]{WordPerfect beeps and displays the "* Not found *" message.}[F7]nn   [7.2]

4. Aeneades was a Trojan prince. He was the son of Diomedes and Achilles. Aeneades married Lavinia.[ALT-F2]n[UP ARROW]Aeneades[CTRL-END][F2] Aeneas[F2]   [7.3]

INTEGRATING SKILLS CHECK

[4.1, 4.3, 4.4, 7.1]   **1.** [SHIFT-F6][F8]<u>Proposal</u>[F8][ENTER][ENTER]The Quick Time division of New Men's Look, Inc., would like to expand their product line to include pocket watches. Adding pocket watches would fit into the division's current production capacity. The plant is operating 30% below capacity. The technology required is already available. This product would also complement the suits produced by another subsidiary, the Taylor division. [ENTER][HOME][HOME][UP ARROW][F2][F8][F2][ALT-F3]

[7.3]   **2.** [ALT-F2]nQuick Time[F2]QUICK TIME[F2]

[7.3]   **3.** [ALT-F2]nTaylor[F2]Tailor[F2]

[6.1]   **4.** [HOME][HOME][UP ARROW][SHIFT-F8]pcy{omit the y in 5.0}[F7]

[3.3]   **5.** [SHIFT-F7]v[F7]

8   SKILLS CHECK

[5.1, 6.2]   **1.** [SHIFT-F8]lm2[ENTER]2[ENTER][F7][SHIFT-F8]pm2[ENTER]2 [ENTER][F7]

[6.3]   **2.** [SHIFT-F8]pn{omit the n in 5.0}p1[F7]

[5.4]   **3.** [SHIFT-F8]lt[HOME][HOME][LEFT ARROW][CTRL-END]1,1[ENTER] [F7][F7]

[4.7]   **4.** Dale Thompson[ENTER]Birds of a Feather[ENTER] 2398 Manzanita Park[ENTER]Stanford, CA 94321

[ENTER] [ENTER]Dear Dale,[ENTER][ENTER]According to your advertisement in Feathered Friends, you are interested in purchasing two white cockatoos. I own several and would like to sell them. Please contact me at (813)212-2634.[ENTER][ENTER][TAB][TAB] [TAB][TAB] Sincerely,[ENTER][ENTER][ENTER][ENTER][TAB] [TAB][TAB][TAB] Byron Wilson[ENTER]{Move to the "F" in "Feathered."}[ALT-F4][CTRL-RIGHT ARROW][CTRL-RIGHT ARROW][LEFT ARROW][LEFT ARROW][F8]

5. [HOME][HOME][UP ARROW][ALT-F2]nwhite cockatoos [F2]parakeets[F2]   [7.3]

6. [SHIFT-F7]f[HOME][HOME][UP ARROW][SHIFT-F8]pcy{omit   [3.1, 6.1]
the y in 5.0}[F7][SHIFT-F7]f

7. [HOME][HOME][UP ARROW][ALT-F3][BACKSPACE][BACKSPACE]   [4.5]
[BACKSPACE][BACKSPACE][ALT-F3]

EXERCISES _____ 8.1

1. A complex sentence consists of an independent clause, which can stand alone, and one or more dependent clauses. A compound sentence is two or more simple sentences joined by a conjunction, such as "and," "or," "but," or "for." A simple sentence expresses a single action or thought. [SPACEBAR][SPACEBAR][ENTER]{Move the cursor to a character in the first sentence.}[CTRL-F4]sm{Move the cursor past the end of the last sentence.} [ENTER]{Move the cursor to a character in what is

now the middle sentence.}[CTRL-F4]sm{Move the cursor to the top of the document.}[ENTER] {Reformat the paragraph}.

2. [TAB]The sun's temperature is 11,000 degrees Fahrenheit at the surface and 35,000,000 degrees in the center. It releases 1.94 calories per square centimeter per minute.[ENTER][TAB]The diameter of the sun is 865,000 miles. It is small by comparison to other stars. The sun's proximity to the earth makes it appear larger than other stars.[ENTER][UP ARROW] [CTRL-F4]pm[HOME][HOME][UP ARROW][ENTER]

3. A nebula is a mass of gas in space.[CTRL-ENTER]A meteoroid is a small object in space.[CTRL-ENTER]A constellation is a group of stars.[CTRL-ENTER][HOME] [HOME][UP ARROW][CTRL-F4]am[HOME][HOME][DOWN ARROW][ENTER]

4. [TAB]Keyboards usually come in two types. A standard keyboard has ten function keys at the side. An enhanced keyboard has 12 function keys across the top.[ENTER][TAB]With WordPerfect, if you have an enhanced keyboard, you can use F11 in place of ALT-F3. You can also use F12 in place of ALT-F4.[ENTER]{Move the cursor to the second sentence.}[CTRL-F4]sm[DOWN ARROW][SPACEBAR] [SPACEBAR][ENTER][CTRL-F4]pm[DOWN ARROW][DOWN ARROW][ENTER][ENTER]

EXERCISES ————————————————— 8.2

1. See 'N' Draw, XY Graphics' new product, should capture a large part of the graphics market for first-time users.[ENTER][UP ARROW][UP ARROW][ALT-F4][CTRL-RIGHT ARROW][CTRL-RIGHT ARROW][CTRL-RIGHT ARROW][CTRL-F4]bm[CTRL-RIGHT ARROW][CTRL-RIGHT ARROW][CTRL-RIGHT ARROW][CTRL-RIGHT ARROW][ENTER]

2. The new machinery funnels the cake mix into preprinted boxes, weighs a predetermined amount of the cake mix, and seals the bag. [ENTER]{Move to the "w" in "weigh."}[ALT-F4]{Move to the "a" in "and."}[CTRL-F4]bm[HOME][HOME][UP ARROW][CTRL-RIGHT ARROW][CTRL-RIGHT ARROW][CTRL-RIGHT ARROW][ENTER]

3. Review meeting agenda.[ENTER]Nominate potential candidates for new director position.[ENTER]Review financial statements.[ENTER]Review minutes from the last meeting.[ENTER]Introduce new corporate treasurer to board.[ENTER][UP ARROW][UP ARROW][ALT-F4][DOWN ARROW][DOWN ARROW][CTRL-F4]bm[UP ARROW][UP ARROW][ENTER]

4. When you move a block, you should check to include any hidden codes in your text. WordPerfect moves all of the codes within the block. If the text that you move is part of a larger block of text that

has special print attributes (for example, bold or underline), the special print characteristics appear in both the moved text and the original. To view the codes, press the Reveal Codes (ALT-F3) key. [ENTER]{Move to the "W" in "WordPerfect."}[ALT-F4]..[RIGHT ARROW][RIGHT ARROW][CTRL-F4]bm[PGUP][ENTER]

8.3   EXERCISES

1. The Office of Human Resources reports that hiring has increased by 14%. This increase is a result of last year's expansion of the Largo division. The increased hiring, which created 1000 new jobs, should not affect next year's personnel needs. [ENTER]{Move the cursor to the period at the end of the first sentence.}[ALT-F4][CTRL-RIGHT ARROW][CTRL-RIGHT ARROW][CTRL-RIGHT ARROW][CTRL-RIGHT ARROW][LEFT ARROW] [CTRL-F4]bd

2. As of May 15, the corporation must increase sales by 15,000 units per month, renovate the corporate offices, and divest itself of its Romper division to meet its 1990 objectives.[ENTER]{Move the cursor to the "r" in "renovate."}[ALT-F4]{Move the cursor to the "a" in "and."}[DEL]y

3. Today's Projects[ENTER]Prepare capital budget request for two computers.[ENTER]Review receivables older than 90 days.[ENTER]Prepare next year's forecast.[ENTER][ALT-F4][UP ARROW][UP ARROW][CTRL-F4]bd

4. Last February, the widget assembler became jammed. While the cause was poor maintenance, the machine's condition requires above-normal maintenance to prevent the problem from recurring. To prevent this problem from recurring, the company should purchase a new machine.[ENTER] {Move the cursor to the second sentence.}[CTRL-F4] sd

EXERCISES _____ 8.4

1. Name: Patrick Rabbit[ENTER]Address: 777 Carrot Lane[ENTER][ALT-F4][UP ARROW][UP ARROW][CTRL-F4]bc [DOWN ARROW][DOWN ARROW][ENTER]{Move to the "P" in "Patrick" in the copy.}[INS]Nancy[DEL][DEL] {Move to the first 7 in 777 in the copy.}515[INS] [DOWN ARROW] [CTRL-F4]rb

2. First, put the correct pens in the plotter. This is an important step. Next, put the paper or transparency in the plotter.[ENTER]{Move the cursor to the second sentence.}[CTRL-F4]sc{Move the cursor to the end of the third sentence.}[SPACEBAR][SPACEBAR] [ENTER]

3. Current Month:[ESC]7.[ENTER]Sales:[ESC]7.[ENTER]Cost of Goods Sold:[ESC]7.[ENTER][UP ARROW][UP ARROW][UP ARROW][ALT-F4][DOWN ARROW][DOWN ARROW][DOWN ARROW] [CTRL-F4]bc[ENTER][CTRL-F4]rb[CTRL-F4]rb[CTRL-F4]rb

4. Directions to the Cloverleaf Hall: Take the interstate to the Bay Street exit. At the exit, turn right,

and take the next left after the light. Stay on this road until you pass the shopping mall on the right. After passing the shopping mall,[SPACEBAR]{Move to the "t" in "take."}[ALT-F4].[CTRL-F4]bc[HOME][DOWN ARROW][END][ENTER]

MASTERY SKILLS CHECK

[8.1]

1. The cost of goods sold is $2,363,782. The beginning inventory is $689,578. The ending inventory is $234,245.[ENTER][HOME][UP ARROW][CTRL-F4]sm[CTRL-RIGHT ARROW][CTRL-RIGHT ARROW][CTRL-RIGHT ARROW][CTRL-RIGHT ARROW][CTRL-RIGHT ARROW][ENTER]

[8.2]

2. The new and improved widget maker has several features. One of these features is the internal painter. This feature evenly coats each widget and limits the fumes, which reduces the number of employees needed to operate the machine. [ENTER]{Move the cursor to the comma in the third sentence.}[ALT-F4].[LEFT ARROW][CTRL-F4]bm{Move the cursor to the period ending the second sentence.} [ENTER]

[8.1, 8.3]

3. Tuesday, the heads of the accounting, production, and MIS departments will review the steps that they can take to reduce the time between the receipt of an order and its completion.[ENTER]{Move the cursor to the beginning of the word "that."} [ALT-F4][CTRL-RIGHT ARROW][CTRL-RIGHT ARROW][CTRL-RIGHT ARROW][CTRL-RIGHT ARROW][DEL]y[CTRL-F4]pd

4. Today's weather will be lovely. The temperature   [8.4]
   will rise to 82 and will cool to an evening low of
   70. The low humidity will contribute to the day's
   pleasant weather.[ENTER][UP ARROW][CTRL-F4]pc[ENTER]
   [CTRL-F4]rb[CTRL-F4]rb

INTEGRATING SKILLS CHECK

1. {Type the text as shown.}[CTRL-ENTER][UP ARROW]   [1.4, 8.1]
   [CTRL-F4]pm[DOWN ARROW][ENTER]

2. [F4][HOME][HOME][DOWN ARROW][F7]nn   [5.2]

3. Marketing Strategy[ENTER][CAPS LOCK]ABC WID-   [1.4, 6.1]
   GETS[CAPS LOCK][ENTER]Prepared on July 7, 1990
   [ENTER][UP ARROW][CTRL-BACKSPACE][CTRL-BACKSPACE]
   [HOME][HOME][UP ARROW][SHIFT-F8]pcy{omit the y in
   5.0}[F7][SHIFT-F7]v[F7] [F7]nn

4. Date:[ENTER]Name:[ENTER]Amount:[ENTER]Explana-   [1.4, 8.4]
   tion:[ENTER]Signature:[ENTER][CTRL-ENTER][HOME][HOME]
   [UP ARROW][ALT-F4][PGDN][CTRL-F4]bc[ENTER]

5. [CTRL-F4]rb[CTRL-F4]rb[CTRL-F4]rb   [8.4]

6. [HOME][HOME][UP ARROW][SHIFT-F8]pn{omit the n in   [3.1, 6.3]
   5.0}p2[F7][SHIFT-F7]f

7. [ALT-F2]nExplanation[F2]For[F2]   [7.3]

SKILLS CHECK   9

1. [SHIFT-F8]lm2[ENTER]2[ENTER][F7]   [5.1]

[6.3]   **2.** [SHIFT-F8]pn{omit the n in 5.0}p1[F7]

[7.2]   **3.** {Type the text as shown.}[ENTER][SHIFT-F2]spell[F2]
[SHIFT-F2][F2]

[7.3]   **4.** [HOME][HOME][UP ARROW][ALT-F2]yit[F2]WordPerfect[F2]
ynyn[F7]

[8.3, 8.4]   **5.** [HOME][HOME][DOWN ARROW][LEFT ARROW][SPACEBAR]
[SPACEBAR]{Enter the text shown.}[UP ARROW][UP
ARROW][UP ARROW]{to move to the second sentence}
[CTRL-F4]sc[HOME][HOME][DOWN ARROW][LEFT ARROW]
[SPACEBAR][SPACEBAR][ENTER]{Move to the "w" in
"when" in the last sentence.}[ALT-F4].[LEFT ARROW]
[DEL]y{Type the new text as shown.}

9.1   EXERCISES

1. {Type the words exactly as shown.}[HOME][HOME][UP
ARROW][CTRL-F2]wawwwaww[F7]

2. {Type the text exactly as shown.}[HOME][HOME][UP
ARROW][CTRL-F2]wawwawwwwwdwwcwwwhw[F7]

3. {Type the text exactly as shown.}[HOME][HOME][UP
ARROW][CTRL-F2]w2w2wwdwwb[F7]

4. {Type the text exactly as shown.}[HOME][LEFT
ARROW][CTRL-F2]w4[RIGHT ARROW][RIGHT ARROW][SPACEBAR]
[F7]ww4p[F7]w4[RIGHT ARROW][RIGHT ARROW][SPACEBAR]
[F7]ww4p[DEL][F7]w4[RIGHT ARROW][RIGHT ARROW][RIGHT

ARROW][SPACEBAR][F7]ww4[RIGHT ARROW][RIGHT ARROW]
[RIGHT ARROW][SPACEBAR][F7]w[SPACEBAR]

EXERCISES — 9.2

1. {Type the paragraph as shown.}[CTRL-F2]db2aa
   [ENTER]

2. {Type the paragraph as shown.}[CTRL-F2]dagaa
   [ENTER]

3. {Type the paragraph as shown.}[CTRL-F2]d2aia[F7]

4. {Type the paragraph as shown.}[CTRL-F2]daadd[F7]

EXERCISES — 9.3

1. {Type the paragraph as shown.}[CTRL-F2]d333
   [SPACEBAR]

2. {Type the paragraph as shown.}[CTRL-F2]d333aa3333 [SPACEBAR]

3. {Type the paragraph as shown.}[CTRL-F2]d333333
   [SPACEBAR]

4. WordPerfect does[ENTER]does not[ENTER]not check
   to see if the[ENTER]the last word of one paragraph
   is the same word as the[ENTER]first word word of
   the next paragraph.[ENTER][CTRL-F2]d3{The speller
   finds only the double word in the last two lines.}

9.4   EXERCISES

1. {Type the names and addresses as shown.}[CTRL-F2]d33333[ENTER]

2. {Type your name.}[CTRL-F2]d{Type **3** to add any part of your name to the dictionary if Word-Perfect does not recognize it.}[ENTER]

3. Abbreviations[ENTER]ATMOS - Atmosphere[ENTER] IDP - Integrated Data Processing[ENTER]OCS - Officer Candidate School[ENTER]SWAZ - Swaziland [ENTER][CTRL-F2]d3333[SPACEBAR]

4. {Type the paragraph as it appears.}[CTRL-F2]d333 [SPACEBAR]

9.5   EXERCISES

1. [SHIFT-F10]wp{wp}us.sup{en.sup in 5.0}[ENTER]{Position the cursor on the first character in a word you wish to remove.}[CTRL-BACKSPACE][DEL]{For each word you wish to remove, move the cursor to the word, and repeat the keystrokes.[F10][ENTER]y

2. [F7]nn[SHIFT-F10]wp{wp}us.sup[ENTER]{Press the DOWN ARROW key to move the cursor to "ATMOS" if it is not already there.}[CTRL-BACKSPACE][DEL]{Press the DOWN ARROW key to move the cursor to "IDP."} [CTRL-BACKSPACE][DEL]{Press the DOWN ARROW key to move the cursor to "OCS."}[CTRL-BACKSPACE][DEL]

{Press the DOWN ARROW key to move the cursor to "SWAZ."}[CTRL-BACKSPACE][DEL][F10][ENTER]y

3. [F7]nn[SHIFT-F10]wp{wp}us.sup[ENTER]{Press the DOWN ARROW key to move the cursor to "Aphrodite" if it is not already there.}[CTRL-BACKSPACE][DEL]{Press the DOWN ARROW key to move the cursor to "Audrey."} [CTRL-BACKSPACE][DEL]{Press the DOWN ARROW key to move the cursor to "Galatea."}[CTRL-BACKSPACE][DEL] {Press the DOWN ARROW key to move the cursor to "Pygmalion."}[CTRL-BACKSPACE][DEL][F10][ENTER]y

EXERCISES _____ 9.6

1. The fair four the bridge to get to the fare is for dollars.[ENTER][ALT-F2]y[UP ARROW]fair[CTRL-END] [F2]fare[F2]y[HOME][LEFT ARROW][ALT-F2]yfare[F2]fair [F2]ny[HOME][LEFT ARROW][ALT-F2]yfor[F2]four[F2]y [HOME][LEFT ARROW][ALT-F2]yfour[F2]for[F2]yn

2. Their demonstrating there new product over they're.[ALT-F2]ythere[UP ARROW][F2]their[F2]y[HOME] [LEFT ARROW][ALT-F2]ythey're[F2]there[F2]y[HOME][LEFT ARROW] [ALT-F2]ytheir[F2]they're[F2]yn

EXERCISES _____ 9.7

1. [ALT-F1]table[ENTER][F7]

2. [ALT-F1]adjoining[ENTER][F7]

3. rich[ALT-F1]c[F7]

4. [ALT-F1]limit[ENTER][RIGHT ARROW]d[RIGHT ARROW]ehdd
[LEFT ARROW][LEFT ARROW]44[F7]

9.8   EXERCISES

1. {Type the sentence as shown.}[CTRL-LEFT ARROW][ALT-F1]1j

2. {Type the sentence as shown. Then, move the cursor to "division."}[ALT-F1]1m

3. {Type the sentence as shown. Then, move the cursor to "Business."}[ALT-F1][RIGHT ARROW]1a

4. {Type the paragraph.}[ENTER][UP ARROW][UP ARROW]
[CTRL-RIGHT ARROW][ALT-F1]1k[CTRL-RIGHT ARROW] [CTRL-RIGHT ARROW][CTRL-RIGHT ARROW][ALT-F1]1n[CTRL-RIGHT ARROW][CTRL-RIGHT ARROW][CTRL-RIGHT ARROW][CTRL-RIGHT ARROW][ALT-F1]1l[CTRL-RIGHT ARROW][CTRL-RIGHT ARROW]
[CTRL-RIGHT ARROW][CTRL-RIGHT ARROW][CTRL-RIGHT ARROW][CTRL-RIGHT ARROW][ALT-F1]1m

MASTERY SKILLS CHECK

[9.1]   1. {Type each word as shown, pressing ENTER at the end of each one.}[HOME][HOME][UP ARROW][CTRL-F2]
wawawaw[F7]

[9.2]   2. {Type the paragraph as shown.}[ENTER][CTRL-F2]
d2c3b3[SPACEBAR]

3. {Type the letter as shown.}[CTRL-F2]d{Type a 3 for   [9.4]
   each proper name suggested as a misspelling to
   add it to the dictionary.}[SPACEBAR]

4. [SHIFT-F10]wp{wp}us.sup[ENTER]{Move the cursor to   [9.5]
   the first name; press CTRL-BACKSPACE and the DEL
   key. Repeat this process for each name that you
   added.}[F10][ENTER]y

5. {Type the paragraph as shown.}[HOME][HOME][UP   [9.6]
   ARROW][ALT-F2]yfor[F2]four[F2]y{Repeat the replace
   process for the homonyms "it's" and "its,"
   "moor" and "more," "too" and "to," and "two"
   and "to."}

6. [ALT-F1]bar[ENTER]e3light[ENTER][F7]   [9.7]

7. {Type the sentence as shown.}[HOME][HOME][UP   [9.8]
   ARROW][CTRL-RIGHT ARROW][CTRL-RIGHT ARROW][ALT-F1]1e

INTEGRATING SKILLS CHECK

1. [SHIFT-F8]lm3[ENTER]3[ENTER][ENTER]pm3[ENTER]3[ENTER]   [5.1, 6.2]
   [F7]

2. {Type the paragraph as shown.}[ENTER][CTRL-F2]   [9.2]
   daaaaa[SPACEBAR]

3. {Type the paragraph as shown.}[CTRL-F2]   [9.2, 9.4]
   d33a[SPACEBAR]

4. [CTRL-F4]pm[HOME][HOME][UP ARROW][ENTER]   [8.1]

[8.4]   5. {Move to the beginning of the second paragraph.}[ALT-F4][ENTER][CTRL-F4]bc[ENTER][CTRL-F4]
rb[CTRL-F4]rb

[9.8]   6. {Type the sentence; then move the cursor to the
word "light."}[ALT-F1]1m

[3.1]   7. [SHIFT-F7]f

[2.2]   8. [F10]words[ENTER]

[9.5]   9. [F7]nn[SHIFT-F10]wp{wp}us.sup[ENTER]{Move the cursor to "Howard."}[CTRL-BACKSPACE][DEL]{Repeat this
procedure for "Moore."}[F10][ENTER]y

10   SKILLS CHECK

[9.2]   1. {Type the paragraph as shown.}[CTRL-F2]daa

[9.8]   2. {Move the cursor to "decides."}[ALT-F1]1as{The "s"
changes the verb tense to fit the context of the
sentence.}

[8.1]   3. [HOME][HOME][UP ARROW][CTRL-F4]sm[HOME][HOME][DOWN
ARROW][LEFT ARROW][SPACEBAR][SPACEBAR][ENTER]

[7.1]   4. [HOME][HOME][UP ARROW][F2]date[F2]{Repeat the F2
sequence until the "* Not found *" message
appears.}

[8.3]   5. {Move the cursor to the last sentence.}[CTRL-F4]sd

EXERCISES ———————————— 10.1

1. [SHIFT-F8]pm5[ENTER]5[ENTER][F7]{Type the paragraphs as shown.}[HOME][HOME][UP ARROW][SHIFT-F8]lwy[F7] {Move the cursor down the screen.}

2. [SHIFT-F8]pm5[ENTER]5[ENTER][F7]{Type the paragraph as shown.}[HOME][HOME][UP ARROW][SHIFT-F8]lwy[F7] {Move the cursor to the bottom of the document to reformat the paragraph.}[F7]ylifo[ENTER]n

3. [SHIFT-F10]lifo[ENTER][ALT-F3][LEFT ARROW][BACKSPACE][ALT-F3][SHIFT-F8]pm[ENTER]9[ENTER][F7]{Press the DOWN ARROW key until you reach the bottom of the document.} [F7][ENTER][ENTER]y[ENTER]

4. [SHIFT-F10]lifo[ENTER][SHIFT-F8]lm3[ENTER]3[ENTER][F7] {Press the DOWN ARROW key until you reach the bottom of the document.}[F7][ENTER][ENTER]y[ENTER]

EXERCISES ———————————— 10.2

1. [SHIFT-F8]phapAcme Inc. Income Statement [F7][F7][SHIFT-F7]v1[F7]

2. [SHIFT-F8]pfap[F6]{Type your name.}[F6][F7][F7][SHIFT-F7]v{Press the DOWN ARROW key repeatedly until the footer appears on the screen.}[F7]

3. [SHIFT-F8]phap[SHIFT-F6]-[CTRL-B]-[F7][F7][SHIFT-F7]v[F7]

4. [SHIFT-F8]phao[CTRL-B][F7]hbv{Type your name.} [F7][F7][CTRL-ENTER][SHIFT-F7]v[PGDN][F7]

10.3   EXERCISES

1. {Type the sentence as shown.}[CTRL-F7]fc[SPACEBAR] {Type the footnote text.}[F7][F7]nn

2. Once upon a time, . . . [CTRL-F7]fc[SPACEBAR]Grimm Brothers Fairy Tales[F7][ENTER]Mary had a little lamb[CTRL-F7]fc[SPACEBAR]Mother Goose[F7][ENTER]The Goose That Laid a Golden Egg[CTRL-F7]fc[SPACEBAR] Aesop's Fables[F7][ENTER]

3. [HOME][HOME][UP ARROW][CTRL-F4]pm[HOME][HOME][DOWN ARROW][ENTER]{You may need to press the DOWN ARROW key to make WordPerfect renumber the footnote.}

4. [CTRL-F7]fe3[ENTER]{Make the changes specified.}[F7]

MASTERY SKILLS CHECK

[10.1]   **1.** [SHIFT-F8]pm[ENTER]9[ENTER][F7]{Type the text as shown.}[ENTER][HOME][HOME][UP ARROW][SHIFT-F8]lwy[F7] {You may need to press the DOWN ARROW key to make WordPerfect reformat the paragraph.}

[10.3]   **2.** {Place the cursor before the tab at the beginning of the paragraph.}[CTRL-ENTER][HOME][HOME][DOWN ARROW][LEFT ARROW][CTRL-F7]fc[SPACEBAR]{Type the footnote text.}[F7]

3. {Move the cursor to the end of the second   [10.3]
   sentence.}[CTRL-F7]fc[SPACEBAR]{Type the footnote
   text.}[F7]

4. [CTRL-F7]fe1[ENTER]{Make the changes shown.}[F7]   [10.3]

5. [HOME][HOME][UP ARROW][SHIFT-F8]phapPreparing a   [10.2]
   Trial Balance[F7][F7][CTRL-END][DEL][DEL]

6. [SHIFT-F8]pfao{Type your name.}[F7][F7][SHIFT-F7]   [10.2]
   v{Page through the document with the PGUP and
   PGDN keys.}

INTEGRATING SKILLS CHECK

1. {Type the address labels as shown. Move to the   [1.4]
   end of the first ZIP code.}[CTRL-ENTER]{Repeat for
   the other addresses.}

2. {Move to the bottom of the first page, press ENTER   [9.7]
   twice, and type the letter text as shown.}{Move
   the cursor to "continue."}[ALT-F1][F7]{Move the cursor to "receive."}[ALT-F1][F7]

3. [CTRL-F2]p{The only words the Spell feature should   [9.2]
   highlight are "Johann," "Sebastian," and "Elsie;"
   you can skip them or add them to the dictionary.}

4. {Move the cursor to the space after the comma   [10.3]
   following "publication."}[CTRL-F7]fc[SPACEBAR]{Type
   the footnote text.}[F7]

5. [CTRL-F7]fe1[ENTER]{Make the change shown.}[F7]   [10.3]

[8.4]   6. {Move the cursor to the beginning of the letter.}[ALT-F4]{Move the cursor to the bottom of the letter.}[CTRL-F4]bc{Move the cursor to the end of the ZIP code in Karl Davis's address.}[ENTER] [ENTER][ENTER]{Move the cursor to the end of the ZIP code in Angus Fuller's address.}[ENTER][ENTER] [CTRL-F4]rb

[10.2]   7. [HOME][HOME][UP ARROW][SHIFT-F8]phap[ALT-F6]{Type your name.}[F7][F7]

11   SKILLS CHECK

[8.1]   1. {Type the paragraphs, pressing ENTER after each one.}[UP ARROW][CTRL-F4]pm[UP ARROW][UP ARROW][UP ARROW][ENTER]

[9.2]   2. [CTRL-F2]d{Fix any spelling errors as WordPerfect finds them; the original had none.}

[9.8]   3. {Move to "redeem."}[ALT-F1]1l

[6.2]   4. [HOME][HOME][UP ARROW][SHIFT-F8]pm5[ENTER]5[ENTER] [F7]

[10.1]   5. [SHIFT-F8]lwy[F7]

[10.3]   6. {Move to the end of the convertible bonds paragraph.}[CTRL-F7]fcUsually in exchange for common stock[F7]

[2.2]   7. [F7][ENTER]stocks[ENTER][ENTER]

EXERCISES ————————————— 11.1

1. The pension plan is expected to earn 6% per year. New employees become vested in the plan after five years with the company.[ENTER][F10]plan [ENTER][F7]nn[F5][ENTER]{Move the highlight to the PLAN filename.}cearn[ENTER][F7]

2. {Place a disk in drive A.}[F5][ENTER]{Move the highlight to the PLAN filename.}ca:plan[ENTER][F7]

3. [SHIFT-F10]plan[ENTER][F10]vested[ENTER]

4. [F5][ENTER]{Move the highlight to the EARN filename.}cpenplan[ENTER][F7]

5. [SHIFT-F10]vested[ENTER]{Place a disk in drive A.} [F10]a:vested[ENTER]

EXERCISES ————————————— 11.2

1. [F5] = \finance[ENTER]y

2. [F5] = letters[ENTER]y

3. [F5] = \finance\finc1989[ENTER]y

4. [F5] = \finance\finc1990[ENTER]y

11.3   EXERCISES

1. [F5]=\finance[ENTER][F1]

2. [F5]=\wp51{\wp50 in 5.0}\letters[ENTER][F1]

3. [F5]=\finance\finc1990[ENTER][F1]

4. [F5]=\finance\finc1991[ENTER][F1]

5. [F5]=\wp51{\wp50 in 5.0}[ENTER][F1]

11.4   EXERCISES

1. {Put the disk containing the PLAN file in drive A.}[F5]a:[ENTER]{Move the highlight to the PLAN file.}dy[F7]

2. [F5][ENTER]{Move the highlight to the LETTERS subdirectory.}dy[F7]

3. [F5]\finance[ENTER]{Move the highlight to the FINC1990 subdirectory.}dy[F7]

4. [F5]\finance[ENTER]{Move the highlight to the FINC1991 subdirectory.}dy[F7]

11.5   EXERCISES

1. [F5][ENTER]{Move the highlight to the PLAN file.} mpension3[ENTER][F7]

2. [F5][ENTER]{Move the highlight to the EARN file.}m[END]ed[ENTER][F7]

3. [SHIFT-F10]EARNED[F10]ERN＿INC[ENTER][F7]n[ENTER][F5] [ENTER]{Move the highlight to the ERN＿INC filename.}m{Move the cursor to the "R" in "ERN."}a[ENTER][F7]

EXERCISES _____ 11.6

1. {In 5.1, do the following:}
[SHIFT-F8]dsnBlank Quit Claim Sales Contract
[ENTER]Contract[ENTER]tJonas Smith[ENTER]Karen
Polk[ENTER]sUndeveloped Real Estate[ENTER]kForm
Contract Quit Claim[ENTER]aThis blank contract
covers most undeveloped land sales in the state
of Florida. This contract has four Xs where you
must fill in information. Paragraphs contained in
braces are optional. Remove them if they are unnecessary for a particular contract.[F7][F7][F7][ENTER]
contract[ENTER]n
{In 5.0, do the following:}
[SHIFT-F8]dsdBlank Quit Claim Sales Contract
[ENTER]sUndeveloped Real Estate[ENTER]aJonas
Smith[ENTER]tKaren Polk[ENTER]cThis blank contract
covers most undeveloped land sales in the state
of Florida. This contract has four Xs where you
must fill in information. Paragraphs contained in
braces are optional. Remove them if they are unnecessary for a particular contract.[F7][F7][F7][ENTER]
contract[ENTER]n

2. {In 5.1, do the following:}
[SHIFT-F8]dsnAugust 17th meeting notes[ENTER]
[ENTER]SHIFT-F10]y[F7][F10]issues[ENTER]
{In 5.0, do the following:}
The August 17th meeting discussed the following
issues:[ENTER]Installation of new parking lot
lights[ENTER]Hiring of security personnel to patrol
the parking lots after dark[ENTER]Completion of
new research and development building[ENTER]Im-
proved insurance benefits[ENTER][SHIFT-F8]dsdAugust
17th meeting notes[ENTER][F7][F10]issues[ENTER]

3. WordPerfect's Graphics features are among the
mostadvanced in the industry. Investing some
time in mastering these features could offer a significant payoff for our company. Outside service
costs for creating newsletters and brochures can
be reduced significantly.[ENTER]
{In 5.1, do the following:}
[SHIFT-F8]dsnCut costs with WordPerfect's
Graphics[ENTER]Product[ENTER][SHIFT-F10]ya[CTRL-PGDN]
Reduce newsletter and brochure development
costs with Graphics features. We can recover the
cost of the upgrade to 5.1 with the first job.[F7][F7]
[F7][ENTER]saving[ENTER][ENTER]
{In 5.0, do the following:}
[SHIFT-F8]dsdCut costs with WordPerfect's
Graphics[ENTER]c[CTRL-PGDN]Reduce newsletter and
brochure development costs with Graphics fea-
tures. We can recover the cost of the upgrade to
5.1 with the first job.[F7][F7][F7][ENTER]saving[ENTER]
[ENTER]

4. [SHIFT-F10]issues[ENTER][SHIFT-F8]dst[ENTER]{omit[ENTER]in 5.0}[CTRL-END]Martha King[ENTER][F7]

EXERCISES 11.7

1. [F5][ENTER]f{w in 5.0}dAugust[ENTER]{The ISSUES file will be listed; additional files may be included (in 5.0, ISSUES will have an asterisk next to it).} [F7]

2. [F5][ENTER]f{w in 5.0}p{f in 5.0}Acme Corporation [ENTER]{The PENSCONT file will be listed; additional files may be included (in 5.0, PENSCONT will have an asterisk next to it).}[F7]

3. [F5][ENTER]f{w in 5.0}eplan[ENTER]{The EARNED, EARN_INC, PENSION, PENSCONT, PENSION3, and VESTED files will be listed (in 5.0, they will have asterisks next to them).}[F7]

4. [F5][ENTER]f{w in 5.0}e{Type your first name.} [ENTER]{Various files may be listed{in 5.0, they will have asterisks next to them.}we{Type your last name.}[ENTER]{Various files may have asterisks next to them.}we{Type your first name, a semi-colon, and your last name.}[ENTER]{Various files may have asterisks next to them.}we{Type your first name, a comma, and your last name.}[ENTER] {Various files may have asterisks next to them.}[F7]

5. [F5][ENTER]f{w in 5.0}dcompany;product[ENTER][F7]

6. [F5][ENTER]f{w in 5.0}epension,contract[ENTER][F7]

11.8 EXERCISES

1. [F5][ENTER]{Move the highlight to the EARNED filename.}[ENTER]{Look through the file.}[F7][F7]

2. [F5][ENTER]{Move the highlight to the CONTRACT file.}[ENTER]{Look through the file.}[F7][F7]

3. [F5][ENTER]{Move the highlight to the ISSUES filename.}[ENTER]{Look through the file.}[F7][F7]

4. [F5][ENTER]{Move the highlight to the PENPLAN filename.}[ENTER]{Look through the file.}[F7][F7]

5. [F5][ENTER]{Move the highlight to the STOCKS filename.}[ENTER]{Look through the file.}[F7][F7]

MASTERY SKILLS CHECK

[11.2]   1. [F5][ENTER]obudget91[ENTER]y[F7]

[11.1]   2. Acme Corporation - 1991 Budget[ENTER][ENTER]Estimated Sales[TAB][TAB]$1,000,000[ENTER]Fixed Costs[TAB][TAB][TAB]$[SPACEBAR][SPACEBAR]400,000[ENTER]Variable Costs[TAB][TAB][TAB]$[SPACEBAR][SPACEBAR]400,000[ENTER]Gross Profit[TAB][TAB][TAB]$[SPACEBAR][SPACEBAR]

200,000[ENTER][F10]BUDGET[ENTER][F7]nn[F5][ENTER]
{Move the highlight to the BUDGET filename.}
cbudget91[ENTER][F7]

3. [F5]=budget91[ENTER][F1]   [11.3]

4. [F5][ENTER]{Move the highlight to the BUDGET   [11.1]
   filename.}cbdgt1991[ENTER][F7]

5. [F5][ENTER]{Move the highlight to the BUDGET   [11.4]
   filename.}dy[F7]

6. [F5][ENTER]{Move the highlight to the BDGT1991   [11.5]
   filename.}m[END][LEFT ARROW][LEFT ARROW]
   [BACKSPACE][BACKSPACE][ENTER][F7]

7. {In 5.1, do the following:}   [11.6]
   [SHIFT-F8]dsnBudget1991[ENTER]Budget[ENTER]tJane
   Smith[ENTER]John Dow[ENTER]sAcme Corporation
   [ENTER]c10023[ENTER]aMichael McCormick must
   have this report by September 30, 1990.[F7][F7]
   {In 5.0, do the following:}
   [SHIFT-F10]bdgt91[ENTER][SHIFT-F8]dsdBudget
   1991[ENTER]sAcme Corporation[ENTER]aJane Smith
   [ENTER]tJohn Dow[ENTER]cMichael McCormick
   must have this report bySeptember 30,
   1990.[F7][F7]

8. [F10][ENTER]y   [11.6]

9. [F5][ENTER]f{w in 5.0}dBudget[ENTER][F7]   [11.7]

10. [F7]nn[F5][ENTER]{Move the highlight to the   [11.8]
    BDGT90 filename.}[ENTER]{Use the cursor move-
    ment keys to look at the file.}[F7][F7]

[11.3]   **11.** [F5] =\wp51{\wp50 in 5.0}[ENTER][F1]

INTEGRATING SKILLS CHECK

[9.2]   **1.** {Type the paragraphs, pressing ENTER at the end of each one.}[CTRL-F2]d{Fix any spelling errors as WordPerfect finds them; the original has none.}

[2.2]   **2.** [F10]prefer[ENTER]

[11.1]   **3.** [F5][ENTER]}{Move the highlight to the PREFER filename.}cpreferrd[ENTER][F7]

[11.3]   **4.** [F5][ENTER]ostock[ENTER]y[F7]

[1.3]   **5.** [F7]nn

[11.1]   **6.** [F5][ENTER]}{Move the highlight to the PREFERRD filename.}cstock[ENTER][F7]

[11.3]   **7.** [F5] = stock[ENTER][F1][SHIFT-F10]preferrd[ENTER]

[8.1]   **8.** {This answer moves "participation" to the bottom and "conversion" between "callable" and "cumulative;" there are other methods to accomplish this.}[HOME][HOME][UP ARROW][DOWN ARROW] [DOWN ARROW][CTRL-F4]pm[PGDN][ENTER][UP ARROW] [CTRL-F4]pm[UP ARROW][UP ARROW][UP ARROW][ENTER]

[6.2]   **9.** [HOME][HOME][UP ARROW][SHIFT-F8]pm5[ENTER]5[ENTER][F7]

[10.1]   **10.** [SHIFT-F8]lwy[F7]

[2.2]   **11.** [F10][ENTER]y

12. [F5]c:\wp51{\wp50 in 5.0}[ENTER]{Move the cursor [11.4] to the PREFER filename.}dy[F7]

13. [F2]dividend[F2]{"Dividend" first occurs in the [7.1] explanation of "Cumulative."}

14. {Move the cursor to "fluctuates."}[ALT-F1]{Look at [9.7] the synonyms.}[F7]{Move the cursor to "extent."} [ALT-F1]{Look at the synonyms.}[F7]

SKILLS CHECK

12

1. {Type the paragraph as shown.}[CTRL-F2] [9.2] da3aa{Press any key.}

2. {Move the cursor to the word "customize."} [9.8] [ALT-F1]1f

3. [HOME][HOME][UP ARROW][SHIFT-F8]phapWordPerfect [10.2] Print Features[F7]fap[SHIFT-F6]Page[SPACEBAR][CTRL-B] [F7][F7][SHIFT-F7]v3[F7]

4. {In 5.1, do the following:} [11.6] [SHIFT-F8]dsnDescribing WordPerfect's Print features[ENTER][ENTER]t{Type your name} [ENTER]{Type your name}[ENTER]sTeach Yourself WordPerfect [ENTER][SHIFT-F10]y {In 5.0, do the following:} [SHIFT-F8]dsdDescribing WordPerfect's Print fea- tures[ENTER]sTeach Yourself WordPerfect[ENTER] a{Type your name.}[ENTER]t{Type your name.} [ENTER][F7]

5. [F10]advprint[ENTER][F5][ENTER]{Move the highlight [11.1, 11.4, 11.5] to the ADVPRINT file.}cprintadv[ENTER]

mprntfeat[ENTER][F7]{Since WordPerfect does not refresh the screen when you copy files, you must leave List Files and reenter it.}[F5][ENTER]{Move the highlight to the PRINTADV file.}dy[F7]

12.1   EXERCISES

1. {Type the paragraph as shown.}[ENTER][SHIFT-F7] n3[ENTER]f[F7][ENTER]filedel[ENTER]n

2. {Type the paragraph as shown.}[ENTER][SHIFT-F7] n2[ENTER]f[F7][ENTER]rename[ENTER]n

3. [SHIFT-F7]n3[ENTER]dprintopt[ENTER][ENTER][F7]

4. [SHIFT-F7]n2[ENTER]dwpset[ENTER][ENTER][F7]

5. [SHIFT-F7]dfiledel[ENTER][ENTER]n1[ENTER]dwpset [ENTER][ENTER][F7]

12.2   EXERCISES

1. [SHIFT-F7]n3[ENTER]drename[ENTER][ENTER]c[F7]

2. [SHIFT-F7]drename[ENTER][ENTER]n2[ENTER]dfiledel [ENTER] [ENTER]n1[ENTER]dwpset[ENTER][ENTER]c{Wait until WordPerfect finishes all three jobs.}[F7]

EXERCISES ———————————————— 12.3

1. [SHIFT-F7]n5[ENTER]drename[ENTER][ENTER]cc{Type the number of the RENAME print job}[ENTER][F7]

2. [SHIFT-F7]n3[ENTER]drename[ENTER][ENTER]dfiledel [ENTER] [ENTER]dwpset[ENTER][ENTER]cc*y[F7]

3. {Turn the printer off.}[SHIFT-F7]n1[ENTER]dfiledel [ENTER][ENTER]cc{Type the number of the FILEDEL print job.}[ENTER][F7]

4. [SHIFT-F7]dwpset[ENTER][ENTER]dfiledel[ENTER][ENTER] drename[ENTER][ENTER]cc{Type the number of the WPSET print job.}[ENTER]c{Type the number of the RENAME print job.}[ENTER][F7]{Turn the printer on.}

EXERCISES ———————————————— 12.4

1. [SHIFT-F7]drename[ENTER][ENTER]dfiledel[ENTER][ENTER] dprintopt[ENTER][ENTER]cr{Type the number of the PRINTOPT print job.}[ENTER]y[F7]

2. {Turn the printer off.}[SHIFT-F7]dwpset[ENTER][ENTER] dfiledel[ENTER][ENTER]drename[ENTER][ENTER]cr{Type the number of the RENAME print job.}[ENTER] {Since the first one has not started printing, the third print request will print before the first one,

and WordPerfect will not prompt you for interrupting the current print job.}{Turn the printer
on.}g[F7]

12.5   EXERCISES

1. [SHIFT-F10]wpset[ENTER][SHIFT-F7]tmf

2. [SHIFT-F7]thf

3. [SHIFT-F7]tdf

12.6   EXERCISES

1. When you change the font, all characters after the
font change are affected.[CTRL-F8]f{Move the highlight to a font that has a smaller CPI, smaller
pitch, or larger point size than the one originally
highlighted.}[ENTER]Characters before the font
change use the initial setting of your printer.[SHIFT-
F7]v1[F7]

2. Fonts can also be proportionally spaced.[CTRL-F8]f{If
your printer has a proportionally spaced font,
move the highlight to a font that has a "PS" after
it, preferably with the same CPI, pitch, or point
size as the one originally highlighted; if your
printer does not have a proportionally spaced
font, move the highlight to a font that has a
smaller point size, smaller pitch, or higher CPI.}In
proportionally spaced fonts, each character uses a
different amount of space. For example, an "i"
takes less space than an "m."[SHIFT-F7]v[F7]

EXERCISES _____ 12.7

1. {Type the paragraph as shown.}[HOME][HOME]
[UP ARROW][ALT-F4].[CTRL-F8]sf[SHIFT-F7]v[F7]

2. H[CTRL-F8]sb2[RIGHT ARROW]O[ENTER][ENTER]E = mc[CTRL-
F8]sp2[RIGHT ARROW][ENTER][ENTER]Subscripted text
appears[CTRL-F8]sbbelow the normal text.[RIGHT
ARROW][ENTER][ENTER]Super-scripted text appears
[CTRL-F8]spabove the normal text.[RIGHT ARROW]
[ENTER][ENTER][SHIFT-F7]v[F7]

3. [CTRL-F8]seYour printer prints Extra Large text like
this.[RIGHT ARROW][ENTER][CTRL-F8]svYour printer
prints Very Large text like this.[RIGHT ARROW]
[ENTER][CTRL-F8]slYour printer prints Large text like
this.[RIGHT ARROW][ENTER][CTRL-F8]ssYour printer
prints Small text like this.[RIGHT ARROW][ENTER][CTRL-
F8]sfYour printer prints Fine text like this.[RIGHT
ARROW][SHIFT-F7]v[F7]

MASTERY SKILLS CHECK

1. {Type the paragraph as shown.}[HOME][HOME][UP   [12.6]
ARROW][CTRL-F8]f{Move the highlight to another font
that has the same PT or pitch as the first one
highlighted and has "italics" following it; if italic
is not available, select another font.}

2. {Move the cursor to the "C" in "CPI."}[ALT-   [12.7]
F4][RIGHT ARROW][RIGHT ARROW][RIGHT ARROW][CTRL-
F8]sl{Move the cursor to the "P" in "PT."}[ALT-
F4][RIGHT ARROW][RIGHT

ARROW][CTRL-F8]sl{Move the cursor to the "P" in "Pitch."}[ALT-F4][CTRL-RIGHT ARROW][LEFT ARROW][CTRL-F8] sl

[12.1, 12.5] **3.** [SHIFT-F7]n4[ENTER]tdf

[12.3] **4.** [SHIFT-F7]cc{Type the number that appears next to "(Screen)."}[ENTER][F7]

[12.1, 12.4, 12.5] **5.** [SHIFT-F7]n2[ENTER]thf[SHIFT-F7]n4[ENTER]tdf[SHIFT-F7] cr{Type the number that appears next to the print job that displays the "Text=Draft" message under Print Options.}[ENTER][F7]

INTEGRATING SKILLS CHECK

[9.2] **1.** {Type the paragraph as shown.}[CTRL-F2]d{The original paragraph has no spelling mistakes; correct any typing mistakes that WordPerfect finds. Press any key to return to the document.}

[11.1, 11.4] **2.** [F10]wordwrap[ENTER][F10]fontadj[ENTER][F5][ENTER]{Move the highlight to the WORDWRAP file.}dy[F7]

[12.7] **3.** {Move to the "f" in "fine."}[ALT-F4][CTRL-RIGHT ARROW] [LEFT ARROW][CTRL-F8]sf[RIGHT ARROW][ALT-F4][CTRL-RIGHT ARROW][LEFT ARROW][CTRL-F8]se[CTRL-RIGHT ARROW][CTRL-RIGHT ARROW][ALT-F4][CTRL-RIGHTARROW][LEFT ARROW][CTRL-F8]ss[SHIFT-F7]v[F7]

[12.6] **4.** [HOME][HOME][UP ARROW][CTRL-F8]f{Move the highlight to a font that has a smaller CPI, smaller pitch, or

larger point size than the one originally highlighted.}[ENTER]{Move to the beginning of the last
sentence.}[CTRL-F8]f{Move the highlight to a font
that has a larger CPI, larger pitch, or smaller
point size than the one originally highlighted.}
[ENTER][SHIFT-F7]v[F7]

5. {Move to the end of the first sentence.}[CTRL-F7]   [10.3]
   fc[SPACEBAR]Changing the font does not change
   WordPerfect's other default settings, such as margins and page size.[F7]

6. [SHIFT-F7]thn4f[SHIFT-F7]n3f[SHIFT-F7]tdn2f[SHIFT-F7]cr   [12.1, 12.4, 12.5]
   {Type the job number of the draft print request.}
   [ENTER]y[F7]

7. [F5][ENTER]{Move the highlight to the FONTADJ   [11.8]
   file.}[ENTER][F7][F7]

SKILLS CHECK ──────────────────────── 13

1. {Type the text as shown.}[ENTER]{Move the cursor   [10.3]
   to the first space after the period at the end of
   the first sentence.}[CTRL-F7]fc[SPACEBAR]These bonds
   were originally issued to upgrade production
   facilities.[F7]

2. [HOME][HOME][UP ARROW][SHIFT-F8]pfap{Type your   [10.2]
   name.}[F7][F7]

3. [SHIFT-F8]phapPage[SPACEBAR][CTRL-B][F7][F7]   [10.2]

4. [SHIFT-F7]td[F7]   [12.5]

[12.6, 12.7]   5. {If your printer has an italic base font:}
[CTRL-F8]f {Move the highlight to a font that is fol-
lowed by the word "Italic."}[ENTER][F7]yxtragain
[ENTER]n
{If your printer does not have an italic base
font:}
[ALT-F4][HOME][HOME][DOWN ARROW][CTRL-F8]ai[F7]
yxtragain[ENTER]n

[11.2]   6. [F5][ENTER]onotes[ENTER]y[F7]

[11.1]   7. [F5][ENTER]{Move the highlight to XTRAGAIN.}
cnotes[ENTER][F7]

[3.4]   8. [SHIFT-F7]d\notes\xtragain[ENTER][ENTER][F7]

[11.4]   9. [F5]notes[ENTER]{Move the highlight to
XTRAGAIN.}dy[F7]

[11.4]   10. [F5][ENTER]{Move the highlight to the NOTES subdirectory.}dy[F7]

13.1   EXERCISES

1. Production used 1200 ball bearings to replace the
machinery's worn ones.[ENTER][SHIFT-F3][SHIFT-F10]
final[ENTER]{Move the cursor to the end of the
letter.}[CTRL-ENTER][F7][ENTER][ENTER]yy[F7][ENTER]
skates[ENTER]n.

2. {Type the text as shown.}[ENTER][F10]stmt1[ENTER]
[SHIFT-F3][SHIFT-F10]stmt1[ENTER]{Move to the end of
the paragraph, and type the text as shown.}
[F10]stmt2[ENTER][F7]ny[F7]nn

3. [SHIFT-F10]stmt2[ENTER][SHIFT-F3][SHIFT-F10]stmt1
[ENTER][F7]ny[F7]nn

EXERCISES ——————————— 13.2

1. [CTRL-F3]w10[ENTER][CTRL-F3]w24[ENTER]

2. [CTRL-F3]w8[ENTER][CTRL-F3]w18[ENTER]

3. [SHIFT-F3][CTRL-F3]w14[ENTER]

4. [CTRL-F3]w8[ENTER]

EXERCISES ——————————— 13.3

1. The discrepancy between the amount due and
what the client believes is the proper amount is
the sales tax of[SHIFT-F3][SHIFT-F10]final[ENTER][SHIFT-F3]
$31.50.{Type the remaining text.}

2. The president, Amanda Williams, started with the
company as chief production officer fifteen years
ago.[SHIFT-F3]Ms. Williams' experience includes
chief production officer, divisional vice president,
production vice president, and president.[SHIFT-F3]
[SPACEBAR][SPACEBAR]After four years as production
officer, she was promoted to divisional vice president of the appliance division.[F7]ypresidnt
[ENTER]y[F7]ypresresu.me[ENTER]n

13.4 EXERCISES

1. [TAB]Peter Sullivan is production vice president. He has held this position for the past three years. [ENTER][TAB]Paula Atchinson is the financial vice president. She has held this position for the past five years.[ENTER][UP ARROW][UP ARROW][UP ARROW][UP ARROW][CTRL-F4]pm[SHIFT-F3][ENTER][F7]ny[F7]nn

2. Terry Kesley[ENTER]Kesley Associates[ENTER]496 Berry Avenue[ENTER]Newport, Rhode Island 03563[ENTER][ALT-F4][HOME][HOME][UP ARROW][CTRL-F4] bc[SHIFT-F3][ENTER]

MASTERY SKILLS CHECK

[13.1]   1. {Type the text as shown.}[SHIFT-F3]

[13.2]   2. [CTRL-F3]w12[ENTER]

[13.2]   3. [SHIFT-F3][CTRL-F3]w8[ENTER]

[13.4]   4. [HOME][UP ARROW][DOWN ARROW][CTRL-F4]pc[SHIFT-F3] [ENTER]

[13.4]   5. [SHIFT-F3][CTRL-F4]pm[SHIFT-F3][ENTER]

INTEGRATING SKILLS CHECK

[11.1]   1. [TAB]The company leases most of its office space and mainframe computer equipment. It owns all of its production facilities.[ENTER][TAB]Total rental expense is $1,709,000 for the current year,

$998,000 for 1989, and $923,000 for 1988.
[ENTER][F10]leases[ENTER][F10]leases.bak[ENTER]

2. [SHIFT-F3][SHIFT-F10]leases.bak[ENTER]   [13.1]

3. [HOME][DOWN ARROW]{Type the text as shown.}
[ENTER][UP ARROW][CTRL-F4]pc[SHIFT-F3][ENTER]

4. [F7][ENTER]leases.new[ENTER]y   [13.1]

5. [SHIFT-F8]dsn{d in 5.0}Notes for financial   [11.6]
statements[ENTER][ENTER]{omit[ENTER] in 5.0}t{a in
5.0}s {Type your name.}[ENTER]{t in 5.0}{Type your
name.}[ENTER]sFor 1990 financial statements[F7]

6. [F5][ENTER]{Move the highlight to the LEASES.BAK   [11.4]
file.}dy[F7]

7. [HOME][HOME][UP ARROW][SHIFT-F8]phapFinancial State- [10.2]
ment Notes[F7][F7]

8. [SHIFT-F8]pfap{Type your name.}[F7][F7]   [10.2]

9. {Turn the printer off.}[SHIFT-F7]n2[ENTER]f[SHIFT-F7]cc [12.1,12.3]
{Type the job number shown under "Current
Job."}[F7]{Turn the printer on.}

SKILLS CHECK   14

1. [SHIFT-F8]lt[CTRL-END]0.5{1.5 in 5.0}[ENTER]3{4 in 5.0} [9.2]
[ENTER][F7][F7]{Type the text as shown, pressing the
TAB key twice for the address and closing lines.}
[CTRL-F2]d{Spelling as shown is correct. Press any

key to end the spelling check when WordPerfect displays the word count.}

[8.2]   **2.** {Move to the "M" in "Mark."}[ALT-F4]{Move to the line below the address.}

[13.4]   **3.** [CTRL-F4]bc[SHIFT-F3][ENTER]

[13.1, 13.2]   **4.** [SHIFT-F3][CTRL-F3]w12[ENTER]

[2.2]   **5.** [F10]request[ENTER]

[12.1]   **6.** [SHIFT-F7]n2[ENTER]f

[12.1, 12.3]   **7.** [SHIFT-F7]f[SHIFT-F7]f[SHIFT-F7]cc*y[F7]

[1.4, 9.2]   **8.** {Move the cursor to the blank line between the letter body and the closing.}[TAB]I have enclosed a list of the sales representatives who will be attending the forum.[ENTER][HOME][HOME][DOWN ARROW][CTRL-ENTER]Jim Styverson[ENTER]Karen Acermann[ENTER]Julie Greenlowe[ENTER]Paul Hatterfield[ENTER][CTRL-F2]p33333{Press any key.}

[10.2]   **9.** {Move the cursor to the top of the page.}[SHIFT-F8]phapForum Attendees[F7][F7]

[11.1]   **10.** [F5][ENTER]{Move to the REQUEST filename.} cletter.bk[ENTER][F7]

[10.2, 13.4]   **11.** [SHIFT-F3][SHIFT-F8]phapBooth Assignments[F7][F7] [SHIFT-F3][ALT-F4][HOME][HOME][DOWN ARROW][CTRL-F4]bc[SHIFT-F3][HOME][HOME][DOWN ARROW][ENTER]

12. [SHIFT-F8]lt[HOME][LEFT ARROW][CTRL-END]3{4 in   [5.4]
5.0}[ENTER][F7][F7][END][TAB]8:00 - 10:00[DOWN
ARROW][TAB]10:00 - 1:00[DOWN ARROW][TAB]1:00 -
3:00[DOWN ARROW][TAB]3:00 - 5:30

13. [SHIFT-F7]n1[ENTER]drequest[ENTER][ENTER]drequest   [12.1, 12.4]
[ENTER][ENTER]p[SHIFT-F7]cr{Type the number of the
"(Screen)" print job.}[ENTER][F7]

14. [F10]times[ENTER][F5][ENTER]{Move the highlight to   [2.2, 11.5]
the TIMES filename.}mbooth[ENTER][F7]

15. [F5][ENTER]f{w in 5.0}eKaren[ENTER]{BOOTH will be   [11.7]
listed (marked with an asterisk in 5.0); others
may also be.}[F7]

16. [F7]ny[F7]nn[F5][ENTER]{Move the highlight to the   [11.8]
BOOTH filename.}[ENTER]{View the file.}[F7][F7]

17. [SHIFT-F10]booth[ENTER][SHIFT-F8]dsn{d in 5.0}{Type a   [11.6]
descriptive filename.}[ENTER]a{Type an author
name.}[ENTER]t{Type a typist name.}[ENTER][F7]

18. {if you have a hard disk}[F5]=\[ENTER][ENTER][F7]{if   [11.3]
you are using floppy disks}[F5]a:[ENTER][F7]

19. {if you have a hard disk}[F5][ENTER]otrdeshow   [11.2, 11.4]
[ENTER]y[F7][F5][ENTER]{Move the highlight to the
TRDESHOW subdirectory.}dy[F7][F5]=wp51{wp50
in 5.0}[ENTER][F1]{if you are using floppy disks}
[F5][ENTER]o\trdeshow[ENTER]y[F7][F5][ENTER]{Move
the highlight to the TRDESHOW subdirectory.}
dy[F7]

[10.2, 13.2]   **20.** [SHIFT-F8]pfap{Type today's date.}[ALT-F6]Page
[SPACEBAR][CTRL-B][F7][F7][F7][ENTER][ENTER]yn[CTRL-
F3]w24[ENTER]

[9.5]   **21.** [SHIFT-F10]wp{wp}us.sup[ENTER]{Move the cursor to
"Acermann."}[CTRL-END][DEL]{Move the cursor to
"Greenlowe."}[CTRL-END][DEL]{Move the cursor to
"Hatterfield."}[CTRL-END][DEL]{Move the cursor to
"Julie."}[CTRL-END][DEL]{Move the cursor to
"Styverson."}[CTRL-END][DEL][F7][ENTER][ENTER]yn

14.1   EXERCISES

1. B. J. Smith[F9]231-46-4232[F9][SHIFT-F9]eCarroll
Lawrence[F9]564-90-5327[F9][SHIFT-F9]e{Follow the
same pattern to enter the last two records.}

2. [SHIFT-F10]names[ENTER][HOME][HOME][DOWN ARROW]
{Type the text as shown, pressing F9 to end the
first, second, third, fifth, sixth, and seventh
lines.}[SHIFT-F9]e

3. {Type your name.}[F9]{Type your title.}[F9]{Type
your company's name.}[F9]{Type your street
address.}[ENTER]{Type your city, state, and ZIP
code.}[F9]{Type your social security number.}
[F9]{Type your first name.}[F9][SHIFT-F9]e[F10][ENTER]y

EXERCISES — 14.2

1. The Association of Computer Graphic Artists wishes to thank[SPACEBAR][SHIFT-F9]f1[ENTER][SPACEBAR] from[SPACEBAR][SHIFT-F9]f3[ENTER][SPACEBAR]for his or her assistance with the Taking Computer Graphics One Step Further forum.[ENTER][F7][ENTER]thanks [ENTER]n

2. [SHIFT-F9]f1[ENTER][ENTER][SHIFT-F9]f2[ENTER][ENTER] [SHIFT-F9]f3[ENTER][ENTER][SHIFT-F9]f4[ENTER][ENTER] [ENTER] Dear [SPACEBAR][SHIFT-F9]f6[ENTER],[ENTER] [ENTER]{Type the paragraph as shown.}[SHIFT-F9] f3[ENTER][ENTER][SHIFT-F9]f4[ENTER][ENTER][SHIFT-F9] f5[ENTER][ENTER]Contact:[TAB][SHIFT-F9]f1[ENTER][ENTER][TAB][TAB][SHIFT-F9]f2[ENTER][ENTER] {Type the last paragraph and the closing.}[F7] [ENTER]cards[ENTER]n

EXERCISES — 14.3

1. [CTRL-F9]mthanks[ENTER]names[ENTER][F10]thanks.out [ENTER]

2. [CTRL-F9]mcards[ENTER]names[ENTER][F10]cards.out [ENTER]

EXERCISES — 14.4

1. [SHIFT-F7]dthanks.out[ENTER][ENTER]

2. [SHIFT-F7]dcards.out[ENTER][ENTER]

MASTERY SKILLS CHECK

[14.1]

1. Karen Simon[F9]34220 Euclid Avenue[F9]Cleveland, OH 44134[F9][SHIFT-F9]eJim Darcy[F9]12353 Carnegie Avenue[F9]Lakewood, OH 44116[F9][SHIFT-F9] e[F10] names2[ENTER]

[14.2, 14.3, 14.4]

2. [SHIFT-F9]f1[ENTER][ENTER][SHIFT-F9]f2[ENTER][ENTER][SHIFT-F9]f3[ENTER][F7][ENTER]lbls[ENTER]n[CTRL-F9]mlbls[ENTER] names2[ENTER][SHIFT-F7]f

[14.1]

3. [SHIFT-F10]names2[ENTER][DOWN ARROW][DOWN ARROW] [DOWN ARROW]Karen[F9][DOWN ARROW][DOWN ARROW] [DOWN ARROW][DOWN ARROW]Jim[F9][F7][ENTER][ENTER]y [ENTER]

[14.2, 14.3, 14.4]

4. [SHIFT-F9]f1[ENTER][ENTER][SHIFT-F9]f2[ENTER][ENTER][SHIFT-F9]f3[ENTER][ENTER][ENTER][SPACEBAR]Dear[SPACEBAR] [SHIFT-F9]f4[ENTER],[ENTER][ENTER]{Type the text as shown.}[F7][ENTER]photos[ENTER]n[CTRL-F9]mphotos [ENTER]names2[ENTER][SHIFT-F7]f

[14.2, 14.3, 14.4]

5. [SHIFT-F10]photos[ENTER]{Move to the "w" in "we."} [SHIFT-F9]f4[ENTER],[SPACEBAR][F7][ENTER][ENTER]y [ENTER] [CTRL-F9]mphotos[ENTER]names2[ENTER][SHIFT-F7]f

INTEGRATING SKILLS CHECK

[14.1]

1. Thomas Douglas[F9]Dept. Manager, Accounting [F9]X3963[F9][SHIFT-F9]eTanya Smith[F9]Dept. Manager, Data Processing[F9]X3959[F9][SHIFT-F9]e[F7] [ENTER]names.two[ENTER][ENTER]

2. Memo[ENTER]To:[TAB][TAB][SHIFT-F9]f1[ENTER][ENTER]   [14.2]
[TAB][TAB][SHIFT-F9]f2[ENTER][ENTER][TAB][TAB][SHIFT-F9]
f3[ENTER][ENTER]{Type the remainder of the memo
as shown, including the date and your name
where indicated.}

3. [PGUP][SHIFT-F6]   [4.6, 4.7]

4. [END][ENTER][ESC]65-   [1.4]

5. [F10]smokers[ENTER][F7]nn   [1.3, 2.2]

6. [CTRL-F9]msmokers[ENTER]names.two[ENTER]   [14.3]

7. [SHIFT-F7]n2[ENTER]f   [12.1, 14.4]

8. [F7]n[ENTER][SHIFT-F10]names.two[ENTER][SHIFT-F3]   [1.3, 2.3, 13.1, 13.2]
[SHIFT-F10]smokers[ENTER][CTRL-F3]w12[ENTER]

SKILLS CHECK — 15

1. [SHIFT-F8]lt[HOME][LEFT ARROW][CTRL-END]1.5 [ENTER]2   [5.4]
[ENTER]4[ENTER][F7][F7][SHIFT-F8]lt[CTRL-END]0,.5[F7][F7]

2. We have written several times to inquire about   [4.1, 4.2]
the status of[F6]order number 98754[F6]. Please
check the status of the backorder items. If you
are unable to fill the remainder of the order
within[F8]10 days[F8], please notify us so that we
can contact other suppliers.[ENTER]

[1.4]

3. 150[ENTER][SPACEBAR]50[ENTER]100[ENTER][ESC]3-[ENTER]
300[ENTER]

[4.2, 12.1]

4. You can use an[F6]'s[F6]to create the plural of letters, numbers, symbols, and words. For example,
you could write that there are four[F6]s's[F6]and
four[F6]i's[F6]in[F6]Mississippi[F6].[SHIFT-F7]n2[ENTER]f

[8.4]

5. Errors, like straws, upon the surface flow;[ENTER]
He who would search for pearls, must dive be-
low. [ENTER][ENTER][TAB][TAB][TAB][TAB]John Dryden
[ENTER][ALT-F4][PGUP][CTRL-F4]bc[ENTER][CTRL-F4]rb

[12.1]

6. [SHIFT-F7]n1[ENTER][F7]

15.1   EXERCISES

1. [SHIFT-F8]lt[CTRL-END]3[ENTER]d[F7][F7][ALT-F7]mo{omit
the o in 5.0}Salaries[TAB]50,000[ENTER]Benefits[TAB]
8,500 [ENTER]Travel[TAB]18,000[ENTER]Rent[TAB]
120,000[ENTER][TAB] + [ALT-F7]mc{a instead of mc in
5.0}[ALT-F7]mf{omit the f in 5.0}

2. {Move the cursor to the 5 in the "Benefits"
amount.}[INS]9[INS][ALT-F7]mc{a in 5.0}

15.2   EXERCISES

1. [SHIFT-F8]lt[CTRL-END]0.5{1.5 in 5.0}[ENTER]4.0[ENTER]
d[F7][F7][ALT-F7]ind{e in 5.0}1[DOWN ARROW][DOWN

ARROW]0[F7]o{m in 5.0}Machine repairs[ENTER]
[ENTER]Model 5210[ENTER][TAB]Factory 1[TAB]10[ENTER]
[TAB]Factory 2[TAB]5[ENTER]Total Repairs 5210[TAB] +
[ENTER][ENTER]Model 6511[ENTER][TAB]Factory 1[TAB]48
[ENTER][TAB]Factory 2[TAB]9[ENTER]Total Repairs 6511
[TAB] + [ENTER][ENTER]TOTAL ALL MODELS[TAB]
[TAB] = [ALT-F7]mc{a in 5.0}{The subtotals should be
15 and 57; the total should be 72.}[ALT-F7]mf{omit
the f in 5.0}

2. EMPLOYEE BENEFIT PARTICIPATION[ENTER]
[SHIFT-F8]lt[CTRL-END]0.3{1.3 in 5.0}[ENTER]0.5{1.5 in
5.0}[ENTER]4.5[ENTER]d5.5[ENTER]d6.5[ENTER]d[F7][F7]
[ALT-F7]md{e in 5.0}1123[DOWN ARROW][DOWN ARROW]
[LEFT ARROW]00[F7]o{m in 5.0}[TAB]Employees
in Savings Plan[ENTER][TAB][TAB]Thrift[TAB]
500[ENTER][TAB][TAB]S&L[TAB]250[ENTER][TAB][TAB]
Bonds[TAB]250[ENTER][TAB]Total in Savings[TAB]
+ [ENTER][TAB]Employees in Stock Option Plan
[ENTER][TAB][TAB]Plan A[TAB]100[ENTER][TAB][TAB]Plan
B[TAB]100[ENTER][TAB]Total in Stocks[TAB] + [ENTER]
[TAB]Total Employees in Investment Plans[TAB] =
[ENTER][ENTER][TAB]Employees in Medical Plan[ENTER]
[TAB][TAB]White Cross[TAB]500[ENTER][TAB][TAB]Cheap
Docs[TAB]500[ENTER][TAB]Total Medical[TAB] + [ENTER]
[TAB]Employees in Life Insurance Plan[ENTER]
[TAB][TAB] Quick Save[TAB]100[ENTER][TAB][TAB]High
Risk[TAB]100[ENTER][TAB]Total Life[TAB] + [ENTER]
[TAB]Total Employees in Insurance Plans[TAB] =
[ENTER][ENTER]TOTAL NUMBERS IN BENEFIT
PLANS[TAB][TAB][TAB]*[ALT-F7]mc{a in 5.0}[ALT-F7]
mf{omit the f in 5.0}

MASTERY SKILLS CHECK

[15.1]

1. [SHIFT-F8]lt[CTRL-END]2.8[ENTER]d[F7][F7][ALT+F7]md{e in 5.0}[DOWN ARROW][DOWN ARROW]0[F7]o{m in 5.0} HEADCOUNT BY LOCATION[ENTER][ENTER] Chicago[TAB]120[ENTER]Dallas[TAB]38[ENTER]Denver[TAB] 105[ENTER]New York[TAB]302[ENTER][ENTER]TOTAL [TAB]+[ALT-F7]mc{a in 5.0}[ALT-F7]mf{omit the f in 5.0}

[15.1]

2. {Move the cursor to the "T" in "TOTAL."} U.S. [SPACEBAR][ALT-F3]{Move the cursor to the [Math Off] code.}[ALT-F3][ENTER][ENTER]Paris[TAB]82[ENTER]London [TAB]106[ENTER]Lisbon[TAB]34[ENTER]Frankfort[TAB]192 [ENTER][ENTER]FOREIGN TOTAL[TAB]+[ALT-F7]mc{a in 5.0}

[15.2]

3. [SHIFT-F8]lt[CTRL-END]0.5{1.5 in 5.0}[ENTER]3.5[ENTER] d4.5[ENTER]d[F7][F7][ALT-F7]md{e in 5.0}12[DOWN AR-ROW][DOWN ARROW][LEFT ARROW]0[F7].{m in 5.0}Product 1 Sales[ENTER][TAB]Jim[TAB]12,500[ENTER][TAB]Fred [TAB]38,900[ENTER][TAB]Harry[TAB]23,500[ENTER]Total Product 1[TAB]+[ENTER][ENTER]Product 2 Sales[ENTER] [TAB]Jim[TAB]23,450[ENTER][TAB]Fred[TAB]56,750[ENTER] [TAB]Harry[TAB]78,900[ENTER]Total Product 2[TAB]+ [ENTER][ENTER]Total Products 1 & 2[TAB][TAB]=[ALT-F7] mc{a in 5.0}[ALT-F7]mf{omit the f in 5.0}

[15.2]

4. [SHIFT-F8]lt[CTRL-END]3.7[ENTER]d4.7[ENTER]d5.7[ENTER]d [F7][F7][ALT-F7]md{e in 5.0}23[F7]o{m in 5.0}Office Supplies[ENTER][TAB]10.00[ENTER][TAB]15.50[ENTER] [TAB]25.60[ENTER]Total Supplies[TAB]+[ENTER]Office Furniture[ENTER][TAB]345.00[ENTER][TAB]545.00[ENTER] Total Furniture[TAB]+[ENTER]Total Office Products

[TAB][TAB] = [ENTER][ENTER]Coffee Supplies[ENTER]
[TAB]25.00[ENTER][TAB]15.80[ENTER]Total Coffee[TAB] +
[ENTER]Paper Products[ENTER][TAB]115.00[ENTER]Total
Paper[TAB] + [ENTER]Total Miscellaneous[TAB][TAB] =
[ENTER][ENTER]TOTAL PURCHASES[TAB][TAB][TAB]*
[ALT-F7]mc{a in 5.0}[ALT-F7]mf{omit the f in 5.0}

INTEGRATING SKILLS CHECK

1. {Type the text as shown.}[ENTER][HOME][HOME][UP   [4.3, 5.5, 10.2]
ARROW][SHIFT-F8]phapABC COMPANY[ALT-F6][SHIFT-
F5]t[SHIFT-F8]pfap[SHIFT-F6]Page[SPACEBAR][CTRL-B][F7][F7]

2. [PGDN][ENTER][SHIFT-F8]lt[CTRL-END]3[ENTER]3.5[ENTER]   [4.1, 5.4, 15.1]
d4.5[ENTER]5[ENTER]d[F7][F7][ALT-F7]md{e in 5.0}121
[DOWN ARROW][DOWN ARROW][LEFT ARROW][LEFT ARROW]
0[RIGHT ARROW]0[F7]o{m in 5.0}[TAB][F8]Last[TAB]
[TAB]This[ENTER][TAB]Year[TAB][TAB]Year[F8]
[ENTER][ENTER]Travel[TAB][TAB]52,900[TAB][TAB]
86,900[ENTER]Consultants[TAB][TAB]104,585[TAB][TAB]
190,800[ENTER]Entertainment[TAB][TAB]3,900[TAB][TAB]
9,800[ENTER]Supplies[TAB][TAB]1,200[TAB][TAB]15,900
[ENTER]Phone[TAB][TAB]25,000[TAB][TAB]49,000[ENTER]
[ENTER]TOTALS[TAB][TAB] + [TAB][TAB] + [ALT-F7]mc{a in
5.0}

3. [ALT-F7]mf{omit the f in 5.0}[ENTER][SHIFT-F8]lt   [5.4, 15.1]
[CTRL-END]0.5{1,.5 in 5.0}[ENTER][F7][F7][TAB]{Type
the text as shown.}[ENTER]

4. [SHIFT-F7]n2[ENTER]f   [12.1]

16

SKILLS CHECK

[11.2]   **1.** [F5]\[ENTER]oaccount[ENTER]y[F7]

[11.2]   **2.** [F5][ENTER]oletters[ENTER]y[F7]

[1.4]   **3.** [ESC]55*

[4.1, 4.2, 4.3]   **4.** [ENTER][SHIFT-F6][F6][F8]{Type the text as shown.} [F8][F6][ENTER]

[3.3]   **5.** [SHIFT-F7]v̄

[8.2]   **6.** {Move the cursor to the first asterisk.}[CTRL-F4] pm{Move the cursor to the line below the text.} [ENTER]

16.1

EXERCISES

1. {Type the first paragraph.}[ENTER][CTRL-F3]L2[ESC] 40[RIGHT ARROW][F7][RIGHT ARROW][ENTER]{Type the second paragraph.}

2. [CTRL-F3]L1[DOWN ARROW][DOWN ARROW][DOWN ARROW] 2[RIGHT ARROW][RIGHT ARROW][RIGHT ARROW][RIGHT ARROW] [RIGHT ARROW][RIGHT ARROW][DOWN ARROW][DOWN ARROW] [DOWN ARROW][DOWN ARROW][DOWN ARROW][F7][SHIFT-F7] v12[F7]

EXERCISES ——————————— 16.2

1. First Name:[SPACEBAR][CTRL-F3]L1[DOWN ARROW][DOWN
ARROW][DOWN ARROW][ESC]15[RIGHT ARROW][UP ARROW]
[UP ARROW][UP ARROW][ESC]15[LEFT ARROW][F7][END][DOWN
ARROW][DOWN ARROW][DOWN ARROW][ENTER]Last Name:
[SPACEBAR][CTRL-F3]l[DOWN ARROW][DOWN ARROW]
[DOWN ARROW][ESC]15[RIGHT ARROW][UP ARROW][UP
ARROW][UP ARROW][ESC]15[LEFT ARROW][F7]{This makes
boxes 3 rows by 15 columns. Your boxes may be
a different size.}

2. [CTRL-F3]l[ESC]14[RIGHT ARROW][ESC]5[DOWN ARROW][ESC]
14[LEFT ARROW][ESC]5[UP ARROW][F7][ALT-F4][PGDN][CTRL-
F4]rc[PGUP][END][TAB][TAB][ENTER][PGDN][ENTER][ENTER]
[ENTER][TAB][TAB][TAB][TAB][TAB][CTRL-F4]rr[ESC]7[RIGHT
ARROW][CTRL-F3]L[ESC]3[UP ARROW][ESC]7[LEFT ARROW][UP
ARROW][UP ARROW][UP ARROW][ESC]11[LEFT ARROW][F7]

EXERCISES ——————————— 16.3

1. [CTRL-F3]L2[ESC]6[RIGHT ARROW]5[ESC]6[LEFT ARROW][F7]

2. [CTRL-F3]L1[ESC]4[DOWN ARROW][ESC]5[RIGHT ARROW][ESC]
4[UP ARROW][ESC]5[LEFT ARROW][RIGHT ARROW][RIGHT
ARROW]5[RIGHT ARROW][DOWN ARROW][DOWN ARROW]
[DOWN ARROW][DOWN ARROW][LEFT ARROW][F7]

16.4   EXERCISES

1. [CTRL-F3]L2[ESC]4[DOWN ARROW][ESC]15[RIGHT ARROW][ESC]
   4[UP ARROW][ESC]15[LEFT ARROW]6[ESC]20[RIGHT ARROW]
   2[DOWN ARROW][DOWN ARROW][ESC]12[RIGHT ARROW]
   [UP ARROW][UP ARROW][ESC]12[LEFT ARROW][F7]

2. [CTRL-F3]L1[ESC]10[RIGHT ARROW]6[ESC]5[LEFT ARROW]1
   [ESC]10[DOWN ARROW]6[ESC]5[LEFT ARROW]1[ESC]10[RIGHT
   ARROW]6[ESC]10[RIGHT ARROW]1[ESC]10[RIGHT ARROW]
   6[ESC]5[LEFT ARROW]1[ESC]10[UP ARROW]6[ESC]5[LEFT
   ARROW]1[ESC]10[RIGHT ARROW]6[ESC]10[RIGHT ARROW]
   1[ESC]10[RIGHT ARROW]6[ESC]5[LEFT ARROW]1[ESC]10[DOWN
   ARROW]6[ESC]5[LEFT ARROW]1[ESC]10[RIGHT ARROW][F7]

16.5   EXERCISES

1. [CTRL-F3]L49[SHIFT-3][ESC]10[DOWN ARROW][ESC]20[RIGHT
   ARROW][ESC]10[UP ARROW][ESC]20[LEFT ARROW][F7]

2. [CTRL-F3]L44[ESC]30[RIGHT ARROW][F7]

16.6   EXERCISES

1. {Answer assumes that you draw the boxes and
   then type the text. This answer creates boxes that
   are 3 rows by 20 columns. If you use different
   numbers, replace the 3 and the 20 in the answers

with the numbers that you use.}[TAB][TAB][TAB][TAB]
[TAB][CTRL-F3]L2[ESC]3[DOWN ARROW][ESC]20[RIGHT
ARROW][ESC]3[UP ARROW][ESC]20[LEFT ARROW][F7][DOWN
ARROW][DOWN ARROW][DOWN ARROW][END][ENTER][ENTER]
[ENTER][HOME][UP ARROW][CTRL-RIGHT ARROW][ALT-F4][DOWN
ARROW][DOWN ARROW][DOWN ARROW][END][CTRL-F4]rc
[DOWN ARROW][DOWN ARROW][DOWN ARROW][ENTER][ALT-F4]
[DOWN ARROW][DOWN ARROW][DOWN ARROW][END][CTRL-F4]
rc[UP ARROW][UP ARROW][UP ARROW][END][SPACEBAR]
[ENTER][ALT-F4][DOWN ARROW][DOWN ARROW][DOWN ARROW]
[END][CTRL-F4]rc[UP ARROW][UP ARROW][UP ARROW][END]
[SPACEBAR][ENTER][ESC]10[RIGHT ARROW][CTRL-F3]L1
[UP ARROW][ESC]43[LEFT ARROW][DOWN ARROW][UP ARROW]
[ESC]21[RIGHT ARROW][DOWN ARROW][UP ARROW][UP ARROW]
[UP ARROW][F7][INS][UP ARROW][UP ARROW][CTRL-LEFT
ARROW][RIGHT ARROW][RIGHT ARROW]Root Directory
[DOWN ARROW][DOWN ARROW][DOWN ARROW][DOWN ARROW]
[DOWN ARROW][DOWN ARROW][CTRL-LEFT ARROW]
[CTRL-LEFT ARROW][CTRL-LEFT ARROW][RIGHT ARROW][RIGHT
ARROW]BUDGET[CTRL-RIGHT ARROW][CTRL-RIGHT ARROW]
[RIGHT ARROW][RIGHT ARROW]PRODUCT[CTRL-RIGHT
ARROW][CTRL-RIGHT ARROW][RIGHT ARROW][RIGHT ARROW]
REPORTS[INS]

2. [CTRL-F3]L1[ESC]4[DOWN ARROW][ESC]50[RIGHT ARROW][ESC]
4[UP ARROW][ESC]50[LEFT ARROW][F7][INS][DOWN ARROW]
[RIGHT ARROW][RIGHT ARROW]All of the paintings displayed in this[DOWN ARROW][CTRL-LEFT ARROW][RIGHT
ARROW][RIGHT ARROW]restaurant are for sale on a
consignment[DOWN ARROW][CTRL-LEFT ARROW][RIGHT
ARROW][RIGHT ARROW]basis. For more details, see the
manager. [INS]

MASTERY SKILLS CHECK

[16.1, 16.3, 16.4]   **1.** [CTRL-F3]L1[ESC]40[RIGHT ARROW]6[ESC]20[LEFT ARROW]
5[ESC]3[RIGHT ARROW][F7][F7]nn

[16.1, 16.2, 16.6]   **2.** [SPACEBAR][SPACEBAR][SPACEBAR][CTRL-F3]L1[ESC]3[DOWN
ARROW][ESC]10[RIGHT ARROW][ESC]3[UP ARROW][ESC]10
[LEFT ARROW][ESC]3[DOWN ARROW][ESC]5[RIGHT ARROW]
[DOWN ARROW][ESC]5[LEFT ARROW][ESC]5[DOWN ARROW]
[ESC]10[RIGHT ARROW][ESC]5[UP ARROW][ESC]5[LEFT
ARROW]6[ESC]5[DOWN ARROW]1[DOWN ARROW][ESC]5[RIGHT
ARROW][ESC]3[DOWN ARROW][ESC]10[LEFT ARROW][ESC]3[UP
ARROW][ESC]5[RIGHT ARROW][F7][INS][ESC]9[UP ARROW][LEFT
ARROW][LEFT ARROW][LEFT ARROW]Receive[ESC]7[LEFT
ARROW][DOWN ARROW]Invoice[DOWN ARROW][DOWN
ARROW][DOWN ARROW][ESC] 7[LEFT ARROW]Compare
[DOWN ARROW][ESC]7[LEFT ARROW] to[DOWN ARROW]
[LEFT ARROW][LEFT ARROW]Purchase[ESC]8[LEFT
ARROW][DOWN ARROW]Order[ESC]5[LEFT ARROW]
[DOWN ARROW][DOWN ARROW][DOWN ARROW]Prepare
[ESC]7[LEFT ARROW][DOWN ARROW]Voucher[INS][F7]nn

[16.5]   **3.** [CTRL-F3]l49:[F7]

[16.1, 16.4]   **4.** [ENTER][SPACEBAR][SPACEBAR]Construction Schedule
[TAB][TAB]Dates[ENTER][ENTER][SPACEBAR][SPACEBAR]Start
renovation[ENTER][ENTER][SPACEBAR][SPACEBAR]Start in-
terior remodeling[ENTER][ENTER][SPACEBAR][SPACEBAR]
Start repaving parking lot[ENTER][ENTER][SPACEBAR]
[SPACEBAR]End repaving parking lot[ENTER][ENTER]
[SPACEBAR][SPACEBAR]End interior remodeling
[ENTER][ENTER][SPACEBAR][SPACEBAR]End renovation
[ENTER][ESC]5[UP ARROW][END][CTRL-F3]L1[ESC]20[RIGHT
ARROW][UP ARROW][UP ARROW][ESC]18[LEFT ARROW]6
[UP ARROW][UP ARROW][LEFT ARROW]1[ESC]21[RIGHT ARROW]

[ESC]6[DOWN ARROW][ESC]23[LEFT ARROW]6[DOWNARROW]
[DOWN ARROW][ESC]9[LEFT ARROW]1[ESC]34[RIGHT
ARROW][ESC]10[UP ARROW][ESC]32[LEFT ARROW][F7]

5. [CTRL-F3]L6[ESC]17[RIGHT ARROW]5[ESC]5[RIGHT ARROW]   [16.3, 16.4]
[DOWN ARROW][DOWN ARROW][ESC]5[LEFT ARROW][DOWN
ARROW][DOWN ARROW][ESC]5[RIGHT ARROW][DOWN
ARROW][DOWN ARROW][ESC]5[LEFT ARROW][DOWN ARROW]
[DOWN ARROW][ESC]5[RIGHT ARROW][DOWN ARROW]
[DOWN ARROW][ESC]5[LEFT ARROW][F7][ESC]10[UP ARROW]
[INS][RIGHT ARROW]5/1[DOWN ARROW][DOWN ARROW]
[ESC]3[LEFT ARROW]6/15[DOWN ARROW][DOWN ARROW]
[ESC]4[LEFT ARROW]7/1[DOWN ARROW][DOWN ARROW][ESC]
3[LEFT ARROW]7/31[DOWN ARROW][DOWN ARROW][ESC]4
[LEFT ARROW]8/30[DOWN ARROW][DOWN ARROW][ESC]4[LEFT
ARROW]9/30[INS]

6. [PGUP]{If you do not have a blank line above the   [16.5]
construction schedule, press ENTER and the UP
ARROW key.}[CTRL-F3]L3[ESC]14[DOWN ARROW][ESC]52
[RIGHT ARROW][ESC]14[UP ARROW][ESC]51[LEFT ARROW][F7]

INTEGRATING SKILLS CHECK

1. Last name:[SPACEBAR][CTRL-F3]L1[DOWN ARROW][DOWN   [16.2]
ARROW][ESC]20[RIGHT ARROW][UP ARROW][UP ARROW][ESC]
20[LEFT ARROW][F7][DOWN ARROW][DOWN ARROW][END]
[ENTER]First name:[SPACEBAR][CTRL-F3]l[DOWN ARROW]
[DOWN ARROW][ESC]20[RIGHT ARROW][UP ARROW][UP ARROW]
[ESC]20[LEFT ARROW][F7][DOWN ARROW][DOWN ARROW]
[END][ENTER]Department:[SPACEBAR][CTRL-F3]l[DOWN
ARROW][DOWN ARROW][ESC]20[RIGHT ARROW][UP ARROW][UP
ARROW][ESC]20

[LEFT ARROW][F7][DOWN ARROW][DOWN ARROW][END][ENTER]
Years with the company:[SPACEBAR][CTRL-F3]l[DOWN ARROW][DOWN ARROW][ESC]20[RIGHT ARROW][UP ARROW]
[UP ARROW][ESC]20[LEFT ARROW][F7][DOWN ARROW][DOWN ARROW][END][ENTER]

[4.1, 16.1]
2. [F8]Acme's Main Product Line[F8][ENTER]Solder
[ENTER]Silver necklaces[ENTER]Silver flatware[ENTER]
[UP ARROW][END][CTRL-F3]L1[ESC]10[RIGHT ARROW][ESC]3
[UP ARROW][DOWN ARROW][ESC]19[LEFT ARROW]6[DOWN ARROW][ESC]10[RIGHT ARROW]1[ESC]9[RIGHT ARROW]

[11.4]
3. [F5]\[ENTER]{Move the highlight to the ACCOUNT subdirectory.}dy[F7]

[11.4]
4. [F5][ENTER]{Move the highlight to the LETTERS sub-directory.}dy[F7]

[4.2, 4.3, 16.2, 16.5, 16.6]
5. [CTRL-F3]L49*[ESC]10[DOWN ARROW][ESC]50[RIGHT ARROW]
[ESC]10[UP ARROW][ESC]50[LEFT ARROW][F7][INS][DOWN ARROW][DOWN ARROW][RIGHT ARROW][RIGHT ARROW][TAB]
[TAB][F6]Clark Corporation is Moving[DOWN ARROW]
[DOWN ARROW][CTRL-LEFT ARROW][RIGHT ARROW][RIGHT ARROW]On Friday the 23rd, Clark Corporation
is[DOWN ARROW][CTRL-LEFT ARROW][RIGHT ARROW][RIGHT ARROW]closing its Lakewood offices. Its new[DOWN ARROW][CTRL-LEFT ARROW][RIGHT ARROW][RIGHT ARROW]
headquarters are in Barlow, Florida. It is[DOWN ARROW][CTRL-LEFT ARROW][RIGHT ARROW][RIGHT ARROW]
moving there to move closer to its prospering
[DOWN ARROW][CTRL-LEFT ARROW][RIGHT ARROW][RIGHT ARROW]land-development subsidiary.[INS]

[4.7]
6. [PGUP][ALT-F4][PGDN][SHIFT-F6]y

SKILLS CHECK 17

1. {Type the text as shown.}[ENTER][HOME][HOME][UP [4.7]
ARROW][CTRL-RIGHT ARROW][ALT-F4][CTRL-RIGHT ARROW]
[CTRL-RIGHT ARROW][CTRL-RIGHT ARROW][CTRL-RIGHT ARROW]
[LEFT ARROW][F8][F10]graphbox[ENTER]

2. [SHIFT-F3][SHIFT-F10]graphbox[ENTER][HOME][HOME][DOWN [13.3]
ARROW][ENTER]{Type the text as shown.}

3. [HOME][HOME][UP ARROW][SHIFT-F8]phapWordPerfect's [10.2]
Graphics Features[F7][F7]

4. {Move to the beginning of the word "captions."} [4.7]
[ALT-F4][CTRL-RIGHT ARROW][LEFT ARROW][F6]{Repeat the
procedure for each of the other two words.}

5. [SHIFT-F7]v[F7][SHIFT-F3][SHIFT-F7]v[F7] [3.3, 13.3]

EXERCISES 17.1

1. [ALT-F9]uc[F7]{Press ENTER 21 times.}

2. [ALT-F9]fc[F7]{Type the paragraph as shown.}

3. [ALT-F9]tc[F7][SHIFT-F7]v[F7]

4. [ALT-F9]bc[F7][ENTER][ENTER][ENTER][ENTER][ENTER][ALT-F9]
fc[F7][SHIFT-F7]v[F7]

5. [ALT-F9]tc[F7][ALT-F9]fc[F7]{Press ENTER 23 times.}[SHIFT-
F7]v[F7]

17.2   EXERCISES

1. [ALT-F9]tce[F8]Project[F8][TAB][TAB][TAB][TAB]{omit one [TAB] in 5.0}[F8]Date[F8][ENTER]Systems analysis[TAB][TAB]{omit one [TAB] in 5.0}5/1[ENTER]Order equipment[TAB][TAB]6/15[ENTER]Design software[TAB][TAB]7/1[ENTER]Test software[TAB][TAB][TAB]{omit one [TAB] in 5.0}7/31[ENTER]Implement software[TAB][TAB]{omit one [TAB] in 5.0}8/30[ENTER]Evaluation[TAB][TAB][TAB]9/30[ENTER][F7][F7][SHIFT-F7]v[F7]

2. {Type the paragraph as shown.}[F7][ENTER]picture [ENTER]n[ALT-F9]bcfpicture[ENTER][F7][SHIFT-F7]v[F7]

3. [ALT-F9]tce{Type the text as shown, pressing ENTER after the heading and after each step.}[F7][F7][SHIFT-F7]v[F7]

17.3   EXERCISES

{If your graphics images are not in the WordPerfect subdirectory, type a backslash, the subdirectory name, a backslash, and the filename where the answers provide only the filename.}

1. [ALT-F9]tcfstar-5.wpg{mapsymbl.wpg in 5.0} [ENTER][F7][SHIFT-F7]v[F7]

2. [ALT-F9]bcfarrow-22.wpg{arrow1.wpg in 5.0} [ENTER][F7][SHIFT-F7]v[F7]

3. [ALT-F9]fcfborder-8.wpg{border.wpg in 5.0}
[ENTER][F7][SHIFT-F7]v[F7]

4. [ALT-F9]ucfgavel.wpg[ENTER][F7][SHIFT-F7]v[F7]

EXERCISES ———————————— 17.4

1. [ALT-F9]bcc[SPACEBAR]To be filled in later[F7][F7][SHIFT-F7]v[F7]

2. [ALT-F9]tceinsert Ms. Mitchell's picture here [F7]
c[SPACEBAR]Susan Mitchell, President[F7][F7][SHIFT-F7]
v[F7]

3. [ALT-F9]fcftelephone.wpg{phone.wpg in 5.0}[ENTER]
c[SPACEBAR]When It Rings, We Answer[F7][F7][SHIFT-F7]v[F7]

4. [ALT-F9]fcftrophy.wpg{no1.wpg in 5.0}[ENTER]
c[SPACEBAR]First in the Business[F7][F7][SHIFT-F7]v[F7]

EXERCISES ———————————— 17.5

1. [ALT-F9]bcv.4[ENTER][F7]{Type the paragraph as
shown.}[SHIFT-F7]v[F7]

2. [ALT-F9]fchl[F7][SHIFT-F7]v[F7]

3. [ALT-F9]ucfchkbox-1.wpg{check.wpg in 5.0}
[ENTER]sh5[ENTER][F7][SHIFT-F7]v[F7]

4. [ALT-F9]tce{Type the paragraph as shown.}[F7][F7]
[SHIFT-F7]v[F7][ALT-F9]te1[ENTER]sw2.5[ENTER][F7][SHIFT-F7]
v[F7][ALT-F9]te1[ENTER]sb3[ENTER]2[ENTER][F7][SHIFT-F7]
v[F7]

5. [ALT-F9]fcfhands-3.wpg{applause.wpg in 5.0}
[ENTER]sh4[ENTER]hc[F7][SHIFT-F7]v[F7]

17.6   EXERCISES

1. [ALT-F9]tcfarrow-22.wpg{arrow1.wpg in 5.0}[ENTER]
[F7][SHIFT-F7]v[F7][ALT-F9]te1[ENTER]fchkbox-1.wpg
{check.wpg in 5.0}[ENTER]y[F7][SHIFT-F7]v[F7]

2. [ALT-F9]bcfcertif.wpg{confiden.wpg in 5.0}[ENTER][F7]
[SHIFT-F7]v[F7][ALT-F9]be1[ENTER]f[CTRL-END][ENTER]y[F7]
[SHIFT-F7]v[F7]

3. [ALT-F9]tc[F7][ALT-F3][LEFT ARROW][DEL][ALT-F3]

4. [ALT-F9]fcfnews.wpg{newspapr.wpg in 5.0}[ENTER]
[F7]{Press ENTER 16 times (19 in 5.0).}[ALT-F9]
fcfbulb.wpg{present.wpg in 5.0}[ENTER][F7]{Press
ENTER 16 times (25 in 5.0).}[HOME][HOME][UP ARROW]
[ALT-F3][BACKSPACE][HOME][HOME][DOWN ARROW][F1]r
[HOME][HOME][UP ARROW]{Press DEL 16 times (19 in
5.0).}[SHIFT-F7]v[F7][ALT-F3]

17.7   EXERCISES

1. {assumes that your printer can print graphics and
text simultaneously}[ALT-F9]tcfbicycle.wpg{and.wpg
in 5.0}[ENTER][F7][SHIFT-F7]gdf

2. {assumes that your printer can print graphics and text simultaneously}[ALT-F9]bcfpc-1.wpg{key.wpg in 5.0}[ENTER][F7]{Type the paragraph as shown, allowing WordPerfect to wrap the text around the text box.}[SHIFT-F7]gmthf

3. {assumes that your printer can print graphics and text simultaneously}[ALT-F9]ucfcntrct-2.wpg {quill.wpg in 5.0}[ENTER][F7]{Type the paragraph as shown, allowing WordPerfect to wrap the text around the user-defined box.}[SHIFT-F7]ghf

4. {assumes that your printer can print graphics and text simultaneously}[ALT-F9]fcfbulb.wpg{pencil.wpg in 5.0}[ENTER][F7][ALT-F9]fcffloppy.wpg{book.wpg in 5.0}[ENTER][F7]{Type the paragraph as shown, allowing WordPerfect to wrap the text around the two figures.}[SHIFT-F7]gmf

MASTERY SKILLS CHECK

1. [ALT-F9]fc[F7][SHIFT-F7]v[F7]   [17.1]

2. [ALT-F9]fchl[F7][SHIFT-F7]v[F7]   [17.1, 17.5]

3. [ALT-F9]fe1[ENTER]fmailbag.wpg{quill.wpg in 5.0}   [17.3, 17.6]
[ENTER][F7][SHIFT-F7]v[F7]

4. [ALT-F9]fe2[ENTER]e{Type the text as shown, pressing   [17.2, 17.6]
ENTER after the colon and after each author.}
[F7][F7][SHIFT-F7]v[F7]

[17.6]   **5.** [ALT-F9]fe1[ENTER]fdiploma.wpg{thinker.wpg in 5.0} [ENTER]y[F7][SHIFT-F7]v[F7]

[17.4]   **6.** [ALT-F9]fe1[ENTER]c[SPACEBAR]A few thoughts to ponder[F7][F7][SHIFT-F7]v[F7]

[17.5]   **7.** [ALT-F9]fe1[ENTER]sh2[ENTER][F7][SHIFT-F7]v[F7]

[17.5]   **8.** [ALT-F9]fe2[ENTER]sw3.5{4 in 5.0}[ENTER][F7][SHIFT-F7]v[F7]

[17.2, 17.6]   **9.** [ALT-F9]fe2[ENTER]e[DOWN ARROW][ENTER][DOWN ARROW] [DOWN ARROW][ENTER][DOWN ARROW][DOWN ARROW] [ENTER][F7][F7][SHIFT-F7]v[F7]

[17.7]   **10.** [SHIFT-F7]tmghf[F7]nn

[17.3, 17.4, 17.5]   **11.** [ALT-F9]h1tcfchkbox-1.wpg{arrow1.wpg in 5.0} [ENTER]c[SPACEBAR]Read This! It Is Important![F7][F7] [SHIFT-F7]v[F7]

INTEGRATING SKILLS CHECK

[17.2]   **1.** {Type the paragraph as shown.}[F7]yimages[ENTER] n[ALT-F9]bcfimages[ENTER][F7]{Press ENTER 18 times (17 in 5.0).}[SHIFT-F7]v[F7]

[17.3, 17.4]   **2.** [ALT-F9]tcfclock.wpg[ENTER]c[SPACEBAR]A stitch in time saves nine[F7][F7][SHIFT-F7]v[F7]

[17.5]   **3.** [ALT-F9]te1[ENTER]sb4[ENTER]4[ENTER][F7][SHIFT-F7]v[F7]

[13.3]   **4.** [SHIFT-F3][SHIFT-F10]images[ENTER][DOWN ARROW][DOWN ARROW][DOWN ARROW][CTRL-F4]sd[F10][ENTER]y[SHIFT-F7]v[F7]

5. [SHIFT-F3][ALT-F9]be1[ENTER]f[ENTER]y[F7][SHIFT-F7]v[F7]   [13.3, 17.6]

6. [ALT-F9]be1[ENTER]e{Move to the "W" in "Word-   [4.7, 17.6]
Perfect 5.1 Made Easy."}[ALT-F4]y[F8][F7][F7][SHIFT-F7]
v[F7]

7. [SHIFT-F7]gdtdf[SHIFT-F7]v[F7]   [17.7]

8. [ALT-F3][HOME][HOME][DOWN ARROW][BACKSPACE][ALT-F3]   [17.6]
[SHIFT-F7]v[F7]

9. [ALT-F9]fcfhands-3.wpg{announce.wpg in 5.0}   [17.3]
[ENTER][F7]{Press ENTER 16 times (19 in 5.0).}
[SHIFT-F7]v[F7]

10. [ALT-F3][HOME][HOME][UP ARROW][BACKSPACE][HOME]   [17.6]
[HOME][DOWN ARROW][F1]r[HOME][HOME][UP ARROW]
{Press the DEL key until the [Fig Box:1;HANDS-3
.WPG;]([Figure:1;ANNOUNCE.WPG;] in 5.0)
code is at the beginning of the document.}[ALT-
F3][SHIFT-F7]v[F7]

11. [SHIFT-F8]phap[ALT-F9]ucfglobe2-m.wpg{airplane.wpg   [10.2, 17.3, 17.5]
in 5.0}[ENTER]hf{b in 5.0}[F7][F7][F7][SHIFT-F7]v[F7]

12. [SHIFT-F7]ghf[SHIFT-F7]v[F7]   [17.7]

SKILLS CHECK _____ 18

1. [F4]{Type the paragraph as shown.}   [5.2]

2. [SHIFT-F4]{Type the paragraph.}   [5.2]

3. [SHIFT-F8]lt[CTRL-END]4[ENTER][F7][F7]Joe Jones[TAB]   [5.4]
Accounting[ENTER]Paul Balber[TAB]Finance[ENTER]
Norlin

Rugers[TAB]Management[ENTER]Mary Rogers[TAB]
Accounting[ENTER]

[5.1, 12.1]   **4.** [SHIFT-F8]lm2[ENTER]2[ENTER][F7]{Type the text as
shown.}[SHIFT-F7]n2[ENTER]f

18.1   EXERCISES

1. [CAPS LOCK]high school sports[ENTER][SHIFT-F5]oo{omit
one o in 5.0}[ENTER][SPACEBAR][TAB]baseball[ENTER]
[SPACEBAR][TAB]football[ENTER][SPACEBAR]swimming
[ENTER][SPACEBAR][TAB]hockey[SHIFT-F5]of{omit the f in
5.0}[CAPS LOCK][F7][ENTER]sports[ENTER][ENTER]

2. [CAPS LOCK]breeds of dogs[CAPS LOCK][ENTER][SHIFT-F5]
oo{omit one o in 5.0}[ENTER][F4]Hounds[ENTER][TAB]
[F4]Greyhound[ENTER]{and [TAB] in 5.0}[F4]Whippet
[ENTER][SHIFT-TAB]{omit [SHIFT-TAB] in 5.0}[F4]Sporting
Dogs[ENTER][TAB][F4]Labrador Retriever[ENTER]{and
[TAB] in 5.0}[F4]Irish Setter[ENTER][SHIFT-TAB]{omit
[SHIFT-TAB] in 5.0}[F4]Terriers[ENTER][TAB][F4]Airedale
[ENTER]{and [TAB] in 5.0}[F4]Welsh Terrier[ENTER]
[SHIFT-TAB]{omit [SHIFT-TAB] in 5.0}[F4]Working
Dogs[ENTER][TAB][F4]Collie[ENTER]{and [TAB] in
5.0}[F4]Siberian Husky[SHIFT-F5]of{omit the f in
5.0}[F7][ENTER]dogs[ENTER][ENTER]

18.2   EXERCISES

1. [SHIFT-F10]sports[ENTER][SHIFT-F5]oo{omit one o in 5.0}
[HOME][HOME][DOWN ARROW][ENTER][SPACEBAR][TAB]BASKET-
BALL[ENTER][SPACEBAR][TAB]TRACK{Move the cursor

after the final "L" in "BASEBALL."}[ENTER][TAB]
[SPACEBAR][TAB]John Doe[ENTER]{and [TAB] in 5.0}
[SPACEBAR][TAB]Bill Black[DOWN ARROW]{Repeat the
process, entering the names of the captains for
the other sports.}

2. [SHIFT-F10]dogs[ENTER]{Move the cursor to the first
"I" in "II."}[ALT-F4][DOWN ARROW][DOWN ARROW][DOWN
ARROW][CTRL-F4]bm[PGDN][ENTER][ENTER]{You may
need to press the DEL key if WordPerfect inserts
an extra number before "Sporting Dogs."}
[RIGHT ARROW]

EXERCISES 18.3

1. [SHIFT-F5]dl[F7]oo{omit one o in 5.0}[ENTER][F4]Estate
Planning[ENTER][TAB][F4]Trust[ENTER]{and [TAB] in 5.0}
[F4]Will[SHIFT-F5]of{omit the f in 5.0}

2. [SHIFT-F5]db[F7]oo{omit one o in 5.0}The following
employees are being honored for 25 years of
service:[ENTER][TAB][TAB][TAB][F4]Jane Parker[ENTER]
{[TAB][TAB][TAB] in 5.0}[F4]Bill Black[SHIFT-F5]of{omit
the f in 5.0}

MASTERY SKILLS CHECK

1. [SHIFT-F5]do[F7]oo{omit one o in 5.0}[CAPS LOCK]port-   [18.1]
folio holdings[CAPS LOCK][ENTER][F4]Zero coupon
bonds[ENTER][F4]Treasury bills[ENTER][F4]Blue chip
stocks[ENTER][F4]Mutual fund shares

[18.2]

2. {Move the cursor to the second outline entry.}
[CTRL-F4]pm{Move the cursor to the end of the last
outline entry.}[ENTER][ENTER]{You may need to
press the DEL key if WordPerfect inserts an extra
number before "Treasury bills."}[RIGHT ARROW]

[18.1]

3. [END][ENTER][F4]Stock options[SHIFT-F5]of{omit the f in
5.0}[F7][ENTER]invest[ENTER]y[ENTER]

[18.1]

4. [SHIFT-F5]oo{omit one o in 5.0}[ENTER][F4]New Con-
struction[ENTER][TAB][F4]Mayfield Village[ENTER]{and
[TAB] in 5.0}[F4]Highland Heights[ENTER][TAB]
{another [TAB] in 5.0}[F4]1114 Miner Road[ENTER]
{[TAB][TAB] in 5.0}[F4]4811 Highland Ave.[ENTER]
[SHIFT-TAB][SHIFT-TAB]{omit both [SHIFT-TAB]'s in 5.0}
[F4]Remodeling Projects[ENTER][TAB][F4]Gates
Mills[ENTER][TAB]{[TAB] in 5.0}[F4]112 Sherman
Road[ENTER]{[TAB][TAB] in 5.0}[F4]230 Saddleback
Lane[ENTER][SHIFT-TAB]{[TAB] instead in 5.0}[F4]
Chagrin Falls

[18.2]

5. [ENTER]{[TAB] in 5.0}[F4]Solon{Move the cursor to
after the period in "Highland Ave."}[ENTER]{[TAB]
[TAB] in 5.0}[F4]5311 Wilson Mills Road[HOME][DOWN
ARROW][SHIFT-F5]of{omit the f in 5.0}[F7][ENTER]jobs
[ENTER][ENTER]

INTEGRATING SKILLS CHECK

[1.4, 3.1, 18.3]

1. {Type the top of the memo and the first paragraph as shown.}[SHIFT-F5]db[F7]oo{omit one o in
5.0}[ENTER][TAB][TAB][TAB][F4]Jim Miller[ENTER]{[TAB]
[TAB][TAB] in 5.0}[F4]Mary Parker[ENTER]{[TAB][TAB]
[TAB] in 5.0}[F4]Paul Drake[SHIFT-F5]of{omit the f in
5.0}

{Move the cursor to after the period in the last sentence.}[CTRL-ENTER][SHIFT-F7]f

2. [SHIFT-F5]dl[F7]oo{omit one o in 5.0}[ENTER][F4]   [18.1, 18.3]
WordPerfect's Math Features[ENTER][TAB][F4]
Add numbers [ENTER][TAB]{another [TAB] in 5.0}
[F4]Produce a subtotal for a column of numbers
[ENTER]{[TAB][TAB] in 5.0}[F4]Add subtotals to
produce totals[ENTER]{[TAB][TAB] in 5.0}[F4]Add totals
to produce a grand total[ENTER][SHIFT-TAB]{[TAB]
instead in 5.0}[F4]Perform formula calculations
across columns[SHIFT-F5]of{omit the f in 5.0}[F7]
[ENTER]math[ENTER][ENTER]

3. [SHIFT-F5]do[F7]oo{omit one o in 5.0}[ENTER][F4]   [4.1, 12.1, 18.1,
WordPerfect Books[ENTER][TAB][F4][F8]WordPerfect   18.2]
Made Easy[F8][ENTER]{[TAB] in 5.0}[F4][F8]Word-
Perfect: The Complete Reference[F8][ENTER][SHIFT-
TAB]{omit [SHIFT-TAB] in 5.0}[F4]1-2-3 Books[ENTER][TAB]
[F4][F8]1-2-3 Made Easy[F8][ENTER]{and [TAB] in 5.0}
[F4][F8]1-2-3: The Complete Reference[F8]{Move to
the end of the last entry in the first section.}
[ENTER]{and [TAB] in 5.0}[F4][F8] Teach Yourself
WordPerfect[F8][SHIFT-F5]of{omit the f in 5.0}
[SHIFT-F7]n2[ENTER]f

4. [SHIFT-F5]oo{omit one o in 5.0}[ENTER][F4]Vacation   [8.2, 18.1, 18.2]
days[ENTER][F4]Sick leave[ENTER][F4]Holidays
[ENTER][TAB][F4]Christmas[ENTER]{and [TAB] in 5.0}
[F4]Thanksgiving[ENTER]{and [TAB] in 5.0}[F4]
Memorial Day[ENTER]{and [TAB] in 5.0}[F4]
Halloween[ENTER]{and [TAB] in 5.0}[F4]
Independence Day[ENTER]{and [TAB] in 5.0}[F4]
Labor Day{Move the cursor to the first "I" in
"III."}[ALT-F4][HOME][HOME][DOWN ARROW][CTRL-F4]bm

[HOME][HOME][UP ARROW][ENTER]{Move to the beginning of the line for "Halloween."}[CTRL-END][DEL]
[HOME][HOME][DOWN ARROW]

19

[4.1, 4.2]

SKILLS CHECK

1. [F6]WordPerfect allows you to change several
settings.[F6]You can set WordPerfect to back up
files automatically. You can also change the
screen's appearance by selecting the colors Word-
Perfect uses.[F8]These are just a few of the selections available.[F8]

[2.2]

2. [F10]default[ENTER]

[11.5]

3. [F5][ENTER]{Move the cursor to the DEFAULT file.}
msettings[ENTER][F7]

[4.4]

4. [ALT-F3]{Soft returns appear as **[SRt]**.}

19.1

EXERCISES

1. [SHIFT-F1]e{omit the e in 5.0}bty120[ENTER][F7]

2. [SHIFT-F1]e{omit the e in 5.0}bty30[ENTER][F7]

EXERCISES ——————————————— 19.2

1. [SHIFT-F1]dcs[DOWN ARROW][DOWN ARROW][DOWN ARROW]
[DOWN ARROW]{Press the RIGHT ARROW key if you have
a Font column.}a[F7][F7]

2. [SHIFT-F1]dcs[DOWN ARROW][DOWN ARROW][DOWN ARROW]
[DOWN ARROW][DOWN ARROW][DOWN ARROW][DOWN ARROW]
[DOWN ARROW]{Press the RIGHT ARROW key if you have
a Font column.}{Type the letter for the normal
font in the Foreground column.}[RIGHT ARROW]
{Type the letter for the normal font in the Background column.}[F7][F7]

3. [SHIFT-F1]de{omit the e in 5.0}h < [F7]

4. [SHIFT-F1]de{omit the e in 5.0}h[SPACEBAR][F7]

5. [SHIFT-F1]de{omit the e in 5.0}fy[F7]

EXERCISES ——————————————— 19.3

1. [SHIFT-F1]e{i in 5.0}e{b in 5.0}en[F7]

2. [SHIFT-F1]id6,[SPACEBAR]3[SPACEBAR]1[ENTER][F7]

3. On[SHIFT-F5]t, the Okra Vegetable company begins
marketing its new product line, the Seeing Green
frozen foods.

MASTERY SKILLS CHECK

[19.1]　　**1.** [SHIFT-F1]e{omit the e in 5.0}bty20[ENTER][F7]

[19.2]　　**2.** [SHIFT-F1]dcs{Press the RIGHT ARROW key if you have a Font column.}[RIGHT ARROW]a[F7][F7]

[19.3]　　**3.** [SHIFT-F1]id3[SPACEBAR]4[ENTER][F7]

[19.3]　　**4.** Acme Corporation projects that its personnel will increase 5% during[SHIFT-F5]t.

[19.3]　　**5.** [SHIFT-F1]e{i in 5.0}e{b in 5.0}sn[F7]

INTEGRATING SKILLS CHECK

[1.3, 11.5, 19.1]　　**1.** [SHIFT-F1]e{omit the e in 5.0}bty1[ENTER][F7]Testing Backups{Wait until WordPerfect backs up the document.}[F5][ENTER]{Move the highlight to the WP{WP}.BK1 file.}mbckuptst[ENTER][F7][F7]nn

[19.1]　　**2.** [SHIFT-F1]e{omit the e in 5.0}btn[ENTER][F7]

[19.3]　　**3.** [SHIFT-F1]id3[SPACEBAR]1,[SPACEBAR]4[ENTER][F7]

[19.3]　　**4.** [TAB]The company picnic is on[SHIFT-F5]t.[ENTER] [TAB]Each person should bring one dish. Please review the schedule, which breaks down the type of dish based upon the person's last name.[ENTER]

[4.7]　　**5.** [HOME][HOME][UP ARROW][ALT-F4][END][F6]{Move to the "o" in "one."}[CTRL-LEFT ARROW][ALT-F4]h[F8]

[19.2]　　**6.** [SHIFT-F1]de{omit the e in 5.0}h*[F7]

7. [SHIFT-F1]dcs{Press the RIGHT ARROW key if you have   [19.2]
   a Font column.}[DOWN ARROW][DOWN ARROW][RIGHT
   ARROW] e{assuming e is the selection for red}[DOWN
   ARROW][DOWN ARROW]d{assuming d is the selection
   for light blue}[F7]

8. {for a hard disk system}[F5][ENTER]{Move the high-   [11.4]
   light to the WP{WP}.SET file.}dy{for a floppy disk
   system}[F5]a:[ENTER]{Move the highlight to the
   WP{WP}.SET file.}dy

9. [F7][ENTER]dish[ENTER]y{for a hard disk system}   [1.1, 1.2, 19.1]
   wp[ENTER]{for a floppy disk system: Place the
   WordPerfect 1 disk in drive A.}a:wp[ENTER]{Place
   the WordPerfect 2 disk in drive A when Word-
   Perfect prompts you, and press any key to continue.}[SHIFT-F1]e{omit the e in 5.0}bty30[ENTER][F7]

SKILLS CHECK _____ 20

1. {Type the heading and the three paragraphs.}

2. [SHIFT-F7]v[F7]

3. [HOME][HOME][UP ARROW][ALT-F4][END][F6][ALT-F4][CTRL-
   LEFT ARROW][SHIFT-F6]y

4. [DOWN ARROW][SHIFT-F8]ls2[ENTER][F7][CTRL-HOME][SHIFT-;]
   [SHIFT-F8]ls1[ENTER][F7]{Move the cursor to the "A"
   in the beginning of the third paragraph.}[SHIFT-
   F8]ls2 [ENTER][F7]

5. [SHIFT-F2][SHIFT-'][F2][BACKSPACE][SHIFT-F2][F2]
[BACKSPACE][SHIFT-F4]

6. {Move the cursor to the "M" in "Mary."}[ALT-F4]
[CTRL-RIGHT ARROW][CTRL-RIGHT ARROW][LEFT ARROW][F8]

7. [SHIFT-F7]v[F7]

8. [F7]ystyl.doc[ENTER]n

20.1   EXERCISES

1. [ALT-F8]cnHeader[SPACEBAR]lvl[SPACEBAR]1[ENTER]c
[SHIFT-F6][F6][RIGHT ARROW][ENTER][SHIFT-F6][ESC]45
[ENTER][F7][F7][F7]

2. [ALT-F8]cnHeader[SPACEBAR]lvl[SPACEBAR]2
[ENTER]c[F8][RIGHT ARROW][ENTER][F7]ef[F7][F7]

3. [ALT-F8]cnLong[SPACEBAR]Quotes[ENTER]c[SHIFT-F8]ls1
[ENTER][F7][SHIFT-F4][F7][F7][F7]

4. [F7]ystyle2.doc[ENTER]n

20.2   EXERCISES

1. [SHIFT-F10]style2.doc[ENTER][SHIFT-F8]ls2[ENTER][F7][ALT-F8]
{Highlight Header lvl 1.}oDepartment Comments
and Concerns[DOWN ARROW][ALT-F8]{Highlight Head-

er lvl 2.}oAccounting Department[ENTER]{Type the first paragraph and press ENTER.}[ALT-F8] {Highlight the Long Quotes style.}o{Type the quote.}[RIGHT ARROW][ENTER][ALT-F8]{Highlight Header lvl 2.}oSales Department[ENTER]{Type the last paragraph.}[F7]ydeptnews.ltr[ENTER]n

2. [SHIFT-F10]style2.doc[ENTER]{Type the text; then move the cursor to the "W" in the first "Welcome."}[ALT-F4][END][ALT-F8]{Highlight Header lvl 1.}o{Move the cursor to the "J" in "John Smith."}[ALT-F4][END][ALT-F8]{Highlight Header lvl 2.}o{Move to the "J" in "Jane Brown."}[ALT-F4] [END][ALT-F8]{Highlight Header lvl 2.}o[F7] ywelcome[ENTER]n

EXERCISES   20.3

1. [SHIFT-F10]style2.doc[ENTER][ALT-F8]cnLetters[ENTER] todGeneral Correspondence[ENTER]c[SHIFT-F8]lm1.5 [ENTER][ENTER]t[HOME][HOME][LEFT ARROW][CTRL-END]0.5 {2 in 5.0}[ENTER][F7][F7][SHIFT-F6]{Type your name.} [ENTER][SHIFT-F6]{Type your street address.}[ENTER] [SHIFT-F6]{Type your city, state, zip.}[ENTER][ENTER] [SHIFT-F6][SHIFT-F5]c[ENTER][ENTER][ENTER][ENTER][F7][F7] [F7][F7]yletter2.doc[ENTER]n

2. [SHIFT-F10]style2.doc[ENTER][ALT-F8]cnNewsletter [ENTER]toc[SHIFT-F8]ls2[ENTER][F7][SHIFT-F6]Acme Corpo- ration Newsletter[F7][F7][F7][F7]ynews.ltr[ENTER]n

20.4   EXERCISES

1. [SHIFT-F10]letter2.doc[ENTER][ALT-F8]{Highlight the style named Letters.}o{Type the text of the letter.} [F10]travel.ltr[ENTER]

2. [SHIFT-F10]news.ltr[ENTER][ALT-F8]{Highlight the style named Newsletter.}o[ENTER][ALT-F8]{Highlight the style named Header Lvl 2.}o[CAPS LOCK]new equipment for sales department[CAPS LOCK][ENTER]{Type the rest of the text as shown.}[F10]newsvol1.doc [ENTER]

20.5   EXERCISES

1. [SHIFT-F10]newsvol1.doc[ENTER][HOME][HOME][DOWN ARROW][ENTER]Ron Adams, MIS coordinator states that:[ENTER][ALT-F8]{Highlight the Long Quotes style.}oAll systems are go. All equipment and cabling has been received, assembled and tested. We anticipate no problems.[RIGHT ARROW][ENTER] Training sessions are planned for the next three Fridays at 1:00 pm.[SHIFT-F7]v[F7][F10][ENTER]y

2. [ALT-F8]{Highlight the Newsletter style.}ec[DEL][F6] [HOME][RIGHT ARROW][ENTER][SHIFT-F6][ESC]27-[F7][F7] {Highlight the Long Quotes style.}ec[RIGHT ARROW][SHIFT-F4][F7][F7][F7][SHIFT-F7]v[F7][F7] ynewsvol1.fin[ENTER]n

EXERCISES ————————————— 20.6

1. [SHIFT-F10]newsvol1.doc[ENTER][ALT-F8]snewsltr.dft
[ENTER][F7]

2. [SHIFT-F10]newsvol1.fin[ENTER][ALT-F8]snewsltr.fin
[ENTER][F7]

EXERCISES ————————————— 20.7

1. [F7]nn[ALT-F8]rnewsltr.dft[ENTER]y{Highlight the
Newsletter style.}o[ENTER]{Type the paragraph as
shown.}[SHIFT-F7]f

2. [ALT-F8]rnewsltr.fin[ENTER]y[F7][SHIFT-F7]f[F7]nn

MASTERY SKILLS CHECK

1. [ALT-F8]cnTitle[ENTER]c[SHIFT-F6][ESC]54*[ENTER][SHIFT-F6]
[RIGHT ARROW][ENTER][SHIFT-F6][ESC]54*[ENTER][F7][F7][F7]

2. [ALT-F8]cnAnnouncement[ENTER]toc[SHIFT-F8]lm1.5
[ENTER]1.5[ENTER][ENTER]pm1.5[ENTER]1.5[ENTER][F7][F7]
[F7][F7]

3. [ALT-F8]{Highlight the Announcement style.}o[ALT-
F8]{Highlight the Title style.}oNew Medical Reimbursement Procedures[RIGHT ARROW][ENTER]{Type
the paragraph as shown.}[F10]announce.doc[ENTER]

4. [ALT-F8]sstyle.ann[ENTER][F7][F7]nn

5. {Type the document as shown.}[HOME][HOME][UP
ARROW][ALT-F8]rstyle.ann[ENTER]y{Highlight the Announcement style.}o{Move the cursor to the "N"
in "New."}[ALT-F4][END][ALT-F8]{Highlight the Title
style.}o

6. [ALT-F8]{Highlight the Title style.}ec[CTRL-END]
[DEL][F6][F7][F7][F7][F7]nn

INTEGRATING SKILLS CHECK

1. {Type the text as shown.}

2. [ALT-F8]cnPress Rel.[ENTER]toc[SHIFT-F8]ls2[ENTER]
[ENTER]pfap[SHIFT-F6]PRESS RELEASE — PRESS
RELEASE — PRESS RELEASE[F7][F7][F7][F7][F7]

3. [ALT-F8]cnMain Heading[ENTER]c[F6][SHIFT-F6][RIGHT
ARROW][ENTER][F7]ef[F7][F7]

4. [HOME][HOME][UP ARROW][ALT-F8]{Highlight the Press
Rel. style.}o

5. [ALT-F8]{Highlight the Main Heading style.}oData-
Blaster Blasts the Competition[ENTER]

6. [SHIFT-F7]f

7. [ALT-F8]{Highlight the Press Rel. style.}ec[SHIFT-F8]
   phap[SHIFT-F6]PRESS RELEASE — PRESS RELEASE
   — PRESS RELEASE[F7][F7][F7][F7][F7]

8. [SHIFT-F7]f[F7]nn

SKILLS CHECK   21

1. [SHIFT-F8]pm2[ENTER]3[ENTER][F7]

2. [SHIFT-F8]ljl{n in 5.0}[F7]

3. [SHIFT-F6]Memory Upgrades Available[ENTER]

4. [SHIFT-F6][ESC]35-[ENTER][ENTER]

5. The memory chips we ordered three months ago
   have[F8]finally[F8]arrived. Those of you who
   have been waiting to upgrade your system
   should schedule a time with MIS Services for
   swapping memory chips at your earliest convenience.

6. [CTRL-F2]d{Skip for MIS and press any key to
   continue.}

7. [F7]ymemory[ENTER]n

21.1 EXERCISES

1. [ALT-F7]c{omit in 5.0}d[F7][F7][SHIFT-F8]pm[ENTER]8
[ENTER][F7][SHIFT-F6][CAPS LOCK]acme corporation[CAPS
LOCK][ENTER][ESC]65 = [ENTER][ENTER][F7]ynewsltr.doc
[ENTER]n

2. [SHIFT-F8]pm[ENTER]8[ENTER][F7][SHIFT-F6][F6][CAPS
LOCK]north coast community news[CAPS LOCK]
[F6][ENTER][SHIFT-F6][ESC]26 = [ENTER][ALT-F7]c{omit in
5.0}dn3[ENTER][F7][F7][F7]ycommnews[ENTER][ENTER]

21.2 EXERCISES

1. [SHIFT-F10]newsltr.doc[ENTER][HOME][HOME][DOWN
ARROW][ALT-F7]co{omit in 5.0}[SHIFT-F6][F8][CAPS
LOCK]safety seminar[CAPS LOCK][F8][ENTER][ENTER]
{Type the first paragraph.}[ENTER][ENTER]{Type the
second paragraph.}[F7]y[ENTER]y[ENTER]

2. [SHIFT-F10]commnews[ENTER][HOME][HOME][DOWN
ARROW][ALT-F7]co{omit in 5.0}[SHIFT-F6][CAPS LOCK]
kiddie calendar[CAPS LOCK][ENTER][ENTER]{Type the
first paragraph.}[ENTER][ENTER]{Type the second
paragraph.}[ENTER][ENTER]{Type the third paragraph.}[F7]y[ENTER]y[ENTER]

3. [ALT-F7]c{omit c in 5.0}d[F7]o{c in 5.0}Paragraph
1[ENTER][ENTER]This is the first paragraph of this
exercise.[CTRL-ENTER]Paragraph 2[ENTER][ENTER]This is
the second paragraph of this exercise. It appears

in column 2.[ALT-F7]cf{omit f in 5.0}Paragraph 3[ENTER][ENTER]This is the third paragraph of this exercise. It should appear below the first two paragraphs.[SHIFT-F7]v[F7][F7]ycolumns[ENTER][ENTER]

EXERCISES ———————————————— 21.3

1. [ALT-F7]c{omit in 5.0}dtpm[ENTER]2.5[ENTER]3[ENTER] [ENTER][F7][F7][SHIFT-F6][CAPS LOCK]meeting new friends[CAPS LOCK][ENTER][ENTER][SHIFT-F6]A Play Presented By:[ENTER][SHIFT-F6]Ms. Walker's First Grade Class[ENTER][ENTER][F7]yplay.doc[ENTER][ENTER]

2. [SHIFT-F8]pm[ENTER]8[ENTER][F7][SHIFT-F6][F6]Name & Address Listing[F6][ENTER][ENTER][ALT-F7]c{omit in 5.0}dtbn3[ENTER]m[ENTER]2.5[ENTER]3[ENTER]6[ENTER]6.5 [ENTER][ENTER][F7][F7][F7]yn&a.lst[ENTER][ENTER]

3. [SHIFT-F8]pm[ENTER]8.5[ENTER][F7][ALT-F7]c{omit in 5.0}dtbn3[ENTER]m[ENTER]1.8[ENTER]2.2[ENTER]4[ENTER] 4.4[ENTER][ENTER][F7][F7][SHIFT-F6][CAPS LOCK]acme corporation[CAPS LOCK][ENTER][SHIFT-F6]Equipment Inventory[ENTER][ENTER][F7]yinvty.doc[ENTER][ENTER]

EXERCISES ———————————————— 21.4

1. [SHIFT-F10]play.doc[ENTER][HOME][HOME][DOWN ARROW] [ALT-F7]co{omit o in 5.0}[SHIFT-F6][F8]Character[F8] [CTRL-ENTER][SHIFT-F6][F8]Lines[F8][CTRL-ENTER]{Type the script using CTRL-ENTER to move to the next column.}[F7]y[ENTER]y[ENTER]

2. [SHIFT-F10]n&a.lst[ENTER][HOME][HOME][DOWN ARROW]
[ALT-F7]co{omit o in 5.0}Sandy Clark[CTRL-ENTER]
121 S. Main St.[ENTER]Cleveland, OH 44114
[CTRL-ENTER]287-1120[CTRL-ENTER]Joe Kent[CTRL-ENTER]
2780 Bluebird Lane[ENTER]North Oak, OH 44013
[CTRL-ENTER]452-7655[CTRL-ENTER]Sally Jones[CTRL-
ENTER]5891 Sunny Vale[ENTER]Little Creek, OH
44410[CTRL-ENTER]552-1732[F7]y[ENTER]y[ENTER]

3. [SHIFT-F10]invty.doc[ENTER][HOME][HOME][DOWN
ARROW][ALT-F7]co{omit o in 5.0}[CAPS LOCK]part no
[CTRL-ENTER]product name[CTRL-ENTER]descrip-
tion[CTRL-ENTER][CAPS LOCK]{Type the remaining
text using CTRL-ENTER to move to the next column.}
[F7]y[ENTER]y[ENTER]

21.5   EXERCISES

1. [SHIFT-F10]commnews[ENTER][DOWN ARROW][DOWN
ARROW][DOWN ARROW][CTRL-HOME][RIGHT ARROW][CTRL-
HOME][RIGHT ARROW][DOWN ARROW][DOWN ARROW][DOWN
ARROW][DOWN ARROW][DOWN ARROW][DOWN ARROW]{The
cursor should now be on the "1" in "12:00."}
[DEL][CTRL-HOME][LEFT ARROW][CTRL-HOME][LEFT ARROW]
[UP ARROW][UP ARROW][UP ARROW][UP ARROW][UP ARROW]
[CTRL-RIGHT ARROW][CTRL-RIGHT ARROW][CTRL-BACKSPACE]
[CAPS LOCK]notes[CAPS LOCK][F7]y[ENTER]y[ENTER]

2. [SHIFT-F10]n&a.lst[ENTER][DOWN ARROW][DOWN ARROW]
[CTRL-HOME][RIGHT ARROW][CTRL-HOME][RIGHT ARROW]
[DOWN ARROW][DOWN ARROW][CTRL-BACKSPACE]555-5555
[CTRL-HOME][LEFT ARROW][CTRL-HOME][LEFT ARROW]

[DOWN ARROW][DOWN ARROW][CTRL-RIGHT ARROW]
[CTRL-BACKSPACE]Smith[F7]y[ENTER]y[ENTER]

3. [SHIFT-F10]play.doc[ENTER][ALT-F3]{Make sure the cursor is just to the right of the [Col Def:] code.}[ALT-F3][ALT-F7]c{omit in 5.0}dm[ENTER]2[ENTER]2.4[ENTER]
[ENTER][F7][F7][SHIFT-F7]v[F7][F7]y[ENTER]
y[ENTER]

MASTERY SKILLS CHECK

1. [SHIFT-F6]The Greenville Library[ENTER][SHIFT-F6]Eager Reader Club[ENTER][ENTER][ALT-F7]c{omit in 5.0}d
[F7][F7]

2. [ALT-F7]co{omit o in 5.0}[SHIFT-F6]Story Hour[ENTER]
[ENTER]Eager readers can take part in story hour every Monday from 10:00 to 11:00 am. Every week, we will feature a new story read by everyone's favorite, Mr. Rabbit. After the reading, the children are encouraged to participate in a lively discussion about the story. Mr. Rabbit tries to teach a valuable lesson from every story he reads to our Eager Readers.[ENTER][ENTER]Mr. Rabbit is looking forward to seeing you next week.[CTRL-ENTER]

3. [ALT-F7]cf{omit f in 5.0}[ENTER][ENTER]

4. [SHIFT-F6]The Top Four Favorites[ENTER][ENTER][ALT-F7]c{omit in 5.0}dtpn3[ENTER]m[ENTER]3[ENTER]3.5
[ENTER]6[ENTER]6.5[ENTER][ENTER][F7][F7]

5. [ALT-F7]co{omit o in 5.0}[SHIFT-F6]Title[CTRL-ENTER]
[SHIFT-F6]Author[CTRL-ENTER][SHIFT-F6]Rating[CTRL-ENTER]
{Type the columns using CTRL-ENTER to move to the
next column.}

6. [ALT-F7]cf{omit f in 5.0}[ENTER][SHIFT-F6]Book Sale
[ENTER][ENTER][F4]On May 5th, the Greenville
Teen Readers will be sponsoring a book sale of
books donated by various members of the community. All are welcome to browse and pick up a
few favorites at very low prices. If you have
books you would like to donate, please bring
them to the library on May 4th during business
hours.[ENTER]

7. [SHIFT-F7]v[F7][F7]nn

INTEGRATING SKILLS CHECK

1. [SHIFT-F8]ljl{n instead of final l in 5.0}m1.5[ENTER]
1.5[ENTER][ENTER]pm1.5[ENTER]1.5[ENTER][F7]

2. [ALT-F7]c{omit in 5.0}dd.4[ENTER][F7][F7]

3. [SHIFT-F6][F6]Looking for the Perfect Candy Bar?
[F6][ENTER][ENTER]

4. [ALT-F7]co{omit o in 5.0}

5. Capital Foods announces the release of their first
no-calorie, no-cholesterol candy bar called[F8]
Perfect-Bar[F8].[CTRL-ENTER]The product received

rave reviews during its test-marketing. Now you can eat a delicious candy bar guilt free!

6. [ALT-F7]cf{omit f in 5.0}[ENTER][ENTER]

7. [SHIFT-F6][F6]Perfect-Bar Taste Testers Survey [F6][ENTER][ENTER]

8. Capital Foods test marketed Perfect-Bar in three different areas of the country. The customer comments were generally favorable. Some of the comments are reproduced below:[ENTER][ENTER]

9. [ALT-F7]c{omit in 5.0}dtpm[ENTER]2.5[ENTER]2.9 [ENTER][ENTER][F7]o{c in 5.0}

10. Area A[CTRL-ENTER]Tasty nougat center. The chocolate coating is rich and creamy.[CTRL-ENTER]Area B[CTRL-ENTER]Where did you put the calories? This tastes just like the stuff I'm not supposed to have.[CTRL-ENTER]Area C[CTRL-ENTER]Anything that tastes this good has to have something wrong with it.

SKILLS CHECK 22

1. [SHIFT-F8]lt[CTRL-END]0[ENTER]0.5[ENTER]5[ENTER]d6 [ENTER]d[F7][F7]

2. [SHIFT-F6]Acme Corporation[ENTER][SHIFT-F6] Statement[ENTER][SHIFT-F6][SHIFT-F5]c[ENTER][ENTER]

3. Previous Balance[TAB][TAB]$1,234.56[ENTER]Expenses
[ENTER][TAB]Rent[TAB]400.00[ENTER][TAB]Utilities[TAB]
[F8]119.00[F8][ENTER]Total Expenses[TAB][TAB](519.90)
[ENTER]Income[ENTER][TAB]Client 012[TAB]150.00
[ENTER][TAB]Client 110[TAB][F8]1,210.00[F8][ENTER]Total
Income[TAB][TAB][F8]1,360.00[F8][ENTER]Current
Balance[TAB][TAB]$[CTRL-F8]ad2,074.66[RIGHT ARROW]
[ENTER]

4. [F7]nn

22.1   EXERCISES

1. [F6]Office Supplies Inventory - Top Shelf [F6][ENTER]
[ENTER][ALT-F7]tc3[ENTER]4[ENTER][F7][HOME][HOME]
[DOWN ARROW][ENTER][F6]Office Supplies Inventory -
Bottom Shelf[F6][ENTER][ENTER][ALT-F7]tc3[ENTER]5
[ENTER][F7][F7]ysupplies[ENTER]n

2. [SHIFT-F6][F6]Faculty Evaluation Form[F6][ENTER]
[ENTER]{Type the paragraph.}[ENTER][ENTER][ALT-
F7]tc4[ENTER]5[ENTER][F7][HOME][HOME][DOWN ARROW]
[ENTER]Return this form to the department's fac-
ulty secretary.[F7]yfaculty.tbl[ENTER]n

3. Attachment C:[ENTER][ENTER][ALT-F7]tc2[ENTER]4
[ENTER][F7][HOME][HOME][DOWN ARROW][ENTER]See
page 14-7 for more details.[F7]yattach.c[ENTER]n

4. [ALT-F7]tc12[ENTER]15[ENTER][F7][HOME][HOME][UP ARROW]
[ALT-F3][ALT-F4][HOME][HOME][DOWN ARROW][DEL]y[ALT-F3]

5. [ALT-F7]tc2[ENTER]4[ENTER][F7][F7]ybill.sht[ENTER]n

EXERCISES ——————————————— 22.2

1. [SHIFT-F10]supplies[ENTER][DOWN ARROW][DOWN ARROW]
[DOWN ARROW]ITEM[TAB]TOTAL[TAB]UNITS[TAB]
Pencils[TAB]10[TAB]Boxes[TAB]Pens[TAB]8[TAB]Boxes
[TAB]Note Pads[TAB]15[TAB]Dozen[DOWN ARROW]
[DOWN ARROW][DOWN ARROW][DOWN ARROW][DOWN
ARROW][SHIFT-TAB][SHIFT-TAB]ITEM[TAB]TOTAL[TAB]
UNITS[TAB]Letterhead[TAB]3[TAB]Boxes[TAB]Second
Sheet Paper[TAB]4[TAB]Boxes[TAB]Bond Paper[TAB]15
[TAB]Reams[TAB]Laser Labels[TAB]2[TAB]Packages
[SHIFT-F7]f[F7]y[ENTER]y[ENTER]

2. [SHIFT-F10]faculty.tbl[ENTER][DOWN ARROW][DOWN
ARROW][DOWN ARROW][DOWN ARROW][DOWN ARROW]
[DOWN ARROW][DOWN ARROW][DOWN ARROW][DOWN
ARROW][DOWN ARROW]{The actual number of down
arrows may differ due to word-wrap differences.}
STATEMENT[TAB]AGREE[TAB]NEUTRAL[TAB]
DISAGREE[TAB]1. He/she comes prepared to class.
[DOWN ARROW]2. He/she has command of the subject matter.[DOWN ARROW]3. He/she seems genuinely
concerned with whether students learn the course
material.[DOWN ARROW]4. The course's contents
were taught in a manner that promoted learning
of the course material.[SHIFT-F7]f[F7]y[ENTER]y[ENTER]

3. [SHIFT-F10]attach.c[ENTER][DOWN ARROW][DOWN
ARROW][DOWN ARROW][DOWN ARROW]1988 MACRS deduction: $12,000 × .20 = [TAB]2,400.00[TAB]1989

MACRS deduction: $12,000 $\times$ .32 $\times$ 1/2 year
=[TAB]1,920.00[TAB]Total MACRS deduction:[F7]
y[ENTER]y[ENTER]

4. [SHIFT-F10]supplies[ENTER][DOWN ARROW][DOWN ARROW]
[DOWN ARROW][DOWN ARROW][DOWN ARROW] [DOWN
ARROW][DOWN ARROW][DOWN ARROW][DOWNARROW]
[DOWN ARROW][ALT-F3]{cursor is on Tbl Def code}
[SHIFT-F8]lt[CTRL-END]2.2[ENTER]4.4 [ENTER][F7][F7]
[DEL][ALT-F3][F7]ytopshelf[ENTER][ENTER]

5. [SHIFT-F10]bill.sht[ENTER][DOWN ARROW][DOWN ARROW]
[DOWN ARROW][DOWN ARROW]Total Charges:[F7]
y[ENTER]y[ENTER]

22.3   EXERCISES

1. [SHIFT-F10]supplies[ENTER][DOWN ARROW][DOWNARROW]
[DOWN ARROW][ALT-F7][TAB][CTRL-LEFT ARROW][CTRL-LEFT
ARROW][CTRL-LEFT ARROW][CTRL-LEFT ARROW][CTRL-LEFT
ARROW][CTRL-LEFT ARROW][CTRL-LEFT ARROW][CTRL-LEFT
ARROW][CTRL-LEFT ARROW][CTRL-LEFT ARROW][TAB][CTRL-LEFT
ARROW][CTRL-LEFT ARROW][CTRL-LEFT ARROW][CTRL-LEFT
ARROW][CTRL-LEFT ARROW][F7][DOWN ARROW][DOWN
ARROW][DOWN ARROW][DOWN ARROW][DOWN ARROW]
[DOWN ARROW][DOWN ARROW][DOWN ARROW][SHIFT-TAB]
[ALT-F7]flw1.17[ENTER][TAB]flw1.57[ENTER][F7][SHIFT-F7]
v[F7][F7]y[ENTER]y[ENTER]

2. [SHIFT-F10]faculty.tbl[ENTER][DOWN ARROW][DOWN
ARROW][DOWN ARROW][DOWN ARROW][DOWN ARROW]
[DOWN ARROW][DOWN ARROW][DOWN ARROW][DOWN

ARROW][DOWN ARROW]{The actual number of down
arrows may differ due to word wrap differences.}
[ALT-F7][TAB][TAB][TAB]flw1.1[ENTER][LEFT ARROW]flw.9
[ENTER][LEFT ARROW]flw.7[ENTER][LEFT ARROW]flw3.8
[ENTER][F7][SHIFT-F7]f[F7]y[ENTER]y[ENTER]

3. [SHIFT-F10]attach.c[ENTER][DOWN ARROW][DOWN ARROW]
[DOWN ARROW][ALT-F7][CTRL-RIGHT ARROW][CTRL-RIGHT
ARROW][CTRL-RIGHT ARROW][CTRL-RIGHT ARROW][CTRL-RIGHT
ARROW][CTRL-RIGHT ARROW][CTRL-RIGHT ARROW][CTRL-RIGHT
ARROW][CTRL-RIGHT ARROW][CTRL-RIGHT ARROW][CTRL-RIGHT
ARROW][CTRL-RIGHT ARROW][CTRL-RIGHT ARROW][CTRL-RIGHT
ARROW][CTRL-RIGHT ARROW]{The number of times you
must press CTRL-RIGHT ARROW may differ depending
on the word wrap on your screen.}[F7][SHIFT-F7]f[F7]
y[ENTER]y[ENTER]

4. [SHIFT-F10]bill.sht[ENTER][DOWN ARROW][ALT-F7][CTRL-RIGHT
ARROW][CTRL-RIGHT ARROW][CTRL-RIGHT ARROW][CTRL-RIGHT
ARROW][CTRL-RIGHT ARROW][CTRL-RIGHT ARROW][CTRL-RIGHT
ARROW][CTRL-RIGHT ARROW][CTRL-RIGHT ARROW][CTRL-RIGHT
ARROW][CTRL-RIGHT ARROW][CTRL-RIGHT ARROW][CTRL-RIGHT
ARROW][CTRL-RIGHT ARROW][CTRL-RIGHT ARROW]{The
number of times you must press CTRL-RIGHT ARROW
may differ depending on the word wrap on your
screen.}[F7][SHIFT-F7]v[F7][F7]y[ENTER]y[ENTER]

EXERCISES
22.4

1. [SHIFT-F10]supplies[ENTER][DOWN ARROW][DOWN
ARROW][DOWN ARROW][ALT-F7][TAB][INS]c1[ENTER][F7]
[DOWN ARROW][DOWN ARROW][DOWN ARROW][DOWN

ARROW][DOWN ARROW][DOWN ARROW][DOWN ARROW]
[DOWN ARROW][ALT-F7][INS]c1[ENTER][DOWN ARROW]
[DOWN ARROW][DOWN ARROW][INS]r1[ENTER][F7][PGUP]
[DOWN ARROW][DOWN ARROW][DOWN ARROW]ORDER
NO.[DOWN ARROW]PX-3[DOWN ARROW]ST-2[DOWN
ARROW]RX-5[DOWN ARROW][DOWN ARROW][DOWN
ARROW][DOWN ARROW][DOWN ARROW]ORDER NO.
[DOWN ARROW]345[DOWN ARROW]23[DOWN ARROW]X35
[DOWN ARROW]RX-34[DOWN ARROW]RX-1[UP ARROW]
[UP ARROW][SHIFT-TAB]Envelopes[TAB][TAB]4[TAB]
Boxes[SHIFT-F7]v[F7][F7]y[ENTER]y[ENTER]

2. [SHIFT-F10]faculty.tbl[ENTER][DOWN ARROW][DOWN
   ARROW][DOWN ARROW][DOWN ARROW][DOWN ARROW]
   [DOWN ARROW][DOWN ARROW][DOWN ARROW]
   [DOWN ARROW][DOWN ARROW][ALT-F7]sr6[ENTER][F7]5. As
   a student, you were interested in learning the
   course material.[SHIFT-F7]f[F7]y[ENTER]y[ENTER]

3. [SHIFT-F10]topshelf[ENTER][DOWN ARROW][DOWN
   ARROW][DOWN ARROW][ALT-F7]sc4[ENTER][F7]
   REORDER[SHIFT-F7]v[F7][F7]y[ENTER]y[ENTER]

22.5 EXERCISES

1. [SHIFT-F10]attach.c[ENTER][DOWN ARROW][DOWN
   ARROW][DOWN ARROW][ALT-F7][ALT-F4][RIGHT ARROW]
   jy[F7]Acme Corporation of North America
   [ENTER]MACRS deduction calculation for XYZ
   Gizmo[ENTER]April 1, 1990[SHIFT-F7]v[F7][F7]
   y[ENTER]y[ENTER]

2. [SHIFT-F10]bill.sht[ENTER][DOWN ARROW][ALT-F7][ALT-F4]
[RIGHT ARROW]jy[F7]Service Bill[ENTER]Please pay
upon receipt.[F7]y[ENTER]y[ENTER]

EXERCISES ——————————————— 22.6

1. [SHIFT-F10]supplies[ENTER][DOWN ARROW][DOWN
ARROW][DOWN ARROW][ALT-F7][TAB][ALT-F4][TAB]
[TAB]fcjc[ALT-F4][LEFT ARROW][LEFT ARROW][LEFT
ARROW]fcaab[TAB][TAB][DOWN ARROW][ALT-F4][DOWN
ARROW][DOWN ARROW]fcjd[F7][DOWN ARROW][DOWN
ARROW][DOWN ARROW][DOWN ARROW][DOWN ARROW]
[SHIFT-TAB][ALT-F7][ALT-F4][TAB][TAB]fcjc[ALT-F4][LEFT
ARROW][LEFT ARROW][LEFT ARROW]fcaab[TAB][TAB][DOWN
ARROW][ALT-F4][DOWN ARROW][DOWN ARROW][DOWN
ARROW][DOWN ARROW]fcjd[F7][UP ARROW][UP ARROW][UP
ARROW][UP ARROW][DEL]10[SHIFT-F7]f[F7]y[ENTER]y[ENTER]

2. [SHIFT-F10]faculty.tbl[ENTER][DOWN ARROW][DOWN
ARROW][DOWN ARROW][DOWN ARROW][DOWN ARROW]
[DOWN ARROW][DOWN ARROW][DOWN ARROW][DOWN
ARROW][DOWN ARROW]{The actual number of DOWN
ARROWS may differ due to word wrap differences.}
[ALT-F7][ALT-F4][TAB][TAB][TAB]fcaab[F7][F7]y[ENTER]y
[ENTER]

3. [SHIFT-F10]attach.c[ENTER][DOWN ARROW][DOWN
ARROW][DOWN ARROW][ALT-F7]fcaabfcjc[DOWN
ARROW][TAB][ALT-F4][DOWN ARROW][DOWN ARROW]
fcjd[F7][SHIFT-F7]v[F7][F7]y[ENTER]y[ENTER]

4. [SHIFT-F10]bill.sht[ENTER][DOWN ARROW][ALT-F7]
fcaabfcjc[DOWN ARROW][TAB][ALT-F4][DOWN
ARROW][DOWN ARROW]fcjd[F7][UP ARROW][UP ARROW]
[SHIFT-TAB]4.3 hours of typing services[TAB]
55.90[TAB]1 diskette[TAB]2.50[SHIFT-F7]v[F7][F7]y
[ENTER]y[ENTER]

22.7 EXERCISES

1. [SHIFT-F10]attach.c[ENTER][DOWN ARROW][DOWN
ARROW][DOWN ARROW][ALT-F7][DOWN ARROW][DOWN
ARROW][DOWN ARROW][TAB]m4[UP ARROW][UP ARROW]
[UP ARROW]fcttmc[F7][SHIFT-F7]f[F7]y[ENTER]y[ENTER]

2. [SHIFT-F10]bill.sht[ENTER][DOWN ARROW][ALT-F7]sr6[ENTER]
[UP ARROW][UP ARROW][TAB]mfb2 + b3[ENTER][DOWN
ARROW]mfb4*.07[ENTER][DOWN ARROW]mfb4 + b5
[ENTER][F7][UP ARROW][SHIFT-TAB]Sales Tax:[DOWN
ARROW]Total Amount Due:[SHIFT-F7]f[F7]y[ENTER]
y[ENTER]

MASTERY SKILLS CHECK

1. [ALT-F7]tc2[ENTER]8[ENTER]

2. [ALT-F4][TAB]jyfcjcfctt

3. [TAB][ALT-F4][TAB]fcjcfctt

4. [DOWN ARROW][ALT-F4][DOWN ARROW][DOWN ARROW]
[DOWN ARROW][DOWN ARROW][DOWN ARROW]fcjd

5. mfb6 + b7[ENTER]{0.00 appears in the cell}fcaad

6. [UP ARROW]mfb6*.07[ENTER]{0.00 appears in the cell}fcaau

7. [UP ARROW]m4{0.00 appears in the cell}[F7]

8. [UP ARROW][UP ARROW][UP ARROW][UP ARROW]
[UP ARROW]JOE'S HARDWARE[TAB]Item[TAB]
Amount[TAB]Nails[TAB]9.00[TAB]Hammer[TAB]
5.00[TAB]Screwdriver[TAB]7.00[TAB]Subtotal
[TAB]21.00[TAB]Tax @ 7%[TAB]1.47[TAB]Total
[ALT-F7]mc

9. [F7][SHIFT-F7]v[F7][F7]nn

INTEGRATING SKILLS CHECK

1. [ALT-F7]tc3[ENTER]6[ENTER]

2. [ALT-F4][TAB][TAB]jyfcjcfctt

3. [DOWN ARROW][ALT-F4][TAB][TAB]fcjc[ALT-F4][LEFT
ARROW]fctt

4. [DOWN ARROW][ALT-F4][TAB][DOWN ARROW][DOWN
ARROW][DOWN ARROW]fcjr

5. m4{0.00 appears in the cell}

6. [LEFT ARROW]m4{0.00 appears in the cell}

7. [UP ARROW][ALT-F4][TAB]fcaau[F7]

8. [UP ARROW][UP ARROW][UP ARROW][UP ARROW]SALES BY
   DEPARTMENT[TAB]DEPT[TAB]JAN[TAB]FEB[TAB]
   Clothing[TAB]25,000.00[TAB]20,000.00[TAB]Shoe[TAB]
   15,000.00[TAB]12,000.00[TAB]Housewares[TAB]40,000.00
   [TAB]42,000.00[TAB]Total[ALT-F7]mc

9. sc4[ENTER][ALT-F4][LEFT ARROW]jjy[TAB][TAB][CTRL-LEFT
   ARROW][CTRL-LEFT ARROW][CTRL-LEFT ARROW][CTRL-LEFT
   ARROW][CTRL-LEFT ARROW][CTRL-LEFT ARROW][TAB][CTRL-
   RIGHT ARROW][CTRL-RIGHT ARROW][CTRL-RIGHT ARROW][TAB]
   [CTRL-RIGHT ARROW][CTRL-RIGHT ARROW][CTRL-RIGHT
   ARROW][F7]MAR[DOWN ARROW]23,000.00[DOWN ARROW]
   14,000.00[DOWN ARROW]37,000.00[ALT-F7]mc

Menu Answers

The following conventions have been used throughout the answer sections:

Menu selections and keystrokes are listed in the order they should be entered. Comments and instructions are enclosed in braces { } to distinguish them from keystrokes. Special keys, such as the function keys, are enclosed in brackets [].

References to sections covering the material tested in the skills checks, mastery skills checks, and integrating skills checks are provided in brackets in the margin beside each answer. In the answers for Chapter 1, spaces are indicated by [SPACEBAR]. After Chapter 1, spaces are indicated either by a space in the text or by [SPACEBAR]; the answers use [SPACEBAR] when using a space would cause confusion.

(Menu selections are preceded by the ALT key. If you follow the directions in Appendix A, you will be able to invoke the menu with ALT and then type the highlighted letters to complete your menu selections. Some lower level selections can be made by typing either a letter or a number; the answer gives the letter.

Some exercises have more than one possible solution. Any solution that produces the desired results can be considered correct.

1.1   EXERCISES

1. {for a hard disk system using WordPerfect 5.1}cd\wp51[ENTER]wp[ENTER] {for a hard disk system using WordPerfect 5.0}cd\wp50[ENTER] wp[ENTER]{for a floppy disk system: Place the WordPerfect 1 disk in drive A and a formatted disk for documents in drive B.}b:[ENTER]a:wp [ENTER]{Place the WordPerfect 2 disk in drive A when WordPerfect prompts you, and press any key to continue.}

1.2   EXERCISES

1. {for a hard disk system using WordPerfect 5.1}cd\wp51[ENTER]wp[ENTER][ALT]File Exit ny {for a hard disk system using WordPerfect 5.0}cd\ wp50 [ENTER]wp[ENTER][ALT]File Exit ny{for a floppy disk system: Place the WordPerfect 1 disk in drive A and a formatted disk for documents in drive B}b: [ENTER] a:wp

[ENTER]{Place the WordPerfect 2 disk in drive A when WordPerfect prompts you, and press any key to continue.} [ALT]File Exit ny

EXERCISES ————————— 1.3

1. accounting [ALT]File Exit nn

2. trees [ALT]File Exit nn

3. 1989[SPACEBAR]holidays [ALT]File Exit nn

4. bills,[SPACEBAR]bills,[SPACEBAR]and[SPACEBAR]more [SPACEBAR]bills [ALT]File Exit nn

EXERCISES ————————— 1.4

1. [ENTER][ENTER][ENTER][ENTER][ENTER][ENTER][UP ARROW] [UP ARROW][UP ARROW][UP ARROW][UP ARROW][UP ARROW] [DOWN ARROW][DOWN ARROW] [DOWN ARROW][DOWN ARROW][DOWN ARROW][DOWN ARROW][ALT]File Exit nn

2. [ESC]10aaaaaaaaaaa{Press the LEFT ARROW and RIGHT ARROW keys as many times as you like.}[END][ENTER] [ALT]File Exit nn

3. [TAB][TAB][TAB][TAB][LEFT ARROW][LEFT ARROW][LEFT ARROW] [LEFT ARROW][ALT]File Exit nn

4. [CTRL-ENTER][CTRL-ENTER][CTRL-ENTER][CTRL-ENTER]{Press PGUP and PGDN as many times as you like.} [CTRL-HOME]{Type a number from 1 to 5.}[ENTER] {Repeat until you are comfortable with the CTRL-HOME key combination.} [ALT]File Exit nn

5. the[SPACEBAR]early[SPACEBAR]bird[SPACEBAR]gets-[SPACEBAR]the[SPACEBAR]worm.[ENTER][UP ARROW]{Press the CTRL-LEFT ARROW and CTRL-RIGHT ARROW key combinations as many times as you like.} {Press the HOME-LEFT ARROW key combination and the END key as many times as you like.} [ALT]File Exit nn

6. [ENTER][ENTER][ENTER][ENTER][CTRL-ENTER][ENTER][ENTER] [ENTER][ENTER][CTRL-ENTER][ENTER][ENTER][ENTER][ENTER] [CTRL-ENTER][ENTER][ENTER][ENTER][ENTER][CTRL-ENTER] [ENTER][ENTER][ENTER][ENTER][CTRL-ENTER][ENTER][ENTER] [ENTER][ENTER][GREY-][GREY-][GREY +][GREY +][HOME] [HOME][UP ARROW][HOME][HOME][DOWN ARROW][ALT] File Exit nn

7. [NUM LOCK]123456789[NUM LOCK][ALT]File Exit nn

8. abc[BACKSPACE][LEFT ARROW][LEFT ARROW][DEL]

1.5   EXERCISES

1. [ALT]Help Help s{for screen} {[ENTER]or [SPACEBAR]to exit Help}

2. he [SPACEBAR] suddenly [SPACEBAR] left.[CTRL-LEFT ARROW][CTRL-LEFT ARROW][LEFT ARROW][DEL] [DEL][DEL][DEL][DEL][DEL][DEL][DEL][END][LEFT ARROW] [ALT]**Edit Undelete** 1 [ALT]**File Exit** nn

3. [ALT]**Help Template** [ENTER]

4. [ALT]**Help Help** d[ENTER]

5. it[SPACEBAR]was[SPACEBAR]a[SPACEBAR]cold,[SPACEBAR] dark,[SPACEBAR]scary[SPACEBAR]evening[CTRL-LEFT ARROW][CTRL-LEFT ARROW][CTRL-LEFT ARROW][DEL][DEL] [DEL][DEL][DEL][DEL][DEL][CTRL-LEFT ARROW][ALT]**Edit Undelete** r [ALT]**File Exit** nn

EXERCISES _____ 1.6

1. [SHIFT-j][SHIFT-q][SHIFT-l][SHIFT-y][SHIFT-z][SHIFT-b][SHIFT-e] [SHIFT-a][SHIFT-n][SHIFT-l][ALT]**File Exit** nn

2. [SHIFT-t]he[SPACEBAR][SHIFT-a][SHIFT-b][SHIFT-c] [SPACEBAR][SHIFT-c]orporation[SPACEBAR]makes [SPACEBAR][SHIFT-t]iger[SPACEBAR]sedans. [ALT]**File Exit** nn

3. [SHIFT-t]he[SPACEBAR]lending[SPACEBAR]rate[SPACEBAR] is 15[SHIFT-5]. [ENTER][SHIFT-9]16[SHIFT-8]2[SHIFT-0] [SHIFT-=]7 = 39[ENTER][SHIFT-p]rofit[SPACEBAR][SHIFT-7] [SPACEBAR][SHIFT-L]oss[SPACEBAR][SHIFT-s]tatement[ALT] **File Exit** nn

4. [CAPS LOCK]capitalization[SPACEBAR]can[SPACEBAR]
emphasize[SPACEBAR]text[ENTER]wordperfect[CAPS
LOCK][SPACEBAR]makes[SPACEBAR]typing[SPACEBAR]
[CAPS LOCK]fun.[CAPS LOCK][ALT]**File Exit nn**

5. [CAPS LOCK]the[SPACEBAR]local[SPACEBAR]car[SPACEBAR]
dealership[SPACEBAR]is[SPACEBAR]offering[SPACEBAR]
16[SHIFT-5][SPACEBAR]apr.[ENTER]company[SPACEBAR]
picnic[SPACEBAR]8/19/89[CAPS LOCK][ALT]**File Exit nn**

1

MASTERY SKILLS CHECK

[1.2]

1. [ALT]**File Exit ny**

[1.1]

2. {for a hard disk system using WordPerfect
5.1}cd\wp51[ENTER]wp[ENTER] {for a hard disk system using WordPerfect 5.0}cd\wp50[ENTER]
wp[ENTER]{for a floppy disk system: Place the
WordPerfect 1 disk in drive A and a formatted
disk for documents in drive B.}b:[ENTER]a:wp
[ENTER]{Place the WordPerfect 2 disk in drive A
when WordPerfect prompts you, and press any
key to continue.}

[1.4, 1.6]

3. [SHIFT-a]ugust[SPACEBAR]15th[SPACEBAR]or[SPACEBAR]
[CAPS LOCK]september[SPACEBAR]3rd[CAPS LOCK][ENTER]
3[SHIFT-6]2[SHIFT-=][SHIFT-9]8[SHIFT-8]9[SHIFT-0]

[1.5]

4. [ALT]**Help Help** e{Press ENTER or SPACEBAR to leave
Help.}

[1.3]

5. [ALT]**File Exit nn**

6. 10[SHIFT-;]34[SPACEBAR][SHIFT-a][SHIFT-m][ENTER][CAPS   [1.4, 1.6]
   LOCK]acme[SPACEBAR]corporation[CAPS LOCK]

7. [ALT]**File Exit** ny   [1.2]

SKILLS CHECK   2

1. [CAPS LOCK]a penny saved is a[CAPS LOCK]penny   [1.3, 1.6]
   earned.[ALT]**File Exit** n[ENTER]

2. [CAPS LOCK]to[SHIFT-;][SPACEBAR]j[CAPS LOCK]ohn   [1.4, 1.6]
   [SPACEBAR][SHIFT-s]mith[ENTER][CAPS LOCK]from[SHIFT-;]
   [SPACEBAR]m[CAPS LOCK]ary[SPACEBAR][SHIFT-b]rown
   [ENTER][CAPS LOCK]subject[SHIFT-;][SPACEBAR][CAPS LOCK]
   1990[SPACEBAR][SHIFT-h]oliday[SPACEBAR][SHIFT-s]chedule

3. [ENTER][ESC]65-   [1.4]

4. [ENTER][ENTER][ENTER][ENTER][TAB]{Type the text as   [1.4]
   shown, using the SHIFT key and SPACEBAR where
   appropriate.}

5. [ALT]**Layout Align Hard Page**[SHIFT-j]anuary   [1.4, 1.6]
   [SPACEBAR]1[TAB][TAB][SHIFT-n]ew[SPACEBAR][SHIFT-y]ear's
   [SPACEBAR][SHIFT-d]ay[ENTER][SHIFT-j]anuary[SPACEBAR]12
   [TAB]{Note that only one tab was required, since
   the cursor was already at the first tab stop.}[SHIFT-f]
   ounders'[SPACEBAR][SHIFT-d]ay[ENTER]{The remaining
   entries follow the same pattern. The lines for November 28 and December 25 will each require
   only one tab.}

[1.4]   6. [CTRL]-[HOME] 1

[1.4]   7. [HOME][HOME][DOWN ARROW]

[1.4]   8. [HOME][HOME][UP ARROW]

[1.3]   9. [ALT]File Exit nn

[1.5]   10. [ALT]Help Help e[ENTER]

[1.2]   11. [ALT]File Exit ny

2.1   EXERCISES

1. {Type the lines as shown, pressing ENTER at the end of the first line and after each sentence.}

2. {Type the paragraph as shown, pressing ENTER only at the end of the paragraph.}

3. {Type the text as shown, pressing ENTER after the words "Descriptions," "light," "black," "translucent," and "diamond."}

4. [TAB]{Type the first paragraph as shown.}[ENTER] [TAB]{Type the second paragraph as shown.}[ENTER]

2.2   EXERCISES

1. [SHIFT-a][SPACEBAR]stitch in time saves nine. [ALT]File Save stitch[ENTER]

2. [SHIFT-j]im[SPACEBAR][SHIFT-a]llen[ENTER]1123[SPACEBAR]
[SHIFT-f]ork[SPACEBAR][SHIFT-r]d.[ENTER][SHIFT-b]
altimore,[SPACEBAR][SHIFT-m]aryland[SPACEBAR]
21237[ALT]File Save name[ENTER][ALT]File Exit
yname2[ENTER][ENTER]

3. {Type the quote as shown.}[ENTER][ENTER][TAB]
[TAB][TAB][TAB]Sam Levenson[ALT]File Exit
[ENTER]kids[ENTER][ENTER]

4. {Type the quote as shown.}[ENTER][ENTER][TAB]
[TAB][TAB][TAB]Theodore Roosevelt[ALT]File Save te-
ddy[ENTER][ALT]File Exit[ENTER]school[ENTER]
[ENTER]

EXERCISES —————————— 2.3

1. [ALT]File Retrieve stitch[ENTER]

2. [ALT]File Retrieve name[ENTER][ALT]File Retrieve
stitch[ENTER]

3. [ALT]File Retrieve teddy[ENTER][ALT]File Retrieve
teddy[ENTER][ALT]File Exit n[ENTER]

4. Favorite Quotes[ENTER][ALT]File Retrieve kids[ENTER]
[ALT]File Retrieve teddy[ENTER][ALT]File Exit nn

2.4   EXERCISES

1. {Type the sentence as shown.}[HOME][HOME][LEFT ARROW][CAPS LOCK]abc[SPACEBAR][CAPS LOCK]

2. {Type the sentence as shown.}[CTRL-LEFT ARROW][LEFT ARROW],975

3. {Type the sentences as shown.}[CTRL-LEFT ARROW] [CTRL-LEFT ARROW][CTRL-LEFT ARROW][CTRL-LEFT ARROW] [CTRL-LEFT ARROW][CTRL-LEFT ARROW]{Type the new sentence.}[SPACEBAR][SPACEBAR]

4. She served cake for dessert.[CTRL-LEFT ARROW][CTRL-LEFT ARROW][CTRL-LEFT ARROW]rich, warm, chocolate [SPACEBAR][CTRL-RIGHT ARROW]and creamy, rich, vanilla ice cream[SPACEBAR]

5. {Type the quote as shown.}[ENTER][ENTER][TAB][TAB] [TAB][TAB]Philip Guedalla{Move to the "a" in "and."}on the east by obituary,[SPACEBAR]

2.5   EXERCISES

1. {Type the sentences as shown; then use the arrow keys to move to the "C" in "Carol."}[INS][SHIFT-e] llen[INS]

2. {Type the sentence as shown.}[CTRL-LEFT ARROW] [CTRL-LEFT ARROW][INS]4[CTRL-LEFT ARROW][CTRL-LEFT

ARROW][CTRL-LEFT ARROW][CTRL-LEFT ARROW][CTRL-LEFT
ARROW][CTRL-LEFT ARROW]answers the phone[DEL][INS]

3. {Type the sentences as shown; then move to the
"c" in "company" in the first sentence.}[INS][CAPS
LOCK]j. l. m[INS][CAPS LOCK]cGregor Corporation

4. The new prices for copies are[ENTER]1 to 100[TAB]
[TAB].08 each[ENTER]101 to 500[TAB].05 each[ENTER]
501 + [TAB][TAB][TAB].02 each[INS]{Move to each
price, typing the new figures over the old.}[INS]

5. Your current balance is $789.95.[CTRL-LEFT ARROW]
[RIGHT ARROW][INS]3[INS]

EXERCISES ——————————— 2.6

1. {Type the sentence as shown; then use the arrow
keys to move to the "t" in "together"}[DEL][DEL]
[DEL][DEL][DEL][DEL][DEL][DEL][DEL]{Move to the
period at the end of the sentence.}[BACKSPACE]
[BACKSPACE][BACKSPACE][BACKSPACE][BACKSPACE]
[BACKSPACE][BACKSPACE][BACKSPACE][BACKSPACE]
[BACKSPACE][BACKSPACE]

2. {Type the sentences as shown; then move to the
word "name" in the first sentence.}[CTRL-BACKSPACE]
[CTRL-BACKSPACE]{Move to "purses."}[CTRL-BACKSPACE]

3. {Type the lines as shown; then move to the beginning of the second slogan.}[CTRL-END][DEL]

4. {Type the text as shown. Move to the beginning of the third line (before the tab).}[CTRL-END][DEL]

5. {Type the text as shown, using the TAB key to place data in columns. Move to the word "SALARY."}[CTRL-BACKSPACE]{Move to the first salary figure.}[CTRL-BACKSPACE]{Repeat this process for the remaining two salary entries.}

MASTERY SKILLS CHECK

[2.1]   1. {Type the paragraph as shown. Do not press ENTER until the end of the paragraph.}

[2.4]   2. {Move to the "X" in "XY."}June 17,[SPACEBAR]

[2.6]   3. {Move to the "I" in "Inc."}[DEL][DEL][DEL][DEL][DEL]

[2.5]   4. {Move to the "n" in "June."}[INS]ly[INS]

[2.4]   5. {Move to the "T" in "This."}[ENTER]

[2.2]   6. [ALT]File Exit[ENTER]seendraw[ENTER]n

[2.3]   7. [ALT]File Retrieve seendraw[ENTER]

[2.6]   8. {Move to "both."}[CTRL-BACKSPACE]

[2.6]   9. {Move to the beginning of the second sentence.} [CTRL-END][DEL]

[2.2]   10. [ALT]File Save draw[ENTER]

INTEGRATING SKILLS CHECK

1. {Type the lines as shown, using CAPS LOCK for the first line.} [1.6]

2. [ALT]Help Help s{Press ENTER to exit help} [1.5]

3. [ALT]File Save cookie[ENTER] [2.2]

4. [ALT]File Exit n[ENTER] [1.3]

5. {Type the line as shown.}[ENTER][ESC]65-[ENTER] [1.4]

6. [ALT]File Retrieve cookie[ENTER] [2.3]

7. {Use the arrow keys to move to the "C" in "COOKIES."}[CAPS LOCK]and butterscotch chip [CAPS LOCK][SPACEBAR] [1.6, 2.4]

8. {Move to the beginning of the last line.}[CTRL-END][DEL]

9. [ALT]File Save list[ENTER] [2.2]

10. [ALT]File Exit ny [1.2]

SKILLS CHECK 3

1. Fourscore and seven years ago our fathers brought forth on this continent, a new nation, [1.4, 1.6, 2.1]

conceived in liberty, and dedicated to the propsition that all men are created equal. [ENTER][ENTER][TAB][TAB][TAB][TAB]Gettysburg Address[ENTER]

[2.4, 2.6]   **2.** {Move to "Fourscore."[CTRL-BACKSPACE][CTRL-BACKSPACE][CTRL-BACKSPACE]87[SPACEBAR]

[1.4, 1.5]   **3.** [HOME][LEFT ARROW][ALT]**Edit Undelete** r[CTRL-BACKSPACE]

[1.4, 2.4]   **4.** {Move to the "s" in "propsition."}o

[2.5]   **5.** {Move to the "G" in "Gettysburg."}[INS]Abraham [SPACEBAR]Lincoln[DEL][DEL][DEL][INS]

[2.2]   **6.** [ALT]**File Save** lincoln[ENTER]

[1.2]   **7.** [ALT]**File Exit** ny

[1.1, 2.3]   **8.** {for a hard disk system using WordPerfect 5.1} cd\wp51[ENTER]wp[ENTER][ALT]**File Retrieve** lincoln [ENTER{for a hard disk system using WordPerfect 5.0}cd\wp50[ENTER]wp[ENTER][ALT]**File Retrieve** lincoln[ENTER]{for a floppy disk system: Place the WordPerfect 1 disk in drive A and a disk for documents in drive B.}b:[ENTER]a:wp[ENTER]{When prompted to do so, replace the Word Perfect 1 disk with the WordPerfect 2 disk, and press any key.}[ALT]**File Retrieve** lincoln[ENTER]

[1.3]   **9.** [ALT]**File Exit** nn

EXERCISES ——————————— 3.1

1. [ALT]File Retrieve lincoln[ENTER][ALT]File Print f

2. [TAB][TAB][TAB][TAB]12345 Commerce Parkway
[ENTER][TAB][TAB][TAB][TAB]Beachwood, OH 44123
[ENTER][TAB][TAB][TAB][TAB]December 1, 1990[ENTER]
[ENTER][ENTER]Samantha Koln[ENTER]Small Business
Administration of Cleveland[ENTER]1235 Public
Square[ENTER]Cleveland, OH 44115[ENTER][ENTER]
Dear Ms. Koln,[ENTER][TAB]I am starting a business
to manufacture mechanical pencils. Can you pro-
vide information on the services that your organi-
zation provides to new companies?[ENTER][ENTER]
[TAB][TAB][TAB][TAB]Sincerely,[ENTER][ENTER][ENTER]
[ENTER][TAB][TAB][TAB][TAB]Tom Lu[ENTER][TAB][TAB]
[TAB][TAB]President, Various Sundries, Inc.[ENTER]
[ALT]File Print f[ALT]File Save sba[ENTER]

3. {Type the quote as shown.}[ENTER][ENTER]
[TAB][TAB][TAB][TAB]John Ruskin[ALT]File Print f

4. [ENTER][ENTER]{Type the quote.}[ENTER][ENTER][TAB]
[TAB][TAB][TAB]Herbert Hoover[ALT]File Print f

EXERCISES ——————————— 3.2

1. [ALT]File Retrieve sba[ENTER][ALT]File Print f {Move
to the end of the paragraph.}[ENTER][TAB]I have en-

closed a notice of our upcoming open house for your monthly newsletter.[HOME][HOME][DOWN ARROW] [CTRL-ENTER]Attend the Open House Celebration at Various Sundries, Inc., on May 15 from 7:30 to 9:30 P.M.[ALT]File Print p

2. Significant Accomplishments 1990 - John Smith [ENTER][CTRL-ENTER]Significant Accomplishments 1990 - Mary Brown[ENTER][CTRL-ENTER]Significant Accomplishments 1990 - Nancy Caster[ENTER][ALT] File Print p

3. [PGUP][ALT]File Print p[PGUP][ALT]File Print p

4. {Type the quotation.}[ENTER][ENTER][TAB][TAB][TAB] [TAB]John Heywood[ENTER][CTRL-ENTER]{Type the second quotation.}[ENTER][ENTER][TAB][TAB][TAB][TAB] Robert Burns[ENTER][PGUP][ALT]File Print p

3.3   EXERCISES

1. [ALT]File Retrieve lincoln[ENTER][ALT]File Print v12

2. To: Sarah Graham, Chief Financial Officer[ENTER] From: Bob Kelly, Chief Accounting Officer [ENTER]Re: Financial Statements[ENTER][ESC]65 = [ENTER]Sarah,[ENTER][ENTER][TAB]Enclosed are the preliminary financial statements. The attached text includes all of the footnotes. If you find any corrections or additions, please contact me immediately.[ENTER][ALT]File Print v312

3. {Type the data as shown.}[ALT]File Print v[F7]
{Position the cursor after the period at the end of
the first sentence.}[ALT]Layout Align Hard Page
{Position the cursor after the period at the end of
the second sentence.}[ALT]Layout Align Hard Page
{Position the cursor after the period in the third
sentence.}[ALT]Layout Align Hard Page[ALT]File
Print v{Use PGUP and PGDN to view the document.}

4. {Type the quotes, ending each entry with[ALT]
Layout Align Hard Page to start a new page.}
[ALT]File Print v4{use PGUP and PGDN to move
within the document.}[F7][ALT]File Save quotes
[ENTER]

EXERCISES _____ 3.4

1. [ALT]File Print dsba[ENTER][ENTER][F7]

2. [CAPS LOCK]residents opposed to road paving[ENTER]
b[CAPS LOCK]lack[ENTER][SHIFT-s]mith[ENTER][SHIFT-c]
ampbell[ENTER][SHIFT-g]ilbert[ENTER][SHIFT-l]ong[ENTER]
[SHIFT-j]ackson[ALT]Layout Align Hard Page[CAPS
LOCK]residents supporting road paving[ENTER]
w[CAPS LOCK]ilson[ENTER][SHIFT-b]oswell[ENTER][SHIFT-d]
ike[ENTER][ALT]File Exit[ENTER] road[ENTER]n[ALT]File
Print droad[ENTER][ENTER]droad[ENTER]2[ENTER][F7]

3. [ALT]File Print dquotes[ENTER]2[ENTER][F7]

4. [ALT]File Print dquotes[ENTER]2-4[ENTER][F7]

5. [ALT]File Print dquotes[ENTER]1,4[ENTER][F7]

MASTERY SKILLS CHECK

[3.3]

1. To: All Managers[ENTER]From: Fred Jones, Director of Human Services[ENTER]Subject: Meetings on the New Benefit Package[ENTER][ENTER][TAB]The Human Services Department will be conducting a one-hour information meeting on the new benefit package. We have attempted to schedule these meetings at convenient times. Please route the sign-up sheets to your employees and encourage everyone to attend one of these sessions.[ENTER][ALT]Layout Align Hard Page Benefit Package meeting - April 5 9:30 A.M.[ALT]Layout Align Hard Page Benefit Package meeting - April 5 2:30 P.M.[ALT]Layout Align Hard Page Benefit Package meeting - April 6 8:30 A.M.[ALT]Layout Align Hard Page Benefit Package meeting - April 6 4:00 P.M.[ENTER][ALT]File Print v3412

[3.1]

2. [ALT]File Print f

[3.2]

3. [HOME][HOME][UP ARROW][ALT]File Print p

[3.4]

4. [ALT]File Exit[ENTER]benefits[ENTER][ENTER][ALT]File Print dbenefits[ENTER]2-5[ENTER][F7]

INTEGRATING SKILLS CHECK

1. [TAB]A meeting is scheduled at 5 PM on January   [1.4, 1.6]
20 to discuss the company's participation in the
[CAPS LOCK]cleveland corporate olympics.[CAPS LOCK]
The meeting will be held in the fourth-floor conference room.[ENTER][ENTER][TAB]This year, we need
a slogan for the banner and a T-shirt design. We
also need a list of the employees participating in
each activity. Please encourage your staff members to participate.[ENTER][ENTER][TAB]Interested individuals unable to attend the scheduled meeting
should contact Steve Spear. His extension is 3963.
[ENTER]

2. {Move to the "H" in "His."}[CTRL-END]   [2.6]

3. {Move to the "0" in "20."}[INS]5[INS]   [1.4, 2.5]

4. [ALT]**File Print f**   [3.1]

5. [HOME][HOME][DOWN ARROW]   [1.4]

6. [ALT]**Layout Align Hard Page**   [1.4]

7. Name[TAB][TAB][TAB][TAB][TAB]Activity[ENTER][ESC]   [1.4]
8-[TAB][TAB][ESC]10-[ENTER]Sue Marianetti[TAB][TAB]
[TAB]Bike Race[ENTER]Sharon Campbell[TAB][TAB]
Tug-of-War[ENTER]John Peterson[TAB][TAB][TAB]Tug-
of-War[ENTER]Tim Smith[TAB][TAB][TAB][TAB]5K Race
[ENTER]Ted McGregor[TAB][TAB][TAB]Tug-of-War
[ENTER]Brandon Leidy[TAB][TAB][TAB]Swimming

[ENTER]Marge Thomas[TAB][TAB][TAB]5K Race[ENTER]
Anne Kettlewood[TAB][TAB]Bike Race[ENTER]

[3.3]   8. [ALT]File Print v3{Use the PGUP and PGDN keys to
view both pages.}

[3.2]   9. {Position the cursor on page 2.}[ALT]File Print p
[ENTER]

[2.2]   10. [ALT]File Exit[ENTER]olympics[ENTER][ENTER]

[1.4, 3.4]   11. [CAPS LOCK]corporate slogan suggestions[ENTER]o
[CAPS LOCK]ur Team's the Best[ENTER][ALT]File Print
dolympics[ENTER]1[ENTER][F7]The Best at All We Do
[ENTER]Scientific Services Employees Have Brains
and Brawn[ENTER]Sticks and Stones Won't Break
Our Bones[ENTER]

4

SKILLS CHECK

[1.4, 1.6]   1. The next meting of the WordPerfect User's
Group will be January 5. Each attendeee will receive a free on the use of the new graphics features.

[1.4, 2.4]   2. {Move to the "e" in "meting."}e{Move to the last
"e" in "attendeee."}[DEL]{Move to the "o" in
"on."}handout[SPACEBAR]

[1.5]   3. [ALT]Help Template[ENTER]

[2.2]   4. [ALT]File Save meeting[ENTER]

[1.3]   5. [ALT]File Exit n[ENTER]

6. [ALT]File Print dmeeting[ENTER][ENTER][F7]   [3.4]

EXERCISES _____ 4.1

1. Acerson, Karen L.,[SPACEBAR][F8]WordPerfect 5.1:
The Complete Reference[F8], Osborne/McGraw-
Hill, 1990.[ENTER]Alderman, Eric, and Lawrence J.
Magid,[SPACEBAR][F8]Advanced WordPerfect, Series
5 Edition[F8], Osborne/McGraw-Hill, 1988.[ENTER]
Mincberg, Mella,[SPACEBAR][F8]WordPerfect 5.1
Made Easy[F8]. Osborne/McGraw-Hill, 1990.

2. We will honor employees with more than
[SPACEBAR][F8]twenty-five years[F8][SPACEBAR]of ser-
vice at the annual appreciation dinner. The fol-
lowing employees are honorees at this year's
dinner:[ENTER][ENTER][F8][CAPS LOCK]employee[F8][TAB]
[TAB][F8]years of service[F8][CAPS LOCK][ENTER]J. Smith
[TAB][TAB]25[ENTER]R. Taylor[TAB][TAB]35[ENTER]
P. Volker[TAB][TAB]31

3. Cost per square foot[SPACEBAR] = [SPACEBAR][F8]Total
cost[F8][ENTER][TAB][TAB][TAB][TAB][SPACEBAR][SPACEBAR]
[SPACEBAR]Square feet

4. [TAB]{Type the first paragraph as shown.}[ENTER]
[TAB][F8] Aconteus[F8][SPACEBAR]looked at[F8]
Medusa's[F8][SPACEBAR]head and turned into
stone.[SPACEBAR][SPACEBAR][F8]Medusa[F8][SPACEBAR]was
a monster whose hair was made of serpents.
[SPACEBAR][SPACEBAR][F8]Perseus[F8], the son of
[SPACEBAR][F8]Danae[F8][SPACEBAR]and[SPACEBAR][F8]

Jupiter[F8], killed[SPACEBAR][F8]Medusa[F8]. To make himself invisible to[SPACEBAR][F8]Medusa[F8], he wore[SPACEBAR][F8]Pluto's[F8][SPACEBAR]helmet and a pair of winged shoes.

4.2   EXERCISES

1. [CAPS LOCK]account[TAB]balance[CAPS LOCK][ENTER]Rent [TAB][TAB] $5,125[ENTER]Utilities[TAB][F6](1,250)[F6] [ENTER]Phone[TAB][F6]([SPACEBAR][SPACEBAR]950)[F6]

2. Your account balance is[SPACEBAR][F6]more than 90 days past due[F6]. Unless you contact us[SPACEBAR] [F6]immediately[F6], we will begin legal action to collect the balance of your account.

3. [F6][F8][CAPS LOCK]dept[TAB][TAB]head count[F6][F8] [ENTER]acct[TAB][TAB]14[ENTER]fin[TAB][TAB]10[ENTER] mfg[TAB][TAB]84[CAPS LOCK]

4. Foreign words can add variety to your writing. When you select foreign phrases, you will want to be certain that both you and your readers understand their meaning.[SPACEBAR][SPACEBAR][F6]Deo gratias[F6][SPACEBAR]means thanks to God.[SPACEBAR] [SPACEBAR][F6]Dei gratia[F6][SPACEBAR]means by the grace of God.[SPACEBAR][SPACEBAR][F6]Deo volente [F6][SPACEBAR]means by God's will.[SPACEBAR] [SPACEBAR][F6]Dieu vous garde[F6][SPACEBAR]means God protect you.

5. Noble by birth, yet nobler by great deeds.[ENTER]
[TAB][TAB][F6]Henry Wadsworth Longfellow,
[SPACEBAR][F8]Tales of a Wayside Inn[F6][F8][ENTER]
Who fears t'offend takes the first step to please.
[ENTER][TAB][TAB][F6]Colley Cibber,[SPACEBAR][F8]Love
in a Riddle[F6][F8][ENTER]The art of praising is the
beginning of the art of pleasing.[ENTER][TAB][TAB]
[F6]Voltaire,[SPACEBAR][F8]La Pucelle[F6][F8]

EXERCISES

4.3

1. {Substitute your own name and address for the
ones in this answer.}[ALT]Layout Align Center
John Smith[ENTER][ALT]Layout Align Center 111
North Ave.[ENTER][ALT]Layout Align Center Cleveland, OH 44040[ENTER]

2. [ALT]Layout Align Center[F6]Tinsel Company[F6]
[ENTER]

3. [ALT]Layout Align Center This text is too long for
one line. WordPerfect cannot fit the entire entry
on one line. When you print the text, you will
notice that WordPerfect centers only the text in
the first line.[ENTER]

4. [CAPS LOCK][ALT]Layout Align Center abc company
[ENTER][ALT]Layout Align Center performance report[ENTER][ALT]Layout Align Center for the quarter ending june 30, 1990[ENTER][CAPS LOCK]

4.4   EXERCISES

1. [ALT]Layout Align Center[CAPS LOCK]abc company
   [ENTER][ALT]Layout Align Center budget report
   [ENTER][ALT]Layout Align Center fiscal 1991[ENTER]
   [CAPS LOCK][ALT]Edit Reveal Codes {Look at the
   codes that cause WordPerfect to center the text.}
   [ALT]Edit Reveal Codes

2. New Sunday store hours are[SPACEBAR][F6]Noon to
   5 P.M.[F6][ALT]Edit Reveal Codes

3. [ALT]Edit Reveal Codes[F6][F8]Overdue Accounts
   [F6][F8]

4. [ALT]Layout Align Center I think, therefore I am.
   [ENTER][ALT]Layout Align Center Rene Descartes
   [ENTER][ALT]Edit Reveal Codes[ALT]File Save
   THINK[ENTER]

4.5   EXERCISES

1. [F6]Quality Corporation[F6][SPACEBAR]is pleased to
   announce the following Christmas bonus struc-
   tures:[ENTER][ALT]Layout Align Center Less than 2
   years of service - 2% bonus[ENTER][ALT]Layout
   Align Center 2 years or more of service - 5%
   bonus[ENTER]Checks will be available for distribution on[SPACEBAR][F8]December 23[F8].[ALT]Edit Reveal Codes {Use the arrow keys to move around
   and view the codes. Position the cursor on the

first Center code ([CNTR] or[C/A/FLRT] in 5.0) and press DEL. Repeat for the second centered line.}

2. [ALT]Edit Reveal Codes[HOME][HOME][HOME]
[UP ARROW][ALT]Search Forward[F6][F2][ALT]File Exit
nn

3. [ALT]File Retrieve THINK[ENTER][ALT]Edit Reveal
Codes {Move to the Center code ([CNTR] or[C/A/FLRT]
in 5.0) on the first line and press the DEL key.
Repeat for the second line.}

EXERCISES ———————————— 4.6

1. {Type the text as shown. Move to the "I" in "In."}
[ALT]Edit Block.

2. An excuse uncalled for becomes an obvious ac-
cusation.[ENTER][TAB][TAB][TAB][TAB]Law Maxim[ENTER]
{Move to the first "e" in "excuse."}[ALT]Edit Block
[CTRL-RIGHT ARROW][F1][ALT]File Save EXCUSE[ENTER]

3. You must submit expense reports by the 15th of
the month following travel.{Move to the "1" in
"15th."}[ALT]Edit Block[RIGHT ARROW][RIGHT ARROW]
[RIGHT ARROW][RIGHT ARROW][F1]

4. {Move to the "m" in "month."}previous[SPACEBAR]
[ALT]Edit Block[CTRL-LEFT ARROW][ALT]Edit Delete y

5. [ALT]File Retrieve THINK[ENTER][DOWN ARROW][ALT]
Edit Block[END][ALT]Edit Delete y

4.7   EXERCISES

1. {Type the text as shown. Move to the "W" in "WordPerfect" in the first sentence.}[ALT]Edit Block y[F8]

2. {Move to the "W" in "WordPerfect" in the second sentence.}[ALT]Edit Block tt[F6]

3. [CAPS LOCK]accounts receivable aging[CAPS LOCK] [ALT]Edit Block[CTRL-LEFT ARROW][CTRL-LEFT ARROW] [CTRL-LEFT ARROW][F8][ALT]Edit Block[CTRL-RIGHT ARROW] [CTRL-RIGHT ARROW][CTRL-RIGHT ARROW][ALT]Layout Align Center y

4. [ALT]File Retrieve EXCUSE[ENTER][HOME][HOME][DOWN ARROW][ENTER]A bad excuse is better, they say, than none at all.[ENTER][TAB][TAB][TAB][TAB]Stephen Gosson{Move to the first "e" in the word "excuse" in the first quotation}[ALT]Edit Block[CTRL-RIGHT ARROW][F6]{Move to the first "e" in "excuse" in the second quotation.}[ALT]Edit Block[CTRL-RIGHT ARROW][F6]

5. {Type the quotation as shown.}{Move to the "w" in either occurrence of "wheels."}[ALT]Edit Blocks [F6][ALT]Edit Block[CTRL-LEFT ARROW][F8]{Repeat the process for the other occurrence of "wheels."}

MASTERY SKILLS CHECK

[4.1]

1. [F8]Bylaws of the WordPerfect Users Group[F8] [ALT]File Exit nn

2. [F6]ABC Company[F6][SPACEBAR]will hold its annual   [4.2]
picnic at the[SPACEBAR][F6]Loch Raven Pavilion
[F6][SPACEBAR]on[SPACEBAR][F6]July 17th[F6].

[4.4, 4.5]

3. [ALT]Edit Reveal Codes {Move to the "L" in
"Loch."}[BACKSPACE]

[4.1, 4.3]

4. [HOME][HOME][HOME][UP ARROW][ALT]Layout Align
Center[F8][CAPS LOCK]company picnic announcement[F8][CAPS LOCK]

[4.4, 4.5]

5. [ENTER][ENTER][ENTER][ALT]Edit Reveal Codes[HOME]
[HOME][HOME][UP ARROW][ALT]Search Forward[F8][F2]
[ALT]File Print f[ALT]File Exit nn

[4.2, 4.4, 4.5]

6. [ALT]Layout Align Center[F6][CAPS LOCK]abc company[ENTER][ALT]Layout Align Center internal
memorandum[ENTER][ENTER]to[SHIFT-;][F6][SPACEBAR]
a[CAPS LOCK]ll staff[ENTER][F6][CAPS LOCK]from[SHIFT-;]
[F6][SPACEBAR]j[CAPS LOCK]ohn[SPACEBAR][SHIFT-s]mith
[ENTER][F6][CAPS LOCK]subject[SHIFT-;][F6][SPACEBAR]c
[CAPS LOCK]ompletion of parking lot resurfacing
[ENTER][F6][CAPS LOCK]date[SHIFT-;][F6][SPACEBAR]f[CAPS
LOCK]ebruary 15, 1990[ENTER][ENTER]The resurfacing
of parking lots A and B is complete. Resurfacing
of parking lot C is scheduled to begin Monday,
February 20. Your[ENTER]continued cooperation is
appreciated.[ALT]Edit Reveal Codes {Move to the
"c" in "continued."}[BACKSPACE][SPACEBAR][ALT]File
Save PARKING[ENTER]

[4.6, 4.7] **7.** {Move to the "c" in "complete."}[ALT]**Edit Block** ee[F6]{Move to the beginning of the second sentence.}[ALT]**Edit Block.**[ALT]**Edit Delete** y[ALT]**File Exit** nn

[4.6, 4.7] **8.** [CAPS LOCK]acct no[TAB]balance[CAPS LOCK][ENTER]1204 [TAB][TAB][SHIFT-4]12,350[ENTER]1567[TAB][TAB][SHIFT-4] 17,865[ENTER]2569[TAB][TAB][SHIFT-4]23,789[ENTER] {Move to the "A" in "ACCT."}[ALT]**Edit Block**[END] [F6][ALT]**Edit Block**[CTRL-HOME][CTRL-HOME][F8]

INTEGRATING SKILLS CHECK

[1.4, 4.3] **1.** [ALT]**Layout Align Center**[CAPS LOCK]abc books[CAPS LOCK][ENTER][ALT]**Layout Align Center** 1115 Warren Avenue[ENTER][ALT]**Layout Align Center** Cleveland, OH 44017[ENTER][ENTER]{Type the remainder of the text as shown.}

[1.3, 2.2, 3.4] **2.** [ALT]**File Exit**[ENTER]myers[ENTER][ENTER][ALT]**File Print** dmyers[ENTER][ENTER][F7]

[2.5, 4.6, 4.7] **3.** [ALT]**File Retrieve** myers[ENTER]{Move to the "N" in "North."}[INS]Sou[INS]{Move to the "S" in "Successful."}[ALT]**Edit Block** t[F8]{Move to the "O" in "October."}[ALT]**Edit Block** 2[F6]

[4.6, 1.5] **4.** [END][ALT]**Edit Block**[UP ARROW][HOME][LEFT ARROW][F1] [2.2, 3.1, 3.3]

  5. [ALT]**File Save**[ENTER]y[ALT]**File Print** v[F1]f

SKILLS CHECK   5

1. [ALT]Layout Align Center Bibliography[ENTER]   [4.1, 4.3]
[ENTER]Mincberg, Mella,[SPACEBAR][F8] WordPerfect
5.1 Made Easy[F8], Osborne/McGraw-Hill, 1072
pages.[ENTER]Campbell, Mary,[SPACEBAR][F8]1-2-3
Made Easy[F8], Osborne/McGraw-Hill, 526 pages.
[ENTER]

2. {Move to the 4 in 492.}1990,[SPACEBAR]{Move to the   [1.4, 2.4]
4 in 400.}1989,[SPACEBAR]

3. [ALT]File Save biblio[ENTER]   [2.2]

4. [HOME][HOME][HOME][UP ARROW][ALT]Search Forward   [4.5]
[F8][F2][BACKSPACE]y[ALT]Search Forward[F2]
[BACKSPACE]y

5. [ALT]File Exit nn   [1.3]

6. [ALT]File Print dbiblio[ENTER][ENTER][F7]   [3.4]

EXERCISES   5.1

1. Some are born great, some achieve greatness, oth-
ers have greatness thrust upon 'em.[ENTER][TAB]
[TAB][TAB][TAB] William Shakespeare[ENTER][HOME]
[HOME][UP ARROW][ALT]Layout Line m2[ENTER]1.5
[ENTER][F7]

2. What makes us discontented with our condition is the absurdly exaggerated idea we have of the happiness of others.[ENTER][TAB][TAB][TAB][TAB]Prov-erb[ENTER][HOME][HOME][UP ARROW][ALT]Layout Line m2[ENTER]2[ENTER][F7][ALT]Edit Reveal Codes {The code for the margin change is[L/R Mar:2,2].}[ALT] Edit Reveal Codes[ALT]Layout Line m1.5[ENTER] 1.5[ENTER][F7]{Press the DOWN ARROWkey to make WordPerfect reformat the paragraph with the new margins.}

3. The plural of most compound nouns is formed by adding "s" or "es" to the main word in the grouping. For example:[ENTER][TAB]mothers-in-law [ENTER][TAB]runners-up[ENTER][TAB]daughters-in-law [ENTER][HOME][HOME][UP ARROW][ALT]Layout Line m2.5 [ENTER]1.5[ENTER][F7]{Press the DOWN ARROW key to make WordPerfect reformat the paragraph with the new margins.}

4. [CAPS LOCK]abc company - memo[ENTER]d[CAPS LOCK] ate: Friday, Sept 10, 1990[ENTER][ESC]65-[ENTER] When using the copier by the coffee machine, use only the paper stacked next to the machine. Since the machine is old, if you use different paper (en-velopes, letterheads, etc.), the machine jams.[HOME] [HOME][UP ARROW][ALT]Layout Line m3[ENTER]3[ENTER] [F7][ALT]File Print v[F7][HOME][HOME][HOME][UP ARROW] [DEL]y

EXERCISES
5.2

1. [ALT]Layout Align Indent → ←[ALT]Layout Align Indent → ←[ALT]Layout Align Indent → ←[ALT] Layout Align Indent → ←{Type the paragraph as shown.}[ENTER]

2. [ALT]Layout Align Indent →{Retype the paragraph from exercise 1.}[ENTER]The meeting is scheduled for 9:00 a.m. in the board room.[ENTER]

3. [ALT]Edit Reveal Codes[HOME][HOME][HOME][UP ARROW][DEL][ALT]Edit Reveal Codes

4. [ALT]Layout Align Indent → ←[ALT]Layout Align Indent → Frequently saving work in progress is a good habit that all computer users should acquire. It avoids the potential for loss of large amounts of work due to power outages, someone tripping over a power cord, etc.[ENTER]

EXERCISES
5.3

1. [ALT]Layout Align Margin Rel←[ALT]Layout Align Margin Rel←You can use the Margin Release feature to make an indented paragraph begin at the left margin. You can also use it to fit additional characters on a line.

2. Name:[ENTER][ALT]Layout Align Margin Rel◄—
[SPACEBAR][SPACEBAR]Address:[ENTER][ALT]Layout
Align Margin Rel◄—[ALT]Layout Align Margin
Rel◄—{Depending on the printer: 0, 1 or 2
[SPACEBAR]'s}Phone Number:[ENTER][ALT]Layout
Align Margin Rel◄—[ALT]Layout Align Margin
Rel◄—{Depending on the printer: 1, 2, or 3
[SPACEBAR]'s}Soc. Sec. #:

5.4   EXERCISES

1. [ALT]Layout Line t3.3[ENTER][F7][F7]

2. [ALT]Layout Line t6[ENTER][SPACEBAR][CTRL-END][F7][F7]

3. [ALT]Layout Line t4[ENTER]r[F7][F7]

4. [ALT]Layout Line t2.5[ENTER]d[F7][F7]

5. [ALT]Layout Line t[HOME][HOME][LEFT ARROW][CTRL-END]
2[ENTER]4.5[ENTER][F7][F7][TAB]Jones[TAB]17,850[ENTER]
[TAB]Culver[TAB]23,489[ENTER][TAB]Walker[TAB]32,500
[ENTER][ALT]File Exit nn

6. [ALT]Layout Line t[HOME][HOME][LEFT ARROW][CTRL-
END]2,.75[ENTER][F7][F7]

7. [ALT]Layout Line t[HOME][HOME][LEFT ARROW][CTRL-
END]-1,.5[ENTER][F7][F7]

EXERCISES — 5.5

1. [ALT]Layout Align Flush Right[ALT]Tools Date Text[ENTER]

2. [ALT]Layout Align Flush Right ABC COMPANY [ENTER]

3. MEMO[ENTER]To: All Employees[ALT]Layout Align Flush Right Date:[SPACEBAR][ALT]Tools Date Text [ENTER]From: Arnold Smith[ALT]Layout Align Flush Right Re: Cleaning Computer Screens[ENTER][ESC] 65[SHIFT–][ENTER][ENTER]Do not use alcohol-based window cleaners to clean your computer screen. Use the special cleaner that is stored with the blank disks.[ENTER]

EXERCISES — 5.6

1. A sense of humor sharp enough to show a man his own absurdities will keep him from the commission of all sins, or nearly all, except those that are worth committing.[ENTER](Samuel Butler from Life and Habit)[ENTER][HOME][HOME][UP ARROW][ALT] Layout Line s2[ENTER][F7][ALT]Layout Line s3[ENTER][F7][ALT]Layout Line sl[ENTER][F7]

2. [TAB]The new Widget maker will expand our current capacity to meet expected demand levels for the next five to ten years. It has a present net value of $25,687.[ENTER][ALT]Layout Line s2[ENTER]

[F7][TAB]The manufacturer gives a 10% trade-in value on its old Widget maker. This is a slightly lower price than expected in the open market. The capital budgeting plan contains the lower trade-in value, but the company will probably sell the used machine in the second-hand market. [ENTER][ALT]Layout Line s3[ENTER][F7][TAB]The new Widget maker has many new features. One of these, a free one-year service contract, will save the company $50,000 in the first year.[ENTER] {Reveal the codes, and delete the line-spacing codes at the beginning of paragraphs 2 and 3. There is no code for paragraph 1, since the defaults are being used.}[HOME][HOME][HOME][UP ARROW] [ALT]Layout Line s2[ENTER][F7]{Move to the beginning of the second paragraph.}[ALT]Layout Line s3[ENTER][F7]}Move to the beginning of the third paragraph.}[ALT]Layout Line s2[ENTER][F7]

3. When you set the line spacing, WordPerfect uses it for all lines after the code in the document.[ALT] Layout Line s2[ENTER][F7]If you change the spacing to double spacing in the middle of a paragraph, the lines above the change are single spaced, and the lines after the change are double spaced. [ENTER]

5.7   EXERCISES

1. The Accounts Receivable computer system was installed last January. Due to this new system, the average daily accounts receivable amount dropped

by $50. Also, the percentage of bad accounts has dropped from 4% to 2%, mostly due to quicker action on overdue accounts.[ENTER][ALT]**File Print v** [F7][HOME][HOME][UP ARROW][ALT]**Layout Line jl**[F7] [ALT]**File Print v**[F7][ALT]**Layout Line jf**[F7]

2. [TAB]When a paragraph is fully justified, Word-Perfect inserts additional space in lines of the printed copy of the document. This creates even left and right margins. The extra spaces appear only in the printed copy and do not appear on the screen.[ENTER][ALT]**Layout Line jl**{n in 5.0}[F7] [TAB]When a paragraph is left justified, Word-Perfect does not insert additional space. The right margin has a jagged appearance.[ENTER][ALT]**File Print v**[F7]

MASTERY SKILLS CHECK

1. {assumes left and right margins are currently 1}   [5.1]
   [ALT]**Layout Line m2**[ENTER]**2**[ENTER][F7]Disks store information using magnetized material to hold information. The basic unit of storage is a byte. A byte stores one character of information.[ENTER] [ALT]**File Exit ydisk**[ENTER]**n**

2. [ALT]**Layout Align Indent** →[ALT]**Layout Align In-**   [5.2]
   dent → Disk drives read information from a disk. The disk drive spins the disk quickly. A read/write head above the disk reads the information as it spins past the head.[ENTER][ALT]**File Exit ydisk read**[ENTER]**n**

[5.4]

3. [ALT]Layout Line t[HOME][HOME][LEFT ARROW][CTRL-END]4[ENTER][F7][F7][TAB]Acme Corporation[ENTER][TAB]496 Prospect Road[ENTER][TAB]Cleveland, Ohio 44115[ENTER][TAB]January 3, 1990[ENTER]

[5.6]

4. [ALT]File Retrieve disk[ENTER][ALT]Layout Line s2[ENTER][F7][ALT]File Save[ENTER]y

[5.7]

5. [ALT]File Retrieve diskread[ENTER][ALT]Layout Line jl{n in 5.0}[F7][ALT]File Save[ENTER]y

[5.5]

6. [ALT]Layout Align Flush Right ACC-9876[ENTER][ALT]Layout Align Flush Right HDG-3218[ENTER][ALT]Layout Align Flush Right CRC-9873[ENTER][5.2,5.3]

7. [ALT]Layout Align Indent →[ALT]Layout Align Margin Rel ← Campbell, Mary,[SPACEBAR][F8]Teach Yourself WordPerfect 5.1[F8], Osborne/McGraw-Hill, 1990.[ENTER]

INTEGRATING SKILLS CHECK

[4.1, 5.1, 5.3]

1. [ALT]Layout Line m1.5[ENTER][ENTER][F7][ALT]Layout Align Margin Rel ← Crosby, Samuel, "Mergers and Acquisitions,"[SPACEBAR][F8]Business Yearly[F8], (OMB Publishing, 1983), June, p. 46-49. [ENTER][ALT]Layout Align Margin Rel ← Lee, Jane, and Lifeson, Tom, "Effectively Combining Companies,"[SPACEBAR][F8]Journal of Business Results[F8], (AMBA, 1987), vol 36, Fall, p. 101-9. [ENTER]

2. [ALT]Layout Align Margin Rel ←[ALT]Layout   [4.3, 4.7, 5.3]
Align Margin Rel ← Acme Corporation[ALT]
Layout Align Center 1560 Main Street[ALT]Layout
Align Flush Right Cleveland, Ohio 44103[ALT-F4]
[HOME][HOME][HOME][LEFT ARROW][F8]

3. Joan Smith[ENTER]President, Widgets Inc.[ENTER]   [3.1, 4.7, 5.7]
7946 Madison Avenue[ENTER]New York, New York
10061[ENTER][ENTER]Dear Ms. Smith:[ENTER][ENTER]
Enclosed is the pamphlet you requested, Wrapping Consumer Goods. Our products can shrink-
wrap any product. If you send the dimensions of
the products that you want to shrink-wrap, one
of our representatives will prepare a list of the
materials and equipment you will need.[ENTER]
[ENTER][TAB][TAB][TAB][TAB]Sincerely,[ENTER][ENTER]
[ENTER][ENTER][TAB][TAB][TAB][TAB]Larry Kennedy
[ENTER][TAB][TAB][TAB][TAB]Plastic Covering Co.
[ENTER][HOME][HOME][UP ARROW][ALT]Layout Line jl{n
in 5.0}[F7]{Move to the "W" in "Wrapping."}[ALT]
Edit Block[CTRL-RIGHT ARROW][CTRL-RIGHT ARROW][CTRL-
RIGHT ARROW][LEFT ARROW][LEFT ARROW][LEFT ARROW][F8]
[ALT]Edit Reveal Codes[BACKSPACE][ALT]Edit Reveal
Codes[ALT]File Print f

4.   1.   j   [1.4, 2.1, 4.1, 4.2,
    2.   e   4.3, 4.4, 4.7, 5.1,
    3.   g   5.2, 5.3, 5.4, 5.5,
    4.   b   5.6, 5.7]
    5.   c
    6.   i
    7.   l
    8.   a

9.   d
10.   k
11.   m
12.   h
13.   f

[4.5, 5.5]   **5.** [ALT]**Layout Align Flush Right**[ALT]**Tools Date Text**
[HOME][HOME][HOME][UP ARROW][ALT]**Search Forward**
[ALT-F6][F2][BACKSPACE]

6

SKILLS CHECK

[1.4, 4.2]   **1.** John Doe[ENTER]23405 Lander Road[ENTER]Cleve-
land, Ohio 44130[ENTER](216)229-8976[ENTER]
[ENTER][F6]Education:[F6][SPACEBAR][SPACEBAR]Cleveland
State University, Cleveland, Ohio[ENTER] Business
Administration, August 1983[ENTER]
Dean's List 7 Quarters, GPA 3.75[ENTER]

[4.6, 4.7]   **2.** [HOME][UP ARROW][ALT]**Edit Block**[DOWN ARROW][DOWN
ARROW][DOWN ARROW][DOWN ARROW][ALT]**Layout Align
Center y**

[4.6, 4.7]   **3.** [HOME][UP ARROW][ALT]**Edit Block**[END][F6]

[4.6, 4.7]   **4.** [DOWN ARROW][DOWN ARROW][DOWN ARROW][DOWN
ARROW][DOWN ARROW][HOME][LEFT ARROW][ALT]**Edit
Block**[CTRL-RIGHT ARROW][LEFT ARROW][LEFT ARROW][LEFT
ARROW][F8]

[5.4]   **5.** [HOME][HOME][UP ARROW][ALT]**Layout Line t.5{1.5 in
5.0}**[ENTER][DEL]1[ENTER][DEL]1.2[ENTER][F7][F7]

6. [DOWN ARROW][DOWN ARROW][DOWN ARROW][DOWN   [5.2]
ARROW][DOWN ARROW][HOME][HOME][LEFT ARROW][ALT]
Layout Align Indent[DOWN ARROW][HOME][LEFT
ARROW][ALT]**Layout Align Indent**[DOWN ARROW][HOME]
[LEFT ARROW][ALT]**Layout Align Indent**

7. [UP ARROW][UP ARROW][ALT]**Layout Align Margin Rel**   [5.3]

8. [ALT]**File Print f**   [3.1]

EXERCISES ———————— 6.1

1. [ALT]**Layout Page cy**[F7][ALT]**Layout Align Center**
Investigation into the Physical Properties of Rust
[ENTER][ALT]**Layout Align Center** Dissertation[ENTER]
[ALT]**Layout Align Center** Angus McPhearson
[ENTER] {To view the centered text:[ALT] **File Print**
v.}

2. {The letter body may be different, and the name
at the bottom should be your own.}[ALT]**Layout
Page cy**[F7]Jules McBride[ENTER]234 Main Street
[ENTER]Lawrence, PA 28634[ENTER][ENTER]Dear Jules,
[ENTER][ENTER]Thank you for promptly sending the
information I requested.[ENTER][ENTER]Sincerely,
[ENTER][ENTER][ENTER][ENTER]John Doe[ENTER]{To view
the centered text:[ALT]**File Print v.**}

3. [ALT]**Layout Page cy**[F7][ALT]**Layout Align Center**
1990 Financial Statements[ENTER][ALT]**Layout Align
Center** Acme Corporation[ENTER][ALT]**File Print**
v[F7]

4. [ALT]Layout **Page** cy[F7]MEMO:[ENTER]To: All Employees[ENTER]Re: Paychecks[ENTER][ENTER][TAB]To receive a paycheck September 10th, submit your time card to payroll by September 3rd.[ENTER][ALT]**File Print** v[F7]

6.2 EXERCISES

1. [ALT]Layout **Page** m3[ENTER]3[ENTER][F7]{You can press[ENTER] approximately 54 times before WordPerfect inserts a page break. The exact number depends upon your printer.}

2. [ALT]Layout **Page** m0[ENTER]0[ENTER][F7]{You can press[ENTER] approximately 65 times before WordPerfect inserts a page break. The exact number depends upon your printer.}

3. [ALT]Layout **Page** m9.5[ENTER][ENTER][F7]{Type the paragraphs as shown. WordPerfect inserts page breaks.}[ALT]**File Print** v{Press[PGUP] and[PGDN] to switch among the pages.}[F7]

6.3 EXERCISES

1. [ALT]Layout **Page** n p6[F7]Travel Expenses[ALT]Layout **Align Hard Page** Benefits[ALT]Layout **Align Hard Page** Salary Expense[ENTER][ALT]**File Print** v{Press[PGUP] and[PGDN] to switch among the three pages.}[F7]

2. [ALT]Layout Page n p6[F7]1[ALT]Layout Align Hard Page 2[ALT]Layout Align Hard Page 3[ALT]Layout Align Hard Page 4[ALT]Layout Align Hard Page 5[ALT]File Print v{Press[PGUP] and[PGDN] to switch among the pages.}[F7]{Press[PGDN] until the Pg indicator displays 5.}[ALT]Layout Page nn1[ENTER] [F7][PGUP][ALT]Layout Page nn2[ENTER][F7][PGUP] [ALT]Layout Page nn3[ENTER][F7][PGUP][ALT]Layout Page nn4[ENTER][F7][PGUP][ALT]Layout Page nn5 [ENTER][F7]

EXERCISES ——————————— 6.4

1. [ALT]Layout Page s[ALL OTHERS]Legals[F7]Legal-Size Paper[ALT]Layout Align Hard Page[ALT]Layout Page sStandard{s in 5.0}s[F7]Standard-Size Paper[ALT]File Print v{Press[PGDN] and[PGUP] to see how WordPerfect will print the two pages.} [F7]

2. [ALT]Layout Page s[ALL OTHERS]Half Sheet s[F7]Jim Adler[ENTER]514 Washington Avenue[ENTER-]Columbus, OH 43213[ENTER][ALT]File Print v[F7]

MASTERY SKILLS CHECK —————————

1. [ALT]Layout Page cy[F7][ALT]Layout Align Center   [4.3, 6.1] Wilbur Horse Supplies[ENTER][ALT]Layout Align Center Financial Statements[ENTER][ALT]Layout Align Center For the Year Ending December 31, 1990[ENTER][ALT]File Print v[F7]

[6.2] **2.** [HOME][HOME][HOME][UP ARROW][ALT]Layout Page m3 [ENTER][ENTER][F7][ALT]File Print v[F7]

[6.3] **3.** [HOME][HOME][UP ARROW][ALT]Layout Page np2[F7]

[6.3] **4.** [HOME][HOME][DOWN ARROW][ALT]Layout Align Hard Page[ALT]Layout Page n10[ENTER][F7]

[6.4] **5.** [ALT]Layout Page s[ALL OTHERS]Half Sheet s[F7]

INTEGRATING SKILLS CHECK

[4.3] **1.** [ALT]Layout Align Center Archie's California Grapes[ENTER][ALT]Layout Align Center Production Records[ENTER][ALT]Layout Align Center For the season ending September 30, 1990[ENTER]

[6.1] **2.** [HOME][HOME][HOME][UP ARROW][ALT]Layout Page cy[F7]

[4.7] **3.** [ALT]Edit Block[END][F6][CTRL-RIGHT ARROW][ALT]Edit Block[END][F8]

[6.3] **4.** [HOME][HOME][DOWN ARROW][ALT]Layout Align Hard Page[ALT]Layout Page np3n1[ENTER][F7]

[5.6] **5.** [ALT]Layout Lines2[ENTER][F7][TAB]This year's crop is the largest in the last 20 years. It is primarily due to improved fertilization methods and increased rainfall. The plants damaged by last year's drought were replaced.[ENTER]

[5.7] **6.** {Move to the beginning of the paragraph.}[ALT]Layout Line jl[F7]

7. [ALT]File Print f   [3.1]

SKILLS CHECK   7

1. Product Announcement[ENTER][ENTER][TAB]The XY   [1.4]
Graphics Company has announced the release of
its new product, See 'N' Draw. This package creates custom pictures by combining existing drawings and advanced graphics features. Since each
new feature added to an image is considered a
unique layer, you can edit one layer without affecting the others. The print options offer features
unavailable in any competing product.[ENTER]

2. [HOME][HOME][UP ARROW][ALT]Edit Block[END][F6]   [1.4, 4.7]

3. [ALT]Edit Block[HOME][LEFT ARROW][ALT]Layout Align   [4.7]
Center y

4. [ALT]Edit Reveal Codes[UP ARROW]{Highlight the   [4.5]
[BOLD] code.}[DEL]

5. [DOWN ARROW][DOWN ARROW][ALT]Layout Align Indent   [5.2]
→ ←{Press the[DOWN ARROW] key to make Word-
Perfect reformat the paragraph.}

6. [HOME][HOME][HOME][UP ARROW][ALT]Layout Line s2   [5.6]
[ENTER][F7]

7. [ALT]Layout Page cy[F7]   [6.1]

8. [ALT]File Print p   [3.1]

7.1   EXERCISES

1. On Saturday, May 16, XY Graphics is holding a press conference for their new product, See 'N' Draw. At this conference, the public relations director, Jill Smith, will reveal the company's marketing strategy for the product.[ENTER][HOME] [HOME][UP ARROW][ALT]Search Forward Jill Smith[F2]

2. Memory Requirements: 512K[ENTER]Storage Space Required: 200K[ENTER]Number of Disks: 5[ENTER] Tutorial: Yes[ENTER]Demo: Yes[ENTER][HOME][HOME] [UP ARROW][ALT]Search Forward 5[ENTER][F2] {or[ALT] Search Forward Disks: 5[F2]}

3. {Type the text as shown.}[HOME][HOME][UP ARROW][ALT]Search Forward forgive[F2][ALT]Search Forward[F2][ALT]Search Forward[F2][ALT]Search Forward[F2]{If you search again, WordPerfect will display the message "Not found" in the status line.}

4. {Type the text as shown.}[HOME][HOME][UP ARROW][ALT]Search Forward sea[F2]{Press[ALT]Search Forward[F2]. Repeat until WordPerfect displays the "Not found" message. WordPerfect will find "Searching," "seashells," "seashore," "sea," and "season."}[HOME][HOME][UP ARROW][ALT]Search Forward[SPACEBAR]sea[SPACEBAR][F2] {WordPerfect will only find "sea" in the last sentence. If you press[ALT]Search Forward[F2] once more, Word-Perfect will display the "Not found" message.}

EXERCISES ———————————————— 7.2

1. The entire project was moved to Tobler Hall under the direction of John Tomita.[ALT]Search Backward to[F2]{The cursor moves to the "m" in "Tomita."}[ALT]Search Backward[F2]{The cursor moves to the "b" in "Tobler."}[ALT]Search Backward[F2]{The cursor moves to the space between "to" and "Tobler."}[ALT]Search Backward[F2] {WordPerfect displays the "Not found" message, and the cursor remains in place.}

2. The meeting is Friday, August 11th.[SPACEBAR] [SPACEBAR][F8]All must attend.[F8]Discuss previous commitments with Carol Stevens.[ALT]Search Backward[F8][F8][LEFT ARROW][BACKSPACE][F2]{The cursor moves to the space after the period at the end of the second sentence.}

3. {Type the text as shown.}[ALT]Search Backward for[F2]{Press[ALT]Search Backward and[F2] again, and repeat until WordPerfect displays the "Not found" message. WordPerfect will find "forty," "foreigners," "for," and "forum."}[HOME][HOME] [DOWN ARROW][ALT]Search Backward[SPACEBAR]for [SPACEBAR][F2]{WordPerfect will find "for" in the first sentence. If you press[ALT]Search Backward and[F2] again, WordPerfect will display the "Not found" message.}

7.3 EXERCISES

1. Sam Cook is the production manager. He has five years' experience in this position. Prior to this position, Sam Cook was a sergeant in the army. Sam Cook succeeded Thomas MacNamara in his current position.[ENTER][ALT]Search Replace n[UP ARROW]{This sets the search and replace to operate from the end. Press[DEL] to remove any previous search string.}Sam Cook[F2]Daniel Jones[F2]{The paragraph now reads: Daniel Jones is the production manager. He has five years' experience in this position. Prior to this position, Daniel Jones was a sergeant in the army. Daniel Jones succeeded Thomas MacNamara in his current position.}

2. WordPerfect's Replace feature allows you to selectively replace one string of characters with another character string. You can have WordPerfect prompt you before completing each replacement, or you can have it make the changes automatically.[ENTER][ALT]Search Replace n[UP ARROW] WordPerfect[F2]WordPerfect 5.1[F2]

3. The Public Relations Director for your area is XX. XX has been with the company for many years and can answer your questions.[ENTER][ALT]Search Replace n[UP ARROW]XX[F2]Nancy Clark[F2][ALT] Search Replace nNancy Clark[F2]Martin Smith[F2]

4. You can use WP's Replace feature to shorten typing in a ms or doc. In a ms or doc, you type the abbreviations in place of the words and have WP replace the abbreviations with the words they represent.[ENTER][ALT]Search Replace n[UP ARROW]ms [F2]manuscript[F2][ALT]Search Replace ndoc[F2]document[F2][HOME][HOME][UP ARROW][ALT]Search Replace nWP[F2]WordPerfect[F2]

MASTERY SKILLS CHECK

1. WordPerfect lets you search for text. You can search either backward or forward. This means that you do not have to move the cursor to a specific location before you can use this feature. [ENTER][HOME][HOME][UP ARROW][ALT]Search Forward search[F2][ALT]Search Forward[F2] [7.1]

2. [HOME][HOME][UP ARROW][ALT]Search Forward you[F2] [ALT]Search Forward[F2][ALT]Search Forward[F2] [ALT]Search Forward[F2][ALT]Search Forward[F2] {WordPerfect displays the "Not found" message after finding "you" four times.} [7.1]

3. [HOME][HOME][DOWN ARROW][ALT]Search Backward for [F2]{The cursor moves to the second "e" in "before" in the second sentence.}[ALT]Search Backward[F2]{The cursor moves to the "w" in "forward."} [ALT]Search Backward[F2]{The cursor moves to the space between "for" and "text" in the first sentence.}[ALT]Search Backward[F2] {WordPerfect displays the "Not found" message.} [ALT]File Exit]nn [7.2]

[7.3]   4. Aeneades was a Trojan prince. He was the son of Diomedes and Achilles. Aeneades married Lavinia.[ALT]Search Replace n[UP ARROW]Aeneades [CTRL-END][F2]Aeneas[F2]

INTEGRATING SKILLS CHECK

[4.1, 4.3, 4.4, 7.1]   1. [ALT]Layout Align Center[F8]Proposal[F8][ENTER][ENTER]The Quick Time division of New Men's Look, Inc., would like to expand their product line to include pocket watches. Adding pocket watches would fit into the division's current production capacity. The plant is operating 30% below capacity. The technology required is already available. This product would also complement the suits produced by another subsidiary, the Taylor division.[ENTER][HOME][HOME][UP ARROW][ALT]Search Forward[F8][F2][ALT]Edit Reveal Codes

[7.3]   2. [ALT]Search Replace nQuick Time[F2]QUICK TIME[F2]

[7.3]   3. [ALT]Search Replace nTaylor[F2]Tailor[F2]

[6.1]   4. [HOME][HOME][UP ARROW][ALT]Layout Page cy[F7]

[3.3]   5. [ALT]File Print v[F7]

8

SKILLS CHECK

[5.1, 6.2]   1. [ALT]Layout Line m2[ENTER]2[ENTER][F7][ALT]Layout Page m2[ENTER]2[ENTER][F7]

2. [ALT]Layout Page np1[F7]   [6.3]

3. [ALT]Layout Line t[HOME][HOME][LEFT ARROW][ALT]   [5.4]
    Layout **Align Hard Page** 1,1[ENTER][F7][F7]

4. Dale Thompson[ENTER]Birds of a Feather[ENTER]   [4.7]
    2398 Manzanita Park[ENTER]Stanford, CA 94321
    [ENTER][ENTER]Dear Dale,[ENTER][ENTER]According to
    your advertisement in Feathered Friends, you are
    interested in purchasing two white cockatoos. I
    own several and would like to sell them. Please
    contact me at (813)212-2634.[ENTER][ENTER][TAB][TAB]
    [TAB][TAB]Sincerely,[ENTER][ENTER][ENTER][ENTER][TAB]
    [TAB][TAB][TAB]Byron Wilson [ENTER]{Move to the
    "F" in "Feathered."}[ALT]Edit **Block**[CTRL-RIGHT
    ARROW][CTRL-RIGHT ARROW][LEFT ARROW] [LEFT ARROW][F8]

5. [HOME][HOME][UP ARROW][ALT]**Search Replace** nwhite-   [7.3]
    cockatoos[F2]parakeets[F2]

6. [ALT]**File Print** f[HOME][HOME][UP ARROW][ALT]Layout   [3.1, 6.1]
    Page cy[F7][ALT]**File Print** f

7. [HOME][HOME][UP ARROW][ALT]**Edit Reveal Codes**   [4.5]
    [BACKSPACE][BACKSPACE][BACKSPACE][BACKSPACE][ALT]Edit
    Reveal Codes

EXERCISES ──────────────── 8.1

1. A complex sentence consists of an independent
    clause, which can stand alone, and one or more
    dependent clauses. A compound sentence is two

or more simple sentences joined by a conjunction, such as "and," "or," "but," or "for." A simple sentence expresses a single action or thought. [SPACEBAR][SPACEBAR][ENTER]{Move the cursor to a character in the first sentence.}[ALT]Edit Select Sentence m{Move the cursor past the end of the last sentence.}[ENTER]{Move the cursor to a character in what is now the middle sentence.}[ALT]Edit Select Sentence m{Move the cursor to the top of the document.}[ENTER]{Reformat the paragraph.}

2. [TAB]The sun's temperature is 11,000 degrees Fahrenheit at the surface and 35,000,000 degrees in the center. It releases 1.94 calories per square centimeter per minute.[ENTER][TAB]The diameter of the sun is 865,000 miles. It is small by comparison to other stars. The sun's proximity to the earth makes it appear larger than other stars.[ENTER][UP ARROW] [ALT]Edit Select Paragraph m[HOME][HOME][UP ARROW] [ENTER]

3. A nebula is a mass of gas in space.[ALT]Layout Align Hard Page A meteoroid is a small object in space.[ALT]Layout Align Hard Page A constellation is a group of stars.[ALT]Layout Align Hard Page[HOME][HOME][UP ARROW][ALT]Edit Select Page m [HOME][HOME][DOWN ARROW][ENTER]

4. [TAB]Keyboards usually come in two types. A standard keyboard has ten function keys at the side. An enhanced keyboard has 12 function keys across the top.[ENTER][TAB]With WordPerfect, if you have an enhanced keyboard, you can use F11 in

place of ALT-F3. You can also use F12 in place of ALT-F4.[ENTER]{Move the cursor to the second sentence.}[ALT]**Edit Select Sentence** m[DOWN ARROW][SPACEBAR][SPACEBAR][ENTER][ALT]**Edit Select Paragraph** m[DOWN ARROW][DOWN ARROW][ENTER] [ENTER]

EXERCISES

8.2

1. See 'N' Draw, XY Graphics' new product, should capture a large part of the graphics market for first-time users.[ENTER][UP ARROW][UP ARROW][ALT]**Edit Block**[CTRL-RIGHT ARROW][CTRL-RIGHT ARROW][CTRL-RIGHT ARROW][ALT]**Edit Move (Cut)**[CTRL-RIGHT ARROW][CTRL-RIGHT ARROW][CTRL-RIGHT ARROW][CTRL-RIGHT ARROW] [ENTER]

2. The new machinery funnels the cake mix into preprinted boxes, weighs a predetermined amount of the cake mix, and seals the bag.[ENTER] {Move to the "w" in "weighs."}[ALT]**Edit Block** {Move to the "a" in "and."}[ALT]**Edit Move (Cut)** [HOME][HOME][UP ARROW][CTRL-RIGHT ARROW][CTRL-RIGHT ARROW][CTRL-RIGHT ARROW][ENTER]

3. Review meeting agenda.[ENTER]Nominate potential candidates for new director position.[ENTER]Review financial statements.[ENTER]Review minutes from the last meeting.[ENTER]Introduce new corporate treasurer to board.[ENTER][UP ARROW][UP ARROW][ALT] **Edit Block**[DOWN ARROW][DOWN ARROW][ALT]**Edit Move (Cut)**[UP ARROW][UP ARROW][ENTER]

4. When you move a block, you should check to include any hidden codes in your text. WordPerfect moves all of the codes within the block. If the text that you move is part of a larger block of text that has special print attributes (for example, bold or underline), the special print characteristics appear in both the moved text and the original. To view the codes, press the Reveal Codes (ALT-F3) key [ALT]Edit Reveal Codes.[ENTER]{Move to the "W" in "WordPerfect."}[ALT]Edit Block..[RIGHT ARROW][RIGHT ARROW][ALT]Edit Move (Cut)[PGUP][ENTER]

8.3   EXERCISES

1. The Office of Human Resources reports that hiring has increased by 14%. This increase is a result of last year's expansion of the Largo division. The increased hiring, which created 1000 new jobs, should not affect next year's personnel needs. [ENTER]{Move the cursor to the period at the end of the first sentence.}[ALT]Edit Block[CTRL-RIGHT ARROW][CTRL-RIGHT ARROW][CTRL-RIGHT ARROW][CTRL-RIGHT ARROW][LEFT ARROW][ALT]Edit Delete y,

2. As of May 15, the corporation must increase sales by 15,000 units per month, renovate the corporate offices, and divest itself of its Romper division to meet its 1990 objectives.[ENTER]{Move the cursor to the "r" in "renovate."}[ALT]Edit Block {Move the cursor to the "a" in "and."}[DEL]y

3. Today's Projects[ENTER]Prepare capital budget request for two computers.[ENTER]Review receivables older than 90 days.[ENTER]Prepare next year's forecast.[ENTER][ALT]Edit Block[UP ARROW][UP ARROW] [ALT]Edit Delete y

4. Last February, the widget assembler became jammed. While the cause was poor maintenance, the machine's condition requires above-normal maintenance to prevent the problem from recurring. To prevent this problem from recurring, the company should purchase a new machine.[ENTER] {Move the cursor to the second sentence.}[ALT] Edit Select Sentence d

EXERCISES

8.4

1. Name: Patrick Rabbit[ENTER]Address: 777 Carrot Lane[ENTER][ALT]Edit Block[UP ARROW][UP ARROW][ALT] Edit Copy[DOWN ARROW][DOWN ARROW][ENTER]{Move to the "P" in "Patrick" in the copy.}[INS]Nancy [DEL][DEL]{Move to the first "7" in "777" in the copy.}515[INS][DOWN ARROW][ALT]Edit Paste b

2. First, put the correct pens in the plotter. This is an important step. Next, put the paper or transparency in the plotter.[ENTER]{Move the cursor to the second sentence.}[ALT]Edit Select Sentence c{Move the cursor to the end of the third sentence.}[SPACEBAR][SPACEBAR][ENTER]

3. Current Month:[ESC]7.[ENTER]Sales:[ESC]7.[ENTER]Cost of Goods Sold:[ESC]7.[ENTER][UP ARROW][UP ARROW][UP ARROW][ALT]**Edit Block**[DOWN ARROW][DOWN ARROW] [DOWN ARROW][ALT]**Edit Copy**[ENTER][ALT]**Edit Paste** b [ALT]**Edit Paste** b[ALT]**Edit Paste** b

4. Directions to the Cloverleaf Hall: Take the interstate to the Bay Street exit. At the exit, turn right, and take the next left after the light. Stay on this road until you pass the shopping mall on the right. After passing the shopping mall,[SPACEBAR] {Move to the "t" in "take."}[ALT]**Edit Block.**[ALT] **Edit Copy**[HOME][DOWN ARROW][END][ENTER]

MASTERY SKILLS CHECK

[8.1]

1. The cost of goods sold is $2,363,782. The beginning inventory is $689,578. The ending inventory is $234,245.[ENTER][HOME][UP ARROW][ALT]**Edit Select Sentence** m[CTRL-RIGHT ARROW][CTRL-RIGHT ARROW][CTRL-RIGHT ARROW][CTRL-RIGHT ARROW][CTRL-RIGHT ARROW] [ENTER]

[8.2]

2. The new and improved widget maker has several features. One of these features is the internal painter. This feature evenly coats each widget and limits the fumes, which reduces the number of employees needed to operate the machine. [ENTER]{Move the cursor to the comma in the third sentence.}[ALT]**Edit Block.**[LEFT ARROW][ALT]**Edit Move (Cut)** {Move the cursor to the period ending the second sentence.}[ENTER]

3. Tuesday, the heads of the accounting, production, [8.1, 8.3]
   and MIS departments will review the steps that
   they can take to reduce the time between the receipt of an order and its completion.[ENTER]{Move
   the cursor to the beginning of the word "that."}
   [ALT]**Edit Block**[CTRL-RIGHT ARROW][CTRL-RIGHT ARROW]
   [CTRL-RIGHT ARROW][CTRL-RIGHT ARROW][DEL]y[ALT]**Edit
   Select Paragraph** d

4. Today's weather will be lovely. The temperature [8.4]
   will rise to 82 and will cool to an evening low of
   70. The low humidity will contribute to the day's
   pleasant weather.[ENTER][UP ARROW][ALT]**Edit Select
   Paragraph** c[ENTER][ALT]**Edit Paste** b[ALT]**Edit Paste** b

INTEGRATING SKILLS CHECK

1. {Type the text as shown.}[ALT]**Layout Align Hard** [1.4, 8.1]
   Page[UP ARROW][ALT]**Edit Select Paragraph** m[DOWN
   ARROW][ENTER]

2. [ALT]**Layout Align Indent** → [HOME][HOME][DOWN [5.2]
   ARROW][F7]nn

3. Marketing Strategy[ENTER][CAPS LOCK]ABC WIDG- [1.4, 6.1]
   ETS[CAPS LOCK][ENTER]Prepared on July 7, 1990
   [ENTER][UP ARROW][CTRL-BACKSPACE][CTRL-BACKSPACE]
   [HOME] [HOME][UP ARROW][ALT]**Layout Page** cy[F7]
   [ALT]**File Print** v[F7][F7]nn

4. Date:[ENTER]Name:[ENTER]Amount:[ENTER]Explana- [1.4, 8.4]
   tion:[ENTER] Signature:[ENTER][ALT]**Layout Align
   Hard**

Page[HOME][HOME][UP ARROW][ALT]Edit Block[PGDN]
[ALT]Edit Copy c[ENTER]

[8.4]   **5.** [ALT]Edit Paste b[ALT]Edit Paste b[ALT]Edit Paste b

[3.1, 6.3]   **6.** [HOME][HOME][UP ARROW][ALT]Layout Page np2[F7]
[ALT]File Print f

[7.3]   **7.** [ALT]Search Replace nExplanation[F2]For[F2]

9   SKILLS CHECK

[5.1]   **1.** [ALT]Layout Line m2[ENTER]2[ENTER][F7]

[6.3]   **2.** [ALT]Layout Page np1[F7]

[7.2]   **3.** {Type the text as shown.}[ENTER][ALT]Search Backward spell[F2][ALT]Search Backward[F2]

[7.3]   **4.** [HOME][HOME][UP ARROW][ALT]Search Replace yit[F2]
WordPerfect[F2]ynyn

[8.3, 8.4]   **5.** [HOME][HOME][DOWN ARROW][LEFT ARROW][SPACEBAR]
[SPACEBAR] {Enter the text shown.}[UP ARROW][UP
ARROW][UP ARROW]{to move to the second sentence}
[ALT]Edit Select Sentence c[HOME][HOME][DOWN
ARROW][LEFT ARROW][SPACEBAR][SPACEBAR][ENTER]{Move
to the "w" in "when" in the last sentence.}[ALT]
Edit Block.[LEFT ARROW][DEL]y{Type the new text as
shown.}

EXERCISES ———————————— 9.1

1. {Type the words exactly as shown.}[HOME][HOME][UP ARROW][ALT] **Tools Spell** wawwwaww[F7]

2. {Type the text exactly as shown.}[HOME][HOME][UP ARROW][ALT] **Tools Spell** wawwawwwwwdwwcwwwhw[F7]

3. {Type the text exactly as shown.}[HOME][HOME][UP ARROW][ALT]**Tools Spell** w2w2wwdwwb[F7]

4. {Type the text exactly as shown.}[HOME][LEFT ARROW][ALT] **Tools Spell** w4[RIGHT ARROW][RIGHT ARROW][SPACEBAR][F7]ww4p[F7]w4[RIGHT ARROW][RIGHT ARROW][SPACEBAR][F7]ww4p[DEL][F7]w4[RIGHT ARROW][RIGHT ARROW][RIGHT ARROW][SPACEBAR][F7]ww4[RIGHT ARROW][RIGHT ARROW][RIGHT ARROW][SPACEBAR][F7]w[SPACEBAR]

EXERCISES ———————————— 9.2

1. {Type the paragraph as shown.}[ALT] **Tools Spell** db2aa[ENTER]

2. {Type the paragraph as shown.}[ALT] **Tools Spell** dagaa[ENTER]

3. {Type the paragraph as shown.}[ALT] **Tools Spell** d2aia[F7]

4. {Type the paragraph as shown.}[ALT] Tools Spell daadd[F7]

9.3 EXERCISES

1. {Type the paragraph as shown.}[ALT] Tools Spell d333[SPACEBAR]

2. {Type the paragraph as shown.}[ALT] Tools Spell d333aa3333[SPACEBAR]

3. {Type the paragraph as shown.}[ALT] Tools Spell d333333[SPACEBAR]

4. WordPerfect does[ENTER]does not[ENTER]not check to see if the[ENTER]the last word of one paragraph is the same word as the[ENTER]first word word of the next paragraph.[ENTER][ALT] Tools Spell d3{The speller finds only the double word in the last two lines.}

9.4 EXERCISES

1. {Type the names and addresses as shown.}[ALT] Tools Spell d33333[ENTER]

2. {Type your name.}[ALT] Tools Spell d{Type 3 to add any part of your name to the dictionary if WordPerfect does not recognize it.}[ENTER]

3. Abbreviations[ENTER]ATMOS - Atmosphere[ENTER]
   IDP - Integrated Data Processing[ENTER]OCS -
   Officer Candidate School[ENTER]SWAZ - Swaziland
   [ENTER][ALT] **Tools Spell** d3333[SPACEBAR]

4. {Type the paragraph as it appears.}[ALT] **Tools
   Spell** d333[SPACEBAR]

EXERCISES

$$9.5$$

1. [ALT]**File Retrieve** wp{wp}us.sup[ENTER]{Position
   the cursor on the first character in a word you
   wish to remove.}[CTRL-BACKSPACE][DEL]{For each
   word you wish to remove, move the cursor to the
   word, and repeat the keystrokes.[ALT]**File Save**
   [ENTER]y

2. [ALT]**File Exit** nn[ALT]**File Retrieve** wp{wp}us.sup
   [ENTER]{Press the[DOWN ARROW] key to move the cur-
   sor to "ATMOS" if it is not already there.}[CTRL-
   BACKSPACE][DEL]{Press the[DOWN ARROW] key to move
   the cursor to "IDP."}[CTRL-BACKSPACE][DEL]{Press the
   [DOWN ARROW] key to move the cursor to "OCS."}
   [CTRL-BACKSPACE][DEL]{Press the[DOWN ARROW] key to
   move the cursor to "SWAZ."}[CTRL-BACKSPACE][DEL]
   [ALT]**File Save**[ENTER]y

3. [ALT]**File Exit** nn[ALT]**File Retrieve** wp{wp}us.sup
   [ENTER]{Press the[DOWN ARROW] key to move the cursor to "Aphrodite" if it is not already there.}
   [CTRL-BACKSPACE][DEL]{Press the[DOWN ARROW] key to
   move the cursor to "Audrey."}[CTRL-BACKSPACE][DEL]

{Press the[DOWN ARROW] key to move the cursor to "Galatea."}[CTRL-BACKSPACE][DEL]{Press the[DOWN ARROW] key to move the cursor to "Pygmalion."} [CTRLBACKSPACE][DEL][ALT]**File Save**[ENTER]y

9.6   EXERCISES

1. The fair four the bridge to get to the fare is for dollars.[ENTER][ALT]**Search Replace** y[UP ARROW] fair[CTRL-END][F2]fare[F2]y[HOME][LEFT ARROW][ALT] **Search Replace** yfare[F2]fair[F2]ny[HOME][LEFT ARROW] [ALT]**Search Replace** yfor[F2]four[F2]y[HOME] [LEFT ARROW] [ALT]**Search Replace** yfour[F2]for [F2]yn

2. Their demonstrating there new product over they're.[ALT]**Search Replace** ythere[UP ARROW] [F2]their[F2]y[HOME][LEFT ARROW][ALT]**Search Replace** ythey're[F2]there[F2]y[HOME][LEFT ARROW][ALT]**Search Replace** ytheir[F2]they're[F2]yn

9.7   EXERCISES

1. [ALT]**Tools Thesaurus** table[ENTER][F7]

2. [ALT]**Tools Thesaurus** adjoining[ENTER][F7]

3. rich[ALT]**Tools Thesaurus** c[F7]

4. [ALT]**Tools Thesaurus** limit[ENTER][RIGHT ARROW]d [RIGHT ARROW]ehdd[LEFT ARROW][LEFT ARROW]44[F7]

EXERCISES

9.8

1. {Type the sentence as shown.}[CTRL-LEFT ARROW][ALT] Tools Thesaurus 1j

2. {Type the sentence as shown. Then, move the cursor to "division."}[ALT]Tools Thesaurus 1m

3. {Type the sentence as shown. Then, move the cursor to "Business."}[ALT]Tools Thesaurus[RIGHT ARROW]1a

4. {Type the paragraph.}[ENTER][UP ARROW][UP ARROW] [CTRL-RIGHT ARROW][ALT]Tools Thesaurus 1k[CTRL-RIGHT ARROW][CTRL-RIGHT ARROW][CTRL-RIGHT ARROW][ALT]Tools Thesaurus 1n[CTRL-RIGHT ARROW][CTRL-RIGHT ARROW] [CTRL-RIGHT ARROW][CTRL-RIGHT ARROW][ALT]Tools Thesaurus 1l[CTRL-RIGHT ARROW][CTRL-RIGHT ARROW][CTRL-RIGHT ARROW][CTRL-RIGHT ARROW][CTRL-RIGHT ARROW][CTRL-RIGHT ARROW][ALT]Tools Thesaurus 1m

MASTERY SKILLS CHECK

1. {Type each word as shown, pressing[ENTER] at the end of each one.}[HOME][HOME][UP ARROW][ALT]Tools Spell wawawaw[F7]   [9.1]

2. {Type the paragraph as shown.}[ENTER][ALT]Tools Spell d2c3b3[SPACEBAR]   [9.2]

3. {Type the letter as shown.}[CTRL-F2]d{Type a 3 for each proper name suggested as a misspelling to add it to the dictionary.}[SPACEBAR]   [9.4]

[9.5]   4. [ALT]File Retrieve wp{wp}us.sup[ENTER]{Move the cursor to the first name; press[CTRL-BACKSPACE] and the[DEL] key. Repeat this process for each name that you added.}[ALT]File Save[ENTER]y

[9.6]   5. {Type the paragraph as shown.}[HOME][HOME][UP ARROW][ALT]Search Replace yfor[F2]four[F2]y{Repeat the replace process for the homonyms "it's" and "its," "moor" and "more," "too" and "to," and "two" and "to."}

[9.7]   6. [ALT]Tools Thesaurus bar[ENTER]e3light[ENTER][F7]

[9.8]   7. {Type the sentence as shown.}[HOME][HOME][UP ARROW][CTRL-RIGHT ARROW][CTRL-RIGHT ARROW][ALT]Tools Thesaurus 1e

INTEGRATING SKILLS CHECK

[5.1, 6.2]   1. [ALT]Layout Line m3[ENTER]3[ENTER][ENTER]pm3 [ENTER]3[ENTER][F7]

[9.2]   2. {Type the paragraph as shown.}[ENTER][ALT]Tools Spell daaaaa[SPACEBAR]

[9.2, 9.4]   3. {Type the paragraph as shown.}[ALT]Tools Spell d33a[SPACEBAR]

[8.1]   4. [ALT]Edit Select Paragraph m[HOME][HOME][UP ARROW] [ENTER]

5. {Move to the beginning of the second paragraph.} [8.4]
[ALT]Edit Block[ENTER][ALT]Edit Copy[ENTER][ALT]
Edit Paste b[ALT]Edit Paste b

6. {Type the sentence; then move the cursor to the   [9.8]
word "light."}[ALT]Tools Thesaurus 1m

7. [ALT]File Print f   [3.1]

8. [ALT]File Save words[ENTER]   [2.2]

9. [ALT]File Exit nn[ALT]File Retrieve wp{wp}us.sup [9.5]
[ENTER]{Move the cursor to "Howard."}[CTRL-
BACKSPACE][DEL]{Repeat this procedure for
"Moore."}[ALT]File Save[ENTER]y

SKILLS CHECK _____ 10

1. {Type the paragraph as shown.}[ALT]Tools Spell   [9.2]
daa

2. {Move the cursor to "decides."}[ALT]Tools Thesau- [9.8]
rus 1as{The "s" changes the verb tense to fit the
context of the sentence.}

3. [HOME][HOME][UP ARROW][ALT]Edit Select Sentence [8.1]
m[HOME][HOME][DOWN ARROW][LEFT ARROW][SPACEBAR]
[SPACEBAR][ENTER]

4. [HOME][HOME][UP ARROW][ALT]Search Forward date[F2] [7.1]
{Repeat the[F2] sequence until the "Not found"
message appears.}

[8.3]   5. {Move the cursor to the last sentence.}[ALT]Edit
          Select Sentence d

10.1   EXERCISES

1. [ALT]Layout Page m5[ENTER]5[ENTER][F7]{Type the
   paragraphs as shown.}[HOME][HOME][UP ARROW]
   [ALT]Layout Line wy[F7]{Move the cursor down
   the screen.}

2. [ALT]Layout Page m5[ENTER]5[ENTER][F7]{Type the
   paragraph as shown.}[HOME][HOME][UP ARROW]
   [ALT]Layout Line wy[F7]{Move the cursor to the
   bottom of the document to reformat the paragraph.}[ALT]File Exit ylifo[ENTER]n

3. [ALT]File Retrieve lifo[ENTER][ALT]Edit Reveal Codes
   [LEFT ARROW][BACKSPACE][ALT]Edit Reveal Codes[ALT]
   Layout Page m[ENTER]9[ENTER][F7]{Press the[DOWN
   ARROW] key until you reach the bottom of the
   document.}[ALT]File Exit[ENTER][ENTER]y[ENTER]

4. [ALT]File Retrieve lifo[ENTER][ALT]Layout Line m3
   [ENTER]3[ENTER][F7]{Press the[DOWN ARROW] key until
   you reach the bottom of the document.}[ALT]File
   Exit[ENTER][ENTER]y[ENTER]

10.2   EXERCISES

1. [ALT]Layout Page hapAcme Inc. Income Statement
   [F7][F7][ALT]File Print v1[F7]

2. [ALT]Layout Page fap[F6]{Type your name.}[F6][F7]
[F7][ALT]File Print v{Press the[DOWN ARROW] key re-
peatedly until the footer appears on the screen.}
[F7]

3. [ALT]Layout Page hap[ALT]Layout Align Center
[CTRL-B] -[F7][F7][ALT]File Print v[F7]

4. [ALT]Layout Page hao[CTRL-B][F7]hbv{Type your
name.}[F7][F7][ALT]Layout Align Hard Page[ALT]File
Print v[PGUP][F7]

EXERCISES _____ 10.3

1. {Type the sentence as shown.}[ALT]Layout Footnote Create[SPACEBAR]{Type the footnote text.}[F7]
[ALT] File Exit nn

2. Once upon a time,. . .[ALT]Layout Footnote Create
[SPACEBAR]Grimm Brothers Fairy Tales[F7][ENTER]
Mary had a little lamb[ALT]Layout Footnote Create
[SPACEBAR] Mother Goose[F7][ENTER]The Goose That
Laid a Golden Egg[ALT]Layout Footnote Create
[SPACEBAR]Aesop's Fables[F7][ENTER]

3. [HOME][HOME][UP ARROW][ALT]Edit Select Paragraph
m[HOME][HOME][DOWN ARROW][ENTER]{You may need
to press the[DOWN ARROW] key to make WordPerfect
renumber the footnote.}

4. [ALT]Layout Footnote Edit 3[ENTER]{Make the
changes specified.}[F7]

MASTERY SKILLS CHECK

[10.1]   **1.** [ALT]Layout Page m[ENTER]9[ENTER][F7]{Type the text as shown.}[ENTER][HOME][HOME][UP ARROW][ALT]Layout Line wy[F7]{You may need to press the[DOWN ARROW]key to make WordPerfect reformat the paragraph.}

[10.3]   **2.** {Place the cursor before the tab at the beginning of the paragraph.}[ALT]Layout Align Hard Page [HOME][HOME][DOWN ARROW][LEFT ARROW][ALT]Layout Footnote Create[SPACEBAR]{Type the footnote text.} [F7]

[10.3]   **3.** {Move the cursor to the end of the second sentence.}[ALT]Layout Footnote Create[SPACEBAR] {Type the footnote text.}[F7]

[10.3]   **4.** [ALT]Layout Footnote Edit 1[ENTER]{Make the changes shown.}[F7]

[10.2]   **5.** [HOME][HOME][UP ARROW][ALT]Layout Page hapPreparing a Trial Balance[F7][F7][CTRL-END][DEL][DEL]

[10.2]   **6.** [ALT]Layout Page fao{Type your name.}[F7][F7][ALT] File Print v{ge through the document with the [PGUP] and[PGDN] keys.}

INTEGRATING SKILLS CHECK

[1.4]   **1.** {Type the address labels as shown. Move to the end of the first ZIP code.}[ALT]Layout Align Hard Page {Repeat for the other addresses.}

2. {Move to the bottom of the first page, press   [9.7]
   ENTER twice, and type the letter text as shown.}
   {Move the cursor to "continue."}[ALT]Tools
   Thesaurus[F7]{Move the cursor to "receive."}
   [ALT]Tools Thesaurus[F7]

3. [ALT]Tools Spell p{The only words the Spell fea-   [9.2]
   ture should highlight are "Johann," "Sebastian,"
   and "Elsie;" you can skip them or add them to
   the dictionary.}

4. {Move the cursor to the space after the comma   [10.3]
   following "publication."}[ALT]Layout Footnote
   Create[SPACEBAR]{Type the footnote text.}[F7]

5. [ALT]Layout Footnote Edit 1[ENTER]{Make the   [10.3]
   change shown.}[F7]

6. {Move the cursor to the beginning of the letter.}   [8.4]
   [ALT]Edit Block {Move the cursor to the bottom of
   the letter.}[ALT]Edit Copy {Move the cursor to the
   end of the ZIP code in Karl Davis's address.}
   [ENTER][ENTER][ENTER]{Move the cursor to the end of
   the ZIP code in Angus Fuller's address.}[ENTER]
   [ENTER][ALT]Edit Paste b

7. [HOME][HOME][UP ARROW][ALT]Layout Page hap[ALT]   [10.2]
   Layout Align Flush Right{Type your name.}[F7][F7]

SKILLS CHECK   11

1. {Type the paragraphs, pressing ENTER after each   [8.1]
   one.}[UP ARROW][ALT]Edit Select Paragraph m[UP

ARROW][UP ARROW][UP ARROW][ENTER]

[9.2] **2.** [ALT]**Tools Spell** d{Fix any spelling errors as Word-
Perfect finds them; the original had none.}

[9.8] **3.** {Move to "redeem."}[ALT]**Tools Thesaurus** 1l

[6.2] **4.** [HOME][HOME][UP ARROW][ALT]**Layout Page**
m5[ENTER]5[ENTER][F7]

[10.1] **5.** [ALT]**Layout Line** wy[F7]

[10.3] **6.** {Move to the end of the convertible bonds paragraph.}[ALT]**Layout Footnote Create** Usually in exchange for common stock[F7]

[2.2] **7.** [ALT]**File Exit** [ENTER]stocks[ENTER][ENTER]

11.1 EXERCISES

1. The pension plan is expected to earn 6% per year.
New employees become vested in the plan after
five years with the company.[ENTER][ALT]**File Save**
plan[ENTER][ALT]**File Exit** nn [ALT]**File List Files**
[ENTER]{Move the highlight to the PLAN
filename.}cearn[ENTER][F7]

2. {Place a disk in drive A.}[ALT]**File List Files**
[ENTER]{Move the highlight to the PLAN filename.}
ca:plan[ENTER][F7]

3. [ALT]**File Retrieve** plan[ENTER][ALT]**File Save** vested-
[ENTER]

4. [ALT]File List Files [ENTER]{Move the highlight to the EARN filename.}cpenplan[ENTER][F7]

5. [ALT]File Retrieve vested[ENTER]{Place a disk in drive A.}[ALT]File Save a:vested[ENTER]

EXERCISES ————————————————— 11.2

1. [ALT]File List Files = \ finance[ENTER]y

2. [ALT]File List Files = letters[ENTER]y

3. [ALT]File List Files = \ finance \finc1990[ENTER]y

4. [ALT]File List Files = \ finance \finc1991[ENTER]y

EXERCISES ————————————————— 11.3

1. [ALT]File List Files = \ finance[ENTER][F1]

2. [ALT]File List Files = \wp51 letters[ENTER][F1]

3. [ALT]File List Files = \ finance \finc1989[ENTER][F1]

4. [ALT]File List Files = \ finance \finc1991[ENTER][F1]

5. [ALT]File List Files = wp51 [ENTER][F1]

11.4   EXERCISES

1. {Put the disk containing the PLAN file in drive A.} [ALT]File List Files a:[ENTER]{Move the highlight to the PLAN file.}dy[F7]

2. [ALT]File List Files [ENTER]{Move the highlight to the LETTERS subdirectory.}dy[F7]

3. [ALT]File List Files \ finance[ENTER]{Move the highlight to the FINC1989 subdirectory.}dy[F7]

4. [ALT]File List Files \ finance[ENTER]{Move the highlight to the FINC1990 subdirectory.}dy[F7]

11.5   EXERCISES

1. [ALT]File List Files [ENTER]{Move the highlight to the PLAN file.} mpension3 [ENTER][F7]

2. [ALT]File List Files [ENTER]{Move the highlight to the EARN file.}m[END]ed[ENTER][F7]

3. [ALT]File RetrieveEARNED[ENTER][ALT]File Save ERNINC[ENTER][ALT]File Exit n[ENTER][ALT]File List Files [ENTER]{Move the highlight to the ERNINC filename.}m{Move the cursor to the "R" in "ERN,"}a[ENTER][F7]

EXERCISES

11.6

1. [ALT]Layout Document snBlank Quit Claim Sales
   Contract[ENTER]Contract[ENTER]tJonas Smith
   [ENTER]Karen Polk[ENTER]sUndeveloped Real Estate
   [ENTER]kForm Contract Quit Claim[ENTER]aThis
   blank contract covers most undeveloped land
   sales in the state of Florida. This contract has four
   Xs where you must fill in information. Paragraphs
   contained in braces are optional. Remove them if
   they are unnecessary for a particular contract.
   [F7][F7][ALT]File Exit[ENTER]contract[ENTER]n

2. The August 17th meeting discussed the following
   issues:[ENTER]Installation of new parking lot lights
   [ENTER]Hiring of security personnel to patrol the
   parking lots after dark[ENTER]Completion of new
   research and development building[ENTER]Im-
   proved insurance benefits[ENTER][ALT]Layout Document snAugust 17th meeting notes[ENTER]
   [ENTER][SHIFT-F10]y[F7][ALT]File Save issues[ENTER]

3. WordPerfect's Graphics features are among the
   most advanced in the industry. Investing some
   time in mastering these features could offer a significant payoff for our company. Outside service
   costs for creating newsletters and brochures can
   be reduced significantly.[ENTER][ALT]Layout Document snCut costs with WordPerfect's Graphic[ENT-
   ER]Product comment[ENTER][SHIFT-F10]
   ya[CTRL-PG DOWN]Reduce newsletter and brochure
   development costs with Graphics features. We

can recover the cost of the upgrade to 5.1 with
the first job.[F7][F7][ALT]File Exit[ENTER]saving[ENTER]
[ENTER]

4. [ALT]File Retrieve issues[ENTER][ALT]Layout Document st [ENTER][CTRL-END]Martha King
[ENTER][F7]

11.7   EXERCISES

1. [ALT]File List Files [ENTER] fdAugust[ENTER]
{The ISSUES file will be listed; additional files
may be included.} [F7]

2. [ALT]File List Files [ENTER] fpAcme Corporation
[ENTER]{The PENSCONT file will be listed; additional files may be included.} [F7]

3. [ALT]File List Files [ENTER] feplan[ENTER]{The
EARNED, EARNINC, PENSION, PENSCONT,
PENSION3, and VESTED files will be listed.} [F7]

4. [ALT]File List Files[ENTER] fe{Type your first
name.}[ENTER]{Various files may be listed.}
[F7]

5. [ALT]File List Files [ENTER] f dcompany;product
[ENTER][F7]

6. [ALT]File List Files[ENTER] f epension,contract
[ENTER][F7]

EXERCISES ——————————————— 11.8

1. [ALT]**File List Files** [ENTER]{Move the highlight to the EARNED filename.}[ENTER]{Look through the file.}[F7][F7]

2. [ALT]**File List Files** [ENTER]{Move the highlight to the CONTRACT file.}[ENTER]{Look through the file.}[F7][F7]

3. [ALT]**File List Files** [ENTER]{Move the highlight to the ISSUES filename.}[ENTER]{Look through the file.}[F7][F7]

4. [ALT]**File List Files** [ENTER]{Move the highlight to the PENPLAN filename.}[ENTER]{Look through the file.}[F7][F7]

5. [ALT]**File List Files** [ENTER]{Move the highlight to the STOCKS filename.}[ENTER]{Look through the file.}[F7][F7]

MASTERY SKILLS CHECK

1. [ALT]**File List Files** [ENTER]obudget90[ENTER]   [11.2]
y[F7]

2. Acme Corporation - 1991 Budget[ENTER][ENTER]   [11.1]
Estimated Sales[TAB][TAB]$1,000,000[ENTER]Fixed
Costs[TAB][TAB][TAB] $[SPACEBAR][SPACEBAR]400,000
[ENTER]Variable Costs[TAB][TAB][TAB] $[SPACEBAR]
[SPACEBAR]400,000[ENTER]Gross Profit[TAB][TAB][TAB]

$[SPACEBAR][SPACEBAR]200,000[ENTER][ALT]File Save
BUDGET[ENTER][ALT]File Exit nn[ALT]File List Files
[ENTER]{Move the highlight to the BUDGET
filename.}cbudget91[ENTER][F7]

[11.3]   **3.** [ALT]File List Files =budget91[ENTER][F1]

[11.1]   **4.** [ALT]File List Files[ENTER]{Move the highlight to
the BUDGET filename.}cbdgt1991[ENTER][F7]

[11.4]   **5.** [ALT]File List Files [ENTER]{Move the highlight to
the BUDGET filename.} dy[F7]

[11.5]   **6.** [ALT]File List Files[ENTER]{Move the highlight to
the BDGT1991 filename.}m[END][LEFT ARROW][LEFT
ARROW][BACKSPACE][BACKSPACE][ENTER][F7]

[11.6]   **7.** [ALT]File Retrieve bdgt90[ENTER][ALT]Layout Document snBudget 1991[ENTER]Budget[ENTER]tJane
Smith[ENTER]John Dow[ENTER]sAcme Corporation[ENTER]c10023[ENTER]aMichael McCormick
must have this report by September 30, 1990.
[F7][F7]

[11.6]   **8.** [ALT]File Save [ENTER]y

[11.7]   **9.** [ALT]File List Files [ENTER] f dBudget[ENTER]
[F7]

[11.8]   **10.** [ALT]File Exit nn [ALT]File List Files[ENTER]
{Move the highlight to the BDGT91 filename.}
[ENTER]{Use the cursor movement keys to look at
the file.}[F7][F7]

[11.3]   **11.** [ALT]File List Files = \wp51 [ENTER][F1]

INTEGRATING SKILLS CHECK

1. {Type the paragraphs, pressing ENTER at the   [9.2]
end of each one.} [ALT]Tools Spell d{Fix any spelling errors as WordPerfect finds them; the original has none.}

2. [ALT]File Save prefer[ENTER]   [2.2]

3. [ALT]File List Files [ENTER]{Move the highlight to   [11.1]
the PREFER filename.}cpreferrd[ENTER][F7]

4. [ALT]File List Files[ENTER]ostock[ENTER]y[F7]   [11.3]

5. [ALT]File Exit nn   [1.3]

6. [ALT]File List Files[ENTER]{Move the highlight to   [11.1]
the PREFERRD filename.}cstock[ENTER][F7]

7. [ALT]File List Files =stock[ENTER][F1][ALT]File Re-   [11.3]
trieve preferrd[ENTER]

8. {This answer moves "participation" to the bot-   [8.1]
tom and "conversion" between "callable" and
"cumulative;" there are other methods to accomplish this.} [HOME][HOME][UP ARROW][DOWN ARROW]
[DOWN ARROW][ALT]Edit Select Paragraph m[PGDN]
[ENTER][UP ARROW][ALT]Edit Select Paragraph m[UP
ARROW][UP ARROW][UP ARROW][ENTER]

9. [HOME][HOME][UP ARROW][ALT]Layout Page m5   [6.2]
[ENTER]5[ENTER][F7]

10. [ALT]Layout Line wy[F7]   [10.1]

[2.2]   **11.** [ALT]File Save[ENTER]y

[11.4]   **12.** [ALT]File List Files c:\wp51 [ENTER]{Move the cursor to the PREFER filename.}dy[F7]

[7.1]   **13.** [ALT]Search Forward dividend[F2]{"Dividend" first occurs in the explanation of "Cumulative."}

[9.7]   **14.** {Move the cursor to "fluctuates."} [ALT]Tools Thesaurus {Look at the synonyms.}[F7]{Move the cursor to "extent."} [ALT]Tools Thesaurus{Look at the synonyms.}[F7]

SKILLS CHECK

[9.2]   **1.** {Type the paragraph as shown.} [ALT]Tools Spell da3aa{Press any key.}

[9.8]   **2.** {Move the cursor to the word "customize."} [ALT]Tools Thesaurus 1f

[10.2]   **3.** [HOME][HOME][UP ARROW][ALT]Layout Page hap WordPerfect Print Features[F7]fap [ALT] Layout Align Center Page[SPACEBAR][CTRL-B] [F7][F7][ALT]File Print v3[F7]

[11.6]   **4.** [ALT]Layout Document s n Describing WordPerfect's Print features[ENTER]documentation (omit in 5.0)[ENTER]t{Type your name}[ENTER] {Type your name}[ENTER]sTeach Yourself WordPerfect[ENTER][SHIFT-F10]y [F7]

[11.1, 11.4, 11.5]   **5.** [ALT]File Save advprint[ENTER][ALT]File List Files[ENTER]{Move the highlight to the ADV-PRINT file.}cprintadv[ENTER]mprntfeat[ENTER][F7]

{Since WordPerfect does not refresh the screen when you copy files, you must leave List Files and reenter it.} [ALT]File List Files [ENTER]{Move the highlight to the PRINTADV file.}dy[F7]

EXERCISES
12.1

1. {Type the paragraph as shown.}[ENTER][ALT]File Print n3[ENTER]f [ALT]File Exit [ENTER]filedel [ENTER]n

2. {Type the paragraph as shown.}[ENTER][ALT]File Print n2[ENTER]f [ALT]File Exit [ENTER]rename [ENTER]n

3. [ALT]File Print n3[ENTER]dprintopt[ENTER] [ENTER][F7]

4. [ALT]File Print n2[ENTER]dwpset[ENTER][ENTER][F7]

5. [ALT]File Print dfiledel[ENTER][ENTER]n1[ENTER] dwpset[ENTER] [ENTER][F7]

EXERCISES
12.2

1. [ALT]File Print n3[ENTER] drename[ENTER] [ENTER]c[F7]

2. [ALT]File Print drename[ENTER][ENTER]n2[ENTER] dfiledel[ENTER][ENTER]n1[ENTER]dwpset[ENTER][ENTER]c {Wait until WordPerfect finishes all three jobs.}[F7]

12.3 EXERCISES

1. [ALT]**File Print** n5[ENTER]drename[ENTER][ENTER]cc
{Type the number of the RENAME print job}
[ENTER][F7]

2. [ALT]**File Print** n3 [ENTER] drename[ENTER][ENTER]
dfiledel[ENTER][ENTER]dwpset[ENTER][ENTER]ccy[F7]

3. {Turn the printer off.} [ALT]**File Print** n1[ENTER]
dfiledel[ENTER][ENTER]cc {Type the number of the
FILEDEL print job.}[ENTER][F7]

4. [ALT]**File Print** dwpset[ENTER][ENTER]dfiledel
[ENTER][ENTER]drename[ENTER][ENTER]cc{Type the
number of the WPSET print job.}[ENTER]c{Type the
number of the RENAME print job.}[ENTER][F7]{Turn
the printer on.}

12.4 EXERCISES

1. [ALT]**File Print** drename[ENTER][ENTER]dfiledel
[ENTER][ENTER]dprintopt[ENTER][ENTER]cr{Type the
number of the PRINTOPT print job.}[ENTER]y[F7]

2. {Turn the printer off.}[ALT]**File Print** dwpset
[ENTER][ENTER]dfiledel[ENTER][ENTER]drename[ENTER]
[ENTER]cr{Type the number of the RENAME print
job.}[ENTER]{Since the first one has not started
printing, the third print request will print before
the first one, and WordPerfect will not prompt

you for interrupting the current print job.}{Turn
the printer on.}g[F7]

EXERCISES ———————————— 12.5

1. [ALT]File Retrieve wpset[ENTER][ALT]File Print tmf

2. [ALT]File Print thf

3. [ALT]File Print tdf

EXERCISES ———————————— 12.6

1. When you change the font, all characters after the
font change are affected. [ALT]Font Base Font
{Move the highlight to a font that has a smaller
CPI, smaller pitch, or larger point size than the
one originally highlighted.}[ENTER] Characters before the font change use the initial setting of your
printer. [ALT]File Print v1[F7]

2. Fonts can also be proportionally spaced. [ALT] Font
Base Font {If your printer has a proportionally
spaced font, move the highlight to a font that has
a "PS" after it, preferably with the same CPI,
pitch, or point size than the one originally highlighted; if your printer does not have a proportionally spaced font, move the highlight to a font
that has a smaller point size, smaller pitch, or
higher CPI.}In proportionally spaced fonts, each

character uses a different amount of space. For example, an I takes less space than an m. [ALT] File Print v[F7]

12.7   EXERCISES

1. {Type the paragraph as shown.}[HOME][HOME][UP ARROW][ALT]Edit Block. [ALT]Font Fine [ALT]File Print v[F7]

2. H [ALT]Font Subscript 2[RIGHT ARROW]O[ENTER] [ENTER]E = mc [ALT]Font Superscript 2[RIGHT ARROW][ENTER][ENTER]Subscripted text appears [ALT]Font Subscript below the normal text. [RIGHT ARROW][ENTER][ENTER]Superscripted text appears [ALT]Font Superscript above the normal text.[RIGHT ARROW][ENTER][ENTER][ALT]File Print v[F7]

3. [ALT]Font Extra Large Your printer prints Extra Large text like this.[RIGHT ARROW][ENTER][ALT]Font Very Large Your printer prints Very Large text like this.[RIGHT ARROW][ENTER][ALT]Font Large Your printer prints Large text like this.[RIGHT ARROW] [ENTER][ALT]Font Small Your printer prints Small text like this.[RIGHT ARROW][ENTER] [ALT]Font Fine Your printer prints Fine text like this.[RIGHT ARROW] [ALT]File Print v[F7]

MASTERY SKILLS CHECK

[12.6]

1. {Type the paragraph as shown.}[HOME][HOME][UP ARROW][ALT]Font Base Font {Move the high

light to another font that has the same PT or pitch as the first one highlighted and has "italics" following it; if italic is not available, select another font.}

2. {Move the cursor to the "C" in "CPI."} [ALT]
   Edit Block [RIGHT ARROW][RIGHT ARROW][RIGHT ARROW]
   [ALT]Font Large {Move the cursor to the "P" in
   "PT."} [ALT]Edit Block [RIGHT ARROW][RIGHT ARROW]
   [ALT]Font Large {Move the cursor to the "P" in
   "Pitch."} [ALT]Edit Block [CTRL-RIGHT ARROW][LEFT AR-
   ROW][ALT]Font Large   [12.7]

3. [ALT]File Print n4[ENTER]tdf   [12.1, 12.5]

4. [ALT]File Print cc{Type the number that appears
   next to "(Screen)."}[ENTER][F7]   [12.3]

5. [ALT]File Print n2[ENTER]thf [ALT]File Print n4[ENTER]   [12.1, 12.4, 12.5]
   tdf [ALT]File Print cr{Type the number that ap-
   pears next to the print job that displays the
   "Text=Draft" message under Print Options.}
   [ENTER][F7]

INTEGRATING SKILLS CHECK

1. {Type the paragraph as shown.} [ALT]Tools Spell   [9.2]
   d{The original paragraph has no spelling mis-
   takes; correct any typing mistakes that Word-
   Perfect finds. Press any key to return to the
   document.}

2. [ALT]File Save wordwrap[ENTER][ALT]File Save fon-   [11.1, 11.4]
   tadj[ENTER] [ALT]File List Files

[ENTER]{Move the highlight to the WORDWRAP file.}dy[F7]

[12.7]

3. {Move to the "f" in "fine."} [ALT]Edit Block [CTRL-RIGHT ARROW][LEFT ARROW][ALT]Font Fine [RIGHT ARROW][ALT]Edit Block [CTRL-RIGHT ARROW][LEFT ARROW][ALT]Font Extra Large [CTRL-RIGHT ARROW][CTRL-RIGHT ARROW][ALT] Edit Block [CTRL-RIGHT ARROW][LEFT ARROW] [ALT]Font Small[ALT]File Print v[F7]

[12.6]

4. [HOME][HOME][UP ARROW][ALT]Font Base Font {Move the highlight to a font that has a smaller CPI, smaller pitch, or larger point size than the one originally highlighted.}[ENTER]{Move to the beginning of the last sentence.} [ALT]Font Base Font {Move the highlight to a font that has a larger CPI, larger pitch, or smaller point size than the one originally highlighted.}[ENTER][ALT]File Print v[F7]

[10.3]

5. {Move to the end of the first sentence.} [ALT] Layout Footnote Create[SPACEBAR] Changing the font does not change WordPerfect's other default settings, such as margins and page size.[F7]

[12.1, 12.4, 12.5]

6. [ALT]File Print thn4[ENTER]f [ALT]File Print n3[ENTER]f [ALT]File Print tdn2[ENTER]f [ALT]File Print cr{Type the job number of the draft print request.}[ENTER]y[F7]

[11.8]

7. [ALT]File List Files [ENTER]{Move the highlight to the FONTADJ file.}[ENTER][F7][F7]

SKILLS CHECK   13

1. {Type the text as shown.}[ENTER]{Move the cursor   [10.3]
to the first space after the period at the end of the
first sentence.} [ALT]Layout Footnote Create
[SPACEBAR] These bonds were originally issued
to upgrade production facilities.[F7]

2. [HOME][HOME][UP ARROW][ALT]Layout Page fap   [10.2]
{Type your name.}[F7][F7]

3. [ALT]Layout Page hapPage[SPACEBAR][CTRL-b][F7]   [10.2]
[F7]

4. [ALT]File Print td[F7]   [12.5]

5. {If your printer has an italic base font:} [ALT]   [12.6, 12.7]
Font Base Font {Move the highlight to a font that
is followed by the word "Italic."}[ENTER][ALT]File
Exit yxtragain[ENTER]n {If your printer does
not have an italic base font:} [ALT]Edit Block
[HOME][HOME][DOWN ARROW][ALT]Font Appearance
Italics [ALT]File Exit yxtragain[ENTER]n

6. [ALT]File List Files [ENTER]onotes[ENTER]y[F7]   [11.2]

7. [ALT]Files List Files [ENTER]{Move the highlight to   [11.1]
XTRAGAIN.}cnotes[ENTER][F7]

8. [ALT]File Print dnotes\xtragain[ENTER][ENTER][F7]   [3.4]

9. [ALT]File List Files notes[ENTER]{Move the highlight   [11.4]
to XTRAGAIN.}dy[F7]

[11.4]   10. [ALT]File List Files [ENTER]{Move the highlight to the NOTES subdirectory.}dy[F7]

13.1   EXERCISES

1. Production used 1200 ball bearings to replace the machinery's worn ones.[ENTER][ALT]Edit Switch Document[ALT]File Retrieve final[ENTER]{Move the cursor to the end of the letter.} [ALT]Layout Align Hard Page[ALT]File Exit [ENTER][ENTER]yy[ALT] File Exit [ENTER]skates[ENTER]n.

2. {Type the text as shown.}[ENTER][ALT]File Save stmt1[ENTER][ALT]Edit Switch Document[ALT] File Retrieve stmt1[ENTER]{Move to the end of the paragraph, and type the text as shown.} [ALT] File Save stmt2[ENTER][ALT]File Exit ny [ALT] File Exit nn

3. [ALT]File Retrieve stmt2[ENTER][ALT]Edit Switch Document[ALT]File Retrieve stmt1[ENTER][ALT] File Exit ny [ALT]File Exit nn

13.2   EXERCISES

1. [ALT]Edit Window 10[ENTER][ALT]Edit Window 24[ENTER]

2. [ALT]Edit Window 8[ENTER][ALT]Edit Window 18[ENTER]

3. [ALT]Edit Switch Document[ALT]Edit Window
   14[ENTER]

4. [ALT]Edit Window 8[ENTER]

EXERCISES ——————————— 13.3

1. The discrepancy between the amount due and
   what the client believes is the proper amount is
   the sales tax of [ALT]Edit Switch Document[ALT]File
   Retrieve final[ENTER][ALT]Edit Switch Document
   $31.50.{Type the remaining text.}

2. The president, Amanda Williams, started with the
   company as chief production officer fifteen years
   ago. [ALT]Edit Switch Document Ms. Williams' experience includes chief production officer, divisional vice president, production vice president,
   and president. [ALT]Edit Switch Document
   [SPACEBAR][SPACEBAR]After four years as production
   officer, she was promoted to divisional vice president of the appliance division. [ALT]File Exit
   ypresidnt[ENTER]y [ALT] File Exit ypresresu.me
   [ENTER]n

EXERCISES ——————————— 13.4

1. [TAB]Peter Sullivan is production vice president.
   He has held this position for the past three year-
   s.[ENTER][TAB] Paula Atchinson is the financial vice
   president. She has held this position for the past

five years.[ENTER][UP ARROW][UP ARROW][UP ARROW][UP ARROW][ALT]**Edit Select Paragraph m** [ALT]**Edit Switch Document** [ENTER][ALT]**File Exit ny**[ALT]**File Exit nn**

2. Terry Kesley[ENTER]Kesley Associates[ENTER]496 Berry Avenue[ENTER]Newport, Rhode Island 03563[ENTER][ALT]**Edit Block** [HOME][HOME][UP ARROW][ALT]**Edit Copy**[ALT]**Edit Switch Document** [ENTER]

MASTERY SKILLS CHECK

[13.1]   1. {Type the text as shown.} [ALT]**Edit Switch Document**

[13.2]   2. [ALT]**Edit Window 12**[ENTER]

[13.2]   3. [ALT]**Edit Switch Document**[ALT]**Edit Window 8**[ENTER]

[13.4]   4. [HOME][UP ARROW][DOWN ARROW][ALT]**Edit Select Paragraph c** [ALT]**Edit Switch Document** [ENTER]

[13.4]   5. [ALT]**Edit Switch Document**[ALT]**Edit Select Paragraph m** [ALT]**Edit Switch Document** [ENTER]

INTEGRATING SKILLS CHECK

[11.1]   1. [TAB]The company leases most of its office space and mainframe computer equipment. It owns all of its production facilities.[ENTER][TAB]Total rental expense is $1,709,000 for the current year, $998,000 for 1989, and $923,000 for 1988.[ENTER] [ALT]File Save leases[ENTER][ALT]File Save leases.bak[ENTER]

2. [ALT]Edit Switch Document[ALT]File Retrieve leases.bak[ENTER]   [13.1]

3. [HOME][DOWN ARROW]{Type the text as shown.}[ENTER] [UP ARROW][ALT]Edit Select Paragraph c [ALT]Edit Switch Document [ENTER]

4. [ALT]File Exit [ENTER]leases.new[ENTER]y   [13.1]

5. [ALT]Layout Document s nNotes for financial statements[ENTER][ENTER]t{Type your name.} [ENTER]{Type your name.}[ENTER]sFor 1989 financial statements[ENTER][F7]   [11.6]

6. [ALT]File List Files[ENTER]{Move the highlight to the LEASES.BAK file.}dy[F7]   [11.4]

7. [HOME][HOME][UP ARROW][ALT]Layout Paragraph hapFinancial Statement Notes[F7][F7]   [10.2]

8. [ALT]Layout Paragraph fap{Type your name.}[F7] [F7]   [10.2]

9. {Turn the printer off.}[ALT]File Print n2[ENTER]f[ALT] File Print c1{Type the job number shown under "Current Job."}[F7]{Turn the printer on.}   [12.1,12.3]

14

SKILLS CHECK

1. [ALT] Layout Line t[CTRL-END]0.5[ENTER]3[ENTER] [F7][F7]{Type the text as shown, pressing the[TAB] key twice for the address and closing lines.}[ALT] Tools Spell d{Spelling as shown is correct. Press any key to end the spelling check when Word-Perfect displays the word count.}

[8.2]

2. {Move to the "M" in "Mark."}[ALT]Edit Block {Move to the line below the address.}

[13.4]

3. [ALT]Edit Copy[ALT]Edit Switch Document[ENTER]

[13.1, 13.2]

4. [ALT]Edit Switch Document[ALT]Edit Window 12 [ENTER]

[2.2]

5. [ALT]File Save request[ENTER]

[12.1]

6. [ALT]File Print n2[ENTER]f

[12.1, 12.3]

7. [ALT]File Print f[ALT]File Print f[ALT]File Print cc*y[F7]

[1.4, 9.2]

8. {Move the cursor to the blank line between the letter body and the closing.}[TAB]I have enclosed a list of the sales representatives who will be attending the forum.[ENTER][HOME][HOME][DOWN ARROW] [CTRL-ENTER]Jim Styverson[ENTER] Karen Acermann [ENTER]Julie Greenlowe[ENTER]Paul Hatterfield [ENTER][ALT]Tools Spell p33333{Press any key.}

[10.2]

9. {Move the cursor to the top of the page.}[ALT] Layout Page hapForum Attendees[F7][F7]

10. [ALT]File List Files[ENTER]{Move to the REQUEST   [11.1]
filename.}cletter.bk[ENTER][F7]

11. [ALT]Edit Switch Document[ALT]Layout Page hap   [10.2, 13.4]
Booth Assignments[F7][F7][ALT]Edit Switch Docu-
ment[ALT]Edit Block[HOME][HOME][DOWN ARROW]
[ALT]Edit Copy[ALT]Edit Switch Document
[HOME][HOME][DOWN ARROW][ENTER]

12. [ALT]Layout Line t[HOME][LEFT ARROW][CTRL-END]   [5.4]
3[ENTER][F7][F7][END][TAB]8:00 - 10:00[DOWN ARROW]
[TAB]10:00 - 1:00[DOWN ARROW][TAB]1:00 - 3:00
[DOWN ARROW][TAB]3:00 - 5:30

13. [ALT]File Print n1[ENTER]drequest[ENTER][ENTER]   [12.1, 12.4]
drequest[ENTER][ENTER]p[ALT]File Print cr{Type the
number of the "(Screen)" print job.}[ENTER][F7]

14. [ALT]File Save times[ENTER][ALT]File List Files   [2.2, 11.5]
[ENTER]{Move the highlight to the TIMES
filename.}mbooth[ENTER][F7]

15. [ALT]File List Files[ENTER]feKaren[ENTER]{BOOTH   [11.7]
will be listed; others may also be.}[F7]

16. [ALT]File Exit ny[ALT]File Exit nn[ALT]File List   [11.8]
Files[ENTER]{Move the highlight to the BOOTH
filename.}[ENTER]{View the file.}[F7][F7]

17. [ALT]File Retrieve booth[ENTER][ALT]Layout Docu-   [11.6]
ment sn{Type a descriptive filename.}[ENTER]
{Type a descriptive document type.}[ENTER]t{Type

an author name.}[ENTER]{Type a typist
name.}[ENTER][F7]

[11.3]

18. {if you have a hard disk}[ALT]File List Files
=\[ENTER][ENTER][F7]{if you are using floppy
disks}[ALT]File List Files a:[ENTER][F7]

[11.2, 11.4]

19. {if you have a hard disk}[ALT]File List Files
[ENTER]otrdeshow[ENTER]y[F7][ALT]File List
Files[ENTER]{Move the highlight to the TRDE-
SHOW subdirectory.}dy[F7][ALT]File List Files
=wp51[ENTER][F1]{if you are using floppy disks}
[ALT]File List Files[ENTER]otrdeshow[ENTER]y[F7][ALT]
File List Files[ENTER]{Move the highlight to the
TRDESHOW subdirectory.}dy[F7]

[10.2, 13.2]

20. [ALT]Layout Page fap{Type today's date.}[ALT]
Layout Align Flush Right Page[SPACEBAR][CTRL-B]
[F7][F7][ALT]File Exit[ENTER][ENTER]yn[ALT]Edit Win-
dow 24[ENTER]

[9.5]

21. [ALT]File Retrieve wp{wp}us.sup[ENTER]{Move the
cursor to "Acermann."}[CTRL-END][DEL]{Move the
cursor to "Greenlowe."}[CTRL-END][DEL]{Move the
cursor to "Hatterfield."}[CTRL-END][DEL]{Move the
cursor to "Julie."}[CTRL-END][DEL]{Move the cursor
to "Styverson."}[CTRL-END][DEL][ALT]File Exit[ENTER]
[ENTER]yn

14.1   EXERCISES

1. B. J. Smith[F9]231-46-4232[F9][ALT]Tools Merge
Codes End Record Carroll Lawrence[F9]564-90-

5327[F9][ALT]Tools Merge Codes End Record {Follow the same pattern to enter the last two records.}

2. [ALT]File Retrieve names[ENTER][HOME][HOME][DOWN ARROW]{Type the text as shown, pressing[F9] to end the first, second, third, fifth, sixth, and seventh lines.}[ALT]Tools Merge Codes End Record

3. {Type your name.}[F9]{Type your title.}[F9]{Type your company's name.}[F9]{Type your street address.}[ENTER]{Type your city, state, and ZIP code.}[F9]{Type your social security number.}[F9] {Type your first name.}[F9][ALT]Tools Merge Codes End Record[ALT]File Save[ENTER]y

EXERCISES
14.2

1. The Association of Computer Graphic Artists wishes to thank[SPACEBAR][ALT]Tools Merge Code Field 1[ENTER][SPACEBAR]from[SPACEBAR][ALT]Tools Merge Code Field 3[ENTER][SPACEBAR]for his or her assistance with the Taking Computer Graphics One Step Further forum.[ENTER][ALT]File Exit[ENTER] thanks[ENTER]n

2. [ALT]Tools Merge Code Field 1[ENTER][ENTER] [ALT]Tools Merge Code Field 2[ENTER][ENTER] [ALT]Tools Merge Code Field 3[ENTER][ENTER] [ALT]Tools Merge Code Field 4[ENTER][ENTER] [ENTER]Dear[SPACEBAR][ALT]Tools Merge Code Field

6[ENTER],[ENTER][ENTER]{Type the paragraph as shown.}[ALT]**Tools Merge Code Field 3**[ENTER] [ENTER][ALT]**Tools Merge Code Field 4**[ENTER] [ENTER][ALT]**Tools Merge Code Field 5**[ENTER] [ENTER]Contact:[TAB][ALT]**Tools Merge Code Field 1**[ENTER][ENTER][TAB][TAB][ALT]**Tools Merge Code Field 2**[ENTER][ENTER]{Type the last paragraph and the closing.}[ALT]**File Exit**[ENTER]cards[ENTER]n

14.3   EXERCISES

1. [ALT]**Tools Merge** thanks[ENTER]names[ENTER][ALT] **File Save** thanks.out[ENTER]

2. [ALT]**Tools Merge** cards[ENTER]names[ENTER][ALT]**File Save** cards.out[ENTER]

14.4   EXERCISES

1. [ALT]**File Print** dthanks.out[ENTER][ENTER]

2. [ALT]**File Print** dcards.out[ENTER][ENTER]

MASTERY SKILLS CHECK

[14.1]   **1.** Karen Simon[F9]34220 Euclid Avenue[F9]Cleveland, OH 44134[F9][ALT]**Tools Merge Codes End Record** Jim Darcy[F9]12353 Carnegie Avenue[F9]Lakewood, OH 44116[F9][ALT]**Tools Merge Codes End Record** [ALT]**File Save** names2[ENTER]

2. [ALT]Tools Merge Code Field 1[ENTER][ENTER][ALT]   [14.2, 14.3, 14.4]
   Tools Merge Code Field 2[ENTER][ENTER][ALT]
   Tools Merge Code Field 3[ENTER][ALT]File Exit
   [ENTER]lbls[ENTER]n[ALT]Tools Merge lbls[ENTER]
   names2[ENTER][ALT]File Print f

3. [ALT]File Retrieve names2[ENTER][DOWN ARROW][DOWN   [14.1]
   ARROW][DOWN ARROW]Karen[F9][DOWN ARROW][DOWN
   ARROW][DOWN ARROW][DOWN ARROW]Jim[F9][ALT]File Exit
   [ENTER][ENTER]y[ENTER]

4. [ALT]Tools Merge Code Field 1[ENTER][ENTER]   [14.2, 14.3, 14.4]
   [ALT]Tools Merge Code Field 2[ENTER][ENTER]
   [ALT]Tools Merge Code Field 3[ENTER][ENTER]
   [ENTER]Dear[SPACEBAR][ALT]Tools Merge Code Field
   4[ENTER],[ENTER][ENTER]{Type the text as shown.}
   [ALT]File Exit[ENTER]photos[ENTER]n[ALT]Tools Merge
   photos[ENTER]names2[ENTER][ALT]File Print f

5. [ALT]File Retrieve photos[ENTER]{Move to the "w"   [14.2, 14.3, 14.4]
   in "we."}[ALT]Tools Merge Code Field 4[ENTER],
   [SPACEBAR][ALT]File Exit[ENTER][ENTER]y[ENTER][ALT]
   Tools Merge photos[ENTER]names2[ENTER][ALT]File
   Print f

INTEGRATING SKILLS CHECK

1. Thomas Douglas[F9]Dept. Manager, Accounting   [14.1]
   [F9]X3963[F9][ALT]Tools Merge Codes End Record
   Tanya Smith[F9]Dept. Manager, Data Processing
   [F9]X3959[F9][ALT]Tools Merge Codes End Record
   [ALT]File Exit[ENTER]names.two[ENTER][ENTER]

[14.2]   **2.** Memo[ENTER]To:[TAB][TAB][ALT]Tools Merge Code Field 1[ENTER][ENTER][TAB][TAB][ALT]Tools Merge Code Field 2[ENTER][ENTER][TAB][TAB][ALT]Tools Merge Code Field 3[ENTER][ENTER]{Type the remainder of the memo as shown, including the date and your name where indicated.}

[4.6, 4.7]   **3.** [PGUP][ALT]Layout Align Center

[1.4]   **4.** [END][ENTER][ESC]65-

[1.3, 2.2]   **5.** [ALT]File Save smokers[ENTER][ALT]File Exit nn

[14.3]   **6.** [ALT]Tools Merge smokers[ENTER]names.two[ENTER]

[12.1, 14.4]   **7.** [ALT]File Print n2[ENTER]f

[1.3, 2.3, 13.1, 13.2]   **8.** [ALT]File Exit n[ENTER][ALT]File Retrieve names.two [ENTER]   [ALT]Edit Switch Document[ALT]File Retrieve smokers[ENTER][ALT]Edit Window 12[ENTER]

15   SKILLS CHECK

[5.4]   **1.** [ALT]Layout Line t[HOME][LEFT ARROW][CTRL-END]1.5 [ENTER]2[ENTER]4[ENTER][F7][F7][ALT]Layout Line t[CTRL-END]0,.5[F7][F7]

[4.1, 4.2]   **2.** We have written several times to inquire about the status of[F6]order number 98754[F6]. Please check the status of the backorder items. If you are unable to fill the remainder of the order within[F8] 10 days[F8], please notify us so that we can contact other suppliers.[ENTER]

3. 150[ENTER][SPACEBAR]50[ENTER]100[ENTER][ESC]   [1.4]
   3[ENTER]300[ENTER]

4. You can use an[F6]'s[F6] to create the plural of   [4.2, 12.1]
   letters,numbers, symbols, and words. For example,
   you could write that there are four[F6]s's[F6]and
   four[F6]i's[F6]in[F6]Mississippi[F6].[ALT]File Print
   n2[ENTER]f

5. Errors, like straws, upon the surface flow;[ENTER]   [8.4]
   He who would search for pearls, must dive be-
   low.[ENTER][ENTER][TAB][TAB][TAB][TAB]John Dryden
   [ENTER][ALT]Edit Block[PGUP][ALT]Edit Copy[ENTER]
   [ALT]Edit Pasteb

6. [ALT]File Print n1[ENTER][F7]   [12.1]

EXERCISES   15.1

1. [ALT]Layout Line t[CTRL-END]3[ENTER]d[F7][F7][ALT]
   Layout Math On Salaries[TAB]50,000[ENTER]
   Benefits[TAB]8,500[ENTER] Travel[TAB]18,000[ENTER]
   Rent[TAB]120,000[ENTER][TAB][RIGHT ARROW] + [ALT]
   Layout Math Calculate][ALT]Layout Math Off

2. {Move the cursor to the 5 in the "Benefits"
   amount.}[INS]9[INS][ALT]Layout Math Calculate]

EXERCISES   15.2

1. [ALT]Layout Line t[CTRL-END]0.5[ENTER]4.0[ENTER]
   d[F7][F7][ALT]Layout Math Define 1[DOWN ARROW]

[DOWN ARROW]0[F7]oMachine repairs[ENTER][ENTER]
Model 5210[ENTER][TAB]Factory 1[TAB]10[ENTER]
[TAB]Factory 2[TAB]5[ENTER]Total Repairs 5210[TAB]
[RIGHT ARROW] + [ENTER][ENTER]Model 6511[ENTER][TAB]
Factory 1[TAB]48[ENTER][TAB]Factory 2[TAB]9[ENTER]
TotalRepairs 6511[TAB][RIGHT ARROW] + [ENTER][ENTER]
TOTAL ALLMODELS[TAB] = [ALT]Layout Math
Calculate{The subtotals should be 15 and 57; the
total should be 72.}[ALT]Layout Math Off

2. EMPLOYEE BENEFIT PARTICIPATION[ENTER]
[ALT]Layout Line t[CTRL-END]0.3[ENTER]0.5[ENTER]
4.5[ENTER]d5.5[ENTER]d[F7][F7][ALT]Layout Math
Define 1123[DOWN ARROW][DOWN ARROW][LEFT ARROW]
[LEFT ARROW]00[F7]o[TAB]Employees in Savings
Plan[ENTER][TAB][TAB]Thrift[TAB]500[ENTER][TAB][TAB]S&L
[TAB]250[ENTER][TAB][TAB]Bonds[TAB]250[ENTER][TAB]
Total in Savings[TAB][RIGHT ARROW] + [ENTER][TAB]
Employees in Stock Option Plan[ENTER][TAB][TAB]
Plan A[TAB]100[ENTER][TAB][TAB]Plan B[TAB]100
[ENTER][TAB]Total in Stocks[TAB][RIGHT ARROW] + [ENTER]
[TAB]Total Employees in Investment Plans[TAB] =
[ENTER][ENTER][TAB]Employees in Medical Plan[ENTER]
[TAB][TAB]White Cross[TAB]500[ENTER][TAB][TAB]Cheap
Docs[TAB]500[ENTER][TAB]Total Medical[TAB][RIGHT
ARROW] + [ENTER][TAB]Employees in Life Insurance
Plan[ENTER][TAB][TAB]Quick Save[TAB]100[ENTER][TAB]
[TAB]High Risk[TAB]100[ENTER][TAB]Total Life[TAB]
[RIGHT ARROW] + [ENTER][TAB]Total Employees in In-
surance Plans[TAB] = [ENTER][ENTER] TOTAL NUM-
BERS IN BENEFIT PLANS[TAB][TAB]* [ALT]
Layout Math Calculate][ALT]Layout Math Off

MASTERY SKILLS CHECK

1. [ALT]Layout Line t[CTRL-END]2.8[ENTER]d[F7][F7]   [15.1]
[ALT]Layout Math Define [DOWN ARROW][DOWN
ARROW]0[F7] o HEADCOUNT BY LOCATION
[ENTER][ENTER] Chicago[TAB]120[ENTER]Dallas[TAB]38
[ENTER]Denver[TAB]105[ENTER]New York[TAB]302
[ENTER][ENTER]TOTAL[TAB][RIGHT ARROW] + [ALT]
Layout Math Calculate][ALT]Layout Math Off

2. {Move the cursor first to the "T" in "TOTAL."}   [15.1]
U.S.[SPACEBAR][ALT]Edit Reveal Codes {Move the
cursor to the[MATH OFF]code.} [ALT]Edit Reveal
Codes [ENTER][ENTER]Paris[TAB]82[ENTER]London
[TAB]106[ENTER]Lisbon[TAB]34[ENTER]Frankfurt[TAB]
192[ENTER][ENTER]FOREIGN TOTAL[TAB][RIGHT
ARROW] + [ALT]Layout Math Calculate]

3. [ALT]Layout Line t[CTRL-END] 0.5[ENTER]4.0[ENTER]   [15.2]
d[F7][F7][ALT]Layout Math Define 12[DOWN ARROW]
[DOWN ARROW][LEFT ARROW]0[F7] o Product 1 Sales
[ENTER][TAB]Jim[TAB]12,500[ENTER][TAB]Fred[TAB]
38,900[ENTER][TAB]Harry[TAB]23,500[ENTER] Total
Product 1[TAB][RIGHT ARROW] + [ENTER][ENTER]
Product 2 Sales[ENTER][TAB]Jim[TAB]23,450[ENTER]
[TAB]Fred[TAB]56,750[ENTER][TAB]Harry[TAB]78,900
[ENTER] Total Product 2[TAB][RIGHT ARROW] + [ENTER]
[ENTER]Total Products 1 & 2[TAB] = [ALT]Layout
Math Calculate][ALT]Layout Math Off

4. [ALT]Layout Line t[CTRL-END]4.7[ENTER]d5.7   [15.2]
[ENTER]d[F7][F7][ALT]Layout Math Define 23

[F7] o Office Supplies[ENTER][TAB]10.00[ENTER]
[TAB]15.50[ENTER][TAB]25.60[ENTER]Total Supplies[TAB]
[RIGHT ARROW] + [ENTER]Office Furniture[ENTER][TAB]
345.00[ENTER][TAB]545.00[ENTER]Total Furniture[TAB]
[RIGHT ARROW] + [ENTER]Total Office Products[TAB] =
[ENTER][ENTER]Coffee Supplies[ENTER][TAB]25.00[ENTER]
[TAB]15.80[ENTER]Total Coffee[TAB][RIGHT ARROW]
+ [ENTER]Paper Products[ENTER][TAB] 115.00[ENTER]
Total Paper[TAB][RIGHT ARROW] + [ENTER]Total Miscel-
laneous[TAB] = [ENTER][ENTER]TOTAL PURCHASES
[TAB][TAB]* [ALT]Layout Math Calculate[ALT]Layout
Math Off

INTEGRATING SKILLS CHECK

[4.3, 5.5, 10.2]   **1.** {Type the text as shown.}[ENTER][HOME][HOME][UP
ARROW][ALT]Layout Page hapABC COMPANY
[ALT]Layout Align Flush Right [ALT]Tools Date
Text F7 fap [ALT]Layout Align Center Page
[SPACEBAR][CTRL-B][F7][F7]

[4.1, 5.4, 15.1]   **2.** [PGDN][ENTER][ALT]Layout Line t[CTRL-END]3[ENTER]
3.5[ENTER]d4.5[ENTER]5[ENTER]d[F7][F7][ALT]Layout
Math Define 121[DOWN ARROW][DOWN ARROW][LEFT
ARROW][LEFT ARROW]0[RIGHT ARROW]0[F7] o [TAB][F8]
Last[TAB][TAB]This[ENTER][TAB]Year[TAB][TAB]Year[F8]
[ENTER][ENTER]Travel[TAB][TAB]52,900[TAB][TAB]86,900
[ENTER]Consultants[TAB][TAB]104,585[TAB][TAB]190,800
[ENTER]Entertainment[TAB][TAB]3,900[TAB][TAB] 9,800
[ENTER]Supplies[TAB][TAB]1,200[TAB][TAB]15,900[ENTER]
Phone [TAB][TAB]25,000[TAB][TAB]49,000[ENTER][ENTER]
TOTALS[TAB][TAB][RIGHT ARROW] + [TAB][TAB][RIGHT
ARROW] + [ALT]Layout Math Calculate]

3. [ALT]Layout Math Off [ENTER][ALT]Layout Line   [5.4, 15.1]
   t[CTRL-END] 0,.5 [ENTER][F7][F7][TAB]{Type the text as
   shown.}[ENTER]

4. [ALT]File Print n2[ENTER]f   [12.1]

SKILLS CHECK   16

1. [ALT]File List Files C:[ENTER]oaccount[ENTER]y[F7]   [11.2]

2. [ALT]File List Files [ENTER]oletters[ENTER]y[F7]   [11.2]

3. [ESC]55*   [1.4]

4. [ENTER][ALT]Layout Align Center [F6][F8]{Type the   [4.1, 4.2, 4.3]
   text as shown.}[F8][F6][ENTER]

5. [ALT]File Print vF7   [3.3]

6. {Move the cursor to the first asterisk.} [ALT]Edit   [8.2]
   Select Paragraph m{Move the cursor to the line
   below the text.}[ENTER]

EXERCISES   16.1

1. {Type the first paragraph.}[ENTER][ALT]Tools Line
   Draw 2[ESC]40[RIGHT ARROW][F7][RIGHT ARROW]
   [ENTER]{Type the second paragraph.}

2. [ALT]Tools Line Draw 1[DOWN ARROW][DOWN
   ARROW][DOWN ARROW]2[RIGHT ARROW][RIGHT ARROW]
   [RIGHTARROW][RIGHT ARROW][RIGHT ARROW][RIGHT ARROW]
   [DOWN ARROW][DOWN ARROW][DOWN ARROW][DOWN ARROW]

[DOWN ARROW][F7][SHIFT-F7]v12[F7]

16.2   EXERCISES

1. First Name:[SPACEBAR][ALT]**Tools Line Draw** 1[DOWN ARROW][DOWN ARROW][DOWN ARROW][ESC]15 [RIGHT ARROW][UP ARROW][UP ARROW][UP ARROW][ESC] 15[LEFT ARROW][F7][END][DOWN ARROW][DOWN ARROW] [DOWN ARROW][ENTER]Last Name:[SPACEBAR][ALT] **Tools Line Draw** [DOWN ARROW][DOWN ARROW] [DOWN ARROW][ESC]15[RIGHT ARROW][UP ARROW][UP ARROW][UP ARROW][ESC]15[LEFT ARROW][F7]{This makes boxes 3 rows by 15 columns. Your boxes may be a different size.}

2. [ALT]**Tools Line Draw** [ESC]14[RIGHT ARROW][ESC]5 [DOWN ARROW][ESC]14[LEFT ARROW][ESC]5[UP ARROW] [F7][ALT]**Edit Block**[PGDN][ALT]**Edit Select Rectangle** c[PGUP][END][TAB][TAB][ENTER][PGDN] [ENTER][ENTER][ENTER][TAB][TAB][TAB][TAB][TAB] [ALT]**Edit Paste** r[ESC]7[RIGHT ARROW][ALT] **Tools Line Draw** [ESC] 3 [UP ARROW][ESC]7 [LEFT ARROW][UP ARROW][UP ARROW][UP ARROW][ESC] 11[LEFT ARROW][F7]

16.3   EXERCISES

1. [ALT]**Tools Line Draw** 2[ESC]6[RIGHT ARROW] 5[ESC]6[LEFT ARROW][F7]

2. [ALT]**Tools Line Draw** 1[ESC]4[DOWN ARROW]
[ESC]5[RIGHT ARROW][ESC]4[UP ARROW][ESC]5[LEFT ARROW]
[RIGHT ARROW][RIGHT ARROW]5[RIGHT ARROW][DOWN
ARROW][DOWN ARROW][DOWN ARROW][DOWN ARROW][LEFT
ARROW][F7]

EXERCISES ————————— 16.4

1. [ALT]**Tools Line Draw** 2[ESC]4[DOWN ARROW]
[ESC]15[RIGHT ARROW][ESC]4[UP ARROW][ESC]15
[LEFT ARROW]6[ESC]20[RIGHT ARROW]2[DOWN ARROW]
[DOWN ARROW][ESC]12[RIGHT ARROW][UP ARROW]
[UP ARROW][ESC]12[LEFT ARROW][F7]

2. [ALT]**Tools Line Draw** 1[ESC]10[RIGHT ARROW] 6
[ESC]5[LEFT ARROW]1[ESC]10[DOWN ARROW] 6[ESC]5[LEFT
ARROW]1[ESC]10[RIGHT ARROW]6[ESC]10[RIGHT ARROW]
1[ESC]10[RIGHT ARROW]6[ESC]5[LEFT ARROW] 1[ESC]10[UP
ARROW]6[ESC]5[LEFT ARROW] 1[ESC]10[RIGHT ARROW]
6[ESC]10[RIGHT ARROW] 1[ESC]10[RIGHT ARROW] 6[ESC]5
[LEFT ARROW] 1[ESC]10[DOWN ARROW] 6[ESC]5[LEFT ARROW]
1[ESC]10[RIGHT ARROW][F7]

EXERCISES ————————— 16.5

1. [ALT]**Tools Line Draw** 49[SHIFT-3][ESC]10[DOWN
ARROW][ESC]20[RIGHT ARROW][ESC]10[UP ARROW]
[ESC]20[LEFT ARROW][F7]

2. [ALT]**Tools Line Draw** 44[ESC]30[RIGHT ARROW][F7]

16.6   EXERCISES

1. {Answer assumes that you draw the boxes and then type the text. This answer creates boxes that are 3 rows by 20 columns. If you use different numbers, replace the 3 and the 20 in the answers with the numbers that you use.}
[TAB][TAB][TAB][TAB][TAB][ALT]Tools Line Draw 2[ESC]3[DOWN ARROW][ESC]20[RIGHT ARROW][ESC]3[UP ARROW][ESC]20[LEFT ARROW][F7][DOWN ARROW][DOWN ARROW][DOWN ARROW][END][ENTER][ENTER][ENTER] [HOME][UP ARROW][CTRL-RIGHT ARROW][ALT]Edit Block [DOWN ARROW][DOWN ARROW][DOWN ARROW] [END][ALT]Edit Select Rectangle c[DOWN ARROW] [DOWN ARROW][DOWN ARROW][ENTER][ALT]Edit Block [DOWN ARROW][DOWN ARROW][DOWN ARROW][END] [ALT] Edit Select Rectangle c[UP ARROW][UP ARROW] [UP ARROW][END][SPACEBAR][ENTER][ALT]Edit Block [DOWN ARROW][DOWN ARROW][DOWN ARROW][END] [ALT]Edit Select Rectangle c[UP ARROW][UP ARROW][UP ARROW][END][SPACEBAR][ENTER][ESC]10 [RIGHT ARROW][ALT]Tools Line Draw 1[UP ARROW] [ESC]43[LEFT ARROW][DOWN ARROW][UP ARROW] [ESC]21[RIGHT ARROW][DOWN ARROW][UP ARROW][UP ARROW][UP ARROW][F7][INS][UP ARROW][UP ARROW][CTRL-LEFT ARROW][RIGHT ARROW][RIGHT ARROW]Root Directory [DOWN ARROW][DOWN ARROW][DOWN ARROW][DOWN ARROW] [DOWN ARROW][DOWN ARROW][CTRL-LEFT ARROW][CTRL-LEFT ARROW][CTRL-LEFT ARROW][RIGHT ARROW][RIGHT ARROW] BUDGET[CTRL-RIGHT ARROW][CTRL-RIGHT ARROW] [RIGHT ARROW][RIGHT ARROW]PRODUCT[CTRL-RIGHT

ARROW][CTRL-RIGHT ARROW][RIGHT ARROW][RIGHT
ARROW]REPORTS[INS]

2. [ALT]**Tools Line Draw** 1[ESC]4[DOWN ARROW][ESC]
50[RIGHT ARROW][ESC]4[UP ARROW][ESC]50[LEFT ARROW]
[F7][INS][DOWN ARROW][RIGHT ARROW][RIGHT ARROW]
All of the paintings displayed in this[DOWN ARROW]
[CTRL-LEFT ARROW][RIGHT ARROW][RIGHT ARROW] restau-
rant are for sale on a consignment[DOWN ARROW]
[CTRL-LEFT ARROW][RIGHT ARROW][RIGHT ARROW]
basis. For more details, see the manager.[INS]

MASTERY SKILLS CHECK

1. [ALT]**Tools Line Draw** 1[ESC]40[RIGHT ARROW]   [16.1, 16.3, 16.4]
6[ESC]20[LEFT ARROW]5[ESC]3[RIGHT ARROW][F7]
[ALT]**File Exit nn**

2. [SPACEBAR][SPACEBAR][SPACEBAR][ALT]**Tools Line Draw**   [16.1, 16.2, 16.6]
1[ESC]3[DOWN ARROW][ESC]10[RIGHT ARROW][ESC]3
[UP ARROW][ESC]10[LEFT ARROW][ESC]3[DOWN ARROW][ESC]
5[RIGHT ARROW][DOWN ARROW][ESC]5[LEFT ARROW][ESC]
5[DOWN ARROW][ESC]10[RIGHT ARROW][ESC]5[UP
ARROW][ESC]5[LEFT ARROW] 6[ESC]5[DOWN ARROW]1
[DOWN ARROW][ESC]5[RIGHT ARROW][ESC]3[DOWN
ARROW][ESC]10[LEFT ARROW][ESC]3[UP ARROW][ESC]5[RIGHT
ARROW][F7][INS][ESC]9[UP ARROW][LEFT ARROW][LEFT
ARROW][LEFT ARROW]Receive[ESC]7[LEFT ARROW][DOWN
ARROW]Invoice[DOWN ARROW][DOWN ARROW]
[DOWN ARROW][ESC]7[LEFT ARROW]Compare[DOWN
ARROW][ESC]7[LEFT ARROW]to[DOWN ARROW][LEFT
ARROW][LEFT ARROW]Purchase[ESC]8[LEFT ARROW][DOWN

ARROW]Order[ESC]5[LEFT ARROW][DOWN ARROW][DOWN ARROW][DOWN ARROW]Prepare[ESC]7[LEFT ARROW][DOWN ARROW] Voucher[INS][ALT]File Exit nn

[16.5]   **3.** [ALT]Tools Line Draw 49:[F7]

[16.1, 16.4]   **4.** [ENTER][SPACEBAR][SPACEBAR]Construction Schedule [TAB][TAB][TAB]Dates[ENTER][ENTER][SPACEBAR][SPACEBAR] Startrenovation[ENTER][ENTER][SPACEBAR][SPACEBAR] Startinterior remodeling[ENTER][ENTER][SPACEBAR] [SPACEBAR]Start repaving parking lot[ENTER][ENTER] [SPACEBAR][SPACEBAR]End repaving parking lot[ENTER] [ENTER][SPACEBAR][SPACEBAR]End interior remodeling [ENTER][ENTER][SPACEBAR][SPACEBAR]End renovation [ENTER][ESC]5[UP ARROW][END][ALT] Tools Line Draw 1[ESC]20[RIGHT ARROW][UP ARROW][UP ARROW][ESC] 18[LEFT ARROW]6[UP ARROW][UP ARROW][LEFT ARROW] 1[ESC]21[RIGHT ARROW][ESC] 6[DOWN ARROW][ESC] 23[LEFT ARROW]6[DOWN ARROW][DOWN ARROW][ESC] 9[LEFT ARROW]1[ESC]34[RIGHT ARROW][ESC]10[UP ARROW][ESC]32[LEFT ARROW][F7]

[16.3, 16.4]   **5.** [ALT]Tools Line Draw 6[ESC]17[RIGHT ARROW] 5[ESC]5[RIGHT ARROW][DOWN ARROW][DOWN ARROW] [ESC]5[LEFT ARROW][DOWN ARROW][DOWN ARROW] [ESC]5[RIGHT ARROW][DOWN ARROW][DOWN ARROW] [ESC]5[LEFT ARROW][DOWN ARROW][DOWN ARROW] [ESC]5[RIGHT ARROW][DOWN ARROW][DOWN ARROW] [ESC]5[LEFT ARROW][F7][ESC]10[UP ARROW][INS][RIGHT ARROW]5/1[DOWN ARROW][DOWN ARROW][ESC]3[LEFT ARROW]6/15[DOWN ARROW][DOWN ARROW][ESC]4[LEFT ARROW]7/1[DOWN ARROW][DOWN ARROW][ESC]3[LEFT ARROW]7/31[DOWN ARROW][DOWN ARROW][ESC]4[LEFT

ARROW]8/30[DOWN ARROW][DOWN ARROW][ESC]4[LEFT
ARROW]9/30[INS]

6. [PGUP]{If you do not have a blank line above the   [16.5]
construction schedule, press ENTER and the UP
ARROW key.} [ALT]**Tools Line Draw** 3[ESC]14[DOWN
ARROW][ESC]52[RIGHT ARROW][ESC]14[UP ARROW]
[ESC]51[LEFT ARROW][F7]

INTEGRATING SKILLS CHECK

1. Last name:[SPACEBAR][ALT]**Tools Line Draw** 1   [16.2]
[DOWN ARROW][DOWN ARROW][ESC]20[RIGHT ARROW][UP
ARROW][UP ARROW][ESC]20[LEFT ARROW][F7][DOWN ARROW]
[DOWN ARROW][END][ENTER]First name:[SPACEBAR]
[ALT]**Tools Line Draw**[DOWN ARROW][DOWN ARROW]
[ESC]20[RIGHT ARROW][UP ARROW][UP ARROW][ESC]20[LEFT
ARROW][F7][DOWN ARROW][DOWN ARROW][END][ENTER] De-
partment:[SPACEBAR][ALT]**Tools Line Draw**
[DOWN ARROW][DOWN ARROW][ESC]20[RIGHT ARROW]
[UP ARROW][UP ARROW][ESC]20[LEFT ARROW][F7][DOWN
ARROW][DOWN ARROW][END][ENTER]Years with the
company:[SPACEBAR][ALT]**Tools Line Draw**
[DOWN ARROW][DOWN ARROW][ESC]20[RIGHT ARROW]
[UP ARROW][UP ARROW][ESC]20[LEFT ARROW][F7][DOWN
ARROW][DOWN ARROW][END][ENTER]

2. [F8]Acme's Main Product Line[F8][ENTER]Solder   [4.1, 16.1]
[ENTER]Silver necklaces[ENTER]Silver flatware
[ENTER][UP ARROW][END][ALT]**Tools Line Draw**
1[ESC]10[RIGHT ARROW][ESC]3[UP ARROW][DOWN
ARROW][ESC]19[LEFT ARROW]6[DOWN ARROW][ESC]10
[RIGHT ARROW]1[ESC]9[RIGHT ARROW]

[11.4] **3.** [ALT]File List Files c:[ENTER]{Move the highlight to the ACCOUNT subdirectory.}dy[F7]

[11.4] **4.** [ALT]File List Files [ENTER]{Move the highlight to the LETTERS subdirectory.}dy[F7]

[4.2, 4.3, 16.2, 16.5, 16.6] **5.** [ALT]**Tools Line Draw** 49*[ESC]10[DOWN ARROW] [ESC]50[RIGHT ARROW][ESC]10[UP ARROW][ESC]50[LEFT ARROW][F7][INS][DOWN ARROW][DOWN ARROW][RIGHT ARROW][RIGHT ARROW][TAB][TAB]Clark Corporation is Moving[DOWN ARROW][DOWN ARROW][CTRL-LEFT ARROW] [RIGHT ARROW][RIGHT ARROW]On Friday the 23rd, Clark Corporation is[DOWN ARROW][CTRL-LEFT ARROW][RIGHT ARROW][RIGHT ARROW]closing its Lakewood offices. Its new[DOWN ARROW][CTRL-LEFT ARROW][RIGHT ARROW][RIGHT ARROW] headquarters are in Barlow, Florida. It is [DOWN ARROW][CTRL-LEFT ARROW][RIGHT ARROW][RIGHT ARROW]moving there to move closer to its prospering[DOWN ARROW][CTRL-LEFT ARROW][RIGHT ARROW] [RIGHT ARROW]land-development subsidiary.[INS]

[4.7] **6.** [PGUP][ALT]**Edit Block** [PGDN][ALT]**Layout Align Center** y

17 SKILLS CHECK

[4.7] **1.** {Type the text as shown.}[ENTER][HOME][HOME][UP ARROW][CTRL-RIGHT ARROW][ALT]**Edit Block** [CTRL-RIGHT ARROW][CTRL-RIGHT ARROW][CTRL-RIGHT ARROW][CTRL-RIGHT ARROW][LEFT ARROW][F8][ALT]**File Save** graphbox[ENTER]

2. [ALT]Edit Switch Document [ALT]File Retrieve   [13.3]
   graphbox[ENTER][HOME][HOME][DOWN ARROW]
   [ENTER]{Type the text as shown.}

3. [HOME][HOME][UP ARROW][ALT]Layout Page   [10.2]
   hapWordPerfect's Graphics Features[F7][F7]

4. {Move to the beginning of the word "captions."}   [4.7]
   [ALT]Edit Block [CTRL-RIGHT ARROW][LEFT ARROW]
   [F6]{Repeat the procedure for each of the other
   two words.}

5. [ALT]File Print v[F7][ALT]Edit Switch Document   [3.3, 13.3]
   [ALT]File Print v[F7]

EXERCISES   17.1

1. [ALT]Graphics User Box Create [F7]{Press
   ENTER 21 times.}

2. [ALT]Graphics Figure Create [F7]{Type the paragraph as shown.}

3. [ALT]Graphics Table Box Create [F7][ALT]
   File Print v[F7]

4. [ALT]Graphics Text Box Create [F7][ENTER]
   [ENTER][ENTER][ENTER][ENTER][ALT]Graphics Figure
   Create [F7][ALT]File Print v[F7]

5. [ALT]Graphics Table Box Create [F7][ALT]
   Graphics Figure Create [F7]{Press ENTER 23
   times.} [ALT]File Print v[F7]

17.2   EXERCISES

1. [ALT]Graphics Table Box Create e[F8]Project[F8]
[TAB][TAB][TAB][F8]Date[F8][ENTER]Systems analysis
[TAB][TAB] 5/1[ENTER]Order equipment[TAB][TAB]
6/15[ENTER]Design software[TAB][TAB]7/1[ENTER]
Test software[TAB][TAB][TAB]7/31[ENTER]Imple-
ment software[TAB][TAB] 8/30[ENTER]Evaluation
[TAB][TAB][TAB]9/30[ENTER][F7][F7][ALT]File Print
v[F7]

2. {Type the paragraph as shown.} [ALT]File Exit
[ENTER]picture[ENTER]n [ALT]Graphics Text Box
Create fpicture[ENTER][F7][ALT]File Print v[F7]

3. [ALT]Graphics Table Box Create e{Type the text as
shown, pressing ENTER after the heading and after
each step.}[F7][F7][ALT]File Print v[F7]

17.3   EXERCISES

{If your graphics images are not in the WordPerfect
subdirectory, type a backslash, the subdirectory name,
a backslash, and the filename where the answers
provide only the filename.}

1. [ALT]Graphics Table Box Create f star-5.wpg
[ENTER][F7][ALT]File Print v[F7]

2. [ALT]Graphics User Box Create f arrow
22.wpg [ENTER][F7][ALT]File Print v[F7]

3. [ALT]Graphics Figure Create f border-8.wpg
[ENTER][F7][ALT]File Print v[F7]

4. [ALT]Graphics User Box Create fgavel.wpg
[ENTER][F7][ALT]File Print v[F7]

EXERCISES ——————————— 17.4

1. [ALT]Graphics Text Box Create c[SPACEBAR]To be
filled in later[F7][F7][ALT]File Print v[F7]

2. [ALT]Graphics Table Box Create einsert Ms.
Mitchell's picture here[F7]c[SPACEBAR]Susan Mitchell,
President[F7][F7][ALT]File Print v[F7]

3. [ALT]Graphics Figure Create f telephone.wpg
[ENTER]c[SPACEBAR]When It Rings, We Answer[F7]
[F7][ALT]File Print v[F7]

4. [ALT]Graphics Figure Create f trophy.wpg
[ENTER]c[SPACEBAR]First in the Business[F7][F7]
[ALT]File Print v[F7]

EXERCISES ——————————— 17.5

1. [ALT]Graphics Text Box Create v.4[ENTER][F7]{type
the paragraph as shown.} [ALT]File Print v[F7]

2. [ALT]Graphics Figure Create hl[F7][ALT]File Print
v[F7]

3. [ALT]Graphics User Box Create f chkbox
1.wpg [ENTER]sh5[ENTER][F7][ALT]File Print
v[F7]

4. [ALT]Graphics Table Box Create e{Type the para-
graph as shown.}[F7][F7][ALT]File Print v[F7]
[ALT]Graphics Table Box Edit 1[ENTER]sw2.5
[ENTER][F7][ALT]File Print v[F7][ALT]Graphics Table
Box Edit 1[ENTER] sb3[ENTER]2[ENTER][F7][ALT]File
Print v[F7]

5. [ALT]Graphics Figure Create f hands-3.wpg
[ENTER]sh4[ENTER]hc[F7][ALT]File Print v[F7]

17.6   EXERCISES

1. [ALT]Graphics Table Box Create f arrow
22.wpg [ENTER][F7][ALT]File Print v[F7][ALT]
Graphics Table Box Edit 1[ENTER] f
chkbox-1.wpg [ENTER]y[F7][ALT]File Print v[F7]

2. [ALT]Graphics Text Box Create f certif.wpg
[ENTER][F7][ALT]File Print v[F7][ALT]Graphics Text Box
Edit 1[ENTER] f[CTRL-END][ENTER]y[F7][ALT]File Print
v[F7]

3. [ALT]Graphics Table Box Create [F7]
[ALT]Edit Reveal Codes [LEFT ARROW][DEL]
[ALT]Edit Reveal Codes

4. [ALT]Graphics Figure Create fnews.wpg
[ENTER][F7]{Press ENTER 16

times.} [ALT]Graphics Figure Create f bulb.wpg
[ENTER][F7]{Press ENTER 16 times.}[HOME][HOME][UP
ARROW][ALT]EditReveal Codes [BACKSPACE][HOME]
[HOME][DOWN ARROW][ALT]Edit Undelete
r[HOME][HOME][UP ARROW]{Press DEL 16 times.}
[ALT]File Print v[F7][ALT]Edit Reveal Codes

EXERCISES ————————————————— 17.7

1. {assumes that your printer can print graphics and
   text simultaneously} [ALT]Graphics Table Box Create f bicycle.wpg [ENTER][F7][ALT]File Print gdf

2. {assumes that your printer can print graphics and
   text simultaneously} [ALT]Graphics Text Box Create f pc-1.wpg [ENTER][F7]{Type the paragraph as
   shown, allowing WordPerfect to wrap the text
   around the text box.} [ALT]File Print gmthf

3. {assumes that your printer can print graphics and
   text simultaneously} [ALT]Graphics User Box Create f cntrct-2.wpg [ENTER][F7]{Type the paragraph
   as shown, allowing WordPerfect to wrap the text
   around the user-defined box.} [ALT]File Print ghf

4. {assumes that your printer can print graphics and
   text simultaneously} [ALT]Graphics Figure Create f
   bulb.wpg [ENTER][F7][ALT]Graphics Figure Create f
   floppy-2.wpg [ENTER][F7]{Type the paragraph as

shown, allowing WordPerfect to wrap the text
around the two figures.} [ALT]File Print gmf

MASTERY SKILLS CHECK

[17.1]   **1.** [ALT]Graphics Figure Create [F7][ALT]File Print v[F7]

[17.1, 17.5]   **2.** [ALT]Graphics Figure Create hl[F7][ALT]File Print
v[F7]

[17.3, 17.6]   **3.** [ALT]Graphics Figure Edit 1[ENTER]f mail-bag.wpg
[ENTER][F7][ALT]File Print v[F7]

[17.2, 17.6]   **4.** [ALT]Graphics Figure Edit 2[ENTER]e{Type the text
as shown, pressing ENTER after the colon and after
each author.}[F7][F7][ALT]File Print v[F7]

[17.6]   **5.** [ALT]Graphics Figure Edit 1[ENTER]f diplo-
ma.wpg [ENTER]y[F7][ALT]File Print v[F7]

[17.4]   **6.** [ALT]Graphics Figure Edit 1[ENTER]c[SPACEBAR]
A few thoughts to ponder[F7][F7][ALT]File Print
v[F7]

[17.5]   **7.** [ALT]Graphics Figure Edit 1[ENTER]sh2[ENTER]
[F7][ALT]File Print v[F7]

[17.5]   **8.** [ALT]Graphics Figure Edit 2[ENTER]sw 3.5
[ENTER][F7][ALT]File Print v[F7]

9. [ALT]Graphics Figure Edit 2[ENTER]e[DOWN   [17.2, 17.6]
   ARROW][ENTER][DOWN ARROW][DOWN ARROW][ENTER]
   [DOWN ARROW][DOWN ARROW][ENTER][F7][F7][ALT]File
   Print v[F7]

10. [ALT]File Print tmghf [ALT]File Exit nn   [17.7]

11. [ALT]Graphics Table Box Create f chkbox   [17.3, 17.4, 17.5]
    1.wpg [ENTER]c[SPACEBAR]Read This! It Is
    Important![F7][F7][ALT]File Print v[F7]

INTEGRATING SKILLS CHECK

1. {Type the paragraph as shown.} [ALT]File Exit   [17.2]
   yimages[ENTER]n [ALT]Graphics Text Box Create
   fimages[ENTER][F7]{Press ENTER 18 times.}
   [ALT]File Print v[F7]

2. [ALT]Graphics Table Box Create fclock.wpg   [17.3, 17.4]
   [ENTER]c[SPACEBAR]A stitch in time saves nine.[F7][F7]
   [ALT]File Print v[F7]

3. [ALT]Graphics Table Box Edit 1[ENTER]sb4   [17.5]
   [ENTER]4[ENTER][F7][ALT]File Print v[F7]

4. [ALT]Edit Switch Document [ALT]File Retrieve   [13.3]
   images[ENTER][DOWN ARROW][DOWN ARROW]
   [DOWN ARROW][ALT]Edit Select Sentence d [ALT]
   File Save [ENTER]y [ALT]File Print v[F7]

5. [ALT]Edit Switch Document[ALT]Graphics   [13.3, 17.6]
   Text Box Edit 1[ENTER]f[ENTER]y[F7][ALT]File Print
   v[F7]

[4.7, 17.6]   **6.** [ALT]Graphics Text Box Edit 1[ENTER]e{Move to the "W" in "WordPerfect Made Easy."} [ALT] Edit Block y[F8][F7][F7][ALT]File Print v[F7]

[17.7]   **7.** [ALT]File Print gdtdf [ALT]File Print v[F7]

[17.6]   **8.** [ALT]Edit Reveal Codes [HOME][HOME][DOWN ARROW][BACKSPACE][ALT]Edit Reveal Codes [ALT]File Print v[F7]

[17.3]   **9.** [ALT]Graphics Figure Create f hands-3.wpg [ENTER][F7]{Press ENTER 16 times.}[ALT] File Print v[F7]

[17.6]   **10.** [ALT]Edit Reveal Codes[HOME][HOME][UP ARROW] [BACKSPACE][HOME][HOME][DOWN ARROW][ALT]Edit Undelete r[HOME][HOME][UP ARROW]{Press the DEL key until the [FIG BOX:1;HANDS-3.WPG;] code is at the beginning of the document.} [ALT]Edit Reveal Codes [ALT]File Print v[F7]

[10.2, 17.3, 17.5]   **11.** [ALT]Layout Page hap [ALT]Graphics User Box Create f globe2-m.wpg [ENTER]h f[F7][F7] [F7][ALT]File Print v[F7]

[17.7]   **12.** [ALT]File Print ghf [ALT]File Print v[F7]

18

SKILLS CHECK

[5.2]   **1.** [ALT]Layout Align Indent→{Type the paragraph as shown.}

2. [ALT]Layout Align Indent → ←{Type the para-   [5.2]
graph.}

3. [ALT]Layout Line t[CTRL-END]4[ENTER][F7][F7]Joe Jones   [5.4]
[TAB]Accounting[ENTER]Paul Balber[TAB]Finance
[ENTER]Norlin Rugers[TAB] Management[ENTER]Mary
Rogers[TAB]Accounting[ENTER]

4. [ALT]Layout Line m2[ENTER]2[ENTER][F7]{Type the   [5.1, 12.1]
text as shown.} [ALT] File Print n2[ENTER]f

EXERCISES ——————————— 18.1

1. [CAPS LOCK]high school sports[ENTER][ALT]Tools
Outline On[ENTER][SPACEBAR][TAB]baseball[ENTER]
[SPACEBAR][TAB]football[ENTER][SPACEBAR]swimming
[ENTER][SPACEBAR][TAB]hockey [ALT]Tools Outline
Off [CAPS LOCK][ALT]File Exit [ENTER]sports[ENTER]
[ENTER]

2. [CAPS LOCK]breeds of dogs[CAPS LOCK][ENTER][ALT]
Tools Outline On [ENTER][ALT]Layout Align
Indent → Hounds[ENTER][TAB][ALT]Layout Align
Indent → Greyhound[ENTER][ALT]Layout Align
Indent → Whippet[ENTER][SHIFT-TAB][ALT]Layout
Align Indent → Sporting Dogs[ENTER][TAB]
[ALT]Layout Align Indent → Labrador Retriever
[ENTER][ALT]Layout Align Indent → Irish
Setter[ENTER][SHIFT-TAB][ALT]Layout Align Indent→
Terriers[ENTER][TAB][ALT]Layout Align Indent→
Airedale[ENTER][ALT]Layout Align Indent →
Welsh Terrier[ENTER][SHIFT-TAB][ALT]Layout

Align Indent → Working Dogs[ENTER][TAB][ALT]
Layout Align Indent → Collie[ENTER][ALT]Layout
Align Indent → Siberian Husky[ALT]Tools Outline
Off [ALT]File Exit [ENTER]dogs[ENTER][ENTER]

18.2   EXERCISES

1. [ALT]File Retrieve sports[ENTER][ALT]Tools Outline
   On [HOME][HOME][DOWN ARROW][ENTER] [SPACEBAR]
   [TAB]BASKETBALL[ENTER][SPACEBAR][TAB]TRACK
   {Move the cursor after the final "L" in "BASE-
   BALL."}[ENTER][TAB][SPACEBAR][TAB]John Doe
   [ENTER][SPACEBAR][TAB]Bill Black[DOWN ARROW]
   {Repeat the process, entering the names of the
   captains for the other sports.}

2. [ALT]File Retrieve dogs[ENTER]{Move the cursor to
   the first "I" in "II."} [ALT]Edit Block[DOWN ARROW]
   [DOWN ARROW][DOWN ARROW][ALT]Edit Move (Cut)
   [PGDN][ENTER][ENTER]{You may need to press the DEL
   key if WordPerfect inserts an extra number before
   "Sporting Dogs."}[RIGHT ARROW]

18.3   EXERCISES

1. [ALT]Tools Define 1[F7]o o [ENTER][ALT]Layout Align
   Indent → Estate Planning[ENTER][TAB][ALT]Layout
   Align Indent → Trust[ENTER][ALT]Layout Align

Indent→Will [ALT]Tools Outline Off

2. [ALT]Tools Define b[F7]o o The following employees are being honored for 25 years of service: [ENTER][TAB][TAB][TAB][ALT]Layout Align Indent→ Jane Parker[ENTER][ALT]Layout Align Indent→ Bill Black [ALT]Tools Outline Off

MASTERY SKILLS CHECK

1. [ALT]Tools Define o[F7]o o [CAPS LOCK]portfolio   [18.1] holdings[CAPS LOCK][ENTER][ALT]Layout Align Indent→Zero coupon bonds[ENTER][ALT]Layout Align Indent→Treasury bills[ENTER][ALT]Layout Align Indent→Blue chip stocks[ENTER][ALT]Layout Align Indent→Mutual fund shares

2. {Move the cursor to the second outline entry.}   [18.2] [ALT]Edit Select Paragraph m{Move the cursor to the end of the last outline entry.}[ENTER][ENTER] {You may need to press the DEL key if Word-Perfect inserts an extra number before "Treasury bills."}[RIGHT ARROW]

3. [END][ENTER][ALT]Layout Align Indent→Stock op-   [18.1] tions [ALT]Tools Outline Off [ALT]File Exit [ENTER] invest[ENTER][ENTER]

4. [ALT]Tools Outline On [ENTER][ALT]Layout Align   [18.1] Indent→New Construction[ENTER][TAB] [ALT]Layout Align Indent→Mayfield Village

[ENTER][ALT]Layout Align Indent→Highland Heights[ENTER][TAB][ALT]Layout Align Indent→ 1114 Miner Road[ENTER][ALT]Layout Align Indent→4811 Highland Ave.[ENTER][SHIFT-TAB] [SHIFT-TAB][ALT]Layout Align Indent→Remodeling Projects[ENTER][TAB][ALT]Layout Align Indent → Gates Mills[ENTER][TAB][ALT]Layout Align Indent → 112 Sherman Road[ENTER][ALT]Layout Align Indent→230 Saddleback Lane[ENTER][SHIFT-TAB][ALT]Layout Align Indent→Chagrin Falls

[18.2]   **5.** [ENTER][ALT]Layout Align Indent→Solon{Move the cursor to after the period in "Highland Ave."} [ENTER][ALT]Layout Align Indent→5311 Wilson Mills Road [HOME][DOWN ARROW][ALT]Tools Outline Off [ALT]File Exit[ENTER]jobs[ENTER][ENTER]

INTEGRATING SKILLS CHECK

[1.4, 3.1, 18.3]   **1.** {Type the top of the memo and the first paragraph as shown.} [ALT]Tools Define b[F7]o o [ENTER][TAB][TAB][TAB][ALT]Layout Align Indent → Jim Miller[ENTER][ALT]Layout Align Indent → Mary Parker[ENTER][ALT]Layout Align Indent → Paul Drake [ALT]Tools Outline Off {Move the cursor to after the period in the last sentence.} [CTRL-ENTER][ALT]File Print f

[18.1, 18.3]   **2.** [ALT]Tools Define l[F7]o o [ENTER][ALT]Layout Align Indent→WordPerfect's Math Features [ENTER][TAB][ALT]Layout Align Indent→Add

numbers[ENTER][TAB][ALT]Layout Align Indent→
Produce a subtotal for a column of numbers
[ENTER][ALT]Layout Align Indent→Add subtotals to
produce totals[ENTER][ALT]Layout Align Indent→
Add totals to produce a grand total[ENTER][SHIFT-
TAB][ALT]Layout Align Indent→Perform formula
calculations across columns [ALT]Tools Outline
Off[ALT]File Exit [ENTER]math[ENTER][ENTER]

3. [ALT]Tools Define o[F7]o o [ENTER][ALT]Layout Align   [4.1, 12.1, 18.1,
Indent→WordPerfect Books[ENTER][TAB]   18.2]
[ALT]Layout Align Indent→[F8] WordPerfect Made
Easy[F8][ENTER][ALT]Layout Align Indent→
[F8]WordPerfect: The Complete
Reference[F8][ENTER][SHIFT-TAB][ALT]Layout Align
Indent→1-2-3 Books[ENTER][TAB][ALT]
Layout Align Indent→[F8]1-2-3 Made Easy
[F8][ENTER][ALT]Layout Align Indent→[F8]
1-2-3: The Complete Reference[F8]{Move to the
end of the last entry in the first section.}[ENTER]
[ALT]Layout Align Indent→[F8]Teach Yourself
WordPerfect 5.1[F8][ALT]Tools Outline Off
[ALT]File Print n2[ENTER]f

4. [ALT]Tools Outline On [ENTER][ALT]Layout Align   [8.2, 18.1, 18.2]
Indent→Vacation days[ENTER][ALT]Layout
Align Indent→Sick leave[ENTER][ALT]Lay-
out Align Indent→Holidays[ENTER][TAB][ALT]
Layout Align Indent→Christmas[ENTER][ALT]
Layout Align Indent→Thanksgiving[ENTER]
[ALT]Layout Align Indent→Memorial Day[ENTER]
[ALT]Layout Align Indent→Halloween[ENTER]

[ALT]Layout Align Indent→Independence Day
[ENTER][ALT]Layout Align Indent→Labor Day
{Move the cursor to the first "I" in "III."}
[ALT]Edit Block[HOME][HOME][DOWN ARROW]
[ALT]Edit Move (Cut)][HOME][HOME][UP ARROW]
[ENTER]{Move to the beginning of the line for
"Halloween."}[CTRL-END][DEL][HOME][HOME][DOWN
ARROW]

19

[4.1, 4.2]

SKILLS CHECK

1. [F6]WordPerfect allows you to change several settings.[F6] You can set WordPerfect to back up files automatically. You can also change the screen's appearance by selecting the colors Word-Perfect uses.[F8]These are just a few of the selections available.[F8]

[2.2]

2. [ALT]File Save default[ENTER]

[11.5]

3. [ALT]File List Files[ENTER]{Move the cursor to the DEFAULT file.}msettings[CTRL-END][ENTER][F7]

[4.4]

4. [ALT]Edit Reveal Codes{Soft returns appear as[SRt].}

19.1

EXERCISES

1. [ALT]File Setup Environment bty120[ENTER][F7]

2. [ALT]File Setup Environment bty30[ENTER][F7]

EXERCISES ——————————— 19.2

1. [ALT]**File Setup Display** cs[DOWN ARROW][DOWN ARROW][DOWN ARROW][DOWN ARROW] {Press the RIGHT ARROW key if you have a Font column.}a[F7][F7]

2. [ALT]**File Setup Display** cs[DOWN ARROW][DOWN ARROW][DOWN ARROW][DOWN ARROW][DOWN ARROW][DOWN ARROW][DOWN ARROW][DOWN ARROW]{Press the RIGHT ARROW key if you have a Font column.}{Type the letter for the normal font in the Foreground column.}[RIGHT ARROW]{Type the letter for the normal font in the Background column.}[F7][F7]

3. [ALT]**File Setup Displaye** h < [F7]

4. [ALT]**File Setup Displaye** h[SPACEBAR][F7]

5. [ALT]**File Setup Displaye** fy[F7]

EXERCISES ——————————— 19.3

1. [ALT]**File Setup Environmente** en[F7]

2. [ALT]**File Setup Initial Settings** d6,[SPACEBAR] 3[SPACEBAR]1[ENTER][F7]

3. On[ALT]**Tools Date Text**, the Okra Vegetable company begins marketing its new product line, the Seeing Green frozen foods.

MASTERY SKILLS CHECK

[19.1]   **1.** [ALT]File Setup Environment bty20[ENTER][F7]

[19.2]   **2.** [ALT]File Setup Display cs{Press the RIGHT ARROW
            key if you have a Font column.}[RIGHT ARROW]a[F7]
            [F7]

[19.3]   **3.** [ALT]File Setup Initial Settings d3[SPACEBAR]4
            [ENTER][F7]

[19.3]   **4.** Acme Corporation projects that its personnel will
            increase 5% during[ALT]Tools Date Text.

[19.3]   **5.** [ALT]File Setup Environmente sn[F7]

INTEGRATING SKILLS CHECK

[1.3, 11.5, 19.1]   **1.** [ALT]File Setup Environment bty1[ENTER][F7]
            Testing Backups{Wait until WordPerfect backs
            up the document.}[ALT]File List Files[ENTER]
            {move the highlight to the WP{WP}.BK1 file.}
            mbckuptst[ENTER][F7][F7]nn

[19.1]   **2.** [ALT]File Setup Environment btn[ENTER][F7]

[19.3]   **3.** [ALT]File Setup Initial Settings d3[SPACEBAR]
            1,[SPACEBAR]4[ENTER][F7]

[19.3]   **4.** [TAB]The company picnic is on[ALT]Tools Date
            Text.[ENTER][TAB]Each person should bring one
            dish. Please review the schedule, which breaks

down the type of dish based upon the person's
last name.[ENTER]

5. [HOME][HOME][UP ARROW][ALT]**Edit Block**[END]   [4.7]
   [F6]{Move to the "o" in "one."}[CTRL-LEFT ARROW]
   [ALT]**Edit Block** h[F8]

6. [ALT]**File Setup Display** h*[F7]   [19.2]

7. [ALT]**File Setup Display** cs{Press the RIGHT ARROW   [19.2]
   key if you have a Font column.}[DOWN ARROW][DOWN
   ARROW][RIGHT ARROW]e{assuming e is the selection
   for red}[DOWN ARROW][DOWN ARROW]d{assuming d is
   the selection for light blue}[F7][F7]

8. {for a hard disk system}[ALT]**File List Files**   [11.4]
   [ENTER]{Move the highlight to the WP{WP}.SET
   file.}dyF7{for a floppy disk system}[ALT]**File List**
   Files a:[ENTER]{Move the highlight to the WP{WP}
   .SET file.}dy[F7]

9. [ALT]**File Exit**[ENTER]dish[ENTER]y{for a hard disk   [1.1, 1.2, 19.1]
   system}wp[ENTER]{for a floppy disk system: Place
   the WordPerfect 1 disk in drive A.}a:wp
   [ENTER]{Place the WordPerfect 2 disk in drive A
   when WordPerfect prompts you, and press any
   key to continue.}[ALT]**File Setup Environment**
   bty30[ENTER][F7]

SKILLS CHECK
_____ 20

1. {Type the heading and the three paragraphs.}

2. [ALT]**File Print** v[F7]

3. [HOME][HOME][UP ARROW][ALT]**Edit Block**[END][F6] [ALT]**Edit Block**[CTRL-LEFT ARROW][ALT]**Layout Align** Centery

4. [DOWN ARROW][ALT]**Layout Lines**2[ENTER][F7][CTRL-HOME][SHIFT-;][ALT]**Layout Lines**1[ENTER][F7]{Move the cursor on the "A" in the beginning of the third paragraph.}[ALT]**Layout Lines**2[ENTER][F7]

5. [ALT]**Search Backward**[SHIFT-'][F2][BACKSPACE][ALT] **Search Backward**[F2][BACKSPACE][ALT]**Layout Align** Indent→ ←

6. {Move the cursor on the "M" in Mary}[ALT]**Edit Block**[CTRL-RIGHT ARROW][CTRL-RIGHT ARROW][LEFT ARROW] [F8]

7. [ALT]**File Print** v[F7]

8. [ALT]**File Exit** ySTYL.DOC[ENTER]n

20.1 EXERCISES

1. [ALT]**Layout Styles**cnHeader[SPACEBAR]lvl[SPACEBAR]1 [ENTER]c[ALT]**Layout Align Center**[F6][RIGHT ARROW] [ENTER][ALT]**Layout Align Center**[ESC]45[SHIFT-8] [ENTER][F7][F7][F7]

2. [ALT]**Layout Styles** cnHeader[SPACEBAR]lvl[SPACEBAR] 2[ENTER]c[F8][RIGHT ARROW][ENTER][F7]ef[F7][F7]

3. [ALT]Layout StylescnLong[SPACEBAR]Quotes[ENTER]c
   [ALT]Layout Lines1[ENTER][F7][ALT]Layout Align
   Indent→ ←[F7]ef[F7][F7]

4. [ALT]File Exit ySTYLE2.DOC[ENTER]n

EXERCISES ———————————————— 20.2

1. [ALT]File Retrieve style2.doc[ENTER][ALT]Layout
   Lines 2[ENTER][F7][ALT]Layout Styles{Highlight
   Header lvl 1.}oDepartment Comments and Con-
   cerns[DOWN ARROW][ALT]Layout Styles{Highlight
   Header lvl 2.}oAccounting Department[ENTER]
   {Type the first paragraph and press ENTER.}[ALT]
   Layout Styles{Highlight Long Quotes.}o{Type the
   quote.}[RIGHT ARROW][ENTER][ALT]Layout Styles{High-
   light Header lvl 2.}oSales Department[ENTER]{Type
   the last paragraph.}[ALT]File Exit ydeptnews.ltr
   [ENTER]n

2. [ALT]File Retrievestyle2.doc[ENTER]{Type the text;
   then move the cursor to the "W" in "Welcome."}
   [ALT]Edit Block[END][ALT]Layout Styles{Highlight
   Header lvl 1.}o{Move the cursor to the "J" in
   "John Smith."}[ALT]Edit Block[END][ALT]Layout
   Styles{Highlight Header lvl 2.}o{Move to the "J"
   in "Jane Brown."}[ALT]Edit Block[END][ALT]Layout
   Styles{Highlight Header lvl 2.}o[ALT]File Exit
   ywelcome[ENTER]n

20.3   EXERCISES

1. [ALT]File Retrieve style2.doc[ENTER][ALT]Layout Styles cnLetters[ENTER]todGeneral Correspondence [ENTER]c[ALT]Layout Line m1.5[ENTER][ENTER]t[HOME] [HOME][LEFT ARROW][CTRL-END]0.5[ENTER][F7][F7][ALT] Layout Align Center{Type your name.}[ENTER][ALT] Layout Align Center{Type your street address.} [ENTER][ALT]Layout Align Center{Type your city, state, zip.}[ENTER][ENTER][ALT]Layout Align Center [ALT]Tools Date Code[ENTER][ENTER][ENTER][ENTER][F7] [F7][F7][ALT]File Exit yletter2.doc[ENTER]n

2. [ALT]File Retrieve style2.doc[ENTER][ALT]Layout Styles cnNewsletter[ENTER]toc[ALT]Layout Lines2 [ENTER][F7][ALT]Layout Align Center Acme Corpora- tion Newsletter[F7][F7][F7][ALT]File Exitynews.ltr [ENTER]n

20.4   EXERCISES

1. [ALT]File Retrieve letter2.doc[ENTER][ALT]Layout Styles{Highlight the style named Letters.}o{Type the text of the letter.}[ALT]File Save travel.ltr[ENTER]

2. [ALT]File Retrieve news.ltr[ENTER][ALT]Layout Styles{Highlight the style named Newsletter.}o [ENTER][ALT]Layout Styles{Highlight the style named Header Lvl 2.}o[CAPS LOCK]new equipment for sales department[CAPS LOCK][ENTER]{Type the rest of the text as shown.}[ALT]File Save news- vol1.doc[ENTER]

EXERCISES ————————————— 20.5

1. [ALT]File Retrievenewsvol1.doc[ENTER][HOME][HOME]
   [DOWN ARROW][ENTER]Ron Adams, MIS coordinator
   states that:[ENTER][ALT]Layout Styles{Highlight the
   Long Quotes style.}oAll systems are go. All equipment and cabling has been received, assembled
   and tested. We anticipate no problems.[RIGHT
   ARROW][ENTER]Training sessions are planned for
   the next three Fridays at 1:00 pm.[ALT]File Printv
   [F7][ALT]File Save[ENTER]y

2. [ALT]Layout Styles{Highlight the Newsletter
   style.}ec[DEL][F6][HOME][RIGHT ARROW][ENTER][ALT]
   Layout Align Center[ESC]27-[F7][F7]{Highlight
   the Long Quotes style.}ec[RIGHT ARROW][ALT]Lay-
   out Align Indent→ ←[F7][F7][F7][ALT]File Print
   v[F7][ALT]File Exit ynewsvol1.fin[ENTER]n

EXERCISES ————————————— 20.6

1. [ALT]File Retrieve newsvol1.doc[ENTER][ALT]Layout
   Styles snewsltr.dft[ENTER][F7]

2. [ALT]File Retrieve newsvol1.fin[ENTER][ALT]Layout
   Styles snewsltr.fin[ENTER][F7]

EXERCISES ————————————— 20.7

1. [ALT]File Exit nn[ALT]Layout Styles rnewsltr.dft
   [ENTER]Y{Highlight the Newsletter style.}o[ENTER]

{Type the paragraph as shown.}[ALT]File Print f

2. [ALT]Layout Stylesrnewsltr.fin[ENTER]y[F7][ALT]File
   Printf[ALT]File Exit nn

MASTERY SKILLS CHECK

1. [ALT]Layout Styles cnTitle[ENTER]c[ALT]Layout Align
   Center[ESC]54[SHIFT-8][ENTER][ALT]Layout Align Cen-
   ter[RIGHT ARROW][ENTER][ALT]Layout Align Center
   [ESC]54[SHIFT-8][ENTER][F7][F7][F7]

2. [ALT]Layout Styles cnAnnouncement[ENTER]toc[ALT]
   Layout Line m1.5[ENTER]1.5[ENTER][ENTER]pm1.5
   [ENTER]1.5[ENTER][F7][F7][F7][F7]

3. [ALT]Layout Styles{Highlight the Announcement
   style.}o[ALT]Layout Styles{Highlight the Title
   style.}oNew Medical Reimbursement Procedures
   [RIGHT ARROW][ENTER]{Type the paragraph as
   shown.}[ALT]File Save announce.doc[ENTER]

4. [ALT]Layout Styles sstyle.ann[ENTER][F7][ALT]File Exit
   nn

5. {Type the document as shown.}[HOME][HOME][UP
   ARROW][ALT]Layout Styles rstyle.ann[ENTER]y{High-
   light the Announcement style.}o{Move the cursor
   to the "n" in the New.}[ALT]Edit Block[END][ALT]
   Layout Styles{Highlight the Title style.}o

6. [ALT]Layout Styles{Highlight the Title style.}ec
[CTRL-END][DEL][F6][F7][F7][F7][ALT]File Exit nn

INTEGRATING SKILLS CHECK

1. {Type the text as shown}

2. [ALT]Layout Styles cnPress Rel.[ENTER]toc[ALT]Lay-
out Lines 2[ENTER][ENTER]pfap[ALT]Layout Align
Center PRESS RELEASE — PRESS RELEASE —
PRESS RELEASE[F7][F7][F7][F7][F7]

3. [ALT]Layout Styles cnMain Heading[ENTER]c[F6]
[ALT]Layout Align Center[RIGHT ARROW][ENTER]
[F7]ef[F7][F7]

4. [HOME][HOME][UP ARROW][ALT]Layout Styles{Highlight
the Press Rel. style.}o

5. [ALT]Layout Styles{Highlight the Main Heading
style.}oDataBlaster Blasts the Competition[ENTER]

6. [ALT]File Print f

7. [ALT]Layout Styles{Highlight the Press Rel. style.}
ec[ALT]Layout Pagehap[ALT]Layout Align Center
PRESS RELEASE — PRESS RELEASE — PRESS
RELEASE[F7][F7][F7][F7][F7]

8. [ALT]File Print f[ALT]File Exit nn

21   SKILLS CHECK

1. [ALT]**Layout Page** m2[ENTER]3[ENTER][F7]

2. [ALT]**Layout Line**jl[F7]

3. [ALT]**Layout Align Center** Memory Upgrades Available[ENTER]

4. [ALT]**Layout Align Center**[ESC]35-[ENTER][ENTER]

5. The memory chips we ordered three months ago have[F8]finally[F8] arrived. Those of you who have been waiting to upgrade your system should schedule a time with MIS Services for swapping memory chips at your earliest convenience.

6. [ALT]**Tools Spell** d{skip for MIS and press any key to continue}

7. [ALT]**File Exit** ymemory[ENTER]n

21.1   EXERCISES

1. [ALT]**Layout Columns Define**[F7][F7][ALT]**Layout Page**m[ENTER]8[ENTER][F7][ALT]**Layout Align Center** [CAPS LOCK]acme corporation[CAPS LOCK][ENTER][ESC] 65=[ENTER][ENTER][ALT]**File Exit**ynewsltr.doc[ENTER]n

2. [ALT]**Layout Page** m[ENTER]8[ENTER][F7][ALT]**Layout Align Center**[F6][CAPS LOCK]north coast community

news[CAPS LOCK][F6][ENTER][ALT]Layout Align Center
[ESC]26 = [ENTER][ALT]Layout Columns Define n3
[ENTER][F7][F7][ALT]File Exit ycommnews[ENTER]
[ENTER]

EXERCISES ————————————— 21.2

1. [ALT]File Retrieve newsltr.doc[ENTER][HOME][HOME]
   [DOWN ARROW][ALT]Layout Columns On[ALT]Layout
   Align Center[F8][CAPS LOCK]safety seminar[CAPS
   LOCK][F8][ENTER][ENTER]{Type the first paragraph}
   [ENTER][ENTER]{Type the second paragraph}[ALT]File
   Exit y[ENTER]y[ENTER]

2. [ALT]File Retrieve commnews[ENTER][HOME][HOME]
   [DOWN ARROW][ALT]Layout Columns On[ALT]Layout
   Align Center[CAPS LOCK]kiddie calendar[CAPS LOCK]
   [ENTER][ENTER]{Type the first paragraph}[ENTER]
   [ENTER]{Type the second paragraph}[ENTER][ENTER]
   {Type the third paragraph}[ALT]File Exit y[ENTER]
   y[ENTER]

3. [ALT]Layout Columns Define[F7]oParagraph 1
   [ENTER][ENTER]This is the first paragraph of this
   exercise.[CTRL-ENTER]Paragraph 2[ENTER][ENTER]This is
   the second paragraph of this exercise. It appears
   in column 2.[ALT]Layout Columns Off Paragraph
   3[ENTER][ENTER]This is the third paragraph of this
   exercise. It should appear below the first two
   paragraphs.[SHIFT-F7]v[F7][ALT]File Exit ycolumns
   [ENTER][ENTER]

21.3   EXERCISES

1. [ALT]Layout Columns Definetpm[ENTER]2.5[ENTER]3
[ENTER][ENTER][F7][F7][ALT]Layout Align Center
[CAPS LOCK]meeting new friends[CAPS LOCK][ENTER]
[ENTER][ALT]Layout Align Center A Play Presented
By:[ENTER][ALT]Layout Align Center Ms. Walker's
First Grade Class[ENTER][ENTER][ALT]File Exit
yplay.doc[ENTER][ENTER]

2. [ALT]Layout Page m[ENTER]8[ENTER][F7][ALT]Layout
Align Center[F6]Name & Address Listing[F6][ENTER]
[ENTER][ALT]Layout Columns Definetbn3[ENTER]m
[ENTER]2.5[ENTER]3[ENTER]6[ENTER]6.5[ENTER][ENTER]
[F7][F7][ALT]File Exit yn&a.lst[ENTER][ENTER]

3. [ALT]Layout Page m[ENTER]8.5[ENTER][F7][ALT]Layout
Columns Define tbn3[ENTER]m[ENTER]1.8[ENTER]2.2
[ENTER]4[ENTER]4.4[ENTER][ENTER][F7][F7][ALT]Layout
Align Center[CAPS LOCK]acme corporation[CAPS LOCK]
[ENTER][ALT]Layout Align Center Equipment Inven-
tory[ENTER][ENTER][ALT]File Exit yinvty.doc[ENTER]
[ENTER]

21.4   EXERCISES

1. [ALT]File Retrieve play.doc[ENTER][HOME][HOME][DOWN
ARROW][ALT]Layout Columns On[ALT]Layout Align
Center[F8]Character[F8][CTRL-ENTER][ALT]Layout Align
Center[F8]Lines[F8][CTRL-ENTER]{Type the script
using[CTRL-ENTER] to move to the next column.}[ALT]
File Exit y[ENTER]y[ENTER]

2. [ALT]**File Retrieve** n&a.lst[ENTER][HOME][HOME][DOWN ARROW][ALT]**Layout Columns On** Sandy Clark[CTRL-ENTER]121 S. Main St.[ENTER]Cleveland, OH 44114 [CTRL-ENTER]287-1120[CTRL-ENTER]Joe Kent[CTRL-ENTER] 2780 Bluebird Lane[ENTER]North Oak, OH 44013 [CTRL-ENTER]452-7655[CTRL-ENTER]Sally Jones[CTRL-ENTER]5891 Sunny Vale[ENTER]Little Creek, OH 44410[CTRL-ENTER]552-1732[ALT]**File Exit** y[ENTER]y [ENTER]

3. [ALT]**File Retrieve** invty.doc[ENTER][HOME][HOME] [DOWN ARROW][ALT]**Layout Columns On**[CAPS LOCK] part no[CTRL-ENTER]product name[CTRL-ENTER] description[CTRL-ENTER][CAPS LOCK]{Type the remaining text using[CTRL-ENTER] to move to the next column.}[ALT]**File Exit** y[ENTER]y[ENTER]

EXERCISES ——————————————— 21.5

1. [ALT]**File Retrieve** commnews[ENTER][DOWN ARROW] [DOWN ARROW][DOWN ARROW][CTRL-HOME][RIGHT ARROW] [CTRL-HOME][RIGHT ARROW][DOWN ARROW][DOWN ARROW] [DOWN ARROW][DOWN ARROW][DOWN ARROW][DOWN ARROW] {The cursor should now be on the "1" in "12:00."} [DEL][CTRL-HOME][LEFT ARROW][CTRL-HOME][LEFT ARROW] [UP ARROW][UP ARROW][UP ARROW][UP ARROW][UP ARROW] [CTRL-RIGHT ARROW][CTRL-RIGHT ARROW][CTRL-BACKSPACE] [CAPS LOCK]notes[CAPS LOCK][ALT]**File Exit** y[ENTER]y [ENTER]

2. [ALT]**File Retrieve** n&a.lst[ENTER][DOWN ARROW][DOWN ARROW][CTRL-HOME][RIGHT ARROW][CTRL-HOME][RIGHT

ARROW][DOWN ARROW][DOWN ARROW][CTRL-BACKSPACE]555-5555[CTRL-HOME][LEFT ARROW][CTRL-HOME][LEFT ARROW][DOWN ARROW][DOWN ARROW][CTRL-RIGHT ARROW][CTRL-BACKSPACE]Smith[ALT]File Exit y[ENTER]y[ENTER]

3. [ALT]File Retrieve play.doc[ENTER][ALT]Edit Reveal Codes{Make sure the cursor is just to the right of the[Col Def:] code.}[ALT]Edit Reveal Codes[ALT]Layout Columns Define m[ENTER]2[ENTER]2.4[ENTER][ENTER][F7][F7][ALT]File Print v[F7][ALT]File Exit y[ENTER]y[ENTER]

MASTERY SKILLS CHECK

1. [ALT]Layout Align Center The Greenville Library[ENTER][ALT]Layout Align Center Eager Reader Club[ENTER][ENTER][ALT]Layout Columns Define [F7][F7]

2. [ALT]Layout Columns On[ALT]Layout Align Center Story Hour[ENTER][ENTER]Eager readers can take part in story hour every Monday from 10:00 to 11:00 am. Every week, we will feature a new story read by everyone's favorite, Mr. Rabbit. After the reading, the children are encouraged to participate in a lively discussion about the story. Mr. Rabbit tries to teach a valuable lesson from every story he reads to our Eager Readers.[ENTER][ENTER]Mr. Rabbit is looking forward to seeing you next week.

3. [ALT]Layout Columns Off[ENTER][ENTER]

4. [ALT]Layout Align Center The Top Four Favorites [ENTER][ENTER][ALT]Layout Columns Define tpn3 [ENTER]m[ENTER]3[ENTER]3.5[ENTER]6[ENTER]6.5 [ENTER][ENTER][F7][F7]

5. [ALT]Layout Columns On[ALT]Layout Align Center Title[CTRL-ENTER][ALT]Layout Align Center Author [CTRL-ENTER][ALT]Layout Align Center Rating[CTRL-ENTER]{Type the columns using[CTRL-ENTER] to move to the next column.}

6. [ALT]Layout Columns Off[ENTER][ALT]Layout Align Center Book Sale[ENTER][ENTER][ALT]Layout Align Indent→On May 5th, the Greenville Teen Readers will be sponsoring a book sale of books donated by various members of the community. All are welcome to browse and pick up a few favorites at very low prices. If you have books you would like to donate, please bring them to the library on May 4th during business hours.[ENTER]

7. [ALT]File Print v[F7][ALT]File Exit nn

INTEGRATING SKILLS CHECK

1. [ALT]Layout Line jlm1.5[ENTER]1.5[ENTER][ENTER] pm1.5[ENTER]1.5[ENTER][F7]

2. [ALT]Layout Columns Define d.4[ENTER][F7][F7]

3. [ALT]Layout Align Center[F6]Looking for the Perfect Candy Bar?[F6][ENTER][ENTER]

4. [ALT]Layout Columns On

5. Capital Foods announces the release of their first no-calorie, no-cholesterol candy bar called[F8] Perfect-Bar[F8].[CTRL-ENTER]The product received rave reviews during its test-marketing. Now you can eat a delicious candy bar guilt free!

6. [ALT]Layout Columns Off[ENTER][ENTER]

7. [ALT]Layout Align Center[F6]Perfect-Bar Taste Testers Survey[F6][ENTER][ENTER]

8. Capital Foods test marketed Perfect-Bar in three different areas of the country. The customer comments were generally favorable. Some of the comments are reproduced below:[ENTER][ENTER]

9. [ALT]Layout Columns Define tpm[ENTER]2.5[ENTER] 2.9[ENTER][ENTER][F7]o

10. Area A[CTRL-ENTER]Tasty nougat center. The chocolate coating is rich and creamy.[CTRL-ENTER]Area B[CTRL-ENTER]Where did you put the calories? This tastes just like the stuff I'm not supposed to have.[CTRL-ENTER]Area C[CTRL-ENTER]Anything that tastes this good has to have something wrong with it.

22   SKILLS CHECK

1. [ALT]Layout Line t[CTRL-END]0[ENTER]0.5[ENTER]5 [ENTER]d6[ENTER]d[F7][F7]

2. [ALT]Layout Align Center Acme Corporation[ENTER]
[ALT]Layout Align Center Statement[ENTER][ALT]
Layout Align Center[ALT]Tools Date Code[ENTER]
[ENTER]

3. Previous Balance[TAB][TAB]$1,234.56[ENTER]Expenses
[ENTER][TAB]Rent[TA B]400.00[ENTER][TAB]Utilities[TAB]
[F8]119.00[F8][ENTER]Total Expenses[TAB][TAB](519.90)
[ENTER]Income[ENTER][TAB]Client 012[TAB]150.00
[ENTER][TAB]Client110[TAB][F8]1,210.00[F8][ENTER]Total
Income[TAB][TAB][F8]1,360.00[F8][ENTER]Current
Balance[TAB][TAB]$[ALT]Font Appearance Double
Underline 2,074.66[RIGHT ARROW][ENTER]

4. [ALT]File Exit nn

EXERCISES   22.1

1. [F6]Office Supplies Inventory - Top Shelf[F6]
[ENTER][ENTER][ALT]Layout Tables Create 3[ENTER]4
[ENTER][F7][HOME][HOME][DOWN ARROW][ENTER][F6]Office
Supplies Inventory - Bottom Shelf[F6][ENTER][ENTER]
[ALT]Layout Tables Create 3[ENTER]5[ENTER][F7][ALT]
File Exit ysupplies[ENTER]n

2. [ALT]Layout Align Center[F6]Faculty Evaluation
Form[F6][ENTER][ENTER]{Type the paragraph}[ENTER]
[ENTER][ALT]Layout Tables Create 4[ENTER]5[ENTER][F7]
[HOME][HOME][DOWN ARROW][ENTER]Return this form to
the department's faculty secretary.[ALT]File Exit
yfaculty.tbl[ENTER]n

3. Attachment C:[ENTER][ENTER][ALT]Layout Tables Create2[ENTER]4[ENTER][F7][HOME][HOME][DOWN ARROW][ENTER]See page 14-7 for more details.[ALT]File Exit yattach.c[ENTER]n

4. [ALT]Layout Tables Create 12[ENTER]15[ENTER][F7][HOME][HOME][UP ARROW][ALT]Edit Reveal Codes[ALT]Edit Block[HOME][HOME][DOWN ARROW][DEL]y[ALT]Edit Reveal Codes

5. [ALT]Layout Tables Create 2[ENTER]4[ENTER][F7][ALT]File Exit ybill.sht[ENTER]n

22.2   EXERCISES

1. [ALT]File Retrieve supplies[ENTER][DOWN ARROW][DOWN ARROW][DOWN ARROW]ITEM[TAB]TOTAL[TAB]UNITS[TAB]Pencils[TAB]10[TAB]Boxes[TAB]Pens[TAB]8[TAB]Boxes[TAB]Note Pads[TAB]15[TAB]Dozen[DOWN ARROW][DOWN ARROW][DOWN ARROW][DOWN ARROW][DOWN ARROW][SHIFT-TAB][SHIFT-TAB]ITEM[TAB]TOTAL[TAB]UNITS[TAB]Letterhead[TAB]3[TAB]Boxes[TAB]Second Sheet Paper[TAB]4[TAB]Boxes[TAB]Bond Paper[TAB]15[TAB]Reams[TAB]Laser Labels[TAB]2[TAB]Packages[ALT]File Print f[ALT]File Exit y[ENTER]y[ENTER]

2. [ALT]File Retrieve faculty.tbl[ENTER][DOWN ARROW][DOWN ARROW][DOWN ARROW][DOWN ARROW][DOWN ARROW][DOWN ARROW][DOWN ARROW][DOWN ARROW][DOWN ARROW][DOWN ARROW]STATEMENT[TAB]AGREE[TAB]NEU-TRAL[TAB]DISAGREE[TAB]1. He/she comes pre-

pared to class.[DOWN ARROW]2. He/she has command of the subject matter.[DOWN ARROW]3. He/she seems genuinely concerned with whether students learn the course material.[DOWN ARROW]4. The course's contents were taught in a manner that promoted learning of the course material.[ALT]File Print f[ALT]File Exit y[ENTER]y[ENTER]

3. [ALT]File Retrieve attach.c[ENTER][DOWN ARROW][DOWN ARROW][DOWN ARROW][DOWN ARROW]1988 MACRS deduction: $12,000 × .20 = [TAB]2,400.00[TAB]1989 MACRS deduction: $12,000 × .32 x 1/2 year = [TAB]1,920.00[TAB]Total MACRS deduction:[ALT] File Exit y[ENTER]y[ENTER]

4. [ALT]File Retrieve supplies[ENTER][DOWN ARROW][DOWN ARROW][DOWN ARROW][DOWN ARROW][DOWN ARROW][DOWN ARROW][DOWN ARROW][DOWN ARROW][DOWN ARROW][DOWN ARROW][ALT]Edit Reveal Codes{cursor is on TAB DEF code}[ALT]Layout Line t[CTRL-END]2.2[ENTER]4.4 [ENTER][F7][F7][DEL][ALT]Edit Reveal Codes[ALT]File Exity topshelf[ENTER][ENTER]

5. [ALT]File Retrieve bill.sht[ENTER][DOWN ARROW][DOWN ARROW][DOWN ARROW][DOWN ARROW]Total Charges:[ALT] File Exit y[ENTER]y[ENTER]

EXERCISES _____ 22.3

1. [ALT]File Retrieve supplies[ENTER][DOWN ARROW][DOWN ARROW][DOWN ARROW][ALT]Layout Tables Edit[TAB]

[CTRL-LEFT ARROW][CTRL-LEFT ARROW][CTRL-LEFT ARROW]
[CTRL-LEFT ARROW][CTRL-LEFT ARROW][CTRL-LEFT ARROW]
[CTRL-LEFT ARROW][CTRL-LEFT ARROW][CTRL-LEFT ARROW]
[CTRL-LEFT ARROW][TAB][CTRL-LEFT ARROW][CTRL-LEFT ARROW]
[CTRL-LEFT ARROW][CTRL-LEFT ARROW][CTRL-LEFT ARROW]
[F7][DOWN ARROW][DOWN ARROW][DOWN ARROW][DOWN
ARROW][DOWN ARROW][DOWN ARROW][DOWN ARROW]
[DOWN ARROW][SHIFT-TAB][ALT]**Layout Tables Edit**
flw1.17[ENTER][TAB]flw1.57[ENTER][F7][ALT]**File Print**
v[F7][ALT]**File Exit** y[ENTER]y[ENTER]

2. [ALT]**File Retrieve** faculty.tbl[ENTER][DOWN ARROW]
   [DOWN ARROW][DOWN ARROW][DOWN ARROW][DOWN ARROW]
   [DOWN ARROW][DOWN ARROW][DOWN ARROW][DOWN ARROW]
   [DOWN ARROW][ALT]**Layout Tables Edit**[TAB][TAB][TAB]
   flw1.1[ENTER][LEFT ARROW]flw.9[ENTER][LEFT ARROW]flw.7
   [ENTER][LEFT ARROW]flw3.8[ENTER][F7][ALT]**File Printf**
   [ALT]**File Exit** y[ENTER]y[ENTER]

3. [ALT]**File Retrieve** attach.c[ENTER][DOWN ARROW][DOWN
   ARROW][DOWN ARROW][ALT]**Layout Tables Edit**[CTRL-
   RIGHT ARROW][CTRL-RIGHT ARROW][CTRL-RIGHT ARROW][CTRL-
   RIGHT ARROW][CTRL-RIGHT ARROW][CTRL-RIGHT ARROW][CTRL-
   RIGHT ARROW][CTRL-RIGHT ARROW][CTRL-RIGHT ARROW][CTRL-
   RIGHT ARROW][CTRL-RIGHT ARROW][CTRL-RIGHT ARROW][CTRL-
   RIGHT ARROW][CTRL-RIGHT ARROW][CTRL-RIGHT ARROW][F7]
   [ALT]**File Print** f[ALT]**File Exit** y[ENTER]y[ENTER]

4. [ALT]**File Retrieve** bill.sht[ENTER][DOWN ARROW][ALT]
   Layout Tables Edit[CTRL-RIGHT ARROW][CTRL-RIGHT
   ARROW][CTRL-RIGHT ARROW][CTRL-RIGHT ARROW][CTRL-RIGHT
   ARROW][CTRL-RIGHT ARROW][CTRL-RIGHT ARROW][CTRL-RIGHT
   ARROW][CTRL-RIGHT ARROW][CTRL-RIGHT ARROW][CTRL-RIGHT

ARROW][CTRL-RIGHT ARROW][CTRL-RIGHT ARROW][CTRL-RIGHT ARROW][CTRL-RIGHT ARROW][F7][ALT]**File Print** v[F7][ALT] **File Exit** y[ENTER]y[ENTER]

EXERCISES ——————————— 22.4

1. [ALT]**File Retrieve supplies**[ENTER][DOWN ARROW][DOWN ARROW][DOWN ARROW][ALT]**Layout Tables Edit**[TAB][INS] c1[ENTER][F7][DOWN ARROW][DOWN ARROW][DOWN ARROW] [DOWN ARROW][DOWN ARROW][DOWN ARROW][DOWN ARROW] [DOWN ARROW][ALT]**Layout Tables Edit**[INS]c1[ENTER] [DOWN ARROW][DOWN ARROW][DOWN ARROW][INS]r1[ENTER] [F7][PgUp][DOWN ARROW][DOWN ARROW][DOWN ARROW] ORDER NO.[DOWN ARROW]PX-3[DOWN ARROW]ST-2 [DOWN ARROW]RX-5[DOWN ARROW][DOWN ARROW][DOWN ARROW][DOWN ARROW][DOWN ARROW]ORDER NO.[DOWN ARROW]345[DOWN ARROW]23[DOWN ARROW]X35[DOWN ARROW]RX-34[DOWN ARROW]RX-1[UP ARROW][UP ARROW] [SHIFT-TAB]Envelopes[TAB][TAB]4[TAB]Boxes[ALT] **File Print** v[F7][ALT]**File Exit** y[ENTER]y[ENTER]

2. [ALT]**File Retrieve faculty.tbl**[ENTER][DOWN ARROW] [DOWN ARROW][DOWN ARROW][DOWN ARROW][DOWN ARROW][DOWN ARROW][DOWN ARROW][DOWN ARROW][DOWN ARROW][DOWN ARROW][ALT]**Layout Tables Edit** sr6 [ENTER][F7]5. As a student, you were interested in learning the course material.[ALT]**File Print**f[ALT] **File Exit** y[ENTER]y[ENTER]

3. [ALT]**File Retrieve topshelf**[ENTER][DOWN ARROW][DOWN ARROW][DOWN ARROW][ALT]**Layout Tables Edit** sc4

[ENTER][F7]REORDER[ALT]File Print v[F7][ALT]File Exit y[ENTER]y[ENTER]

22.5   EXERCISES

1. [ALT]File Retrieve attach.c[ENTER][DOWN ARROW][DOWN ARROW][DOWN ARROW][ALT]Layout Tables Edit[ALT-F4] [RIGHT ARROW]jy[F7]Acme Corporation of North America[ENTER]MACRS deduction calculation for XYZ Gizmo[ENTER]April 1, 1990[ALT]File Print v[F7][ALT]File Exit y[ENTER]y[ENTER]

2. [ALT]File Retrieve bill.sht[ENTER][DOWN ARROW][ALT] Layout Tables Edit[ALT-F4][RIGHT ARROW]jy[F7]Service Bill[ENTER]Please pay upon receipt.[ALT]File Exit y[ENTER]y[ENTER]

22.6   EXERCISES

1. [ALT]File Retrieve supplies[ENTER][DOWN ARROW][DOWN ARROW][DOWN ARROW][ALT]Layout Tables Edit[TAB][ALT-F4][TAB][TAB]fcjc[ALT-F4][LEFT ARROW][LEFT ARROW][LEFT ARROW]fcaab[TAB][TAB][DOWN ARROW][ALT-F4][DOWN ARROW][DOWN ARROW]fcjd[F7][DOWN ARROW][DOWN ARROW][DOWN ARROW][DOWN ARROW][DOWN ARROW][SHIFT-TAB][ALT]Layout Tables Edit[ALT]Edit Block[TAB][TAB] fcjc[ALT-F4][LEFT ARROW][LEFT ARROW][LEFT ARROW]fcaab [TAB][TAB][DOWN ARROW][ALT-F4][DOWN ARROW][DOWN ARROW][DOWN ARROW][DOWN ARROW]fcjd[F7][UP ARROW] [UP ARROW][UP ARROW][UP ARROW][DEL]10[ALT]File Print f[ALT]File Exit y[ENTER]y[ENTER]

2. [ALT]**File Retrieve faculty.tbl**[ENTER][DOWN ARROW]
[DOWN ARROW][DOWN ARROW][DOWN ARROW][DOWN
ARROW][DOWN ARROW][DOWN ARROW][DOWN ARROW][DOWN
ARROW][DOWN ARROW][ALT]**Layout Tables Edit**[ALT-F4]
[TAB][TAB][TAB]fcaab[F7][ALT]**File Exit** y[ENTER]y
[ENTER]

3. [ALT]**File Retrieve attach.c**[ENTER][DOWN ARROW]
[DOWN ARROW][DOWN ARROW][ALT]**Layout Tables Edit**
fcaabfcjc[DOWN ARROW][TAB][ALT-F4][DOWN ARROW][DOWN
ARROW]fcjd[F7][ALT]**File Print** v[F7][ALT]**File Exit** y
[ENTER]y[ENTER]

4. [ALT]**File Retrieve bill.sht**[ENTER][DOWN ARROW][ALT]
Layout Tables Edit fcaabfcjc[DOWN ARROW][TAB]
[ALT-F4][DOWN ARROW][DOWN ARROW]fcjd[F7][UP ARROW]
[UP ARROW][SHIFT-TAB]4.3 hours of typing services[TAB]
55.90[TAB]1 diskette[TAB]2.50[ALT]**File Print** v[F7][ALT]
File Exit y[ENTER]y[ENTER]

EXERCISES

22.7

1. [ALT]**File Retrieve attach.c**[ENTER][DOWN ARROW][DOWN
ARROW][DOWN ARROW][ALT]**Layout Tables Edit**[DOWN
ARROW][DOWN ARROW][DOWN ARROW][TAB]m4[UP ARROW]
[UP ARROW][UP ARROW]fcttmc[F7][ALT]**File Print** f[ALT]
File Exit y[ENTER]y[ENTER]

2. [ALT]**File Retrieve bill.sht**[ENTER][DOWN ARROW][ALT]
Layout Tables Edit sr6[ENTER][UP ARROW][UP ARROW]
[TAB]m4[DOWN ARROW]mfb4*.07[ENTER][DOWN ARROW]
mfb4[RIGHT ARROW] + b5[ENTER][F7][UP ARROW][SHIFT-TAB]

Sales Tax:[DOWN ARROW]Total Amount Due:[ALT]File Print f[ALT]File Exit y[ENTER]y[ENTER]

MASTERY SKILLS CHECK

1. [ALT]Layout Tables Create 2[ENTER]8[ENTER]

2. [ALT-F4][TAB]jyfcjcfctt

3. [TAB][ALT-F4][TAB]fcjcfctt

4. [DOWN ARROW][ALT-F4][DOWN ARROW][DOWN ARROW][DOWN ARROW][DOWN ARROW][DOWN ARROW]fcjd

5. mfb6[RIGHT ARROW] + b7[ENTER]{0.00 appears in the cell.}fcaad

6. [UP ARROW]mfb6*.07[ENTER]{0.00 appears in the cell.} fcaau

7. [UP ARROW]m4{0.00 appears in the cell.}[F7]

8. [UP ARROW][UP ARROW][UP ARROW][UP ARROW][UP ARROW] JOE'S HARDWARE[TAB]Item[TAB]Amount[TAB] Nails[TAB]9.00[TAB]Hammer[TAB]5.00[TAB]Screw Driver[TAB]7.00[TAB]Subtotal[TAB]21.00[TAB]Tax @ 7%[TAB]1.47[TAB]Total[TAB]22.47[ALT]Layout Tables Edit mc

9. [F7][ALT]File Print v[F7][ALT]File Exit nn

INTEGRATING SKILLS CHECK

1. [ALT]Layout Tables Create 3[ENTER]6[ENTER]

2. [ALT-F4][TAB][TAB]jyfcjcfctt

3. [DOWN ARROW][ALT-F4][TAB][TAB]fcjc[ALT-F4][LEFT ARROW] fctt

4. [DOWN ARROW][ALT-F4][TAB][DOWN ARROW][DOWN ARROW] [DOWN ARROW]fcjr

5. m4{0.00 appears in the cell.}

6. [LEFT ARROW]m4{0.00 appears in the cell.}

7. [UP ARROW][ALT-F4][TAB]fcaau[F7]

8. [UP ARROW][UP ARROW][UP ARROW][UP ARROW]SALES BY DEPARTMENT[TAB]DEPT[TAB]JAN[TAB]FEB[TAB] Clothing[TAB]25,000. 00[TAB]20,000.00[TAB]Shoe[TAB] 15,000.00[TAB]12,000.00[TAB]Housewares[TAB]40,000.00 [TAB]42,000.00[TAB]Total[ALT]Layout Tables Edit mc

9. sc4[ENTER][ALT-F4][LEFT ARROW]jy[TAB][TAB][CTRL-LEFT ARROW][CTRL-LEFT ARROW][CTRL-LEFT ARROW][CTRL-LEFT ARROW][CTRL-LEFT ARROW][CTRL-LEFT ARROW][TAB][CTRL-RIGHT ARROW][CTRL-RIGHT ARROW][CTRL-RIGHT ARROW][TAB] [CTRL-RIGHT ARROW][CTRL-RIGHT ARROW][CTRL-RIGHT ARROW] [F7]MAR[DOWN ARROW]23,000.00[DOWN ARROW] 14,000.00[DOWN ARROW]37,000.00[ALT]Layout Tables Edit mc

▶ Index ◀

C

D